Guide to the 1987
National Electrical Code®

Guide to the 1987
National
Electrical Code®

by Roland E. Palmquist

Joseph A. Tedesco
NEC Consultant and Technical Editor

Macmillan Publishing Company
New York

Collier Macmillan Publishers
London

Copyright © 1972, 1975, and 1978 by Howard W. Sams & Co., Inc.
Copyright © 1982 and 1984 by The Bobbs-Merrill Co., Inc.
Copyright © 1986 and 1987 by Macmillan Publishing Company, a division of
Macmillan, Inc.

Macmillan Publishing Company
866 Third Avenue, New York, N.Y. 10022
Collier Macmillan Canada, Inc.

Library of Congress Cataloging-in-Publication Data
Palmquist, Roland E.
    Guide to the 1987 National Electrical Code.
    Includes index.
    1. Electric engineering—Insurance requirements.
    2. National Fire Protection Association. National
Electrical Code, 1987.   I. National Fire Protection
Association.   National electrical code, 1987.
II. Title.
TK260.P33 1988   621.319'24'0218   88-5183
ISBN   0-02-594560-2

Macmillan books are available at special discounts for bulk purchases for sales
promotions, premiums, fund-raising, or educational use. For details, contact:

> Special Sales Director
> Macmillan Publishing Company
> 866 Third Avenue
> New York, N.Y. 10022

10 9 8 7 6 5 4 3 2 1

Printed in the United States of America

While every precaution has been taken in the preparation of
this book, the Publisher assumes no responsibility for errors
or omissions. Neither is any liability assumed for damages
resulting from the use of the information contained herein.

National Electrical Code® and NEC® are Registered Trademarks of the National
Fire Protection Association, Inc., Quincy, MA.

Contents

Foreword   ix

Information about the *NEC*   1

Article
90   Introduction   1

Chapter 1 General

100	Definitions	7
110	Requirements for Electrical Installations	9

Chapter 2 Wiring Design and Protection

200	Use and Identification of Grounded Conductors	22
210	Branch Circuits	26
215	Feeders	45
220	Branch-Circuit and Feeder Calculations	48
225	Outside Branch Circuits and Feeders	61
230	Services	68
240	Overcurrent Protection	98
250	Grounding	112
280	Surge Arresters	152

Chapter 3 Wiring Methods and Materials

300	Wiring Methods	155
305	Temporary Wiring	170
310	Conductors for General Wiring	172
318	Cable Trays	181
320	Open Wiring on Insulators	193
321	Messenger-Supported Wiring	197
324	Concealed Knob-and-Tube Wiring	198
325	Integrated Gas Spacer Cable—Type IGS	201
326	Medium Voltage Cable—Type MV	202
328	Flat Conductor Cable—Type FCC	203
330	Mineral-Insulated Metal-Sheathed Cable—Type MI	208
331	Electrical Nonmetallic Tubing	211
333	Armored Cable—Type AC	213
334	Metal-Clad Cable—Type MC	216
336	Nonmetallic-Sheathed Cable—Types NM and NMC	218
337	Shielded Nonmetallic-Sheathed Cable—Type SNM	222
338	Service-Entrance Cable—Types SE and USE	223
339	Underground Feeder and Branch-Circuit Cable—Type UF	226
340	Power and Control Tray Cable—Type TC	228
342	Nonmetallic Extensions	229
344	Underplaster Extensions	234
345	Intermediate Metal Conduit	235
346	Rigid Metal Conduit	237
347	Rigid Nonmetallic Conduit	242
348	Electrical Metallic Tubing	245
349	Flexible Metallic Tubing	247
350	Flexible Metal Conduit	249
351	Liquidtight Flexible Metal and Nonmetallic Conduits	250
352	Surface Metal and Nonmetallic Raceways	254
353	Multioutlet Assembly	256
354	Underfloor Raceways	258
356	Cellular Metal Floor Raceways	263
358	Cellular Concrete Floor Raceways	265
362	Wireways	265
363	Flat Cable Assemblies	267
364	Busways	269
365	Cablebus	274
370	Outlet, Device, Pull, and Junction Boxes, Conduit Bodies, and Fittings	274
373	Cabinets and Cutout Boxes	290
374	Auxiliary Gutters	295
380	Switches	299
384	Switchboards and Panelboards	306

Chapter 4 Equipment for General Use

400	Flexible Cords and Cables	314
402	Fixture Wires	319
410	Lighting Fixtures, Lampholders, Lamps, Receptacles, and Rosettes	320
422	Appliances	342
424	Fixed Electrical Space Heating Equipment	349
426	Fixed Outdoor Electric De-Icing and Snow-Melting Equipment	367
427	Fixed Electric Heating Equipment for Pipelines and Vessels	373
430	Motors, Motor Circuits, and Controllers	379
440	Air-Conditioning and Refrigerating Equipment	414
445	Generators	427
450	Transformers and Transformer Vaults	427
460	Capacitors	442
470	Resistors and Reactors	446
480	Storage Batteries	447

Chapter 5 Special Occupancies

500	Hazardous (Classified) Locations	448
501	Class I Locations	455
502	Class II Locations	471
503	Class III Locations	484
510	Hazardous (Classified) Locations—Specific	489
511	Commercial Garages, Repair and Storage	490
513	Aircraft Hangars	495
514	Gasoline Dispensing and Service Stations	499
515	Bulk Storage Plants	504
516	Spray Application, Dipping and Coating Processes	507
517	Health Care Facilities	512
518	Places of Assembly	540
520	Theaters and Similar Locations	541
530	Motion Picture and Television Studios and Similar Locations	546
540	Motion Picture Projectors	546
545	Manufactured Building	546
547	Agricultural Buildings	548
550	Mobile Homes and Mobile Home Parks	551
551	Recreational Vehicles and Recreational Vehicle Parks	557
553	Floating Buildings	557
555	Marinas and Boatyards	558

Chapter 6 Special Equipment

600	Electric Signs and Outline Lighting	559
604	Manufactured Wiring Systems	559

605	Office Furnishings	559
610	Cranes and Hoists	561
620	Elevators, Dumbwaiters, Escalators, and Moving Walks	561
630	Electric Welders	561
640	Sound-Recording and Similar Equipment	561
645	Electronic Data Processing Systems	562
650	Organs	562
660	X-ray Equipment	562
665	Induction and Dielectric Heating Equipment	562
668	Electrolytic Cells	562
669	Electroplating	562
670	Industrial Machinery	562
675	Electrically Driven and Controlled Irrigation Machines	562
680	Swimming Pools, Fountains, and Similar Installations	563
685	Integrated Electrical Systems	581
690	Solar Photovoltaic Systems	581

Chapter 7 Special Conditions

700	Emergency Systems	583
701	Legally Required Standby Systems	591
702	Optional Standby Systems	593
705	Interconnected Electric Power Production Sources	595
710	Over 600 Volts, Nominal	595
720	Circuits and Equipment Operating at Less than 50 Volts	607
725	Class 1, Class 2, and Class 3 Remote-Control, Signaling, and Power-Limited Circuits	608
760	Fire Protective Signaling Systems	608
770	Optical Fiber Cables	608
780	Closed-Loop and Programmed Power Distribution	611

Chapter 8 Communication Systems

800	Communication Circuits	612
810	Radio and Television Equipment	612
820	Community Antenna Television and Radio Distribution Systems	612

Chapter 9 Tables and Examples

Tables and Examples	613

Appendix A

614

Index

615

Foreword

Many persons whose job it is to make installations or designs, or to inspect electrical wiring installations, or to operate electrical equipment have often expressed a desire for further interpretation or clarification of certain parts of the *National Electrical Code*® *(NEC).** This book has been written in an attempt to fill this need.

The *National Electrical Code* is published by the National Fire Protection Association as one of numerous codes, standards, and recommended practices prepared by NFPA Technical Committees. Because of the complexity of all possible installation of electrical wiring and equipment and the necessity for covering any possible contingency the *NEC* becomes a little complicated in certain areas. For this reason, this Guide has been written to simplify the intent of the Code where needed most. In no way am I suggesting that the *NEC* is inadequate; nevertheless, my experience has been that people using it often need further guidance.

Interpretations are often made that are not the intent of the *NEC*. I have attempted in this book to clarify interpretations in the manner in which I would explain them in the field. You will not find direct quotations, tables, and so forth here. The *Guide to the 1987 National Electrical Code* is intended to be used concurrently with the *National Electrical Code*.

The *NEC* is revised every three years to keep up to date with new methods and new materials that are constantly being developed. This Guide

---

**National Electrical Code*® and *NEC*® are Registered Trademarks of the National Fire Protection Association, Inc., Quincy, MA.

is based on the 1987 revision of the *NEC*. The interpretations in this Guide are those of the author and are in no manner to be considered as official NFPA Electrical Code Committee interpretations. This book has been written and revised with the permission of the National Fire Protection Association.

As the code is changed, proposals or changes are sent to the NFPA and will be printed in what is commonly termed the "Preprint." Each proposal is numbered and labeled "accept" or "reject," depending on the decisions of the code-making panel. These are then made available for comments from the electrical industry. What changes are then made will come out in print and be sent to the correlating committee for their approval. From this the next edition of the *National Electrical Code* will be prepared.

The NFPA prints a multitude of fire codes. As you read this book reference will be made to many of these other codes. For your information, these publications may be purchased in total, in loose-leaf binders, or in individual booklets. Those that are referred to in this book are useful in conjunction with the *NEC*, and it is pertinent that they are used with the *NEC*.

The NFPA has an electrical section membership. All of these, plus the current *NEC* and *NEC* handbook, are available from NFPA, Quincy, Mass.

My sincere thanks to Frank Stetka (deceased), who was secretary to the *NEC* Correlating Committee for ten years, George Tryon, Technical Secretary of the National Fire Protection Association for many years, and Anthony R. O'Neill, Vice President, and Dennis J. Berry, Associate General Counsel of NFPA, for their kindness in granting me permission to write this book. I also wish to acknowledge the part that my wife, Elsie, has played in this matter. Her patience and extreme tolerance in permitting me to devote so much time to this venture must not go unrewarded. I therefore wish to dedicate this book to her. My sincere thanks to my grandson, Michael Fisk, for assisting me in the 1987 revision.

Roland E. Palmquist, C.E.T.
Senior Engineering Technician

Information about the NEC

Your copy of the *NEC* contains a complete history of the growth of the Code. The Code is set up as a minimum standard for electrical interpretations for the protection of life and property.

The *NEC*, as it now exists, is very complete. However, local conditions may dictate some variations; and as we proceed with the text, you will see that, in most instances, these variations have been anticipated and planned for in the Code.

Please study the official NFPA definitions of "Approved," "Authority Having Jurisdiction," "Labeled," "Listed," and "Shall," as they will be helpful in understanding passages from the *NEC*.

The proposed new *NEC* was available early enough so that members of the Electrical Section of NFPA who agree or disagree with parts of it could vote at the May finalizing meeting, which was held in Atlanta, Georgia, for the 1987 *NEC* on May 19–22, 1986.

After the Code had been finalized, it was sent to ANSI for adoption. The 1987 *National Electric Code* was available in September 1986. It may be purchased from the NFPA or from ANSI.

ARTICLE 90—INTRODUCTION

90-1. Purpose.

(a) Electricity may be hazardous, if proper precautions are not taken. This Code was intended to give guidelines for the proper installations, so as to safeguard personnel and property.

(b) This Code's provisions are those essential for safety, and compliance herewith may not necessarily result in efficient, convenient, or good

1

service and may not provide for future expansion of electrical usage. It is however essentially free from hazards that may be encountered. Nonconformity to the rules of the NEC may result in hazards or overloading of wiring systems. Most of these problems result from not taking into consideration the increasing usages of electricity. If future needs are taken into consideration at the time of the original installation and adequate measures are taken to provide for the increased usage of electricity, these hazards and overloading may be greatly eliminated.

(c) In no manner is this Code intended to be used for design specifications or as an instruction manual for untrained persons. The rules of this Code will, however, add materially to proper design. It is also adopted as the regulations governing wiring installations by most government agencies. Most governmental authorities enforcing the 1987 Code will no doubt adopt it effective January 1, 1987. There may be additional requirements by the local agencies and these should be checked out.

90-2. Scope.

(a) **Covered.** This Code covers:

(1) Electric conductors and equipment installed in or on: public or private buildings or other structures, mobile homes and recreational vehicles, floating buildings, and other premises, such as yards, carnivals, parking and other lots, and industrial substations.

Additional information concerning installations in multibuilding complexes or industrial buildings is found in the National Electrical Safety Code, ANSI C2-1984.

(2) The installation of conductors on a premise outside of a premise is covered.

(3) The installation of conductors outside of a premise is covered.

(4) Optical fibers are relatively new. Article 770 directly covers optical fibers.

(b) **Not Covered.** This Code does not cover:

(1) Ships, watercraft, trains, aircraft, automobiles, or trucks, although mobile homes and recreational vehicles are covered.

(2) Installation of conductors is not covered in the NEC for underground mines. This does not exempt the above-ground installation of wiring.

(3) Railroad generation, transformation, and transmission or distribution, if used only for signaling devices, and railroad trains are not covered in the NEC.

(4) Communication equipment located outdoors or indoors, if used exclusively by utilities, is not covered in the NEC.

(5) Electric utilities exclusively under their control for communication, metering, generation, transformation, and distribution of electricity, whether indoors or outdoors on property owned or leased by the utility, whether out of doors by established rights on private property and public highways, streets, or roads, are not covered by the *NEC*. The above does not cover any metering, wiring, buildings, or structures on any premise that is not owned or leased by the utility. The *NEC* does cover all wiring other than utility metering equipment ahead of service equipment through building structures or any other place not owned or leased by the utility. The Code also covers utility office buildings, warehouses, machine shops, recreational buildings, and garages—even those that may be part of a generating plant for a substation, etc.

(c) **Special Permission.** Conditions and usages vary in different localities; therefore, the authority having jurisdiction for the enforcement of the Code must be able to grant exemptions for the installation of the wiring system equipment not under the control of the utilities. This occurs whenever utilities are connecting service-entrance conductors of the building or structure that they are serving. If such installations are outside the building or terminate just inside the building, special permission should be granted in writing.

There has been an abundance of work done by utilities, and often the work becomes a part of the Code. Should the installation of service laterals, for example, be deemed good engineering practice by utilities and acceptable by the enforcing authority, this practice may, by special permission, be permitted under the Code. This special permission does not eliminate the Special Permission under Article 100; it applies only to Section 90-2.

90-3. Code Arrangement—The Code is divided into an introduction and chapters. Chapters 1 through 4 deal with general applications of the Code to wiring and installations. Chapters 5, 6, and 7 supplement or amend the first four chapters, and deal with special occupancies and installations that involve special equipment or special conditions. Chapter 8 deals with communication circuits, and with the equipment and installation of radio and television. Chapter 9 deals with tables not included in, but to be used in conjunction with, the first eight chapters. Also included are examples for figuring minimum requirements for installation. These examples are extremely valuable in the understanding of the preceding chapters.

Familiarity with the various Code chapters makes it easy to find what you want in the Code. The chapters from 4 on are special chapters and refer back to the previous three chapters. An "x" before a section number indicates excerpts from other NFPA documents that will be found in Appendix A. See Section 514-2, for an example.

90-4. Enforcement—The *NEC* is written so that it can be enforced when adopted by agencies having the rights of inspection. The Code's enforcement and interpretation is placed in the hands of the enforcing agency or authority. They decide the answers, but of course good judgment is essential in the interpretations. In many instances, the Code puts the entire responsibility of interpretation on the enforcing authority. For example, you will often find the phrase *by special permission*; this means special permission, in writing, by the Code-enforcing authority.

The enforcing authority is vested with the right to decide on the approval of equipment and materials. However, listings from the Underwriters' Laboratory or other independent testing laboratories are used for this purpose in many instances. One of the deterrents to Code understanding can be lack of communication between the inspector and the installer. Actually the inspector is the installer's friend, and all he wants is a good safe job. The best advice to offer in this respect is—get acquainted with your inspector. Take your problems to him; you will find him understanding and helpful in most cases.

Many industries have established procedures for installation and maintenance that are very effective and in many cases far more safety oriented than the Code installations. This gives the authority enforcing the latitude to okay such installations.

90-5. Formal Interpretations—An *NEC* committee is set up to render official Code interpretations when these are necessary. In the majority of questions arising on the Code, the interpretations are under the inspector's jurisdiction, as will be seen in the next section. However, there may be instances when official interpretations are required. No official interpretations will be made unless the Formal Interpretation Procedures outlined in the Code are followed.

90-6. Examination of Equipment for Safety—Most equipment and materials have been tested by electrical testing laboratories such as Underwriters' Laboratories (UL), and carry their label. This is increasingly the case; however, there are times when the testing agency will not find such labeling and will have to make its own judgment as to the safety of the equipment involved. Extreme caution or care should be taken by the inspection authority in judging the safety instability of devices, equipment, or material, and ensuring that it is used only for the purpose for which it was designed. Section 110-3 and Article 100 cover examination of equipment and the meaning of "Listed."

90-7. Wiring Planning—In the design of electrical systems by electrical engineers, ample provision should be made in the raceways for adequate wiring, as well as distribution and load centers which should be laid out in practical locations, keeping in mind their accessibility. The number of wires in enclosures and boxes should adhere to Code requirements in order to avoid fires and breakdowns and the inconveniences that accompany such troubles.

In reaching the goal of good wiring and installation, there is one requirement—good workmanship. Insulation damage, too many wires, and overfusing are the points that must be carefully watched. Regardless of how good the design of the installation, cutting corners will defeat the intended product.

(a) **Future Expansion and Convenience.** Until recently it was customary to have only one circuit in homes and a minimum of wiring in industrial locations. We have all seen the use of electricity increased in all aspects of our lives. Therefore, in designing wiring systems consideration should be given to large enough raceways and in some cases spare raceways to accommodate the changes—future uses of electricity or expansion of operations—that are certain to come. At this time it will be well to review Sections 110-16 and 240-24, which describe the necessary clearance distances and accessibility for future additions.

(b) **Number of Circuits in Enclosure.** You will find later in the *NEC* that there is a maximum number of conductors and circuits that you can put in a single enclosure such as raceways, boxes, and so on. These limitations for single raceways and boxes will reduce problems with short circuits and ground faults in a circuit.

Severe damage could be done to conductor insulation by pulling in to raceways and the like too many conductors, or around too many bends. There are even times, when pulling large sizes of conductors, that the 360 degrees in total bends between pull boxes and the like could be too many. Since the Code is not intended to be a design manual, it is up to the designer and the inspection authority to watch for these things. The Code has taken into account (derated), as you will find in Article 310, certain numbers of current carrying conductors in raceways to avoid overheating of conductors and raceways.

90-8. Metric Units of Measurement—Metric units, together with our own units of measurement, will assist us as we make increased use of the international system of units (SI). The SI units are not used everywhere. Omitted will be horsepower, wire sizes, box sizes, and conduit sizes.

CHAPTER I

General

ARTICLE 100—DEFINITIONS

Refer to your copy of the *NEC* for definitions. Occasionally, however, as you go through the Code you will find some additional definitions that may not appear in Article 100, as they are more applicable to the particular part you are covering.

The following figures are useful in understanding the definitions. For a branch circuit, see Fig. 100-1. For a multiwire branch circuit, see Fig. 100-2. For an illustration of service drop, see Fig. 100-3. Service lateral and service entrance equipment are illustrated in Figs. 100-4 and 100-5 respectively.

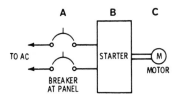

Fig. 100-1. A motor circuit. The branch circuit extends from point **A** to point **C**.

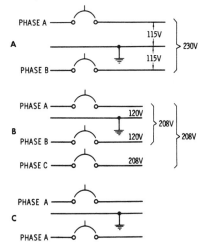

Fig. 100-2. Variations of a multiwire branch circuit. Circuit **C** is not a multiwire branch circuit because it utilizes two wires from the same phase in conjunction with the neutral conductor.

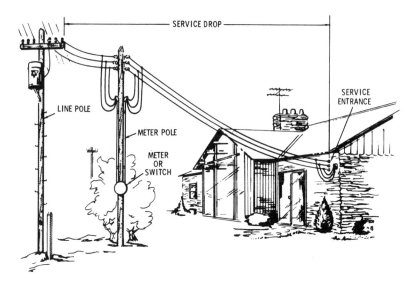

Fig. 100-3. Illustrating the service drop attached to a building or other structure.

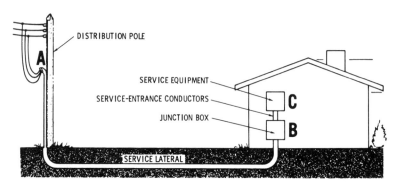

Fig. 100-4. Illustrating the service lateral extending from point **A** to point **B**. The service entrance is from point **B** to point **C**.

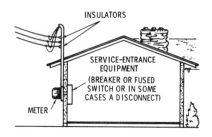

Fig. 100-5. Showing the service-entrance equipment that will serve as the electrical disconnect supply.

ARTICLE 110—REQUIREMENTS FOR ELECTRICAL INSTALLATIONS

This article is by-passed in the study of the Code more often than any other article. It is short, but it is actually the foundation upon which the Code is written, as it contains provisions that are used throughout the entire Code.

A. General

110-1. Mandatory Rules and Explanatory Material—In the Code, one will find both mandatory and advisory rules. The mandatory rules are characterized by the word "shall." This means that the rules must be strictly followed. Explanatory material is in the form of Fine Print Notes (FPN).

110-2. Approval—See definition of "approved" under Article 100.

110-3. Examination, Identification, Installation, and Use of Equipment.

(a) **Examination.** Observe the following considerations for the evaluation of equipment:

(1) Wiring devices and equipment that are suitable for use must be provided with identification of the product and of the use intended—environmental application. The identification, in most cases, is by labeling or listing.

If the above information is not available, it becomes the responsibility of the authority having jurisdiction to decide on the suitability of the equipment.

(2) The wiring material and equipment must have its parts properly designed so that the enclosure will protect other equipment.

(3) Adequate splice wire bending is required. This will be found in a table in your *NEC*.

(4) Electrical insulation may be checked.

(5) Heating effects must be taken into consideration, on conductors. In Article 310 will be found tables reducing the ampacity of a conductor as ambient temperatures rise. The author finds that few are familiar with high-altitude rating of motors, which starts at 3500 feet above sea level. In higher altitudes the air is thinner and therefore has less cooling effect on the motor. For instance a 5-horsepower motor at a high altitude cannot be expected to carry as much load as the same 5-horsepower motor at sea level.

(6) The equipment must be designed for minimal index from arcing.

(7) The use of voltage currents must all be taken into consideration.

(8) Other factors which affect safety to persons that will have occasion to come in contact with this equipment.

(b) **Installation and Use.** Labeling or listing will only amount to as much as the precautions taken in following the installation and use instructions included with the labeling or listing service. Alteration of equipment in the field voids any labeling or listing.

110-4. Voltages—The voltages referred to in the Code are the supply voltages, regardless of their source. The supply may be a battery, generator, transformer, rectifier, or a thermopile. When considering ac voltages, the voltage is the rms voltage as explained in the Definitions. There are really three general classifications of voltages in the Code—0 to 50 volts; 50 to 600 volts; and voltages that exceed 600 volts. Each is dealt with in separate parts of the Code. If wires having different voltages are run in the same raceway, there are specific rules to be followed.

110-5. Conductors—Unless the material of which the conductor is made is specifically identified, it is assumed to be copper. Any other material of which a conductor shall be made, such as aluminum, shall be identified as such.

Copper and aluminum conductors have different ampacities. These are covered in Article 310. Copper-clad aluminum has the same ampacity as aluminum conductors.

110-6. Conductor Sizes—In dealing with wire sizes, the Code always refers to the American Wire Gage (AWG). At one time, this was known as the B&S Gage. Sizes of conductors larger than 4/0 are measured in MCMs.

110-7. Insulation Integrity—All wiring installed shall be installed free of shorts and grounds. This does not cover conductors potentially grounded, as covered in Article 250.

Shorts or grounds may be located before energizing circuits by use of a Megger® (Biddle Co.).

Conductors of the same circuit and in the same raceway must be insulated with the same type material, etc. They should therefore have insulation resistance tests on each conductor that are very close to being the same values. A case in point: six–500 MCM, THW, conductors in the same conduit, read approximately 1500 megohms on four conductors and in the vicinity of 300 megohms on the other two conductors. The 300 megohms would have been a good value, but the difference in the readings indicated problems. The low reading cables were pulled out, and it was found that the insulation had been cut in many places. With time and condensation moisture, a fault would have occurred.

110-8. Wiring Methods—Only recognized and suitable wiring methods are included in the Code. Basically, Chapter 3 covers approved wiring methods; Chapters 5 through 8 cover specific conditions and occupancies. For instance, the question of whether plastic or flexible tubing is permitted often arises. The tubing referred to comes in rolls, such as flexible water pipe. Rigid nonmetallic conduit (Article 347) and electrical metallic tubing (Article 331) are the only types in the plastics category that are approved at the present time.

110-9. Interrupting Capacity—Interrupting capacity is far different from the rating of the amperes that is required by a load. We are faced with what is known as fault currents. A fault current is the amount of current that might develop under a dead-short condition. At one time, this was not much of a problem, but with increased electrical use and larger generating and distribution capacities, the problem of fault currents has increased. As you read the Code, you will find that this is taken more into consideration now than in the past, and will no doubt become an increasingly important factor. If a piece of equipment is rated at X number of amperes, this does not necessarily mean that it can be disconnected under load or faults without damage. Equipment is rated in carrying capacity as well as interrupting capacity.

110-10. Circuit Impedance and Other Characteristics—The fault currents are limited only by the capacity of the electrical supply, the impedance of the supplying circuits, and the wiring. As an example, the fault current will be much larger in circuits supplied from a large-capacity transformer supplying a heavily loaded city block than the fault current from a transformer serving a 5-horsepower irrigation pump in a rural area. The impedance of the supply to the 5-horsepower motor will be high in comparison to the impedance of the supply to the city block.

It is necessary to understand fault currents, circuit impedances, and component short-circuit withstanding ratings. Fuse and breaker manufacturers have available easy-to-understand literature on fault currents and impedances to make it simple to check whether the equipment will withstand available fault currents.

110-11. Deteriorating Agents—Environmental factors, such as wetness, dampness, fumes, vapors, gases, liquids, temperatures, and any other deteriorating effects, must also be noted; conductors and equipment used shall be approved for the specific conditions of operation. The inspection authority is often faced with the responsibility of deciding in which category the installation belongs; it most certainly is beyond the scope of the Code to define and specify for every possible condition that will have to be met. The NFPA National Fire Codes will be of great value in this respect.

Protection shall be given to equipment, such as control equipment, utilization equipment, and busways during construction, if this equipment is approved for dry locations only. It shall not be permanently damaged by weather during the building construction. Section 300-6 further discusses protection from corrosion.

110-12. Mechanical Execution of Work—Electricians are required to install all electrical work in a neat and workmanlike manner. Materials are not the only items to be watched; workmanship is also important. Not only is this necessary for safety, but an electrician is recognized by the work that he or she performs.

110-13. Mounting and Cooling of Equipment.

(a) **Mounting.** Mounting of equipment is an item directly related to workmanship. Wooden plugs driven into holes in masonry, plaster, concrete, etc., will shrink and rot, thereby allowing the equipment to become loose. Therefore, only approved methods of mounting and special anchoring devices may be used.

(b) **Cooling.** Electricity produces heat. Electrical equipment shall be so installed that circulation of air and convection methods of cooling will not be interfered with, by mounting too close to walls, ceilings, floors, or other items which will interfere with the cooling of the electric equipment, by means for which it was designed. Ventilation openings in the electric equipment shall be free to permit natural circulation.

One should also watch the amount of total space of the room where the equipment is mounted. If it is inadequate to permit a low enough ambient temperature, means must be taken to permit the lowering of high ambient temperatures by natural or other means.

110-14. Electrical Connections—Because values of electrolysis vary among metals, and since fundamentally we are using copper or aluminum conductors, copper, being the more noble on the electrolysis series, will corrode the aluminum away. Therefore you must be sure when making splices of terminations that the lugs or connectors be listed for the purpose for which you are using them. When using solder fluxes or inhibitors, make sure they are listed for the job you are doing. Wherever values for tightening torques are given they shall be adhered to.

The author has found very little information on torquing values available. Therefore it might be appropriate to insert some torquing values in this

Tightening Torque in Pound-Feet—Screw Fit

Wire Size, AWG	Driver	Bolt	Other
18–16	1.67	6.25	4.2
14–8	1.67	6.25	6.125
6–4	3.0	12.5	8.0
3–1	3.2	21.00	10.40
0–2/0	4.22	29	12.5
AWG 200MCM	—	37.5	17.0
250–300	—	50.0	21.0
400	—	62.5	21.0
500	—	62.5	25.0
600–750	—	75.0	25.0
800–1000	—	83.25	33.0
1250–2000	—	83.26	42.0

Screws

Screw Size, Inches Across Hex Flats	Torque, Pound-Feet
1/8	4.2
5/32	8.3
3/16	15
7/32	23.25
1/4	42

book. Many breakdowns and possible fires might result from poor workmanship in not adhering to proper torquing values, so the tables here are presented as guidelines for tightening connections. It might also be mentioned that dies on compression tools do wear; and to avoid breakdowns, The Biddle Co.'s Ducter can prevent this problem, as it will read down to one-half millionth of an ohm. This instrument has been invaluable to me.

You will find additional torquing pressures in mechanical engineering handbooks. Loose connections can be a hazard, causing breakdowns and possibly fires. If the authority having jurisdiction so wishes, they may require torquing tests during inspections.

Bolts

Size	Duronze	Steel	Aluminum
Standard, Unlubricated			
3/8	20	15	16
1/2	40	25	35
5/8	70	50	50
3/4	100	90	70
Lubricated			
3/8	15	10	13
1/2	30	20	25
5/8	50	40	40
3/4	85	70	60

(a) **Terminals.** Connections to terminals shall ensure a good electrical and mechanical contact without injury to the conductors; connection shall be by approved pressure connectors, solder lugs, or splices to flexible wires. The exception to the regulation is that No. 10 or smaller stranded conductors can be connected by means of clamps or screws

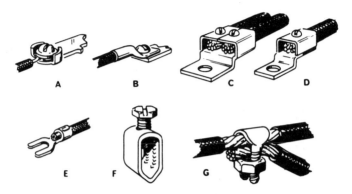

Fig. 110-1. Various types of approved pressure connectors. (A) Terminal plate; (B) Soldered lug; (C) Double pressure-type lug; (D) Single pressure-type lug; (E) Open-end crimp-type lug; (F) Pressure-type connector; (G) Split-bolt clamp.

with terminal plates having upturned lugs (Fig. 110-1). Terminals for more than one conductor must be of the approved type for this purpose. When permitted to place a wire under a terminal screw, wrap it in such a direction that when you tighten the screw the wire will not be squeezed out from under the head of the screw.

Compression-type connections are extremely good if the proper compression tool is used and it is in good shape.

Exception: No. 10 or smaller conductors may be used for screws, studs, or nuts that have upturned lugs or equal design to keep the wire connection in place.

Any terminal or lug intended for use with aluminum shall be so marked.

When permitted to place a wire under a terminal screw, wrap it in such a direction that when you tighten the screw the wire will not squeeze out from under the head of the screw. On the smaller sizes of conductors, especially cord conductors, it is well to twist the conductor strands and apply some solder to them.

(b) **Splices.** Splices in wires are permissible in the proper places. When making a splice, the wires must be clean and a good electrical and mechanical connection must be made. The wires may then be soldered, provided a suitable solder and flux are used. The soldering temperature should be carefully controlled since a cold solder joint is of no value; also, if the wires become too hot, the heat will damage the insulation. Remember that soldering is not permitted on conductors used for grounding. Approved connectors may also be used for splices, making sure the wires are clean and free from corrosion. After splicing, insulation at least equivalent to that on the wire must be applied to the splice. In general, this applies to all splices, but on high-voltage splicing, the specifications supplied with the high-voltage cables should be followed.

This is extremely important. Many electrical connections fail because they are improperly made. Many troubles have been due to electrolysis between different metals; that is, the more noble metal depleting the less noble metal. Also, the oxidation of aluminum conductors (and this oxidation occurs practically instantly) creates a layer having a very high resistance.

Another problem is the coefficient of expansion of different metals, creeping, and the difference in deformation of different metals. A copper-clad aluminum has appeared on the market. This has been approved, but precautions must be taken in its use, especially with copper or plain aluminum. Be certain that you use connectors approved for use with this new product.

Inhibitors for use with aluminum are very important. Do not rely on the inhibitor alone, but thoroughly brush the aluminum conductor to remove the oxide film and then immediately apply the inhibitor to prevent the recurrence of the oxide film.

110-16. Working Space about Electric Equipment (600 Volts, Nominal, or Less)—Adequate space for safety must be maintained for easy maintenance of equipment.

(a) **Working Clearances.** Tables appearing in the *NEC* will not appear in this book. For working clearances, refer to Table 110-16(a) in your *NEC*.

(1) In this portion, insulated wire or busbars are not considered live parts. Any exposed energized parts or those parts that are grounded on the opposite side from the working space, or if there are exposed live parts on both sides of the equipment, suitable or other insulating materials must be installed for protection only the live parts described above.

From this we might look at such a panel that will have to be worked on from time to time, as coming under Condition 1 and give a minimum of 3 feet clearance. This will apply to busbars and conductors as well.

(2) In part Condition 1 the panel was used as an example; but since the panel is usually contained in a metal enclosure, we must also look at part Condition 2, where we find that this part might be used under certain conditions.

(3) Condition 1 might be an electrical closet, where panels are on two walls, then 3- and 4-ft. conditions will prevail.

Exception No. 1: See the *NEC.*

Exception No. 2: The inspection authority has the right to make exceptions for smaller spaces where it seems appropriate. These judgments pertain if the particular arrangement of the installation shows it will provide sufficient accessibility or if all insulated parts do not carry more than 30 volts RMS or 42 volts dc.

Concrete, brick, or tile walls very definitely are to be considered as grounds.

(b) **Clear Spaces.** See the *NEC.*

(c) **Access and Entrance to Working Space.** This portion is very important for persons working in the area discussed above. There shall be at least one entrance that is large enough to give adequate working space to the electrical equipment therein. Where switchboards and control panels are located with a rating of 1200 amperes or more and 6 feet or more in width, it is required that one entrance be at least 24 inches in width and 6.5 feet in height at each end. (Thus, in cases such as this at least two entrances are required.)

Exception No. 1: This allows for a continuous unobstructed way of exit wherever switchboards or panelboards are located.

Exception No. 2: See the *NEC.*

(d) **Front Working Space.** See the *NEC.*

(e) **Illumination.** See the *NEC.*

(f) **Headroom.** See the *NEC.*

110-17. Guarding of Live Parts (600 Volts, Nominal, or Less)—

This section applies to parts supplied with 600 volts or less.

(a) **Live Parts Guarded Against Accidental Contact.** This covers the guarding or protecting of live parts of electrical equipment that are operated at 50 volts or more, so as to prevent accidental contact with them. Approved cabinets or enclosures shall be used, according to the requirements in other portions of the Code. The following are the means by which this shall be accomplished.

(1) Many references are made to qualified persons only having access to rooms, vaults, etc. It is recommended that the reader turn back to Article 100 and review the definition of qualified persons.

(2) So that only qualified persons may have access to live parts, suitable partitions or screens shall be installed to keep away unqualified persons. Openings to live parts shall be of such a size that unqualified persons will be kept from accidentally contacting with live parts. Again, qualified persons are mentioned. Their safety is thought of in making the equipment accessible without obstruction and giving attention to the contact of conducting materials such as conduit or pipes.

(3) Balconies, galleries, or platforms shall have sufficient elevations and be so arranged that unqualified persons have no access to live parts.

(4) Any live parts of equipment that are elevated a minimum of 8 feet or more above the floor or other accessible places are considered accessible to qualified persons only.

(b) **Prevent Physical Damage.** Many times electrical equipment is located in a work area where the activity around it might damage the equipment. In such a case, the enclosures or guards shall be of such strength as to prevent any damage to the electrical equipment.

(c) **Warning Signs.** Warning signs shall be posted at entrances to rooms or other guarded locations, giving warning that only qualified personnel are permitted to enter. Although not specifically covered here, posting of dangers that might exist in any situation is always good safety practice.

Motors are covered in Sections 430-132 and 420-133, and if over 600 volts, refer to Section 110-34.

110-18. Arcing Parts—Making and breaking of contacts usually cause sparking or arcing. Also, the white-hot filament of a lightbulb broken while in operation takes a little time to cool. Any parts that normally cause arcing or sparking are to be enclosed unless they are isolated or separated from combustible material. Lightbulbs were mentioned, but additional information will be given in the articles covering hazardous areas, along with the specific requirements for switches, outlets, and other devices in hazardous locations.

Hazardous areas are covered in Sections 500 through 517.

110-19. Light and Power from Railway Conductors—It is not permissible to connect any circuits for light or power to any trolley wires that use a ground return signal.

The exceptions to this include car houses or any other freight station, etc., that operates with the electric railways.

110-21. Marking—See the *NEC.*

110-22. Identification of Disconnecting Means—It is essential that disconnecting means for appliances, motors, feeders, and branch circuits be properly identified as to what the disconnect serves. Such markings shall be legible and durable. Panels usually have a card with the circuit numbers marked, which should be filled out in its entirety as a permanent record. The author has found this to be one of the most frequent violations of the Code.

B. Over 600 Volts, Nominal

110-30. General—Since 1975, throughout the Code at the end of various Articles, additions have been made to cover over 600 volts, nominal. It is the intent that conductors and equipment used on volts higher than

600 volts, nominal, comply with this article and with all applicable Articles. It is not intended that provisions of this article apply to equipment on the supply side of the service conductors.

110-31. Enclosure for Electrical Installations—In areas where access is controlled by lock and key or other approved means, these areas shall be considered as accessible to qualified persons only. Involved are: vault installations, room or closet installations, and areas surrounded by walls, screens, or fences.

The design and construction of enclosures shall be suitable to the nature and degree of hazard involved.

Any wall or fence less than 8 feet in height is not considered as preventing access. An 8-foot fence or wall is considered to be adequate. Fences or walls of lower height must have additional protection to the 8-foot limit.

Transformer vaults are covered by Article 450.

(a) **Indoor Installations.**

    (1) **In Places Accessible to Unqualified Persons.** This covers indoor installations to which unqualified persons might have access. The equipment shall be made with metal enclosures or a vault that is accessible only by lock and key.

        Unit substations and any pullboxes or other means of connection associated with the equipment must be permanently marked with caution signs. Dry-type transformers must be ventilated so that they have openings in the equipment, but they shall be designed in such a manner that foreign objects inserted through the ventilating holes will have something to deflect them from the live parts.

    (2) **In Places Accessible to Qualified Persons Only.** Sections 110-34, 710-34, and 710-33 are to be used in compliance when indoor electrical installations are considered accessible to qualified persons. A number of these rulings formerly appeared in Article 710. These have been deleted and appear in other articles and sections of the Code.

(b) **Outdoor Installations.**

    (1) **In Places Accessible to Unqualified Persons.** Article 225 covers outdoor installations that are accessible to unqualified persons.

        The National Electrical Safety Code (ANSI) C2-1984 covers the clearance of conductors that are over 600 volts nominal.

    (2) **In Places Accessible to Qualified Persons Only.** Sections 110-34, 710-32, and 710-33 cover places of outdoor electrical installations where exposed live parts may be accessible to qualified persons. These sections mentioned deal with voltages over 600, nominal, and need not be repeated here.

(c) **Metal-Enclosed Equipment Accessible to Unqualified Persons.** Where equipment requires ventilation or other openings, the design of the equipment shall be such that foreign objects that might be inserted into ventilating openings will be deflected so as not to contact any live parts. Any such equipment that is in a position where it may be physically damaged from passing traffic shall be protected by a suitable guard. Sometimes metal-enclosed equipment has to be located outdoors, where it might be damaged by the general public. If so, the design of such equipment shall be such that any exposed bolts, nuts, and so forth cannot easily be removed by the public, and if such electrical equipment is located outdoors and is less than 8 feet from floor or ground, any doors or covers shall be hinged and capable of being locked.

110-32. Work Space about Equipment—There shall be sufficient clear space about high-voltage equipment to permit ready and safe operation of such equipment.

If any energized parts are exposed, they shall not be less than 6½ feet measured vertically from any floor or platform, or less than 3 feet wide, measurement being parallel to the equipment. In all cases the width shall not be less than the space required for doors or hinge panels to open to a position of at least 90 degrees.

110-33. Entrance and Access to Work Space.

(a) **Entrance.** The requirements for the entrance are to be not less than 6½ feet in height and not less than 2 feet in width. Adequate space must be provided for access to the working space around electrical equipment. If the switchboard or controller panels are more than 6 feet wide, entrance at each end will be required for both panel boards.

See the *NEC* for Exceptions Nos. 1 and 2.

When only one entry is provided, it shall be so located that the distance from switchboard to panel board meets the minimum requirements for distance away from the equipment given in Table 110-34(a).

If bare or insulated parts of more than 600 volts, nominal, are located adjacent to such entrances, there shall be suitable means taken to guard them.

(b) **Access.** When electric equipment is installed on platforms, balconies, mezzanine floors, or in attic or roof rooms or spaces, there shall be permanent ladders or stairways installed for access. (There is an OSHA regulation which requires ladders to extend 3 feet above the platform, etc., to which they give access.)

110-34. Work Space and Guarding.

(a) **Working Space.** The minimum clear working space in front of electric equipment such as switchboards, control panels, switches, circuit breakers, motor controllers, relays, and similar equipment shall not be less than specified in Table 110-34(a) in the *NEC* unless otherwise specified in this Code. Distances shall be measured from the live parts if such are exposed, or from the enclosure front or opening if such are enclosed.

(1) Insulated wire or insulated busbars, if they do not have over 300 volts, shall not be considered to be live parts. If live parts are exposed on any one side and the parts on the other side are grounded in the working space, or if suitable guards, made of wood or other insulating materials, are in place, then the live parts shall be considered suitably protected.

(2) See the *NEC*.

(3) See the *NEC*.

Exception: The deenergized parts are to be worked from the back on enclosed equipment. The required work space is 30 inches nominal. If dead-front switchboards or control assemblies are in use, there are no fuses or breakers or adjustable parts on the back, and all connections are accessible from places other than the back, then the above 30-inch requirement will apply.

(b) **Separation from Low-Voltage Equipment.** When there is any low-voltage equipment in the room or enclosure, such as switches, cut-outs, or other equipment that operates at 600 volts, nominal, or less, all exposed live parts or exposed wiring that operates at more than 600 volts, nominal, must be separated effectively from the low-voltage equipment and wiring by suitable partitions, screens, or fences.

Many utility companies will not permit low voltage in transformer vaults with high voltage, with the exception of low-voltage buses. This does not include lighting and other low voltage that might be required in the operation of the high-voltage equipment.

Exception: When 600 volts or less for switches or other equipment servicing only equipment within the high-voltage room, vault, or enclosure. Such equipment in use in conjunction therewith at a voltage of 600 or less, nominal, may be installed in the room that is accessible to qualified persons only.

(c) **Locked Rooms or Enclosures.** When there are live parts or exposed conductors that operate at over 600 volts, nominal, the entrances to any such building shall be locked. There is an exception: Such locked entrances must be under the observation of qualified persons at all times. Permanent and conspicuous caution signs are to be installed conspicuously where the voltage exceeds 600 volts, nominal, and contain the message "WARNING—HIGH VOLTAGE—KEEP OUT."

(d) **Illumination.** Adequate illumination shall be provided to properly illuminate the high-voltage area for safe working and the fixtures are to be installed so that there will be no danger to anyone changing bulbs or working on the illumination system. The switching points for this illumination shall be readily accessible and in such a place that, in operating the controls for the illumination, there is no danger of coming into contact with any live parts.

(e) See Table 110-34(e) for elevation of unguarded live parts.

CHAPTER 2

Wiring Design and Protection

ARTICLE 200—USE AND IDENTIFICATION OF GROUNDED CONDUCTORS

200-1. Scope—Grounding is very important, and the conductors that are grounded intentionally must have identification to indicate for what grounding purpose they are used. This also indicates that terminals to which grounded conductors are attached shall be identified. There are a number of definitions pertaining to grounding in Article 100. These seem to confuse some wiremen. This will be covered further in Article 250.

200-2. General—All premise wiring shall have a grounded conductor, and this conductor shall be identified by white or natural gray insulation as covered in Section 200-6.

There are exceptions to all systems having a grounded conductor, and these exceptions are covered in Sections 210-10, 215-7, 250-3, 250-5, 250-7, 503-13, 517-104, 668-11, 668-21, and 690-41 Exception.

For identification, the conductors that are purposely grounded when they are insulated must have insulation of a different color from that of ungrounded conductors, when the circuit voltage is 1000 volts or less. Circuits not rated less than 600 volts up to 1000 volts and over will be described in Section 250-152(a).

Be sure to read Section 200-6, which covers neutral conductors that are insulated. Section 200-6(b) takes into consideration that in sizes larger than No. 6 it is impossible to find white or natural gray insulation and makes provisions for this.

200-3. Connection to Grounded System—If there is a grounded conductor in the interior wiring system, it shall not be electrically connected to a supply system that does not have a corresponding conductor grounded.

This condition could be dangerous and could cause many varied difficulties that most certainly would not be considered as safe wiring procedures. Electrically connected means that the connections are capable of carrying current. Electromagnetic induction, such as the windings on an isolating transformer, would not be considered electrically connected. Connections capable of carrying current and electromagnetic induction must be separated in one's mind. Later, the text will deal with isolation transformers and give further clarification of how and what parts of the wiring system must be grounded.

200-6. Means of Identifying Grounded Conductors—Insulated conductors of No. 6 or smaller wire, when used as identified, grounded conductors, shall have a white or natural gray colored insulation. Conductors of color other than white or natural gray that have any color trace in the braid and that identify the source of manufacture will be considered as meeting the requirement of Section 200-6. If the insulated conductors are larger than No. 6, they shall be identified by a white or natural gray colored insulation, or by a distinctive marking (white) at the terminals while they are being installed. Type MI cable has bare conductors, so identification of the grounded conductors shall be marked generally by sleeving during the installation; the sleeving shall be white or natural gray, as indicated in Fig. 200-1.

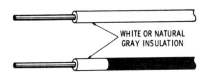

WHITE OR NATURAL
GRAY INSULATION

#6 OR SMALLER WIRE SHALL HAVE
WHITE OR NATURAL GRAY INSULATION

WIRE LARGER THAN #6 MAY HAVE
WHITE TAPE OR PAINT TO INDICATE
GROUNDED CONDUCTORS

Fig. 200-1. Method of identifying grounded conductors.

The insulated conductor which is intended to be used in flexible cords for the grounded conductor shall be white or natural gray insulation. In Section 400-22, there are some other means of identification permitted.

Where maintenance supervision will be done only by qualified persons, grounded conductors in multiconductor cables may, at time of installation, be identified with a distinctive white marking, or any other equally effective means.

Grounded Conductors of Different Systems. It is sometimes necessary to run different systems with the grounded conductor for each system in the same raceway or other type of enclosure. Therefore it becomes necessary for each grounded conductor for each of the systems involved to have its own identification. One grounded conductor may be white and others may be white with color tracers, provided the color tracer is not green.

200-7. Use of White or Natural Gray Color—White or natural gray is to be used only for the identification of grounded conductors. There are a few exceptions made necessary by the use of cords and cables, such as types AC, NM, and UF. These cables must always carry a white or natural gray conductor. If a cable with a white or gray conductor is used on a multiwire circuit in a circuit connected to the two *hot* legs of a 3-wire circuit (as in Fig. 200-2), or if 3-wire cable is used on a 3-phase system, the white or natural gray conductor shall be reidentified at its terminals.

When two or three wires are used for a single-pole or three-way switch, conductors in a cable assembly do not have to be reidentified, providing the wire feeding the switch is white or natural gray and is connected to the black wire at the source. The black wire will be connected from the switch to the load as shown in Fig. 200-3.

When a flexible cord is permitted for connecting an appliance and the cord used has a white or natural gray conductor or other means permitted in Section 400-22, this conductor may be used even though it is not connected to a receptacle which has a grounded circuit.

If a circuit is less than 50 volts, a white or natural gray conductor must be grounded if required by Section 250-5(a).

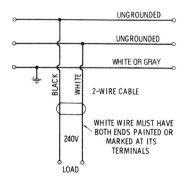

Fig. 200-2. A 2-wire cable connected to the two hot wires of a 3-wire circuit.

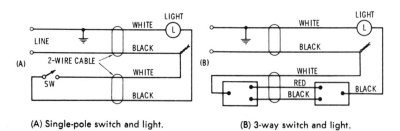

(A) Single-pole switch and light.   (B) 3-way switch and light.

Fig. 200-3. Method of connecting a common light and switch.

200-9. Means of Identification of Terminals—Terminals used by grounded conductors shall be substantially white in color. Other terminals not used for grounded conductors shall be colors other than white.

Where maintenance is done only by qualified persons, grounded conductors may be permanently marked at the time of installation by effective means; for instance, grounded conductors shall be marked with white or natural gray, and equipment grounding conductors shall be bare or marked with green.

200-10. Identification of Terminals.

(a) **Device Terminals.** All devices and equipment that have terminals with which to attach conductors to more than one conductor of a circuit shall be permanently marked so as to distinguish between the ungrounded conductor, the grounded conductor, and equipment grounding conductors.

This would not apply to a single pole toggle switch that opens or closes one conductor of a circuit. Terminals of lighting appliance branch-circuit panel boards are also an exception, because it is obvious where hot conductors, grounded conductors, and equipment-grounding conductors shall be attached. On devices having over 30 amperes normal current capacity, unless they are polarized attachment plugs or polarized receptacles for attachment—which are to be shown in (b) below—the terminals need not be identified.

(b) **Receptacles, Plugs, and Connectors.** The terminals intended for attaching the grounded conductor (white or natural gray) on receptacles, polarized attachment plugs and cord connectors for plugs and polarized plugs is required to have the terminal that is intended to be used for connecting the grounded conductor colored substantially white in color, such as chrome plated, etc., by a metal or metal coating, white in color, or the word "white" shall be located by this terminal.

Should the terminal not be visible, the hole where the conductor is inserted must be either white in color or engraved with the word "white." This indicates that the terminal is for use with either a white-colored or natural gray-colored conductor.

The terminal for attaching equipment grounding conductors must be a green, hexagonal, nonremovable screw or terminal nut, or a green pressure connector. If, instead of attaching the conductors under screws, the conductor is pushed into a hole with pressure connection, the entrance for the equipment grounding conductor must be a distinctive green color.

Exception: Two-wire nonpolarized attachment plugs need no terminal identification. The use of 2-wire nonpolarized attachment plugs becomes less and less frequent as Code changes are made. Their use is principally on existing wiring installations or on approved double-insulated tools.

(c) **Screw Shells.** For devices such as lamp sockets, the shells or thread part of the socket must be connected only to the grounded conductor. An example of this may be seen in Fig. 200-4. This is true of all devices having screw shells, with the exception of screw-shell (edison base) fuseholders.

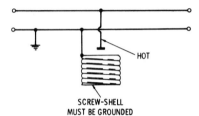

SCREW-SHELL
MUST BE GROUNDED

Fig. 200-4. Illustrating the grounding of a screw-shellbase.

(d) **Screw-Shell Devices with Leads.** This part covers items commonly known as pigtail sockets; the lead that connects to the shell must be white or natural gray. The same will be true of lighting fixtures that have the leads attached.

(e) **Appliances.** Appliances to be connected (1) by permanent wiring methods or (2) by field-installed plugs and cords with three or more wires shall have marking to identify the terminal for the grounded circuit conductor. Appliances that have a single-pole switch or a single-pole overcurrent device in the line or any screw-shell lampholder shall meet (1) or (2) of this paragraph, and an equipment grounding conductor shall be included.

This should be called to your attention in more detail. An electric range or electric dryer circuit which is supplied from the service-equipment panel may have the grounded conductor (neutral) connected to the range or dryer frame as an equipment grounding conductor also. If these circuits are from a feeder panel, the grounded conductor shall NOT be used as the equipment grounding conductor and it shall be insulated, but a fourth conductor of green color or bare shall be used as the equipment grounding conductor. Refer to Section 250-60, which also refers you to Sections 250-57 and 250-59.

200-11. Polarity of Connections—See the *NEC*.

ARTICLE 210—BRANCH CIRCUITS

A. General Provisions

210-1. Scope—Branch circuits are defined and explained in Article 100. This article applies to branch circuits supplying lighting or appliance loads or combinations of such loads. Motor branch circuits will be covered under Article 430.

See Section 668-3(c)—the exceptions for electrolytic cells—for exceptions to the above.

210-2. Other Articles for Specific-Purpose Branch Circuits—There are a number of exceptions or supplemental provisions of this article on branch circuits. The listings of many of these exceptions are given in the Code under Section 210-2. Changes have been made in the *NEC* amending or supplementing the provisions therein. They are not quoted here because the article and section that apply are in the Code. Refer to the *NEC* for a listing of additional systems and the sections in which they are to be found.

210-3. Classifications—In general, branch circuits will be classified by the maximum permitted ampere rating or setting of the overcurrent device. Otherwise, they will be classified as 15, 20, 30, 40, and 50 amperes. If conductors of higher ampacity are used, the ampere rating or setting of the specified overcurrent device shall determine the classification of the branch circuit.

As an illustration, if there is a 15-ampere protective device in a circuit wired with No. 12 conductors, this will be a 15-ampere branch circuit; you cannot make a 20-ampere branch circuit out of it merely because it uses No. 12 conductors. In all probability, the No. 12 wire was installed to handle a voltage drop which was too great, or, if installed in a raceway, it is possible that derating was required because of the fill. Derating will be thoroughly covered in Article 310.

Exception: In industrial premises that are maintained and supervised by qualified persons servicing the equipment outlet circuits, greater than 50 amperes will be permitted. Note that this will be an exception rather than a general rule.

210-4. Multiwire Branch Circuits—The definition of a multiwire branch circuit was covered in Article 100. So that multiwire circuits will be thoroughly understood and the terminology used properly, diagrams are included to explain them more fully. On a delta-connected, 4-wire system, only two ungrounded conductors and the neutral will be considered as the multiwire branch circuit. Fig. 210-1 shows a multiwire branch circuit from a 4-wire delta system; note that the ungrounded conductors extend from phases A and B. Phases A and B and the neutral satisfy the condition of a multiwire branch circuit since there are 120 volts from A to the neutral,

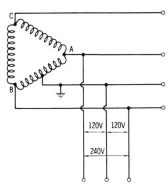

Fig. 210-1. One type of multiwire circuit from a 4-wire delta system.

120 volts from B to the neutral, and 240 volts from A to B. There is an equal potential difference between each phase wire and the neutral, and a difference of potential between the two phase wires.

A multiwire circuit shall be considered as multiple circuits, and it is required that all conductors of such a circuit shall originate from the same panel.

Fig. 210-2 does not satisfy the multiwire branch circuit conditions; both ungrounded phases are connected to the same phase, and so there is no difference of potential between the phase wires. Fig. 210-3 does not satisfy the definition of a multiwire branch circuit; there is a voltage between the phase wires, but the same potential difference does not exist between each phase wire and the neutral. On the wye system, shown in Fig. 210-4, the three phase conductors and the neutral satisfy the requirements for a multiwire branch circuit. Any two phase wires and the neutral satisfy the conditions; therefore, this is a multiwire branch circuit.

Fig. 210-5, which is a 3-wire, 120/240-volt single-phase circuit, is also a multiwire circuit. Fig. 210-6 does not satisfy the requirements of a multiwire branch circuit because there is no potential difference (zero voltage) between the two ungrounded phase conductors. Multiwire branch circuits are often misinterpreted. When the conditions of multiwire branch circuits are

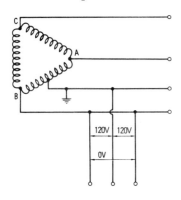

Fig. 210-2.   This is not a multiwire circuit from a 4-wire delta system.

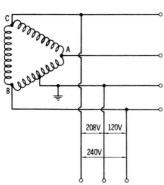

Fig. 210-3.   This is not a multiwire circuit from a 4-wire delta system.

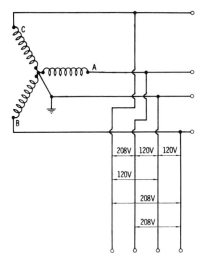

Fig. 210-4. A multiwire circuit from a 4-wire wye system.

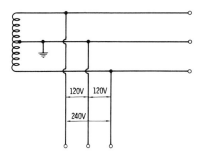

Fig. 210-5. A 3-wire, 120/240-volt, multiwire circuit.

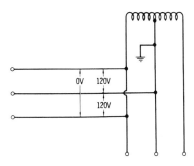

Fig. 210-6. This is not a multiwire circuit.

misapplied, the neutral may be forced to carry a heavy current, and this heavy current will result in heating and damage to the conductor insulation. There is no illustration of a 277/480-volt wye system, but the same would apply as with the 120/208-volt wye system.

A device with a means of disconnecting simultaneously all ungrounded conductors at the panel board where the multiwire branch circuit originates, is required in dwelling units if multiwire circuits supply more than one device or equipment on the same yoke.

If only one piece of utilization equipment is on a multiwire circuit, the above does not apply.

All multiwire branch circuits should have a breaker that opens both hot conductors at the same time.

The above exceptions are for the reason that if one overcurrent device wire opened and multiwire circuit supplied a circuit with only the hot conductors being used, a very severe safety hazard could result.

The continuity of the grounded conductor on multiwire circuits must be maintained. This will be covered later in Section 300-13(b).

210-5. Color Code for Branch Circuits.

(a) **Grounded Conductor.** When a branch circuit has a grounded conductor, and this grounded conductor may be a neutral or one phase of a delta supply which is grounded, the grounded conductor shall have insulation (continuous) that is white or natural gray color. See Fig. 210-7.

Where there is a raceway, box, gutter, or any other type enclosure, with conductors from more than one system and neutrals or grounded conductors involved, one system shall use a white or natural gray

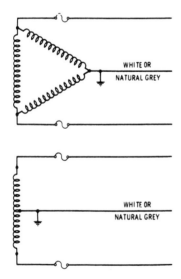

WHITE OR
NATURAL GREY

WHITE OR
NATURAL GREY

Fig. 210-7. Showing a grounded conductor in a branch circuit.

color for its neutral—a second system shall use the other color and more systems with neutrals will use a white conductor with a colored stripe for neutral. Thus, each system neutral may be easily identified. This colored stripe should not be green since green always indicates equipment grounding conductors. It is up to the authority having jurisdiction to accept or reject the other means of identification.

Exception No. 1: Since mineral-insulated cable consists of bare conductors surrounded by insulating powder and the entirety encased in a metal sheath, it becomes necessary at terminations to identify the neutral conductor. This is generally done by slipping the wide insulating sheath over one bare conductor.

Exception No. 2: More color coding insulated neutrals will be covered in Exception No. 2 of Section 200-6(a) and the exception with Section 200-6(b).

(b) **Equipment Grounding Conductor.** If a conductor is used as a grounding conductor, it may be a continuous green color or a continuous green color with one or more yellow stripes, or bare. Green, green with yellow stripes, and bare are used only as grounding conductors. There is an exception to the bare conductor under services, and with SE Cable.

Exception No. 1: The exception will be found in other sections later in the Code under grounding and conductors.

Exception No. 2: When equipment is internally wired, green conductors may be used for current carrying conductors, but we must stop where the lead wires from a branch circuit attach to the equipment. Green, green with yellow stripes, and in most cases bare shall never be used as the grounded conductor.

210-6. Branch Circuit Voltage Limitations.

(a) **Occupancy Limitation.** There have been major additions to this section. It includes all dwelling units, which in turn could include guest rooms, hotels, motels, etc., where the voltage shall not exceed 120 volts, nominal. When the conductor supply terminals of the following:
See numbers 1 and 2 in the *NEC.*

(b) **120 Volts Between Conductors.** Voltages exceeding 120 volts, nominal, between conductors are permitted to supply the following:
See numbers 1, 2, and 3 in the *NEC.*

(c) **277 Volts to Ground.** Circuits not exceeding 277 volts to ground, but lower than 120 volts to ground, nominal, are permitted to supply the following:
See numbers 1, 2, and 3 in the *NEC.*

(d) **600 Volts Between Conductors.** Circuits having 600 volts and more than 277 volts, nominal, between conductors are permitted to supply the following:

The alternative equipment supplies electric discharge fixtures if they are mounted according to one of the following:

(a) On poles or similar structures used to light outdoor areas that include streets, roads, bridges, highways, athletic fields, or parking lots, provided they are mounted a minimum of 22 feet in height.

(b) **A minimum height of 18 feet on structures such as tunnels.**
Permanently connected utilization of cord and plug equipment.

See *NEC* Section 410-78 for auxiliary equipment limitations.

Exception No. 1: Section 422-15(c) covers lampholders for infrared or industrial heating appliances. This exception applies to (b), (c), and (d) above. This applies to railroad properties as described in Section 110-19 and covers (b), (c), and (d) above.

210-7. Receptacles and Cord Connectors.

(a) **Grounding Type.** Grounding-type receptacles and cord connectors shall be installed on 15- and 20-ampere branch circuits. The voltage class and current rating of receptacles must be adhered to in installing grounding type receptacles. Exceptions to this are covered in Tables 210-21(b)(2) and (b)(3).

In Section 210-7(d) there will be an exception covering nongrounding-type receptacles.

Example: There may be a case where one wishes to use a 30-ampere twist-lock receptacle on a 30-ampere branch circuit, which is quite permissible. But it would not be permissible to use a 20-ampere twist-lock receptacle on a 30-ampere branch circuit.

(b) **To Be Grounded.** Effective grounds must be supplied to receptacles before connectors that have grounding contacts. The nongrounding type receptacle is only being used for some replacement purposes.

Exception No. 1: In order to take care of receptacles that are mounted on portable and vehicle-mounted generators an exception is granted if the requirements of Section 250-6 are met.

Section 210-7(d) exception permits ground-fault circuit interrupters as replacement receptacles. Where a nongrounding receptacle appears and there is a chance of an unqualified person coming in contact with it, the author highly recommends replacing the nongrounding receptacle with a GFCI.

(c) **Methods of Grounding.** Grounding-type receptacles and cord connectors with grounding contacts shall be effectively grounded. This shall be accomplished by means of a grounding conductor or metallic raceway in lieu thereof, which shall be connected to the grounding screw of the receptacle or other approved means. Section 250-91(b) will cover the acceptable means of grounding.

An exception has been inserted to take care of additions to existing systems that do not have a grounded raceway or a grounding conductor. The grounding-type receptacle may be connected to a water pipe near the receptacle. See Fig. 210-8. The Code specifically states a grounded water pipe; make certain that the pipe is grounded before using it under this exception. The connection illustrated in Fig. 210-8 is covered in Section 250-50 in the exception for (a) and (b).

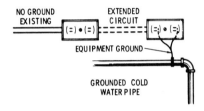

NO GROUND
EXISTING

EXTENDED
CIRCUIT

EQUIPMENT GROUND

GROUNDED COLD
WATER PIPE

Fig. 210-8. Grounding equipment on an existing circuit that is not grounded.

(d) **Replacements.** When nongrounding-type receptacles are being replaced, they shall be replaced by grounding-type receptacles and in equipment grounding conductor provided as covered in (c) above.

Where there is no existing equipment grounding conductor to supply a receptacle enclosure, either a nongrounding or a GFCI type of receptacle must be used. But the GFCI cannot supply other receptacles.

(e) **Cord- and Plug-Connected Equipment.** The fact that a grounding-type receptacle is installed does not necessarily mean that all equipment plugged into this grounding-type receptacle need be of the grounded type of equipment. Section 250-45 covers the types of portable equipment which are to be of the grounded type.

(f) **Noninterchangeable Types.** Occasionally circuits having different voltages for ac or dc, or different frequencies are found on the same premises. This very seldom happens, but the circuitry shall be designed so that the plugs are not interchangeable.

NEMA configurations for receptacles and plugs should be followed. Receptacles rated 20 amperes or less directly connected to aluminum conductors shall be identified for the purpose and marked CO/ALR.

210-8. Ground-Fault Protection for Personnel.

(a) **Dwelling Units.** Ground-fault circuit protection may be used in any location, circuits, or occupancies and will provide additional protection from line-to-ground shock hazards.

(1) For personnel protection, ground-fault circuit-interrupter protection is a requirement for all 125-volt, single-phase, 15- and 20-ampere receptacle outlets installed in bathrooms.

(2) GFCI protection for personnel is required on all 125-volt single-phase, 15- or 20-ampere receptacles, installed in garages. Garages usually have cement or dirt floors, which are always considered to be ground potential.

If a receptacle is not readily accessible, a GFCI is not required. Exceptions to *NEC* Section 210-8(a)(2) are not to be considered as meeting the requirement of Section 210-52(a). In a garage where you have the receptacles without GFCI protection for specific purposes, electric drills or other tools could be easily plugged into one of the receptacles. Since the floors of garages are usually concrete or dirt and the walls brick, unless a GFCI is installed in those outlets it could be hazardous. The exceptions to 210-8(a)(2) do not actually meet the requirements of Section 210-52(f).

(3) Code requires that all 125-volt single-phase 15- and 20-ampere receptacles, which are installed outdoors and are readily accessible to grade level, shall have GFCI protection.

Grade level access means located not more than 6 feet, 6 inches above ground level of dwelling units.

(4) In the basement, at least one 125-volt, 15- or 20-ampere receptacle shall be installed with a GFCI.

(5) Any receptacle in the kitchen over the counter top that is mounted 6 feet or less from the kitchen sink shall have a GFCI for protection of the people.

Note: Receptacles for refrigerators and freezers are exempt from GFCI protection for people. However, if these are within the 6-foot limit from the sink, a shock hazard might still be present.

(6) Boathouse receptacles also require GFCI protection.

(b) **Hotels and Motels.** In the bathrooms or guestrooms of hotels and motels, GFCIs shall be installed for the protection of personnel. This will include all 125-volt, 15- and 20-ampere circuits in the bathroom.

Bathroom—As stated earlier, definitions appear throughout the Code. This is the definition of a bathroom: It is an area including a basin and at least one of the following: a tub, a toilet, or a shower.

It would appear to the author that a ground-fault circuit interrupter would be the least expensive and the most positive protection, for the overall picture.

210-9. Circuits Derived from Autotransformers—An autotransformer is a transformer with only one winding and tap to give different voltages. It shall not be used to supply branch circuits.

Autotransformers are transformers whose windings are common to both primary and secondary. There shall be no autotransformer connected to a system unless there is a grounded conductor solidly connected to a similar grounded conductor of the supply system.

Fig. 210-9 shows three autotransformer connections. Fig. 210-9A and B are both approved connections; Fig. 210-9C is not approved since there is no common ground between the supply and the output of the autotransformer. Fig. 210-10A represents an autotransformer dimmer circuit and is approved by the *NEC*.

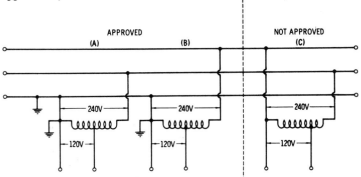

Fig. 210-9. Autotransformer connections.

The above will not apply if the autotransformer is supplied from a system where the ground is connected to the ground supplying the autotransformer.

Autotransformers may be used to extend or add on to a branch circuit in an installation for which equipment is already installed and does not have a connection to a grounded conductor. An example would be changing a 208 volts, nominal, supply to a 240 volts, nominal, supply, or the reverse.

See Fig. 210-10B. The second exception permits autotransformers to be used as booster transformers from 208 to 240 volts, or reducers from 240 to 208 volts. The neutral or grounded conductor that is ordinarily required when autotransformers are used is not required in this case.

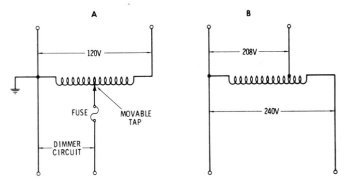

Fig. 210-10. An autotransformer dimmer circuit (A) and a voltage booster (B).

210-10. Ungrounded Conductors Tapped from Grounded System —This section permits two or more ungrounded conductors to be tapped from ungrounded conductors of circuits that have a grounded neutral. One must be careful that these taps are not being made from a multiwire circuit because of feedbacks. It will be recalled that under multiwire circuits this was prohibited.

Two-wire dc circuits and ac circuits of two or more ungrounded conductors may be thus tapped. Switching devices in these tapped circuits shall have a switching pole in each ungrounded conductor and all poles of multipole switching devices shall be manually switched together where such switching devices serve as disconnecting means as covered in Sections 422-21(b) for an appliance; 424-20 for a fixed electric space heating unit; 426-51 for electric de-icing and snow melting equipment; 430-85 for a motor controller; and 430-103 for a motor.

B. Branch-Circuit Ratings

210-19. Conductors—Minimum Ampacity and Size.

(a) **General.** The branch-circuit rating is governed by the breaker size. Conductors shall not be less than the rating of the overcurrent protection, and not less than the maximum load to be served. This also applies to conductors serving branches with more than one receptacle that are to be used for cord and plug loads. These shall have an ampacity that is at least as great as the branch circuit protection. Cable assemblies, if the neutral conductor is smaller than the ungrounded conductors, shall be legibly so marked.

The ampacity ratings of conductors is covered in Tables 310-6 through 310-31. Motor branch-circuit conductor sizing is covered in Part B of Article 430. Chapter 3 will cover temperature limitations. This part was added to the Code in 1965. The conductors for branch circuits shall be so sized that the voltage drop to the farthest outlet used for power, heating, lighting, or combinations of any of these, shall not exceed 3 percent. The maximum allowable voltage drop for combinations of feeder and branch circuits shall not exceed 5 percent. Special noting of this is necessary since it is the first time that branch circuits have been taken into consideration when calculating voltage drop. Voltage drop on feeder conductors is covered in Section 215-2.

(b) **Household Ranges and Cooking Appliances.** There is a table covering range loads in Article 220. However, for range loads of 8¾ kW or more, the minimum branch-circuit rating shall be 40 amperes. This may have to be increased for ranges of larger capacity. The above covers conductors supplying household ranges or other cooking equipment that is wall-mounted or counter-mounted.

In Table 220-19, you will find demand factors for ranges. Most inspection authorities consider that the branch circuit shall not be loaded in excess of 80 percent, as covered elsewhere in the Code, and since this Table covers derating they are very careful as to the ampacity of conductors serving ranges.

Exception No. 1: Branch-circuit conductors to ranges, etc., of 8¾ kW and more are permitted to be smaller than the ungrounded conductors of the circuit. Column A of Table 220-19 computes the ampacities. Neutrals shall not be less than 70 percent of the branch circuit rating, and shall never be smaller than No. 10 AWG.

Exception No. 2: On taps supplying wall-mounted ovens or cooking top units that are supplied by 50-ampere branch circuit, the taps to the additional units shall not be less than 20-ampere capacity, but shall not be less than sufficient to cover the load the taps serve, and these taps shall be no longer than necessary to provide servicing of the equipment involved.

(c) **Other Loads.** When branch-circuit conductors are supplying other than cooking appliances that are covered in (b) above and are listed in Section 210-2, the ampacity of the conductors shall never be less than No. 14 AWG copper or No. 12 aluminum. Of course the branch circuit overcurrent protection shall not be sized over the ampacity of the conductor it serves.

Exception: Tap conductors for 15-ampere circuits, from a circuit rated less than 40 amperes; if the tap conductor comes from a circuit rated at 40 or 50 amperes, the tap conductors shall not be less than 20 amperes. This applies to tap conductors that supply any of the following loads:

(1) Shall not be longer than 18 inches where they serve individual lampholders or fixtures with this tap to the lampholder or fixture.
(2) Tap conductors covered by Section 410-67 to a fixture.
(3) Shall not be over 18 inches longer to outlets served by the tap.
(4) Industrial heating appliances serving infrared lamp.
(5) Deicing and snow-melting cables or mats may have smaller tap conductors serving only the nonheating modes.
Section 240-4, covering fixtures and cords, is an exception.

210-20. Overcurrent Protection—The overcurrent device supplying branch-circuit conductors and equipment shall have a rating or setting: (1) see Section 240-3 for the rating specified therein for conductors; (2) the specified rating or not exceeding the rating for applicable articles. These will be referred to in Section 240-2 for equipment; and (3) Section 210-21 provides for outlet devices.

Exception No. 1: Section 210-18(c) covers tap conductors to be permitted by the overcurrent device.

Exception No. 2: Section 240-4 will cover fixture wires and cords permitted.

For further information on overcurrent protection, see Section 240-1 covering the purpose of overcurrent protection and Sections 210-22 and 220-3 for the coverage of overcurrent protection for continuous loads.

210-21. Outlet Devices—(See Article 100 for the definition of "outlet.") Outlet devices shall conform to (a) and (b) below and the ampere rating shall not be less than that of the load being served.

(a) **Lampholders.** Branch circuits of over 20 amperes shall have heavy-duty lampholders, and heavy-duty lampholders of the medium base type shall be rated at not less than 660 watts and not less than 750 watts for other types.

(b) **Receptacles.** A single receptacle is a single contact device with no other contact device on the same yoke. A multiple receptacle is a single device containing two or more receptacles.

(1) Where a branch circuit serves a single receptacle that is the only receptacle in the branch circuit, the receptacle shall have a rating of not less than that of the branch circuit.

(2) Where two or more receptacles or outlets are on the same branch circuit, Table 210-21(b)(2) tells us that receptacles shall not supply a total cord- and plug-connected load greater than that specified in the Table.

(3) You are referred to Table 210-21(b)(3) when a branch circuit supplies two or more receptacles or outlet receptacles. If the branch circuit is larger than 50 amperes, the branch-circuit rating applies to the rating of the receptacle. The rating of the receptacle shall not be less than the branch circuit overcurrent protection for over 50 amperes.

(4) Table 220-19 shall be used to apply to the rating of a receptacle or the single range specified, so follow Table 220-19 for this purpose.

210-22. Maximum Loads—Be cautioned that the total load shall not exceed the rating of the branch circuit that is covered by the branch circuit overcurrent section, and shall not exceed the maximum load specified below in (a) through (c) where the conditions are specified.

(a) **Motor-Operated and Combination Loads.** If an appliance consists of motor load only, Article 430 will apply. Branch-circuit calculations for appliances (other than portable) which use a motor larger than ⅛ horsepower plus additional loads such as heating elements, lighting, etc., make it necessary to figure the motor load at 125 percent, with the additional loads added to this figure. For example, a dishwasher uses a ⅓-horsepower motor which draws 7.2 amperes. This would be figured at 125 percent, or 9 amperes. In addition, there is a heating element that draws 840 watts at 120 volts, or 7 amperes. The figure used in calculating the branch circuit would be 9 amperes + 7 amperes, or 16 amperes. In Section 210-21(b), a 20-ampere branch circuit that serves two or more outlets should supply no more than 16 amperes. From this it may readily be seen that an outlet to supply the above dishwasher should be on a 20-ampere circuit of its own.

Circuits supplying only air-conditioning and/or refrigeration equipment are now covered in Article 440.

(b) **Inductive Lighting Loads.** The computed load for circuits supplying lighting units having ballasts, autotransformers, or transformers will be based on the total ampere rating of such units, but not on the total watts of the lamps.

There are several factors that enter into this, such as there are losses in ballasts, transformers, and autotransformers, as well as power factor which might be a lagging power factor. Thus the amperes drawn will be more than the wattage of the lamps would indicate.

(c) **Other Loads.** A load where the maximum current is expected to continue for three hours or more. Continuous loads operating for 3 or more hours shall not exceed 80 percent of the rating of the branch circuit. In considering such loads, store lighting, office lighting, and numerous types of loads must be considered, taking into account the definition of continuous loads.

Exception No. 1: Motor loads having demand factors (and demand factors are usually considered as the consumption in 15-minute periods) will be covered in Article 430.

Exception No. 2: If the overcurrent devices are rated for continuous operation at 100 percent of their ratings, then the circuits they supply will follow suit.

Range loads are covered by demand factors in Table 220-19, including Note 4, and it will be acceptable to use these demand factors.

210-23. Permissible Loads—The branch circuit overcurrent rating shall never be exceeded. Branch circuits shall only carry the load for which they are rated. Those consisting of two or more outlets shall supply loads according to the sizes of branch circuit overcurrent protection that is covered in (a) through (c) below and is summarized in Section 210-24 and Table 210-24.

(a) **15- and 20-Ampere Branch Circuits.** Lighting units, other utilization equipment, or a combination of both may be supplied from 15- or 20-ampere branch circuits. The branch circuit supplying one cord- and plug-connected utilization equipment shall not be loaded to more than 80 percent of the branch-circuit rating.

Where lighting units, cord- and plug-connected utilization equipment, or both are supplied by a branch circuit, the total rating of utilization equipment fastened in place on that circuit shall not exceed 50 percent of the branch-circuit rating.

Exception: Dwellings shall have a minimum of two small appliance circuits. These are 20-ampere circuits and are covered in Section 220-4(b), which will specify where they are to be located. They are to be used for no other purpose.

(b) **30-Ampere Branch Circuits.** Fixed lighting units with heavy-duty lampholders in other than dwelling unit(s) or utilization equipment in any occupancy may be supplied from 30-ampere branch circuits. The rating of any cord- and plug-connected utilization equipment shall not, however, exceed 80 percent of the branch circuit ampere rating.

(c) **40- or 50-Ampere Branch Circuits.** This category includes fixed or stationary cooking appliances. In other than dwelling units, it might also include fixed lighting units with heavy-duty lampholders, infrared heating units, or other utilization equipment. An electric range may be a fixed appliance or a stationary appliance, depending upon whether or not it was built in, or permanently connected to the branch circuit or plugged in. It is recommended that a minimum of 40 amperes be used to supply clothes dryers as too many will not meet the requirements of a 30-ampere branch circuit.

(d) **Branch Circuits Larger than 50 Amperes.** Branch circuits 50 amperes or larger are never to supply lighting loads. They are to supply only nonlighting loads.

210-24. Summary of Branch-Circuit Requirements—Table 210-24 summarizes branch circuits in dwelling units, and a branch circuit shall not be connected to serve more than one dwelling unit. The above requirements are for circuits having two or more outlets, but do not include the special circuits covered in 220-4(b).

In two-family or multifamily dwelling units that are under the same management, a branch circuit is permitted to serve more than one of the dwelling units. They shall also be permitted to serve central alarm systems, signals, or similar functions.

Refer to the *NEC* for Table 210-24, Summary of Branch-Circuit Requirements.

C. Required Outlets

210-50. General—Sections 210-52 through 210-63 cover the installation of receptacle outlets.

(a) **Cord Pendants.** A cord connected, permanently installed, is to be considered the same as a receptacle outlet.

(b) **Cord Connections.** Where flexible cords with a receptacle outlet are used, a receptacle outlet shall be installed. In the event that flexible cords are permitted, it will be permissible for the omission of receptacle outlets for such cords. This might be interpreted that extension-cord lamps, with receptacles in the lamp head, shall be required to have a receptacle outlet for plugging in the extension cord. The author suggests that long cords should not be permitted to be solidly connected instead of being plugged into a receptacle outlet. The authority having jurisdiction may make this interpretation.

(c) **Laundry Outlet.** Where outlets are installed in dwellings for specific appliances such as laundry equipment, there shall be a maximum of 6 feet or less from the appliance they serve.

210-52. Dwelling Unit Receptacle Outlets.

(a) **General Provisions.** For all practical purposes, this covers all rooms in a residence that are used for living space. It does not cover bathrooms or hallways. The installation of receptacle outlets shall be such that no point along the floor line in any wall space is more than 6 feet, measured horizontally from an outlet in that space. To clarify this, many outlets may be 12 feet apart.

It also includes any isolated wall space that is 2 feet or more in width, and wall space occupied by sliding panels, or panel doors on exterior walls. If a room is divided by a fixed room divider, such as a standing bar counter, it shall also be included in the 6-foot rule. (See Fig. 210-11.)

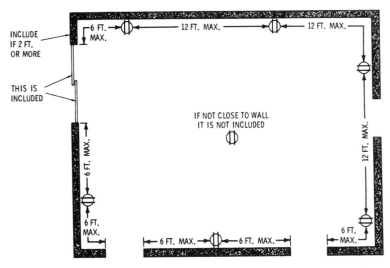

Fig. 210-11. Proper wall receptacle outlet spacing for residential housing.

The wall space includes all wall space that is unbroken along the floor line. This would eliminate counting wall spaces with doorways, fireplaces, and similar openings. Any wall space 2 feet or more in width shall be considered separately. The wall space will include corners of rooms along the floor line. The exclusion of fireplaces and so forth will prevent the use of cords across such potentially hazardous openings.

Outlets that are not close to the wall shall not be counted as fulfilling the requirements. Practical receptacles should be equally spaced along the wall line.

There has been considerable confusion in inspections on these matters, and the above should clarify many problems that formerly existed.

(FPN): The purpose of this requirement is to minimize the use of cords across doorways, fireplaces, or similar openings.

The pertinent points to remember are that at no point around the room shall a receptacle outlet be more than 6 feet from what is to be plugged into it, and no cords shall cross doorways, fireplaces, and similar things placed in wall spaces.

By no means does this mean that you are required to start measuring 6 feet from a door and 12 feet between receptacle outlets. The intent is that, insofar as is practical, receptacle outlets shall be spaced equal distances apart so that there are no more than 6 feet from a receptacle outlet to the appliance plugged into the outlet. Also, floor-installed receptacles are permitted to be counted if they are located close to a wall. This occurs often when older houses are being rewired.

With electric baseboard heating being used frequently, it is not advisable, and may not be permitted by the manufacturer's instructions, to install receptacle outlets above the baseboard heaters because the heat will tend to deteriorate the cord installation. The receptacle outlets would be much better placed in the floor in front of any baseboard heater. Electric baseboard heaters are now available with built-in receptacle outlets in the baseboard electric heaters to eliminate deterioration of the cord insulation. Such receptacle outlets shall not be connected to the heater circuits.

Any receptacles in lighting fixtures or appliances within cabinets or cupboards are not to be counted in the receptacles required by the section if they are over 5½ feet above the floor.

Exception: Where there is baseboard heating, this heating can be obtained already equipped with factory-installed outlets or separate assemblies provided by the manufacturer. These outlets are permitted as fulfilling the outlet and wall space rule. These special outlets shall not be connected to the heater circuit itself. The purpose is to prevent outlets from being installed above heating and prevent the cord from being placed over the hot baseboard heater, causing the deterioration of the cord.

(b) **Counter Tops.** Counter tops in kitchen and dining areas are of various widths and are often cut up by sinks, ranges, refrigerators, etc. When this is the case, any portion of the counter-top space that is wider than 12 inches (305 mm) shall have a receptacle outlet installed. See

Fig. 210-12. Any receptacle covered by appliances fastened in place or appliances occupying dedicated space adjacent to the basin shall have at least one receptacle outlet installed. This is to be used for electric appliances such as electric razors, toothbrushes, and hair dryers. Further information was given in Section 210-8(a)(1).

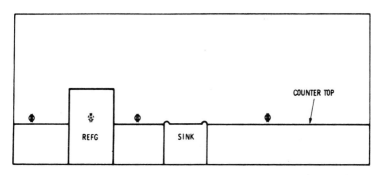

Fig. 210-12. Proper wall receptacle outlet spacing for countertops in kitchen or dining areas.

(c) **Bathrooms.** Section 210-8(a)(1) covers outlets in bathrooms. There shall be at least one receptacle installed near the basin, and this should be a GFCI type of receptacle.

GFCI's can be obtained as receptacles or as breakers and the service entrance equipment covering an entire circuit.

(d) **Outdoor Outlets.** See Section 210-8(a)(3). A one-family dwelling must have at least one receptacle outlet that may be reached from ground level, and it shall be installed outdoors. In a two-family dwelling, each dwelling must have an outdoor receptacle, and in either case they shall have GFCI protection.

(e) **Laundry Areas.** Laundry areas shall have at least one receptacle outlet installed.

Exception No. 1: In apartments or multifamily dwellings that share laundry facilities that are furnished in a common location on the premises and are available to all occupants, a laundry receptacle is not required in each dwelling occupancy.

In other than one-family dwellings, laundry facilities are often not permitted. When this is the case, no laundry receptacle need be installed.

(f) **Basements and Garages.** See the *NEC.*

210-60. Guest Rooms—Hotels, motels, and similar occupancies have been interpreted as coming under this category, and the receptacle outlet spacing is the same as for dwelling units covered in Section 210-52. However, since many hotels and motels have beds, dressers, and other furniture permanently attached to the walls, receptacles by necessity must be permitted to be located so that they will be convenient for the permanent fixtures that have been installed. See Section 210-8(a)(2).

210-62. Show Windows—Screw-shell lampholders have been used for many years to attach extension cords for floodlighting and the like. The Code now requires that at least one receptacle outlet be installed directly above the window. The receptacle outlets shall be installed for each 12 feet (3.66 m) of linear length or major portion thereof. It also requires that the show window be measured horizontally at its maximum width.

210-63. Rooftop Heating, Air-Conditioning, and Refrigeration Equipment Outlet—These items from time to time require servicing. Therefore, 125-volt, single-phase, 15- or 20-ampere-rated receptacle outlets are a necessity for the service man to plug in his service equipment. This shall be readily accessible to the unit requiring services at the same roof level not over 75 feet from the equipment being serviced. Never connect the service receptacle to the load side of the disconnecting means for the equipment; the service receptacle will be hot, and the equipment being serviced may be entirely disconnected. The above does not apply to one- and two-family dwellings.

210-70. Lighting Outlets Required—The lighting outlet installation is covered in (a) and (b) below.

(a) **Dwelling Units.** This requires at least one wall switched lighting outlet to be installed in every habitable room: in hallways, bathrooms, stairways, attached garages, and at outdoor entrances. There was confusion about installing a switched light at the vehicle door entrance to the garage. This is clarified: Because this is not considered an outside entrance, no switched light is required.

Also, at least one lighting outlet shall be installed in the attic, utility room, underfloor space and in basement only when these spaces are used for storage or contain equipment that will require servicing.

Exception No. 1: In habitable rooms one or more receptacles may be controlled by a switch—where they control lighting outlets such as where a lamp will be turned on. This does not apply to kitchen and bathrooms. This will permit controlling of floor lamps and the like by means of a switch for entering the room, thus providing illumination.

Exception No. 2: Remote control or automatic control in lighting is permitted for hallways, stairways, and outdoor entrances. Remember, this does not cover lighting by a garage door. This will allow the prescribed lighting in these areas, if properly installed.

(b) **Guest Rooms.** This requires at least one wall switch-controlled lighting outlet or receptacle for a lamp in guest rooms of hotels, motels, etc.

ARTICLE 215—FEEDERS

215-1. Scope—This article covers the minimum size of feeder conductors supplying branch circuits. A feeder conductor here would have to go to a panel covering branch circuits, and loads to the feeder circuit shall be computed in accordance with Article 220.

Exception: Section 668-3(c), Exceptions Nos. 1 and 4 will cover feeders at that point for electrolytic cells.

215-2. Minimum Rating and Size—Parts B, C, and D of Article 220 cover the calculations for feeder ampacities, and they shall not be of lower ampacity than thus computed, with minimum sizes as covered in (a) and (b) below. In the calculation of feeder sizes, voltage drops must be considered.

Feeder conductors need not be larger than the service entrance conductors when serving dwellings or mobile homes. By referring to Note 3 of Table 310-16, the conductor size can be determined.

(a) **For Specified Circuits.** Conductors with a minimum ampacity of 30 are the minimum size permitted for loads consisting of the following types and numbers of circuits: (1) two or more 2-wire branch circuits supplied by a 2-wire feeder; (2) more than two 2-wire branch circuits supplied by a 3-wire feeder; and (3) two or more 3-wire branch circuits supplied by a 3-wire feeder.

(b) **Ampacity Relative to Service-Entrance Conductors.** Where feeder conductors handle the entire load supplied by service-entrance conductors with an ampacity of 55 or less, the feeder conductors shall not be smaller than the service-entrance conductors.

Unlike ordinary houses, mobile homes never have service entrance conductors attached to them. The service entrance conductors are mounted away from the mobile home, and feeders run from there to the mobile home.

Voltage drop was mentioned above. Feeders shall have no more than a 3 percent voltage drop at the furthest outlet, and combined branch circuits and feeders shall not exceed a 5 percent voltage drop. This to a certain degree was covered in Section 210-19(a), which discussed voltage drop for branch circuits. Further examples of this may be seen in examples 1 through 8 in Chapter 9.

The formula for voltage drop is as follows:

$$V_d = \frac{2L \times 12 \times I}{CM}$$

where V_d = voltage drop
L = length of the circuit, feet, one way
I = current, amperes
CM = area of the conductors, circular mils

To arrive at the voltage drop in percent, the voltage supplied to the circuit is divided into the voltage drop.

Branch-circuit voltage drop was also covered previously in Section 210-19(a).

215-3. Overcurrent Protection—Part A of Article 240 covers how feeders shall be protected from overcurrent.

215-4. Feeders with Common Neutral—A common neutral feeder may be used for two or three sets of 3-wire feeders or two sets of 4- or 5-wire feeders, providing that the neutral is large enough to take care of the unbalanced current that it may be required to carry, and that, when these are installed in a metal raceway or enclosure, all conductors are enclosed within the same raceway as required in Section 300-20. This is necessary to counteract induction that might be set up, which will cause heating and possibly unbalance.

Caution should be taken when current-carrying conductors and the neutral are brought into a large panel. The conductors should be run side by side (parallel) whenever possible, since a voltage unbalance might be caused by induction. Running the conductors side by side tends to cancel out the induction. This explanation does not appear in the Code, but is of vital importance.

At a Code panel session of questions and answers, a question arose: If you have conductors parallel of the same size and length, why is it required that they have the same type of insulation? The answer to this is that different types of insulation have different insulating qualities at different temperatures. As an example, if you had USE-RHW conductors on two and a THW on the third, the USE-RHW insulation resistance is much more stable under fluctuations of heat than the THW is. Therefore you could possibly cause an imbalance of the impedance of the circuit to the lower insulation resistance of the THW, which would in turn cause a mismatch of the impedances at the end of the circuit.

215-5. Diagrams of Feeders—The enforcing authority may require diagrams showing feeder details, and they should show the area in square feet, total connected load before applying demand factors, demand factors selected, computed load after applying the demand factors, and size and type of conductors to be used. A wiring job of any size should have the feeder diagram supplied to the owner since it is a great assistance in determining where the feeders go and what they serve.

215-6. Feeder Conductor Grounding Means—If grounding conductors are required in branch circuits fed from feeders to a branch-circuit panel, there shall be a grounding means provided to which the grounding conductors may be attached. Also, in service-entrance equipment, the grounding bus must be grounded to the enclosure. In feeder panels, the grounding bus shall be grounded to the enclosures. This often brings up the question of where to attach the grounding conductor when it is required. The grounding conductor shall not be connected to the neutral bus of a feeder panel, but shall be connected to a separate grounding bus for the grounding conductors, or to the enclosure by approved lugs. Do not confuse a "grounded" conductor and a "grounding" conductor.

If the feeder panel is supplied by a metallic raceway which serves as a grounding conductor, the grounding conductors are attached to the enclosure and not the neutral bus since the neutral bus is isolated from the enclosure. If there is a grounding conductor but no metallic raceway, it is attached to the enclosure as are the grounding conductors that leave the feeder panel. The latter part is not in the Code under this section, but is very appropriate.

215-7. Ungrounded Conductors Tapped from Grounded Systems —There are places where it will be necessary to tap into 2-wire dc or ac circuits of two or more grounded conductors. Such a place might be a 240-volt single-phase motor to be tapped from a 3-wire 240/125 volt system. It can easily be seen that you would have no use for the grounded conductor going to the motor, so such a 2-wire tap on ungrounded conductors is permitted. Any switching device on this tap circuit shall open both ungrounded conductors, and one should be able to search the two ungrounded conductors simultaneously. However, there should be an equipment grounding conductor either in the metal raceway of the separate green color or a bare conductor installed with the two ungrounded conductors so that the motor would be at ground protection.

215-8. Means of Identifying Conductor with the Higher Voltage to Ground—There are many 4-wire delta-connected systems, the fourth wire being the tap of one phase to ground. Refer to Fig. 215-1A. From this illustration, you can see that two ungrounded conductors of the delta system will give 120 volts to ground, but notice that the third ungrounded conductor gives us a voltage of 208 volts to ground. In the field this is often referred to as the wild leg. This leg of the delta must have some kind of clear and permanent identification. The conductor can be orange in color, tagged or permanently and effectively colored orange at any point where it could be used with the neutral. This identification shall be placed at any point where

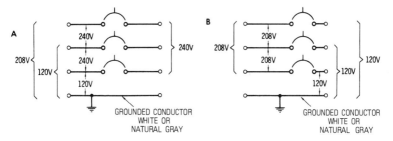

(A) 4-wire system with a neutral.   (B) Grounded 4-wire wye system.

Fig. 215-1.   Voltage relationship on grounded 4-wire systems.

there might be connection made to the neutral or grounded conductor when it is present.

Fig. 215-1B shows the voltage relationships on a grounded 4-wire wye system. On this system, 120 volts to neutral can be obtained from any ungrounded conductor and neutral.

215-9. Ground-Fault Protection for Personnel—There is nothing to prevent using GFCI's on a feeder supplying 15- or 20-ampere receptacle branch circuits. Section 210-8 covers some specifics, and Article 305 will cover others. The point is that nothing prevents them from being used on 15 or 20 ampere circuits.

ARTICLE 220—BRANCH-CIRCUIT AND FEEDER CALCULATIONS

A. General

220-1. Scope—In this article, the basic calculations for feeders, branch circuits, loads, and the method of determining the number of branch circuits will be discussed. This article might well be called "Fundamentals of Design" because it contains the minimum requirements for a particular design or application. This does not mean that in designing a wiring system one should not take into consideration whether or not the minimum will be sufficient or whether allowances for future expansion should be provided for. This, of course, is very hard to anticipate with much accuracy, but definitely should be considered. A good and proper design always provides for at least the immediate future requirements that can be foreseen.

220-2. Voltages—The following voltages shall be used in calculations involving branch circuits and feeders. This will hold true unless other voltages are specifically specified. These voltages to be used are 120, 120/240, 208Y/120, 240, 480Y/277, 480, and 600 volts, nominal.

220-3. Computation of Branch Circuits.

(a) **Continuous Loads.** This section is to be used in the computation of branch circuits. In the calculation of loads for stores and similar occupancies, the minimums specified in this article shall not exceed 80 percent of the branch-circuit rating.

Exception: The alternative to this 80 percent would be for overcurrent devices listed for continuous operation at 100 percent rating.

(b) **Lighting Load for Listed Occupancies.** The calculations for loads in various occupancies are based on watts (volt-amperes) per square foot. This is a minimum basis and consideration should be given to the ever increasing trend toward higher levels of illumination. Each installation should be examined and not figured entirely on the watts-per-square-foot basis, but on the anticipated figure demands upon the system.

In figuring the watts per square foot (0.093 sq m), the outside dimensions of the building are to be used. They do not include the area of open porches and attached garages with dwelling occupancies. If there is an unused basement, it should be assumed that it will be finished later, thus it should be included in the calculations so that the capacity of the wiring system will be adequate to serve at a later date. Conduit or EMT should be installed in concrete basement walls during construction since the cost will be much lower than at the time of finishing the basement.

The unit values given are based on 100 percent factor for the minimum requirements, so any low power factors should be taken into account in the calculations. If high-power-factor discharge lighting is not used, allowance should be made for the increased amperage due to the lower-power factor.

See Table 220-3(b) in the *NEC*. The unit load calculation shall not be less than shown in this table.

In calculation for dwellings, when figuring the area to be covered, porches, garages, and—if not adaptable for future use—unused or unfinished spaces are not to be included.

Author's Note: If unfinished spaces are adaptable for future use, the area should be included in your calculations.

The load values used here are considered at 100 percent power factor. If less than 100 percent power factor, equipment is installed with sufficient capacity figured in to take care of the additional current values.

(c) **Other Loads—All Occupancies.** For any lighting other than general illumination, and for appliances other than motors, a minimum unit load per outlet is given in the table listed under this section of the Code.

In the *NEC* under this part you will find five categories that will be necessary in making calculations. Receptacle outlets, whether single or multiple, are to be considered at not less than 180 volt-amperes. Section 220-4(b) above, for items covered in the Code, shall not be applicable. This will cover duplex receptacles or receptacles on the same mounting strap in an outlet box.

Exception No. 1: Multiple outlet assemblies are available, and if the multiple outlets are 5 feet or less from each other, then the continuous length of the multiple outlet assembly shall be considered as one outlet and figured at 180 volt-amperes capacity. Where a number of appliances will be used simultaneously, each foot (305 mm) will be considered as an outlet of not less than 180-volt-amperes capacity. These requirements shall not apply to either dwellings or guest rooms in hotels. A location where 1 foot might be considered as 180 volt-ampere capacity could be an appliance sales floor where a number of appliances might be connected for demonstration. Another location might be in a school lab where a number of experiments using electrical apparatus would be used at the same time.

Exception No. 2: Household electric ranges are not subject to this regulation, but their minimum loads may be determined by using Table 220-19.

Exception No. 3: For show-window lighting, a minimum of 200 volt-amperes per linear foot (305 mm) of show window, measured horizontally along the base of the window, shall be used.

Exception No. 4: See the *NEC.*

Exception No. 5: Section 220-18 is an acceptable method of computing electric clothes dryer loads.

(d) **Loads for Additions to Existing Installations.** Additional installations to existing electrical systems shall conform to the following:

(1) **Dwelling Units.** When computing additional loads, for structural additions onto an existing dwelling unit, (b) or (c) above shall be used in the computation of the additional new load. Loads for structural additions to an existing dwelling unit or to a previously unwired portion of an existing dwelling that exceeds 500 square feet (46.5 sq m) shall be computed in accordance with (b) above.

It is necessary that the existing electrical systems be checked to make certain that the circuit or circuits being added have sufficient current-carrying capacity to take care of the additional load.

(2) **Other than Dwelling Units.** When adding new circuits or extensions of circuits in other than dwelling units, either volt-amperes per square foot or amperes per outlet may be used as covered in (b) and (c) above.

220-4. Branch Circuits Required—Section 220-3 covers branch circuits for lighting and for appliances, including motor-operated appliances. There will be branch circuits required elsewhere in the Code, which are not covered in Section 220-3. Small appliance loads are covered in (b) below; laundry loads are covered in (c) below.

(a) **Number of Branch Circuits.** The total computed load and the size or rating of the branch circuits used will determine the number of branch circuits required. The maximum load on any branch circuit should not exceed the maximum specified in Section 210-22 and it is good practice to leave some spare capacity, as in most cases additional load will be needed at some time.

(b) **Small Appliance Branch Circuits—Dwelling Unit.**

(1) In addition to the branch-circuit requirements of (a) above, there shall be a minimum of two or more 20-ampere small appliance branch circuits to cover the receptacle outlets as required by Section 210-52. These are for small appliances including refrigeration equipment. These circuits shall have no other outlets on

them and they shall cover receptacle outlets in the kitchen, pantry, breakfast room, and dining room of dwelling units. The above does not cover disposals or dishwashers.

Exception No. 1: Receptacles installed in any of the rooms above and used solely for the support and supply of an electric clock. A 3-wire 120/240-volt branch circuit would be the equivalent of two 120-volt receptacle branch circuits. On this type of circuit, the split-type receptacle would be used which would aid in balancing the load; each receptacle would be the equivalent of two circuits.

Exception No. 2: Outdoor receptacles.

Exception No. 3: Section 210-70(a) Exception No. 1 permits switched receptacles supplied by a general-purpose branch circuit as defined in Section 210-70(a), and covers the additional switched receptacles that were specified in Section 210-52 from general branch circuits.

(2) Counter-top receptacle outlets that are installed in the kitchen shall be connected to not less than two small appliance 20-ampere circuits, covered previously, supplying the kitchen and other specified rooms. This does not mean that only two small appliance circuits may be used in wiring a dwelling; in fact, more than two will certainly prove an extra asset.

(c) **Laundry Branch Circuits—Dwelling Unit.** In addition to the number of branch circuits required, including the small appliance circuits, there shall be a minimum of at least one 20-ampere branch circuit to supply laundry receptacle outlet(s) required by Section 210-52. There shall be nothing else on this circuit.

(d) **Load Evenly Proportioned Among Branch Circuits.** When computing on a volt-amperes-per-square-foot (0.093 sq m) basis, the load should be distributed as evenly as possible between the required circuits, and according to their capacities.

Examples of computations are found in Chapter 9 of the *NEC*.

B. Feeders

220-10. General.

(a) **Ampacity and Computed Loads.** In no case shall the ampacity of the feeders be smaller than required to serve the load, and also in no case shall it be smaller than the sum of the loads of the branch circuits which it supplies, as computed in Part A of this article. This statement is subject to applicable demand factors which may apply in Parts B, C, and D of this Article.

See examples in Chapter 9, and see Section 210-22(b) for maximum load permitted, at 100 percent power factor, for lighting units.

(b) **Continuous and Noncontinuous Loads.** Where a feeder supplies continuous loads or any combination of continuous and noncontinuous loads, *neither* the rating of the overcurrent device *nor* the ampacity of feeder conductors shall be the ampacity of the noncontinuous load plus 100 percent of any continuous load on the feeders.

The service conductors serving the ungrounded conductors are to be not less than the continuous load plus 125 percent of any continuous load that will be served.

Exception: If the overcurrent devices that protect feeders are listed at 100 percent operation of their rating, the ampacity of the overcurrent protection and feeder shall be not less than the ampacity of the noncontinuous load plus the sum of the continuous load. In addition, 125 percent of the continuous load must be added to the ampacity of the overcurrent devices and feeders.

This will eliminate the confusion as to increases to the unit load of Table 220-3(b) in the Code. It recognizes the overcurrent devices are not normally rated for continuous duty at full load and allows the use of overcurrent devices rated for continuous duty at full load. Also, it separates the required derating of conductors from the required derating of overcurrent devices.

220-11. General Lighting—The demand factors listed in Table 220-11 cover that portion of the total branch-circuit loads that are computed for lighting loads. These demand factors are only for the purpose of determining feeders to supply lighting loads, and are not for the purpose of figuring the number of branch circuits. The number of branch circuits has been covered in the preceding part, and will also be covered in Chapter 9 of the Code, as well as in following parts of this coverage of Article 220.

Each installation should be specifically analyzed, since the demand factors listed in this section of the Code are based only on the minimum requirements of load conditions and for 100 percent power-factor conditions. There will be conditions of less than unity power factor and conditions where these demand factors would be wrong. With the trend to higher illumination intensities and the increased use of fixed and portable appliances, the loads imposed on the system are very likely to be greater than the minimums. Also, electric discharge lighting should be of the high-power-factor type; if not, additional provisions should be made for the low-power factor involved.

Demand factors for small appliances for laundry equipment in dwellings is covered in 220-16.

Author's Note: See *NEC*, Table 220-11, Lighting Load Feeder Demands.

220-12. Show-Window Lighting—Show-window lighting is a separate load from that calculated on the volt-ampere-per-square-foot basis. This lighting is to be figured at a minimum of 200 volt-amperes per linear foot (305 mm), measured horizontally along the base.

Branch circuits supplying show windows are covered in Exception No. 3 of Section 220-3(c).

220-13. Receptacle Loads—Nondwelling Units—In other than nondwelling units, lighting load demand factors are covered in Table 220-11, and those shown in Table 220-13 shall be permitted for calculating receptacle loads. The rating of a receptacle shall not be more than 180 amperes per outlet, as covered in Section 220-3(c)(5).

This is to say that if receptacle outlets are computed at not more than 180 volt-amperes per receptacle, the demand factors may be used in the calculation of the feeder loads.

220-14. Motors—The computing of motor loads is covered in Sections 430-24, 430-25, and 430-26.

Author's Note: See the *NEC*, Table 220-13, Demand Factors for Non-dwelling Receptacle Loads.

220-15. Fixed Electric Space Heating—With two exceptions, the computed load on a feeder that serves fixed electrical space heating shall be equal to the total of the electrical space heating load on all of the branch circuits. There is no demand factor. The feeder load current rating shall never be computed at less than the rating of the largest branch circuit supplied.

Exception No. 1: The inspection authority enforcing the code may grant special permission to issue a demand factor for electrical space heating where they have duty-cycling or where all units will not be operating at the same time. The feeders are required to be of sufficient current-carrying capacity to carry the load as so determined.

Exception No. 2: There are optional calculations for single-family dwellings, etc., in Sections 220-30 and 220-31. These optional calculations shall be permitted for fixed space heating in single-family dwellings or in individual apartments of multifamily dwellings. Where the calculations are for a multifamily dwelling, Section 220-32 will be permitted to be used.

220-16. Small Appliance and Laundry Loads—Dwelling Unit.

(a) **Small Appliance Circuit Load.** The requirements for small-appliance receptacle outlets in single-family dwellings, multifamily dwellings with individual apartments having cooking facilities, and in hotels or motels having serving-pantries facilities or other cooking facilities, shall be a minimum of not less than 2-wire small appliance circuits, as required in Section 220-4(b). The calculated load for each circuit shall not be less than 1500 volt-amperes. These loads may be included with the general lighting load which makes it subject to the demand factors as set forth in Table 220-11 in the Code.

(b) **Laundry Circuit Load.** A minimum of one 20-ampere laundry circuit is required in the laundry room, but a feeder load of not less than 1500 volt-amperes shall be included for each 2-wire laundry branch circuit installed as required in Section 220-4(c). These circuit(s) may be included with the general lighting load and subjected to the demand factors provided in Section 220-11.

220-17. Appliance Load—Dwelling Unit(s)—A demand factor of 75 percent of the nameplate rating is permitted where there is a load of four or more fixed appliances served by the same feeder in a single-family dwelling or a multifamily dwelling.

Exception: The demand factors above do not apply to electric ranges, clothes dryers, air-conditioning, or space heating equipment.

220-18. Electric Clothes Dryers—Dwelling Unit(s)—When the wiring is installed, the clothes dryer is practically never available to check the nameplate rating so the feeder circuit which shall feed the dryer may be sized properly.

Electric clothes dryer units shall be calculated at 5000 watts (volt-amperes) or the nameplate rating on the dryer, whichever is larger. When a house is being wired the wireman cannot be certain what the rating of the clothes dryer to be purchased will be. This is why Code has placed the 5000-watt minimum. Table 220-18 in your *NEC* is permitted to arrive at the demand factors. See Table 220-18 in your *NEC*.

Many inspectors have insisted on No. 8 copper or the equivalent for dryers, as most dryers draw 30 amperes, or more. Nameplate rating and a branch circuit should not be loaded to exceed 80 percent of its capacity.

220-19. Electric Ranges and Other Cooking Appliances—Dwelling Unit(s)—In calculating feeder loads for electric ranges or other cooking appliances in dwelling occupancies, any that are rated over 1¾ kW shall be calculated according to Table 200-19 in the *NEC*. The Notes following Table 220-19 are a part of the Table and are very important in the calculation of feeder and branch-circuit loads.

Due to the increased wattages being used in modern electric ranges, it is recommended that the maximum demands for any range of less than 8¾ kW rating be figured using Column A in Table 220-19.

Three-phase, 4-wire wye systems are often used. When calculating the current in such systems, it is necessary to use a demand of twice the maximum number of ranges that will be connected between any two phase wires. An example of this is shown under Example 6, Chapter 9.

Refer to the *NEC* for Table 229-19, Demand Loads for Household Electric Ranges, Wall-Mounted Ovens, Counter-Mounted Cooking Units, and Other Household Cooking Appliances over 1¾ kW Rating. Column A is to be used in all cases except as otherwise permitted in Note 3.

There are five notes and two exceptions following Table 220-19 in the *NEC*. These are very clear and must be adhered to in some calculations of load. Please do not overlook these items. The Code panel has done an excellent job on these items and the Examples in Chapter 9.

For loads computed under this section, kVA shall be considered equivalent to kW. Heating loads are 100 percent power factor.

220-20. Kitchen Equipment—Other than Dwelling Unit(s)—Table 220-20 in your *NEC* is permitted to be used for load computation for commercial electric cooking equipment, dishwashers, booster heaters, water heaters, and other kitchen equipment. The demand factors shown in that Table are applicable to all equipment that is thermostatically controlled or is only intermittently used as part of the kitchen equipment. In no way do the demand factors apply to the electric heating, ventilating, or air-conditioning equipment. In figuring the demand, note that it shall never be less than the sum of the two largest kitchen equipment loads.

Author's Note: Refer to *NEC* for Table 220-20, Feeder Demand Factors for Kitchen Equipment—Other than Dwelling Units.

220-21. Noncoincidental Loads—When adding the branch-circuit loads, the smaller of two loads may be omitted if it is not likely that they will be used at the same time.

220-22. Feeder Neutral Load—The maximum unbalanced load controls the feeder neutral load ampacity.

Neutral feeder load must be considered wherever a neutral is used in conjunction with one or more ungrounded conductors. On a single-phase feeder using one ungrounded conductor and a neutral, the neutral will carry the same amount of current as the ungrounded conductor. A two-wire feeder is rare, so in considering the neutral feeder current, we will assume that there is a neutral and two or more ungrounded phase conductors. If there are two ungrounded conductors that are connected to the same phase, and a neutral, the neutral would be required to carry the total current from both phase wires, which would not be accepted practice.

On 5-wire two-phase systems, the neutral shall carry 140 percent of the unbalanced load. On feeders that supply electric ranges, wall-mounted ovens, counter-mounted cooking tops, etc., the maximum unbalanced load shall be considered to be 70 percent of the load on the ungrounded conductor. Therefore, the neutral supplying these may be 70 percent as large as the ungrounded conductors, providing that the neutral is no smaller than No. 10. The capacity of the ungrounded conductors is figured by Table 220-19 for ranges and Table 220-18 for dryers. For 3-wire dc or single-phase ac, 4-wire 3-phase, and 5-wire 2-phase systems, a further demand factor of 70 percent may be applied to that portion of the unbalanced load in excess of 200 amperes. There shall be no reduction of the neutral capacity for that portion of the load which consists of electric discharge lighting, data processing, or similar equipment. See Fig. 220-1.

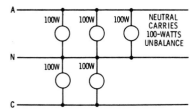

Fig. 220-1.

The question is often asked why a neutral that serves discharge lighting cannot be derated. This is because of a third harmonic frequency produced by the discharge lighting and its ballast. This third harmonic may load the neutral to the maximum or higher allowable current. Fig. 220-2 shows the effect of the third harmonic on a three-phase system, how the harmonics are in phase and will thus be added together.

As an example in figuring the neutral feed load, a 4-wire, 3-phase wye system of 120/208 volts will be used. Assume the following loads:

Discharge lighting	150 amperes per phase
Electric ranges	200 amperes per phase
Other loads [incandescent lighting,	
motor (3φ), miscellaneous]	<u>295</u> amperes per phase
Total	645 amperes per phase

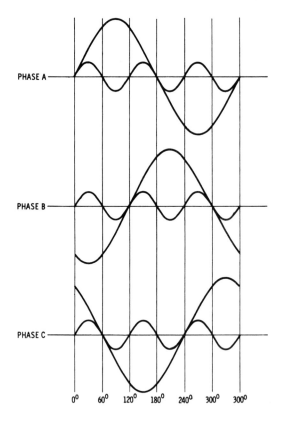

Fig. 220-2. The effect of a third harmonic.

On 3φ motor loads a neutral is not involved, and so it will not enter into the calculation of the neutral sizing.

The neutral current is calculated as follows:

Ranges, 200 amperes @ 70%	140 amperes
Other loads	295 amperes
	435 amperes
200 amperes @ 100%	200 amperes
235 amperes @ 70%	164.5 amperes
	364.5 amperes
Discharge lighting	150 amperes
Total calculated neutral current	514.5 amperes

In the preceding case, it may be seen that the phase currents are 645 amperes per phase, while the neutral current may be derated to 514.5 amperes. These figures are based on demand-factor ratings.

As another example, assume a 50-unit apartment house using a 4-wire, 3-phase, 120/208-volt wye system, with fifty 3-wire electric ranges and a gross area of 1000 square feet per apartment:

General lighting, 50 × 3 × 1000	150,000 volt-amperes
Small-appliance loads, 50 × 2 × 1500	150,000 volt-amperes
	300,000
3000 volt-amperes @ 100%	3,000 volt-amperes
117,000 volt-amperes @ 35%	40,950 volt-amperes
300,000-120,000 volt-amperes @ 35%	45,000 volt-amperes
Minimum feeder capacitor for general lighting and appliances	88,950

For the 50 ranges, this will put 16 ranges on one phase and 17 ranges on each of the other two phases. From Table 220-19 in the *NEC*, the indicated demand will be as follows: There will be a maximum demand of 17 + 17 ranges on any phase, or 34 ranges connected at the same time. According to Table 220-19, however, this will be 15,000 + 34,000 volt-amperes, or 49,000 watts.

From Table 220-19	49,000 volt-amperes
General lighting and small-appliance loads	88,950 volt-amperes
Total	137,950 volt-amperes

Maximum feeder demand:

$$\frac{137.950}{1.73 \times 208} = 384 \text{ amperes}$$

To size the neutral:

General lighting and small appliances	88,950 volt-amperes
Electric ranges, 49,000 @ 70%	34,300 volt-amperes
Total	123,250 volt-amperes

Total neutral current:

$$\frac{123,250}{1.73 \times 208} = 342 \text{ amperes}$$

Thus:

200 amperes @ 100%	200 amperes
142 amperes @ 70%	99.4 amperes
Total	299.4 amperes

After figuring the phase load and neutral load in amperes, use the wire size necessary to carry that amount of current. In most cases, you will find that a conductor capable of carrying the exact number of amperes required will not be available, so use the next larger size.

C. Optional Calculations for Computing Feeder and Service Loads

220-30. Optional Calculation—Dwelling Unit(s).

(a) **Feeder and Service Loads.** This takes into consideration the load calculations for single-family dwellings or an individual apartment of a multifamily dwelling served by a single 3-wire 120/240 volt or 120/208 volt set of service conductors or feeder conductors, with an ampacity of 100 amperes or more. It is permitted to use Table 220-30 instead of the method outlined in Part B of this article. If service-entrance conductors or feeder conductors are calculated by this section, it will be permitted to calculate the neutral load using Section 220-22.

See Table 220-30 for optional calculation for dwelling unit loads in kVA.

(b) **Loads.** Take note of Table 220-30. Loads that are identified as "other loads" and "remainder of other loads" are shown below:

(1) Each 20-ampere small appliance branch circuit and laundry circuit that was specified in Section 220-16 shall be calculated at 1500 volt-amperes.

(2) The same square footage, namely 3 volt-amperes per square foot, shall be used for general lighting and also for receptacles.

(3) For mounted-in-place cooking units, including ranges, wall-mounted ovens, counter-mounted tops, you shall use the nameplate rating in the calculations.

(4) Lower-power-factor loads, including motors, shall use the ampere rating on the load.

220-31. Optional Calculation for Additional Loads in Existing Dwelling Unit—If the present dwelling added onto is served by existing 120/240 volt or 208Y/120, 3-wire service, you may use the Table in your *NEC* for calculations. Also, the 3 watts per square foot and the 1500 volt-amperes for each 20-ampere small appliance circuit shall be used. Ranges and wall-mounted or counter-mounted cooking equipment that is connected or fastened in place should use the nameplate rating.

Where space heating equipment or air-conditioning is to be installed, at this point in your *NEC* you will find a listing of how to calculate these loads. Other loads shall include the same items that were covered above for small appliance circuits and receptacles. Where there are other appliances fastened in place, including four or more separately controlled space heating units, use the nameplate rating.

220-32. Optional Calculation—Multifamily Dwelling.

(a) **Feeder and Service Load.** Table 220-32 instead of Part B of this article may be used to compute feeder or service load for multifamily dwellings that have three or more units. The following conditions shall be met:

(1) There cannot be more than one feeder serving a dwelling unit.

(2) Electrical cooking equipment is supplied in each unit.

Exception: In Part B of this article, if the multifamily dwelling load does not have electric cooking, and is more than the computed load in Part C for the identical load plus electric cooking using 8 kW for each dwelling cooking unit, the smaller of the two loads shall be used.

(3) Where each dwelling unit has electric space heating equipment or air-conditioning or both.

When this optional method is used to compute the loads for feeders or services, the neutral load may be computed as was covered in Section 220-22.

(b) **House Loads.** Part B of Article 220 shall be used for computing house loads. In addition, Table 220-32 shall be used in computing dwelling unit loads.

(c) **Connected Loads.** Demand factors for the connected loads are covered in Table 220-32, and shall include the following:

(1) Each small appliance branch circuit of 2-wire, 20 amperes and its laundry branch circuit is covered in Section 220-16 and is figured at 1500 volt-amperes for each circuit.

(2) General lighting or general-use receptacles are figured at 3 volt-amperes per square foot.

(3) For appliances that are fastened in place or permanently connected on a specific circuit, the nameplate rating is to be used. Such appliances would include ranges and other cooking equipment, all wall-mounted or counter-top units, clothes dryers, space heating, and water heaters.

Some water heaters are designed so that only one element at a time can come on, the top heating unit first and the bottom heating unit last. Here the maximum possible load shall be considered as the nameplate load. See in the *NEC* for Table 220-32, Optional Calculation—Demand Factors for Three or More Multifamily Dwelling Units.

(4) For motors and all low-power factor loads, the nameplate ampere or kVA rating shall be used.

(5) Where both air-conditioning or space heating equipment are installed, the one with the larger rating shall be used.

220-33. Optional Calculations—Two Dwelling Units—When the word "feeder" is used in these cases, it may also refer to the service. Where two dwellings are supplied by a single feeder or service and the load is computed under Part B of Article 220, and if this computed load exceeds that under Section 220-32 for three identical units, you may use the lesser of the two loads.

220-34. Optional Method—Schools—Table 220-34 may be used in lieu of Part B of this article in the calculation of the service or feeder loads for schools if they are equipped with electric space heating or air conditioning or both. The demand factors in Table 220-34 apply to both interior and exterior lighting, power, water heating, cooking, other loads, and the larger of the space heating load or the air-conditioning load.

When using this optional calculation, the neutral of the service or feeder loads may be calculated as outlined in Section 220-22. Feeders within the building or structure where the load is calculated by this optional method and calculated in Part B of Article 220 may use the ampacity as computed, but the ampacity of any feeder as calculated in Part B of Article 220 need not be larger than the individual ampacity for the entire building (this would mean the service entrance). Portable classrooms or buildings are not included in this Section.

See the *NEC* for Table 220-34, Optional Method—Demand Factors for Feeders and Service-Entrance Conductors for Schools.

220-35. Optional Calculations for Additional Loads to Existing Installations—When additional loads are added to existing facilities having feeders and service as originally figured, you are permitted to use the maximum kVA figures in determining the load on the existing feeders and service if the following conditions are met:

(1) If the maximum data of the demand in kVA is available for a minimum of one year, such as demand meter ratings.

(2) If the demand ratings for that period of one year at 125 percent and the addition of the new load does not exceed the rating of the service. Where demand meters are used, in most cases the load as calculated will probably be less than the demand meter indications.

(3) If the overcurrent protection meets Sections 230-90 and 240-3 for feeder or service.

D. Method for Computing Farm Loads

220-40. Farm Loads—Buildings and Other Loads.

(a) **Dwelling Unit.** Part B or C of Article 220 shall be used for computing the service or feeder load of a farm dwelling.

(b) **Other than Dwelling Unit.** The load for feeder, service-entrance conductors or service equipment is to be computed in accordance with the farm dwelling load and the demand factors which are specified in Table 220-40. This is for each farm building or load supplied by two or more branch circuits.

The conductors from the service pole to buildings or other structures are services, and this is covered in Section 230-21.

220-41. Farm Loads—Total—The farm dwelling load and the demand factors in Table 220-41 are to be used in computing the load on service-entrance conductors and service equipment. Remember, the dwelling load is computed as per computations for dwellings and added to the other loads. If there is equipment in two or more farm equipment buildings or if loads have the same function, these loads are to be calculated with Table 220-40, and they shall also be allowed to be combined as a single load for computing the total load. See Table 220-41, Method for Computing Total Farm Load, and see the *NEC* for Table 220-40, Method for Computing Farm Loads for Other Than Dwelling Unit. Again, service drops, etc., are calculated as per Section 230-21.

ARTICLE 225—OUTSIDE BRANCH CIRCUITS AND FEEDERS

225-1. Scope—This article covers any electrical equipment or wiring that is attached to the outside or located on public premises. It also covers the conductors running between the buildings, structures, or poles that are involved with the premises that are being served.

Exception: See Section 668-3(c) for outside branch circuits or feeders to electrolytic cells.

There is also the National Electrical Safety Code (ANSI C2-1984); it is used primarily by utility companies, but may be also involved in outdoor wiring of other property.

225-2. Other Articles—See the *NEC* for listing of other article requirements for specific cases.

225-3. Calculation of Load.

(a) **Branch Circuits.** The provisions of Article 220, covering the calculation of loads on branch circuits, will apply to this article. In calculating loads for branch circuits, the ampacities allowable for single conductors in free air must be considered. These ampacities are given in Table 310-17 for insulated conductors, and in Table 310-19 for insulated conductors and for bare or covered conductors.

(b) **Feeders.** The provisions covering feeders in Part B of Article 220 apply to outdoor feeders also; and Tables 310-17 and 310-19 apply for feeders for the ampacity of single conductors in free air.

225-4. Conductor Covering—This section covers the insulation of conductors and where such conductors are required. It must be remembered that these conductors are exposed to the elements and therefore must have an insulation that will withstand these conditions, including ultraviolet light.

Open conductors supported on insulators shall be insulated or covered when located within 10 feet (3.05 m) of a building or structure. Conductors that are in the form of a cable or are in raceways, with the exception of Type MI Cable, shall be of the rubber-covered or the thermoplastic type. In addition, where they are exposed to water or moisture, they shall comply with Section 310-8, which states that they shall be resistant to moisture. There must be a "W" in the designation of the type of insulation. Festoon lighting conductors shall be rubber-covered or have a thermoplastic covering.

225-5. Size of Conductors—The loads on the branch circuit and feeder conductors determine the ampacity of conductor required. Loads will be determined as per Section 220-3 and Part B of Article 220. The ampacity will determine the size conductor to use and this will be found in Tables 310-16 through 310-31.

225-6. Minimum Size of Conductor.

(a) **Overhead Spans.** The following are the minimum sizes permitted for overhead conductors:

(1) No. 10 copper or No. 8 aluminum of 600 volts, nominal, or less for spans up to 50 feet (15.2 m) in length, and No. 8 copper or No. 6 aluminum for a longer span.

(2) For over 600 Volts, nominal, No. 6 copper or No. 4 aluminum are the minimum sizes where open individual conductors are used, and No. 8 or No. 6 aluminum where in cable.

(b) **Festoon Lighting.** No. 12 is the minimum size permitted for festoon lighting.

Exception: This covers conductors supported by messenger wire.

See Section 225-24 for outdoor lampholders.

Definition of festoon lighting: This is a string of outdoor lighting with support points more than 15 feet apart.

225-7. Lighting Equipment Installed Outdoors.

(a) **General.** Article 210 and (b) through (d) below cover branch circuits supplying lighting equipment out of doors.

(b) **Common Neutral.** If a neutral is used in multiwire branch circuits having a maximum of eight ungrounded conductors, the neutral shall be sized by calculating the sum of the currents in all ungrounded conductors that are connected to one phase of the involved circuit.

(c) **277 Volts to Ground.** For branch circuits of more than 120 volts, nominal, between conductors, and not over 277 volts, nominal to ground, are used to supply electric lighting where outdoor fixtures are located for illumination around industrial establishments, office buildings, schools, stores, and any other public or commercial buildings. The fixtures shall be 3 feet or more from any window, fire escape, stairs, platforms, and similar structures where a person may come in contact with the 277-volt conductors by ordinary means.

(d) **600 Volts Between Conductors.** Section 210-6(d)(1) covers auxiliary equipment supplying electric discharge lamps, and this where conductors exceeding 227 volts, nominal, to ground, but not exceeding 600 volts, nominal, between conductors are permitted.

225-8. Disconnection—See Section 240-40 of the *NEC*.

25-9. Overcurrent Protection—The overcurrent protection of branch circuits shall be governed by Section 210-20 for branch circuits. The overcurrent protection for feeders is covered by Part A of Article 240.

225-10. Wiring on Buildings—Wiring for circuits of 600 volts, nominal, or less may be installed on the outside of buildings as open wiring on insulated supports, as multiconductor cable, as type MC or MI cable, in rigid metal conduit, messenger-supported wiring, cable trays, cable bus,

wireways, flexible metal conduit, liquidtight flexible metal conduit in intermediate metal conduit, in electrical metallic tubing, in rigid nonmetallic conduit (see Section 347-2), in busways (see Article 364).

Circuits of over 600 volts, nominal, are to be treated the same as were the services in Section 230-202. Circuits for sign and outline lighting are covered in Article 600.

225-11. Circuit Exits and Entrances—Where outside branch and feeder circuits enter or leave a building, they are to be treated as service entrances as covered in Sections 230-43, 230-52, and 230-54. There is actually no difference except for classification of the purpose for which they are used.

225-12. Open-Conductor Supports—See the *NEC*.

225-13. Festoon Supports—It is required that any spans of festoon lighting that are more than 40 feet (12.2 m) long shall be supported by messenger wire which shall have approved strain insulators. Neither the conductors nor the messenger wire shall be attached to any fire escape, downspout, or plumbing equipment.

225-14. Open-Conductor Spacings.

(a) **600 Volts, Nominal, or Less.** Table 230-51(c) covers the spacing provided for conductors 600 volts, nominal, or less.

(b) **Over 600 Volts, Nominal.** Part D in Article 710 covers spacing of conductors over 600 volts, nominal.

(c) **Separation from Other Conductors.** Open conductors shall be spaced not less than 4 inches. This applies to circuits (electrical) such as TV leads, telephone lines, etc. Of course, attention must be paid to the voltages involved and the separation spaced accordingly. There will be instances where 4 inches (102 mm) might not be sufficient due to higher voltages involved.

(d) **Conductors on Poles.** A 1-foot minimum spacing is required where racks or brackets are used. This again is determined by the voltages involved, with the spacing increased as required for higher voltages.

On conductors on poles the horizontal climbing space will be found in this section of the *NEC*.

225-15. Support over Buildings—These require the same procedure as for service conductors covered in Section 230-29.

225-16. Point of Attachment to Buildings—This is covered in Section 230-26. Section 230-26 refers you to Section 230-24, where you will notice that (b) calls for a minimum of 10 feet (3.05 m) at the height of service entrance to building or at the drip-loop of the building electric entrance. Please note there are two 10-foot (3.05 m) dimensions. Where there is a drip-loop, this dimension should be used. Also, remember the dimension is from final grade level or above areas or sidewalks accessible only to people.

225-17. Means of Attachment to Buildings—This is covered in Section 230-27 of the *NEC*.

225-18. Clearance from Ground—The following shall be conformed for open conductors not over 600 volts, nominal:

If the conductors do not exceed 150 volts to ground and are accessible to pedestrians only, they shall be a minimum of 10 feet above finished grade, sidewalks, or any other object from which they might be reached.

Here it would be well to follow the instructions given in Section 225-16.

If the voltage is limited to 300 volts to ground, the conductors may be a minimum of 12 feet over residential driveways and those commercial areas that do not have truck traffic.

If the voltage exceeds over 300 volts to ground, the minimum height of the conductors shall be 15 feet instead of the 12 feet for voltages less than 300 volts to ground.

An 18-foot minimum is required over public streets and alleys, roads, and parking areas when involved with truck traffic. This also applies for driveways on other than residential driveways, and for areas such as forests, orchards and farmland, or cattle grazing areas.

Clearances of conductors over 600 volts are not covered in the *NEC*. You are referred to the National Electrical Safety Code (C2-1984), which the utility companies used.

For an illustration of the above clearances, see Fig. 225-1.

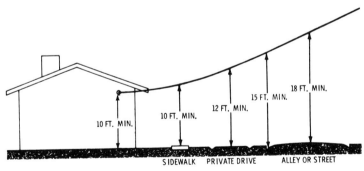

Fig. 225-1. Minimum service-drop clearance.

225-19. Clearances from Buildings for Conductors of Not Over 600 Volts, Nominal—Many changes have been made over previous Codes for clearances over buildings for feeder and branch-circuit conductors. The ambient temperature affects conductor lengths; this should be considered because cold temperatures reduce the conductor length, giving more clearance than in the heat of the summer when the conductors increase in length.

(a) **Above Roofs.** The vertical or diagonal clearance over roofs for conductors that are not fully insulated for the operating voltage shall have a clearance of not less than 10 feet (3.05 m) from the roof surface.

Exception No. 1: This permits insulated conductors to have vertical or diagonal clearances of 3 feet or more. This should be checked carefully, because of sagging caused by accumulation of ice in sleet storms and the increase in length in the hot weather, causing more sagging.

Exception No. 2: When conductors cross roofs and are accessible to pedestrians, the vertical clearance for uninsulated conductors shall be a minimum of 18 feet, but if the conductors are insulated the minimum clearance must be 8 feet.

Exception No. 3: Above a roof accessible to vehicle traffic, a minimum of 18 feet will be required.

Exception No. 4: Where the voltages are less than 300 volts, the slope of the roof shall be taken into consideration. If it has a rise of 4 inches or more in 12 inches of the roof, the reduction of the clearance above the roof may be a minimum of 3 feet.

Exception No. 5: See Fig. 230-4, which illustrates this exception; where the conductors do not exceed 300 volts to ground, the clearance is reduced for the overhanging portion of the roof only. This reduction is to be not less than 18 inches, provided that point is not more than 4 feet where conductors pass above the roof overhang, and where they are supported by a service mast or through-the-roof raceway or other approved support.

Author's Note: The through-the-roof raceway or other approved support must be capable of standing the strain of the service drop or be guyed or otherwise sufficiently supported.

(b) **From Nonbuilding or Nonbridge Structures.** This involves clearance both vertically and horizontally from signs, chimneys, antennas, tanks, or anything that is a nonbuilding or nonbridge structure. The clearance for uninsulated conductors shall be not less than 5 feet, and the clearance for insulated conductors shall be not less than 3 feet.

(c) **Horizontal Clearances.** See the *NEC*.

(d) **Final Spans.** Branch circuits and feeders to a building may supply from where they originate. You are permitted to attach these to the building, but they shall be kept a minimum of 3 feet from points from where they can be reached by persons, such as windows, doors, and fire escapes.

There is an exception that will permit them to be less than 3 feet above a window.

(e) **Zone for Fire Ladders.** It is essential that when a building exceeds 3 stories or 50 feet in height, overhead lines shall leave at least a 6-foot clearance for fire ladders. When adjacent to buildings, an 8-foot clearance should be left for the fire fighters.

This is followed by a fine-print note referring to the National Electrical Safety Code, which is used for high voltages or by utilities.

225-20. Mechanical Protection of Conductors—Refer to Section 230-50 in the *NEC*.

225-21. Multiconductor Cables on Exterior Surfaces of Buildings—The requirements are the same as for service entrance cable covered in Section 230-51. Also refer to Section 338-3, which covers service entrance cable used for branch circuits and feeders. It is almost certain that it will be necessary to carry an equipment ground or otherwise satisfy the safety requirement of grounding to the satisfaction of the Code enforcing authority.

225-22. Raceways on Exterior Surfaces of Buildings—See the *NEC*.

225-23. Underground Circuits—The requirements for underground branch circuits and feeders are the same as those covered in Section 300-5. However, remember that provisions must be made for an equipment or grounding conductor for feeders and branch circuits. This is important because the neutral of a feeder circuit is isolated from the cabinet and equipment, so the continuity of grounding must be provided or the purpose for this isolation will be defeated. If in doubt, check with the inspector before installation.

225-24. Outdoor Lampholders—With outdoor lampholders, connections to the conductors shall be staggered. Also where the lampholders are of the pin-type, which puncture the insulation, that the conductors to which they are fastened be stranded type conductors.

225-25. Location of Outdoor Lamps—For safety's sake, the location of lamps for outdoor lighting are required to be installed below all live conductors, electrical utilization equipment, transformers, and primary fuses. This will prevent persons changing the lamps from being endangered by hot equipment.

Exception No. 1: Where relamping operations are provided with safeguards and proper clearances.

Exception No. 2: Where the equipment described above is controlled by a disconnect that can be locked, so that live parts can be killed, putting it in the open position.

225-26. —Live trees cannot be used for the support of any equipment or conductor span run overhead except for temporary wiring covered by Article 305.

From the above, one may realize that safety is of the utmost importance, and regulations are thus given for maintaining this safety.

ARTICLE 230—SERVICES

A. General

230-1. Scope—This article gives a complete coverage of service conductors and equipment for the control and protection of all services. In Article 100 covering definitions, these were the conductors and equipment from the source of power through the service-entrance equipment. The source might be distribution lines, transformers, or generators.

A thorough knowledge of this article is very important since a good service is the keystone of the entire installation. Services may be overhead or underground. A review of Article 100 and the following definitions pertaining to services is essential. Service; service cable; service conductors; service drop; service-entrance conductors, overhead system; service-entrance conductors, underground systems; service equipment; service lateral; service raceway.

Although it is not a Code requirement, the local utility company should always be consulted as to the location for the service entrance.

230-2. Number of Services—Fundamentally, there is to be only one set of services to a building or premises. Should more than one service to a building or structure be required, as permitted in the Exceptions that follow, some means, such as a plaque or directory clearly indicating locations where other services to the building or structure are, must be installed at each service drop or service lateral, or at each service-equipment location. This is essential to protect personnel should one service be disconnected and people be led to believe that all electrical service to the building or structure had been disconnected.

See the *NEC* for Diagram 230-1, Services.

Exception No. 1: Separate services may be required for fire pumps. This would indicate an instance where a fire pump is being served from a separate transformer. It would accomplish nothing if the fire pump and the other service came from one transformer.

Exception No. 2: A separate service may be installed for emergency lighting and power. One would be a standby in the event of failure of the other service. An example of this might be a hospital where two separate services are installed, each being served from a different distribution feeder. In the event that one source failed, the other service might be fed from an emergency standby generator. This applies when there is a legal requirement for emergency services, standby or optimal standby systems.

Exception No. 3: By special permission (in writing), more than one service may be run to a building if there is no space available for service equipment that is accessible to all occupants.

Exception No. 4: Capacity Requirements. By special permission or where capacity requirements are in excess of 3000 amperes at a supply voltage of 600 volts or less, two or more services may be installed.

When we get into large ampacity services, it is felt that it is better to run two or more services than merely one service for the entire capacity requirement. Note "by special permission."

Exception No. 5: Buildings on Large Areas. For buildings covering large areas, by special permission, it may be necessary to have more than one service. This exception is not as prevalent as it was at one time, due to the increases in voltages and the use of transformer vaults and dry types of transformers.

Exception No. 6: Additional services may be required for different voltages, different frequencies, different phases, different classes of use, such as lighting rate and power rate, and controlled water-heater service.

The last exception is for *NEC* Section 230-40, Exception No. 2 only. If the ungrounded conductors are of size 1/0 or larger and are connected together at their supply end but go to the same location, and the service entrance end is not tied together so that it will become a parallel circuit, then they shall be considered one service lateral. This would mean that each set of individual service laterals could terminate in separate service entrances because they are in no way parallel.

230-3. One Building or Other Structure Not to Be Supplied Through Another—Service drop or laterals are defined as the conductors that supply electricity to the point of usage. Service conductors that supply a building or structure shall never be allowed to be run through one building to another unless the buildings are under single occupancy or management. Section 230-6 explains when conductors are considered to be outside a building. Even when under the same occupancy or management, one should be careful in permitting conductors to be run through the buildings. See Figs. 230-1 and 230-2.

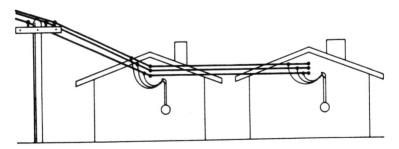

Fig. 230-1. The service entrance for two buildings under the same ownership.

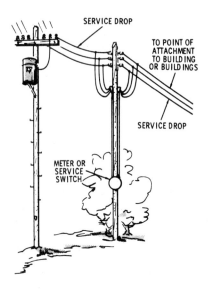

SERVICE DROP

TO POINT OF
ATTACHMENT
TO BUILDING
OR BUILDINGS

SERVICE DROP

METER OR
SERVICE
SWITCH

Fig. 230-2. A metering pole.

In Fig. 230-2, please note that the conductors to the meter and from the meter to supply the premises are separate conduits. You are never allowed to run metered and unmetered conductors in the same conduit. Some utilities that install these metering poles do, but that comes under the exception for utilities by Code.

(FPN): The minimum sizes for service conductors are given in the following references:

For Service Drops—See Section 230-23
For Underground Service Conductors—See Section 230-31
For Service-Entrance Conductors—See Section 230-41
For Farmstead Service Conductors—See Part D of Article 220

B. Overhead Services

230-21. Overhead Supply—See Figs. 230-1 and 230-2. Overhead supplies are commonly referred to as service drops and are the conductors to a building or other structure. This drop could also be to a service pole where metering for a disconnect has been placed. On mobile home meters you will find that if the metering and disconnect are on a pole (because they may not be mounted on a mobile home), the service drop stops at that point, and the overhead conductors from the pole to the mobile home are called "feeders." An example of this will be found not only in the section on mobile homes, but also in Part D of Article 220, which covers loads on farms.

230-22. Insulation or Covering—Service conductors have to withstand exposure to atmospheric conditions or any other conditions that will cause leakage between conductors. The insulation for service conductors that are individually insulated is usually covered with extruded thermoplastic or thermosetting insulating material. There is an exception to the insulation. Where multiconductor cable such as duplex, triplex, or fourplex cables are used, the neutral conductor may be an uninsulated conductor.

See *NEC* tables in Article 310 for the ampacity of service drop conductors, run in cable or as open conductors. If covered with extruded thermoplastic or thermosetting insulation, the ampacity shall be the same as if they were bare conductors of the same size.

230-23. Size and Rating—The first requirement shall always be that service-drop conductors shall be of sufficient size to carry the load. They shall not be smaller than No. 8 copper or the equivalent, except for limited loads as covered in Section 230-42. Exception permits service-entrance conductors to be small as No. 12 hard-drawn copper or No. 10 aluminum, providing that they only furnish a single circuit, such as a small polyphase motor, controlled water heaters, or similar loads, and providing they are hard-drawn copper or equivalent.

Figs. 100-1 and 230-2 show the service drops when the structure is a pole. The same condition could be a building with the meter on the building and/or a disconnecting means and other buildings or structures from said meter and/or disconnecting means. The grounded conductor of service drops shall be sized as per Section 250-23(b) in the *NEC*.

230-24. Clearances—As previously mentioned, temperature allows conductors to lengthen, therefore clearances are given: In the Code, 60°F (15°C), no wind, and this book mentions ice-loading sag of conductors. The *NEC* has taken care of this in this section. This section pertains to services that are not readily accessible, do not exceed 600 volts, nominal, and must conform to the following:

(a) **Above Roofs.** The basic requirement is that conductors shall have a vertical clearance of not less than 8 feet (2.44 m) from the highest point of the roofs above which they pass, but the following exceptions may also apply:

Exception No. 1: Services that do not exceed 300 volts between conductors. Formerly, services above roofs that were not readily accessible were permitted to have a clearance of not less than 3 feet (914 mm). It was a very debatable question as to what was not readily accessible. The 1965 Code clarified this:

If the voltage does not exceed 300 volts and the roof slope meets requirements noted earlier of a slope not less than 4 inches in 12 inches, then the clearance may be reduced to not less than 3 feet.

Exception No. 2: Service drop conductors of 300 volts or less which do not pass above other than a maximum of 4 feet (1.22 m) of the overhang portion of the roof for the purpose of terminating at a (through-the-roof) service raceway or approved support may be maintained at a minimum of 18 inches (457 mm) from any portion of the roof above which it passes. This exception does not mention the slope of the overhang, but does clear up the height of the point of attachment to the mast. Fig. 230-3 shows where this exception is applicable.

Exception No. 3: Section 230-24(b) gives the vertical clearance when the area above a roof's clearance is subject to vehicular traffic.

Section 230-28 covers mast supports.

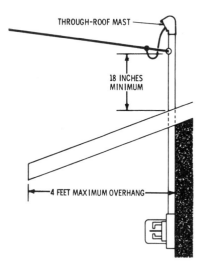

THROUGH-ROOF MAST

18 INCHES MINIMUM

4 FEET MAXIMUM OVERHANG

Fig. 230-3. A service-drop mast mounted through the roof.

(b) **Vertical Clearance from Ground.** This pertains to voltages not in excess of 600 volts, nominal, and covers clearances of service drops.

Refer to Fig. 230-4 for ground clearances over the various areas where vehicles are used.

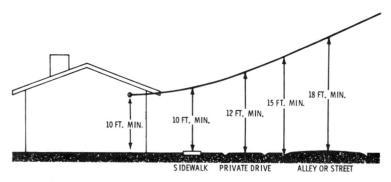

10 FT. MIN.   10 FT. MIN.   12 FT. MIN.   15 FT. MIN.   18 FT. MIN.

SIDEWALK   PRIVATE DRIVE   ALLEY OR STREET

Fig. 230-4. Minimum service-drop clearance.

(c) **Clearance from Building Openings.** Again, this is for service conductors not exceeding 600 volts, nominal. (For clearances of conductors of over 600 volts, nominal, see the *National Electrical Safety Code,* available from the IEEE.) There is to be a clearance of not less than 3 feet (914 mm) from windows, doors, porches, fire escapes, or similar locations. Conductors above windows may be less than the 3 feet (914 mm) requirement.

(d) **Clearance from Swimming Pools.** See Section 680-8.

230-26. Point of Attachment—The point of attachment of conductors (service drop) to a building or structure shall meet all the requirements of Section 230-24. The minimum is 10 feet (3.05 m) above finished grade, but in going back to Section 230-24(b), note that the drip loop is mentioned as well as service-drop cables supported and/or cabled together with a grounded bare messenger.

When sufficient attachment height for service drops cannot be obtained due to the construction of the building, a mast type of riser (Fig. 230-5) may be used providing it is capable of withstanding the strain that might be imposed upon it. In considering the strain that might be imposed, the prevailing weather conditions should be considered. Each locality will no doubt have specifications which should be met.

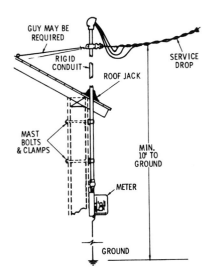

Fig. 230-5. Mast installation for proper service-drop height.

230-27. Means of Attachment—In attaching multiconductor cables to buildings or other structures, only approved devices shall be used. In the attachment of open conductors, only approved, noncombustible, nonabsorptive types of fittings shall be used.

230-28. Service Masts as Supports—All fittings for service mast shall be properly identified; this means listed for the purpose for which they are used. Any braces or guys supporting the mast shall be adequate for the purpose. See Section 230-26 in this book and Fig. 230-5.

230-29. Supports Over Buildings—Substantial structures shall be used to securely support conductors that pass over roofs. They shall be of substantial construction and independent of the building where practicable.

C. Underground Service-Lateral Conductors

230-30. Insulation—The insulation on service-lateral conductors must be adequate for the voltage being carried, and the insulation also must be approved for direct burial so that there will not be detrimental leakage of current. In Article 300 you will find that service lateral cables generally are noted by USE and most of the average conductors we use in wiring carry a 600-volt rating, which in most cases will be more than adequate to cover the applied voltage. An exception for grounded uninsulated conductors is given; check your *NEC* for this. It is very important to know the electrolytic qualities of the earth in which they are being installed, if they are used. Also note that aluminum conductors or copper-clad aluminum conductors that are grounded are to be used only when part of a cable that is listed for direct burial.

Take note of the bare copper for direct burial; also take note of the fact that the soil conditions must be judged suitable and this judgment is up to the authority having jurisdiction, as provided in Section 90-4.

230-31. Size and Rating—As with all conductors, they shall have sufficient ampacity to carry the load and they shall not be smaller than No. 8 copper or No. 6 aluminum or copper-clad aluminum. The grounded (neutral) conductor shall not be smaller than the minimum size as permitted by Section 250-23(b).

Exception: When supplying loads with a limited demand and a single branch circuit, such as small polyphase motors, controlled water heaters and the like, it will be permitted to use conductors not smaller than No. 12 copper or No. 10 aluminum or copper-clad aluminum, provided they have the proper ampacity to carry the load.

230-32. Protection Against Damage—It is very important to see that ungrounded service laterals shall not be subject to damage. See Section 300-5. The above refers to service-laterals not enclosed in raceways. It would not be amiss, if they are enclosed in metallic or plastic raceways, to encase them in concrete of a red color, added, and the author recommends 2000 pound concrete with a 7-inch slump and not larger than ⅜ inch aggregate. Where service lateral conductors enter a building, Section 230-6 applies, or raceway may be used as identified in Section 230-43.

D. Service-Entrance Conductors

230-40. Number of Service-Entrance Conductor Sets—Only one set of service drops or service laterals shall supply the service entrance conductors.

Exception No. 1: Buildings such as shopping centers that have more than one occupancy will be permitted to have more than one set of service-entrance conductors run to each occupancy, or they may be grouped so that more occupancies can be served by more than one set of service conductors by means of auxiliary gutters, etc.

Fig. 230-6. Two sets of service-entrance conductors tapped to one service drop.

Exception No. 2: This exception covers places where two to six disconnecting means are located in separate enclosures that must be grouped at one location supplying separate loads. From where we only have one service drop or service lateral, a separate set of service-entrance conductors is permitted to supply each or several of these service equipment enclosures. Note that the disconnecting means shall be grouped.

230-41. Insulation of Service-Entrance Conductors—Service-entrance conductors entering buildings or other structures shall be insulated. Where only on the exterior of buildings or other structures the conductors shall be insulated or covered: The attachment of service entrance conductors shall be installed so that water will not be siphoned into the service entrance conductors.

Exception: Uninsulated grounded conductors are permitted to be used in service-entrances as follows:

Check your *NEC* in this section for (a) to (d) where ungrounded conductors are permitted or not permitted.

It would be well to note the similarity of this section and Section 230-30; the same notation applies here.

(a) **General.** The first requirement, as always, is that the service-entrance conductors be of sufficient ampacity to carry the required load. The determination of the sizing was covered in Article 220, and the ampacity of the conductors is to be determined by Tables 310-16 through 310-31 and the applicable notes that accompany these tables shall apply.

(b) **Ungrounded Conductors.** The ampacity of ungrounded conductors shall not be less than those covered below:

(1) One-family dwellings with six or more 2-wire branch circuits shall have a minimum of 100 ampere 3-wire service.

Nowadays it is practically impossible to find a residence that would have only six 2-wire circuits, as there would be a minimum of two for small appliances and one for the laundry, which would leave only three circuits for other uses.

(2) One-family dwellings where the computed load is 10 kVA or more shall have a minimum of 100-ampere 3-wire service.

(3) Other than those covered in (1) and (2), there may be loads that can have 60-ampere services.

Do not take the 100-ampere capacity as the maximum that is required. The computed load may require higher ampacity for the service conductors.

Exception No. 1: Where the load computed has not more than two 2-wire branch circuits, the service conductors may be No. 6 aluminum or No. 8 copper.

Exception No. 2: Some wiring is now done with demand-limiting equipment at the source of supply. If the maximum demand permits No. 8 copper, No. 6 aluminum, or No. 6 copper-clad aluminum.

Exception No. 3: If the load is limited to one single branch circuit—and this could be on such as an illuminated advertising sign—No. 12 copper, No. 10 aluminum, or copper-clad aluminum may be used, but never shall it be permitted to be less than the branch circuits covered.

(c) **Grounded Conductors.** Section 250-23(b) sets the minimum size that will be permitted for the grounded (neutral) conductor, and this size shall not be less than as covered in that section.

230-43. Wiring Methods for 600 Volts, Nominal, or Less—Code
covers (later) what conditions service-entrance conductors may be installed,

but the requirements of Code limit wiring methods used. For these methods, check this section in your *NEC*. You will also find that it covers installation around flexible metal conduit according to the provisions of Section 250-79(a), (b), (c), and (e). See Section 350-2 as well.

Permission is granted with approved cable tray systems to support cables for use as service-entrance conductors. This is covered in Article 318.

230-46. Unspliced Conductors—Splices are not permitted in service-entrance conductors.

Excludes metering equipment and enclosures where by necessity clamp or bolted connections must be used.

Where service-entrance conductors enter such an auxiliary gutter to supply two to six separate disconnecting means and these means are grouped in one location, tapping will be required.

Where an underground service conductor enters a building, a splice may be made in an approved enclosure for connecting to approved service raceway or cable. (See Fig. 230-7.)

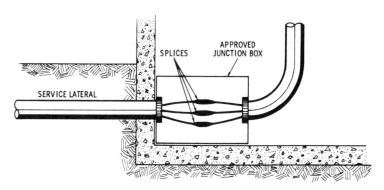

Fig. 230-7. A splice in an underground service.

On existing installations, a connection will be permitted where service conductors are extended from a service drop to an outside meter and returned to connect to the service-entrance conductors of an existing installation.

Where the service-entrance conductors are buses, the only method of getting continuity is by bolting the different pieces of busbars to fit the various sections and fittings.

230-49. Protection Against Damage—Underground—Section 300-5 covers the protection required for underground conductors, which applies also to underground service entrance conductors.

In areas where frost and freezing are problems, if the soil is of a rocky nature that frost heave can cause physical damage to the insulation of underground conductors, whether they are service conductors, feeders, or branch-circuit conductors. As a precautionary measure, one should lay a sand bed, install the conductors, and then cover them with a sand cover and then back-fill with the earth that was removed. There should also be a loop at the point where they leave the ground, so that if the earth settles, the conductors will not be subjected to pulling out of terminations, etc. Experience has also shown that if the conduit leaving the conductors at the point of their emergence from the earth is straight down, with an insulated bushing on the end of the conduit, that frost will not cut the insulation as badly as if a 90-degree ell is put on the end of the conduit. These are not Code requirements, but merely good procedures.

230-50. Protection of Open Conductors and Cables Against Damage—Aboveground—(a) and (b) below provide information about what is necessary to prevent physical damage to service-entrance conductors installed aboveground.

(a) **Service-Entrance Cables.** It is possible that service-entrance cables be installed where they may be exposed to physical damage, such as near driveways or coal shutes, or where subject to contact with awnings, shutters, swinging signs, or similar objects; if so, they shall be protected by one or more of the following means: (1) by rigid metal conduit; (2) by intermediate metal conduit; (3) by rigid nonmetallic conduit suitable for the location; (4) by electrical metallic tubing; (5) by other approved means.

(b) **Other than Service-Entrance Cable.** Open cables other than service-entrance cables and open conductors shall have a minimum clearance of 10 feet above grade level to protect them from physical damage.

230-51. Mounting Supports—(a), (b), or (c) below cover mounting supports for individual open service conductors or cables.

(a) **Service-Entrance Cable.** Support service-entrance cables by straps or other approved means within 12 inches (305 mm) of the service head, gooseneck, or connection to a raceway or enclosure; otherwise support the cables at intervals not to exceed 30 inches (763 mm).

(b) **Other Cables.** If the cables are not approved for mounting in contact with the building, they are to be mounted on insulators at intervals not to exceed 15 feet (4.57 m) and must have a minimum clearance of 2 inches (50.8 mm) from the surface over which they pass. (See Fig. 230-8.)

(c) **Individual Open Conductors.** Table 230-51(c) covers mounting of individual conductors. When exposed to weather, mounted on insulating supports, or attached to racks, brackets, insulators, or any other means, they shall be approved by authority having jurisdiction or shall have a listing such as UL. If the conductors are not exposed to weather, you are permitted to mount them on glass or porcelain

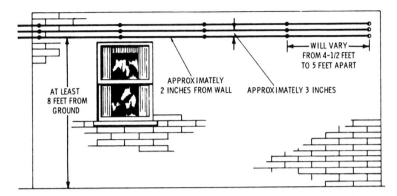

Fig 230-8. Service conductors run on an outside wall.

mounts. See Table 230-51(c) for supports and clearances for Individual Open Service Conductors in your *NEC*.

230-52. Individual Conductors Entering Buildings or Other Structures—Where individual conductors enter buildings, they are required to pass inward and upward through noncombustible and nonabsorptive insulating tubes, or through roof busings. The Code calls for drip loops. However, one should consider Section 230-54, which requires the service head to be above the service drop to prevent the entrance of moisture.

230-53. Raceways to Drain—Service-entrance raceways, when exposed to weather, shall be raintight and arranged to drain. If embedded in concrete they shall also be arranged to drain.

This brings to mind an applicable case that should be mentioned here. A large building housing turkeys had a service mast and service-entrance equipment. The service entrance was mounted in the enclosure where the turkeys were kept. The service mast had a raintight cap. However, the humidity was extremely high in the building and the temperature warm, so the moisture entered the service-entrance equipment, and as the warm air rose in the service mast it came in contact with the cold. The moisture condensed and ran back down the service mast into the service equipment, causing some shorts. The author solved the problem by having duct seal placed at both ends of the service mast to stop the moisture from moving up the mast, and thus eliminated these shorting problems.

230-54. Connections at Service Head.

(a) **Raintight Service Head.** Always be sure that service-entrance raceways are equipped with approved raintight service heads.

(b) **Service Cable Equipment with Raintight Service Head or Gooseneck.** Unless service cable is continuous from the meter enclosure or service equipment to the pole serving same, raintight service heads shall be used or a gooseneck shall be formed. The connections shall then be taped and painted unless thermoplastic tape—that is, self-sealing—is used. This is to stop the siphoning of water down the cable.

(c) **Service Heads Above Service-Drop Attachment.** To prevent water from entering the conductor, which has caused some troubles due to siphoning between the conductor and its insulation, service entrance heads or goosenecks are always to be located above the service drop.

There are, as usual, exceptions to this which might be required if it is impractical to meet the above requirements. Where necessary to locate the service head below the service-drop conductors, this service head may be located at a point not to exceed 24 (610 mm) inches from the point of attachment.

There should also be a mechanical connector at the lowest point to prevent siphoning of water by the service-entrance conductors, as shown in Fig. 230-9.

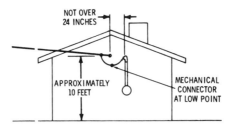

Fig. 230-9. A connection to prevent siphoning of water into the service-drop head.

(d) **Secured.** It is essential where service cables are used that they are securely fastened in place to avoid possible damage.

(e) **Opposite Polarity Through Separate Bushed Holes.** (See Fig. 230-10.) Service conductors brought through holes in the service-entrance head shall have the conductors of different polarities brought out through separate holes, thus avoiding a possible short between different phase conductors.

(f) **Drip Loops.** The drip loops required shall be formed on all conductors to prevent siphoning of moisture into the service equipment. Service conductors may be connected to service-entrance conductors in several ways. In one the service drop conductors shall be below the service-entrance head. In another the service drop conductors shall be below the termination of service-entrance cable sheath.

(g) **Arranged so that Water Will Not Enter Raceway or Equipment.** In all cases service drop conductors must be arranged to prevent water

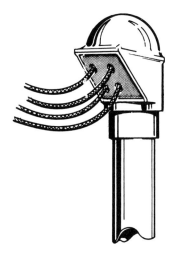

Fig. 230-10. Separation and insulation of the service-entrance conductors to the service head.

entering the service-entrance or the service-entrance equipment. (This has been discussed just previous to this section.)

230-55. Terminations at Service Equipment—Service-entrance raceway or cable must be terminated in service-entrance equipment such as box, cabinet, auxiliary gutters, or other effective means that resistantly enclose live parts to easy access. An exception permits a switchboard, having busbars exposed on the back of the service equipment disconnecting means mounted on the switch board a raceway, to terminate at a bushing.

230-56. Service-Entrance Conductor with the Higher Voltage-to-Ground—If a 4-wire delta with a midpoint of one grounded phase is used, one phase point to ground will give a higher voltage than the other phase of 208 volts, nominal, to ground. In the field we often refer to this as the wild leg, and every precaution must be taken to identify the wild leg on the outer finish that is orange in color or by other effective means if approved by the authority having jurisdiction. This marking shall show up at every location or other connection place where it would be possible to connect the wild leg to the neutral.

E. Service Equipment—General

230-62. Service Equipment—Enclosed or Guarded—(a) below covers live parts or service equipment that are enclosed, and (b) below covers guarded parts as specified therein.

(a) **Enclosed.** With service equipment the live parts shall be enclosed so as not to permit accidental contact. Thus service-entrance equipment usually has a dead front so that breaker panels are exposed only, and then a hinged door or removable cover to cover these breaker handles; or as stated before, live parts in this equipment may be guarded as in (b) following:

(b) **Guarded.** Live parts not enclosed such as might be installed on switch boards panel boards or control boards may be guarded as covered in Sections 110-17 and 110-18. Means shall be provided for locking or sealing doors that would give access to live parts.

230-63. Grounding and Bonding—Grounding of service equipment, raceways, cable armor, cable sheaths, etc., and service conductors that are required to be grounded shall be in accordance with the following parts of Article 250:

See the *NEC* for Parts B, D, F, G, H, and J, which show portions covering certain parts of grounding.

See Figs. 230-11 through 230-13.

230-64. Working Space—Section 110-16 covers working space. There shall always be working space provided in the vicinity of service equipment so that repairs, inspection, and operation may be conducted in a safe manner.

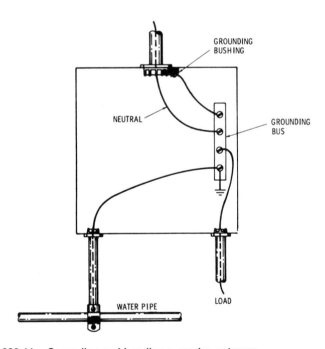

Fig. 230-11. Grounding and bonding a service entrance.

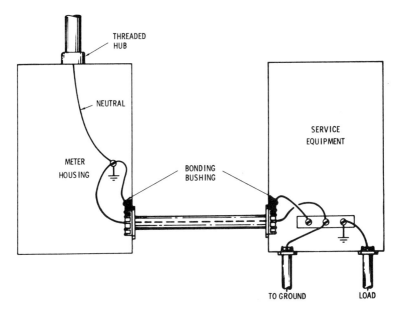

Fig. 230-12. Grounding and bonding a typical service entrance.

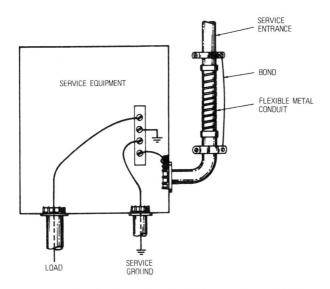

Fig. 230-13. Bonding flexible metal conduit in a service entrance.

230-65. Available Short-Circuit Current—Every supply has what we call available fault currents that are much larger than the overcurrent protection usually provided in service-entrance equipment. Many pamphlets are available from fuse and breaker manufacturers for calculating available fault current; or you should consult the electric utility supply for the available fault current supplying the structure being served.

F. Service Equipment—Disconnecting Means

230-70. General—A separate means shall be provided for disconnecting the service-entrance conductors from the building or structure wiring proper.

(a) **Location.** The service disconnecting means is to be located in a readily accessible point near the closest point of entrance of the service-entrance conductors. It may be a separate piece of equipment or a part of the service-entrance equipment panel where there are also branch circuits. The location of this disconnect may be either on the outside of the building or structure or inside the closest point where the service-entrance conductors enter.

Many inspectors require that the disconnecting means be set at a height of not to exceed 6½ feet above where a person would be standing when using the disconnecting means. Check with the inspection authority for the location. Some inspectors consider bathrooms and bedrooms to be not readily accessible, as they may be considered as private locations. The author would not accept a disconnecting means located in the basement unless there was an en-

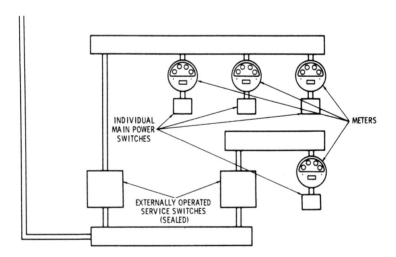

Fig. 230-14. Typical service disconnect switches.

trance to the basement at ground level. In case of fire, the basement would not be a readily accessible place.

(b) **Marking.** It is very important that the service disconnecting means be legibly marked so that it may be easily identified in case of electrical trouble or fire.

(c) **Suitable For Use.** It shall also be suitable for use for the prevailing conditions; for example, if it is outdoors, it shall be raintight. If service equipment is installed in hazardous (classified) locations it shall comply with requirements of Articles 500 through 517.

230-71. Maximum Number of Disconnects.

(a) **General.** Section 230-2 covered disconnecting means for each service permitted under this section. Each set of service-entrance conductors that were permitted by Section 230-40, Exception No. 1, shall consist of not more than a disconnecting means in a single enclosure, but this is expanded to include also a group of separate enclosures for more disconnecting means. Remember, the maximum is six disconnecting means that are grouped together or on a switchboard.

Exception: A disconnecting means that is used solely for control of ground-fault protection that has been installed as part of the equipment for ground-fault protection, shall not be considered one of the not more than six disconnecting means.

(b) **Single-Pole Units.** On two- or three-pole services, single switches or breakers may be used, provided they have the capacity and are equipped with handle ties or master handle (this would be a two or three breaker controlled by one handle) so that all disconnecting means to the service equipment shall open the ungrounded conductors with not more than six operations of the hand. The six operations of the hand are included to cover situations where you have up to six disconnecting means. More will be covered in Section 384-16(a), where the service equipment is in the panelboard.

This is commonly known as the "six operations of the hand rule." Note the mention of multiwire circuits, and refer to the definition of a multiwire circuit in Article 100.

See Figs. 230-13 and 230-15 through 230-17.

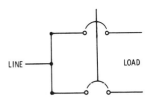

LINE — LOAD **Fig. 230-15. A two-pole circuit-breaker switch which cannot be used as a service disconnect.**

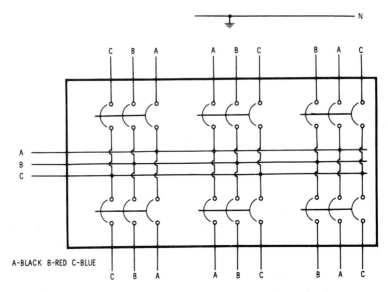

Fig. 230-16. Illustrating eighteen circuit breakers tied together in groups of three.

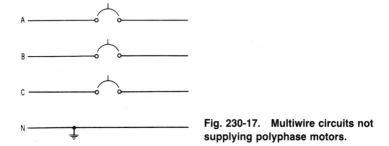

Fig. 230-17. Multiwire circuits not supplying polyphase motors.

230-72. Grouping of Disconnects.

(a) **General.** The two to six disconnecting means just covered in Section 230-71 again are to be grouped, and each separate one of the two to six disconnecting means shall be plainly marked as to what load each serves.

If one of the disconnecting means of Section 230-71 is used for fire protection only, it does not have to be grouped with the other disconnecting means, but may be in a remote place. This, as one can readily see, is in the event of fire. The fire disconnecting means should not be as readily disconnected as the rest of the disconnecting means because of its importance for fire protection.

(b) **Additional Service Disconnecting Means.** To be compatible with Sections 700-12(d) and (e) where one or more additional service disconnecting means for fire pumps or for emergency services are installed, they shall be sufficiently remote from the one to six service disconnecting means for normal services so that there will be no chance or at least minimal chance of simultaneous interruption of supply.

(c) **Access to Occupants.** In multiple-occupancy buildings it is essential that each occupant of the building have ready access to the disconnecting means serving their apartment.

Exception: In a multiple-occupancy building, if the building and electrical maintenance are provided by the management and this service is under continual supervision, it is not necessary that the disconnecting means be accessible to each occupant, because management has continuous service available.

230-74. Simultaneous Opening of Poles—All ungrounded service conductors shall be capable of simultaneously disconnecting from the building or structure wiring.

230-75. Disconnecting of Grounded Conductor—The disconnecting means may be so designed that it also opens the grounded conductor simultaneously with the ungrounded conductors. Where the disconnect does not accomplish this, there shall be other means provided in the service cabinet for disconnecting the grounded conductor from the interior wiring. This is usually accomplished by pressure-type connectors for the grounded conductor. The service-entrance ground shall always be attached to the service side of the disconnecting means. This is required so that there will be ground on the service, even though the grounded conductors on the interior wiring have been disconnected.

230-76. Manually or Power Operable—A manually operable switch for disconnecting means of ungrounded service conductors or a circuit breaker with common trip or equipped with a handle that will operate the opening of all ungrounded conductors may be used, or a power-operated switch or circuit breaker may be used as a disconnecting means, provided such equipment can also be operated by hand in case of trouble or power failure.

230-77. Indicating—Service disconnecting means must be plainly marked to show whether it is open or closed.

230-78. Externally Operable—All enclosed service disconnecting means are required to be such that they are operable by an external means so that anyone operating them will not be exposed to live parts.

Exception: When a disconnecting means is power operable, it is not necessary to have an external means of hand-closing the switch or circuit breaker.

When a single circuit or group of circuits is separately metered, as in apartment-house installations, it is recommended that the devices (disconnecting means) be installed in a convenient location to control each separately metered installation. These devices (main disconnects) are to be enclosed and the switch or circuit breaker be externally operable.

In this type of installation, a maximum of six main disconnects shall be maintained or a main disconnect must be installed to take care of all the circuits. In the installation, it should be remembered that the main disconnects shall be accessible to the occupants of the apartments. This is a condition that causes much concern, although it need not if all the requirements that must be met are considered.

Fig. 230-14 illustrates a typical example of such a condition. This installation may use a wiring trough or gutter, or a combination meter installation and trough or gutter. The illustration shown will, of course, not meet all installation requirements, but is an example of the intent in this matter. The one point to bear in mind is that there are to be no more than six main disconnects in service-entrance equipment. It would be suggested that when this type of installation is anticipated, the authorities be consulted and the installation worked out before the work is done.

230-79. Rating of Disconnect—Article 220 covered calculation of load. The service disconnecting means shall not be less than the load that is calculated, and in no case shall the service disconnecting means be rated smaller than required in (a), (b), and (c) below:

(a) **One-Circuit Installation.** When limited loads are served by a single branch circuit, the rating of the service disconnecting means shall not be lower than 15 amperes.

(b) **Two-Circuit Installations.** For installations that do not supply more than two 2-wire circuits, the minimum size of service disconnecting means shall not be less than 30 amperes.

(c) **One-Family Dwelling.** Single-family dwellings shall have a service disconnecting means of not less than 100 amperes, 3-wire, where either of the following conditions exists: (1) If the calculated load is 10 kilo volt-amperes or more, or (2) where six or more 2-wire branch circuits are installed on the original installation.

   The preceding conditions in no manner prohibit the installation of larger services and service disconnecting means to take care of any future added loads.

(d) **All Others.** Sixty amperes is the smallest service disconnecting means that may be used for all other installations.

230-80. Combined Rating of Disconnects—Where more than one switch or circuit breaker is used as a disconnecting means in accordance with Section 230-71, the combined ratings of the switches or circuit breakers that are used shall be no less than what would be required had only one switch or circuit breaker been used.

230-81. Connection to Terminals—Soldered connections are never to be used for connecting service conductors to service disconnecting means. The conductors shall be connected by means of pressure connectors, clamps, or other approved means.

230-82. Equipment Connected to the Supply Side of Service Disconnecting—Ordinarily no circuits shall be connected ahead of the disconnecting means. There of course are 8 exceptions to the above, as follows:

Exception No. 1: Any current-limiting device, including cable limiters.

Exception No. 2: This will be used a great deal in the article covering mobile homes. Used as disconnecting means or circuit breaker that conforms to the use as service equipment and meter pedestals or otherwise provided such as on the service pole and in series with the ungrounded service conductors, they are permitted, and in mobile home installations are a requirement. They may be located away from the building supplied.

Exception No. 3: Meter installations on less than 600 volts, nominal, and housed in a metal enclosure if the metal enclosures are grounded as covered in Article 250.

Exception No. 4: Among the items that may be connected ahead of the disconnecting means are instrument transformers, consisting of current transformers and voltage transformers, and high-impedance shunts; in many places you will find that surge protection devices are also required. One such place is a grain elevator. These must be connected ahead of the disconnecting means. With surge protection you will later find places where capacitors are used and fed through a fuse disconnecting means. These are connected on the load side of the service disconnecting means. Lightning arresters have to be connected ahead of any fusing or service disconnecting means. They are often mounted where the service drop and service conductors are spliced together or sometimes out of the disconnecting means. These take care of such surges as lightning surges, etc.

Exception No. 5: This is an exception for connecting what I call load-management devices, and consists of essential circuits for emergency systems. Among these emergency systems, fire pumps and fire sprinkler alarms, if provided from the service equipment (many places, such as hospitals and places where electrical service must be maintained, have stand-by power systems that come on to pick up the load when power fails), they are to be connected ahead of the disconnecting means so that they don't come on accidentally. See Figs. 230-18 and 230-19 on page 90.

Exception No. 6: See Article 690 for situations in which power is interconnected to the source.

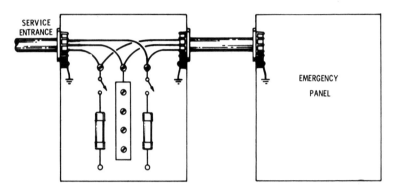

Fig. 230-18. Unapproved means of connecting an emergency panel.

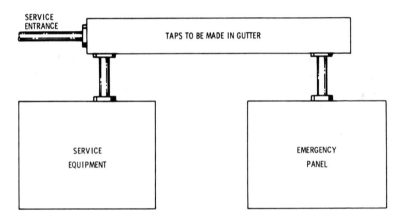

Fig. 230-19. Approved means of connecting an emergency panel.

Exception No. 7: Where suitable overcurrent protection and disconnecting means may be provided and may be connected ahead of the regular service disconnecting means, if it is operated from the regular power. This exception covers control circuits for such.

Exception No. 8: If suitable overcurrent protection and disconnecting means are provided on ground-fault protection systems that are listed as part of the equipment, their installation may be connected ahead of the main service disconnecting means.

230-83. Transfer Equipment—On transfer equipment, such as equipment transfer from one source of power to another, it shall be designed so that all ungrounded conductors from the source supply are disconnected before any ungrounded connectors from the second source are connected.

Exception No. 1: When two or more power services, whether manually or automatically operated, are utilized, they may be connected in parallel. This of course must take into account phase relationships and synchronization.

Exception No. 2: Parallel operation of transfer equipment is permitted where suitable control equipment is used.

230-84. More than One Building or Other Structure.

(a) **Disconnect Required for Each.** When more than one building or structure is located on property under single management, a means for disconnecting all ungrounded conductors is required at each building.

See Section 230-70, which covers locations.

Exception No. 1: For more coverage on this exception, see Section 230-91(b). As to Exception No. 1 itself, refer to your *NEC.*

Exception No. 2: See your *NEC* for provisions under Article 685.

(b) **Suitable for Service Equipment.** Any disconnecting means covered specifically in (a) above must be listed for service equipment or be approved by the authority having jurisdiction.

Exception: For garages and outbuildings on residential property, the disconnecting means may consist of a snap switch or a set of 3-way or 4-way snap switches suitable for use on branch circuits.

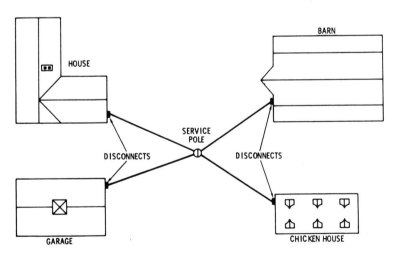

Fig. 230-20.   A group of farm buildings showing a service drop to each building.

G. Service Equipment—Overcurrent Protection

230-90. Where Required—Every ungrounded service conductor shall have overcurrent protection. The various locations where this may be mounted were covered earlier.

(a) **Ungrounded Conductor.** This overcurrent protection is to be in series with the ungrounded service conductor it is protecting. The ampere rating or setting of adjustable overcurrent protection is never permitted to be rated over the ampacity of the service conductors it protects.

An example of the above would be that a 100-ampere service should have No. 3 THW conductors or larger, and a 300-ampere service would have 350 MCM THW or larger conductors. Any derating that might be applicable in Article 310 must always be considered.

Exception No. 1: Motor-starting currents will have to be dealt with separately, and the ratings must be in conformity with Sections 430-52, 430-62, or 430-63. Although not stated in this section of the Code, you should always take into consideration what might be added in the future, and, if possible, make allowances for this at the time of the installation.

Exception No. 2: Where nonadjustable circuit breakers do not conform to the ampacity of the conductor, the next larger size may be used provided that it is 800 amperes or less. If the breaker is adjustable, it shall not be set at a rating of more than 125 percent of the ampacity of the conductor. When fuses are used, if there is not a standard size to fit the ampacity of the conductor, the next larger size may be used provided that it is 800 amperes or less. See Section 240-3, Exception No. 1, and Section 240-6.

Exception No. 3: As was stated earlier, there shall not be more than six circuit breakers or six sets of fuses for any service disconnecting means. Here, one must remember that a single-pole, a two-pole, or a three-pole breaker may count as one.

Exception No. 4: Fire Pumps. If we have a fire pump room for the service to the fire pump, it may be judged outside of the building, and the provisions above shall not apply. Locked-rotor current of the fire pump motor may be selected to carry the fire pump locked-rotor current indefinitely. Note: Here you are referred to another fire code, NFPA 20-1983, or to the ANSI standards covering Centrifugal Fire Pumps. This is one point where other NFPA fire codes are recommended to be used with the *NEC*.

In considering the overload current protection for fire pumps, a set of fuses protecting all ungrounded conductors of the circuit is adequate. If single-pole breakers are used and grouped together, as previously covered, by a tie handle that opens all the breakers to the ungrounded protection device, they are also permitted. The grounded conductor must be connected to service equipment and grounding electrode ahead of the fuse in the grounded conductor.

(b) **Not in Grounded Conductor.** There is to be no overcurrent device in the grounded service conductor. The exception to this is that the circuit breaker shall simultaneously open all conductors of the circuit. A little explanation of this might be in order. Should the grounded conductor overcurrent device open by itself and the ungrounded conductor overcurrent devices not open, an unbalanced voltage condition would exist that might cause damage to equipment. See Fig. 230-21.

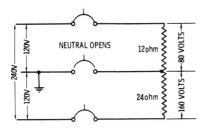

Fig. 230-21. A breaker in the neutral. The neutral circuit breaker must be open simultaneously with the breaker contacts in the phase wires.

230-91. Location of Overcurrent Protection.

(a) **Location.** A no-fuse disconnect may be used, but the service overcurrent device shall be located immediately thereto. Doing it this way just means more expense. Section 230-70(a) tells us that the service disconnecting means must be located either inside or outside of the building or structure at the closest point of entrance.

(b) **More than One Building.** Please refer back to Section 230-84. Where more than one building or structure is under single management, the ungrounded conductors serving each building or structure shall have overcurrent devices of the proper size to protect them. These may be located in the building served or in another building or structure, but in all cases they are to be readily accessible to the occupants of the building being served. A case in point would be a farmstead with a residence and a guest house. Should the overcurrent device be located in the residence, it would be considered as being accessible to the guest house.

(c) **Access to Occupants.** Occupants shall have access to the overcurrent protection devices in multiple-occupancy buildings.

You will find an exception to this in Section 240-24(b).

230-92. Locked Service Overcurrent Devices—If the service overcurrent devices are locked or sealed or otherwise not readily accessible, the branch-circuit overcurrent devices have to be located and readily ac-

cessible on the load side of the service overcurrent device. The circuits in this branch-circuit panel are to be of lower ratings than these service overcurrent devices. Since the branch-circuit devices will have a smaller rating than the inaccessible service overcurrent protection device, there will be less likelihood that it will trip.

230-93. Protection of Specific Circuits—To prevent tampering, it might become necessary to provide a locked or sealed automatic overcurrent device to serve some specific load, such as a water heater. Such a locked or sealed device must be in an accessible location.

230-94. Relative Location of Overcurrent Device and Other Service Equipment—The overcurrent devices are installed for protection, and must protect all circuits and devices.

The service switch may be on the supply side. In fact, it has been repeatedly said that the service disconnecting means shall be on the supply side.

Exception No. 1: As permitted in Section 230-82, the following may be installed on the supply side of the service disconnecting means: high-impedance shunt circuits, lightning arresters, surge protective capacitors, and instrument transformers (current and potential).

Exception No. 2: Where supplied with separate overcurrent protection, such circuits as emergency circuits and time switches may be connected to the supply side of the service overcurrent protection. In fact, emergency systems must be ahead of the service disconnecting means as covered in Article 700 and in NFPA 101 by reference.

Exception No. 3: Circuits for fire alarms and other protective signaling equipment, as well as fire pump equipment, may be connected ahead of the service overcurrent protection provided that they have their own overcurrent protection.

Exception No. 4: If the volts are not over 600 volts, nominal, meters that are provided with metal housing and service enclosures are properly grounded, as described in Article 250.

Exception No. 5: If service disconnecting equipment is operated by power, the control circuit should be mounted ahead of the service equipment with proper overcurrent protection and a disconnecting means provided, so that if overcurrent devices in the service disconnecting means should open, current is still available from an electric control circuit.

230-95. Ground-Fault Protection of Equipment—Fault currents that are available, plus the damaging effects of ground-faults, have made it necessary to do something about injury to personnel and damage to equipment.

Where service disconnecting means is rated 1000 amperes or more, ground-fault protection of equipment must be installed when the system is a solidly grounded wye system having more than 150 volts to ground and not exceeding phase-to-phase voltages of 600 volts.

(a) **Setting.** The ground-fault maximum setting shall be 1200 amperes and the maximum delay shall be only one second where the ground-fault is equal to or greater than 3000 amperes. This ground-fault protection shall operate the service disconnecting means opening all ungrounded conductors of the faulted circuit.

Exception No. 1: On industrial applications the disconnection in a nonorderly shutdown will cause increased hazards. This exception shall not apply to service disconnecting means.

Exception No. 2: Service to fire pumps does not apply with the above provisions.

(b) **Fuses.** Where fuses are used as the overcurrent protection, they shall be capable of interrupting any current higher than the interrupting capacity of the switch involved, at any time when the ground-fault protection system does not cause a switch to be opened. Fuse manufacturers give the fuse rating and the ground-fault capabilities of the fuse interruption.

Note: A service interrupting rating of the disconnecting means shall be based on the current rating of the largest fuse that could be installed therein, even though fuses of lower rating must be used. Circuit breakers that are adjustable for current ratings shall have disconnecting means installed based on the highest setting of the circuit breaker, even though lower rating of the circuit breaker is to be used.

Although 1000 amperes is the requirement in this section, it is recognized that it is desirable to have solidly grounded systems of less than 1000 amperes protected by ground-fault protection when the system is over 150 volts to ground and not exceeding 600 volts phase-to-phase.

"Solidly grounded" as used in this section means the grounded conductor (neutral) is solidly grounded and not grounded through a resistive or impedance device.

Ground-fault protective equipment which opens the service entrance equipment will only protect said equipment and the equipment and conductors on the load side of the service disconnecting means, and will not protect the service entrance conductors.

The addition of ground-fault protective equipment at the service disconnecting means will by necessity require that the overcurrent devices used on the system elsewhere be coordinated by proper selection of the overcurrent devices downstream. Additional ground-fault protection will be needed downstream where the maximum continuity of service is required.

(c) **Performance Testing.** The Code requires that the ground-fault protection system be performance tested when first installed on site. Approved instructions are to be furnished with the equipment and the test run according to the test instructions.

You may be required to make a record of said test in writing and make this written record available to the authority having jurisdiction.

H. Service Exceeding 600 Volts, Nominal

230-200. General—Service conductors and equipment used on circuits over 600 volts, nominal, are covered in the following material, but it shall also be applicable to the previous sections. Where the equipment is on the supply side of the point of service, the provisions of this article shall not apply. There is a definition that will not be found in Article 100 but appears in the *NEC* just after the first part of Section 230-200, for "Service-Point."

Note: For circuits over 600 volts, you should also refer to the National Electrical Safety Code (ANSI C2-1984).

230-201. Service Conductors—The words "primary" and "secondary" are often confused in the field. If the transformer is a step-down transformer, the primary is the high voltage side. If the transformer is a step-up transformer, the primary is the low voltage side.

In most cases, the primary is the high voltage side.

At the service point where the disconnecting means is to be considered, the service conductors may be on either the primary or the secondary side of a step-down transformer. The final decision will probably be made by the authority having jurisdiction.

230-202. Service-Entrance Conductors—The following parts shall be used to identify where service-entrance conductors to a building or separate enclosure are to be installed.

(a) **Conductor Size.** Conductors in a cable shall not be less than No. 8, or if not in a cable shall not be less than No. 6.

(b) **Wiring Methods.** Several methods of installing service entrance conductors are listed in your *NEC*.

Section 710-3(b) will cover underground service-entrance conductors.

Approved cable tray systems shall be permitted to support cables approved for use as service-entrance conductors. See Article 318.

Section 310-6 will cover shielding on conductors.

(c) **Open Work.** See the *NEC*.

(d) **Supports.** In the event of short circuits, extra strain is placed on the supports due to magnetic fields. The supports, including the insulators, shall have sufficient strength to withstand this extra strain.

(e) **Guarding.** Qualified persons only shall be permitted access to open wires, and the necessary guarding to restrict access to such persons shall be installed.

(f) **Service Cable.** Potheads or other suitable means shall be used to protect the conductors where they emerge from a metal sheath or raceway. This protection shall be for moisture and physical damage.

(g) **Draining Raceways.** Unless raceways have conductors that are identified for that use, they shall be arranged to drain where they are embedded in masonry, exposed to the weather, or in wet locations.

(h) **Over 15,000 Volts.** Here, you are referred to Sections 450-41 through 450-48. Conductors are required to enter either a metal enclosure for the switchgear or a transformer vault.

230-203. Warning Signs—High voltage signs shall be posted where unauthorized persons might come in contact with live parts.

230-204. Isolating Switches.

(a) **Where Required.** An air-break isolating switch shall be installed on the supply side of the disconnecting means and any equipment associated with the installation, where oil switches or air or oil circuit breakers are used for the service disconnecting means. Air break switches can be observed to be certain that they are opened, where oil switches and circuit breakers cannot readily be checked for opening.

Exception: Where such equipment is automatically disconnected from circuit breakers and all live parts (this applies to such equipment as is mounted on removable truck panels or metal-enclosed switch gear units that cannot be opened unless the circuit is disconnected).

(b) **Fuses as Isolating Switch.** When fuses are such that they may be operated as a disconnecting switch, a set of fuses is acceptable as the isolating switch if the following conditions are met: (1) the oil disconnecting means is a nonautomatic switch, and (2) the set of fuses disconnects the oil switch and all associated service equipment from the service-entrance conductors.

(c) **Accessible to Qualified Persons Only.** Qualified persons only shall have access to isolating switches.

(d) **Grounding Connection.** See *NEC.* Take note of the grounding, as mentioned. It serves as a precaution should a switch accidentally become energized. Also with shielded-type high-voltage cables of any great length, the cable and the shield become a fair sized capacitor, and the grounding bleeds the charge away, thus preventing what might be a painful shock.

If a duplicate isolating switch is maintained by an electric supply company, a means for grounding need not be installed.

230-205. Disconnecting Means.

(a) **Location.** Sections 230-70 or 230-208(b) give us the location of the disconnecting means.

Exception: This exception applies to places under single management and allows the service disconnecting means to be installed in a separate building on the premises. If the disconnecting means is operated by a control device, the device shall be located as near as possible to where the service-entrance conductors enter the building served. Permanently marked visual identification is required to indicate the ON and OFF position on the remote service disconnect.

Note: Here in the *NEC* you are referred to Sections 230-3, 230-6, 230-70, 230-71(a), and 230-200.

(b) **Type.** All ungrounded conductors shall be capable of being open at the service disconnect at the same time. They shall also be capable of being closed on ground-faults that are equal to or greater than the maximum current available on such a ground-fault.

230-206. Overcurrent Devices as Disconnecting Means—Where in Section 230-208 the circuit breakers or fuses specified therein meet the requirements for service overcurrent devices that were covered in Section 230-205, they will constitute the service disconnecting means.

230-207. Equipment in Secondaries—See the *NEC.*

230-208. Overcurrent Protection Requirements—See the *NEC.*

230-209. Surge Arresters (Lightning Arresters)—Here the requirements in Article 280 for surge protection and lightning arresters or ungrounded overhead service conductors, if required by the authority having jurisdiction, shall be placed on the supply side of this equipment.

This is not very specific, and decisions should be made on the number of lightning disturbances.

230-210. Service Equipment—General Provisions—See the *NEC.*

230-211. Metal-Enclosed Switchgear—See the *NEC.*

ARTICLE 240—OVERCURRENT PROTECTION

240-1. Scope—This article is arranged so that Parts A through G provide the general requirements for overcurrent protection and overcurrent protective devices. These are general requirements, and Part H covers the overcurrent protection for over 600 volts, nominal. Conductors have specific current-carrying capacities (ampacity) for different sizes of conductors, for different insulations, and for different ambient-temperature conditions. The purpose of overcurrent protection is to protect the insulation of the conductors from damage caused by the current reaching too high a value.

You are referred to Sections 110-9 and 110-10 for requirements covering interrupting capacity and protection against fault currents.

A. General

240-2. Protection of Equipment—Equipment shall be protected by over-current devices. The list in this section of the *NEC* covers the equipment that is to be protected. See the *NEC*.

240-3. Protection of Conductors—Other than Flexible Cords and Fixture Wires—It is the intent that conductors shall be protected according to their ampacities. These are given in Tables 310-16 through 310-31 in the *NEC*. Accompanying the tables of ampacities are notes governing deratings that are required under various conditions. In figuring the ampacities of the conductors, these deratings shall be taken into consideration. The following exceptions apply:

Exception No. 1: Next Higher Overcurrent Protective Device Rating. This higher rating of adjustment cannot be used if the rating does not exceed 800 amperes or if the circuit involved is a multiwire branch circuit that supplies cord- and plug-connected receptacles. There are standard ampere ratings for fuses and circuit breakers where the standard rating is not high enough for the ampacity of the conductors. You can use the next higher fuse or circuit breaker rating, or if the circuit breaker has adjustments higher than the standard rating, you may use a higher rating on the circuit breaker.

Exception No. 2: Tap Conductors. If the adjusted rating exceeds 800 amperes, the next lower size adjustable rating for fuse or circuit breaker, provided the overload adjustment does not exceed the rating required for the job. When tap conductors are needed, they are covered in Sections 210-19(c), 240-21, Exceptions 2, 3, 5, 8, 9, and 10; or Sections 364-10 and 364-11, or under Article 430 covering motors in Part D.

Exception No. 3: Motor and Motor-Control Circuits. For this you are referred to Parts C, D, E, and F for motors in Article 430. If they are motor-operated appliance circuit conductors, you are referred to Article 422, Parts B and D. You are referred to the *NEC* for the protection of conductors in Parts C and F of Article 440 covering air-conditioning.

Exception No. 4: Remote-Control Circuits. Article 725 of the *NEC* covers remote-control circuits.

Exception No. 5: Transformer Secondary Conductors. Section 450-3 considered secondary 2-wire single phase supplied by a transformer supplying only 2-wire secondary. The secondary is considered protected on the primary overcurrent protection of the transformer. If the primary overcurrent device does not exceed the value that is found by multiplying a secondary conductor ampacity by the secondary to primary transformer voltage ratio, then the secondary shall be considered to be protected by the overcurrent device of the primary.

Exception No. 6: See Article 460 for compliance with capacitor circuits.

Exception No. 7: See Article 630 for welder circuits.

Exception No. 8: Power Loss Hazard. If power loss will create a hazard, as in circuits handling material with a magnet, conductor overcurrent protection shall not be required. Short-circuit protecting devices shall be provided.

240-4. Protection of Fixture Wires and Cords—In this section the overcurrent protection for tinsel cords and other flexible cords and their ampacities will be covered in Table 400-5. Protection as covered in Section 240-10 shall be permitted and be accessible for supply overcurrent protection for the cords.

You are referred to Exceptions Nos. 1, 2, and 3 of Section 240-4 in your *NEC.*

240-6. Standard Ampere Ratings—Fuses and inverse time circuit breakers come in standard ratings. These are given in your *NEC* at this point.

Exception: There are additional standard ratings for standard Edison plug fuses and S-type plug fuses. More will be covered, but lower than 30-ampere plug fuses (either type) are essential for proper protection of small load.

In referring to standard ratings, I should mention that when using adjustable circuit breakers, where the adjustment is readily accessible, the maximum setting of this overload adjustment shall be considered the maximum load resistance of this circuit breaker.

240-8. Fuses or Circuit Breakers in Parallel—Overcurrent devices consisting of fuses and/or circuit breakers shall not be arranged or installed in parallel.

Exception: If circuit breakers or fuses are assembled at the factory for paralleling and are listed for that purpose, they may be approved as being just one (a unit).

240-9. Thermal Devices—Thermally operated relays and other devices are operated by heat generation and a strip in the device causing them to open. But remember, they are not designed to be used for short-circuits. They may be used for motor protection as explained in Section 430-40. Fuses or circuit breakers having a rating that does not exceed four times the rating of the motor shall be used ahead of the thermal device. (See Fig. 240-1.)

240-10. Supplementary Overcurrent Protection—Any supplementary overcurrent protection that is used in connection with lighting fixtures, appliances, or other utilization equipment, or for internal circuits and components of equipment, does not in any manner take the place of nor is deemed a substitute for the branch-circuit protection. Neither is it the intent that any such supplementary overcurrent protection device be subject to the accessibility required for branch-circuit protective devices. See Article 210.

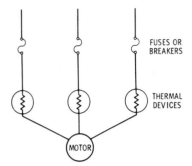

Fig. 240-1. Thermal protection for motors.

240-11. Definition of Current-Limiting Overcurrent Protective Device—See the *NEC*.

240-12. Electrical System Coordination—The coordination of overcurrent devices has always been a problem, which too often has been overlooked. The *NEC* has taken this into consideration.

Often an orderly shutdown is vital to minimize hazard(s) to personnel as well as equipment problems. In this case the following two conditions will be the basis of a system of coordination:

See (1) and (2) in your *NEC* at this point.

Note: Fault current protection shall be so designed that in the case of a fault that is localized at one point of a system, it is taken care of by properly designed fault current protection to open that point only, and thus not shut off the entire service to a building.

One example of such a system is a wye supply to motors with a resistance in the ground circuit, limiting ground-fault current to a predetermined value, such as possibly 10 amperes. A relay is connected across the ground resistor, or in series with it, which actuates an alarm.

A low-amperage ground fault in one phase will not cause a shutdown but will notify personnel that a ground fault has developed, and they can locate the ground and arrange for a proper shutdown for repairs. Two phases with ground faults at the same time of course would cause immediate shutdown.

B. Location

240-20. Ungrounded Conductors.

(a) **Overcurrent Device Required.** An overcurrent device (fuse or overcurrent trip unit of a circuit breaker) shall be placed in each ungrounded conductor. An equivalent overcurrent trip unit may be a combination of a current transformer along with a relay to open the overcurrent.

Note: Article 430, Parts C, D, F, and J.

(b) **Circuit Breaker as Overcurrent Device.** Any circuit breakers shall open all of the ungrounded circuit.

Exception: Individual single-pole circuits breakers may be used for the protection of each ungrounded conductor of 3-wire direct-current or single-phase circuits, or for each ungrounded conductor of light or appliance branch circuits connected to 4-wire, 3-phase systems, or 5-wire, 2-phase systems, provided that lighting or appliance circuits are supplied from a system having a grounded neutral, and that no conductor in such circuits operates at a voltage greater than permitted in Section 210-6. See Figs. 240-2 and 240-3.

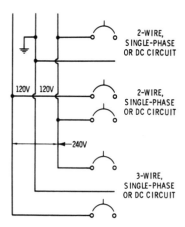

Fig. 240-2. Overcurrent protection for a 3-wire, single-phase system.

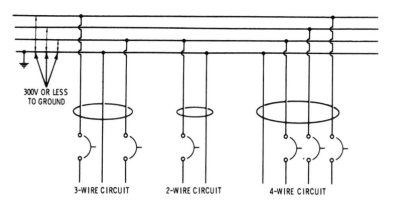

Fig. 240-3. Overcurrent protection for a 4-wire grounded system.

240-21. Location and Circuit—Overcurrent devices of circuits shall be located at the point where the service to those circuits originates.

Smaller Conductor Protected. Tables 310-16 through 310-31 cover overcurrent protection for the larger conductor and provide for smaller conductors.

Exception No. 1: (Take particular note of this Exception, as it is broad in its coverage. Especially note in the first paragraph "feeder or transformer.")

(a) **Feeder Taps Not over 10 Feet (3.05 m) Long.** If all of the following conditions are met, tap conductors from a feeder or a transformer secondary may be used.

(1) Not over 10 feet of tap conductor length.

(2) The ampacity of the tap conductors is:
- (2a) If the tap conductors supply a load computed not less than that for the circuit supplied, and
- (2b) If the taps are not less than the rating of the device involved, or
- (2c) If the tap conductors are not less than the overcurrent device where the tap conductors terminate.

(3) Tap conductors shall not extend beyond any control devices or panelboards they supply.

(4) Where tap conductors supply switchboard, panelboard, or control devices, or the back of an open switchboard, they are to be enclosed in a raceway that extends from where the tap terminates. The only exception to this requirement is at the point of connection to the feeder.

Lighting and branch panelboards are covered in Section 384-16(a).

In explanation of some of the above, see Fig. 240-4. It appears

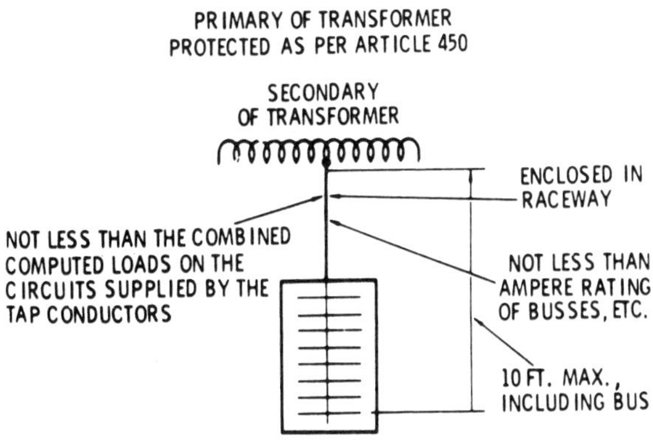

PRIMARY OF TRANSFORMER
PROTECTED AS PER ARTICLE 450

SECONDARY
OF TRANSFORMER

ENCLOSED IN
RACEWAY

NOT LESS THAN THE COMBINED
COMPUTED LOADS ON THE
CIRCUITS SUPPLIED BY THE
TAP CONDUCTORS

NOT LESS THAN
AMPERE RATING
OF BUSSES, ETC.

10 FT. MAX.,
INCLUDING BUS

Fig. 240-4. Illustrating a tap circuit not to exceed 10 feet in length.

that with transformers the only place this might apply is with unit load centers having a transformer with a primary overcurrent device, short busbars and a series of breakers or fuses, which do not serve as a lighting or appliance branch-circuit panelboard. This has been a question for some time and to all appearances is clarified here.

(b) **Feeder Taps Not over 25 Feet (7.62 m) Long.** The following conditions must be met for taps from a feeder where the tap conductors do not exceed 25 feet:

(1) See the origin of this exception.

(2) The ampacity of the taps shall not be less than one-third the ampacity of the feeder conductors or overcurrent protection from which they originate.

(3) The tap conductors shall terminate in a circuit breaker or a single set of fuses to limit the load to the ampacity of the tap conductors. Any such circuit breaker or set of fuses located at the tap load device may supply any number of additional loads from this tap conductor overcurrent device.

(4) The tap conductors are in a raceway suitable for protecting them from physical damage. (See Fig. 240-5.)

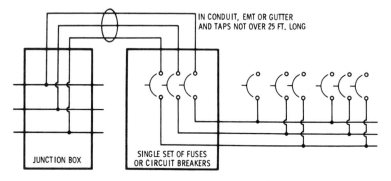

IN CONDUIT, EMT OR GUTTER
AND TAPS NOT OVER 25 FT. LONG

JUNCTION BOX

SINGLE SET OF FUSES
OR CIRCUIT BREAKERS

Fig. 240-5. Illustrating tap circuits not over 25 feet long.

Service Conductors. Section 230-91 provides for service-entrance conductors where protected in the section just mentioned. See Figs. 240-6, 240-7, and 240-8.

(c) **Branch Circuit Taps.** In Sections 210-19, 210-20, and 210-24, taps and outlets for circuits that supply an electric range are considered as being protected by the branch circuit overcurrent protection.

Basically, referring back to Section 210-19(b), Exception No. 2, it states that tap conductors supplying electric ranges, etc., from a 50-

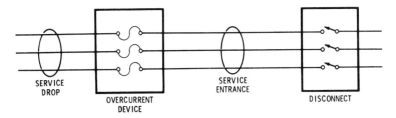

Fig. 240-6. Separate disconnect and overcurrent devices which are separated because of service-entrance length.

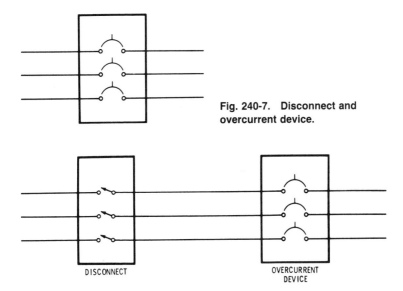

Fig. 240-7. Disconnect and overcurrent device.

Fig. 240-8. Separate disconnect and overcurrent devices which must be adjacent.

ampere branch circuit shall have an ampacity of not less than 20 amperes and the taps shall not be longer than necessary for servicing the equipment.

(d) **Motor Circuit Taps.** Tap conductors for motors are discussed in Section 430-28 and 430-53, and are considered protected as covered in these sections.

(e) **Busway Taps.** Busway taps as covered in Sections 364-10 through 364-14 will be considered as protected.

(f) **Transformer Feeder Taps with Primary Plus Secondary Not over 25 Feet (7.62 m) Long.** A very important Exception No. 8 is added

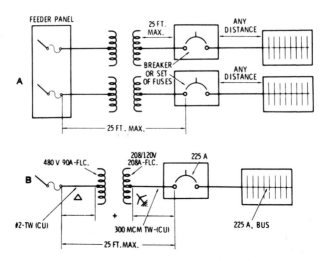

Fig. 240-9. Transformer feed taps not over 25 feet long.

and is somewhat misunderstood at times. It pertains to a separately derived system from transformers. Refer to Fig. 240-9A and B.

An exception covers generator overcurrent protection, and is covered in Section 445-5.

See the *NEC* for Exceptions No. 10 and 11.

240-22. Grounded Conductors—No overcurrent device is ever permitted in series with a circuit that is intentionally grounded.

An exception permits opening the neutral, provided all conductors involved are opened intentionally and the neutral or grounded conductor cannot be opened independently.

Also, Sections 430-36 and 430-37 for motor overload protection permit the fusing of the grounded phase of a delta, but the grounded conductor from the delta must be connected ahead of the disconnecting means, overcurrent device, and proper ground protection.

240-23. Change in Size of Grounded Conductor—See the *NEC*.

240-24. Location in or on Premises.

(a) **Readily Accessible.** Basically the requirement that overcurrent devices be readily accessible is a must. They shall be located so that they may be readily reached in emergencies or for servicing without reaching over objects, climbing on chairs, ladders, etc. There are three exceptions in the *NEC*: One covers busways as provided in Section 364-12, the second covers supplementary overcurrent protection as described in Section 240-10, and the third refers us to Section 230-92.

(b) **Occupant to Have Ready Access.** This was added to the 1971 *NEC* to assure that occupant has ready access to the supply conductors supplying his or her occupancy.

Exception: In a multiple-occupancy building where there is continuous management and supervision of electric service and electrical maintenance, overcurrent devices for services and feeders that supply more than one occupancy are permitted to be accessible only to the full-time management.

(c) **Not Exposed to Physical Damage.** Overcurrent devices shall not be subject to physical damage, and should thus be located with this in mind.

(d) **Not in Vicinity of Easily Ignitible Material.** When an overcurrent protective device opens there will be a spark and possible particles of hot metal which could cause a fire. This explains why most inspection authorities do not permit overcurrent panels in clothes closets and other similar locations.

C. Enclosures

240-30. General—Overcurrent devices shall be in an approved enclosure unless a part of a specially approved assembly which affords equal protection, or unless mounted on switchboards, panelboards or controllers located in rooms or enclosures free from easily ignitible material and dampness.

Most branch circuit panelboards come with a cover over the hot portions of the panel so that the breaker handles can be switched without danger. Here another door is not necessarily required, but in most cases there will be an outside door.

240-32. Damp or Wet Locations—In damp or wet places, there shall be a minimum of ¼ inch (6.35 mm) air space back of the enclosure, between

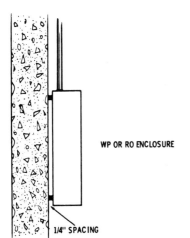

WP OR RO ENCLOSURE

1/4" SPACING

Fig. 240-10. Spacing of enclosures for overcurrent devices in damp or wet locations.

the wall or other mounting space, and the enclosure shall be identified for the location. Many enclosures come with provisions built in to allow the ¼ inch (6.35 mm) air space. See Fig. 240-10, page 107.

240-33. Vertical Position—It is necessary to mount switches in a vertical position so that gravity cannot close the switch unintentionally.

Exception: A case where this is impractical is covered in Section 240-81.

D. Disconnecting and Guarding

240-40. Disconnecting Means for Fuses and Thermal Cutouts—In almost all cases circuit opening devices are installed. There is an exception for thermal cutouts and fuses below 150 volts to ground, and fuse cartridges of any voltage: Each circuit containing fuses or thermal cutouts shall have means of disconnecting them from the electrical supply current.

Recall that plug fuses come under the 125-volt classification and the screw shell of the holder is connected to the load side. Thus, they are not required to have a disconnecting means. Service fuses (fuses at the outer end of the service entrance) may be ahead of the disconnecting means. See Section 230-82. A group of motors may be served by a single disconnecting means providing that the requirements of Section 430-112 are met. The same is permitted for fixed electric space heating equipment, in Section 424-22.

240-41. Arcing or Suddenly Moving Parts—See the *NEC*.

E. Plug Fuses, Fuseholders, and Adapters

240-50. General.

(a) **Maximum Voltage.** Part E of Article 240 is quite important as inspectors find considerable misuse of plug fuses. This is in no manner to indicate that they are to be avoided, but to show proper uses of same.

Plug fuses and fuseholders are intended to be used only on circuits not exceeding 125 volts between conductors. For instance, circuits of 277 volts and two other conductors are definitely not to involve plug-type fuses.

Exception: This approves the use of plug fuses and fuseholders on 120/208 volt wye systems.

(b) **Marking.** Ampere rating shall be plainly marked on every fuse, fuseholder, or adapter.

(c) **Hexagonal Configuration.** You will notice plug fuses with a mica glass on top that has a hexagonal configuration. The hexagonal mica indicates that the fuse is 15 amperes or less, and a round configuration indicates amperages from 15 to 30 amperes.

(d) **No Live Parts.** No live parts shall be exposed after the installation of plug fuses, fuseholders, or adapters.

(e) **Screwshell.** The screwshell of plug fuses shall always be connected to the load side of the circuit. The moment that the current is disengaged even partway, the shell has no voltage. (See Fig. 240-11.)

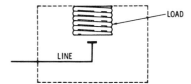

Fig. 240-11.   A screw-shell fuseholder.

240-51. Edison-Base Fuses.

(a) **Classification.** Edison-base fuses shall not be rated at more than 125 volts and 0 to 30 amperes and below.

(b) **Replacement Only.** It states that plug fuses of the Edison-base type are recognized in this Code only as a replacement item in existing installations where there has been no evidence of overfusing or tampering. This means that all inspection authorities can condemn any new installations that use Edison-base fuses, regardless of how they are used or in what type of electrical device. The reason for this ruling is because of the dangerous practice of replacing a blown fuse with one of a higher rating than the ampacity of the conductor they are supposed to protect. This type of fuse also makes it easy to use a penny or other metal disk when a replacement fuse is not available. The proper plug fuse to be used on new installations is covered in Section 240-54.

240-52. Edison-Base Fuseholders—On all new installations requiring plug fuses, the Type S fuse is required to be used. Type S adapters should be installed in all Edison-base fuseholders in old installations to convert them to the new requirements.

240-53. Type S Fuses—Type S fuses are really screw-type fuses, and comply with (a) and (b) below.

(a) **Classification:** S-type fuses, like Edison-type fuses, are not to be on circuits over 125 volts between conductors. We will see in (b) that the different sizes of S-type fuse are not interchangeable with 0 to 30 amperes. One S adapts from 0 to 15 amperes, another 16 to 20. Only a third S adapter takes 21 to 30. (Note these classifications.)

(b) **Noninterchangeable.** With reference to the above classifications, the

16- to 20-ampere and the 21- to 30-ampere classifications shall not be usable in a fuseholder or adapter designed for lower amperages. See Fig. 240-12.

Fig. 240-12. Type-S plug-fuse adapter.

240-54. Type S Fuses, Adapters, and Fuseholders.

(a) **To Fit Edison-Base Fuseholders.** S-type fuseholders are designed to screw into Edison-base fuseholders. (See Fig. 240-12.)

(b) **To Fit Type S Fuses Only.** Any fuseholders made only for S-type fuses or S-type adapters are designed so that the fuseholder itself or the adapter will accept only S-type fuses.

(c) **Nonremovable.** Type S adapters are made so that once screwed into an Edison base fuseholder they cannot be removed.

(d) **Nontamperable.** All precautions have been taken to prevent shunting around S-type fuseholders. (Of course, anyone who is really determined to do it will occasionally succeed.)

(e) **Interchangeability.** The design of S-type fuses and fuseholders shall be standardized by the manufacturer.

F. Cartridge Fuses and Fuseholders

240-60. General.

(a) **Maximum Voltage—300-Volt Type.** This part was new in the 1965 Code. A new fuse (Type SC) has been approved for 300-volt systems. This was a necessity due to the extended use of 277/480-volt wye systems, which before required the use of a 600-volt fuse. These are a noninterchangeable type of cartridge fuse and are made to fit certain devices the size of circuit breakers. This will allow the use of either circuit breakers or fuses in the same panel.

Exception: This applies to conductors having not over 300 volts to ground that are supplied with a grounded neutral.

(b) **Noninterchangeable—0-6000 Ampere Cartridge Fuseholders.** Adapters may be purchased for using lower-current-rated cartridge fuses in a higher-current-rated fuseholder. A 100-ampere-rated fuse switch may be adapted to use a 60-ampere fuse, but a 60-ampere fuse switch is not to be altered to adapt a 100-ampere fuse. Current-limiting fuses, which are covered in Section 240-11, are a special type of fuse and are not to be interchangeable with fuses that are not current limiting.

(c) **Marking.** Fuses shall be plainly marked to show their ampere rating, voltage rating, and interrupting rating, if it is over 10,000 amperes. The name or trademark of the manufacturer shall be marked, and, if the fuses are the current-limiting type, then they shall also be so marked.

240-61. Classification—Fuse cartridges shall be marked with the current ampere rating, but if the voltage rating on the fuse is higher than the circuit rating, it may be used.

G. Circuit Breakers

240-80. Method of Operation—Circuit breakers shall be trip free and capable of being opened and closed by hand without employing other sources of power, even though they are designed to be normally operated by electrical, pneumatic, or other sources of power.

Large circuit breakers which are opened and closed by means of electrical, pneumatic, or other power shall be capable of being closed by hand for the purpose of maintenance and shall also be capable of being opened by hand under load without the use of any other form of power.

240-81. Indicating—The open and closed position of a circuit breaker shall be clearly marked so that it is easy to tell whether the breaker is on or off.

If circuit breakers are mounted in other than the horizontal position, such as a vertical, the "on" position of the handle shall be up.

240-82. Nontamperable—See the *NEC*.

240-83. Marking—See the *NEC*.

H. Overcurrent Protection over 600 Volts, Nominal

240-100. Feeders—Each ungrounded conductor shall have short-circuit protective devices. For Section 230-208(d)(2) or (d)(3), any protecting device or devices used must have the capability of detection and interruption of any currents that occur at their location that are more than the trip setting of the circuit breaker or the melting point of the fuse. A fuse rating in continuous amperes not to exceed three times the ampacity of the conductor or a breaker having a trip setting of not more than six times the ampacity of the conductor shall be considered as providing the required short circuit protection. See Tables 310-69 through 310-84 for ampacities of high-voltage conductors.

This allows tap conductors to be considered protected by the feeder overcurrent device when this device also feeds the tap conductors.

240-101. Branch Circuits—Section 230-208(d)(2) or (d)(3) covers the branch circuits, and they shall have short-circuit protective device on each ungrounded conductor. The protective device(s) also has to be capable of not only detecting but interrupting these overcurrents that may occur there.

ARTICLE 250—GROUNDING

A. General

250-1. Scope—Grounding is very important. You will find some places that are not to be grounded, but in the majority of the cases grounding takes precedence. The reasons for grounding are protection from lightning, safety to people, and safety to property. There is some confusion at times among the definitions covering grounding; be sure to check your definitions of the different groundings. Of the definitions most commonly causing confusion, the distinction between grounding of services and equipment grounding is the most frequent.

In the *NEC* you will find the type of conductors and sizes to be used for each of the above-mentioned groundings. To have equipment grounding there must be service-entrance grounding. As we proceed, various methods of grounding and of bonding equipment grounding will be discussed in detail. You will also find certain places where grounding is not required if proper guarding and isolation are provided. We have mentioned some of the purposes for grounding; it also protects if a circuit comes in contact with higher voltage or if a fault occurs to ground. Then it facilitates the opening of overcurrent devices. See Section 110-10.

250-2. Application of Other Articles—Other articles in the Code list additional grounding requirements for specific conductor and equipment installation other than those covered in this article. A listing to which additional grounding requirements apply is given in this section. In your *NEC* you will find a list of many places where additional information on grounding will be given, along with the section numbers.

B. Circuit and System Grounding

250-3. Direct-Current Systems.

(a) **Two-Wire Direct Current Systems.** Systems supplying 2-wire dc shall be grounded.

There are cases in which this could cause electrolysis on under-grounded pipes, etc., as in the past, when trolley cars had the ground at positive potential one day and negative potential the next day to counteract damage by electrolysis.

Exception No. 1: A system that supplies limited areas of industrial equipment.

Exception No. 2: DC systems operating at 50 volts or less.

Exception No. 3: DC systems operating at 300 volts or over.

Exception No. 4: Section 250-5 covers dc systems obtained from a rectifier supply by ac current where superfluous.

Exception No. 5: Part C of Article 700 exempts signaling devices having a current not over 0.030 amperes.

(b) **Three-Wire Direct-Current Systems.** The neutral conductor sup-plying premises with 3-wire dc supply shall be grounded.

250-5. Alternating-Current Circuits and Systems Less Than 50 Volts to be Grounded—(a), (b), (c), or (d) below covers ac circuits that shall be grounded. Circuits not covered by these four will be permitted to be grounded.

(a) **Alternating-Current Circuits and Systems to Be Grounded.** Any ac circuits of 50 volts or less shall be grounded if they meet any of the following conditions:

(1) If the transformer supplying the 50 volts or less is supplied by voltages in excess of 150 volts to ground, the 50-volt side shall be grounded.

(2) When transformers are supplied from an ungrounded system.

(3) If 50-volt ac conductors run overhead outside of the buildings, then one wire shall be grounded.

(b) **Alternating-Current Systems of 50 Volts to 1000 Volts.** The conditions that follow will require that ac systems of 50 volts to 1000 volts that supply premises wiring systems must be grounded:

(1) If the voltage to ground on ungrounded conductors is 150 volts or less.

(2) On a 4-wire wye system of 480/277 volts, if the neutral is used as a circuit conductor, grounding is required. This would not include a 480/277-volt high resistance grounded system where the mid-point of the Y is grounded through a resistor, but this connection is not used as a circuit conductor.

(3) This is best described by Fig. 250-1E, where the midpoint of one phase of a delta supply is grounded and this midpoint is used as a neutral.

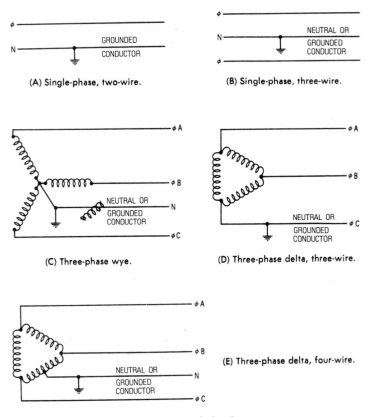

Fig. 250-1. Grounding different types of circuits.

(4) See Sections 230-22, 230-30, and 230-41, where a service conductor is uninsulated, such as a quadraplex.

Exception No. 1: An exception to the grounding of these systems
covers electric furnaces, or any other means of heating metals for
refining, melting, or tempering.

Exception No. 2: Grounding is not required for separately derived
systems used for speed control in industrial plants or for rectifiers.
Nothing else shall be connected to these.
   Ground-fault detectors if used on ungrounded systems will provide additional protection.

Exception No. 3: If all the following conditions are met, separately
derived systems supplied by primary voltage rating less than 1000
volts will not be required to be grounded.

a. See the *NEC*.
b. If qualified persons only maintain service or supervise the installation, grounding will not be required.
c. See the *NEC*.
d. See the *NEC*.

Exception No. 4: Article 517 does not permit a neutral ground in operating rooms; this system is an isolated system and uses a special transformer with a metal barrier between the primary and secondary windings.

Exception No. 5: As mentioned in (b)(2) above, a 4-wire wyes with the resistive ground on the center where the fourth wire was not used as a circuit conductor. This will also apply to impedance grounded neutral systems. The impedance may be a resistor, as mentioned before. The purpose of this is to limit the ground fault current values. Such systems may be used where the voltages run from 480 volts to 1000 volts, three phase if all of the following conditions are met:

a. If qualified persons only will be servicing and maintaining the installation.
b. Where the system being supplied must have continuity of service.
c. To identify grounded phase conductors, ground detecters must be supplied to indicate that there is a grounded phase. This permits operation in most cases until the shutdown can occur, or until repair.
d. In no case shall this high-impedance neutral be used to supply line-to-neutral loads.

(c) **Alternating-Current Systems 1 kV and Over.** It is required that systems which supply mobile portable equipment and are supplied by ac systems of 1 kV or over shall be grounded as covered in Section 250-154. Where not supplying portable equipment, such systems may be grounded. When grounding systems (ac) 1 kV and over, the grounding shall meet the applicable parts of this Article 250.

(d) **Separately Derived Systems.** Where interior wiring systems are supplied by generators not connected to the supply system, such as emergency generators, or where transformers in the supply system are used for other than supply voltage and the primary and secondary are isolated (which also includes converter windings that have no direct connections to the supply source), grounding is required where stated above. Grounding of separate systems will be explained in Section 250-26.

Note: On-site generators are not considered separately derived systems, if the neutral of the generator is solidly connected to the neutral of the supply service. Section 250-26 involves systems that are not separately derived systems and that do not specifically require to be grounded. You are also referred to Section 445-5 for the minimum size of conductors required to carry the fault currents.

250-6. Portable and Vehicle-Mounted Generators.

(a) **Portable Generators.** It is not required that the frame of a portable generator be grounded if the following conditions are met:

(1) If only equipment mounted on the generator and/or cord- and plug-connected to outlets on the generator, and

(2) If any of the metal parts of the equipment being supplied has equipment grounding conductor to the terminals of the outlet of the generator receptacles, which in turn are bonded to the generator frame.

It is to be noted that equipment is to be mounted on the generator, or that a receptacle(s) is to be mounted on the generator and cord and plug connections be made to the equipment for which the power is being supplied. Also, there is to be an equipment grounding conductor in the cord and the receptacles connected as on any system, with the equipment grounding conductor going back to the generator frame.

(b) **Vehicle-Mounted Generators.** A generator mounted on the frame of a vehicle shall be considered as serving as the grounding electrode for the system being supplied.

(1) The generator frame shall be bonded to the frame of the vehicle, and

(2) Current supplies only equipment mounted on the vehicle and/or cord- and plug-connected equipment when supplied from outlets mounted on the vehicle or on the generator, and

(3) In equipment grounding conductor is supplied from the equipment being served to receptacles on the vehicle or generator where they are properly bonded to the generator frame, and

(4) The provisions of this article shall also comply.

(c) **Neutral Conductor Bonding.** Bonding of conductors other than the neutral to the frame is not required.

Refer to Section 250-5, especially (d), for grounding portable generators supplying fixed wiring systems.

250-7. Circuits Not to Be Grounded—See the following for circuits which need not be grounded.

(a) **Cranes.** Electrically operated cranes operating over combustible fibers as provided in Section 503-13, which covers Class III locations.

(b) **Health-Care Facilities.** Circuits in operating rooms, as per Article

517. This will also apply to health-care facilities as provided in the same article. This would be anesthetics locations.

C. Location of System Grounding Connections

250-21. Objectionable Current over Grounding Conductors.

(a) **Arrangement to Prevent Objectionable Current.** In the grounding of electrical systems and circuit conductors, all conducting noncurrent-carrying materials including surge arresters shall be arranged so that objectionable flow of current will be prevented over all grounding paths and grounding conductors.

On occasion, metal-sided houses, with metal water pipes, have started electrical fires because of grounded current flowing through the metal siding to ground.

Sometimes persons are concerned over reading current on the grounding electrode conductor. This is natural as it is a parallel path from the service equipment to the transformer ground. There are other cases which might appear to be of concern, but which are really not. In meeting the requirements of this section, one must carefully analyze whether it is a problem or not.

(b) **Alterations to Stop Objectionable Current.** In using multiple grounding connections, if there is current flowing, check to see if it is a natural condition, or objectionable. If objectionable, one or more of the following steps will help:

For 1, 2, 3, and 4, refer to your *NEC*.

(c) **Temporary Currents Not Classified as Objectionable Currents.** Grounding and grounding conductors have a job to do and it is possible under certain conditions, such as a ground fault, there will be current flowing while they are performing their duty. Such currents are not classified as being objectionable as covered in (a) and (b) above.

250-22. Point of Connection for Direct-Current Systems—On direct-current systems that are to be grounded, the grounding shall be done at one or more supply stations, but not at the individual services. This refers to the grounding of the supply conductors and not to the service equipment itself. The equipment is to be grounded at the service, but the neutral is to be isolated from the equipment at the service-entrance equipment. These requirements are greatly different from those for alternating-current systems because any passage of current between the ground at the supply station and at the service-entrance equipment may cause objectionable electrolysis, which must be avoided.

250-23. Grounding Service-Supplied Alternating-Current Systems.

(a) **System Grounding Connections.** The reason for grounding on the supply side of the service-entrance equipment is because if the supply side is ever disconnected there will still be a ground on the supply system. In the event that the distribution system is ungrounded, there would, of course, be no ground from the primary supply. The ground at the service-entrance equipment shall be connected at an accessible point on the load side. It is preferred that this connection be made in the service-entrance equipment; thus it is accessible without breaking the utilities meter housing seal for checking. See Fig. 250-2. See Section 250-24 for two or more buildings supplied by a single service and Section 250-26 for separately derived systems.

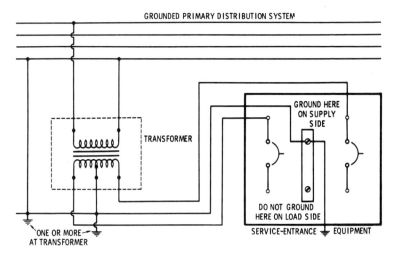

GROUNDED PRIMARY DISTRIBUTION SYSTEM

TRANSFORMER

GROUND HERE ON SUPPLY SIDE

DO NOT GROUND HERE ON LOAD SIDE

ONE OR MORE AT TRANSFORMER

SERVICE-ENTRANCE EQUIPMENT

Fig. 250-2. Grounding on the supply side of the service-entrance equipment will provide a ground on the supply if it is ever disconnected.

Exception No. 1: Provisions of Section 250-26(b) require that separately derived systems meet the requirements of this section, and a grounding electrode conductor is to be connected to the separately derived system.

Exception No. 2: Section 250-24 will cover the necessity of grounding conductor connection where there are separate buildings.

Exception No. 3: Section 250-61 covers the grounding meter enclosing all ranges, wall-mounted ovens, clothes dryers, and counter-mounted cooking units.

As an inspector, the author likes to see the grounding electrode conductor connected in the service equipment enclosures of any size of service. Here it is accessible for service problems

Exception No. 4: See your *NEC.*

Exception No. 5: See your *NEC.*

Exception No. 6: Section 250-27 covers high-impedance grounded neutral systems, and what grounding connections are required.

(b) **Grounded Conductor Brought to Service Equipment.** When an ac system is served by 1000 volts or less and is grounded at any point, you are required to run the grounded conductor to each service. The grounded conductor size is determined and shall not be less than the requirements for grounded conductors covered by Table 250-94 in the *NEC.* This grounded conductor shall also be routed in with the phase conductors. If service conductors are larger than 1100 MCM and made of copper, or 1750 MCM made of aluminum, the table indicated above can not be used. The grounded conductor shall not be smaller than 12½ percent of the area of the largest phase conductor. If the phase conductors are paralleled, the grounded conductor size will be based on the total area of the paralleled conductors.

Exception No. 1: The size of the grounded conductor is not required to be larger than the size of the phase conductors. This means that the conductors, if paralleled or single, are of an individual phase. Of course, remember that if they are paralleled you use the combination of the sizes of the parallel conductors for determining the size of the grounded conductor.

Exception No. 2: Where high-impedance grounding neutral systems are covered in Section 250-27 under connection requirements.

250-24. Two or More Buildings or Structures Supplied from a Common Service.

(a) **Grounded Systems.** This applies to two or more buildings or structures served from one service. Part H describes the grounded system of each building or structure; each of them shall have a grounding electrode that is also connected to the metal enclosure of the disconnecting means that actually would be a feeder, and a grounding electrode is to be provided connected to the disconnecting means as well as the grounded circuit conductor of the ac supply on the supply side of the building or structure disconnecting means.

Exception No. 1: If the building or structure is supplied by only one branch circuit and there will be no equipment used in the building or structure that requires grounding, no grounding electrode will be required. This is a little questionable, as it is inspected when wired, but can be changed by the occupant without the authority having jurisdiction ever knowing about it.

Exception No. 2: In some cases a grounding electrode will not be required for the separate building or structure, if an equipment grounding conductor is run with the current supply wires to the building or structure. This equipment grounding conductor is for grounding noncurrent carrying parts of equipment. It is also used for interior metal piping systems and for building or structural metal frames. It shall also be bonded to the disconnecting means of separate building or structure or grounding electrodes. This will be further described in Part H of this article. When using the equipment grounding conductor, and there are no other grounding electrodes, two or more branch circuits may be used. Be careful where livestock is involved. If the equipment grounding conductor serving in such an area should be run underground in the earth to the disconnecting means, it shall be insulated or covered.

(b) **Ungrounded Systems.** When two or more buildings or structures are supplied in an ungrounded system you are required to install a grounding electrode at each building or structure. This will be further described in Part H. The grounding electrode shall be connected to both metal enclosures of a building or structure as well as to the disconnecting means.

Exception No. 1: See Exception No. 1 of (a).

Exception No. 2: See your *NEC.*

250-25. Conductor to Be Grounded—Alternating-Current Systems—Article 200 covers the use and identification of grounded conductors. Ordinarily, the grounded conductor is commonly known as "the white wire," although it will be recalled that a neutral gray color may also be used. Fig. 250-1 illustrates the different grounding circuits used.

(1) One conductor shall be grounded if the circuit is single phase 2-wire.

(2) The neutral conductor shall be grounded if the circuit is single phase 3-wire.

(3) On a wye system having a center tap common to all phases.

(4) On a delta system having one phase conductor grounded.

(5) In a delta where one phase is used as in (2) above, the mid-tap shall be grounded and be the neutral conductor. Remember not to connect to the wild leg from the neutral.

Article 200 tells us how to identify the grounded conductor.

250-26. Grounding Separately Derived Alternating-Current Systems—Section 250-5 covers separately derived ac systems that are to be grounded, and (a) through (d) specify how they shall be grounded.

(a) **Bonding Jumper.** If bonding jumpers are used, their sizing shall be according Section 250-79(c). This shall be used for connecting the derived phase conductors to the grounded conductor from the derived system to the equipment grounding conductors of said system. There is an exception, No. 4, which is part of Section 250-23(a), which permits this connection to be made at any point of the separately derived system to the grounding source of the first disconnecting means, which can include the overcurrent devices. As an alternative, the separately derived system ground may be made at the source of the separately derived system when it does not have either overcurrent device or disconnecting means.

It would be well to check back to Section 240-21 as to where overcurrent devices are required on separately derived systems.

Exception: Also covered is the size of the bonding jumper on a system of not over 1000 volt-amperes, and which supplies a Class 1 remote-control or signaling system. The bonding jumper shall not be smaller than the derived phase conductors, but in no event shall it be smaller than No. 14 copper or No. 12 aluminum.

(b) **Grounding Electrode Conductors.** Section 250-94 covers the sizing of grounding electrode conductors. The grounding electrode conductor for the derived phase conductors shall be used to connect the grounded conductor of the derived system to the grounding electrode. In (c) below, how to do this is discussed. Unless permitted by Exception No. 4 of Section 250-23(a), the grounding connection may be made at any point on the separately derived system provided it is made from the disconnect of the first system or overcurrent device. It may also be made at the source of a separately derived system when no disconnecting means or overcurrent device is used. This would indicate that it could be made from the secondary of the transformer from which the separately derived system originates.

Exception: An exception does not require a grounding electrode conductor if the system is supplied by a transformer rated not more than 1000 volt-amperes and the system supplies Class 1 remote-control or signal circuit. However, the system grounding conductor must be bonded to the transformer framer or enclosure and the bonding jumper meet the requirements of the Exception in (a) above, and the transformer frame enclosure has to be grounded as required by Section 250-57.

(c) **Grounding Electrode.** The grounding electrode must be as close as practical, and is preferred in the same area as the grounding conductor to the system. Where grounding electrodes are used, they should be: (1) the nearest effectively grounded metal building or structure; or (2) the nearest water pipe that is effectively grounded by sufficient metal water pipe buried in the earth; or (3) made electrodes as specified in Sections 250-81 and 250-83, provided that the electrodes that were specified in (1) and (2) above are not available.

(d) **Grounding Methods.** See the *NEC*.

As to (c)(2), one must be careful in attaching to just any water pipe as it may be opened for repairs, moved, replaced with sections of nonmetallic pipe, or disbanded and a dangerous condition might develop. Be careful!

250-27. High-Impedance Grounded Neutral System Connections —The provisions of (a) through (f) below are to be complied with when high-impedance grounded neutral systems are used.

(a) **Grounding Impedance Location.** When high-impedance grounding is used, it shall be located between the grounding source neutral and the grounding electrode. Where a neutral does not exist, the high-impedance shall be installed from a grounding transformer to the grounding electrode.

(b) **Neutral Conductor.** The neutral conductor from its connection point to the grounding impedance must be fully insulated.

(c) **System Neutral Connection.** The neutral conductor shall only be connected through the grounding impedance to the grounding electrode.

Note: When a circuit is closed, there is a value of charging current that sometimes exceeds the overcurrent protection on that system. The impedance usually is selected not only for ground-fault current slightly greater than or equal to this capacity charging current; impedance grounding also aids in limiting any transient overvoltages to safe values. For more information, refer to ANSI/IEEE Standard 142-1982, which gives recommendations for Industrial Commercial Power Systems. The design of impedance grounding in reality becomes an engineering and design problem.

(d) **Neutral Conductor Routing.** The impedance grounding system from the neutral point of a transformer or generator may be installed in a separate raceway. Thus you can see it is not required to be run in the same raceways as the phase conductors to the disconnecting means or overcurrent device. The impedance grounding limits the ground current so it may be treated from a solidly grounded neutral.

(e) **Equipment Bonding Jumper.** An equipment bonding jumper (connected between equipment grounding conductors and the grounding impedance) must be an unspliced conductor and must run from the first disconnecting means to the grounded side of the impedance.

(f) **Grounding Electrode Conductor Location.** The grounding conductor is to be attached at any point from the grounded side of a grounding impedance to the equipment grounding connection, which may be at the service equipment or disconnecting means of the first system. At first this might sound like paralleling grounding conductors, but the impedance grounding conductor originates from the phase neutral, and the equipment grounding conductor referred to here connects from the grounding electrode to the equipment disconnecting means of the first system.

D. Enclosure Grounding

250-32. Service Raceways and Enclosures—See the *NEC*.

250-33. Other Conductor Enclosures—See the *NEC*.

E. Equipment Grounding

250-42. Equipment Fastened in Place or Connected by Permanent Wiring Methods (Fixed)—The grounding of noncurrent-carrying metal parts of fixed equipment is always subject to becoming energized due to the results of abnormal conditions, and so this section requires the grounding of these noncurrent-carrying parts [see (a) through (f) below]. This should not be taken lightly, and all precautions must be taken to keep these parts, should they become energized, at as near zero potential with surrounding areas as possible.

(a) **Vertical and Horizontal Distances.** Fixed equipment under 8 feet vertically or 4 feet horizontally of ground or grounded metal objects which may be contacted by persons. Concrete is an excellent ground and this should be included.

(b) **Wet or Damp Locations.** Equipment in damp or wet locations that are not isolated.

(c) **Electrical Contact.** See the *NEC*.

(d) **Hazardous (Classified) Locations.** These are covered in Articles 500 through 517 in your *NEC*.

(e) **Metallic Wiring Methods.** See the *NEC*.

(f) **Over 150 Volts to Ground.** Where the voltages are over 150 volts to ground.

Exception No. 1: If switches or circuit breakers are used for other than service equipment and only qualified persons have access.

Exception No. 2: Special permission may be granted for metal frames of electrically heated appliances where the frames are permanently and effectively insulated from ground. Take note of "special permission"; the intent is no doubt that this is not intended to cover house heating in general.

Exception No. 3: If transformers and capacitors are mounted on wooden poles and are over 8 feet from grade or ground level and are used as distribution apparatus. Here again, care must be exercised in judgment to see that this equipment is high enough to avoid persons touching it while standing on grounded objects, etc.

Exception No. 4: Equipment that is double-insulated and effectively marked as such; listed processing; and listed office equipment are not required to be grounded.

250-43. Fastened in Place or Connected by Permanent Wiring Methods (Fixed)—Specific—Equipment described in (a) through (j) below, irrespective of the voltage, shall be grounded. This covers exposed noncurrent-carrying metal parts. For (a) through (j), see the *NEC*.

250-44. Nonelectric Equipment—This section covers grounding of metal parts of nonelectric equipment. Basically any nonelectric equipment which might become accidentally electrically energized must be properly grounded. See the *NEC*.

250-45. Equipment Connected by Cord and Plug—Exposed non-current-carrying metal parts of cord- and plug-connected equipment that may become energized shall be grounded. This is covered by (a) through (d) below:

(a) **In Hazardous (Classified) Locations.** These are covered in Articles 500 through 517.

(b) **Over 150 Volts to Ground.** If they are operated at over 150 volts to ground, guarded motors are exempt. Metal frames of heating appliances that are effectively insulated from ground may be exempted by special permission. Also see Exception No. 4 of Section 250-42.

(c) **In Residential Occupancies.** In residential occupancies:

(1) Refrigerators, freezers, and air-conditioners.

(2) Clothes washing, clothes-drying, dish-washing machines; sump pumps and electrical aquariums.

(3) Hand-held motor-operated tools.

(4) Motor-operated appliances such as hedge clippers, lawn mowers, snow blowers, and wet scrubbers.

(5) Portable hand-held lamps.

The use of ground-fault circuit interrupters will also be a great assistance to personnel safety.

Exception: Hand-held appliances that are doubly insulated or have equivalent protection shall not be required to be grounded. Double-insulated tools, etc., shall be effectively marked as such.

A portable GFCI would give additional protection and assist in personnel safety.

(d) **In Other than Residential Occupancies.**

(1) Refrigerators, freezers, and air-conditioners.

(2) Clothes-washing, clothes-drying, and dish-washing machines.

(3) Electronic computer plant and data-processing equipment.

(4) Sump pumps and electrical aquarium equipment.

(5) Motor-operated hand tools such as hedge clippers, lawn mowers, snow blowers, and wet scrubbers.

(6) Cord- and plug-connected appliances used in damp or wet locations, used by persons that may be standing on concrete ground or metal floors. This could include working inside metal tanks or boilers or concrete metal tanks.

(7) If likely to be used in damp or wet locations or any other conductive location, hand tools are included.

(8) Portable hand lamps.

Portable GFCI's are available and add a great deal of protection.

Exception No. 1: If the source of supply is an isolated transformer with an ungrounded secondary not over 50 volts, tools and hand lamps may be used in wet and conductive places and are not required to be grounded.

Exception No. 2: Double-insulated or distinctively marked, if listed portable tools and listed appliances, may be approved and shall not require grounding.

See the *NEC* for the fine-print note.

250-46. Spacing from Lightning Rods—See the *NEC*.

F. Methods of Grounding

250-50. Equipment Grounding Conductor Connections—The equipment grounding conductor shall be connected on the supply side of the service-entrance disconnecting means and shall be made as required in (a) and (b) below. The equipment grounding conductor from a separately derived system shall be connected at the source as required in Section 250-26(a).

(a) **For Grounded System.** The connection of the equipment grounding conductor shall be made by bonding it to the grounded service conductor or neutral, and also to the grounding electrode. This can usually all take place in the service disconnecting means. See Figs. 250-3 and 250-4 on page 126.

(b) **For Ungrounded System.** You are required to have a grounding electrode, even though no conductor from the supply is grounded, and the equipment grounding conductor (be it the metallic raceways or a conductor) shall be connected to the grounding electrode conductor.

Exception for (a) and (b) above: Nongrounded-type receptacles are to be used only for replacement on ungrounded systems and for branch circuit extensions only where the installations already exist

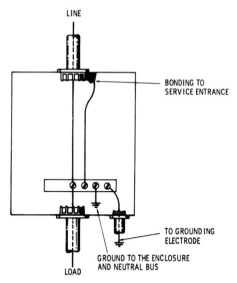

Fig. 250-3. The grounding conductor that grounds the neutral must also be used for all other grounding.

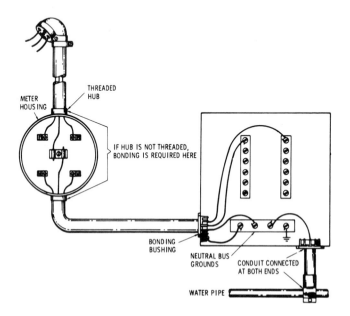

Fig. 250-4. An example of proper bonding.

and do not have equipment grounding conductors in the branch circuits. When adding a grounding-type receptacle to an ungrounded equipment wiring system, you may ground the receptacle-grounding terminal to a metallic water pipe. This is covered in the exception to this section and bonding is covered in Section 250-80(a).

Author's Note: Be sure the water pipe is continuous metal pipe and that there are no insulated couplings or unions separating the piping from ground.

Note: The exception in Section 210-7(d) permits the use of a GFCI type of receptacle on systems that were installed without equipment grounding conductors.

250-51. Effective Grounding Path—Caution must be taken to ensure that the grounding path from circuit equipment and conductor enclosures will be continuous and not subject to damage. They must be capable of safely handling fault currents that may be imposed on it. The impedance must be sufficiently low to keep the voltage ground minimum and facilitates the opening of overcurrent devices covering the circuit.

Grounding conductor cannot use the earth as the only equipment-grounding conductor.

250-53. Grounding Path to Grounding Electrode at Services.

(a) **Grounding Electrode Conductors.** The equipment grounding conductors shall be grounded to the grounding electrode. This may be a means of connecting to the grounding conductor at the service equipment, and if a grounded system is being used, the grounding conductor originates at the same point as the service equipment. See Fig. 250-5 and Section 250-23(a).

(b) **Main Bonding Jumper.** An unspliced jumper shall be used to connect the equipment grounding conductor and the service equipment enclosure to the grounded conductor. This shall be in the service equipment or the service conductor enclosure. (See Fig. 250-3.) Usually in service-entrance equipment there is a grounding bar for attaching the neutral of the service and branch circuits. This is usually connected to the enclosure by means of inserting a screw to the bar into the enclosure. Then an additional bar is bolted or clamped to the service equipment for attaching the equipment grounding conductors. A case such as this constitutes the bonding.

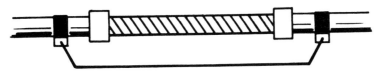

Fig. 250-5. Bonding must extend around any flexible conduit used in conjunction with service-entrance equipment.

250-54. Common Grounding Electrode—This section applies to alternating-current systems and requires that the same grounding electrode in or at the building shall be used to ground the conductor enclosure and equipment in or on that building. See Sections 250-23 and 250-24.

When two or more grounding electrodes are bonded together, they are considered one.

250-55. Underground Service Cable—Where an underground service is supplied by a continuous metal-sheathed or armored cable which is bonded to the underground system, it need not be grounded at the building and may be insulated from the interior conduit. Please note that this is quite different from an overhead system in which the cable sheath or armor and/or conduit shall be grounded at the service entrance.

250-56. Short Sections of Raceway—See the *NEC*.

250-57. Equipment Fastened in Place or Connected by Permanent Wiring Methods (Fixed)—Grounding—This covers the noncurrent-carrying metal parts of equipment. For other enclosures and raceways that are required to be grounded, (a) or (b) below shows two methods of this type of grounding:

Exception: As permitted by Section 250-24, 250-60, and 250-61, equipment, raceways, and enclosures where grounded to the grounded circuit conductor.

(a) **Equipment Grounding Conductor Types.** Section 250-91(b) covers the equipment grounding conductors.

(b) **With Circuit Conductors.** When equipment grounding conductors are contained in the same raceway cable or cord, or run with the circuit conductors, they may be bare, covered, or insulated. Equipment grounding conductors covered or insulated shall have insulation that is continuously of a green color or green with a yellow stripe.

It shall be a part of the cable or cord, or run in the same raceway with the circuit conductors to keep the impedance to the lowest value. When using NM, NMC, or UF cables, these cables are required to contain the equipment-grounding conductor as part of the cable. See *NEC* Section 300-3(b).

Exception No. 1: Should the insulated or covered conductor be larger than No. 6 copper or aluminum, this conductor shall be permanently marked at the time of installation, at each end or any other accessible point. It shall be identified by any one of the following means.

See the *NEC* for (a) through (c).

Exception No. 2: On dc circuits the equipment grounding conductor may be permitted to be run separately from the circuit conductors. The current is steady in dc, while in ac the current fluctuates 120 times per second, causing induction between the conductors. This is allowed because impedance does not enter into dc circuits.

Exception No. 3: Where maintenance and supervision is done only by qualified persons, insulated conductors in a multiconductor cable may at the time of installation be permanently marked to indicate it is equipment grounding conductor. This must be done at both ends and at any point where there is access to the equipment grounding conductor.

  a. By removing the insulation along the entire length of the exposed conductor.

  b. By a painted or otherwise permanent color such as green tape where the equipment grounding conductor is exposed.

  c. Or marking by permanent tags or labels.

Note: Section 250-79 covers bonding jumper and the requirements thereof, and Section 400-7 covers the use of cords for fixed equipment.

250-58. Equipment Considered Effectively Grounded—The non-current-carrying metal parts of equipment, as specified under (a) and (b) below, shall be considered as being effectively grounded.

(a) **Equipment Secure to Grounded Metal Supports.** Even if electrical equipment is secured on a good electrical contact with metal racks or supports, it shall be grounded by one of the means indicated in Section 250-57. Structural steel shall not be used as a conductor for equipment grounding. Recall that it was required that the equipment grounding conductor be in with the circuit conductors.

(b) **Metal Car Frames.** The metal car frames of elevators and similar devices are considered to be adequately grounded if attached to a metal cable running over or attached to a metal drum that is well grounded according to the grounding requirements of the Code. See Section 250-57.

250-59. Cord- and Plug-Connected Equipment—On equipment that has metal noncurrent-carrying parts that are to be grounded, the grounding may be accomplished by the methods (a), (b), or (c) following:

(a) **By Means of the Metal Enclosures.** By means of the metal enclosure of the conductors feeding such equipment, provided an approved grounding type attachment plug is used, one fixed contacting member being for the purpose of grounding the metal enclosure, and provided, further, that the metal enclosure of the conductors is attached to the attachment plug and to the equipment by approved connectors.

  The above means that the outlet shall be of the grounded receptacle type, and that the attachment plug shall be of the type approved for grounding from a grounding-type receptacle, and that the cord shall carry a grounding conductor, one end of which is attached to the grounding terminal of the attachment plug and the other end to the frame of the portable equipment. Since it was found that it is not always possible to attach a portable appliance or equipment to a grounding-type receptacle because the grounding terminal of the attachment plug was often broken off or cut off to fit an old type of receptacle, the following exception has therefore been added:

Exception: The grounding contact member of grounding-type attachment plugs on the power supply cord of portable hand-held, hand-guided, or hand-supported tools or appliances may be of the movable self-restoring type. In other words, there are approved attachment plugs that have a hinged grounding prong with a spring so that it can be folded out of the way and yet will restore itself to the normal position for use on grounding-type receptacles.

(b) **By Means of a Grounding Conductor.** The grounding conductor may be run in the cable or flexible-cord assembly, provided that it terminates in an approved grounding-type attachment plug having a fixed grounding-type contact member. This grounding conductor in the cable or cord assembly may be bare; but if insulated, it shall be green or green with a yellow stripe. You will notice that it says a "fixed grounding contact member"—again there is an exception. This exception is exactly as above: that is, the contact member may be a restoring type.

(c) **Separate Flexible Wire or Strap.** See the *NEC.*

250-60. Frames of Ranges and Clothes Dryers—Frames of electric ranges and electric clothes dryers shall be grounded as provided for in Sections 250-57 and 250-59, that is, by metal raceways or a grounding conductor. Outlet and/or junction boxes shall also be grounded. There is another alternative on 120/240-volt three-wire circuits, or 120/208-volt circuits derived from a three-phase 4-wire supply. This type of circuit may be grounded to the neutral conductor provided that the neutral or grounded circuit conductor is no smaller than No. 10 copper. This applies to wall-mounted ovens and counter-top cooking units as well. This is the one instance where the neutral may be used also as the grounding conductor, providing all other conditions are met.

Where Type SE cable with a bare neutral is used for ranges or dryer branch circuits, it shall originate only for service equipment. If it were permitted to originate from feeder panels, we would have an isolated neutral bus with a bare conductor attached. With a bare conductor, it could easily touch the enclosure and defeat the protection that the isolated neutral affords. This does not apply to mobile homes or recreational vehicles.

If grounding-type receptacles are furnished with the equipment, they shall be bonded to the equipment.

250-61. Use of Grounded Circuit Conductor for Grounding Equipment—This section was rewritten in the 1978 *NEC* to clarify intent.

(a) **Supply-Side Equipment.** In Section 250-24 there was covered supply to a building or buildings having only one branch circuit, and the neutral could be used to ground enclosures on the supply side of the service disconnecting means or main disconnecting means.

(b) **Load-Side Equipment.** The grounded neutral shall not be used for grounding noncurrent-carrying metal parts of equipment, but is supplied from the load side of a service disconnecting means or on the load side of the separately derived system disconnecting means or the overcurrent devices.

Exception No. 1: See the *NEC.*

Exception No. 2: See the *NEC.*

Exception No. 3: Meter enclosures may be grounded to the grounded circuit conductor (neutral) if the grounding is on the supply side of the service disconnecting means, and:

a. Where no ground-fault protection has been installed on the service, and

b. The meter enclosures in the above shall be located near the service disconnecting means.

Exception No. 4: Refer to Sections 710-72(e)(1) and 710-74 in the *NEC.*

250-62. Multiple Circuit Connections—There will be cases where the equipment will be required to be grounded, that is it is supplied by one or more circuits of grounded wiring systems on the premises; in this case, separate equipment-grounding conductors shall be supplied from each system as specified in Sections 250-57 and 250-59.

G. Bonding

250-70. General—To ensure electrical continuity and also sufficient capacity to safely conduct the fault-current likely to occur, bonding shall be required to ensure that necessary electric continuity is provided. This section is very basic and important. Larger available fault currents demand proper means of safely handling this problem.

250-71. Service Equipment—This is an item that has been a part of the Code for many years, but is often overlooked. It is recommended that a careful understanding of the reason for bonding at this location be gained because of its importance. The way in which this bonding is to be done will be covered in Section 250-72. An example of proper bonding is shown in Fig. 250-6.

The parts of equipment required to be effectively grounded are given in (a) and (b) below:

(a) **Bonding of Service Equipment.** Noncurrent-carrying metal parts of equipment shall be effectively bonded as covered in (1), (2), and (3) below:

(1) Section 250-55 gives the exception for service raceways, service cable armor or sheath, or cable trays.

(2) Bonding is required for all service equipment enclosures when service entrance conductors are present. This includes any meter fittings, boxes, auxiliary gutters, etc., that may be connected in the service raceway or armor. Meter socket threaded hubs served by metal conduit will serve as a bond.

(3) Section 250-92(a) covers metal raceways or armor in which the grounding electrode conductor is contained therein. This will be explained more in detail when we come to the aforementioned section.

(b) **Bonding to Other Systems.** See the *NEC*.

See the *NEC* for the fine-print notes as well.

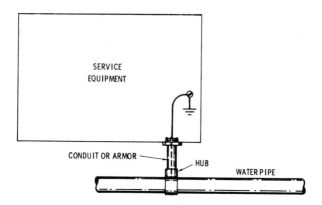

Fig. 250-6. Conduit or armor used to protect the grounding wire shall be bonded to the grounding electrode and to the service-entrance enclosure.

250-72. Method of Bonding Service Equipment—The following is the procedure to be followed to assure continuity at service equipment:

(a) **Grounded Service Conductor.** Section 250-113 requires bonding equipment to the grounded service conductor. See Fig. 250-7.

(b) **Threaded Couplings.** Threaded couplings or threaded bosses when used with rigid or intermediate metal conduit shall be made wrench-tight so that good bonding is made.

(c) **Threadless Couplings and Connectors.** Threadless couplings and connectors are available for rigid metal conduit. They shall be made up

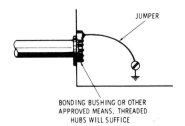

NO SOLDERED CONNECTIONS.
USE APPROVED LUGS, PRESSURE
CONNECTIONS, ETC.

JUMPER

BONDING BUSHING OR OTHER
APPROVED MEANS. THREADED
HUBS WILL SUFFICE

Fig. 250-7.   Equipment shall be bonded to the grounded service entrance.

tight to ensure electrical continuity as required for bonding for this section. Standard locknut or bushing shall not be used for the bonding required.

(d) **Bonding Jumpers.** Where concentric or eccentric knockouts are used in enclosures that have been punched or the bonding security has been otherwise impaired, the electrical connection to ground bonding jumpers meeting other requirements of this article shall be used in such places—for instance, bonding type bushings, or locknuts, or otherwise bonded around.

This requires that, in services and entrance equipment, as well as other points where there are eccentric or concentric knockouts, bonding jumpers be used around concentric or eccentric knockouts. It is also necessary to use bonding around any flexible conduit that might be used in conjunction with service entrances. (See Fig. 250-5.)

(e) **Other Devices.** Lockout and bushings of the conventional type are not approved for continuity at service entrances. Devices shall be approved for the purpose, that is, bonding-type bushings, wedge nuts, etc.

250-73. Metal Armor or Tape of Service Cable—When using service cable with an uninsulated grounding conductor, the armor or metal tape shall be considered as adequately grounded if the armor or metal tape is in continuous electrical contact with the grounding conductor.

250-74. Connecting Receptacle Grounding Terminal to Box—Grounding continuity between a grounded outlet box and the grounding circuit of the receptacle shall be established by means of a bonding jumper between the outlet box and the receptacle grounding terminal. (See Fig. 250-11, page 149.)

Exception No. 1: Where the box such as a handy box is surface mounted, then direct metal contact may be made metal to metal with the handy box or other box and the yokes of the receptacle. This shall be accepted as a ground connection to the receptacle. The above will not apply to mounted receptacles unless you have ensured the positive ground connection between the receptacle yoke and box.

Exception No. 2: There are contact devices and yokes specifically listed for proper grounding when used in conjunction with supporting screws to ensure proper grounding between the yoke and flush-type mounted boxes or receptacles.

Exception No. 3: If floor-mounted boxes are listed and designed specifically for making good electrical contact, when this receptacle is installed, they may be used.

Exception No. 4: When electrical noise (electromagnetic interference) occurs in the grounding circuit, a receptacle on the grounding circuit in which the grounding terminal or receptacle has purposely been insulated from the mounting means or yoke should be permitted. In this case an insulated equipment grounding conductor may run to the isolated terminal with the circuit conductors. This insulated grounding conductor may pass through one or more panelboards without being connected thereto as covered in Section 384-27, Exception No. 1, so it terminates at the equipment grounding terminal at that derived system or service.

See the *NEC* for the fine-print note.

The grounding similar to that described in Exception No. 4 may also be found to be advantageous for grounding computers or solid-state counters on machines. However, if metal conduit is used as the raceway, it should be insulated from the machine in question and then the insulated grounding conductor run back from the equipment to the source as explained in Exception No. 4.

The results of the above established that a grounding jumper shall be used from grounded boxes to the grounding terminal of the receptacle in all cases, including boxes on conduit circuits and EMT circuits, unless the box is surface mounted so that the mounting screws may be tightened to make a secure grounding connection between the device yoke and the box. Of course, if a device is approved for making the proper grounding connection, the bonding will not be necessary. (See Fig. 250-8.)

250-75. Bonding Other Enclosures—When all types of metal raceways, armor cable, cable sheath, enclosures, frames, and other metal non-current-carrying parts that serve as the equipment grounding conductors, whether using a supplementary grounding conductor or not, require bonding to ensure the safe handling of any fault-currents that may be imposed and to ensure electrical continuity. Sometimes you will run into nonconductive paint or similar coatings. These must be removed at the threads or other contact points, and these clean surfaces shall be connected by means of fittings or bonding jumpers designed to make such removal unnecessary for service. On large buildings there are usually expansion joints in the buildings to take care of temperature changes and movements where these joints are crossed by a metal raceway. There are listed fittings to

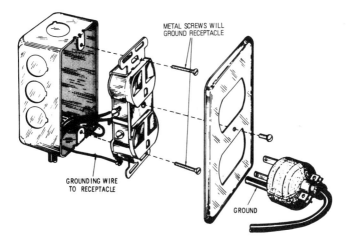

Fig. 250-8. A grounding jumper shall be used from grounded boxes to the grounding terminal of the receptacle.

permit the movement of the building by bonding across the fitting externally so as not to interrupt equipment grounding continuity.

The phrase "shall be effectively bonded where necessary" is the key of this section. It appears to become a design and an inspection problem to pass judgment as to where to bond and where bonding will not be required.

250-76. Bonding for over 250 Volts—Metal raceways and conduits enclosing conductors at more than 250 volts to ground (other than service conductors) shall have the electrical continuity assured by one of the methods outlined in Section 250-72(b) through (e). Recall that this section covered continuity at service equipment.

Exception: Where oversized eccentric or concentric knockouts are not used, the following explanations will be permitted:

(a) **Threadless Fittings.** Threadless couplings may be used with metal sheath cables.

(b) **Two Locknuts.** Two locknuts may be used with rigid metal conduit or intermediate metal conduit, one locknut on the outside of the enclosure and one on the outside when entering boxes or cabinets. You still have to use the appropriate bushings inside the enclosure. On some you will use the metal and on others, as you will see later, you must use insulated bushings.

Grounding connections and circuit conductors that are not made tight cause many electrical faults and some fires. When tightening screws showing inch pounds, pressure should be used, with 12 inch pound pressure as the minimum tightening of device screws. These locknuts are also to be made up tight. Elsewhere in the Code it is permissible to use one locknut and one bushing where it is not practical to use two locknuts and a bushing. Where the voltage exceeds 250 volts to ground, there are to be two locknuts as outlined above.

(c) One locknut on the inside of the boxes or cabinets will suffice where the fitting shoulders seat firmly on the box or cabinet. These include electric metallic tubing connectors, cable connectors, and flexible metal conduit connectors.

250-77. Bonding Loosely Jointed Metal Raceways—This was discussed earlier for covering conduit crossing expansion joints or telescoping sections of raceways and using on bonding jumpers.

Metal trough raceways used in connection with sound recording and reproducing, made up in sections, shall contain a grounding conductor to which each section shall be bonded. In recording and reproducing, the bonding wire will reduce the conditions that affect the quality of recording and reproduction.

250-78. Bonding in Hazardous (Classified) Locations—Regardless of the voltage, the electrical continuity of raceways and boxes shall be assured by one of the methods in Section 250-72(b) through (e). However, this does not cover the continuity in hazardous locations in entirety; the requirement for the specific type of hazardous condition involved should be looked up. These are covered in Sections 500 through 517. In reality, this section is rather broad and does not cover all hazardous locations.

250-79. Main and Equipment Bonding Jumpers.

(a) **Material.** Copper or other noncorrosive material is to be used for main and equipment bonding jumpers. This automatically eliminates aluminum in many places. Remember that if other than copper is used, it shall be sized to an equivalent to what would be required for copper jumpers.

(b) **Attachment.** Section 250-113 specifies the manner in which main and equipment bonding shall be attached for circuits and equipment. Section 250-115 specifies the manner of attachment for grounding electrodes.

Both (a) and (b) should be reviewed, noting that soldering is not permitted. This question of aluminum for common grounding conductors is always arising. This is taken care of in (a), and to my knowledge there is no grounding clamp approved by UL for grounding with aluminum. If it were to go to a made electrode, it could not be run closer than 18″ to the earth; and if to a water pipe, the water piping is subject to sweating and would cause corrosion of the aluminum.

(c) **Size—Equipment Bonding Jumper on Supply Side of Service and Main Bonding Jumper.** See Fig. 250-5. There seems to be considerable confusion in Tables 250-94 and 250-95. By looking at the headings there should be no confusion. Table 250-94 is grounding electrode conductor for AC systems. Table 250-95 is: minimum equipment-grounding conductors for grounding raceway and equipment.

Table 250-94 is for grounding electrode conductors, if the service-entrance phase conductors are larger than 1100 MCM copper or 1700 MCM aluminum. This will require that the bonding jumper circular mill area shall not be less than 12½ percent of the size of the largest phase conductor. See the *NEC* for the remainder of (c).

(d) **Size—Equipment Bonding Jumper on Load Side of Service.** Table 250-95 lists the size of the equipment bonding jumpers on the load side of the service overcurrent devices. The bonding jumper is to be a single conductor sized according to Table 250-95 for the largest overcurrent device that is provided to supply the circuits. If the bonding jumper supplies two or more raceways or cables, the same rulings apply.

Exception: It is not necessary to have the equipment bonding jumper larger than the phase conductors, but in no case shall it be smaller than No. 14 AWG.

(e) **Installation—Equipment Bonding Jumper.** It is permitted to install the equipment bonding jumper either inside or outside of the raceway or enclosure. When it is installed outside of the raceway or enclosure, it shall not be over 6 feet in length and shall be routed with the raceway or enclosure. If the equipment bonding jumper is inside the raceway, refer to Section 310-12(b) for the conductor identification requirements you are to comply with.

250-80. Bonding of Piping Systems.

(a) **Metal Water Piping.** Regardless of whether the water piping is supplied by nonmetallic pipe to the building or structure, you are required to bond the interior metal water piping to the service equipment enclosure. This bonding jumper is sized using Table 250-94. It may be run to the service-entrance equipment where the service grounding conductor is of sufficient size, or it may be run to two or more grounding electrodes, if used.

Exception: In multiple occupancies if the interior piping is metal and the piping systems of all occupancies are tied together, it is required that metal piping be isolated from all other occupancies by the use of nonmetallic pipe. Each individual metal water pipe system is required to be bonded separately to the panelboard or switchboard enclosure, but not to the service-entrance equipment. Bonding jumper points of attachment shall be accessible and sized according to Table 250-95. This ensures that the metal piping system in each occupancy is at ground potential.

(b) **Other Metal Piping.** All interior metal piping which may be subjected to being energized shall be bonded to the service equipment ground at the service enclosure to the common grounding conductor, if it is of sufficient size, or to one or more of the grounding electrodes, and this bonding jumper shall be sized according to Table 250-95. See Fig. 250-9.

With circuit conductors that could cause energizing of piping, you will be permitted to use the equipment ground run with the circuit conductors.

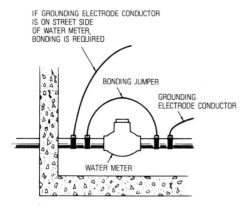

IF GROUNDING ELECTRODE CONDUCTOR
IS ON STREET SIDE
OF WATER METER,
BONDING IS REQUIRED

BONDING JUMPER

GROUNDING
ELECTRODE CONDUCTOR

WATER METER

LEAVE BONDING JUMPER LONG ENOUGH
SO THAT IT WILL NOT HAVE TO BE
REMOVED IN METER REPLACEMENT

Fig. 250-9. Proper bonding of a water meter.

Note: It is a good idea, for additional safety, to bond all metal air ducts and piping on the premises.

H. Grounding Electrode System

250-81. Grounding Electrode System—Grounding electrodes and method have been constantly improved, and when you refer to Section 250-84, you find that the grounding electrode resistance actually has to be measured.

The table opposite may assist you in determining approximate resistivity of various soils. This table does not appear in the *NEC.*

In (a) through (d) below, all shall be bonded together from the grounding electrode service, if available at the building or structure being served. Section 250-92(a) covers the installation of the bonding jumpers, and Section 250-94 covers the size of the bonding jumper to be used and connected as specified in Section 250-115. The unspliced electrode conductor (note *unspliced*) may be run to any available grounding electrode. It shall be sized to the largest conductor required to be run to the grounding electrode.

Resistivities of Different Soils

Soil	Resistivity OHM – CM		
	Average	Min.	Max.
Fills—ashes, cinders, brine wastes	2,370	590	7,000
Clay, shale, gumbo, loam . .	4,060	340	16,300
Same—with varying proportions of sand and gravel	15,800	1,020	135,000
Gravel, sand, stones, with little clay or loam	94,000	59,000	458,000

(a) **Metal Underground Water Pipe.** A buried metal underground water system may be used as a ground electrode if there is 10 feet (3.05 m) or more in direct contact with the earth (including any metal well casing bonded to the water pipe). These shall be electrically continuous or made electrically continuous by bonding around insulated joints or sections of insulating pipe, to the point where the common grounding conductor connects to the pipe and any bonding connection. Water meters should not be relied upon for the grounding path, the grounding should be on the street side of the water meter or the water meter should be effectively bonded around, as shown in Fig. 250-9.

You are required, when using a metal underground water pipe system as a grounding electrode, to supplement it with at least one additional electrode such as that described in Sections 270-81 or 250-83. This ensures some bonding electrode in the event that some outside water system is eventually replaced with nonmetallic water pipe. This supplemental electrode may be supplied from the grounded service-entrance conductor, a grounded service raceway, any grounded service enclosure, or the interior metal water piping at any point that is convenient.

If the building or structure has nonmetallic water piping to it, and metal water piping within the building or structure, this will eliminate the use of the interior water piping as an electrode. However, the Code also requires bonding the equipment grounding electrode to interior metallic water piping, even though supplied by a nonmetallic water piping underground supply.

If the supplemental electrode is one that is described in Section 250-83(c) or (d), the size of the grounding electrode need not be larger than No. 6 copper or No. 4 aluminum.

Author's Note: Aluminum is mentioned, but recall that aluminum is not permitted closer than 18 inches to the earth or in contact with anything corrosive, and the service entrance conductor is to be without a splice.

(b) **Metal Frame of the Building.** The metal frame of a building may be used as a grounding electrode provided it is effectively grounded and would give the same protection as the other methods of grounding.

(c) **Concrete-Encased Electrode.** Concrete-encased steel reinforcing bar of No. 4 AWG copper encased in concrete footings or direct contact with the earth. The criteria for this shall be: (1) not less than 20 feet (6.1 m) of one or more steel reinforcing bars not less than 20 feet (6.1 m) long and not less than ½ inch (12.7 mm) in diameter. In most cases more than 20 feet (6.1 m) will be available, making for a lower resistance ground; or (2) a minimum of 20 feet (6.1 m) of bare copper conductor not smaller than No. 4 AWG.

On a large industrial complex we use the metallic water pipe bonding by exothermic welding across the joints of the cast-iron pipe, plus tying the steel column anchor bolts by exothermic welding to the bolt and then to the rebar in the casson and the rebar in the concrete pudding. These are then all tied together as the grounding electrode for a building. The results are amazing: The ground test is very close to or just a little above zero ohms resistance. Concrete in contact with earth will always draw some moisture, which causes the grounding to be very effective.

(d) **Ground Ring.** The ring of copper conductor not smaller than 2 AWG, buried at a depth of not less than 2½ feet, and in direct contact with the earth can be used as the grounding electrode for buildings or structures.

In encircling the building or structure, you will find that in most cases there will be much more than 20 feet (6.1 m) of conductor. The author has found that a better ground may be obtained by burying the conductor about 3 feet from the building and also by periodically driving ground rods and attaching them to the bare conductor by approved methods.

If the connection is made by exothermic welding, these welds often are deceptive. One sure method to be certain that they make good contact, if it is rebar, is to buff the rust off the rebar and heat it, to drive the moisture out of the pores. Then, to verify the load resistance connection, the load resistance reading ohmmeter that will go down to at least 1/2 ohm resistance should be used to verify the proper weld. This would also apply to exothermic welding to ground rods, except that the buffing and preheating would not be required.

250-83. Made and Other Electrodes—If electrodes as specified in Section 250-81 are not available, you may use one or more electrodes covered in (a) through (d) below. If practical, these made electrodes should reach permanent moisture levels. If one electrode is not long enough to reach permanent moisture, an additional one may be added to lengthen it. There shall be no paint or enamel or nonconductive coatings on the electrode. If more than one made electrode is required (including those used for lightning protection), then they shall be spaced a minimum of 6 feet apart—a greater distance apart would be preferable.

Where two or more made electrodes are used, they are considered and treated as a single electrode system.

(a) **Metal Underground Gas Piping System.** The *NEC* permits grounding to underground gas piping systems that are not insulated and are acceptable to both the supplier and the authority having jurisdiction. Be careful here because NFPA 54, the Code used for gas systems, does not permit the gas pipe to be used as an electrode.

Practically all gas underground services are tarred and wrapped with tarpaper coating to slow down electrolysis, so this system is practically never used.

(b) **Other Metal Underground Systems of Structures.** Other underground systems or structures such as underground tanks or piping.

(c) **Rod and Pipe Electrodes.** When rod or piping electrodes are given they must be a minimum of 8 feet long and shall be installed as covered below. One gross violation of this is the grounding electrodes used on antenna systems where the installer usually uses a 3-foot rod.

(1) When electrodes are pipe or conduit, they shall not be smaller than ¾ inch trade size. When using iron or steel piping, the conduit used shall be galvanized coated or otherwise coated with conductive noncorrosive material.

(2) Rods used as electrodes made of steel or iron shall be at least ⅝ inch in diameter. Nonferrous rods such as solid copper or steel that is copperclad shall not be less than ½ inch in diameter.

(3) The electrodes that are driven shall be driven to the 8-foot minimum or more. In other words, an 8-foot rod shall not be sticking out of the ground. In mountainous areas where bedrock is encountered close to the surface, the rod electrode may be driven at an oblique angle or may be buried in a trench that shall be at least 2½ feet deep. The upper end of the ground rod is to be flush with the surface or below surface level. If this cannot be done, the end above ground shall be protected as described in Section 250-117 from physical damage.

(d) **Plate Electrodes.** Plate electrodes shall be a minimum of 2 square feet, and if made of iron or steel they shall be at least ¼ inch thick. If made of a nonferrous metal such as copper, they may be .06 inch in thickness. These are often used by utilities at the bottom of a pole hole.

250-84. Resistance of Made Electrodes—Made electrodes shall have a resistance to ground of 25 ohms or less, wherever practicable. When the resistance is greater than 25 ohms, two or more electrodes may be connected in parallel or extended to a greater length. It should be noted that a made electrode that measures more than 25 ohms is required to be augmented by one additional electrode of a type permitted by Section 250-83. The Code cannot go into the mechanics of grounding, but good practice indicates that the electrode has a lower resistance when not driven close to a foundation. See Sections 250-81 and 250-83.

Continuous water piping systems usually have a ground resistance of less than 3 ohms. Metal frames of buildings often make a good ground and usually have a resistance of less than 25 ohms. As pointed out in Section 250-81 the metal frame of a building (when effectively grounded) may be used as the ground. Local metallic water systems and well casings also make good grounds in most cases.

Grounding, when made electrodes are used, can be greatly improved by the use of chemicals, such as magnesium sulphate, copper sulphate, or rock salt. A doughnut-type hole may be dug around the ground rod into which the chemicals are put. Another method is to bury a tile close to the rod and fill with the chemical. Rain and snow will dissolve the chemicals and allow them to penetrate the soil. See Fig. 250-10.

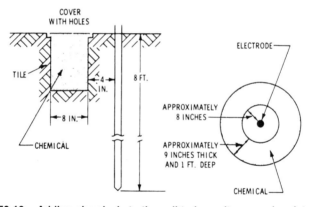

Fig. 250-10. Adding chemicals to the soil to lower its ground resistance.

It is recommended that the resistance of ground rods be tested periodically after installation. This is rarely done, however, except by utility companies who realize the importance of an adequate ground. The testing of ground resistance is a mystery to many electricians. Never attempt to use a common ohmmeter for the testing; the readings obtained are apt to be almost anything due to stray ac or dc currents in the soil or dc currents set up by the electrolysis in the soil. There are many measuring devices on the market, such as the ground megger—a battery-operated ground tester that uses a vibrator to produce pulsating ac current. In recent years, the transistor-type ground tester has appeared on the market.

An example of what you might expect to get by the paralleling of ground rods might be as follows (these figures are general and should not be taken as being the results in every case): Two rods paralleled with a 5-foot spacing between will reduce the resistance to about 65 percent of what one rod would be. Three rods paralleled with a 5-foot spacing between will reduce the resistance to about 42 percent, while four rods paralleled will reduce the resistance to about 30 percent.

In summarizing, there is only one method of telling if the grounding electrode meets these requirements: by testing the ground resistance by means of a good ground resistance tester.

250-86. Use of Lightning Rods—Lightning-rod conductors and made electrodes for grounding of lightning rods shall not be used in place of made electrodes for grounding wiring systems and equipment. However, they may be bonded together; in fact, the Code recommends the bonding of these electrodes to limit the difference of potential that might appear between them. See Sections 250-81 and 250-83.

To assist in the above, see Sections 250-46, 800-31(b)(7), and 820-22(h) for required bonding.

Difference of potential between two different grounding systems on the same building, if tied together, will reduce the potential difference between them—for instance, lightning rods and grounding electrodes.

J. Grounding Conductors

250-91. Material—The material for grounding conductors shall be as specified in (a), (b), and (c) below.

(a) **Grounding Electrode Conductor.** The grounding electrode conductor shall be of copper or other corrosive-resistance material, solid or stranded, insulated or bare, without splices or joints (except in the case of busbars), and electrical resistance per foot (linear) shall not exceed that of the allowable copper conductors that might be used for this purpose. Thus, if aluminum (in cases where permissible) is used, the conductor will have to be larger than copper would have to be for the same purpose. If aluminum is used, see Section 250-92.

There is an exception permitting busbars to be spliced.

There is another exception that covers places where more than a single enclosure is permitted, as described in Section 230-40, Exception No. 2. Here you are permitted to connect taps to the grounding electrode conductor. These taps shall be run into each enclosure. The main grounding electrode conductor is to be sized according to Section 250-94, but the sizing shall be for the largest conductor serving each separate enclosure.

(b) **Types of Equipment Grounding Conductor.** When the equipment grounding conductor encloses the circuit conductors, it shall consist of one or more of the combinations as listed in the *NEC*.

Exception No. 1: Flexible metal conduit is required to have all the fittings listed. This also applies to flexible metallic tubing, but the following conditions must be met:

a. Six feet is the maximum length of the ground return path.
b. The circuit shall be protected by overcurrent devices not to exceed 20 amperes, but that may also be less than 20 amperes.
c. The flexible metal conduit or tubing shall be terminated only in fittings listed for grounding.

Exception No. 2: Liquidtight flexible metal conduit, in sizes up to 1¼ inch, that have a total length not to exceed 6 feet from the ground return path and fitting for terminating the flexible conduit, are also to be listed for grounding. Liquidtight flexible metal conduit ⅜ and ½ inch trade size shall be protected by overcurrent devices at 20 amperes or less, and sizes of ¾ inch through 1¼ inch trade size, protected by overcurrent devices of 60 amperes or less.

Exception No. 3: This covers direct current systems only. With the dc systems, the equipment grounding conductor may be run separately from the circuit conductors.

With dc circuits only resistance is involved, while with ac circuits, resistance, capacitance, and inductance are involved. This is why with ac circuits the equipment grounding conductor must be run with the circuit conductors to lower the total impedances.

(c) **Supplementary Grounding.** Separate grounding electrodes will be permitted to augment grounding conductors as specified in Section 250-91(b). The earth is not to be used as the sole equipment grounding conductor.

It is required that a metallic equipment grounding conductor be used; the earth resistance in almost every case is too high to properly cause the overcurrent devices to operate when a ground fault occurs.

250-92. Installation—Grounding conductors shall be installed as follows:

(a) **Grounding Electrode Conductor.** No. 4 or larger grounding conductors may be attached to the surface—knobs or insulators are not required. Mechanical protection will be required only where the conductor is subject to severe physical damage. No. 6 grounding conductors may be run on the surface of a building if protected from physical damage and rigidly stapled to the building structure. Grounding conductors smaller than No. 6 shall be in conduit, EMT, intermediate metal conduit or cable armor.

The metallic enclosures for the grounding conductor shall be continuous from the cabinet or equipment to the grounding electrode and shall be attached at both ends by approved methods. Articles 345, 346, 347, and 348, shall govern the installation of the enclosure for the grounding conductor. A common error is often made here—

if the system or common grounding conductor is smaller than No. 6, it shall always be in rigid metal conduit, intermediate metal conduit, rigid nonmetallic conduit, electrical metallic tubing, or armor cable. This is often confused with a conductor used for grounding equipment and enclosures only.

Due to corrosion, aluminum grounding conductors shall not be placed in direct contact with masonry, earth, or other corrosive materials. Also, where aluminum grounding conductors are used, they shall not be closer than 18 inches to the earth. Please note that this does not prohibit the use of aluminum for grounding conductors, but merely places certain restrictions on it. One sadly abused use of aluminum grounding conductors is in antenna grounding. Remember also that the grounding conductor is to be without splice. If a metal raceway is used merely as a physical protection for the common grounding conductor, it is often not attached to either the enclosure or the grounding electrode. If this is the case, you are required to bond the common grounding conductor to both ends of the metal protective raceway. This will lower the impedance of the circuit, which is very necessary upon fault.

It is recommended that magnetic metal enclosures, such as steel pipe or armor, not be used where protection from physical damage can be otherwise obtained, such as the size of the conductor itself or by nonmetallic enclosures.

(b) **Enclosures for Grounding Electrode Conductors.** If a metal enclosure is used over the grounding conductor, it shall be electrically continuous from its origin to the grounding electrode. It shall also be securely fastened to the grounding clamp so that there is electrical continuity from where it originates to the grounding electrode. If a metal enclosure is used for physical protection only for the ground conductor and is not continuous from the enclosure to the ground rod bonding, it shall be done from the grounding conductor to the metal enclosure at each end of the metal enclosure used for physical protection. The requirements of Article 345 shall be met for the installation where intermediate metal conduit is used. If rigid metal conduit is used for protection of the grounding conductor, the requirements of Article 346 shall be complied with. If rigid nonmetallic is used for protection, it must meet the requirements of Article 347, and if EMT is used, it must meet the requirements of Article 348.

(c) **Equipment Grounding Conductor.** The following cover the installation of equipment grounding conductors:

(1) When an equipment grounding conductor is used in a raceway, cable tray, cable armor, or cable sheath, and where it is wire in a raceway or cable, the installation must conform to the applicable provisions in the *NEC*. All terminations and joints shall be listed and approved for use in the above. All joints and fittings are to be made up tight by using tools suitable for the purpose.

(2) The exception for Section 250-50(a) and (b) provides for where an equipment grounding conductor is a separate conductor. Instructions just above shall apply to aluminum, and shall also apply to protection from physical damage.

Exception: If the grounding conductors run in the hollow spaces of a building that is protected, sizes smaller than No. 6 shall not be required in raceways.

250-93. Size of Direct-Current System Grounding Conductor—See the *NEC*.

250-94. Size of Alternating-Current Grounding Electrode Conductor—Table 250-94 gives us the size of the grounding electrode conductor where used on a grounded or ungrounded ac system. The size shall not be less than shown in the table.

Exception No. 1: Grounded Systems.

a. In Section 250-83(c) or (d), we were told that if a grounding electrode was the sole means of grounding, the grounding conductor to the electrode need not be any larger than No. 6 copper or No. 4 aluminum.

b. In Section 250-81(c), where portions of the grounding electrode connect to concrete-encased electrode, it need not be larger than No. 4 copper wire.

c. Where we described using a grounding ring as the electrode, the conductor from the grounding ring is not required to be larger than the conductor used for the grounding ring.
Refer to Table 250-94 in the *NEC*—Grounding Electrode Conductor for AC Systems. Also see the fine-print note accompanying the table.

Exception No. 2: Ungrounded Systems.

a. As in Section 250-83(c) or (d), where connection is to a made electrode, that portion of a grounding conductor that is solely connected to the grounding main electrode is not required to be larger than No. 6 or No. 4 aluminum wire.

b. Refer to the *NEC* for this.

c. Refer to the *NEC* for this.

250-95. Size of Equipment Grounding Conductors—Refer to the *NEC* and Table 250-95. Equipment grounding conductors are sized in accordance with the rating or setting of automatic overcurrent device in circuit ahead of equipment, conduit, etc.

If conductors are paralleled in several raceways, which you will find permitted in Section 310-4, if an equipment grounding conductor has to be used, if for instance nonmetallic conduit was used instead of metal, the equipment grounding conductors shall be run in parallel—one in each raceway if more than one raceway is used. Each equipment grounding conductor in parallel circuits is required to meet the requirements of Table 250-95.

Where current-carrying conductors have to be larger to compensate for voltage drop, the equipment grounding conductors shall be adjusted proportionately to the circular metal area.

The intent of this seems to be that the equipment grounding conductor in each paralleled raceway circuit shall be sized to the ampere rating of the overcurrent device protecting these circuits at the service-entrance equipment. Table 250-95 covers the sizing of these equipment grounding conductors.

Where a single equipment grounding conductor is run with multiple circuits in the same raceway, it shall be sized for the largest overcurrent device protecting the conductors in the raceway.

Exception No. 1: If the overcurrent protection of a circuit is 20 amperes or less and flexible cord assemblies are used, the equipment grounding conductor shall not be smaller than the No. 18 copper, or shall not be smaller than the circuit conductors.

Exception No. 2: The equipment grounding conductor shall not be larger than the current-carrying conductors supplying any equipment.

Exception No. 3: See Sections 250-57(a) and 250-91(b) for raceway or cable armor or sheath used as the equipment grounding conductor.

250-97. Outline Lighting—Where a conductor complying with Section 250-95 is used to ground outline lighting systems, the isolated noncurrent-carrying parts of this system may be bonded together with a No. 14 copper or No. 12 aluminum conductor which is protected from physical damage.

250-99. Equipment Grounding Conductor Continuity.

(a) **Separable Connections.** Where separable connections are made to draw out equipment, there are attachment plugs to receptacles to main equipment connectors. Equipment grounding conductor is longer so that it will be the first connection made when plugging.

The main point here is that the grounding terminal on plugs makes contact before the current-carrying conductors do.

Exception: Interlocking plugs, receptacles, equipment, and connectors do provide for grounding continuity first.

(b) **Switches.** You never install a switch or automatic cutout in the equipment grounding conductor where a premise wiring system is involved.

Exception: Where all conductors are disconnected at once.

The main point of all this is that the equipment-grounding conductor is all-important for safety, and all assurances must be taken into account to see that the equipment grounding is intact before energizing circuits.

K. Grounding Conductor Connections

250-112. To Grounding Electrode—This section tells us that the grounding conductor shall be connected to the grounding electrode in such a manner that a *permanent and effective ground* will result. Most inspectors insist that this connection be accessible wherever possible, or cad-welded or brazed. The connection to the grounding electrode shall be accessible.

Where water piping is used as the grounding electrode, any joints that may be disconnected for repairs or replacement shall be bonded around. The same shall be done with insulated coupling, unions, and water meters. This applies to water meters in the house or other buildings where the grounding conductor is connected to the piping on the building side of the meter. It is a common practice to connect the grounding conductor to the street side of the piping ahead of the water meter. Most inspectors prefer it this way when practical to do so. If the meter is at the curb, and there are 10 feet or more of buried water piping (metallic), bonding is not required. See Fig. 250-9.

Exception: Buried connections or encased connections to a buried grounding electrode, concrete-encased grounding electrode, or driven grounding electrode shall not be required to be accessible.

250-113. To Conductors and Equipment—The grounding conductors and bonding jumpers shall be attached to circuits, conduits, cabinets, equipment, and the like, which are to be grounded, by means of suitable lugs, listed pressure connectors, clamps, exothermic welding, or other approved means. Soldering is never permitted—neither is the strap type of grounding clamp. Be certain that the device used is identified as being suitable for the purpose.

250-114. Continuity and Attachment of Branch-Circuit Equipment Grounding Conductors to Boxes—When more than one equipment grounding conductor enters a box, they shall be spliced or connected to any device provided for connecting them to part of the box. Soldering is not permitted. Splices shall be made up to meet the requirements of Section 110-14(b), but no insulation is required. If there is a receptacle connected in that box, a separate pigtail shall be connected where the wires are spliced to serve that receptacle. This is done so that after that receptacle is removed, the grounding continuity will not be interrupted.

This has caused considerable concern in the field. The grounding conductor is to be attached to a screw used for no other purpose or by approved means. Boxes are available with two or more 10-32 tapped holes for this purpose. The clamp screws on loom-wire boxes are not intended to be used as grounding screws. All grounding conductors entering the box are to be made electrically and mechanically secure, and the pigtail made from them is to serve as the grounding connection to the device being installed. Thus, if the device is removed, the continuity will not be disrupted. Soldering is not permitted. Pressure connectors should be used—twisting the wires together is not satisfactory because poor contact may result. Most inspectors

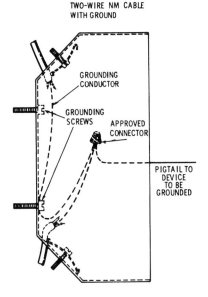

TWO-WIRE NM CABLE
WITH GROUND

GROUNDING
CONDUCTOR

GROUNDING
SCREWS   APPROVED
CONNECTOR

PIGTAIL TO
DEVICE
TO BE
GROUNDED

Fig. 250-11. Illustrating the proper method of grounding boxes and carrying the grounding conductor on to the device to be grounded.

require that all of this be done at the time of the rough-in inspection so that they do not have to open all of the outlets to see that they have been properly made up. See Fig. 250-11.

Where nonmetallic boxes are used, it is not required to attach the equipment grounding conductors to them. The other requirements listed above are to be complied with. [See the *NEC*, parts (a) and (b) of this section.]

250-115. Connection to Electrodes—In connecting grounding conductors to grounding fittings by suitable lugs, pressure connectors, clamps, or other listed means (including exothermic welding). Soldering shall never be used. The ground clamps shall be of a material that is compatible for both the grounding electrode and the grounding conductor. No more than one conductor shall be connected to an electrode unless the connector is listed for the purpose. One of the methods below shall be used and exothermic welding could be added:

(a) **Bolted Clamp.** Listed bolted clamps may be used for connecting the conductor to the made electrode provided they are made of bronze or brass, or of plain or malleable iron. If plain or malleable iron is used and they are not accessible, the copper grounding conductor might cause some electrolysis on the iron.

(b) **Pipe Fitting, Pipe Plug, etc.** See the *NEC*.

(c) **Sheet-Metal-Strap-Type Grounding Clamp.** Ordinary sheet metal grounding clamps are not approved. There is a listed clamp that has a rigid metal base that clamps firmly to the electrode and the strap. Only this strap is of such material and heavy enough that it is very unlikely that it will stretch after being installed.

(d) **Other Means.** See your *NEC*.

Author's Note: In my experience, exothermic welding (Cadwelding) has proved to be an excellent method. However, with Cadwelding you can be fooled about the connections. Eyeballing and hammer testing do not always disclose defects of high-resistance connections. I used a Biddle Ductor, which you can read down to ½ milthant ohms resistance. This is a positive check on the resistance of the connection to the grounding electrode.

250-117. Protection of Attachment—Unless approved for general use without protection, ground clamps and fittings shall:

(1) Be located so that they will not be subject to damage, or

(2) Be enclosed in metal, wood, or equivalent protective covering.

With exothermic welding (Calwelding), checked for the resistance of the connection with a Ductor, you know that the problems of a high-resistance connection are eliminated.

250-118. Clean Surfaces—Good electrical continuity must always be made. If there are any nonconductive paints, lacquers, enamels, or the like on equipment that is to be grounded, it shall be removed from any contact surfaces or threads.

All corrosion shall be removed. If rebar is used as the grounding electrode, thoroughly clean the surface of the rebar by grinding to remove the oxidation. If a Cadweld is used, heat the rebar to drive out the moisture in its pores.

L. Instrument Transformers, Relays, etc.

250-121. Instrument Transformer Circuits—Current transformers (CT) and potential transformers (PT) shall have the secondary windings grounded when the primary windings are connected to 300 volts or more to ground regardless of the primary voltage. The exception to this is when the primary windings are connected to less than 1000 volts with no live parts or wiring exposed or accessible to other than qualified persons.

250-122. Grounding—Where accessible only to qualified persons, instrument transformers, cases, or frames shall be grounded.

Exception: On current transformers where the primary is not over 150 volts to ground, and if they are used exclusively for current meters.

250-123. Cases of Instruments, Meters, and Relays—Operating at Less than 1000 volts—Any instruments, relays, or meters operating with winding or working parts at less than 1000 volts shall be grounded as in (a), (b), or (c) following:

(a) **Not on Switchboards.** All cases and other exposed metal parts of instruments, meters, and relays that are not on switchboards shall be grounded when the windings or working parts operate at 300 volts or more to ground, and when they are accessible to other than qualified persons.

(b) **On Dead-Front Switchboards.** All instruments, meters, and relays that are mounted on a switchboard that has no live parts on the front of the panel shall be grounded, whether direct connected or whether supplied by current and potential transformers.

(c) **On Live-Front Switchboards.** All instruments, meters, and relays that are mounted on a switchboard that has live parts on the front of panels shall not have their cases grounded; but there shall be mats of insulating rubber or other suitable floor insulation wherever the voltage to ground exceeds 150 volts.

250-124. Cases of Instruments, Meters, and Relays—Operating Voltage 1 kV and Over—Any of these listed in the title that are 1 kV or over to ground have to be isolated by elevation or copper guarding, and the cases are to be left ungrounded.

Exception: Where electrostatic ground detectors are used, the internal ground segments of the instrument are connected to the instrument case and grounded. Here, the ground detector shall be isolated by elevation.

250-125. Instrument Grounding Conductor—See the *NEC*.

M. Grounding of Ssytems and Circuits of 1 kV and Over (High Voltage)

250-150. General—High-voltage systems that are grounded shall comply with previous sections of this article, which may be modified and supplemented by future articles or sections.

250-151. Derived Neutral Systems—Where a neutral is derived from a grounding tranformer, permission is granted to use it when grounding high voltage systems.

250-152. Solidly Grounded Neutral Systems—See the *NEC*.

250-153. Impedance Grounded Neutral Systems—See the *NEC*.

250-154. Grounding of Systems Supplying Portable or Mobile Equipment—See the *NEC*.

250-155. Grounding of Equipment—See the *NEC*.

ARTICLE 280—SURGE ARRESTERS

A. General

280-1. Scope—The general requirements are incorporated in this article governing the installation and connection requirements of surge arresters (also called "lightning arresters"). Do not confuse them with "surge capacitors," which are covered in other places in the Code, especially in Section 502-3.

280-2. Definition—Surge arresters are devices to protect equipment from surge line voltages. They absorb some of the surges, but are also capable of stopping the flow of the surge current by absorbing it, and they maintain their capability of repeating such functions.

These surge arresters break down at voltages higher than the supply voltage, allowing the higher voltage and accompanying currents to flow to ground, thus protecting the equipment on the system. After the surge passes to ground, the arrester heals itself, shutting off follow current from the supply system.

A case in point: There was a 7½-horsepower irrigation-pump motor out in a field under a large tree. Because of lightning, we averaged a motor rewind at least every two years. I received permission to install surge arresters and surge capacitors to the service. Approximately 30 years later, there has not been a motor burnout due to lightning.

280-3. Number Required—When using surge arresters, they shall be connected to each ungrounded circuit conductor.

Surge arresters are available in single units to connect to only one ungrounded circuit conductor; here one would be required for each ungrounded conductor. They also are available with three units in one enclosure, which would thus take care of a 3-phase supply. If there are other supply conductors, such as supplied from a farm service pole, as illustrated in Fig. 230-20, one set of surge arresters would be sufficient. But in Fig. 230-20 there are a number of service drops, and so surge arresters should be installed at the load end of each service drop.

280-4. Surge Arrester Selection.

(a) **On Circuits of Less than 1000 Volts.** On circuits of less than 1000 volts, it is required that the voltage rating of the surge arresters be equal to or greater than the maximum voltage of the phase-to-ground voltage available. Thus a service of 480 volts to ground (rms) would be 0.707 of the maximum voltage to ground; so maximum voltage would be 480 divided by 0.707, or 679 volts. By the same token, a 20 volts to ground (rms) would be 170 volts maximum.

(b) **On Circuits of 1 kV and Over.** This requires that the surge arrester have a rating of not less than 125 percent of the maximum phase-to-ground voltage. Again, do not confuse rms voltage and maximum voltage. Use the examples in (a) above.

Note: See ANSI C62.2-1981 for further information. Arresters are usually metal oxide. See the *NEC* for this fine-print note.

B. Installation

280-11. Location—Surge protection of surge arresters may be located in the system either indoors or outdoors, but shall not be accessible to unqualified persons.

In deciding whether to place surge arresters indoors or outdoors, take into consideration that some have exploded. Although this is not a Code requirement, I would suggest that if they are placed indoors, they should be kept away from combustible items.

Exception: There are some surge arresters that are listed to be located in accessible places.

280-12. Routing of Surge Arrester Connections—The connections from the supply system to the surge arresters should be as short as possible. Also, there should be as few bends in the leads and grounding as possible. Lightning takes a direct path to the ground.

C. Connecting Surge Arresters

280-21. Installed at Services of Less than 1000 Volts—See the *NEC*.

280-22. Installation on the Load Side of Services of Less than 1000 Volts—This section tells us that line and grounding conductors shall not be smaller than No. 14 copper or No. 12 aluminum. Some judgment must be used here, and, if possible, check with the authority having jurisdiction as to size of conductors to use.

Surge arresters may be connected to any two ungrounded conductors, grounded conductors, or grounding conductors. The grounded conductors and the grounding conductors are to be interconnected only during normal operation of the surge arrester when a surge occurs.

The shortest method of getting the surge to ground is always the best method. Avoid bends as much as possible.

280-23. Circuits of 1 kV and Over—Surge Arrester Conductors—Here we are limited to No. 6 copper or aluminum for conductors connecting the surge arrester to both the ungrounded conductors and the ground.

280-24. Circuits of 1 kV and Over—Interconnection—Where circuits are supplied by 1 kV and over, the grounding conductor from surge arresters that protect a transformer supplying a secondary distribution system is required to be interconnected as follows.

(a) **Metallic Interconnection.** An interconnection to the secondary neutral may be made if the direct grounding is made to the surge arrester.

(1) The conditions for permitting metallic interconnection, as covered in the paragraph above, are contingent upon meeting the requirements of both (1) and (2). Thus, an interconnection may be made between the surge arrester and the grounded conductor of the secondary if the secondary has the grounded conductor connected elsewhere to a continuous metal underground water piping system. If in urban areas there is a minimum of four water-pipe grounding connections in a distance of one mile, the direct ground from the surge arrester may be eliminated and the secondary neutral used as the grounding for the surge arrester.

(2) In many instances the primary is 4-wire wye, with the neutral grounded periodically. In these cases the secondary neutral is usually interconnected with the primary neutral. If the primary neutral is grounded in a minimum of four places in each mile, plus the secondary service ground, the surge arrester ground may be interconnected with the primary and secondary grounds in addition to the surge arrester grounding electrode.

(b) **Through Spark Gap.** See the *NEC*.

(c) **By Special Permission.** The authority having jurisdiction may grant special permission to an interconnection of the surge arrester ground and the secondary neutral, other than permitted in (a) and (b) of this section.

280-25. Grounding—As is usually the case in grounding, the grounding of surge arresters shall comply with the requirements in Article 250 except as otherwise indicated in this article.

CHAPTER 3

Wiring Methods and Materials

ARTICLE 300—WIRING METHODS

A. General Requirements

300-1. Scope.

(a) **All Wiring Installations.** This article is very broad in its coverage; it discusses the fundamentals that apply to all wiring installations.

Exception No. 1: Class 1, Class 2, and Class 3 circuits as provided for in Article 725.

Exception No. 2: Fire protective signaling circuits as provided for in Article 760.

Exception No. 3: Article 770, covering optical fiber cables.

Exception No. 4: Communication systems as provided for in Article 800.

Exception No. 5: Community antenna television and radio distribution systems will be referenced in Article 8.

(b) **Integral Parts of Equipment.** Wiring that is an integral part of motor controllers, motors, motor control centers, or other factory-assembled control equipment is not covered by this article.

300-2. Limitations.

(a) **Voltage.** Unless there are specific limitations in a section of Chapter 3, the wiring methods in Chapter 3 shall apply to voltage of 600 volts, nominal, or less. Elsewhere in the *NEC* you will find that some voltages over 600 volts, nominal, are specifically permitted under Chapter 3.

(b) **Temperature.** Section 310-10 covers limitations as far as temperature is concerned for conductors.

300-3. Conductors.

(a) **Single Conductors.** The single conductors that were specified in Table 310-13 are only part of a recognized wiring method, if permitted in Chapter 3.

(b) **Conductors of the Same Circuit.** To keep impedance and induction as low as possible, it is necessary that all conductors of the same circuit—including the neutral, if one is used—and the equipment grounding conductor shall be contained in the same raceway, cable tray, cable, trench, or cord. Do not confuse this with requirements for paralleled circuits, but each one of the parallel circuits must abide by the above.

Exception: This is to (a) and (b). See the NEC for the sections that permit this.

(c) **Conductors of Different Systems.**

(1) **600 Volts, Nominal, or Less.** If more than one circuit is involved and each of these circuits is 600 volts, nominal, or less, regardless of whether ac or dc, they may be enclosed together in the same enclosure, whether a cable or raceway. By necessity the voltage rating of the insulation of the conductors shall be equal to the maximum voltage involved, or higher. The equipment grounding conductor may of course be bare or insulated, and identified. When circuits of different voltages occupy the same raceway or enclosure some identification by color of insulation or other appropriate means should be used to identify the difference of voltages of the circuits involved.

Exception: In the case of solar photovoltaic systems, refer to Section 690-4(b) of the NEC.

Note: See Section 725-38(a) (2) for Class 2 and Class 3 circuit conductors in the NEC.

(2) **Over 600 Volts, Nominal.** Any circuits over 600 volts, nominal, cannot be permitted to be involved in the same enclosure with circuits of 600 volts, nominal, or less.

Note: See Section 300-32 of the NEC for coverage of circuits over 600 volts, nominal.

Exception No. 1: Electric-discharge lamps with a secondary voltage of 1000 volts or less may have their conductors in the same fixture enclosure as the branch-circuit conductors, providing that the secondary conductors are insulated for the voltage involved. This takes care of the higher voltages that are encountered in discharge type of lighting fixtures.

Leads of electric discharge lamp ballasts are permitted if the primary leads of the ballast are insulated for the primary voltage to the ballast, and are permitted to occupy the same enclosure of the fixture of the branch-circuit conductors. An example is a

227-volt ballast that might have primary leads rated at 300 volts. These primary leads may be in the same enclosure as the branch-circuit conductors having 600-volt insulation.

Exception No. 2: Conductors such as excitation, control, relay, and ammeter conductors, used in connection with any individual motor or starter may occupy the same enclosure as the motor circuit conductors are also permitted.

300-4. Protection Against Physical Damage—This title is self-explanatory. Additional and corrective action may be required.

(a) **Cables and Raceways Through Wood Members.**

(1) **Bored Holes.** When installing exposed or concealed conductors in insulating tubes, or installing a cable or raceway-type wiring method in holes bored through studs, joists, or rafters, or wood members, the holes shall be drilled as near the center of the wood member as possible, but not less than 1¼ inches (31.8 mm) from the nearest edge. In drilling, notching, etc., the structure shall not be weakened. It is not within the scope of the Code to cover this fully, but all building codes should be adhered to.

If the holes cannot be bored at not less than 1¼ inches from the nearest edge, the cable or raceway shall be protected by a plate or bushing at least 1⁄16 inch (1.59 mm) in thickness, of sufficient size to protect from penetration of nails, etc., and of appropriate length and width to cover the area of wiring.

(2) **Notches in Wood.** If there is no objection because of weakening the structure, notching for cables or raceways of all types is recognized by the Code, provided that the notch is covered by a steel plate at least 1⁄16 inch (1.59 mm) thick to protect the cable from nails. [For the intent of (a) and (b), see Fig. 300-1.]

See the *NEC* for raceways in Articles 345, 346, 347, and 348, which are exceptions.

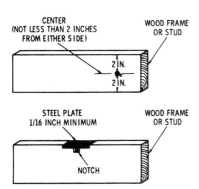

CENTER
(NOT LESS THAN 2 INCHES
FROM EITHER SIDE)

WOOD FRAME
OR STUD

2 IN.

2 IN.

STEEL PLATE
1/16 INCH MINIMUM

WOOD FRAME
OR STUD

NOTCH

Fig. 300-1. Proper drilling and notching procedures.

(b) **Cable and Electrical Nonmetallic Tubing Through Metal Framing Members.**

(1) This part can be extremely important, as metal framing members can cut into nonmetallic-sheathed cables where they pass through any hole in metal framing members, whether factory field punched or made by any other means. Great care shall be taken so that the cable will be thoroughly protected by proper bushings or grommets that will not readily deteriorate and are fastened securely in the metal opening before passing any cable through them.

(2) If there is any chance of penetrating nonmetallic-sheathed cable by nails or screws by the building contractor. This will also apply to electrical nonmetallic tubing. You are required to install a steel sleeve for the cable to pass through or cover the building studs, etc., by means of a steel plate or steel clip. This steel shall be at least $\frac{1}{16}$ inch in thickness to keep the nails or screw from penetrating the cable or tubing.

(c) **Cables Through Spaces Behind Panels Designed to Allow Access.** The cables or raceways are required to be supported according to their applicable articles.

300-5. Underground Installations.

(a) **Minimum Cover Requirements.** Table 300-5 in the *NEC* gives the depths at which buried cables or conduits or other raceways are installed. These are minimum requirements.

See the *NEC* at this point for the definition of "cover."

On buried cables and raceways, it is the author's contention that added protection should be required. For instance, a buried cable should not be buried directly against the rocky bottom of a trench. There should be a layer of fine sand laid on the rocks, and after the cable is laid another layer of fine sand should be added so that the rocks in the backfill will not cut. Personal experience has shown that direct-buried raceways, unless covered by a manufacturer-produced coating of plastic, are very vulnerable to electrolysis. Referring back to the table in this book covering soil resistance, you can see that different soils have different electrolysis characteristics. In soil in the author's area, a tar coating over the raceway does not stand up long. In some cases, therefore, it might be well to consider encasing the raceway in concrete. I suggest 2000-pound concrete with $\frac{3}{8}$ aggregate maximum and a 7-inch slump, which allows it to form readily around the raceway.

See the *NEC* for Table 300-5, Minimum Cover Requirement, 0 to 600 Volts, Nominal.

Exception No. 1: If a 2-inch (50.8 mm) thick pad or equivalent in physical protection is placed in the trench over the underground installation, the minimum cover requirements may be reduced by 6 inches (152 mm). This does not refer to rigid metal conduit or intermediate metal conduit.

Following the Table 300-5 in the NEC there are seven exceptions in addition to Exception No. 1 above. These are all self-explanatory. Please refer to the NEC.

(b) **Grounding.** Grounding and bonding of underground installations shall be by methods that are described in Article 250 on grounding.

(c) **Underground Cables Under Buildings.** Section 230-49 explains the protection of service conductors run underground. Some inspectors will require a sand bed and a sand covering for protecting underground conductors, especially in rocky areas and where freezing temperatures are encountered. They may also require a mechanical protection over the conductors. The mechanical protection required is the inspector's prerogative. Some may require redwood or treated boards; others may require a plastic strip that has the word "Caution" printed along the entire length.

UF cable under concrete floors patios, etc., shall be installed in raceway that extends to points away from or up through the concrete (check for transition and continuity).

Before this sentence was inserted, UF cable could be buried below a cement floor of a building, and conduit used to sleeve it through the concrete. The Code ruling is a very welcome change; most inspectors never considered it good workmanship to pour a floor over a cable because it was not readily replaceable.

(d) **Protection from Damage.** Direct-buried cables and conductors where they emerge from the ground shall be protected by proper raceways as covered in Section 300-5(a) and Table 300-5(a) from a point of below grade to at least 8 feet above grade. In no case shall this requirement of encasing be required to exceed 18 inches.

When conductors are brought from underground to above ground, several factors definitely should be taken into consideration. When direct burial conductors are in a trench they tend to settle, especially if the trench is not properly compacted. Thus, should these be service lateral conductors, entering a conduit, up to a meter enclosure, and should any settling result from the trench, the conductors could be pulled out of the meter enclosure and possibly result in a fire. To avoid this, a loop should be formed at the bottom of the trench to provide slack.

Also, in areas where hard freezing occurs, the conductor insulation is often cut where the conductors enter the conduit underground. This may be prevented by using an insulated bushing on the conduit underground and by not making a 90-degree bend where the conductors enter the conduit underground. Make a bend of more than 90 degrees so that any water that accumulates will flow down into the ground, thus aiding in eliminating damage to the insulation of the buried conductors where they enter the conduit.

You are required to protect conductors that enter a building at the point of entrance.

If the raceway entering a building is subject to physical damage, rigid metal conduit or intermediate metal conduit or Schedule 80 rigid nonmetallic conduit is required, or equivalent.

When using rigid metal conduit, one must consider that it will no doubt be required that it be protected from corrosion in the earth as specified in Section 346-1.

(e) **Splices and Taps.** Boxes are not required to make splices or taps in underground cables, but the splices or taps have to be made by methods and with identified material that have been approved by the electrical inspector.

(f) **Backfill.** Materials removed from the trench excavation may often contain large rocks, paving material, cinders, large or sharply angular substances, or corrosive materials. This shall not be used for backfilling as it may cause damage to cable, ducts or other raceways. As stated earlier, it is often a good idea to use sand bedding and a layer of sand fill to prevent damage from frost heave.

If necessary to prevent physical damage to the raceway or cable, granular selected material may be used for covering, or suitable running boards such as redwood or any other suitable means to protect raceway or cable from damage may be used.

(g) **Raceway Seals.** Sealing will be required at one or both ends of conduits or raceways where moisture may contact energized parts. Earlier in the book a case was cited in which moisture caused a short out of the service-entrance equipment.

Note: Where a raceway enters a building underground, there is always a chance of hazardous gases or other vapors entering the conduit into the building. Therefore, you must seal raceways entering buildings.

(h) **Bushing.** Conduit terminating underground for direct burial wiring methods shall have bushings on the end. The author would recommend the insulating type of bushings. Also the end of the conduit in the earth should be sloped down to drain, as freezing has often caused faults in the conductors. A seal that provides physical protection from damage may be used instead of a bushing.

(i) **Single Conductors.** All conductors of a circuit shall be installed in the same raceway, including the neutral and equipment-grounding conductor as well. Single conductors in a trench shall be installed in close proximity. The purpose of this is to keep the impedance of the circuit as low as possible.

Exception No. 1: Conductors in parallel may be installed in the same raceway if they contain all the conductors of the circuit, including the grounding conductors.

Exception No. 2: As permitted in Section 310-4 and under the conditions of Section 300-20 if met, isolated phase installations will be allowed in nonmetallic raceways enclosed to where conductors are paralleled, as described in the two aforementioned sections.

300-6. Protection Against Corrosion—Metal raceways, armor cable, cable sheathing, cabinets, elbows, couplings, fittings, boxes, and all other metal hardware necessary in the installation must be made of material that will be suitable for the environment encountered.

(a) **General.** Ferrous raceways, cable armor, boxes, cable sheathing, cabinets, and all other fittings of metal, including supports but not including the threads at joints, shall be protected by a coating of material that will resist corrosion—use zinc, cadmium, enamel, or some other material (corrosion-resistant) for coating. If the protective coating is enamel only, they shall not be installed out of doors or in wet locations. This will be further discussed in (c) below. If the boxes or cabinets have approved coatings and are marked or listed for outdoor use, they shall be permitted to be used out of doors.

Exception: Electrically conducting material is permitted to be used on threads at joints.

(b) **In Concrete or in Direct Contact with the Earth.** Ferrous and nonferrous metal raceways, cable armor, boxes, and all other fittings involved in the installation are permitted to be installed in concrete. They may be in direct contact with the earth. If the surrounding has severe corrosive influences, then they may be in direct contact with the earth if judged to be suitably provided with corrosion-resistant material approved for the purpose. Refer to the table (in Article 250 of this book) showing average soil resistances of earth.

The above is rather broad in scope. In one area galvanized rigid conduit will last about one year. Asphalt painting is not adequate and so the decision is up to the inspection authority who is familiar with the earth's ohm/centimeter resistivity in the area.

(c) **Indoor Wet Locations.** Such locations might include dairies, laundries, canneries, and any other indoor locations. Also where walls and floors have to be frequently washed down—so that much of the material that these are made of will absorb moisture. Therefore the entire wiring system, including boxes, fittings, and so forth, must be mounted so that there is at least a ¼-inch air space between them and the wall or other supporting surface.

Meat-packing plants, tanneries, hide cellars, casing rooms, glue houses, fertilizer rooms, salt storage, some chemical works, metal refineries, pulp mills, sugar mills, round houses, some stables, and similar locations are judged to be occupancies where severe corrosive conditions are likely to be present.

It can be seen from the above that precautions have been taken for protection from corrosive elements, including excess moisture. There may be conditions in which the best raceway might be the nonmetallic type. If this type is used, the article covering the installation of same must be adhered to. Plastic coated metal raceways conduit are also available.

Note: In some of the inner areas acids and alkali chemicals are stored or handled that may cause severe corrosion. This is especially true under damp or wet conditions. Some of these locations may be meat-packing plants, tanneries, glue factories, certain stables, areas adjacent to seashores, swimming pools, places where chemical deicers are used, fertilizer storage places, damp cellars, salt or chemical storage places, and of course many others.

300-7. Raceways Exposed to Different Temperatures.

(a) **Sealing.** Where portions of interior raceways may be subject to widely different temperatures, such as conduit going from a normal room to a freezer storage room, circulation of the air can cause the warmer air to rise and flow into the cooler section. At such places the raceway shall be sealed to prevent the flow of air from one temperature to the other, thereby stopping condensation.

While not specifically covered, conditions will be found in which the wireman runs a service mast down an inside wall of a house to the service-entrance equipment. The temperature in the house will run possibly 75 degrees, and the mast exposed to an outside temperature of -10 to -30 degrees. This will cause a chimney effect. The warm air will rise and be cooled, thus causing moisture to run down inside the conduit into the panel.

(b) **Expansion Joints.** These were briefly covered earlier in this book. In many places in large buildings, expansion joints in raceways are required to compensate for the expansion or contraction due to thermal conditions.

Where these joints are to be used will require common sense. In using expansion joints it is necessary to provide bonding jumpers, as required under Section 250-77, so as to make good electrical contact around the expansion joints.

See *NEC* Index for 10 Code sections that cover "expansion joints."

300-8. Installation of Conductors with Other Systems—You are not permitted to enclose electrical conductors in raceways, cable trays, and so

forth, if they contain pipes or tubes or the equivalent to be used with steam water or gas or any service other than the electrical service.

Exception: See the *NEC.*

300-9. Grounding Metal Enclosures—See Article 250—It will be recalled that there are many and varied methods of grounding metal enclosures. In ordinary wiring with conduit, armored cable, MI cable, etc., the metal of the raceway is the grounding conductor. On the service entrance and in hazardous locations, hubs or bonding is required. With NM and UF cables, the grounding conductor is to be placed under a screw used only for grounding purposes. They are to be made electrically and mechanically secure, and soldering is not permitted.

300-10. Electrical Continuity of Metal Raceways and Enclosures —All raceways, armored cable, and other metal enclosures shall be connected to any boxes or other fittings and cabinets so that effective electrical continuity of grounding is acquired.

Locknuts, bushings, and connectors supply this continuity, except where other measures are required to be taken, such as bonding at services, expansion joints, eccentric and concentric knockouts, and in hazardous locations. Where nonmetallic boxes are used, as permitted in Section 370-3, they do not have to make a connection with the metal raceway, but the box must include an integral bonding means.

300-11. Securing and Supporting.

(a) **Secured in Place.** All raceways, boxes, cabinets, and fittings are required to be securely fastened in place. Support wires for drop ceilings, unless securely fastened in place, are not permitted as the sole support, unless it is permitted elsewhere in the Code.

Wooden plugs driven into concrete are not considered acceptable for fastening electrical equipment. Securing of continuous cable-tray supports is covered in Article 318.

(b) **Raceways Used as Means of Support.** Raceways are not to be used as a means of support for other raceways, cables, or nonelectrical equipment.

Exception No. 1: If identified for the purpose, raceways or other means of support may be used.

Note: See Article 318 for cable trays in the *NEC.*

Exception No. 2: Raceways containing Class 2 circuit conductors or cables used strictly for the purpose of connection to the equipment control circuits may be supported from the general circuit raceways.

Exception No. 3: In the *NEC* you are referred for this exception to Sections 370-13 or 410-16 (f).

300-12. Mechanical Continuity—Raceways and Cables—There shall be mechanical continuity between boxes, cabinets, or other fittings and enclosures, or outlets or raceways, or cables, metal or nonmetallic raceways, armored cable, or cable sheaths.

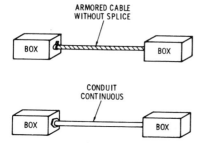

Fig. 300-2. Approved method of connecting conduit and armored cable between boxes.

300-13. Mechanical and Electrical Continuity—Conductors.

(a) **General.** Conductors are to be continuous between outlet devices and shall never be spliced in a raceway, except as permitted for auxiliary gutters in Section 374-8; for wire-ways in Section 362-6; for boxes and fittings in Section 300-15(a), Exception No. 1, and for surface metal raceways Section 352-7. In other words, conductors in raceways shall be in one piece and without splice except as used above.

(b) **Device Removal.** On multiwire circuits, it is not permitted to remove a device such as a lampholder or receptacle, and as a result the grounded conductor that is opened. On multiwire circuits, the grounded conductor or neutral shall always be installed so that if a device is removed, the grounded conductor will remain continuous throughout the entire multiwire circuit.

300-14. Length of Free Conductors at Outlets and Switch Points

—A minimum of 6 inches (152 mm) of free conductor length shall be left at each outlet and switch point, except if a conductor loops through without connection to any device and is without a splice. This ruling is to provide ample conductor length for making connections to the outlet or switch, and to provide some spare length in the event that a piece should break off in the makeup.

Exception: If the conductors are not terminated or spliced at a box or junction point, the above paragraph will not apply.

300-15. Boxes and Fittings—Where Required.

(a) **Box or Fitting.** When connections have to be made, where wiring is run into conduit, EMT, surface raceway, or other raceway where splices have to be made, a box or fitting shall always be installed where the splice connection is being made. This applies as well to outlets, switch points, pull points, and so forth.

Exception No. 1: If the splices are made in surface raceways, header-ducts, multioutlet assemblies, auxiliary gutters, cable trays, or conduit bodies, or have removable covers that are accessible, they are allowed in these raceways.

Exception No. 2: You are permitted by Section 410-31 to splice in a fixture that is used as a raceway.

(b) **Box Only.** A box must always be installed for conductor splices connecting points, outlets, switch points, junction points, or pull points for the connection for Type AC cable, Type MC cable, mineral-insulated metal-sheathed cable, nonmetallic-sheathed cable or any other type of cables that run between two such boxes or fittings. This will also apply at switch or outlet points for concealed knob-and-tube wiring. Knob-and-tube wiring are practically never installed anymore, but you may be required to make additions to them.

Exception No. 1: There is an exception in Section 336-16 that covers nonmetallic-sheathed cable to insulated outlet devices.

Exception No. 2: See Section 410-62 in the *NEC* covering rosettes.

Exception No. 3: If accessible fittings are used, with MI cable or metallic-sheathed cable or straight-through splices.

Exception No. 4: Where conduit or tubing is used only for support or protection from physical damage. The cables entering the conduit or tubing shall have a fitting on the conduit or tubing to prevent damage to the cable installed therein.

Exception No. 5: This applies to devices that are integrally identified for use on walls or ceilings or on-site construction. Devices for use with nonmetallic-sheathed cable are also permitted to be used without a separate box.
See the *NEC* Exception No. 2, 336-15, 545-10; 550-8 (j); and 551-14(e), Exception No. 1.

Exception No. 6: See the *NEC.*

Exception No. 7: If a conduit body meets the requirements of Sections 370-6(c) and 370-18, they may be used in lieu of boxes.

Exception No. 8: See the *NEC.*

Exception No. 9: If a fitting that is identified as usable is permitted in place of a box, and after installation, where the conductors are not spliced or terminated.

300-16. Raceway or Cable to Open or Concealed Wiring.

(a) **Box or Fitting.** When changing from conduit, electrical metallic tubing, nonmetallic-sheathed cable, Type AC cable, Type MC cable, or mineral-insulated, metal-sheathed cable and surface raceway wiring to open wiring or concealed knob-and-tube wiring, a box or fitting with bushed openings or holes for each conductor may be used. The box or fitting shall contain no splices, nor shall it be used at fixture outlets. See Fig. 300-3.

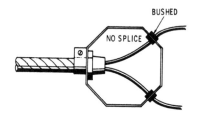

BUSHED

NO SPLICE

Fig. 300-3. Method of transferring from cable to concealed knob-and-tube wiring.

(b) **Bushing.** At the end of a terminal fitting or conduit or electrical metallic tubing where the raceway ends behind an open (unenclosed) switchboard or other uncontrolled or similar equipment, in lieu of a box or terminal fitting at the end, a bushing may be used.

300-17. Number and Size of Conductor in Raceway—The most

commonly used raceways are conduit and EMT. See NEC tables in Chapter 9. Table 1 gives us the percent of cross section of conduit and tubing for conductors. Table 2 gives us fill for fixture wires. Tables 3A, 3B and 3C apply to complete conduit or tubing systems and do not apply to sections of conduit used for physical protection only. Nipples not exceeding 24 inches may be filled to 60 percent.

Note: The fine-print note explains the *NEC* sections applicable, so refer to your *NEC* for this (FPN).

300-19. Supporting Conductors in Vertical Raceways.

(a) **Spacing Intervals—Maximum.** Conductors in vertical raceways shall be supported at the top of the run or as close to the top as practical. There shall also be supports as specified in Table 300-19(a) of the *NEC*.

Exception No. 1: An exception to Table 300-19(a). See your *NEC*.

Exception No. 2: See also Exception No. 2 of this section in the *NEC*.

(b) **Support Methods.** The following covers methods of support used:

(1) On clamping devices of insulating material with insulated wedges inserted in the ends of the conduit, if the clamping does not

adequately support the cable conductor, the wedges should be approved so as not to damage the insulation by wedging it to the conduit. The varnished cambric and thermoplastic insulation is inclined to slip on the conductor. Therefore, wedges might not hold this type of conductor and insulation effectively.

(2) Boxes may be inserted at the required intervals. These boxes are to have insulated supports installed and secured adequately to stand the weight of the conductors to which they are to be attached. The boxes shall be provided with covers.

(3) In addition to the boxes protecting the conductors at not less than 90 degrees, carrying them horizontally to a distance equal to not less than twice the conductor diameter, two or more supports shall be used for carrying these conductors or cables. The support intervals when this method is used shall be at points not greater than 20 percent of the distances mentioned in the preceding table. The necessity of supporting at not more than one-fifth of the distance in the table would seem to make this method less practical, because additional expense would be involved.

(4) Equally effective methods may be used, but approval should be secured from the authority having jurisdiction.

300-20. Induced Currents in Metal Enclosures or Metal Raceways—Please note that prior to the 1965 Code, this section was effective only for circuits carrying 50 amperes or more. The present rule mentions no minimum value of current.

To accomplish the minimizing of heating effects, the phase conductors, neutral, where used, and equipment grounding conductor, where used, shall all be in the same enclosure. See the *NEC* for further clarification.

300-21. Spread of Fire or Products of Combustion—Although we do not often think of electrical installations being responsible for fire spread, it is a definite problem when wiring is installed in hollow spaces, vertical shafts, or ventilation of air-handling equipment ducts, or even up through a ceiling to another floor. All of these installations shall be made so as greatly to decrease the spread of fire penetration through walls, partitions, floors, or ceilings that are fire rated for fire resistance, and only approved methods for installing fire stop at these points shall be used to maintain the fire rating of the building or structure.

Even slight openings will increase the risk of possible fire spread. This section is very important. Many new products have been approved to close these spaces.

300-22. Wiring in Ducts, Plenums, and Other Air-Handling Spaces—This section applies to air-handling spaces and applies to the use and installation of wiring and equipment in ducts, plenums, or any air-handling spaces.

Note: Article 424, Part F covers Electric Duct Heaters

(a) **Ducts or Dust, Loose Stock, or Vapor Removal.** No wiring whatsoever shall be installed in ducts handling flammable vapors or loose stock. No wiring shall be installed in ducts or duct shafts containing only such ducts that are used for vapor removal or for ventilation of commercial-type cooking.

(b) **Ducts or Plenums Used for Environmental Air.** MI cable, intermediate metal conduit, EMT, rigid metal conduit, metal-sheathed cable, type MC cable using a smooth or corrugated impervious metal sheath without an overall nonmetallic covering, and flexible metal tubing. When equipment is permitted in these types of ducts or plenums, flexible metal conduit not to exceed 4 feet (1.22 m) in length may be used to connect physically adjustable equipment and devices.

When flexible metal conduit is used, the fittings shall effectively close any openings or connections only if necessary where there is direct action upon or sensing of the contained air, should any equipment or device be installed in such ducts or chambers. If illumination is required to facilitate repair and maintenance, only gasketed-type fixtures are permitted to be used.

Note: What has been discussed here is only applicable if ducts or plenums are used exclusively for the environmental air.

(c) **Other Space Used for Environmental Air.** Cables of the following types are permitted in space for environmental air: MI cable, metal-sheathed cable, type MC without an overall nonmetallic covering, type AC cable, and other factory-assembled multiconductor control or power cable where specifically listed for the use. Any of the other types of cables or conductors shall be installed in EMT, intermediate metal conduit, rigid metal conduit, wireway with metal covers, metal solid bottom cable tray with solid metal covers, flexible metal conduit, or flexible metallic tubing.

Unless prohibited elsewhere in the Code, electrical equipment in either metal or nonmetal enclosures may be used, provided the nonmetal enclosure is listed for the use, if it is adequately fire resistant and produces very little smoke. Along with the wiring methods that are suitable for this installation other electrical equipment may be permitted in this space when provided with a metal enclosure or with listed nonmetallic enclosures of a type that has adequate fire-resistant and low smoke-producing characteristics where all associated wiring materials are suitable for ambient temperatures that may be involved.

Note: Paragraph (c) includes other spaces such as above hung ceilings that are being used for environmental air-handling purposes.

Exception No. 1: If liquidtight flexible metal conduit is not over 6 feet long, it will be permitted in these spaces.

Exception No. 2: Fans that are specifically approved for such use are permitted.

Exception No. 3: Rooms that are habitable or areas of the building that are not used primarily for air handling are not included in this section.

Exception No. 4: Cable assemblies of metallic manufactured wiring system, if they do not have nonmetallic sheath. If they are listed for this use, they shall be permitted.

Exception No. 5: Joist or stud spaces in dwelling units are not included in this section. If wiring or equipment passes through such places where it is perpendicular to the long dimension of such spaces.

Exception No. 6: Underfloor areas are covered in Section 645-2(c) (3) and are not covered by this section.

(d) **Data Proccessing Systems.** Article 645 will cover spaces under raised floors where there is electrical wiring for air-handling areas of data processing systems.

B. Requirements for Over 600 Volts, Nominal

300-31. Covers Required—Boxes, fittings, and similar enclosures shall have covers suitable for preventing accidental contact with energized parts or physical damage to parts or insulation.

300-32. Conductors of Different Systems—High-voltage and low-voltage systems have conductors that are not permitted to occupy the same enclosure or pull box and junction box.

Exception No. 1: See your *NEC.*

Exception No. 2: When high-voltage and low-voltage have to be in a manhole, it is permitted if they are well separated.

300-34. Conductor Bending Radius—There is a difference in the bending radius of shielded and nonshielded conductors. The radius of bend for nonshielded conductors shall not be less than eight times the diameter of the conductor. For shielded or lead-covered conductors, the radius of a bend shall not be less than twelve times the diameter of the cable during or after installation.

Care should be exercised when pulling conductors off a reel to assure that the reels are placed so that the natural bends of the cable as it leaves the reels will enter the raceways without reversing the natural bends. This is highly important, especially with shield cables, as damage may occur to the shielding if these precautions are not taken.

300-35. Protection Against Induction Heating—Care must be taken in arranging conductors in metal ducts to avoid heating by induction. In other words, all conductors of the same circuit shall be installed in the same raceway. Also, if nonmetallic ducts are used and placed in a bank and poured in concrete, it is necessary to secure them so that the spacing is maintained and flotation will not occur. To accomplish these things, it is often necessary to secure them by tying them together or down in the trench. No metallic wires, etc., should encircle the duct bank. All ties shall be made to eliminate a closed loop around the duct bank.

300-36. Grounding—Article 250 on grounding applies to the wiring of equipment installations.

ARTICLE 305—TEMPORARY WIRING

305-1. Scope—Temporary electrical lighting and wiring methods are covered here. The type of wiring used for temporary wiring is sometimes of lower quality than may be required for a permanent wiring.

This gives the inspection authorities having jurisdiction something to use for decisions.

305-2. Other Articles—All other requirements in this Code for permanent wiring installations will apply except as this Article 305 may modify it.

305-3. Time Constraints.

(a) **During the Period of Construction.** This fundamentally pertains to temporary electrical wiring and lighting installations. They are required and permitted while construction, remodeling, maintenance, repair, or demolition is taking place.

Since its evolution, OSHA, in addition to the authority having jurisdiction, has had a great deal to say about the safety of temporary wiring.

Every one working in this field has seen very dangerous practices used in temporary wiring.

(b) **Ninety Days.** Christmas decorations come under temporary wiring for decorative lighting, as do events such as carnivals. There is a time limit for permitted for this type of temporary wiring that shall not exceed 90 days.

(c) **Emergencies and Tests.** Emergencies and tests or experiments that cover development work are included under temporary electrical wiring installations.

(d) **Removal.** When construction is completed or any other type of temporary wiring is installed, it shall be removed immediately. For instance, wiring for Christmas lighting shall not be permitted to stay year after year.

305-4. General.

(a) **Services.** Article 230 must be followed on temporary services.

(b) **Feeders.** Temporary feeders must conform to Article 240. They must also originate in an approved method for the distribution of current. Multiconductor cord or cable assemblies may be used if they are of a type shown in Table 400-4 for hard usage or extra-hard usage. If the voltage does not exceed 150 volts to ground and the conductors are not subjected to physical damage, they may be run in open wiring, but to meet this requirement they must be supported at intervals of 10 feet or less.

Exception: As specified in Section 305-3(c).

(c) **Branch Circuits.** See your *NEC*.

The three preceding parts are a far cry from the temporary wiring so often used on construction sites. If the overcurrent panels, etc., are exposed to the elements, the same types of equipment shall be used as would be used under similar conditions on permanent wiring.

(d) **Receptacles.** Grounding-type receptacles only shall be used. All branch circuits shall contain an equipment grounding conductor. A grounded metal raceway or grounded metal cable will serve as the equipment grounding conductor, otherwise a separate grounding conductor shall be run. Irrespective of the method of grounding conductor as outlined, every receptacle shall be electrically connected to the equipment grounding conductor. Any branch circuit on temporary construction wiring or lighting shall not have any receptacle installed on it. If the circuit is a multiwire circuit, receptacles are not to be connected to the same ungrounded conductor as the temporary lighting is.

(e) **Disconnecting Means.** Disconnecting means that are suitable for use, such as switches and plug connectors, must be installed so as to permanently disconnect all ungrounded conductors of each of the temporary circuits, the disconnecting means shall disconnect all ungrounded conductors at the same time at the power outlet or panelboard where the branch circuit originated. Approved handle ties will be permitted.

(f) **Lamp Protection.** Lighting fixtures on temporary wiring for illumination must be protected from accidental contact by persons or breakage. To do this, a suitable fixture is to be used, or a suitable guard.

If ordinary brass shell, paper, line sockets, or any other metal-cased sockets are used, the metal encasing shall be grounded.

(g) **Splices.** On construction sites, boxes are not required for splices or junction connections. This applies to circuit conductors or multiconductor cord or cable assemblies or open conductors. Refer to the *NEC* for Sections 110-14(b) and 400-9. If a change is made to a raceway system or cable system that is metal clad or sheathed, a box must be used.

(h) **Protection from Accidental Damage.** All cords or cables must be protected where accidental damage may occur. Any projections or sharp corners make accidental damage likely, and shall be avoided. When cords or cables pass through doorways or any other place where they could be readily damaged, additional protection is required over the cord or cable.

305-5. Grounding—All grounding shall be in accordance with grounding as covered in Article 250.

305-6. Ground-Fault Protection for Personnel—To comply with (a) or (b), below-ground-fault protection for personnel shall be installed on construction sites.

(a) **Ground-Fault Circuit-Interrupters.** 15- and 20-ampere receptacles for 125-volt single-phase, if these outlets are not a part of the permanent building or structure and are for the use of the construction employees, shall have GFCI protection for persons.

Exception: If a 5 kW or less portable generator is vehicle mounted, 2-wire single-phase do not require GFCI protection—if the circuit conductors are insulated from the generator frame and on any other grounded surface.

(b) **Assured Equipment Grounding Conductor Program.** See the *NEC*.

Author's Note: This section is quite necessary as extension cords and portable equipment used on construction sites usually receive rather severe usage and can become dangerous to personnel.

305-7. Guarding—To prevent access to other than authorized and qualified personnel, any temporary wiring over 600 volts, nominal, is required to have suitable fencing or barriers or some other effective means to prevent access by unqualified persons.

ARTICLE 310—CONDUCTORS FOR GENERAL WIRING

310-1. Scope—This article is to assure that conductors for general wiring have mechanical strength, have adequate current-carrying capacity (ampacity), and are adequate for the particular usage to which they are to be put (such as wet or dry locations), for the temperature to which they will be subjected, etc. A large part of this article is in the form of tables, which will be explained as they are covered.

Conductors that are an integral part of a motor, motor controller, or other equipment, or which are provided for elsewhere in the Code, are not covered by this article.

Note: Flexible cords and cables are covered in the *NEC* in Article 400, and fixture wire in Article 402.

310-2. Conductors.

(a) **Insulated.** Conductors shall be insulated, except when covered or bare conductors are specifically permitted elsewhere in the Code.

Note: The *NEC* in Section 250-152 covers insulation for neutrals on high-voltage systems.

(b) **Conductor Material.** Conductors in this article may be copper, copper-clad aluminum, or aluminum, and unless the material is specified, they shall be copper.

310-3. Stranded Conductors—All conductors of No. 8 or larger installed in raceways shall be stranded.

Exception No. 1: This applies only where the conductors are used as busbars or in mineral-insulated cable, or metal-sheathed cable.

Exception No. 2: In the *NEC*, Section 680-22(b) has some requirements for solid bonding conductors.

310-4. Conductors in Parallel—This section applies to aluminum, copper-clad aluminum, or copper conductors connected in parallel so as to in reality form a common conductor. This part is commonly abused. It is recommended that the following conditions for paralleling be followed closely.

When necessary to run equipment grounding conductors with paralleled conductors, these equipment grounding conductors are to be treated the same as the other conductors and sized according to Table 250-95. Size 1/0 or larger, comprising each phase or neutral, will be permitted to be paralleled, that is, both ends of the paralleled conductors electrically connected together so as to form a single conductor.

Exception No. 1: You will find an exception in Section 620-12(a) (1).

Exception No. 2: Conductors smaller than 1/0 AWG may be run in parallel to supply control power to indicating instruments, contactors, relays, solenoids, and similar control devices if the following conditions exist: (a) they are in the same raceway or cable; (b) the ampacity of each conductor is sufficient to carry the entire load shared by the parallel conductors; and (c) if one parallel conductor should happen to become disconnected, the ampacity of each conductor is not exceeded.

Exception No. 3: Conductor sizes smaller than 1/0 may be run in parallel at frequencies of 360 Hertz and higher—if all of the conditions in Exception No. 2 (a), (b), and (c) are met.

The parallel phase conductors or neutral or parallel conductors shall be as follows:

1. All parallel conductors shall be the same length.
2. Parallel conductors shall be made of the same conductive material.

3. Parallel conductors shall all be the same circular mil area.
4. The insulation of all the conductors shall be of the same material.
   Note: The question was asked in a question-and-answer session, why did the insulation of all the parallel conductors have to be of the same type? If you study insulation resistance properties and the effect of different temperatures on the insulating properties of different conductor insulation, the reason will be become apparent. A case in point: On an industrial building, specs called for RHH-USE conductors to be run in conduits above a building exposed to sunlight and temperature variations. The first test of insulation was run early one cool morning, some time before energizing, and the resistance of insulation met the specification requirements. When it came time to energize the insulation, resistance was again measured, and it dropped to a very low figure. Energizing was not permitted at that time, and the inspector began studying insulation resistance. He found that THW had been used instead of the specified type insulation, and when the sunlight raised the ambient temperature, the insulation resistance dropped drastically. The point of this notation is that if different insulation types are used, ambient temperature conditions may have a great deal to do with leakage through the insulation, thus upsetting the impedance of the conductors in parallel.
5. Terminating all parallel conductors in the same manner is essential. If paralleled conductors are run in separate raceways, the conductors in each raceway are required to have the same physical characteristics so that conductors in each paralleled raceway will pull equal amounts of current.

See (FPN) in the *NEC*.

Equipment grounding conductors used in parallel circuits shall meet the requirement of this article, and also be sized as shown in the table in Section 250-95.

Consideration must be given to spacing in enclosures that have parallel circuits run to them. This is for bending radius and space considerations. For further information, refer to Articles 370 and 373.

Note 8 To Tables 310-16 through 310-31 shall be complied with when installing parallel conductors.

The above applies to parallel conductors in the same raceway or cable and will also apply to single conductors or multiconductor cables, which are stacked or bundled together and are not installed in raceways. Unless more than three current-carrying conductors are installed in one raceway, and more than one set of such a raceway and conductors are paralleled together, no derating will be required.

310-5. Minimum Size of Conductors—Conductors shall not be smaller than No. 14 copper or No. 12 aluminum or copper-clad aluminum, whether they are solid or stranded, except:

See Table 310-5 in the *NEC*, which gives minimum sizes of conductors for a number of different voltages, and see Table 310-64, Definitions.

Following the above, there are ten exceptions, which will not be repeated here. Refer to the ten exceptions following Table 310-5 in your *NEC*.

310-6. Shielding—The insulation shall be ozone resistant for solid dielectric insulated conductors if they are being operated over 2000 volts and are in permanent installations. They shall also be shielded. At high voltages ozone is created, and ozone has deteriorating effects on many types of insulation, which is the reason for the above. When cable is shielded metallically, which might be a ribbon of tin-coated copper or bare copper conductor, these shields shall be grounded at both ends and bonded across any splices made in the cables. The requirement of Section 250-51 shall be followed. Shielding contains voltage stresses to the insulation. Stress-cones are used at terminations and splices, and it is well to use the manufacturer's instructions for the cable that you are using.

Exception: If nonshielded insulated conductors are listed by a testing laboratory, they shall be permitted to be used when voltages do not exceed 8000 volts and under the following conditions:

a. High-voltage insulation shall resist electric discharge or surface tracking. If this is not the case, then the insulated conductors must be covered by a material not affected by ozone, electric discharge, or surface tracking.
b. In wet locations the insulated conductors shall have a nonmetallic jacket over all the insulation where there shall be a continuous metallic sheath.
c. See your *NEC*.
d. Table 310-63 covers the thickness of insulation and jacket.

310-7. Direct Burial Conductors—As was stated earlier, cables operating above 2000 volts are required to be shielded. Any cables used for direct burial shall be of a type that has been identified and listed to be used thus.

Exception: Multiconductor, nonshielded cables, 2001–5000 volts will be permitted, but the cable itself is required to have an overall metal sheath or armor.

The requirements of Section 250-51 shall be met for metallic shield, sheath, or armor grounded effectively through the grounding path.

Note: You are referred by the *NEC* to Sections 300-5 and 710-3 (b).

The authority enforcing the Code may require supplemental mechanical protection, such as a covering board, concrete pad, or raceway. In rocky soil, and more especially where frost is prevalent, the inspection authority will in addition usually require that a bed of fine sand be provided both under and over the conductors and the protection board. Rocks subject to frost heave will cause damage to the insulation.

310-8. Wet Locations.

(a) **Insulated Conductors.** The following types of cable may be used in wet locations: (1) lead-covered; (2) RHW, TW, THW, THWN, and XHHW.

Author's Note: In going through these identifications of conductor insulation, you will find that the H's may be used at a higher temperature, the W's for wet locations, the N's are nylon covered, and the two H's are for higher temperatures than one H.

(b) **Cables.** Only types of cable containing one or more conductors shall be used in wet locations unless listed for use in such locations.

Direct burial conductors must be listed for direct burial.

310-9. Corrosive Conditions—Where conductors are exposed to (1) oils, (2) greases, (3) vapors, (4) gases, (5) fumes, (6) liquids, or other substances that might cause deterioration of the conductor insulation, a type approved for the condition shall be required. A case in point is a gasoline dispensing island where lead-covered cable or cable with an approved nylon jacket is required. The conductors may be found in the UL listings to be certain whether or not they are approved for the location.

310-10. Temperature Limitation of Conductors—Table 310-13 lists temperature ratings of various insulations. These are the temperature ratings under load-carrying conditions, not ambient temperature. For instance, it is incorrect to use TW wire for wiring boiler controls—a high-temperature wire is required. Also, TW wire is not generally applicable for running to fluorescent lighting fixtures because of the heat of the ballasts.

No conductor is to be used in any manner which will cause the insulation to reach a temperature greater than the temperature for which the insulation was designed.

Note: See the (FPN) at this location in your *NEC*.

The principal problems of operating temperature are:

(1) Ambient temperature refers to the temperature in the area in which the conductors are run. It may affect certain parts of a run because of a higher room temperature in certain locations, and it may change from time to time: winter to summer, daylight to dark, etc.

(2) Current flow in a conductor will always cause some heat because of the resistance of the conductor.

(3) The amount of heat dissipated by the conductors will depend upon whether the ambient temperature is high or low. When conductors are surrounded with a thermal insulation, it will also affect the rate of heat distribution.

(4) Conductors adjacent to each other will affect the raising of the ambient temperatures and slow up the heat dissipation.

310-11. Marking—See the *NEC*.

310-12. Conductor Identification.

(a) **Grounded Conductors.** If the grounded conductors are No. 6 or smaller, they shall be identified as being grounded conductors or neutral by being white or natural gray color. Multiconductor flat cables No. 4 or larger shall have the grounded or neutral conductor identified by a ridge of the conductor.

As an inspector, the author found attempts made to use other colors than white or natural gray as the grounded or neutral conductor. It is very dangerous to deviate from what is called for by the Code.

Exception No. 1: Multiconductor cables insulated with cambric or varnished cloth.

Exception No. 2: Fixture wires as covered in Article 402.

Exception No. 3: This covers mineral-insulated cable and metal-sheathed cable. Conductors of MI cable are bare, so they must be sleeved with sleeves of proper colors, such as white or natural gray for the grounded conductors and appropriate colors for phase conductors.

Exception No. 4: Section 210-5(a) covers branch circuits. A grounded conductor of different systems must be identified per this section.

Exception No. 5: This allows grounded conductors in multiconductor cable to be identified at their terminations at the time when they are installed by distinctive white markings, which will be permanent, or by other effective means. The main conditions involved here are that maintenance and supervision of such will be done by only qualified persons.

If it is aerial mounted, cable shall be identified as in the above, or by a ridge so located on the outside of the cable as to clearly identify it as a grounded cable.

If conductors have a white or natural gray covering, with a color tracer thread in the braid that identifies the source or manufacturer, They shall meet the requirements of this section.

Tracer threads are sometimes advantageous; for example, when several grounded conductors are in the same location, the threads aid in identifying the source of the grounded conductors.

In Section 200-6 we covered identification requirements for conductors larger than No. 6.

(b) **Equipment Grounding Conductors.** When using insulated equipment grounding conductors, the insulation shall be continuous green or green with one or more yellow stripes. The conductor may, of course, be bare.

Exception No. 1: Insulated or covered conductors larger than No. 6 may be black or other color, but when installing same, the conductor shall be identified at every point where the conductor is accessible by one of the following means:

a. Stripping the insulation or covering from the entire exposed length.

b. Coloring the exposed insulation or covering green.

c. Marking the exposed insulation or covering with green colored tape or green colored adhesive labels.

Exception No. 2: At the time of installation, a multiconductor cable may be permanently identified as being the equipment grounding conductor at each end, and at every point where the conductor needs to be accessible. This applies only where maintenance supervision and qualified persons service the installation and the marks permanently identify it as the grounding conductor. Whenever an end starts or appears as accessible equipment follow the *NEC* requirements in this exception.

(c) **Ungrounded Conductor.** Ungrounded conductors shall be clearly distinguishable from grounded or grounding conductors. This applies whether they are single conductors or in cable form. They shall never be white, natural gray, green, or green with yellow stripes. Ungrounded conductors may be solid colors or colors with stripes in a regularly spaced series of identical marks; such stripes shall not be white, gray, or green and shall not conflict with markings as required in Section 310-11(b)(1).

310-13. Conductor Constructions and Applications—Insulated conductors must meet the requirements of one or more of the following tables: 310-13, 310-61, 310-62, 310-63, 310-64, 310-65, 310-66, and 310-67.

If specified in the respective tables, all of these conductors shall meet wiring methods that are covered by Chapter 3.

Note: Thermoplastic insulation is very susceptible to temperature variations. If temperatures are cooler than minus 10° C (or plus 14° F) during installation, care is required when installing above the temperatures. At normal temperatures thermoplastic insulation may also be deformed by pressure. This requires extra care during the installation and at any point where the conductor is supported.

Insulation resistance will vary a great deal with temperature. The resistance is higher at lower temperatures and steadily decreases as the temperature rises. A case in point: On one job I was testing insulation on 500 MCM THW insulation. The first test was run first thing in the morning. A portion of the conduit run was in the open on a roof, and this insulation test was very high. Later, just before energizing the feeder circuit, another insulation resistance test was run, and the resistance was found to be very much lower than the first test. One question was whether the insulation had been deformed. After analyzing the problem, I realized that the sun's heat was raising the temperature on the outdoor conduit and thus giving a much lower insulation resistance reading.

310-14. Aluminum Conductor Material—When aluminum conductors came into use, many problems arose. Now when solid aluminum conductors Nos. 8, 10, and 12 AWG are installed, they are required to be of an aluminum alloy conductor material. The balance of this is thoroughly covered in the Code at this point. Please refer to your *NEC*.

310-15. Ampacity—The term "electrical ducts" as used in this particular Article 310 recognizes any electrical conduit as covered in Chapter 3 that is suitable for use underground. Other raceways, round in cross section, are listed to be embedded in concrete underground.

(a) **Applications Covered by Tables.** We are about to cover conductors rated at various voltages. Table 310-16 through 310-31 and any notes therewith cover conductors rated 0–2000 volts and conductors rated 2001–5000 volts. The ampacity of these will be covered for Types V, AVA, AVB, and AVL conductors. These ratings will be the same for conductors rated 0–2000 volts. The ampacity for dielectric insulated conductors rated 2001–35000 volts will be found in Tables 310-69 through 310-84 along with the accompanying note.

(b) **Applications Not Covered by Tables.** Some conductors will not be covered by the tables. The calculation of the ampacities may be made under engineering supervision using the following formula: See the *NEC* for this formula.

Note: In these tables the ampacity involves temperature alone. Voltage drops will have to be calculated.

Note: If the voltage drop does not exceed 5 percent, this will allow for reasonable efficiency.

(c) **Selection of Ampacity.** If more than one calculated ampacity is found to be acceptable for a given circuit length, you must use the lowest calculated value.

A very controversial item is whether the neutral conductor of a four-wire wye system has a bearing on derating. It is the author's opinion that this question cannot be answered in a broad sense, but depends upon the types of loads and whether or not the neutral was carrying any appreciable amount of current.

Most of the balance of Article 310 consists of Tables 310-16 through 310-84, which you will find in the *NEC*. The Notes to Tables 310-16 through 310-31 are extremely important and should be adhered to very closely. These will be covered here.

The tables will not be repeated here, but mention will be made of them and what they cover.

Table 310-13, Conductor Application and Insulation.

Tables 310-16 through 310-23 are the tables most used. At the bottom of each table you will find an additional table covering correction to be made in ampacity requirements, giving the temperature in which compensation must be made for ambient temperatures above these temperatures.

These affect not only the resistance of the conductor, such as resistors at lower temperature of less resistance than the same conductor at a higher temperature, but also possibly the insulation of the conductor.

Table 310-24, Ampacities for Bare or Covered Conductors Based on 40° C Ambient, 80° C Total Conductor Temperature, 2 Feet (610 mm) per Second Wind Velocity.

Table 310-25, Ampacities of Single Insulated Conductors, Rated 0 through 2000 Volts, in Nonmagnetic Underground Electrical Ducts (One Conductor per Electrical Duct) Based on Ambient Earth Temperature of 20° C (68° F), Electrical Duct Arrangement as per Fig. 310-1, 100 Percent Load Factor Thermal Resistance (RHO) of 90, Conductor Temperature 75° C (167° F).

Table 310-26, Ampacities of Three Insulated Conductors, etc.

Table 310-27, Ampacities of Three Single Insulated Conductors, etc.

Table 310-28, Ampacities of Two or Three Insulated Conductors, etc.

Table 310-29, Ampacities of Three Triplexed Single Insulated Conductors, etc.

Table 310-30, Ampacities of Three Single Insulated Conductors, etc.

Table 310-31, Ampacities of Multiconductor Cable with not more than three Insulated Conductors, etc.

Refer to the notes following the tables listed above.

See the *NEC* following Note 3. A table there is headed Conductor Types and Sizes. This gives the comparable sizes of copper and aluminum for service ratings in amperes.

Table 310-61, Conductor Application and Insulation.

Table 310-62, Thickness of Insulation for 601–2000 Volt Nonshielded Types RHH and RHW in Mils.

Table 310-63, Thickness of Insulation and Jacket for Nonshielded Solid Dielectric Insulated Conductors Rated 2001 to 8000 Volts, in Mils.

Table 310-64, Thickness of Insulation for Shielded Solid Dielectric Insulated Conductors, etc.

Table 310-65, Thickness of Varnished-Cambric Insulation for Single-Conductor Cable, in Mils.

Table 310-66, Thickness of Varnished-Cambric Insulation for Multi-conductor Cable, in Mils.

Table 310-67, Thickness of Asbestos and Varnished-Cambric Insulation for Single-Conductor Cable, etc.

Table 310-69, Ampacities for Insulated Single Copper Conductor Isolated in Air, etc.

Table 310-70, Ampacities for Insulated Single Aluminum Conductor Isolated in Air, etc.

Table 310-71, Ampacities of an Insulated Three-Conductor Copper Cable Isolated in Air, etc.

Table 310-72, Ampacities of an Insulated Three-Conductor Aluminum Cable Isolated in Air, etc.

Table 310-73, Ampacities of an Insulated Triplexed or Three Single-Conductor Copper Cables in Isolated Conduit in Air, etc.

Table 310-74, Ampacities of Insulated Triplexed or Three Single-Conductor Aluminum Cables in Isolated Conduit in Air, etc.

Table 310-75, Ampacities of an Insulated Three-Conductor Copper Cable in Isolated Conduit in Air, etc.

Table 310-76, Ampacities of an Insulated Three-Conductor Aluminum Cable in Isolated Conduit in Air, etc.

Table 310-77, Ampacities of an Insulated Triplexed or Three Single-Conductor Copper Cables in Underground Raceways, etc.

Table 310-78, Ampacities of Three Single Insulated Aluminum Conductors in Underground Electrical Ducts, etc.

Table 310-79, Ampacities of Three Insulated Copper Conductors Cabled Within an Overall Covering, etc.

Table 310-80, Ampacities of Three Insulated Aluminum Conductors Cabled Within an Overall Covering, etc.

Table 310-81, Ampacities of Single Insulated Copper Conductors Directly Buried in Earth, etc.

Table 310-82, Ampacities of Single Insulated Aluminum Conductors Directly Buried in Earth, etc.

Table 310-83, Ampacities of Three Insulated Copper Conductors Cabled Within an Overall Covering, etc.

Table 310-84, Ampacities of Three Insulated Aluminum Conductors Cabled Within an Overall Covering, etc.

ARTICLE 318—CABLE TRAYS

318-1. Scope—This article covering cable tray systems includes a number of items. Among these are solid bottom trays, troughs, channels, ladders, etc.

318-2. Definitions—See your *NEC*.

318-3. Uses Permitted.

(a) **Wiring Methods.** Continuous rigid cable supports may be used for the following, but the conditions covering the installation of each should be followed as per the articles referred to:

(1) Mineral-insulated, metal-sheathed cable (Article 330).

(2) Armored cable (Article 333).

(3) Metal-clad cable (Article 334).

(4) Power-limited tray cable (Section 725-40).

(5) Nonmetallic-sheathed cable (Article 336).

(6) Shielded, nonmetallic-sheathed cable (Article 337).

(7) Multiconductor service-entrance cable (Article 338).

(8) Multiconductor underground feeder and branch-circuit cable (Article 339).

(9) Power and control tray cable (Article 340).

(10) Other factory-assembled, multiconductor control, signal, or power cables, which are specifically approved for installation in cable trays; or

(11) Any approved conduit or raceway with its contained conductors.

(b) **In Industrial Establishments.** In these establishments, provided that only qualified persons will service the cable tray systems, (1) and (2) below will be permitted in ladder, ventilated trays, channel-type cable trays of 4 inches or 6 inches if ventilated.

(1) **Single Conductor.** Single conductor, 250 MCM or larger, are permitted in listed cable trays. Should the cable trays be exposed to sunlight, they shall be listed for exposure to sunlight.

Exception: Article 630, Part E, tells us where welding cables are permitted.

(2) **Multiconductor.** Type MV multiconductors, as covered in Article 326, if exposed to sun shall be identified for this purpose.

(c) **Equipment Grounding Conductors.** Table 318-7(b)(2) gives minimum cross-sectional area of metal in square inches for different ampere ratings or settings of largest automatic overcurrent device protecting any circuit in the cable tray system. In industrial and commercial establishments only, where continuous maintenance and supervision assure that only competent persons will service the installed cable tray system, the cable trays shall be permitted to be used as equipment grounding conductors.

(d) **Hazardous (Classified) Locations.** Cable tray systems shall be permitted to be used in hazardous locations where the contained cables are specifically approved for such use. See Sections 501-4, 502-4, and 503-3.

Note: Cable trays are permitted in other than industrial use.

(e) **Nonmetallic Cable Tray.** These are permitted with corrosive areas and in areas requiring isolation of different voltages.

318-4. Uses Not Permitted—Cable trays are not permitted where subject to severe physical damage, for example in hoistways.

318-5. Construction Specifications—See the *NEC.*

318-6. Installation.

(a) **Complete System.** Cable trays shall be installed as a complete system from the point of origin to the point of termination, including bends, etc. The electrical continuity shall be maintained throughout the cable tray system and supports. See Figs. 318-1 and 318-2.

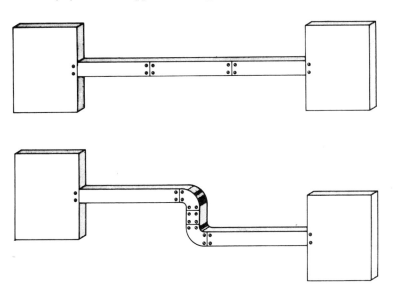

Fig. 318-1. Cable trays shall be continuous as a complete system from the point of origin to the point of termination.

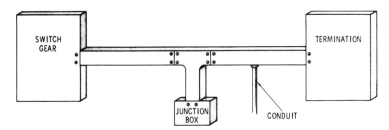

Fig. 318-2. Cable trays shall be mechanically connected to all enclosures or raceways.

(b) **Completed Before Installation.** Conductors cannot be installed in cable trays until the run of the cable tray involved is entirely completed.

(c) **Supports.** Wherever cable for cable trays enters raceways or other enclosures, supports shall be provided where the cables enter the other raceways or enclosures.

(d) **Covers.** Wherever runs of cable trays might require additional protection, covers may be installed of material that is compatible with the material of which the cable tray is made. (See Fig. 318-3.)

(e) **Multiconductor Cables Rated 600 Volts or Less.** Conductors may occupy the same cable tray regardless of the voltage, provided that it is 600 volts or less. See Fig. 318-4.

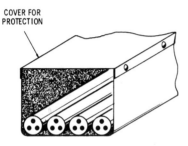

COVER FOR PROTECTION

Fig. 318-3. Covers shall be used where necessary for protection.

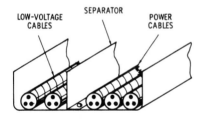

LOW-VOLTAGE CABLES   SEPARATOR   POWER CABLES

Fig. 318-4. Separators shall be used where required.

(f) **Cables Rated over 600 Volts.** You are permitted to install cables rated over 600 volts in the same cable tray with cables rated 600 volts or less.

Exception No. 1: A barrier in the cable tray that is compatible with the cable tray material.

Exception No. 2: If MC cable is used for over 600 volts.

(g) **Through Partitions and Walls.** If the requirements of Section 300-21 are met, portions of cable trays are permitted to pass through partitions, or vertically through platforms or wet or dry locations. (See Figs. 318-5 and 318-6.)

(h) **Exposed and Accessible.** Except as permitted by 318-6(g), cable trays shall be exposed and accessible.

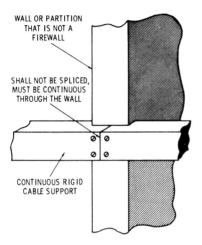

WALL OR PARTITION
THAT IS NOT A
FIREWALL

SHALL NOT BE SPLICED,
MUST BE CONTINUOUS
THROUGH THE WALL

CONTINUOUS RIGID
CABLE SUPPORT

Fig. 318-5. Cable trays shall be continuous through walls or partitions.

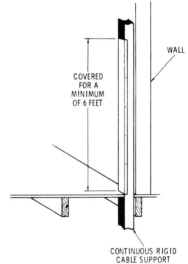

WALL

COVERED
FOR A
MINIMUM
OF 6 FEET

CONTINUOUS RIGID
CABLE SUPPORT

Fig. 318-6. Cable trays shall be covered to a minimum height of 6 feet when run through floors.

(i) **Adequate Access.** Cable trays shall be installed so that there is sufficient space provided to permit access for the installation and maintenance of the cables. This does not give dimensions, but Figs. 318-7 to 318-9 might give some idea of what clearances might be considered as being adequate.

Note: See the *NEC*, Section 310-10, which covers temperature limitations of conductors.

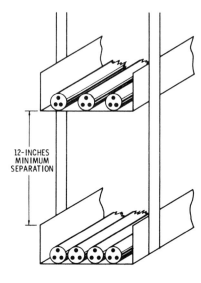

Fig. 318-7. A 12-inch minimum separation shall be maintained between continuous rigid cable supports in tiers.

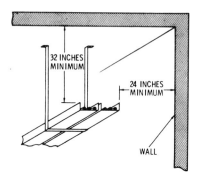

Fig. 318-8. A 24-inch minimum horizontal and a 32-inch minimum vertical working space should be maintained.

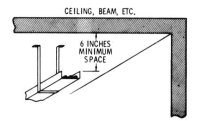

Fig. 318-9. A minimum 6-inch clearance should be provided from the top of the cable support to the ceiling, beams, etc.

318-7 Grounding.

(a) **Metallic Cable Tray Systems.** The grounding of metallic cable trays which support electrical conductors shall meet the same grounding requirements as for other conductor enclosures as covered in Article 250.

(b) **Steel or Aluminum Cable Tray Systems.** If the following requirements are met, cable trays made of steel or aluminum may be used as equipment grounding:

   (1) All the cable trays and fittings must be identified or listed to be used as equipment grounding conductors.

   (2) They shall conform to the requirements in Table 318-7(b)(2) to provide the minimum cross-section area of cables which are used as equipment grounding conductors. See Table 318-7(b)(2).

   (3) Cable tray and fittings must be legibly and durably marked to show the area of the metal and all types of cable trays or ladders.

   (4) Bondings of cable trays and fittings shall be bonded as covered in Section 250-75. This may be bolted mechanically or by bonding jumpers that are to be installed as per Section 250-79.

   See the *NEC*, Table 318-7(b)(2), Metal Area Requirements for Cable Trays Used as Equipment Grounding Conductors.

318-8. Cable Installation.

(a) **Cable Splices.** Splices that are properly insulated and do not project above the sides of cable trays shall be permitted to be made.

(b) **Fastened Securely.** They must be securely fastened or fastened by other approved means of conductors in horizontal runs of cable trays. This keeps them in their proper location, especially if fault currents occur. (See Fig. 318-10.)

(c) **Bushed Conduit.** If conduit has cables with conductors installed in it, junction boxes are not required, but the conduit must be properly bushed and supported from physical damage.

(d) **Connected in Parallel.** Where parallel conductors are installed in cable trays, the phase conductor and neutral of each parallel set shall be permitted as covered in Section 310-4. One of each of the phase conductors in the neutral shall be bound together to prevent unbalanced currents in the parallel conductors due to inductive reactance.

   Thus by grouping and using such tie-wraps to keep three different phase conductors and the neutral together, the currents cancel each other; if this was not done, there would be an unbalance of phase currents at times and cancellation would not take place.

Also single conductors must be bound in circuit groups to contain them to prevent excessive movement in the event of fault-current magnetic forces. See Fig. 318-11.

Exception: Triplex of twisted conductors are an exception.

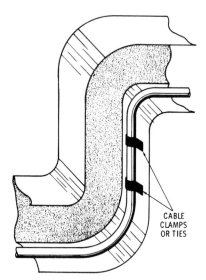

CABLE
CLAMPS
OR TIES

Fig. 318-10. Cables shall be securely fastened by a suitable means when required.

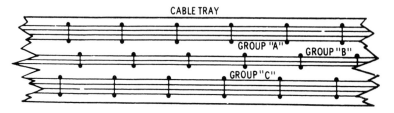

Fig. 318-11. Single-conductor phase groups shall be bound in circuit groups.

318-9. Number of Multiconductor Cables, Rated 2000 Volts, Nominal, or Less, in Cable Trays—This section covers the number of cables of 2000 volts or less that are permitted to be installed in a single cable tray. The conductor sizes that are covered in this section apply to both aluminum and copper conductors.

(a) **Any Mixture of Cables.** For ventilated trough cable trays that contain multiconductors or lighting cables and any mixture thereof of multiconductor power and lighting control and signal conductors, see the following for the maximum number of conductors that will conform to such installations.

(1) If all of the conductor cables are 4/0 AWG or larger, the sum of the cable diameters is not permitted to exceed the width of the cable tray, nor are cables permitted to be installed in multilayers—single layer only is allowed!

Tables giving the diameters of conductors, with various types of insulation, are given in Chapter 9 of the NEC.

(2) Table 318-9 gives the allowable cable fill area for multipleconductor cables in ladder, ventilated trough, or solid bottom cable trays. Where all of the cables are smaller than 4/0 AWG, Table 318-9, Column 1, gives the allowable fill area for the appropriate cable tray width.

(3) Part of this is similar to (2), so it will not repeated here. However, the sum of all cables smaller than 4/0 AWG shall not exceed the maximum allowable fill area. Column 4 of Table 318-9 covers the computation for the proper width of a cable tray. Only a single layer of 4/0 AWG and larger cables shall have no other cables on them. See Fig. 318-12.

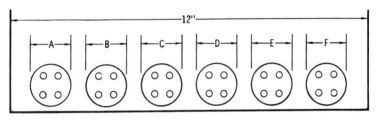

Fig. 318-12. Cables (multiple conductor) diameter A + B + C + D + E + F shall not equal more than 10.8 inches when installed in a 12-inch cable tray. Single layer only.

(b) **Multiconductor Control and/or Signal Cables Only.** Ladder or ventilated trough cable trays that are used for multipleconductor control and/or signal cables *ONLY* and which have a depth of 6 inches (152 mm) or less may have a conductor fill of not to exceed 50 percent of any cross-sectional area of the cable tray. Cable trays with a usable depth of more than 6 inches (152 mm) shall use 6 inches (152 mm) as the depth for fill, and not more than 6 inches (152 mm).

(c) **Solid Bottom Cable Trays Containing Any Mixture.** In solid bottom cable trays for mounted conductor, power, lighting cables, or with control insertion cables, you shall follow (1), (2), and (3):

(1) If all the cables installed are 4/0 AWG or larger, you are only allowed up to 90 percent fill in a single layer. (See Fig. 318-12.)

(2) Column 3 of Table 318-9, where the appropriate cable tray width is to be used where all of the cables are smaller than 4/0 AWG. The sum of the cross-section areas of all cables involved shall comply with the maximum allowable in the above-stated column and section.

(3) Column 4 of Table 318-9 and the appropriate cable tray widths shall be adhered to when 4/0 AWG or larger cables are installed. With cables smaller than 4/0 AWG in the same cable tray, the sum of the cross-section area of all cables smaller than 4/0 AWG shall not exceed the allowable fill area when using the aforementioned column and table for the appropriate tray width, and the cables of 4/0 AWG and larger are to be installed in a single layer. No additional cables are to be placed on them.

Using Column 4 of Table 318-9, this gives the square inches allowable for various sizes of cable trays, for conductors (multiple) smaller than 4/0 AWG. Note the 4/0 AWG and larger conductors are to be in a single layer only.

(d) **Solid Bottom Cable Tray Multiconductor Control and/or Signal Cables Only.** A solid bottom cable tray that has a usable inside depth of 6 inches or less and where it contains multipleconductor control and/or signal cables only, the cross-sectional areas shall be not more than 40 percent of cross-sectional area of the cable tray. If the cable tray depth is over 6 inches, the usable cross-sectional area shall be figured as if the cable tray were 6 inches deep, even though it is deeper.

(e) **Ventilated Channel Cable Trays.** Refer to the *NEC.*

Exception: Refer to your *NEC* and Table 318-9.

318-10. Number of Single Conductor Cables, Rated 2000 Volts or Less, in Cable Trays—When conductors are rated 2000 volts or less, the number of single conductor cables in a single cable tray section is required to abide by the requirements of this section. Single conductors or cable assemblies shall be distributed evenly across the bottom of the cable tray in which they are being installed. This will make it necessary to secure them in place to hold them in the spacing required, and the conductors may be copper or aluminum conductors.

(a) **Ladder or Ventilated Trough Cable Trays.** Cable trays as indicated in the title contain single conductor cables. The following additions to this portion shall be met in determining the maximum single conductors that the particular tray or ladder may hold:

(1) The sum of the diameter of all single conductors 1000 MCM or larger shall not exceed the cable tray width. Refer to Table 318-10. See Fig. 318-13. This will possibly fill the width of the cable tray, but it will permit only one layer of cables.

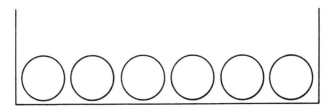

Fig. 318-13. The sum of the diameter of single-conductor 1000 MCM or larger shall not exceed the width of the cable tray.

(2) Where all of the cables are smaller than 1000 MCM, the cable tray fill is governed by Column 1 of Table 318-10, and the sum of the cross-sectional areas of the cables shall not exceed the square inches allowable in Column 1 for the appropriate cable tray width.

(3) If 1000 MCM or larger single-conductor cables are installed in a cable tray with single-conductor cables smaller than 1000 MCM, the total cross-sectional area of the cables smaller than 1000 MCM is controlled by the computation in Column 2 of Table 318-10 for the appropriate cable tray widths.

(b) **Ventilated Channel-Type Cable Trays.** The sum of the diameter of all single conductors in 4-inch or 6-inch-wide ventilated channel-type cable trays shall not exceed the inside width of the channel.

See the *NEC* for Table 318-10, Allowable Cable Fill Area for Single Conductor Cable in Ladder or Ventilated Trough Cable Trays for Cable Rated 2000 Volts or Less.

318-11. Ampacity of Cables Rated 2000 Volts or Less in Cable Trays—The derating factor with Tables 310-16 through 310-31 covers Note 8(a) and does not apply to the ampacity when these conductors are in cable trays.

(a) **Multiconductor Cables.** Tables 310-18 and 310-22 cover the allowable ampacities and will apply to multiconductor cables nominally rated 2000 volts or less, provided that they are installed according to the requirements of Section 318-9.

Exception No. 1: Ampacities must be cut to 95 percent of the ampacity in Tables 310-22 and 310-31 where cable trays are continuously covered for more than 6 feet with a solid cover that is not ventilated.

Exception No. 2: The allowable ambient temperatures and corrected ampacities in Table 310-31 of multiconductor cables when installed in single, in uncovered cable trays, and having a spacing between them of not less than one of the conductor diameters of the conductor cables. The allowable ampacity shall not exceed those covered in Table 310-31.

(b) **Single Conductor Cables.** The following will apply to the ampacity of single-conductor cables or single-conductor cables that are twisted or bound together, such as triplex to quadraplex, etc. This applies to nominally rated 2000 volts or less:

(1) If 600 MCM or larger single-conductor cables are installed as per Section 318-10, and uncovered cable trays shall not exceed 75 percent of the ampacities as shown in Tables 310-17 and 310-19. Where cable trays are contiously covered for more than 4 feet and unventilated covers are used, ampacities for 600 MCM and larger cables shall not exceed the ampacity of 70 percent of the level ampacities shown in Tables 310-17 and 310-19.

Referring to Tables 310-17 and 310-19 in the *NEC*, you will notice that these tables are for Single Conductors in Free Air for Copper and Aluminum, respectively.

(2) When cables are installed according to Section 318-9, single conductor cables from 250 MCM through 500 MCM installed in uncovered cable trays shall have their ampacities calculated as 65 percent of the allowable ampacities in Tables 310-17 and 310-19. If the cable trays are continuously covered for more than six feet with solid unventilated covers, then for 250 MCM through 500 MCM single-conductor cables the ampacities shall not exceed 60 percent of the allowable ampacities as covered in Tables 310-17 and 310-19.

(3) Tables 310-17 and 310-19 give the ampacities of cables that shall not be exceeded under the following: single cables installed in single and uncovered cable trays, and if spacing is maintained of not less than the diameter of one cable between each conductor; this covers cables of 25 MCM and larger.

(4) The ampacity allowable in Table 310-23 will apply to single cables arranged in a triangular form and in uncovered cable trays. The cables shall be spaced not less than 2.15 times the diameter of one cable, between the circuit conductors in a triangular configuration, and the ampacities are for 250 MCM and larger cables.

Note: Remember that we have Correction Tables for Ambient Temperatures over 30°C, 86°F. These appear below Tables in *NEC* Article 310.

318-12. Number of Type MV and Type MC Cables (2001 Volts or Over) in Cable Trays—The number of cables as covered in the title and rated nominal 2001 volts or over in a single tray shall not exceed the requirements of this section.

The sum of the diameters of the load conductor cables for single conductors that are installed in cable trays shall be installed in single layers, and the sum of the diameters shall not exceed the cable tray width at which they are installed. Where single conductors or triplexed or quadraplexed cables are installed they are to be in a single layer only. This can also apply to bundled conductors if they are all of a single circuit group. The cable tray width shall not be exceeded by the sum of the diameter of the covered conductors. These shall be installed in single layer arrangement.

318-13. Ampacity of Type MV and Type MC Cable (2001 Volts or Over) in Cable Trays—The requirements of Section 318-12 shall apply to this type of cable.

(a) **Multiconductor Cables (2001 Volts or Over).** The ampacity of multiconductor cables shall not exceed the ampacities allowable in Tables 310-75 and 310-76.

Exception No. 1: If the cable trays are covered with unventilated covers exceeding 6 feet with solid unventilated covers, the ampacities as shown in Tables 310-75 and 310-76 shall be rated to 95 percent of the ampacities shown in these tables.

Exception No. 2: The allowable ampacity in Tables 310-71 and 310-72 will be allowed for multiconductor cables provided that they are installed in a single layer and the cable trays are uncovered. The spacing of not less than one cable diameter shall be allowed between the multiconductor cables.

(b) **Single Conductor Cables (2001 Volts or Over).** Following this paragraph the ampacity of single conductors or single conductors bundled together, if one circuit (triplexed or quadraplexed), must comply with the following:

(1) Tables 310-69 and 310-70 cover ampacities for cables 250 MCM or larger if they are single conductors and in uncovered cable trays. They shall not exceed 75 percent of the allowable ampacities shown in these tables. If the cable trays are covered more than 6 feet, the same type of conductor shall not exceed 70 percent of the ampacity allowed in the aforementioned tables.

(2) In single-conductor cables, provided the proper spacing is maintained, which is one cable diameter, the ampacities of 250 MCM and larger cables shall be as shown in Table 310-69 and 310-70, and shall not be more than those shown.

(3) Where single conductors of a circuit are in a triangular form, the spacing between the different triangular bundled circuit conductors shall not be less than 2.15 times the conductor diameter between the bundled circuit conductors and the ampacities of 250 MCM or larger cables shall not be allowed to exceed 105 percent of the ampacities covered in Tables 310-71 and 310-72.

ARTICLE 320—OPEN WIRING ON INSULATORS

On this article you are referred to the *NEC*. The author's opinion is that this type of wiring is so seldom used that it need not be covered here section by section. However, illustrations will be presented showing how open wiring is installed.

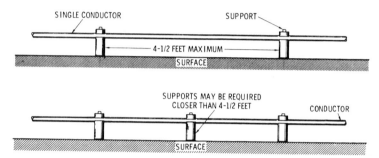

Fig. 320-1.   Spacing of supporting knobs.

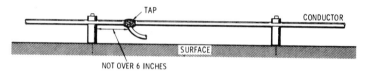

Fig. 320-2.   Distance between a support and a tap should never exceed 6 inches.

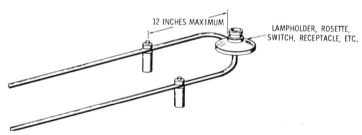

Fig. 320-3.   Distance of supports when connecting receptacles, switches, rosettes, and other devices.

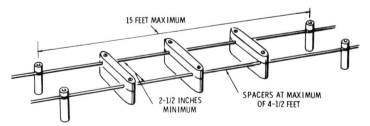

Fig. 320-4.   A 15-foot span requires spacers.

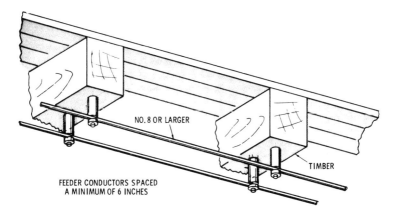

NO. 8 OR LARGER

TIMBER

FEEDER CONDUCTORS SPACED
A MINIMUM OF 6 INCHES

Fig. 320-5.   Mill construction installation.

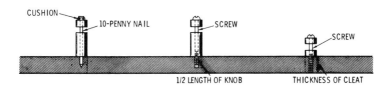

CUSHION

10-PENNY NAIL

SCREW

SCREW

1/2 LENGTH OF KNOB

THICKNESS OF CLEAT

Fig. 320-6.   Length of nails and screws for knobs and cleats.

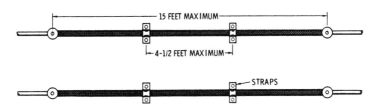

15 FEET MAXIMUM

4-1/2 FEET MAXIMUM

STRAPS

Fig. 320-7.   Use of approved nonmetallic tubing.

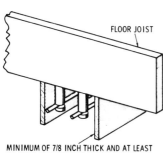

FLOOR JOIST

MINIMUM OF 7/8 INCH THICK AND AT LEAST
AS HIGH AS THE KNOBS WHERE SUBJECT TO
PHYSICAL DAMAGE

**Fig. 320-8.   Protecting conductors
from physical damage.**

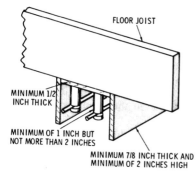

FLOOR JOIST

MINIMUM 1/2 INCH THICK

MINIMUM OF 1 INCH BUT NOT MORE THAN 2 INCHES

MINIMUM 7/8 INCH THICK AND MINIMUM OF 2 INCHES HIGH

Fig. 320-9. Use of running board and sides for protection.

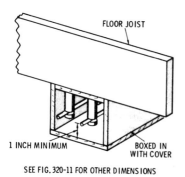

FLOOR JOIST

1 INCH MINIMUM

BOXED IN WITH COVER

SEE FIG. 320-11 FOR OTHER DIMENSIONS

Fig. 320-10. Use of enclosure with cover.

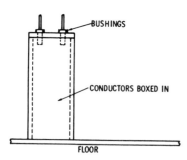

BUSHINGS

CONDUCTORS BOXED IN

FLOOR

Fig. 320-11. Vertical enclosure for conductors.

ARTICLE 321—MESSENGER-SUPPORTED WIRING

321-1. Definition—See your *NEC*.

321-2. Other Articles—Not only must messenger-supported wiring comply with this article, but it shall also comply with any of the provisions that may be applicable in Articles 225 and 300, plus any other applicable articles in the Code.

321-3. Uses Permitted.

(a) **Cable Types.** Cable-type wiring may be permitted to be installed as messenger-supported wiring if it meets all of the conditions of the following articles for each type of cable listed below:

(1) Mineral insulated, metal-sheathed cable (Article 330)

(2) Metal clad cable (Article 334)

(3) Multiconductor service-entrance cable (Article 338)

(4) Multiconductor underground feeder and branch-circuit cable (Article 339)

(5) Power and control tray cable (Article 340)

(6) Section 725-40 covers power-limited tray cable.

(7) Other factory-assembled multiconductor control, signal, or power cable that have been identified for the use.
The use of any of the above for messenger-supported cables shall meet all requirements of the applicable article involved.

(b) **In Industrial Establishments.** If competent individuals only will be servicing installed messenger cable wiring in industrial establishments, the following conditions shall be met:

(1) Conductor types in Table 310-13 or 310-62 may be used.

(2) MV cable may be used.

If the messenger-supported conductors are exposed to a wet location or to sunlight, they shall be listed for wet locations or sunlight or both, if both conditions are prevalent.

(c) **Hazardous (Classified) Locations.** The only hazardous (classified) locations where messenger-supported wiring shall be used—if they are approved—are those covered in Sections 501-4, 502-4, and 503-3.
The use of messenger-supported cable in hazardous (classified) locations is very limited.

321-4. Uses Not Permitted—In hazardous locations such as hoistways or other places where damage may occur, messenger-supported wiring shall not be used.

321-5. Ampacity—Section 310-15 is used to determine the maximum ampacity permissible.

321-6. Messenger Support—Proper and adequate support shall be used for dead-ending the messenger cable. At any location, you are required to eliminate the conductors being put under tension. Conductors shall not come in contact with the messenger cable, points of support, or structure members such as walls or pipes.

321-7. Grounding—Grounding is covered by Sections 250-32 and 250-33 for enclosures, which cover the means of grounding the messenger.

321-8. Conductor Splices and Taps—If approved means are used, splices and taps in conductors, if properly insulated, shall be permitted for messenger-supported wiring.

ARTICLE 324—CONCEALED KNOB-AND-TUBE WIRING

A number of years ago knob-and-tube wiring was the main method used in wiring houses and commercial buildings. Many are still wired that way, and if proper installation had been made, it is a very safe wiring method. The insulators, etc., are now very hard to obtain, but you will be required to make additions to knob-and-tube wiring by adding NM cable, which needs much less time for installation and incoporates an equipment-grounding conductor. In other words, changes in wiring methods have meant changes in the materials used since this method was popular.

324-1. Definition—See your *NEC*.

324-2. Other Articles—As with open wiring in preceding Article 320, other parts of the Code are applicable, especially Article 300, Wiring Methods—General.

324-3. Uses Permitted—This type of wiring is permitted to be used only in extensions to existing installations, and may be used in other places only with special permission—if the following conditions are met:
See the *NEC* for (1) and (2).

324-4. Uses Not Permitted.

(1) In commercial garages.

(2) In theaters and similar locations.

(3) In motion-picture studios.

(4) In hazardous (classified) locations.

324-5. Conductors.

(a) **Type.** See the *NEC*.

(b) **Ampacity.** See your *NEC*.

324-6. Conductor Supports—See your *NEC*.

324-7. Tie Wires—If solid knobs are used, the conductors shall be mounted on these solid supports by means of tie wires made of the same material as the conductors.

324-8. Conductor Clearance—Conductors shall be separated at least 3 inches and maintained at least 1 inch from the surface wired over. Notice that this is different from Article 320. At distributing centers, meters, outlets, switches or other places where space is limited and the 3-inch separation cannot be maintained, each conductor shall be encased in a continuous length of flexible nonmetallic tubing. Where practicable, conductors shall run singly on separate timbers or studding.

Exception: If the space is so limited as not to provide the minimum clearances described above for meters, panelboards, outlets, switch boxes, and so on, the means of protecting conductors shall be a flexible nonmetallic tubing, and this shall extend from the last support continuously to the box and the terminal point.

324-9. Through Walls, Floors, Wood Cross Members, etc.—See Section 320-11 for conductors passing through these points. Also, when conductors pass through cross members in plastered partitions, the conductors must be protected by a nonabsorbent, noncombustible, insulating tube. These tubes shall extend not less than 3 inches beyond the wood member.

324-10. Clearance from Piping, Exposed Conductors, etc.—The same conditions of Section 320-12 are applicable to knob-and-tube wiring. See Figures 320-8 through 320-11.

324-11. Unfinished Attics and Roof Spaces—Conductors in unfinished attics and roof spaces shall comply with the following:

Accessible by Stairway or Permanent Ladder. Conductors in unfinished attics and roof spaces shall be run through or on the sides of joists, studs and rafters, except in attics and roof spaces having head room at all points of not less than 3 feet in buildings completed before the wiring was installed. See Fig. 324-1.

Where conductors in accessible unfinished attics or roof spaces reached by stairway or permanent ladder are run through bored holes in the floor joists or through bored holes in the studs or rafters within 7 feet of the floor or floor joists, such conductors shall be protected by substantial running boards extending 1 inch on each side of the conductors and securely fastened in place. See Fig. 324-2.

Where carried along the sides of rafters, studs or floor joists, neither running boards or guard strips will be required.

Exception: An exception covers buildings being wired after completion that have head room at all points of less than 3 feet.

Fig. 324-1. Running conductors in attics.

RUNNING BOARD
ONE INCH OVER
EACH SIDE

Fig. 324-2. Protection by running boards in attics accessible by stairs or permanent ladder.

324-12. Splices—Splices under strain or in-line are not permitted. Where splices are permitted, they may be soldered (do not use acid core when soldering), or other approved splicing means may be used.

324-13. Boxes—See Article 370 for outlet boxes.

324-14. Switches—See Sections 380-4 and 380-10 (b) for switches that shall comply with this type of wiring.

ARTICLE 325—INTEGRATED GAS SPACER CABLE
Type IGS

A. General

325-1. Definitions—See your *NEC*.

325-2. Other Articles—Other articles in this Code, as well as this article covering IGS cable, shall apply.

325-3. Uses Permitted—IGS-type cable may be used in a number of places such as underground, including direct burial in the earth, and it may also be used in service entrance conductors as well as feeder or branch-circuit conductors.

325-4. Uses Not Permitted—This type of cable shall not be used in direct contact with the building when exposed.

B. Installation

325-11. Bending Radius—Where the nonmetallic conduit is coilable and the cable is bent for any purpose such as shipping or installation, the radius is measured to the inside of the bend, and in no case shall the radius be less than that shown in Table 325-11.
See the *NEC* for Table 325-11, Minimum Radii of Bends.

325-12. Bends—For bends made in IGS cable run between two pull boxes, the total of the bends shall not exceed four 90-degree bends or the equivalent (360 degrees total). This includes bends that may need to be made immediately at terminations and pull boxes.

325-13. Fittings—Since IGS cable is to be under pressure from an inert gas, the fittings shall be approved as suitable for maintaining this pressure within the conduit. There shall be a valve and cap inserted in each length of the cable for checking pressure and adding insert gas to maintain the pressure in the conduit.

325-14. Ampacity—Table 325-14 gives sizes of cables and ampacities for IGS cable for both single conductor or multiple conductor cables. See the *NEC* for Table 325-14, Ampacity Type IGS.

C. Construction Specifications

325-20. Conductors—Solid aluminum rods shall be used as conductors—if they are laid parallel—and may consist of up to 19 rods each of ½ inch diameter.

The maximum size of the conductors together shall not be over 1750 MCM or smaller than 250 MCM.

325-21. Insulation—The insulation is composed of dry kraft paper tapes, which shall be pressurized by sulfur hexafluoride gas (SF_6), and both the paper and the gas shall be approved for electrical use. The pressure of the gas between the taped conductors and the outer nonmetallic conduit shall be 20 pounds per square inch gage (psig) (138 kPagage).

In the *NEC* the thickness of the paper is specified in Table 325-21. See the *NEC* for Table 325-21.

325-22. Conduit—Approved medium-density polyethylene conduit that has been identified for use with natural gas rated pipe may be used in 2-inch, 3-inch, or 4-inch trade sizes. See Table 325-22 in the *NEC* for the percent fill for the conduit.

Table 1, Chapter 9, may be used for calculating for the percent fill, which is not to exceed amount determined in this table.

325-23. Grounding—See Article 250 for grounding-type IGS.

325-24. Marking—See Section 310-11 for the requirements of marking that apply to IGS cable.

ARTICLE 326—MEDIUM VOLTAGE CABLE
Type MV

326-1. Definition—Type MV cable stands for medium voltage. It may be multiconductor or single conductor that is a solid dielectric cable. The insulation rating of MV cable is 2001 volts or higher.

Later in this article you will find this covers Type MV cable rated up to 35,000 volts.

326-2. Other Articles—By necessity to conform to other Code requirements, this article on Type MV cable must also meet other requirements in the Code, especially Articles 300, 305, 310, 318, 501, and 710.

326-3. Uses Permitted—Type MV cable is permitted for many purposes: It can be used for up to 35,000 volts, nominal, for power systems. It may also be used in wet or dry locations, or in raceways or cable trays. This part is covered in Section 318-2(b): It may be used for direct burial if installed as per Section 710-3 (b), and it may also be used in messenger-supported systems.

326-4. Uses Not Permitted—This type of cable shall not be used when exposed to direct sunlight unless specifically identified for that purpose. Unless as specified in Section 318-2(b), it shall not be used in cable trays.

326-5. Construction—Copper, aluminum, or copper-clad aluminum conductors are permitted to be used in MV cable, and the construction shall conform with Article 310.

326-6. Ampacity—Section 310-15 gives the allowable ampacity when Type MV cable is used.

Exception: In Section 318-13, when Type MV cable is installed in cable trays.

326-7. Marking—As with many other cables, the marking on Type MV shall conform to Section 310-11.

ARTICLE 328—FLAT CONDUCTOR CABLE
Type FCC
A. General

328-1. Scope—This article covers cable and the necessary associated accessories, which will be defined in this article. This cable was designed for use under carpet squares.

328-2. Definitions.

Type FCC Cable. Take note of the fact that the conductors are flat and are to be only of copper. Three or more flat copper conductors, which are placed edge to edge and entirely enclosed with an assembly of insulation, make up FCC cable.

FCC System. FCC systems are designed for complete branch circuits, which, as we stated, are to be installed under carpet squares. FCC systems are to be complete with all the necessary fittings, including associated shielding, the connector terminals, adapters, and receptacles that are designed only for this type FCC cable. Standard fittings, etc., are not to be used. All of the items must be properly identified for the purpose for which they are used.

Courtesy The Wiremold Company

Fig. 328-1. Fantom Flex™ Undercarpet Wiring System, illustrating receptacles, top shield, and Flatwire™ Cable with carpet tile in place.

Cable Connector. FCC cable is designed for use where installations join connectors without using junction boxes.

Insulated End. The ends of FCC cable shall have an insulator for the ends designed for the purpose.

Top Shield. The circuit components of an FCC system are required to have a grounded metal shield that covers the flat under-carpet conductors. This is for protection against physical damage.

Bottom Shield. Protective layer installation must be made between the flat conductor cable and the floor. This may or may not be an integral part of the cable; it is required for protection from physical damage.

Transition Assembly. There shall be approved assembly for the connection of the FCC to other approved types of wiring. This may be an approved means of making the interconnection, or it may be a box or covering that will provide electrical safety and protect all conductors from physical damage.

Metal Shield Connections. See your *NEC*.

328-3. Other Articles—Other articles that may be applicable include some of the provisions of Articles 210, 220, 240, 250, and 300.

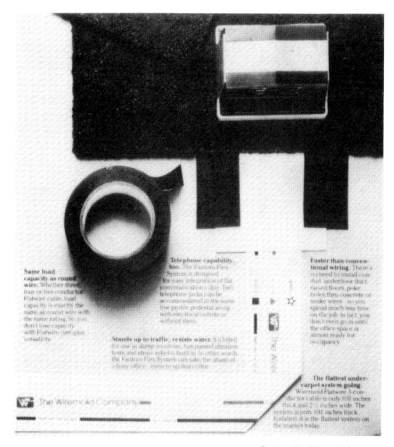

Fig. 328-2. Fantom Flex™ Undercarpet Wiring System.

328-4. Uses Permitted.

(a) **Branch Circuits.** Type FCC installations may be used with individual branch circuits for general purpose and appliance branch circuits.

(b) **Floors.** FCC cable is permitted to be used on floors that are of sound construction and smooth. The continuous floor surface may be made of many different materials, such as ceramic, concrete, wood, or composition flooring, or other similar materials.

(c) **Walls.** If metal surface raceways are used on walls, Type FCC systems will be permitted.

(d) **Damp Locations.** Since rugs are sometimes cleaned with a liquid cleaner, type FCC systems must be approved for damp locations.

(e) **Heated Floors.** If floors are heated in excess of 30° C (86° F), the material used for the heated floors must be identified as being suitable for use at these temperatures.

328-5. Uses Not Permitted—FCC systems shall not be used in the following places: They are not to be installed out of doors, where they will be in wet locations; wherever subject to corrosive vapors; in hazardous (classified) locations; or in residences, hospitals, or schools.

328-6. Branch-Circuit Ratings.

(a) **Voltage** . Ungrounded conductors used in FCC installations shall not be permitted to be over 300 volts between the ungrounded conductors, and not over 150 volts between the ungrounded conductor and the grounded conductor.

(b) **Current.** Individual branch circuits may be rated up to 30 amperes for appliance and general purpose circuits. FCC installations shall not exceed 20 amperes.

B. Installation

328-10 Coverings—The FCC-type insulation, including all parts on the floor, shall be covered by carpet squares that are not larger than 3 feet square. These squares shall have adhesive to hold them down, and this shall be a release type of adhesive.

328-11. Cable Connections and Insulating Ends—All of the FCC cable shall use connectors that are identified for this use. The installation shall have electrical continuity insulation and dampness sealing from spilled liquids; it is up to the installer to see that all of these are provided. Also, the cable ends must be throughly sealed against dampness and spilled liquids. Only listed insulation ends are to be used.

328-12. Shields.

(a) **Top Shield.** See the definition at the beginning of this article in this book. Same as below. Refer to Section 328-3 and you will find that Article 250 is mentioned; this article covers grounding.

(b) **Bottom Shield.** See the definition in Section 328-3.

328-13. Enclosure and Shield Connections—The equipment grounding conductor of the supply branch circuit shall be electrically connected to all shields, boxes, receptacle housings, and self-contained devices. Identified connectors only shall be used for making this electrical continuity. In this electrical equipment grounding that is required, the electrical resistivity of the sealed system shall not be more than the electrical resistivity of one of the regular conductors used in the installation of Type FCC cable.

Here, again, grounding of the shield is mentioned, as in Section 328-12. To properly check the resistivity of the shielding and compare it with the resistivity of one conductor will require a very-low-reading ohmmeter, or ducter.

328-14. Receptacles—All receptacles, including the receptacle housing and self-contained devices that are used in the installation of any FCC system, shall be positively identified for the purpose you are using them for. A good connection shall be made to the Type FCC cable and metal shields. At each receptacle, a connection to the grounding conductor of Type FCC cable shall be made to the grounded shielding at each receptacle.

328-15. Connection to Other Systems—The transition system for connecting the FCC system to other systems where they originate shall be only a system identified for this purpose only.

328-16. Anchoring—For anchoring the FCC system to the floor, adhesive or mechanical anchoring may be used, but it shall be identified for this purpose. The floors shall be in such shape that the FCC system will be firmly anchored to the floor until the carpet squares are properly in place.

328-17. Crossings—Two FCC-type cable runs shall be permitted to be crossed. If the FCC-type system crosses over or under flat telephone cables they shall be permitted, but a grounded-type shielding shall separate the telephone and the FCC-type system.

328-18. System Height—Tapering or feathering at the edges of FCC systems is required if the height above the floor level exceeds 0.090 inches (2.29 mm).

328-19. FCC Systems Alterations—Alterations in FCC systems may be made. Added cable connectors may be used at new connection points if alterations are needed. It shall be permissible to leave unused portions of the FCC-type system in place and they may still be energized, but all cable ends shall be covered with insulation ends.

328-20. Polarized Connections—All connections and receptacles must be installed so that the polarization of the system is maintained.

C. Construction

328-30. Type FCC Cable—Only approved Type FCC cables shall be used when they are approved for use with FCC systems. They may consist of three, four, or five flat copper conductors. One of these shall be the equipment grounding conductor. Only moisture-resistant and flame-retardant insulation shall be used.

For Sections 328-31, Markings; 328-32, Conductor Identification; 328-33, Corrosion-Resistance; 328-24, Insulation; 328-35, Shields; 328-36, Receptacles and Housings; and 328-37, Transition Assemblies, refer to the *NEC*.

ARTICLE 330—MINERAL-INSULATED METAL-SHEATHED CABLE

Type MI

A. General

330-1. Definition—Mineral-insulated, metal-sheathed Type MI cable is composed of one or more conductors insulated by a highly compressed refractory mineral insulation and enclosed in a gastight metal-tube sheath.

The highly compressed refractory mineral insulation is magnesium oxide powder. The conductors are normally copper. MI cable is also made up into a heating cable in which the outside or sheath is a seamless phosphorized copper tubing. As a word of explanation, magnesium oxide is the material used in many range burners as the insulation in the tube elements to enclose and insulate the nichrome elements from the outer sheath of the units (see Fig. 330-1). It is required that MI cable be used only with approved fittings for terminating and connecting boxes, outlets, etc. (see Fig. 330-2).

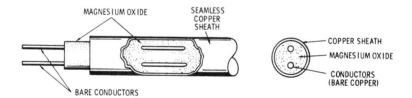

Fig. 330-1.   Construction of MI cable.

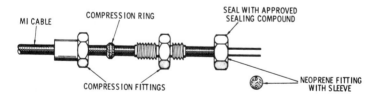

Fig. 330-2.   Fittings for MI cable.

330-2. Other Articles—As with other wiring materials, Type MI cable must comply not only with this article, but also with the provisions of Article 300 in the Code.

330-3. Uses Permitted—Mineral-insulated metal-sheathed MI cable may be used for: (1) services, (2) feeders, (3) branch circuits, (4) open wiring (exposed), (5) concealed wiring, and (6) wet locations.

MI cable may be used in practically all locations except that, if used in a highly corrosive location (such as cinder fill), it shall be protected. It may be used for all of the following: (1) all hazardous areas: Class I, Class II, and Class III locations; (2) under plaster extensions; (3) embedded in plaster finish; (4) on brick or masonry; (5) exposed to weather or continuous moisture; (6) embedded in concrete or fill; (7) buildings under construction; (8) exposed to oils and gasoline; and (9) any other location that will not have a deteriorating effect on the copper sheath.

The following is not a part of the Code, but it is felt that it should be mentioned here as a precaution in the installation of MI cable: Magnesium oxide will draw some moisture when exposed to the air. Therefore, when the cable is cut, the end should be taped. When using a piece of MI cable, about 6 inches should be cut off from the end, or start back from the cut end a couple of feet and heat it with a torch, working toward the cut end, thus driving any moisture out of the cable. See Fig. 330-3. The temperature to which the cable may be heated is limited only by the melting point of the sheath. In Article 310 it is mentioned that MI cable is 90° C cable. This will not prevent the use of a torch in driving out the moisture, however.

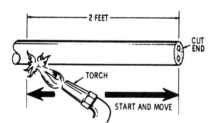

Fig. 330-3. One method of driving out moisture.

330-4. Uses Not Permitted—Where it will be exposed to destructive and corrosive conditions, MI cable may not be used.

Exception: If the MI cable is made of material suitable for the condition.

Exception: Fished-in MI cable.

B. Installation

330-10. Wet Locations—Reference is made to Section 300-6(c), which gives the precautions that must be taken on corrosive locations.

330-11. Through Studs, Joists and Rafters—Reference is made to Section 300-4, permits notching, providing a steel plate of not less than ¹⁄₁₆ inch is provided so as to give protection from nails.

330-12. Supports—Mineral-insulate d metal-sheathed cable shall be securely supported by approved staples, straps, hangers or similar fitting, so designed and installed as not to injure the cable. Cable shall be secured at intervals not exceeding 6 feet (1.83 m) except where cable is fished. Please note the term "approved." Consideration must always be given to electrolysis which is ever present between dissimilar metals.

330-13. Bends—All bends shall be so made that the cable will not be damaged and the radius of the curve of the inner edge of any bend shall be not less than five times the diameter of the cable. See Fig. 330-4.

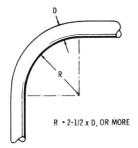

R = 2-1/2 x D, OR MORE

Fig. 330-4. Radius of bends.

330-14. Fittings—Identified fittings shall be used with MI cable for the conditions of service. Type MI cable of single conductor must be used when entering metal boxes, as outlined in Section 300-20, to prevent induced currents from causing heating.

330-15. Terminal Seal—Where MI cable is terminated, approved seals shall be used. Refer to Fig. 330-2. These seals have a compression ring and fittings similar to those used on copper tubing. In addition, there is a neoprene bushing which slips into these fittings and is sealed with an epoxy resin, after which a neoprene bushing with holes for the conductors and the sleeves is inserted. This sealing should be done immediately after stripping or heating so as to prevent the entrance of any moisture. The bare conductors are of course insulated with sleeving, the color of which must be correct for the particular use of the conductor.

MI cable of the heating type is often used for ice and snow melting. When used for these purposes, an insulation tester (Megger®) test should be made to check the insulation resistance of the conductors to the metal shield to see that proper insulation values are maintained. The same test should be run after the cable is embedded in the concrete slab. A case in point found small holes in the metal sheath which permitted moisture to enter the cable. The concrete had to be removed and new cable installed because the installation would be worthless.

C. Construction Specifications

Note: The Code does not specify the sizes that are available in MI cable, and so the following information is included for the reader's convenience:

Cable	Size Available
Single-conductor	No. 16–4/0
Two-conductor	No. 16–No. 4
Three-conductor	No. 16–No. 4
Four-conductor	No. 16–No. 6
Seven-conductor	No. 16–No. 10

Remember that No. 14 wire is the smallest allowable under the Code for general wiring; smaller sizes may be used for low-voltage thermostat wiring, as permitted. There is also MI low-energy cable rated at 300 volts available in two-, three-, four-, and seven-conductor cable, but a check should be made to be certain that this low-energy cable has been tested by UL.

Mention was also made of heating cable. This is not considered a wiring cable, and so it would have to be tested by UL for the purpose to which it is to be used.

330-20. Conductors—Only copper conductors are to be used in MI cable, and they shall be of standard AWG sizes.

330-21. Insulation—The insulation between the conductors and the MI cable must be highly compressed, of a refractory mineral, and provided with proper spacing of the cables.

330-22. Outer Sheath—Copper is used for the outer sheath and shall be of continuous construction, provide mechanical protection, provide moisture seal, and the sheath will be used for grounding purposes, but an adequate continuous path must be maintained.

ARTICLE 331—ELECTRICAL NONMETALLIC TUBING
A. General

331-1. Definition—See your *NEC*.

331-2. Other Articles—Other articles in the Code will apply where appropriate for the installation of electrical nonmetallic tubing. For instance, numerous parts of Article 300 will apply, and since the tubing is nonmetallic it cannot be used as equipment grounding conductor, so equipment grounding conductor as required in Article 250 will have to be installed in the raceways with the circuit conductors.

331-3. Uses Permitted—The uses for electrical nonmetallic tubing are listed below:

(1) It may be used in walls, ceilings, and floors provided that there is a thermal barrier that is composed of material that will have a minimum of a 15 minute rating for finish and is identified in listings of fire rated material.

Exception: It may be installed above suspended ceilings if the material of the ceiling is at least ½ inch gypsum board or equivalent to ½ inch gypsum that is a thermal barrier.

(2) In places such as those covered in Section 300-6, where such places or locations may be subjected to severe corrosive influence. This is where the material of the electrical nonmetallic cable has been specifically approved.

(3) If not prohibited by Section 331-4, it may be used in concealed dry and damp locations.

(4) This type of conduit may be used above suspended ceilings—if this ceiling is provided with a thermal barrier material with at least a 15 minute rating listing of fire rated assemblies.

(5) If fittings are identified for embedding in concrete, flexible nonmetallic tubing may be installed in poured concrete.

Note: Flexible metallic tubing is susceptible to extreme cold temperatures, and at these low temperatures it becomes brittle. For this reason it will become more vulnerable to physical damage, especially during installation.

331-4. Uses Not Permitted—The following (in your *NEC*) covers where nonmetallic electrical tubing is not permitted to be used. It will be more appropriate in covering these seven nonpermitted usages to refer your *NEC*.

Exception: If suspended ceilings consist of at least ½ gypsum board or the equivalent, you may install nonmetallic electrical tubing above installations.

B. Installation

331-5. Size.

(a) **Minimum.** Tubing shall not be smaller than ½-inch electrical trade size.

(b) **Maximum.** Tubing shall not be larger than 1-inch electrical trade size.

331-6. Number of Conductors in Tubing—Table 1, Chapter 9 in the *NEC* will govern the percentage of fill of conductors in nonmetallic flexible conduit.

331-7. Trimming—All cut edges, both inside and outside, shall be trimmed to eliminate rough edges.

331-8. Joints—Only approved fittings, couplings, and boxes shall be used by approved methods.

331-9. Bends—How Made—The radius of the bends in the internal side of the bend shall not be less than covered in Table 346-10 for rigid metal conduit. Also, bends in nonmetallic electrical tubing shall be made so as not to reduce the internal diameter of the tubing. No special tools are required for bending; they are made by hand.

331-10. Bends—Number in One Run—The number of bends between outlet and outlet or outlet and fitting shall be the same as for rigid metal conduit, that is, 360 degrees maximum total, including bends located immediately at outlets or fittings.

331-11. Supports—Nonmetallic electrical tubing installation—the tubing shall be fully installed before pulling wires, and it shall be fastened within 3 feet of any box, junction box, etc., where the ends terminate. Elsewhere the tubing shall be secured every 3 feet.

331-12. Boxes and Fittings—Applicable provisions of Article 370 shall be required for all boxes and fittings.

331-13. Splices and Taps—See Article 370. Splices shall never be made within the tubing, but only at junction boxes, outlet boxes, or conduit boxes.

331-14. Bushings—Where the tubing enters boxes, etc., bushings are required to protect the wiring from abrasion. If the design of the box or fitting is such as to prevent abrasion to the wiring bushings, it will not be required.

Note: It is suggested that you refer to Section 373-6 (c) for the protection required with No. 4 AWG or larger.

C. Construction Specifications

331-15. General—See the *NEC*.

ARTICLE 333—ARMORED CABLE
Type AC

Prior to the 1978 *NEC*, Types MC and AC series were included together in Article 334. They have been separated into two articles, namely, Article 333, which covers Type AC cable, and Article 334, which now covers Type

MC cable. It was felt that an incomplete coverage of the two types of cables were given, and so it was referred to CMP 20. The results are that Article 333 now covers Type AC cable and Article 334 covers Type MC cable.

333-1. Definition—Type AC cable is a flexible metallic enclosure with circuit conductors installed at the time of manufacturing. The *NEC* refers you to Section 333-4.

333-2. Other Articles—Type AC cable of course is subject to other Articles of the *NEC*, but more especially to Article 300.

333-3. Marking—Marking shall be required as described in Section 310-11. The maker of the AC cable must be distinctively marked on the cable sheath throughout its entire length.

333-4. Construction—AC cable is to be approved. It has an acceptable extra metal covering, and insulated conductors inside the metal covering are required to conform with Section 333-5.

AC cable is to be used for branch circuits and feeders. The armor must be flexible metal tape. AC cable shall have a bonding strip that touches the outer flexible metal covering for the full length. This is not required on ACL, which has lead-covered AC cable. Where the bonding strip is required in regular AC cable, it shall make good contact with the outer sheath for the full length.

333-5. Conductors—The type of conductors permitted in AC cable are listed in Table 310-13. If not listed there, they must be identified for use in AC cable. Around all the conductors in the cable a moisture-resistant and fire-retardant covering is to be applied. This is a fibrous-type covering. The ampacity of the conductors will be determined by Section 310-15. If the cable is Type ACT, moisture-resistant fibrous covering shall be wrapped around each conductor.

Exception: See your *NEC*.

333-6. Use.

(a) **Uses Permitted.** Unless otherwise specified in the *NEC* and if not subject to physical damage, Type AC cable shall be permitted in both exposed and concealed work for both branch circuits and feeders. Type AC cable may be used for underplaster extensions (Article 344) or embedded in plaster that is applied to brick or other masonry, provided these are not wet locations. It may be run or fished in air voids of masonry block and tile walls; where such walls are exposed or subject to excessive moisture or dampness or below grade line, Type ACL cable shall be used. Type ACL (cable with lead covered conductors) shall be used when exposed to weather, continuous moisture, exposed to oil, for underground runs in raceways, embedded in masonry or concrete or in fill in buildings under construction and elsewhere where conditions may cause the insulation to deteriorate.

(b) **Uses Not Permitted.** The Code prohibits the use of AC cable in certain other places. Seven prohibited places are shown in the *NEC*. Refer to the *NEC* for these seven.

Exception: There is an exception in Class 1 hazardous areas in Section 501-4(b).

ACL is not permitted for direct burial in the earth.

333-7. Supports—AC Type cable shall be secured at intervals not to exceed 4½ feet and within 12 inches of a box or fitting, except where fished and except that the 12 inches may be extended to not over 24 inches at terminals where there is a necessity for flexibility. See the *NEC* for another exception.

333-8. Bends—For Type AC cable, the bends radius is taken from the inner edge of the bend and shall be not less than five times the diameter of the cable.

333-9. Boxes and Fittings.

(a) Approved fittings suitable for Type AC cable shall be used at all terminals where Type AC cable is used.

(b) For Type AC cable, approved fittings to prevent abrasion of the conductors and their insulation shall be used. In addition to this, an approved insulating bushing is required to be inserted at the end between the conductors and the outer metallic covering. The connection to the fitting or box must be so designed that the insulated bushing will be visible for inspection without removing the fitting. This is an excellent requirement, because it seems that in the haste of installation this bushing is so often overlooked, and it is a vital spot for a breakdown in the insulation. The insulated bushing is not required where a lead covering is used on the conductors, such as ACL type. Any splices or connections to other raceways must be in approved junction boxes.

333-10. Through Studs, Joists, and Rafters—The same protection must be taken as outlined in Section 300-4 to protect the cable from being punctured by nails, etc.

333-11. Exposed Work—The cable on exposed work shall follow the surface of the building finish or of running boards. Please remember the limitations on bends and do not try to form the cable to a right angle as this would damage the cable. The provisions of Section 333-7 also apply.

333-12. In Accessible Attics—Where run across the top of floor joists or within 7 feet of the floor, or floor joists across the face of rafters or studding in the attics and roof spaces that are accessible, the cables are to be protected by substantial guard strips that are as high as the thickness of the cable. Where such spaces are only accessible by scuttle holes, or the equivalent, protection will be required within 6 feet of the scuttle hole. Where cable is run along the sides of rafters, studs, or floor joists, the guard strips or running boards will not be required. This may sound like a lot of extra work for space that will probably not be used. Remember though that plans change. The attic may become a storage space or room, in which case damage to the cable may result and the work will have to be redone.

ARTICLE 334—METAL-CLAD CABLE
Type MC
A. General

334-1. Definition—MC cable is factory-produced and is composed of one or more conductors, each of which is individually insulated. These insulators are enclosed within a metal enclosure or interlocking tape, or a smooth or corrugated tube.

334-2. Other Articles—Metal-clad cable, of course, is subject to any other applicable provisions of the Code, but more especially to Article 300. See Section 300-2(a). Type MC cable is permitted on systems over 600 volts, nominal.

334-3. Uses Permitted—Unless otherwise specified in this Code, and if not subject to physical damage, the following uses for Type MC cable are permitted:

(1) branch circuits, feeders, and services;

(2) for signal circuits, control circuits, and power and lighting;

(3) indoors or outdoors;

(4) when concealed or exposed;

(5) if identified for the use, may be used for direct burial;

(6) installed in cable trays;

(7) it may be installed in any approved raceway;

(8) for open runs of cable;

(9) on messenger cable as an aerial conductor;

(10) as provided in Article 501, 502, and 503 in hazardous (classified) locations;

(11) in dry locations;

(12) if any of the following conditions are met, it may be installed in wet locations:

(a) The metallic covering will not be damaged by moisture.

(b) A water-resistant lead covering is applied under the metallic covering.

(c) The insulation of the conductors is approved for wet locations.

Exception: You are refered by the *NEC* to Section 501-4(b), Exception.

Note: Section 300-6 covers corrosion protection.

Note: The conditions that must be met in (12) above must also apply to (5) above.

334-4. Uses Not Permitted—MC cable shall not be used where corrosive conditions exist. Some of the corrosive conditions are: direct burial in earth, causing electrolysis of the metal sheath or cinder fills, which will consume the metal sheath rather rapidly. Some of the corrosive chemicals are hydrochloric acid, chlorine vapor, strong chlorides, and caustic alkalis.

Exception: If the metal sheath is proved capable of withstanding any of the above corrosive vapors, etc., it may be made of material suitable for the conditions.

It leaves much up to the inspection authority to judge if the material is suitable for the conditions.

B. Installation

334-10. Installation—If applicable, MC cable must be installed to comply with Articles 300, 710, and 725.

(a) **Support.** The intervals of support of MC cable shall not exceed 6 feet.

(b) **Cable Tray.** Cable tray installations shall comply with Article 318.

(c) **Direct Buried.** As appropriate with Sections 300-5 or 710-3, direct buried cable shall comply with these sections.

(d) **Installed as Service-Entrance Cable.** Compliance with Article 230 must be met when MC cable is used for service-entrance cable.

(e) **Installed Outside of Buildings or as Aerial Cable.** Installation of MC cable shall comply with Articles 225 and 321, if installed outdoors or on aerial cables.

334-11. Bending Radius—Bends in MC cable must be made so the cable is not damaged. The radius of the curve of the inside bend shall not be less than is shown below:

(a) **Smooth Sheath.**

(1) MC cable not more than ¾ inch in diameter shall have a bending radius of a minimum of 10 times the diameter of the cable.

(2) For MC cable more than ¾ inch in diameter but not more than 1½ inches in diameter, the bending radius shall be a minimum of 12 times the diameter of the cable.

(3) For MC cable more than 1½ inches in diameter the bending radius shall be a minimum of 15 times the diameter of the cable.

(b) **Interlocked-type Armor or Corrugated Sheath.** The bending radius shall not be less than seven times the diameter of the cable, measured for the radius from the inside of the cable.

(c) **Shielded Conductors.** Bending radius may be twelve times the diameter of one of the individual conductors, or the bending radius seven times the diameter of the multiconductor cable, including the sheath. Whichever one of the two gives the larger bending radius shall be used.

334-12. Fittings—All fittings shall be identified for use in connecting Type MC cable to boxes, cabinets, etc. If single conductor cables enter ferrous metal boxes or cabinets, Section 300-20 shall be complied with to prevent inductive heating. The author questions this where single conductor cables are prohibited in other places in the Code.

334-13. Ampacity—The ampacity of Type MC cable is controlled by Section 310-15.

Exception: Type MC Cables ampacities installed in cable trays are required to be in conformance with Section 318-11 and 318-13.

Note: Temperature limitations of the ampacity of the conductors will be found in Section 310-10.

C. Construction Specifications

Refer to the NEC, Sections 334-20 through 334-24.

ARTICLE 336—NONMETALLIC-SHEATHED CABLE
Types NM and NMC
A. General.

By definition, a nonmetallic-sheathed cable is an assembly of two or more conductors having an outer sheath of moisture-resistant, flame-resistant, nonmetallic material. This is commonly known as Romex.

Nonmetallic-sheathed cable shall be of an approved type. This type of cable is available in sizes from No. 14 to and including No. 2. The No. 2

was an addition in the 1962 Code. This cable may have an uninsulated conductor or a green insulated conductor for equipment grounding purposes in addition to the current-carrying conductors. Table 250-95 in the NEC lists the size of this grounding conductor in reference to the current-carrying conductors.

Type NM cable is the type most commonly used, especially in residential occupancies, but there is an NMC type that has an overall covering that is not only flame-retardant and moisture-resistant, but also fungus-retardant and corrosion-resistant.

There must be a distinctive marking on the exterior of the cable for its entire length that specifies cable type and the name of the manufacturing company. The box in which the cable is packaged will have the UL listing, if any, on it. NM cable is also made in No. 12 through No. 2 sizes for aluminum conductor.

336-2. Other Articles—As with most types of wiring installation, NM and NMC cables, where applicable, shall comply with other parts of this Code, with special reference to Article 300 and 310.

336-3. Uses Permitted—Unless not permitted in Section 336-4, Type NM and NMC cable is permitted to be used in one and two family dwellings and other structures.

Note: Section 310-10 covers temperature limitations for the conductors in NM and NMC cable.

Nonmetallic cable may be used for the following:

(a) **Type NM.** Type NM cable may be used for: concealed or exposed installation; installed or fished in the hollow voids of masonry or tile walls that are not exposed to excessive moisture or dampness; or installed in voids in masonry block or tile walls where such walls are not exposed or subject to excess moisture or dampness.

(b) **Type NMC.** Moisture-and corrosion-resistant Type NMC cable may be used for both exposed and concealed work in dry, moist, damp, or corrosive locations; and in outside or inside walls of masonry block or tile.

336-4. Uses Not Permitted.

(a) **Type NM or NMC.** The uses not permitted include: service-entrance cables, in commercial garages, in theaters and assembly halls (except as provided in Article 518), in motion-picture studios, in storage-battery rooms, in hoistways, in hazardous locations, or embedded in poured cement, concrete, or aggregate.

(b) **Type NM.** Type NM cable may not be used where exposed to corrosive vapors or fumes; embedded in masonry, concrete, fill, or plaster; run in shallow chase in masonry or concrete and covered with plaster or similar finish; for direct burial; in adobe or similar finish.

In the next article, it will be seen that service-entrance cable cannot be used for feeders under certain conditions. However, NM and NMC cable may be used for this purpose, and this was apparently the intent of increasing the size of conductors to No. 2.

B. Installation

336-10. Exposed Work—General—In exposed work, except as provided in Sections 336-12 and 336-13, the cable is to be installed as follows: It shall follow the surface of the building finish or of running boards. It shall be protected from physical damage where necessary by conduit, intermediate metal conduit, pipe, guard strips, or other satisfactory means, and when passing through a floor, it shall be protected by conduit or pipe to a minimum height of 6 inches above the floor.

336-11. Through Studs, Joists, and Rafters—See Section 300-4.

336-12. In Unfinished Basements—If the cable is run at an angle with joists in unfinished basements, assemblies not smaller than two No. 6 or three No. 8 conductors may be fastened directly to the lower edges of the joists. Small assemblies shall be either run through bored holes or on running boards. Cables of any size that are run parallel to the joists may be attached to the sides of the joists or to the face.

336-13. In Accessible Attics—Where run across the top of floor joists, or within 7 feet of the floor, or floor joists across the face of rafters or studding in attics and roof spaces that are accessible, the cables are to be protected by substantial guard strips that are as high as the thickness of the cable. Where such spaces are only accessible by scuttle holes, or the equivalent, protection will be required for any cable within 6 feet of the scuttle hole. Where the cable is run along the sides of rafters, studs, or floor joists, the guard strips or running boards are not required.

This may sound like a lot of extra work for space that will probably not be used. Remember, however, that plans change. The attic may become a storage space or room, in which case damage to the cable may result and the work will have to be redone. See Section 333-12.

336-14. Bends—All bends are to be made so as not to damage the cable or its protective covering, but no bend shall have a radius of less than five times the diameter of the cable.

336-15. Supports—Approved staples, straps, or other fittings shall be used to support nonmetallic-sheathed cable, and shall be so designed and installed so as to not cause damage to the cable. Too often it is the last blow of the hammer that should never be given. Inspectors find much insulation damaged in this fashion. It is also easy to use a nail bent over to secure a cable. This should never be tolerated.

Cables shall be secured at intervals not exceeding 4½ feet and within 12 inches of the box or fitting, except that in concealed work in finished buildings or finished panels of prefabricated buildings, it may be fished into the walls.

Exception No. 1: The cable may be fished between accessible points where installed as concealed, worked in finished panels or when the buildings are prefabricated. You can see that fastening would be impractical.

Exception No. 2: Some fitting devices are identified for installation of NM or NMC cable without outlet boxes. They are equipped with the cable clamp. The cable must be secured in place at intervals not exceeding 4 ½ feet and within 12 inches of this device. There shall also be an unbroken loop of cable 6 inches or more that will become available on the interior side of a finished wall, to provide extra cable if replacements are made and some of the conductors may be broken at the device.

336-16. Devices of Insulating Materials—For exposed work, concealed work for rewiring existing buildings where the cable is concealed or fished, switch, outlet, and tap devices made of insulating materials may be used without the use of boxes if approved types make a close fit around the outer covering of the cable and fully cover the part from which the outer covering has been removed. Also, there shall be one terminal screw for each conductor, or a type of connector that is approved for multiple conductor connections.

336-17. Boxes of Insulating Materials—Nonmetallic outlet boxes are approved for nonmetallic cable and provision for their use is made in Section 370-3.

336-18. Devices with Integral Enclosures—Section 300-15(b), Exception No. 5, covered devices with integral enclosures. This is for use, and they shall be permitted.

C. Construction Specifications.

336-25. Construction—For most of this, see the *NEC*. In copper of small sizes No. 14 AWG and for copper-clad aluminum of small sizes No. 12 AWG, there shall be a equipment grounding conductor in these cables. It may be bare or insulated.

(a) **Type NM.** NM cable is to be flame-retardant and moisture-resistant.

(b) **Type NMC.** With NMC cable the overall covering shall be flame-retardant, moisture-resistant, fungus-resistant, and corrosion-resistant.

336-26. Conductors— The conductors used in these cables are to be of types listed in Table 310-13, where they are suitable for branch-circuit wiring. Other types are permitted if identified for use in the cables.

Although the conductors in the cable shall have a rating of 90°C (194°F), the ampacity of NM and NMC cables shall be rated only at 60°C (140°F), and Section 310-15 shall be complied with.

336-27. Marking—Not only shall these cables meet the provisions of Section 310-11, but the marking on the exterior of the cable sheath shall be for its entire length indicating the cable type.

ARTICLE 337—SHIELDED NONMETALLIC-SHEATHED CABLE
Type SNM

337-1. Definition—See your *NEC*.

337-2. Other Articles—As with many other wiring materials, the installation of SNM cable shall comply with some of the provisions of Articles 300, 318, 501, and 502.

337-3. Uses Permitted—Type SNM cable is permitted for the following uses: In areas where the operating temperature of the cable is maintained at or below the temperature marked on the cable; in cable trays and raceways such as conduit, etc., and in hazardous (classified) locations if it is permitted to be used in these locations in Articles 500 through 517.

Note: The conductors have temperature limitations. These are covered in Section 310-10.

337-4. Bends—The bends shall have a radius from the inner surface of the bend of not less than five times the diameter of the cable. We should also observe the installation of this cable to be sure that it is made without physical damage to either the covering or the cable itself.

337-5. Handling—SNM cable shall be handled, so as not to damage in any way the cable or its covering.

337-6. Fittings—Only fittings that are identified for use with SNM cable for connecting it to enclosures are to be used.
The most practical way that I know of to determine whether fittings are approved or not is to look for listing in the UL books.

337-7. Bonding—The wire shielding shall be properly bonded to frames or enclosures of equipment supplied by this cable, and to the ground bus or other connection at the source of the power supply. Identified fittings were mentioned in Section 337-6. These shall be used, or other methods in Section 501-16(a) approved in the Code for bonding in these sections.

337-8. Construction—The types of conductor insulation for Type SNM cable shall be TFN, TFFN, THHN, or THWN, and they shall come in sizes No. 18 AWG through No. 2 AWG of copper. If aluminum or copper-clad aluminum conductors are used, they shall be No. 12 AWG to No. 2 AWG. Mixing of conductor cable sizes in an individual cable is allowed. The spiraling metal tape shall have overlapping. The shielding wires shall have a total cross-sectional area as required for equipment grounding conductors in Article 250, and shall be not less in size than the largest circuit conductor in the cable.

The outer jacket shall be suitable for mounting these cables in cable trays. The outer jacket shall also be water-, oil-, flame-, corrosion-, fungus-, and sunlight-resistant.

337-9. Marking—Type SNM cable shall meet the general marking that was required in Section 310-11. This marking shall be distinctive on the external surface for the entire length, and shall indicate its type and the maximum temperature at which it will be operated.

Each conductor shall have a marking giving numbers to the conductors on both sides of each conductor (180 degrees apart), and shall be marked every 6 inches. The numbering of the conductors identifies them at each end.

ARTICLE 338—SERVICE-ENTRANCE CABLE
Types SE and USE

There has been considerable misuse of service-entrance cables. It will be attempted here to bring out some of these abuses so that one may secure a better understanding of the uses for which service-entrance cable is intended.

338-1. Definition—Service-entrance cable may be a single conductor or a multiconductor assembly. It is usually supplied with an outer covering, but it may be supplied without the covering. Its primary use is for services. The following are the different types:

(a) **Type SE.** A flame-retardant and moisture-resistant covering is required in Type SE cable. This may be one of two types—one with a bare neutral conductor and the other with all conductors insulated and with or without a grounding conductor for the purpose of grounding equipment. This is mentioned because it is very important as one will see in the following information.

Type SE cable has no inherent mechanical protection against abuse. Therefore, it may be necessary to provide mechanical protection should the Code-enforcing authority require it.

(b) **Type USE.** This is a direct burial cable and is recognized for use underground. The insulation of the USE shall be moisture-resistant, but not flame-retardant. It is intended that USE cable be a conductor assembly provided with a suitable overall covering. This brings up the point of single conductors that might be marked "RHW-USE." Most certainly if the Code enforcing authority approves these conductors for direct burial, they will demand that they be buried side by side and possibly require other provisions in the installation of same, such as mechanical protection. If the conductors are marked USE they are identified for use underground for direct burial.

Single-conductor-type USE cable, which has been recognized for underground use, may have bare copper conductor cabled with it in the assembly. If USE is single-conductor paralleled or cabled conductors recognized for underground burial, a bare copper conductor applied may be. These constructions are not required to have an outer overall cover.

Note: The *NEC* refers us to Section 230-41, Exception (b).

(c) **One Uninsulated Conductor.** When USE cable or SE cable consists of two or more insulated conductors, they are permitted to have a bare conductor. This is wrapped around the insulated conductors, and it will serve as a neutral conductor.

338-2. Uses Permitted as Service-Entrance Conductors—When SE cable is used for service-entrance conductors, the requirements of Article 230 shall be adhered to.

SE cable was primarily used for service-entrances, but has other uses as will be covered in the next Section. It is not a cure-all, but does have definite uses. Check with your inspector for lengths permitted for service entrances.

338-3. Uses Permitted as Branch Circuits or Feeders

(a) **Grounded Conductor Insulated.** SE cables are permitted to be used for branch circuits and feeder on interior wiring, where all of the circuit conductors of the cable are of rubber-covered or thermoplastic type. Where an equipment grounding conductor is required, it may be a bare conductor in the cable.

(b) **Grounded Conductor Not Insulated.** SE cable without individual insulation on the grounded circuit conductor shall not be used for branch circuits or feeders within buildings, except a cable that has a final nonmetallic covering and is supplied by alternating current at not over 150 volts to ground shall be permitted: (1) As a branch circuit to supply only a range, wall-mounted oven, counter-mounted cooking top, or clothes dryer as covered in Section 250-60. Its use in feeder panels will not be permitted; this is covered in Section 250-60. (2) As a feeder to supply only other buildings on the same premises. When it is used for this purpose, care must be taken to properly ground the other buildings as required by Article 250. See Figs. 338-1, 338-2, 338-3, 338-4, and 338-5.

SE cable is allowed for interior use when the fully insulated conductors are used for circuit wiring and the uninsulated conductor is used for equipment grounding only.

(c) **Temperature Limitations.** When service-entrance cable is used to supply appliances, it shall not be used where the temperatures are higher than that specified for the specific insulation in the SE cable.

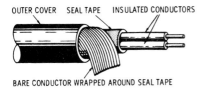

Fig. 338-1. SE cable with bare neutral.

Fig. 338-2. SE cable with all insulated conductors.

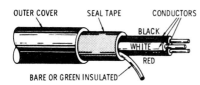

Fig. 338-3. SE cable with insulated conductors and equipment grounding conductor.

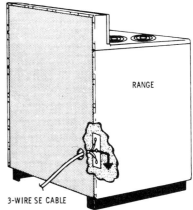

Fig. 338-4. SE cable for ranges and dryers.

ONE CONDUCTOR BARE FOR NEUTRAL WHICH MAY BE USED FOR EQUIPMENT GROUND IF NO. 10 OR LARGER

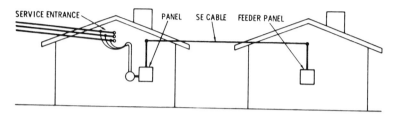

Fig. 338-5. SE cable for feeder or branch circuit to other buildings on the same premises.

338-4. Installation Methods—As with other wiring methods, the installation of this type of cable must not only conform to provisions of this Article, but also to any applicable provision of Article 300. Unarmored cable shall be installed in the same manner as the nonmetallic-sheathed cable requirements in Article 336. Also, if run through or notched into studs, joists, or rafters, protection shall be given from nails, etc., as per Article 300.

338-5. Marking—Marking of cables and of conductors was covered in Section 310-11. This marking will include manufacturer's name, type of cable, size of conductors in the cable, and an indication if the cable contains a derated neutral. See Fig. 338-6. If the neutral conductor is smaller than the ungrounded conductor, the cable shall be so marked.

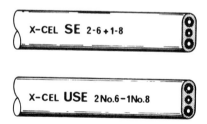

Fig. 338-6. Marking of SE cable.

ARTICLE 339—UNDERGROUND FEEDER AND BRANCH-CIRCUIT CABLE
Type UF

339-1. Description and Marking—This is a cable that is used for underground branch circuits and feeders. It is not to be confused with USE which is a direct burial cable for services. UF is not to be used for services. Approved UF cable comes in conductor sizes from No. 14 copper or No. 12 aluminum through No. 4/0. The conductors within the outer sheath may be TW, RHW, etc., which is identified for this use. Over the conductors and their insulation is placed an outer covering which shall be flame-retardant, moisture-resistant, fungus-resistant, and corrosive-resistant—this outer covering shall be suitable for direct burial in the earth. UF cable may also carry a bare or insulated conductor to be used for an equipment-grounding conductor, providing that it is the proper size.

In addition to the provisions of the insulation, as provided for in Section 310-11, the outer covering shall have distinctive markings along its entire length showing the size of conductors, number of conductors, whether with ground or not, and have the UF marking.

339-2. Other Articles—The provisions of this article not only apply to the use and installation of UF cable, but the provisions covering general wiring methods in Article 300 apply as well in the uses of the insulation as outlined in Section 310-13 and Article 200.

339-3. Uses.

(a) **Uses Permitted.**

(1) UF cable may be used as a direct burial cable for branch circuits and feeders, if installed properly and the conductor sizes are protected by proper overcurrent devices and if all other conditions as outlined are met. It will be well to refer to Section 300-5, which states: When this cable is installed under a building, it is required to be encased in a raceway, and this raceway shall extend through the floor and outside the building. Your attention should be called to the fact that any raceway that is installed or buried in the earth will be subject to electrolysis, unless this was taken into consideration.

(2) UF single-conductor cables may be installed for feeders, subfeeders, and branch circuits, including the neutral. However, they shall be run together in the same trench or raceway. In mentioning the neutral, be assured that in no case will a bare neutral be permitted in direct burial. Also, in running these circuits, in practically every case, and equipment ground will have to be used and one must remember that bare equipment grounding conductors are not permitted for direct burial.

Exception: Refer to the *NEC* Section 690-31 for solar photovoltaic systems.

(3) The Code stipulates a minimum of 24-inch burial unless the conductors or cable are protected by a covering board, concrete pad, raceway, etc. It will also be found that many Code-enforcing authorities will require, in addition to the 24-inch burial (and especially in rocky ground), the protection of a sand bed and covering for the cable. This is easy to understand, for in frost areas, rocks may damage the insulation of the cable. The enforcing authority has the right to require this, as all work shall be done

in a proper and workmanlike manner. See Section 300-5 for UF cable buried underground.

(4) The use of UF cable for interior wiring is not prohibited provided that it meets the requirements of the Code. If used as nonmetallic-sheathed cable, Article 336 will apply. It is very common practice to use UF cable in concrete-block walls (especially basement walls) instead of NMC cable, as it will stand any dampness that is present. When used for interior wiring, UF cable shall consist of multiple conductors, unless it is to be used for nonheating leads of heat cable as allowed in Section 424-43.

Exception: Section 424-43 permits us to use a single conductor UF cable as the nonheating leads at the ends of heat cable. See Section 690-31 when used with solar photovoltaic systems.

When cable trays are used to support UF cable, the cable shall be of a multiconductor type.

Note: Section 310-10 covers temperature limitations for the conductors in UF cable.

(b) **Uses Not Permitted.** There are a number of places where UF cable is not permitted to be used, such as service-entrance cable, theaters, commercial garages, motion picture studios, rooms having storage batteries, in hazardous (classified) locations, and in hoistways, and it shall never be embedded in poured concrete or aggregate (it is, however, permitted to be used as a nonheating lead as covered in Article 424, where it may be embedded in plaster); and it shall not be used in sunlight, unless specifically listed for such use.

Exception: See the *NEC* Section 501-4(b), Exception. This section covers Class I hazardous areas.

339-4. Overcurrent Protection—UF cable must have proper over-current protection as provided in Section 240-3.

339-5. Ampacity—UF cable ampacity is rated according to Table 310-16. The derating notes accompanying these tables shall be used as with any other current-carrying conductor.

ARTICLE 340—POWER AND CONTROL TRAY CABLE Type TC

340-1. Definition—See your *NEC*.

340-2. Other Articles—Again, other articles may apply in addition to this, especially Articles 300 and 318.

340-3. Construction—The following covers Type TC tray cable:
(1) Insulated conductors shall be sizes 18 AWG through 1000 MCM copper; sizes 12 AWG through 1000 MCM aluminum or copper-clad aluminum.

(2) Insulation: Insulated conductors (copper) in sizes 14 AWG and larger and (aluminum) sizes 12 AWG and larger. (This includes copper-clad aluminum) shall have insulation of one of the types listed in Table 310-13. The insulation must be suitable for branch-circuit and feeder conductors. Insulated conductors of size 18 and 16 AWG copper shall be in accordance with Article 726-16.

(3) The outer sheath shall be a flame-retardant, nonmetallic material. Where installed in wet locations, type TC cable shall be resistant to moisture and corrosive agents.

340-4. Use Permitted—Type TC cable is permitted to be used where lighting and power, control and signal, and communication circuits may be used in cable trays and raceways outdoors, where supported by messenger wire. In some cases it may be used as stated above in hazardous (classified) areas; these will be covered in Articles 318 and 501, and they will be for industrial establishments in which maintenance is done only by qualified persons when installing and servicing the installations. It may be used in Class I locations, which will be covered in Article 725.

Note: The temperature limitations of TC cable comes under Section 310-10.

340-5. Uses Not Permitted—Cable tray for TC cable will not be installed where it will be subject to physical damage. It cannot be mounted on cleats or brackets in an attempt to use it for open wiring, which is prohibited. It must be listed for exposure to direct sunlight, if used in such a location. Direct burial is not permitted unless the TC cable is specifically listed for that use.

340-6. Marking—Section 310-11 applies to the marking of TC cable.

340-7. Ampacity—If the TC tray cable is smaller than No. 14 AWG, its ampacity will be covered in Sections 400-5 and 318-11.

ARTICLE 342—NONMETALLIC EXTENSIONS

342-1. Definitions—See your *NEC*.
This is a wiring method that is intended for specific purposes, mainly that of extensions either on the surface or in the form of an aerial cable assembly. Reference to Fig. 342-1 will give an idea of its construction and will facilitate its application. This illustration shows a cross section and how it is mounted on the surface.

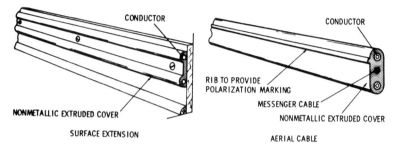

Fig. 342-1. Cross-sectional view of nonmetallic surface extension cable and nonmetallic aerial cable.

342-2. Other Article—Not only do the provisions of this article apply to nonmetallic extensions, but as with other wiring methods, any other applicable provisions of the Code will also apply.

342-3. Use Permitted—The use of nonmetallic extensions is permitted where the following conditions are met:

(a) **From an Existing Current.** These extensions are only permitted from existing 15- to 20-ampere branch circuits that meet all of the requirements in Article 210.

(b) **Exposed and in Dry Locations.** The extension is never to be run concealed and must always be used in dry locations.

(c) **Nonmetallic Surface Extensions.** Nonmetallic surface extensions shall not exceed the height limits specified in Section 336-4(a). They may be used in residential areas or in offices.

(c1) **[Alternate to (c)]** Aerial cable is to be used for industrial purposes where flexibility is required for connecting equipment. It is not intended for use in offices and residences.

Note: Temperature limitations for nonmetallic surface extensions are covered in Section 310-10.

Fig. 342-2 illustrates the use of nonmetallic surface extensions. Fig. 342-3 illustrates the use of aerial nonmetallic cable with fluorescent lighting.

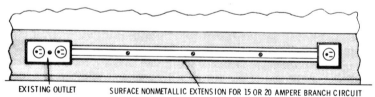

Fig. 342-2. Purpose of nonmetallic surface extensions.

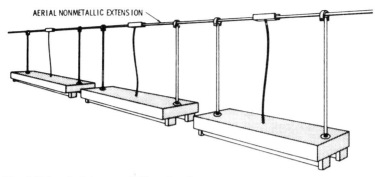

AERIAL NONMETALLIC EXTENSION

Fig. 342-3. Aerial nonmetallic extension.

342-4. Uses Not Permitted—The following are places where nonmetallic surface cable cannot be used:

(a) **Aerial Cable.** This method of wiring is not intended to be used as aerial cable to take the place of other approved methods as provided by the Code.

(b) **Unfinished Areas.** They are never to be used in unfinished basements, attics, or roof spaces, but are intended for use only in finished places and must be exposed.

(c) **Voltage between Conductors.** The maximum voltage shall not exceed 150 volts between conductors for nonmetallic surface extensions and shall not exceed 300 volts between conductors for aerial cables.

(d) **Corrosive Vapors.** They shall not be used where subject to corrosive vapors.

(e) **Through a Floor or Partition.** They are to be installed only within the room in which they originate and are not to be run through walls, floors, or partitions.

342-5. Splices and Taps—Nonmetallic extensions shall be continuous, unbroken lengths. There shall be no splices and no exposed conductors between fittings. If approved coverings are used, taps may be permitted. If used as aerial cable, and approved material is installed for making taps, provision must be made for polarization of the conductors. Taps of the receptacle type shall be provided with locking-type devices, rather than the ordinary receptacle device. Refer to Fig. 342-1, which shows a rib on the aerial cable for polarization. Taps other than by means of devices approved for this purpose are prohibited.

342-6. Fittings—The fittings and devices used with this method of wiring are to be of a type identified for the use and each run shall be terminated so that the end of the assembly is covered and no bare conductors exposed.

342-7. Installation—Nonmetallic extensions shall be installed in conformity with the following requirements:

(a) **Nonmetallic Surface Extensions.**

(1) One, or more than one, extension may be run in any direction from the existing outlet from which it is supplied. This will not apply to extensions run on the floor or within 2 inches of the floor.

(2) Nonmetallic surface extensions shall be secured in place by approved means at intervals not exceeding 8 inches, except that where connection to the supplying outlet is made by means of an attachment plug the first fastening may be placed 12 inches or less from the plug. There shall be at least one fastening between each two adjacent outlets supplied. An extension shall be attached only to woodwork or plaster finish, and shall not be in contact with any metal work or other conductive material except with metal plates on receptacles. See Fig. 342-5.

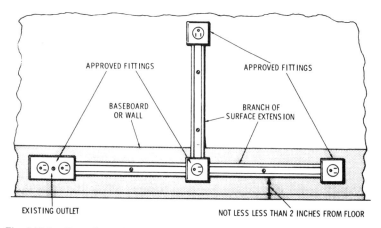

APPROVED FITTINGS   APPROVED FITTINGS

BASEBOARD
OR WALL

BRANCH OF
SURFACE EXTENSION

EXISTING OUTLET   NOT LESS LESS THAN 2 INCHES FROM FLOOR

Fig. 342-4. Branches of nonmetallic surface extensions and clearance.

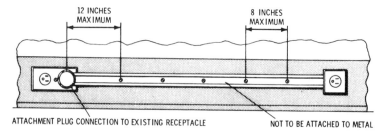

12 INCHES
MAXIMUM

8 INCHES
MAXIMUM

ATTACHMENT PLUG CONNECTION TO EXISTING RECEPTACLE   NOT TO BE ATTACHED TO METAL

Fig. 342-5. Supporting distances for nonmetallic surface extensions.

(3) A cap shall be furnished to protect the assembly from physical damage when bends reduce the normal spacing of conductors.

(b) **Aerial Cable.**

(1) Aerial cable shall be supported by the messenger cable in the assembly, and not by the conductors or insulation. The messenger cable is to be fastened securely at both ends by means of approved cable clamps and turnbuckles for taking up any sag in the assembly. If the span is over 20 feet, the assembly shall be supported by approved hangers at intervals not to exceed 20 feet. The cable shall be so suspended as to eliminate excessive sag and shall clear any metal by a minimum of 2 inches. The assembly is not to contact any metal and the messenger cable is to take the strain of supporting the assembly with added supports as required.

(2) Aerial cable shall have a minimum height of 10 feet above areas of pedestrian traffic only and a minimum height of 14 feet above vehicular traffic. See Fig. 342-7.

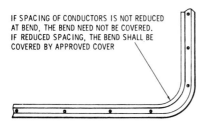

IF SPACING OF CONDUCTORS IS NOT REDUCED AT BEND, THE BEND NEED NOT BE COVERED. IF REDUCED SPACING, THE BEND SHALL BE COVERED BY APPROVED COVER

Fig. 342-6. Bends in nonmetallic surface extensions.

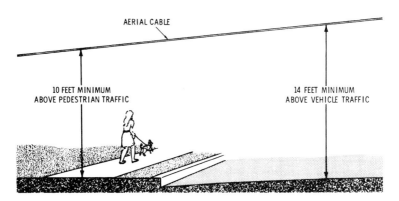

AERIAL CABLE

10 FEET MINIMUM ABOVE PEDESTRIAN TRAFFIC

14 FEET MINIMUM ABOVE VEHICLE TRAFFIC

Fig. 342-7. Clearances above floors for aerial nonmetallic surface extensions.

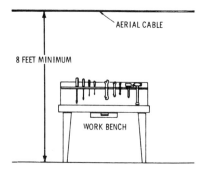

AERIAL CABLE

8 FEET MINIMUM

WORK BENCH

Fig. 342-8. Clearances above workbenches for aerial nonmetallic extensions.

(3) Cable assemblies that are over workbenches, but not over vehicular or pedestrian traffic areas, may have a minimum height of 8 feet. See Fig. 342-8.

(4) Where the strength of the messenger cable is not exceeded, it may also serve to support lighting fixtures. The supporting capabilities of the assembly may be found by contacting the manufacturer for specifications.

(5) If the supporting messenger cable meets the requirement of Article 250 for grounding conductors for grounding of equipment, it may be used for this purpose if all provisions covering same in Article 250 are met, but under no condition is to be used as a grounded or hot conductor of a branch circuit.

342-8. Marking—The *NEC* refers us to Section 110-21.

ARTICLE 344—UNDERPLASTER EXTENSIONS

344-1. Use—It is sometimes necessary to make an extension to an existing receptacle (or similar device) or other branch circuits. This article covers these extensions. They are to be installed only in fire-resistive buildings, such as brick, concrete block, and masonry. It is not necessary to cover extensions in frame buildings as they are covered under other articles of the Code.

344-2. Materials—Underplaster extensions may be run in most of the metallic conduit or tubing, nonmetallic conduit or tubing, Type MI cable, type MC cable, or other metal-raceways. For details of all types covered here, see this Section in your *NEC*.

The cable and raceways shall all be standard size.

Exception: See your *NEC*.

344-3. Box and Fittings—The same provisions that apply to boxes and fittings in Article 370 apply to underplaster extensions.

344-4. Installation—Underplaster extensions are to be laid on the face of masonry or other subsurface material and buried in the plaster finish. The provisions of other articles in the Code which cover the specific material or wiring method to be used will apply in the installation of underplaster extensions.

344-5. Extensions to Another Floor—If an underplaster extension extends from the origin to a floor, it shall be encased for going through the floor and to a point high enough above the floor to protect it from physical damage. Rigid metal conduit, intermediate metallic conduit, EMT, or Type AC or MI cables shall be used for protection against damage.

ARTICLE 345—INTERMEDIATE METAL CONDUIT
A. General

345-1. Definition—This is a metal conduit—similar to rigid metal conduit—that may be threaded and fitted with approved fittings.

345-2. Other Articles—For installations not specifically outlined in this article, Article 300 is to be used.

345-3. Uses Permitted.

(a) **All Atmospheric Conditions and Occupancies.** Use of intermediate metal conduit shall: (1) be permitted under all atmospheric conditions; (2) be permitted in all occupancies; (3) where practicable, dissimilar metals in contact anywhere in the system shall be avoided to eliminate the possibility of galvanic action; (4) be permitted to be used as an equipment grounding conductor. See Section 250-91.

Exception: The Code permits aluminum fittings and enclosures to be used with steel intermediate metal conduit. The author prefers to use steel alone because, in the electrolysis series, steel is more noble than aluminum, and therefore, if any electrolysis takes place, the steel will affect the aluminum.

(b) **Corrosion Protection.** Unless made of material judged suitable for the condition, or unless corrosion protection is provided. Intermediate metal conduit, elbows, couplings, and fittings may be installed in concrete in direct contact with the earth, or in areas subject to severe corrosive influence, but the conduit, etc., shall be protected by corrosion protection if judged protection is suitable for prevailing conditions.

This places considerable responsibility on the inspector to use discretionary powers in its enforcement. It is recommended that if in doubt, the inspection authority be contacted for a decision before installation.

Note: The Code refers you to Section 300-6 for protection against corrosion.

(c) **Cinder Fill.** Cinder fill causes considerable corrosion, therefore, unless intermediate metal conduit is of corrosion-resistant material which will withstand this corrosive condition, it shall not be buried under or in cinder fill unless protected by a noncinder concrete covering of a minimum of 2 inches thickness, or unless it is buried a minimum of 18 inches below the fill. See Figs. 346-1 and 346-2 in the next article. See Section 300-6.

B. Installation

345-5. Wet Locations—All means of support shall be made of corrosion-resistant materials. Referral is made to Section 300-6, which requires ¼ inch air space between the wiring system, including boxes and fitting in damp or wet locations.

Also note that the above requires that screws and bolts used in the installation shall be corrosion-resistant or plated by corrosion-resistant materials. This prohibits the use of common steel nails, screws, and bolts in these locations. Galvanized ¼ inch spacers may be purchased for the purpose of giving the ¼ inch air space required. Common steel washers are not permitted as they are not coated with corrosion-resistant material.

345-6. Size—The minimum size of intermediate metal conduit which is permitted to be used is ½ inch, and the maximum size is 4 inches.

345-7. Number of Conductors in Conduit—Table 1, Chapter 9 will be used for the percentage fill for conductors. Conduit dimensions appear in Table 4, Chapter 9.

345-8. Reaming and Threading—Cut ends of intermediate conduit shall have the inside smoothed by reaming or other satisfactory means, removing all the rough edges to prevent abrasion of conductor insulation. With threaded intermediate metal conduit, taper dies shall be used. See your *NEC* for additional information.

345-9. Couplings and Connectors—This is the same as Section 346-9 in the next article.

345-10. Bends—How Made—This is the same as Section 346-10 of the next article.

345-11. Bends—Number in One Run—This is the same as Section 346-10 of the next article and is covered by Fig. 346-3. See Tables 346-10 and 346-10, Exception.

345-12. Support—As in Article 300, intermediate metal conduit is to be installed and fastened securely in place as a complete system before pulling in conductors. The first fastening from an outlet or junction box shall be not over 3 feet; other support shall be not less than 10 feet apart.

Exception No. 1: If threaded couplings are used in straight runs of intermediate conduit, they shall comply with Table 346-12. This is to be used only at stresses at terminations where the conduit is deflected between supports.

Exception No. 2: If the conduit is made up of threaded couplings and firmly supported at the top and bottom of the vertical run, and if no other visible means of supporting the rigid intermediate conduit is available, you will be permitted to supply supports for the conduit that are not to exceed 20 feet in a vertical run.

345-13. Boxes and Fittings—See the *NEC.*

345-14. Splices and Taps—Splices shall be made only in junction outlet boxes and conduit bodies; there shall be none in the conduit. Article 370 will supplement this.

345-15. Bushings—This is the same as Section 346-8 of the next article. See Section 373-6 for the protection of conductors at bushings.

C. Construction Specifications

345-16. General—Intermediate metal conduit shall comply with the following:

(a) **Standard Lengths.** Standard length in intermediate metal conduit is 10 feet. If specific conditions require it, lengths longer than 10 feet may be shipped with or without couplings.

(b) **Corrosion-Resistant Material.** Intermediate metal conduit that is made of noncorrosive materials or corrosive-resistant materials shall be suitably marked.

(c) **Marking.** This conduit shall be plainly marked at 2 ⅜-feet intervals with the letters "IMC." It shall also be marked as was covered in the first sentence in Section 110-21.

The above construction specifications are quite important to assist the inspection authority in identifying the conduit and to provide assurance that it has approved labeling.

ARTICLE 346—RIGID METAL CONDUIT

346-1. Use—Rigid conduit is the old standby in wiring methods. It may be used in all atmospheric conditions and occupancies, but there are some provisions that cover its use. Ferrous conduit and fittings that have enamel protection from corrosion can only be used indoors and even then shall not be subject to severe corrosive influences. Where practical, ferrous conduit shall be used with ferrous fittings, and nonferrous conduit shall be used with fittings of similar material. This is to avoid galvanic action between the dissimilar metals.

Exception: Steel rigid metal conduit may be permitted to be used with aluminum fittings and enclosures. Also, aluminum rigid metal conduit may be used with steel fittings and enclosures.

Unless made of a material judged suitable for the condition, or unless corrosion protection approved for the condition is provided, ferrous or nonferrous metallic conduit, elbows, couplings, and fittings shall not be installed in concrete or in direct contact with the earth, or in areas subject to severe corrosive influences. This places considerable responsibility upon the inspector to use discretionary powers in its enforcement. It is recommended that, if in doubt, the inspection authority be contacted for a decision before installation. The following item was brought to my attention: A 6-inch galvanized rigid metal conduit was installed in direct contact with the earth in a temporary wiring situation during construction on an industrial building. Less than one year later this conduit was removed, and the portion in contact with the earth was all but eaten away. This can be prevented; rigid steel conduit is now available with a heavy nonmetallic coating that makes it practically noncorrosive.

Note: See Section 300-6, where rigid metal conduit is solely protected by enamel. Conduits, fittings, etc., (solely protected by enamel) are not to be used outdoors or in locations judged corrosive or damp.

Please also refer to Section 346-1 in the Code.

346-2. Other Articles—This article covers many installation problems for rigid metal conduit. However, some of them will be applicable to the provisions found in Article 300.

A. Installation

346-3. Cinder Fill—Cinder fill causes considerable corrosion. Therefore, unless conduit is of a corrosion-resistant material which will withstand this corrosive condition, it shall not be buried under or in cinder fill unless protected by a noncinder concrete covering of a minimum of 2 inches thickness, or unless it is buried a minimum of 18 inches below the fill. See Figs. 346-1 and 346-2.

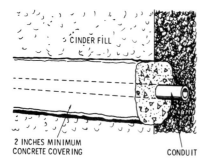

CINDER FILL

2 INCHES MINIMUM
CONCRETE COVERING

CONDUIT

Fig. 346-1. Concrete covering for conduit under cinder fill.

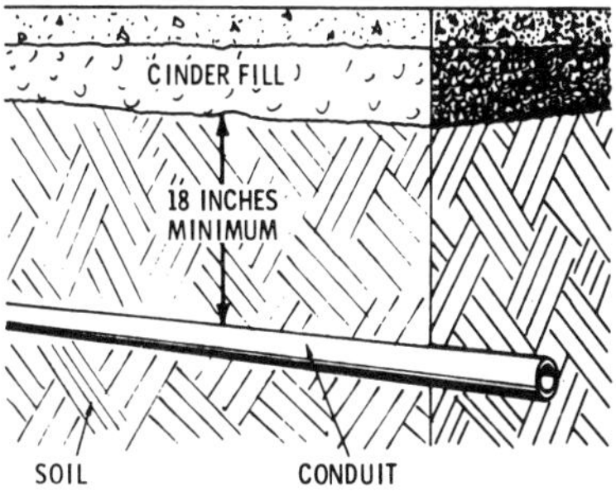

Fig. 346-2. No concrete is required if buried a minimum of 18 inches below cinder fill.

346-4. Wet Locations—All means of support of rigid metal conduit, including bolts, straps, or screws, etc., shall either be protected from corrosion or be of a noncorrosive material.

Referral is made to Section 300-6, which requires a ¼-inch air space between the wiring system, including boxes and fittings in damp or wet locations. Also note that the above requires that screws and bolts used in the installation shall be corrosion-resistant or plated by a corrosion-resistant material. This prohibits the use of common steel nails, screws, and bolts in these locations. Galvanized ¼-inch spacers may be purchased for the purpose of giving the ¼-inch air space required—common steel washers are not permitted as they are not coated with corrosion-resistant material.

346-5. Minimum Size—For practical purposes, ½-inch trade-size rigid conduit is the smallest allowable. However, for underplaster extensions, conduit with a minimum inside diameter of ⁵⁄₁₆ inch is permitted in some cases, and ⅜-inch conduit is permitted in some cases listed in Section 430-145(b).

346-6. Number of Conductors in Conduit—Conduit fill of conductors shall not exceed the fills given in Table 1 of Chapter 9.

346-7. Reaming and Threading.

(a) **Reamed.** All ends of this conduit shall be carefully reamed to remove rough edges that might damage the conductors.

(b) **Threaded.** The die you should use to thread rigid metal conduit is required to have a ¾-inch taper per foot.

Where conduit is threaded in the field, it is assumed that a standard conduit cutting die providing ¾-inch taper per foot will be employed. It must be kept in mind that conduit couplings are different from water-pipe couplings—conduit couplings have no taper in the threads inside the coupling, whereas pipe couplings do have.

346-8. Bushings—Bushings are required on conduits wherever they enter boxes or fittings to protect the wire from abrasion, unless the design of the box or fitting is such that it provides an equivalent protection. Section 373-6(c) requires insulated bushings where No. 4 or larger conductors are used. This may be an insulated bushing, a fiber insert for a metal bushing (provided that it is an approved insert), or it may be a grounding-type bushing which is a combination of metal and insulation, where grounding bushings are required, or the approved fiber insert may be used with a grounding type of bushing.

346-9. Couplings and Connectors.

(a) **Threadless.** Threadless couplings and connectors shall be made tight to insure electrical continuity. Concrete-type fittings only shall be used when rigid metal conduit is buried in concrete, and if it is in wet locations the fittings are required to be of the raintight type. They, or the box they are contained in, will contain the listed marking of the testing laboratory.

(b) **Running Threads.** It was common years ago to use running threads in place of conduit-type unions. For those not familiar with running thread, it is made by threading a piece of the conduit for a considerable length so that a coupling can be screwed down on the running thread, then screwed back to the conduit you are trying to connect to. This is not done now. There is no taper to running threads—all of the thread is the same size throughout its length, tending to make a loose fit. In addition, there is no corrosion-resistant covering on the threaded portion.

346-10. Bends—How Made—Conduit may be bent, but it shall be done in such a way as not to damage the conduit nor reduce its internal diameter. Conduit is often kinked while being bent. Installation of kinked conduit is not permitted, as the internal diameter will be reduced, making the pulling of conductors increasingly difficult and making damage to the insulation more probable. Torches have been used to heat conduit to facilitate the bending, but this will damage the galvanizing or other protective coating and is not permitted.

Table 346-10 lists the minimum radius of the inside bend allowed for various sizes of conduit. Factory ells will have a shorter radius than those listed, but this is permissible as they are approved items.

There is an exception on bends, which we have not had before. This is the permitting of bends of less radius than permitted by Table 336-10, provided that a one-shot bender is used and that it is the type approved for this purpose. Also Table 346-10, Exception has been added to cover these bends.

346-11. Bends—Number in One Run—There is a limit of four 90 degree bends, or the equivalent of 360 degrees between outlet and outlet, between fitting and fitting, or between outlet and fitting. This is to control the number of bends so that pulling of conductors is not made too difficult. See Fig. 346-3.

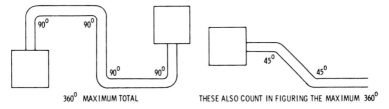

360° MAXIMUM TOTAL   THESE ALSO COUNT IN FIGURING THE MAXIMUM 360°

Fig. 346-3. A maximum of 360 degrees allowed between outlets and/or fittings.

There are times with large conductors that a total of 360 degree bends will be too much. These may be calculated. In these cases damage may be caused to the insulation of the conductors. This is an engineering problem and also up to the authority having jurisdiction.

See the *NEC*, Tables 346-10, and 346-10, Exception.

346-12. Supports—This section was a new addition to the 1965 Code. Rigid metal conduit shall be installed as a complete system as provided in Article 300 and shall be securely fastened in place. Conduit shall be firmly fastened within 3 feet of each outlet box, junction box, cabinet, or fitting. Conduit shall be supported at least every ten feet except that straight runs of rigid conduit made up with approved threaded couplings may be secured in accordance with Table 346-12, provided such fastening prevents transmission of stresses to terminus when conduit is deflected between supports.

On vertical risers from machine tools and the like, the distance between supports may be increased to 20 feet. There are restrictions: (1) the conduit must be provided with threaded couplings; (2) the conduit is firmly attached at the top and the bottom; (3) there is no other means of intermediate support readily available.

See the *NEC*, Table 346-12.

346-13. Boxes and Fittings—See Article 370.

346-14. Splices and Taps—This is the same as Section 345-14 in the preceding article, so need not be repeated. Also see Article 370.

B. Construction Specifications

346-15. General—The requirements of this section are very plain. The requirements of this section are covered in (a) through (d) below:

(a) **Standard Lengths.** Rigid metal conduit is shipped in 10-foot lengths. One coupling is furnished with each length, and it shall come with threads on each end and be properly reamed. If longer lengths are required, the conduit may be ordered in lengths longer than 10 feet with or without couplings or threads. Steel conduit shall have an inferior coating of a character and appearance so as to readily distinguish it from ordinary pipe commonly used for other than electrical purposes. Greater care must be exercised in applying the interior coating on conduit in order that no abrasion to the insulation will result.

(b) **Corrosion-Resistant Material.** If the conduit is of nonferrous corrosion-resistant material, it shall be plainly marked to indicate this.

(c) **Durably Identified.** Each length of rigid metal conduit shall be identified every 10 feet. This also refers to Section 110-12. This is highly important so that it will be easy to identify what type of rigid conduit is being used.

ARTICLE 347—RIGID NONMETALLIC CONDUIT

The use of rigid nonmetallic conduit first became a part of the *NEC* in the 1962 edition, with a number of changes made in the 1965 edition.

347-1. Description—See your *NEC*.

Note: Nonmetallic conduit may be made of a number of different materials. You are refered to the fine-print note after "Description" in the *NEC*.

If in doubt about the application of rigid nonmetallic conduit, it is well to check the UL listings for which the particular type intended to be used is applicable.

347-2. Uses Permitted—The use of rigid nonmetallic conduit and fittings follows, but be sure that the type you are using is listed for the following conditions. Some of the types listed in the fine-print note in the section above are permitted only for certain conditions.

Note: Some nonmetallic conduit becomes very brittle in cold, which would cause it to be more easily damaged.

(a) **Concealed.** Concealed wiring in walls, floors, and ceilings of buildings or structures is permitted.

(b) **Corrosive Influences.** Section 300-6 covers locations that are severely corrosive. Therefore, use the type of rigid nonmetallic conduit that is approved for the specific chemicals in the specific corrosive atmosphere.

(c) **Cinders.** Cinders have corrosive influences; nonmetallic conduit is permitted to be used under cinders where specifically approved.

(d) **Wet Locations.** Dairies, laundries, canneries, etc., are wet locations, requiring frequent washing. For such places, the entire system, including conduits, boxes, and fittings, shall be installed so as to prevent water from entering the conduit system. Straps, bolts, screws, etc., shall be made only of materials that are proved resistant to corrosion.

(e) **Dry and Damp Locations.** Section 347-3 permits installation in dry or damp locations.

(f) **Exposed.** If they will not be subject to physical damage, they may be used for exposed wiring installation when they are approved for exposure.

(g) **Underground Installations.** Referral is made to Sections 300-5 and 710-3(b), where installation of rigid nonmetallic conduit is made underground.

347-3. Uses Not Permitted—Rigid nonmetallic conduit is not permitted to be used in the following:

(a) **Hazardous (Classified) Locations.** In all hazardous (classified) locations except those covered in Sections 514-8 and 515-5. There is an exception to this in Class 1, Division 2 locations as found in the exception to Section 501-4(b). Article 514 covers Gasoline Dispensing and Service Stations. In Section 514-8, rigid metal conduit or, where buried not less than 2 feet in the earth, nonmetallic rigid conduit may be installed. When nonmetallic rigid conduit is installed, there shall be an equipment-grounding conductor installed, conforming in size to Table 250-95, for the purpose of grounding the metal non-current-carrying parts of any equipment. The use of rigid nonmetallic conduit in this type of location will not change the use of seal-offs, as covered elsewhere in Article 514. Also see Section 515-5. See Fig. 347-1.

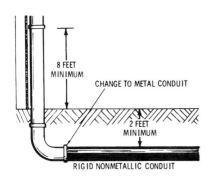

Fig. 347-1. Running nonmetallic conduit above ground. PVC may be run above-ground if approved for the purpose and not subject to physical damage.

(b) **Support of Fixtures.** Rigid nonmetallic conduit shall not be used for supporting fixtures and any other equipment.

(c) **Physical Damage.** It shall not be used unless identified for locations where subject to physical damage.

(d) **Ambient Temperatures.** It shall not be used where subject to ambient temperatures higher that it is approved for.

(e) **Insulation Temperature Limitations.** If the conductor limitations are higher than the temperature limitations for which the conduit is approved, it shall not be used.

347-4. Other Articles—As with all wiring methods, Article 300, covering General Wiring Methods, is always referred to. Where Article 250 requires an equipment grounding conductor, one shall be installed.

A. Installations

347-5. Trimming—Trimming and smoothing the inside and outside of ends to remove rough edges is required. This is for the same reason that rigid metal conduit has to be reamed, namely to prevent damage to the conductor insulation.

347-6. Joints—In the makeup of rigid nonmetallic conduit, various methods are used, depending on the material. The instructions for the particular conduit shall be followed in making up lengths and between conduit and couplings, fittings, and boxes. Use of a solvent or similar substance is to be applied to the joints and fittings before putting them together.

347-8. Supports—Rigid nonmetallic conduit shall be supported within 3 feet (914 mm) of each box, cabinet, or other conduit termination, and elsewhere according to Table 347-8 in the *NEC*.

347-9. Expansion Joints—Where expansion and contraction due to temperature differences might be encountered, approved rigid nonmetallic conduit expansion joints shall be used. Practically all substances expand and contract with temperature changes, which will put undue strain on the conduit. Expansion joints absorb this expansion and contraction, thus avoiding damage to the conduit and fittings.

347-10. Minimum Size—One-half inch electrical trade size is the smallest permissible size of rigid nonmetallic conduit that can be used.

347-11. Number of Conductors—The fill for both new work and re-wire are governed by the same rules as are applicable to rigid metal conduit. This will not be repeated here, but refer back to Section 346-6 of this book. See Table 1, Chapter 9, of the *NEC*.

Note: In the Code you are referred to Chapter 9, Tables 5, 6, 7, and 8, along with the applicable notes to these tables.

347-12. Bushings—This ruling is practically the same as for rigid metal conduit, except that it says bushing or adapter. As with metal conduit [Section 373-6(c)] an insulated bushing is required where No. 4 or larger conductors are used.

347-13. Bends—How Made—See the *NEC*. Note that in the *NEC*, field bends are to be made only by use of a bending machine designed for the purpose, and Table 346-10 governs the radius of the bends. Only identified methods of bending shall be used. Never use flame torches for bending.

In one case the wireman failed to use the bending machine and heated the points he wanted bent with a torch, with the result that the conduit did not bend evenly. There were numerous kinks in it, and he had to replace it all.

347-14. Bends—Number in One Run—See the *NEC* and Article 346.

347-15. Boxes and Fittings—See Article 370.

347-16. Splices and Taps—Splices and taps are never to made in the conduit, only in junction boxes, outlet boxes, or conduit bodies. This is also covered in Article 370.

B. Construction Specifications

347-17. General and Marking—See the *NEC*.

ARTICLE 348—ELECTRICAL METALLIC TUBING

Electrical metallic tubing is commonly known as EMT, thin wall conduit, or merely thin wall.

348-1. Use—EMT may be used for exposed work, and concealed work.

If during or after installation EMT is subject to severe physical damage, it shall not be used. As with rigid metal conduit, it shall not be used if protected by enamel only. In cinder fill or cinder concrete, if subjected to permanent moisture, it shall not be used unless it is encased in regular concrete and has at least a 2-inch casing around it. It may, however, be buried at least 18 inches beneath the surface under a cinder fill. Care shall be taken to keep it from contacting dissimilar metals, to eliminate the possibility of electrolysis. (See the table showing resistivity of soils.) There is a great difference among soils in their reaction to EMT and conduits.

Exception: Aluminum fittings and enclosures are permitted to be used on steel EMT.

348-2. Other Articles—The installation of EMT, as with other wiring methods, shall be governed by Article 300 as well as by this article.

A. Installation

348-4. Wet Locations—See the *NEC*.

348-5. Size.

(a) **Minimum.** Minimum size of EMT shall be ½ inch trade size. Smaller sizes may be used under plaster extensions covered in Section 344-2. In Section 430-145(b) you will find that it can sometimes be used to enclose motor leads.

(b) **Maximum.** The maximum trade size permitted is 4 inches.

348-6. Number of Conductors in Tubing—The requirements for conductors in EMT are exactly the same as for rigid metal conduit as provided in Section 346-6. See Table 1, Chapter 9, for percentage fill permitted in a single tubing.

The cross-sectional area of conductors is covered in Chapter 9 in Tables 5, 6, 7, and 8, and the notes therewith.

348-7. Threads—Basically, EMT is not meant to be connected to boxes or fittings or coupled together by means of threads in the wall of the tubing. An integral coupling is permitted where it is factory threaded.

348-8. Couplings and Connectors—As with all fittings, EMT fittings, couplings, etc., shall be made up tight for electrical continuity. If EMT is buried in masonry or concrete, the fittings shall be concretetight and approved. In wet locations the fitting shall be identified as being raintight. There are a great variety of connectors and couplings available, but regardless of the type used, care should be taken to make up the connection tightly. It will be recalled that EMT will, in most cases, be serving as the equipment ground. Loose connections will not provide proper grounding and could be the cause of a fire or injury.

Where permitted in concrete, couplings and fittings might be damaged during the installation of the concrete, and once buried, repairs are very costly. Care should be taken to make sure that such damage does not occur.

348-9. Bends—How Made—Table 346-10 covers the radius of bends (minimum). In making bends in EMT, care shall be taken not to injure the EMT or decrease the interior dimensions. These are the same requirements as for rigid metal conduit. In making field bends, the proper equipment should always be used. Also see Table 346-10 Exception.

348-10. Bends—Number in One Run—These requirements are the same as for rigid metal conduit—a maximum of the equivalent of four 90 degree bends, or a total of 360 degrees between outlet and outlet, between fitting and fitting, or between outlet and fitting.

348-11. Reaming—All ends of EMT shall be reamed or otherwise finished so as not to leave any rough edges. EMT cuts easily and thus there is a tendency not to worry too much about reaming. Reaming is very important, however, to keep from damaging the insulation of the conductors.

348-12. Supports—EMT shall be installed as a complete system, as was covered in Article 300. EMT shall be fastened securely within 3 feet of boxes, etc., otherwise supports shall not be placed over 10 feet apart. This ruling is a definite asset as there has always been much question as to what constituted properly secured EMT in an installation. As required in Article 300, raceways shall be installed complete before installing the conductors.

348-13. Boxes and Fittings—See Article 370.

348-14. Splices and Taps—Splices and taps shall never be made in the EMT itself, but only in junction boxes, outlet boxes, and conduit bodies. This also is covered in Article 370.

Conductors, including splices and taps, shall not fill a conduit body to more than 75 percent of its cross-sectional area at any point. All splices and taps shall be made by approved methods. Also see Article 370.

Conduit bodies are commonly known as LB condulet, T condulets, etc.

B. Construction Specifications

348-15. General—See the *NEC*.

ARTICLE 349—FLEXIBLE METALLIC TUBING

A. General

349-1. Scope— This is a raceway for electrical conductors. It is circular in cross section, and must be flexible, liquidtight, metallic, and without a nonmetallic covering.

349-2. Other Articles—The applicable provisions of Article 300 shall apply to the installation of flexible metallic tubing.

349-3. Uses Permitted—Flexible metallic tubing shall be permitted to be used in dry locations and in accessible locations, provided it is protected from physical damage. It may be also used for concealed work above a suspended ceiling. It may be used for branch circuits, and also for voltages up to 1000 volts.

349-4. Uses Not Permitted—The following uses are not permitted for flexible metallic tubing: It may not be used underground as a direct burial raceway, nor shall it be embedded in poured concrete or aggregate. It shall not be permitted in hoistways, or battery storage rooms. It shall not be used in hazardous (classified) locations. (It can be used in these locations only where it might be permitted in other articles of the Code.) It is not permitted to be used in lengths over 6 feet or when subject to physical damage.

B. Construction and Installation

349-10. Size.

(a) **Minimum.** ½ electrical trade size flexible metallic tubing is the smallest size permitted.

Exception No. 1: In accordance with Section 300-22(b) and (c), ⅜-inch trade size shall be permitted. In referring to these two Sections, you find that they cover Ducts or Plenums Used for Environmental Air and Other Spaces Used for Environmental Air.

Exception No. 2: See Section 410-67(c). As part of an approved assembly, ⅜-inch trade size is permitted to be used in lengths of not over 6 feet, and it may also be used in lighting fixtures.

(b) **Maximum.** The maximum allowable trade size of flexible metallic tubing is ¾ inch.

349-12. Number of Conductors.

(a) **½-Inch and ¾-Inch Flexible Metallic Tubing.** Table 1, Chapter 9, governs the maximum cross-sectional fill of conductors allowed in flexible metallic tubing.

(b) **⅜-Inch Flexible Metallic Tubing.** Table 350-3 for fill of insulated conductors for ⅜-inch flexible metal conduit also applies to fill for flexible metallic tubing.

Note: For conductor cross-sectional area, see Chapter 9 and its notes. Then refer to Tables 5, 6, 7, and 8 in that chapter.

349-16. Grounding—Exception No. 1 of Section 250-91(b) applies to flexible metallic tubing.

349-18. Fittings—The terminating fittings for flexible metallic tubing shall be listed for the purpose, and shall satisfactorily close any openings in that connection.

Note: Section 300-22(b) and (c) cover use in air ducts, plenums, etc., that are for carrying environmental air.

349-20. Bends—Refer to the *NEC*; (a) is for bends where flexible metallic tubing is infrequently flexed in service after installation and Table 349-20(a) covers this bending.

Fixed Bends. Table 349-20(b) covers bends in flexible metallic tubing for fixed bends.

Refer to Tables 349-20(a) and 349-20(b).

ARTICLE 350—FLEXIBLE METAL CONDUIT

350-1. Other Articles—Not only are sections of this article applicable to flexible metal conduit, but any appropriate provisions of Article 300 (General Wiring Methods), Article 333 (Metal-Clad Cable), and Article 346 (Rigid Metal Conduit) also apply.

350-2. Use—Flexible metal conduit is permitted to be used in wet locations only when the conductors are of types approved for the specific conditions, or if they are lead-covered conductors and there is very little likelihood of water entering under raceways or enclosures that might be connected to the flexible metal conduit. It shall not be used in storage-battery rooms or hoistways, nor shall it be used in hazardous (classified) locations except as permitted in Section 501-4(b). If it is likely to be exposed to oil, gasoline, and other deteriorating materials affecting rubber, then rubber-covered conductors shall not be used. Flexible metal conduit shall not be used underground for direct burial, nor shall it be used embedded in poured concrete or aggregate.

Flexible metal conduit offers a high impedance, having three to four times the impedance of AC cable. Therefore, many inspectors will require bonding or the use of an equipment grounding conductor when using flexible metal conduit.

350-3. Minimum Size—For practical purposes, the minimum metal conduit is ½-inch electrical trade size. There are a few exceptions which will permit ⅜-inch electrical trade size to be used. There is sometimes a tendency to use ⅜-inch conduit in the wrong places and for the wrong purposes.

Exception No. 1: The *NEC* permits it to be used under plaster extensions as covered in Section 344-2.

Exception No. 2: As permitted for motors by Section 430-145(b).

Exception No. 3: If the lengths are not over 6 feet, ⅜-inch, nominal, trade size is permitted by Code. For approved assemblies and as required in Section 410-67(c), flexible metal conduit is permitted for tap connections to lighting fixture, or for lighting fixtures.

Exception No. 4: Section 604-6(a) permits ⅜-inch trade size flexible metal conduit to be used in manufactured wiring systems.

Exception No. 5: The *NEC* refers you to Section 620-21, Exception No. 5.

See Table 350-3 in the *NEC*.

350-4. Supports—Flexible metal conduit is a wiring method and may be used to wire buildings, etc., unless prohibited in certain locations, such as in most hazardous locations. It shall be supported by approved means at least every 4½ feet and within 12 inches on each side of every outlet box or fitting. There, however, are a few exceptions to this:

Exception No. 1: Flexible metal conduit may be fished. Here, of course, it would be impossible to support it within walls, etc.

Exception No. 2: If flexibility is necessary at terminals, the length shall not be over 3 feet.

Exception No. 3: Taps connections are required for fixtures as in Section 410-67(c). Lengths of not more than 6 feet from a fixture terminal are permitted. I am certain that almost any inspection authority would require that the flexible metal conduit not be draped in such a manner as to lay or drop in ceilings, etc.

350-5. Grounding—Flexible metal conduit may be used as a grounding means where both the conduit and the fittings are listed for grounding.

Exception No. 1: Flexible metal conduit may be used as an equipment grounding means if the total length of the conduit (and thus the ground return path) is 6 feet or less. Only fittings listed for grounding for this type of conduit are permitted, and the overcurrent devices protecting the conductors are to be rated not over 20 amperes or less.

Exception No. 2: The grounding shall be installed where flexible metal conduit is connected to equipment where flexibility is required.

Basically, flexible metal conduit is not to be used as an equipment grounding conductor. This exception was put in the Code since there is no way of knowing the problems resulting from the resistance of the conduit in these lengths.

350-6. Bends—See Sections 346-10 and 346-11. In concealed installations, angle connectors shall not be used.

ARTICLE 351—LIQUIDTIGHT FLEXIBLE METAL CONDUIT AND LIQUIDTIGHT FLEXIBLE NONMETALLIC CONDUIT

351-1. Scope—This article covers two types of flexible conduit. One is liquidtight flexible nonmetallic, the other is liquidtight flexible metal conduit.

Liquidtight flexible metal conduit is not intended as a cure-all, but has a very definite purpose. However, when it is used, care must be taken that only approved terminal fittings are employed. When conventional fittings are used, the grounding that is normally provided by the conduit is often destroyed. Section 351-9 will cover grounding.

A. Liquidtight Flexible Metal Conduit

351-2. Definition—This is a raceway of circular cross section with the outside covering being a nonmetallic, sun-resistant, liquidtight jacket over the metal flexible core. Only listed couplings, connectors, and other fittings shall be used.

351-3. Other Articles—This article covers most of the permitted uses; however, some of the provisions in other articles shall apply. These includes the following Articles: 300, 350, 501, 502, 503, and 553.

351-4. Use.

(a) **Permitted.** When listed and marked, it is permissible to be used for direct burial in the earth, and for both concealed and exposed installations:

(1) It may be used in installations where maintenance conditions require not only flexibility, but also protection from liquids, solids, or vapors.

One very practical use for this material might be where there is a service pole located close to a pumphouse. The movement of the pole might prohibit the use of rigid metal conduit as the wiring method. The installation is exposed to the elements, so wiring with liquidtight flexible metal conduit would be very practical, provided that all of the requirements of proper grounding continuity are met.

(2) Sections 501-4(d), 502-4, and 503-3 are referred to. It is permitted to be used as per these sections—if it is listed for approval. It may also be used as covered in Section 553-7(b) for floating buildings.

The aforementioned sections do not give a complete release to use liquidtight flexible metal conduit in all hazardous locations, but there are some places where it will be permitted.

(b) **Not Permitted.** Where not permitted:

(1) Any place that is subject to physical damage.

(2) If ambient temperatures and/or conductor temperature for liquidtight flexible metal conduit are in excess of that for which the material or covering was approved.

351-5. Size—The sizes of liquidtight flexible metal conduit shall be a minimum of size ½ inch to a maximum of 4-inch electrical trade size.

Exception: Section 350-3 permits the use of ⅜-inch size.

351-6. Number of Conductors.

(a) **Single Conduit.** Table 1, Chapter 9 of the *NEC* gives the percentage of conductor fill permitted in a single conduit of ½ inch through 4 inch.

(b) **⅜-Inch Liquidtight Flexible Metal Conduit.** See Table 350-3 of the *NEC* for the maximum number of conductors allowed in ⅜-inch liquidtight flexible metal conduit.

351-7. Fittings—Only listed terminal fittings shall be used with liquidtight flexible metal conduit.

This wiring method has connectors, etc., which are listed for liquidtight flexible metal conduit to give electrical and mechanical continuity; substitutions shall not be permitted.

351-8. Support—Where liquidtight flexible metal conduit is used as a fixed raceway, it shall be secured: (1) by approved methods; (2) at intervals not exceeding 4½ feet (1.37 m); (3) within 12 inches (305 mm) of outlet boxes and fittings.

Exception No. 1: Where liquidtight flexible metal conduit is acceptable for fishing—but of course it cannot be fastened at supportive locations.

Exception No. 2: Where flexibility is required, the length shall not exceed 3 feet.

Exception No. 3: Section 410-67(c) requires that there be not more than 6 feet from the fixture to the terminal connection.

351-9. Grounding—If listed for grounding purposes, the liquidtight flexible metal conduit is permitted for use as the equipment-grounding conductor, and the fittings shall also be listed. Wherever bonding jumpers are required to maintain equipment grounding continuity, Section 250-79 shall be followed.

Exception No. 1: Liquidtight flexible metal conduit of sizes 1 ¼ inch and smaller is permitted to be used as a grounding conductor if the total length does not exceed 6 feet, but the conduit must be terminated in fittings that are listed for grounding. If the overcurrent devices protecting the circuits are rated at 20 amperes or less, they shall be for ⅜- and ½-inch trade sizes, and if 60 amperes or less, they shall be for ¾-inch through 1 ¼-inch trade sizes.

Exception No. 2: If used where flexibility is required and where connected to equipment, an equipment-grounding conductor shall be installed.

Note: The *NEC* refers you to Sections 501-16(b), 502-16(b), and 503-16(b).

351-10. Bends—When this type of conduit extends from outlet to outlet, fitting to fitting, or outlet to fitting, the total bends of the conduit shall not exceed 360 degrees. This includes any offsets or bends that occur immediately at the outlet or fitting.

Concealed raceway installations shall not contain angle connectors.

B. Liquidtight Flexible Nonmetallic Conduit

351-22. Definition—Liquidtight flexible nonmetallic conduit is used as a raceway. It is required to have integrated within it reinforcement within the conduit walls, and it is to have a smooth inner surface. This type of conduit shall be approved for use with approved fittings, and approved for flame-retardancy. Both conduit, and fittings shall be approved for the installation of conductors.

351-23. Use.

(a) **Permitted.** It is permitted to be used in the following locations:

Note: If exposed to extreme cold temperatures, it is more likely to be damaged from physical contact.

(1) It may be used where flexibility is required in installation, maintenance, or operation.

(2) If protection from vapors, liquids, and solids is required for the circuit conductors installed therein, it may be used.

(3) It must be suitably marked and listed if used outdoors.

(b) **Not Permitted:**

(1) Where it can be subjected to physical damage.

(2) If, due to ambient and conductor temperatures, the conduit is subjected to higher temperatures than it has been approved for.

(3) The limitation placed on length is 6 feet.

Exception: If listed for approval on some special installations.

(4) Voltage of the circuit conductors used therein shall be 600 volts, nominal, or less.

351-24. Size—Sizes of liquidtight nonmetallic conduit include ½ inch through 2 inches electrical trade size.

Exception: If approved in Section 430-145(b), ⅜ inch may be used to enclose the leads to motors.

351-25. Number of Conductors—The number of conductors in a single conduit is the same as for regular conduit, as covered for percent of fill in Table 1, Chapter 9.

351-26. Fittings—Terminal fittings shall be identified for the use when used on liquidtight nonmetallic conduit.

351-27. Equipment Grounding—When an equipment grounding conductor is required, which will be in practically all cases, the equipment grounding conductor shall be run in the conduit with the circuit conductors as required by Article 250.

ARTICLE 352—SURFACE METAL RACEWAYS AND SURFACE NONMETALLIC RACEWAYS

A. Surface Metal Raceways

Metal surface raceways provide a wiring method that has many advantages. This wiring method is not intended for new construction, but is quite valuable in additions to existing wiring systems that must be expanded without cutting into the existing building to add conduit and other components. Metal surface raceways have been used for many years and have been found quite satisfactory for the purpose for which they are intended.

352-1. Use—They are permitted to be used in dry locations. They shall not be used as follows: Unless otherwise approved and listed, they shall not be used where subjected to severe physical damage. Unless the metal has a thickness of not less than 0.040 inch, they shall not be used. Where The voltage is 300 volts or more between circuit conductors, they shall not be used. They will not be approved where corrosive vapors are present, nor in any hoistways. Except as permitted in Section 501-4(b), they are not permitted in hazardous (classified) locations, Class I, Division 2. Nor are they permitted where concealed, except as follows:

Exception No. 1: If they are identified or listed for such use, they will be permitted for underplaster extensions.

Exception No. 2: The *NEC* refers us to Section 645-2(c) (2).

Note: See your *NEC*.

352-2. Other Articles—The provisions of Article 300 (General Wiring Methods) shall be used in addition to this article, where applicable.

352-3. Size of Conductors—The size of the raceway determines the size of the conductors that it may be used for. The design of the size of the metal surface raceway is a governing factor. This will make it necessary to know what size conductor the raceway was designed for.

352-4. Number of Conductors in Raceways—The design of the raceway governs the number of conductors that may be installed. Also, the number will depend upon the size of the conductors. The manufacturer of the raceway can be contacted for this information.

If all the following conditions are met, the derating factors in Note 8 (a) accompanying Tables 310-16 through 310-31 shall not apply: if the cross-sectional area of the raceway exceeds 4 square inches; not more than thirty current-carrying conductors shall be installed; the sum of the cross-sectional area of all conductors installed in metal surface raceways does not exceed a maximum of 20 percent of the interior cross-sectional area of the raceway.

Note: The cross-sectional areas of different sizes of conductors and insulation can be found in Tables 5, 6, 7, and 8, and notes 8 at the beginning of Chapter 9.

352-5. Extension through Walls and Floors—Multioutlet assemblies are not to be extended through floors and walls. Metal surface raceways may be extended through dry walls, dry partitions, and dry floors. However, they shall be in unbroken lengths where they pass through, so that no joint will be hidden.

Note: The *NEC* refers you to Section 353-3 for multioutlet assemblies.

352-6. Combination Raceways—Take special note of this section, as it is quite different from conduit systems. Sometimes combinations for signal, lighting, and power circuits may be necessary to run in the same metal surface raceway. Where this is required, two sections shall be made in the raceway by a metal partition, and each separate compartment in the raceway shall be identified by a different color. These colors shall be maintained throughout the premises.

352-7. Splices and Taps—Splices and taps are permitted if the metal surface raceways have removable covers that are readily accessible when the installation is completed. Seventy-five percent of the raceway area is the limitation placed on splices and taps in the area. If there are no removable covers, splices and taps shall be made only in junction boxes. Of course, all splices and taps are to made by approved methods.

352-8. Construction—See your *NEC* for this construction of metal surface raceways and fittings used therewith.

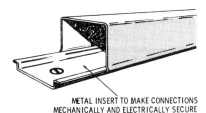

METAL INSERT TO MAKE CONNECTIONS
MECHANICALLY AND ELECTRICALLY SECURE

Fig. 352-1. Connectors shall be electrically and mechanically secure.

SCREW HOLE COUNTERSUNK

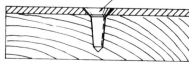

Fig. 352-2. Holes for screws shall be countersunk to protect wire from damage.

B. Surface Nonmetallic Raceways

352-21. Description—This covers a raceway made of nonmetallic material. It is resistant to moisture and chemical atmospheres. Heat resistance is important, as well as resistance to impact and distortion. The temperature under which it is likely to be used shall not cause distortion, and it shall also be resistant to low temperature effects.

352-22. Use—It is to be used in dry locations. It is not to be used in concealed locations, where subject to physical damage. Voltages between conductors shall be 300 volts or less. It is not to be used in hazardous (classified) locations, with the exception of Class 1, Division 2 where permitted in Section 501-4(b). It shall not be used in hoistways. It shall not be used if the ambient temperature exceeds 50° C, or for conductors whose insulation temperature exceeds 75° C.

352-23. Other Articles—The provisions of Article 300 shall be applicable.

352-24. Size of Conductors—The design of the nonmetallic surface raceways will govern the conductor sizes that may be used.

352-25. Number of Conductors in Raceways—The design of the nonmetallic surface raceways and the size of the conductors will govern the number of conductors.

352-26. Combination Raceways—See the *NEC.*

352-27. General—See the *NEC.*

ARTICLE 353—MULTIOUTLET ASSEMBLY

Multioutlet assemblies consist of either a flush or surface raceway which has been designed to hold receptacle outlets and has either been factory assembled or assembled in the field. They are used especially where there are a number of outlets required in a relatively short space, such as in show rooms where the connections for appliances for demonstration, for outlets along a workbench, etc., are necessary.

Some multioutlet assemblies have receptacles that are movable. They make connections with some type of bus and may be slid along to obtain different spacings. Other assemblies are designed with outlets at fixed intervals so as to facilitate the connection of appliances, tools, etc. There are many different makes available, so care should be taken to pick a multioutlet assembly that is approved and to properly install it.

353-1. Other Articles—The use and installation of multioutlet assemblies is governed not only by this article but also by Article 300 (General Wiring Methods).

353-2. Use—Multioutlet assemblies are to be installed only in dry locations. They are not to be installed: (1) where concealed, except that the back and sides of metal multioutlet assemblies may be surrounded by the building finish, and nonmetallic multioutlet assemblies may be recessed in the baseboard (see Figs. 353-1 and -2); (2) where subject to severe physical damage; (3) where the voltage is 300 volts or more between conductors, unless the assembly is of metal having a thickness of at least 0.040 inch; (4) where subject to corrosive vapors; (5) in hoistways; (6) in any hazardous (classified) locations.

It may be used in Class I, Division 2 locations as permitted in Section 501-4(b).

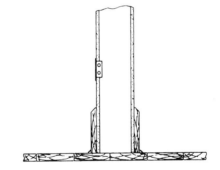

Fig. 353.1. Metal multioutlet assemblies may be installed in building finishes.

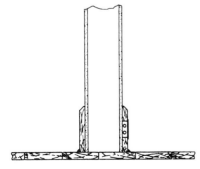

Fig. 353-2. Nonmetallic assemblies may be installed in baseboards.

353-3. Metal Multioutlet Assembly through Dry Partitions—Metal multioutlet assemblies shall not be run in partitions, but may be run through dry partitions providing that the covers outside of the partition are arranged so that they may be removed, and providing that there are no outlets inside the partition. See Fig. 353-3.

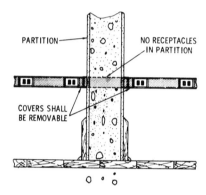

Fig. 353-3. Multioutlet assemblies may pass through dry partitions, provided there are no outlets in the partition and the covers are removable.

ARTICLE 354—UNDERFLOOR RACEWAYS

Underfloor raceways are extensively used in larger buildings, especially those with concrete floors. They have a number of advantages that make them convenient to use where a number of floor outlets are required (as in offices), and where more may be needed at some future date.

354-1. Other Articles—The provisions of this article and of Article 300 (General Wiring Methods) apply to the installation of underfloor raceways.

354-2. Use—Underfloor raceways may be installed beneath the surface of concrete or other flooring material (Fig. 354-1), or in office occupancies, where laid flush with the concrete floor and covered with linoleum or equivalent floor coverings. See Fig. 354-2.

Underfloor raceways shall not be installed: (1) where subject to corrosive vapors; or (2) in any hazardous (classified) location unless made of material judged suitable for the condition. It may be used in Class I, Division 2 locations as permitted in Section 501-4 (b).

Unless corrosion protection approved for the conditions is provided, ferrous or nonferrous metallic underfloor raceways, junction boxes, and fittings shall not be installed in concrete or in direct contact with the earth or in areas subject to severe corrosive influences. Formerly, open-bottom type raceways were permitted where they were installed in a concrete fill. This has now been deleted (Fig. 354-3). These raceways shall be corrosion protected and approved for the purpose where installed in concrete or in contact with the earth. This is the same requirement as for rigid metallic conduit.

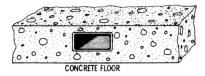

Fig. 354-1. Underfloor raceways may be installed in concrete floors or under other floors.

Fig. 354-2. Underfloor raceways may be laid flush with the surface of the concrete in office occupancies if covered by linoleum or the equivalent.

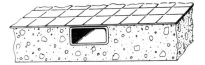

Fig. 354-3. Open-bottom raceways are no longer permitted.

354-3. Covering—Raceway coverings shall comply with (a) through (d) below.

(a) **Raceways Not Over 4 Inches Wide.** Raceways that are half round or flat-top raceways that are not over 4 inches in width shall be covered with ¾ inch of concrete or wood. See Fig. 354-4. There is an exception to this in (c) below for flat-top raceways.

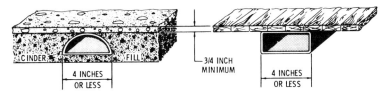

Fig. 354-4. Minimum covering over 4-inch raceways.

(b) **Raceways Over 4 Inches Wide but Not Over 8 Inches Wide.** If underfloor raceways exceed 4 inches in width but are not over 8 inches in width, they are to be covered with concrete of not less than 1 inch thickness. If raceways are spaced less than 1 inch, a concrete covering over the raceway shall be 1½ inches. See Fig. 354-5.

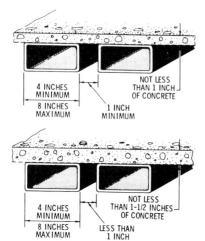

Fig. 354-5. Minimum covering over 4- to 8-inch raceways.

(c) **Trench-Type Raceways Flush with Concrete.** Trench-type under-floor raceways may be flush with the concrete floor or other surface. They shall be approved raceways with cover plates that are rigid and designed to give mechanical protection to the covers.

(d) **Other Raceways Flush with Concrete.** In office occupancies, if flat-top raceways are approved and are not over 4 inches in width, permission is granted to lay them flush with the concrete surface if covered by linoleum that is not less than 1 $\frac{1}{16}$ inch thick. Other equivalent coverings may be used instead of linoleum. When not over three single raceways are installed flush with the concrete, they shall be joined together, thus making a rigid assembly.

354-4. Size of Conductors—The design of the raceway shall govern the maximum conductor size.

354-5. Maximum Number of Conductors in Raceway—To figure the number of conductors for underfloor raceways, the total cross-sectional area of all the conductors is calculated. This total area shall not exceed 40 percent of the cross-sectional area of the interior of the raceway. In arriving at the cross-sectional area of the conductors, use the appropriate Tables in Chapter 9, and see Tables 5, 6, 7, and 8.

354-6. Splices and Taps—Splices and taps are not to be made in the raceway itself but only in junction boxes. For purposes of this section, loop wiring is not a splice or tap. See Fig. 354-6. Your attention is also called to the next section.

Exception: In trench-type flush raceways having removable covers, splices and taps will be permitted if they are accessible after the installation is

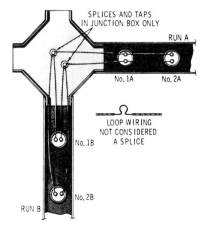

SPLICES AND TAPS
IN JUNCTION BOX ONLY

RUN A

No. 1A   No. 2A

LOOP WIRING
NOT CONSIDERED
No. 1B   A SPLICE

No. 2B

RUN B

**Fig. 354-6.   Splices and taps are
to be made in junction boxes
only.**

complete. When such taps or splices are made, they shall not fill the cross-sectional area of the raceway over 75 percent.

354-7. Discontinued Outlets—When an outlet is removed from underfloor raceways, the conductors supplying that outlet shall also be removed from the raceway. No splices or taps will be allowed when abandoning new outlets, as would be the case on loop wiring.

To illustrate the essential parts of this ruling, refer to Fig. 354-6. Should outlet No. 2B in Run B of the raceway be removed, the wires that served it shall be removed back to the junction box. Should outlet No. 1A also be removed, the conductors to No. 2A would also have to be removed and new conductors run to No. 2A from the junction box.

354-8. Laid in Straight Lines—It is necessary to lay underfloor raceways in a straight line from one junction box to the next, with the centerlines of the two junction boxes coinciding with the centerline of the raceway. This is essential so that the raceways may be located in the event that additional outlets are required later and so that the end markers covered by the next section have some meaning. It is also required that the raceways be held firmly in place by appropriate means to prevent disturbing the alignment during construction.

354-9. Markers at Ends—A suitable number of markers that extend through the floor shall be installed at the end of line raceways, and at other places where the location of the raceway is not apparent, so that future location of the raceway is made possible. It is recommended that these identification markers be indicated on any blueprints of the building for future reference to assist in the locating of the raceways.

354-10. Dead Ends—All dead ends of raceways shall be closed by suitable means that are approved by the inspection authority.

354-13. Junction Boxes—Junction boxes shall be leveled to the floor grade and sealed against the entrance of water. Junction boxes used with metal raceways shall be metal and shall be electrically continuous with the raceways. Metal underfloor raceways, junction boxes, etc., are to be electrically continuous, the same as metallic conduit and electrical metallic tubing. This is one of the most important parts of the installation.

354-14. Inserts—Inserts shall be leveled to the floor grade and sealed against the entrance of water. Inserts used with metal raceways shall be metal and shall be electrically continuous with the raceway. Inserts set in or on fiber raceways before the floor is laid shall be mechanically secured to the raceway. Inserts set in fiber raceways after the floor is laid shall be screwed into the raceway. In cutting through the raceway wall and setting inserts, chips and other dirt shall not be allowed to fall into the raceway, and tools shall be used which are so designed as to prevent the tool from entering the raceway and injuring conductors that may be in place. All of this merely means good workmanship. It might be well to mention here that if fiber raceways are used, it will be necessary to install a separate conductor to be used as a grounding conductor, the same as required with nonmetallic rigid conduit.

354-15. Connections to Cabinets and Wall Outlets—Connection between distribution centers and wall outlets shall be made with flexible metal conduit when not installed in concrete. Rigid metal conduit, intermediate metal conduit, EMT, or approved fittings may be used for connectios between distribution centers and wall outlets.

Under certain conditions nonmetallic raceways are permitted. Also, see this section in the *NEC*.

This article concerns only underfloor raceways—this means that it is not intended to be run up walls to outlets and cabinets. Therefore, conduit or other approved means must be used for this purpose.

ARTICLE 356—CELLULAR METAL FLOOR RACEWAYS

This article is similar in many respects to the preceding article on underfloor raceways.

356-1. Definition—See the *NEC* for the definition of cellular metal floor raceways.

In order to gain a better understanding of cellular metal floor raceways, illustrations will be used. Fig. 356-1 shows a cross section of cellular metal floor raceway. Raceways are made, not only for electrical conductors, but also for telephone lines, signal circuits, steam, and hot and cold water pipes. Fig. 356-2 illustrates a cell. Notice that it is just one single enclosed tubular area. Fig. 356-3 illustrates a header which is transversely connecting two cells. With this arrangement, conductors may be run at right angles to the cells as well as in the cells of the raceway.

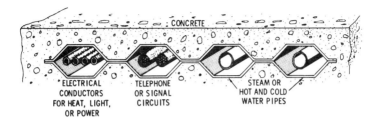

Fig. 356-1. Cross-sectional view of cellular metal floor raceways used for installation of electrical and other systems.

Fig. 356-2. Illustration of a cell.

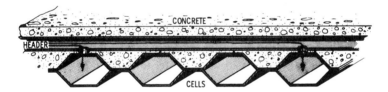

Fig. 356-3. Illustration of a header and cells.

356-2. Use—Conductors are not to be installed in cellular metal floor raceways: (1) where corrosive vapors are present; (2) in any hazardous (classified) locations, except, as indicated in the *NEC*, for Class I, Division 2 locations in some instances as permitted in the Exception to 501-4(b);(3) in commerical garages (except where they supply outlets or extensions to the area below the floor but not above). See Section 300-8 in the *NEC*. See Fig. 356-1.

356-3. Other Articles—The provisions of this article and of Article 300 (General Wiring Methods) apply in the installation of this wiring method.

A. Installation

356-4. Size of Conductors—Except by special permission, conductors larger than ⅙ shall not be installed. Your attention is called to the definition of "special permission" as it appears in Article 100—"the written consent of the authority enforcing this Code."

356-5. Maximum Number of Conductors in Raceway—The fill shall be no more than 40 percent of the cross-sectional area of the raceway. In other words, the total cross-sectional area of all the conductors shall not fill the raceway to over 40 percent of its capacity. Tables in Chapter 9 of the NEC give the cross-sectional area of various conductors and their insulations. These figures are to be used in the calculation of the total cross-sectional area of the conductors. The requirements just mentioned will not apply where Type AC metal-clad cable or nometallic sheathed cables are used in the raceways. The area of the raceway will have to be calculated mathematically unless the specifications are available to the wireman.

356-6. Splices and Taps—These were allowed only in junction boxes with underfloor raceways. With cellular metal floor raceways, they are also permitted in header access boxes. Refer to Fig. 356-3, which shows a header.

356-7. Disconnected Outlets—Conductors that supplied outlets which are being discontinued shall be removed from the raceway back to a junction box. They cannot be merely taped up and left in place.

356-8. Markers—Markers are to be extended through the floor for the purpose of locating the cells and the wiring system in the future. There should be enough markers to properly assist in the location of the raceways. It is also recommended that the location of these markers be indicated on the final set of electrical plans that is to be given to the owner.

356-9. Junction Boxes—Junction boxes are to be installed level with the floor grade and are to be sealed against the entrance of water and dirt. They shall be made of metal and shall be made electrically continuous with the rest of the system. Although not mentioned at this point, the metal of which the junction boxes are made should be such as to not cause corrosion or electrolysis.

356-10. Inserts—Inserts (such as for outlets) shall be made of metal and made electrically continuous with the rest of the system. They shall be installed level with the floor grade and made watertight. When cutting the raceway for the installation of these inserts, no rough spots shall be left, and the dirt and chips removed, so as not to cause abrasion to the insulation of the conductors. When installing inserts, the tools used when cutting through the raceway shall be such as not to cause damage to the conductors that have been installed.

356-11. Connection to Cabinets and Extensions from Cells—Flexible metal conduit may be used for connections from raceways, distribution centers, and wall outlets if they are not concrete. If in concrete, rigid metal conduit, intermediate metal conduit, EMT, or approved fitting shall be used. If provisions have been made for equipment-grounding conductors, nonmetallic conduit or electrical nonmetallic tubing will be permitted.

B. Construction Specifications

356-12. General—See the *NEC*.

ARTICLE 358—CELLULAR CONCRETE FLOOR RACEWAYS

This article is very similar to Article 356 (Cellular Metal Floor Raceways). Because of this similarity, only those points that are treated differently will be covered in order to prevent repetition.

Fig. 358-1 shows the construction of cellular concrete floor raceways. They are constructed of precast concrete with cells or openings provided for the wiring conductors. Since this type of raceway is made of concrete, it cannot be made electrically continuous. Therefore, an equipment ground of the proper size must be used in the installation, and all header ducts, junction boxes, and inserts shall be electrically secured to this grounding conductor.

Refer to the *NEC* for coverage of this article.

Fig. 358-1. Cross-sectional view of a cellular concrete floor raceway.

ARTICLE 362—WIREWAYS

362-1. Definition—See your *NEC*, and see Fig. 362-1.

COVER MAY BE HINGED
OR ATTACHED WITH SCREWS

Fig. 362-1. Illustration of wireway.

362-2. Use—Wireways shall be used only for exposed work, and may be used out of doors if of an approved raintight construction.

Wireways shall not be installed where they can be physically damaged, or where there are corrosive vapors. They cannot be installed in hazardous (classified) locations. There is an exception for Class I, Division 2 and Class II, Division 2 in these sections: 501-4(b) and 502-4(b).

362-3. Other Articles—Wireways and the installation thereof shall conform to the provisions of Article 300.

362-4. Size of Conductors—The design of the wireway shall govern the maximum size conductor that will be permitted.

362-5. Number of Conductors—There is a limit of thirty current-carrying conductors in any wireway, at any cross-sectional area. This is the maximum number of conductors allowed.

For this purpose conductors for signal circuits, or controller circuits between starter and motor, shall not be considered to be current-carrying conductors.

No more than 20% of the cross-sectional area of a wireway may be used for conductors. This is based on the total cross-sectional area of the conductors against the cross-sectional area of the wireway.

There are derating factors with Note 8(a) to Tables 310-16 through 310-31 that will not be applicable when the thirty current-carrying conductors are at the 20 percent fill specified above.

Exception No. 1 is covered in the material above. See your *NEC* for Exception No. 2.

Exception No. 3 pertains to elevators and dumbwaiters with which it is allowable to use up to 50 percent of the cross-sectional area of the wireway.

Note: Cross-sectional area of conductors is covered in Tables 5, 6, 7, and 8 and the notes at the beginning of Chapter 9.

362-6. Splices and Taps—This is one wiring method in which splices and taps are allowed, but with the following restrictions: (1) they shall be accessible; (2) they shall be insulated by approved means; and (3) they shall not fill the wireway to more than 75 percent of its area at that point. If the splices or taps are staggered slightly, more room can be obtained.

362-7. Supports—Wireways may be screwed or bolted to a wall or supported by hangers or any other suitable and acceptable means, but in any case they shall be supported at intervals not to exceed 5 feet (1.52m). In no case shall the distance between supports exceed 10 feet (3.05m).

Exception: Vertical run supports for wireways shall be not over 15 feet apart. There shall not be more than one joint between supports. Any adjoining wireways shall be fastened to the other wireway so as to provide a rigid joint.

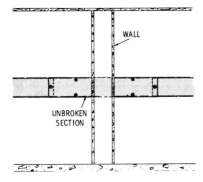

Fig. 362-2. Wireways may
extend transversely through a
wall in unbroken lengths.

362-8. Extensions Through Walls—When passing through walls, the wires shall be in unbroken lengths.

362-9. Dead Ends—Dead ends shall have caps to close the ends of the wireways.

362-10. Extension from Wireways—Extension from wireways may be made with many different types of raceways. We refer you to the *NEC* for this section. However, we are always faced with equipment grounding continuity, and if it is required by some of this type of raceway, continuity must be maintained throughout. See Sections 250-113 and 250-118.

362-11. Marking—The manufacturer's name or trademark must be durably marked on wireways where it shall be visible after installation.

362-12. Grounding—Equipment grounding was just mentioned in Section 362-10, but it is mentioned again here because of its importance. The provisions of Article 250 shall be adhered to.

ARTICLE 363—FLAT CABLE ASSEMBLIES
Type FC

This product was new with the 1971 *NEC*. As an introduction, it might be well to give some of the submitter's supporting comment as it appeared in the 1971 preprint:

> This new article is basically a busway system. In an approved busway system, all of the basic components are factory assembled. In this proposed wiring system, the basic components are intended to be field assembled.
>
> The conductors are formed into a flat cable assembly of three or four conductors and are completely encased in an insulating material,

properly spaced. Special spacing insulation is extruded integrally with the cable assembly to facilitate the location of the cable within the metal raceway. Refer to Section 363-1 of the *NEC*.

Article 362 (Wireways, Chapter 3) more or less completes the requirements for a class of wiring systems intended for use and field assembly of standard components. Article 364-1 (Busways) more or less begins the requirements for wiring systems consisting of completely factory-wired assemblies.

This proposed Article 363 is a transition from the field assembly of standard components to the field of completely wired factory installations.

363-1. Definition—See your *NEC*.

363-2. Other Articles—There are additional provisions other than those referred to in this article for the installation of type FC cable. You will find these in Articles 210, 220, 250, 300, 310, and 352.

363-3. Uses Permitted—Type FC cable is for use only with branch circuits to supply tap devices that are suitable for light, small appliances, or small power loads and is to be used only in installation for exposed work, where not subject to severe physical damage.

363-4. Uses Not Permitted—It shall not be installed where there are corrosive vapors unless it is suitable for the location. It shall not be installed outdoors or in wet or damp locations unless identified. It can not be used in hazardous (classified) locations or hoistways.

363-5. Installation—FC cable shall be installed in the field only in metal surface raceways that are identified for this purpose. The surface metal raceway must be installed as a complete system before any of the FC cable is pulled into the raceway.

363-6. Number of Conductors—FC cable may be in assemblies of two, three, or four conductors.

363-7. Size of Conductors—This comes in only one size, namely No. 10 AWG special stranded copper wires.

363-8. Conductor Insulation—Materials of which the cable is to be made and that forms the insulation for all the conductors shall be material found in Table 310-13 for general-purpose branch-circuit wiring.

363-9. Splices—Splices shall be made only in junction boxes only by approved wiring methods for making the splices.

363-10. Taps—Taps between phase and neutral or other phases are permitted to be made by use of fittings and devices that are approved for the purpose, and tap devices shall be rated not less than 15 amperes and not more than 300 volts. Color coding is required, and is covered in Section 363-20.

363-11. Dead Ends—Dead ends shall be covered with only approved end caps.
The metal raceway dead ends shall be closed only by identified fittings.

363-12. Fixture Hangers—Fixture hangers from flat cable assemblies shall be installed only with identified fittings.

363-13. Fittings—All fittings used with FC cable shall be designed and the insulation made to prevent physical damage to the cable assemblies.

363-14. Extensions—All extensions from flat cable assemblies shall be made from the terminal blocks enclosed within the junction boxes, installed at either end of the flat cable assembly runs.

363-15. Supports—FC cable's special design features are to be used for mounting the FC cable assemblies within the surface metal raceways. Instructions for supporting the surface metal raceways will differ, and only the supporting means for a specific raceway shall be used.

363-16. Rating—Branch-circuit rating shall not be permitted to be over 30 amperes.

363-17. Marking—See the *NEC*.

363-18. Protective Covers—See the *NEC*.

363-19. Identification—See the *NEC*.

363-20. Terminal Block Identification—See the *NEC*.

ARTICLE 364—BUSWAYS

A. General Requirements

364-1. Scope—This article covers busways and associated fittings used as service-entrance feeders and branch circuits.

364-2. Definition—Busway, as covered in this article, means a grounded metal enclosure used to contain bare or insulated conductors, which may be either copper or aluminum, may be bars, rods, or tubes, and are factory-mounted.

Note: For cablebus, the *NEC* refers you to Article 365.

364-3. Other Articles—Installations of busways shall comply with the applicable provisions of Article 300 as well as this article.

364-4. Use.

(a) **Use Permitted.** Busways must be installed in the open, and are to be visible.

Exception: Busways may be installed behind panels, but means of access must be provided. Also, all of the following conditions are to be met:

a. Overcurrent devices, other than for the individual fixture involved, shall not be installed on the busway.

b. They shall not be mounted in access panels if these panels are for air-handling purposes.

c. They shall be nonventilating, and the busways shall be totally enclosed.

d. In the installation of busways, any joints between sections or fitting shall always be accessible for maintenance purposes.

(b) **Use Prohibited.** Busways shall not be installed under the following conditions: where physical damage or corrosive conditions exist, in hoistways, in hazardous (classified) locations (in Sections 501-4 (b) they are approved in these hazardous locations for some specific uses). Unless specifically approved for such use, they may not be installed in wet or damp locations or outdoors.

364-5. Supports—Busways are to be supported at intervals not exceeding 5 feet unless specifically approved for support at greater distances.

364-6. Through Walls and Floors—Busways may be extended through walls transversely (horizontally), providing that they go through dry walls and are in unbroken lengths. See Fig. 364-1.

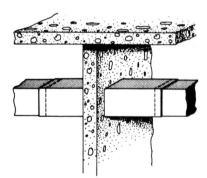

Fig. 364-1. Busways may extend transversely through walls in unbroken lengths.

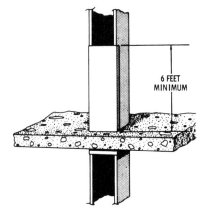

6 FEET
MINIMUM

Fig. 364-2. Busways may extend vertically through floors (dry), if not ventilated, for a minimum height of 6 feet.

Busways may be extended vertically through dry floors when totally enclosed, provided this total enclosure extends for a minimum distance of 6 feet above the floor through which they pass and are adequately protected from physical damage. See Fig. 364-2.

364-7. Dead Ends—A dead end of a busway shall be properly closed.

364-8. Branches from Busways—Branches from busways shall be made with busways, rigid or flexible conduit (metal), electric metallic tubing, surface metal raceways, rigid metal conduit, metal-clad cable, electrical nonmetallic tubing, or with suitable cord assemblies approved for hard usage with portable equipment or to facilitate the connection of stationary equipment to aid in interchanging said equipment.

There are provisions for use of flexible cord assemblies. These connections are permitted to be made directly to the end terminals of a busway that has a plug-in device installed. This is permitted if suitable means are provided to take up the tension on the cord. Again we must bear in mind the continuity of equipment grounding conductors; therefore, if nonmetallic raceways are used, connection to the equipment grounding conductor shall meet the requirements of Sections 250-113 and 250-118.

364-9. Overcurrent Protection—It is necessary to provide overcurrent protection with busways in accordance with Section 364-10 through 364-14.

364-10. Rating of Overcurrent Protection—Feeders and Subfeeders—If the overcurrent protection device does not correspond to the rating of the busway, the next larger size of overcurrent protection may be used.

364-11. Reduction in Size of Busway—Busways may be reduced in size without the use of overcurrent protection at the point of reduction providing that the following condition or conditions are met: (1) the smaller busway does not extend over 50 feet; (2) the smaller busway has a current rating of at least one-third that of the larger busway; (3) the smaller busway is protected by overcurrent capacity of not over three times the rating of the smaller busway; (4) the smaller busway shall not come in contact with combustible material.

364-12. Subfeeder or Branch Circuits—Where busways are to be used as a feeder, devices or plug-in connections for tapping off subfeeders or branch circuits shall contain the overcurrent devices to protect the subfeeder or branch circuit. These may be either externally operated circuit feeders or externally operated usable switches. If these overcurrent devices are not readibly reachable, disconnecting means shall be provided for opening them. This means of opening or disconnecting the overcurrent device may be ropes, chains, or suitable sticks that may be operated from the floor.

Exception No. 1: For the overcurrent protection of taps, refer to Section 240-21, which allows placing the overcurrent protection at various distances from the busway, depending on conditions.

Exception No. 2: On cord-connected fixtures of the fixed or semi-fixed type, the overcurrent device may be a part of the fixture cord plug.

Exception No. 3: The overcurrent protection may be mounted on cordless fixtures that are plugged directly into the busway.

364-13. Rating of Overcurrent Protection—Branch Circuits—Busways may be used as a branch circuit of any type of branch circuit covered in Article 210. When a busway is used as a branch circuit, the overcurrent device protecting the busway usage determines the ampere rating of the branch circuit. Any requirements of Article 210 that applied to busway branch circuits shall be complied with.

364-14. Length of Busways Used as Branch Circuits—Busways when used for branch circuits shall be designed so that loads can be connected at any point and shall be limited to such length that under normal usage the circuits will not be overloaded.

364-15. Marking—See the *NEC*.

B. Requirements for over 600 Volts, Nominal

364-21. Identification—Each run shall have a nameplate permanently marked with the voltage rating and the continuous current rating. If the busway is force-cooled, both the normal forced-cooled current rating and the self-cooled rating shall be marked; the rated frequency, the rated impulse withstanding voltage, the rating at 60 AC Hertz of the voltage it will withstand, and the momentary overcurrent it may withstand shall also be marked.

364-22. Grounding—Metal-enclosed busways that meet the requirements of Article 250 must be installed for equipment grounding continuity.

364-23. Adjacent and Supporting Structures—Busways that are metal enclosed shall be so installed that any temperature rises that may occur from induced currents circulating in any adjacent metallic parts will in no way be hazardous to people or in any manner constitute a fire hazard.

364-24. Neutral—The neutral bus shall be designed to carry any loads that might be placed on it and especially with discharge lighting. Harmonic currents will increase the current in the neutral. Any momentary short circuit requires that the neutral be capable of handling it. See Note 10 in Article 310.

364-25. Barriers and Seals—Any busways installed outside the building that enter the building shall incorporate a vapor seal to prevent the interchange of interior and outdoor air.

Where floors or ceilings are penetrated, or drop ceilings or walls are penetrated, fire barriers will be installed.

Exception: If the busway is forced-cooled, vapor seals will not be required.

364-26. Drain Facilities—For the removal of any condensed moisture at low points in the bus run, drain plugs, filter drains, or other similar methods shall be provided.

364-27. Ventilated Bus Enclosures—Article 710, Part D covers ventilated bus enclosures, unless the design is such that foreign objects cannot be inserted into the energized parts of the busway.

364-28. Terminations and Connections—If the busway enclosures terminate at machines that are cooled by flammable gases, proper seal-off bushings, baffles, or any other means that will keep the flammable gas from entering the bus enclosures are required.

Temperature changes will cause the buses to expand or contract, therefore flexible or expansion connections will be required. If building vibration insulation joints are used, means shall be provided as for temperature changes.

All conductor terminations and any connecting hardware shall be readily accessible for installation, connection, and maintenance.

364-29. Switches—See your *NEC*.

364-30. Low-Voltage Wiring—If secondary control wiring is provided as a part in the bus that is metally enclosed, it shall be insulated from all primary circuit elements by a flame-retardant barrier. This does not include short lengths of secondary conductors such as those running to instrument transformers.

ARTICLE 365—CABLEBUS

See the *NEC.*

ARTICLE 370—OUTLET, DEVICE, PULL, AND JUNCTION BOXES, CONDUIT BODIES, AND FITTINGS

This is one of the most important articles in Chapter 3, and should be carefully examined.

370-1. Scope—This article covers the installation of all boxes, conduit bodies, and fittings that were required in Section 300-15. Those that were covered in Section 300-15 that may be used as pull boxes, junction boxes, or outlet boxes shall conform with the provisions of this article, depending upon the purpose for which you are using them. These boxes, etc., may be made of cast material, sheet metal, or nonmetallic material. Other boxes, such as FS, FD, or larger, are not considered to be conduit bodies. Elbow fittings that are capped, including service-entrance elbows, shall not be classified as conduit bodies. When we speak of conduit bodies, we generally speak of condulets.

Note: Part D of this article will cover systems of over 600 volts.

370-2. Round Boxes—Round boxes create a problem with the use of locknuts, bushings, and connectors. There are usually knockouts in the bottom of the boxes, so where these types of connections are used, they shall not be connected to the sides of the box. Round boxes are usually found on existing jobs. Boxes that are now manufactured are in accordance with the *NEC.*

370-3. Nonmetallic Boxes—Nonmetallic boxes are approved for specific purposes—they may be used only with open wiring on insulators, concealed knob-and-tube work, nonmetallic sheathed cable (NM cable), electrical nonmetallic tubing and with rigid nonmetallic conduit. Nonmetallic boxes have advantages and disadvantages which the wireman must consider and make the decision as to when to use them. They shall not exceed 100 cubic inches.

Nonmetallic boxes over 100 cubic inches are permitted to be used with raceways and metal-sheathed cables. Here again we run into equipment grounding and its continuity, so when nonmetallic boxes are used they shall be bonded from the metal raceway or metal-sheathed cable.

370-4. Metal Boxes—All metal boxes shall be properly installed so as to carry the continuity of the equipment grounding system, which is covered in Article 250.

B. Installation

370-5. Damp or Wet Locations—When used in damp or wet locations, boxes and fittings shall be so installed as to prevent the accumulation of moisture or to prevent water from entering the boxes or fittings. All boxes and fittings that are installed in wet locations shall be weatherproof.

In hazardous (classified) locations, all boxes, in fact the entire wiring system, shall conform to Articles 500 through 517.

Where boxes are mounted in floors, they shall be listed for use in wet locations. The reason for this is that, in scrubbing floors, for example, water may enter these boxes and be a source of trouble. Section 370-17(b) covers boxes in floors. For protection from corrosion, see Section 300-6.

Conduit bodies are also included in this section.

370-6. Number of Conductors in Outlet, Device, and Junction Boxes, and Conduit Bodies—The interior of the boxes, etc., shall be large enough so that there is plenty of free space for the conductors installed in them.

This is a basic and broad statement which, in itself, is quite sufficient; however, a complete analysis of this will be made as it is in the Code. The main point is that in the installation of conductors in boxes, it should be unnecessary to force the conductors into the box as this is a potential source of trouble. The Code spells out what is good practice as well as the minimum requirements. The installer should, however, always bear in mind the intent and, if necessary to do a good job, go even further than the minimum requirements.

The limitations imposed by Section 370-6(a) and (b) are not intended to apply to terminal housings supplied with motors. See Section 430-12.

Conductors No. 4 or larger shall comply with the provisions of Section 370-18 when used in boxes and conduit bodies.

Section 370-18 provides for space to make proper bends without injury to the conductors.

(a) **Standard Boxes.** Table 370-6(a) gives us the maximum number of conductors that are permitted in standard boxes. Section 370-18 covers boxes or conduit bodies when used as junction or pull boxes.

(1) Table 370-6(a) covers the maximum number of conductors that will be permitted in outlet and junction boxes. There has been no allowance in this table for fittings or devices, such as studs, cable clamps, hickeys, switches, or receptacles that are contained in the box. These must be taken into consideration and deductions made for them. A deduction of one conductor shall be made for each of the following: one or more fixture studs, cable clamps,

hickeys. One conductor shall be deducted for one or more grounding conductors that enter the box.

There shall be a further deduction of one conductor for one or several flush devices mounted on the same strap. A conductor that runs through a box is counted as only one conductor. A conductor originating out of the box and terminating in the box is counted as one conductor. Conductors of which no part leaves the box will not be counted.

Boxes are often ganged together with more than one device per strap mounted in these ganged boxes. In these cases, the same limitations will apply as if they were individual boxes.

Please refer to Figs. 370-1 through 370-4 for illustrations concerning this section. Caution shall be taken to use boxes large enough to accommodate the counting of these grounding conductors. This was interpreted in various ways in the past, but it is now very clear. Table 370-6(a) now has the cubic content listed for the popular sizes of boxes, and has also been expanded.

The volume of a wiring enclosure (box) shall be the total volume of the assembled sections, and where used, the space provided by plaster rings, domed covers, extension rings, etc. that are marked with their volume in cubic inches, shall be the total volume to be used for computing box fill.

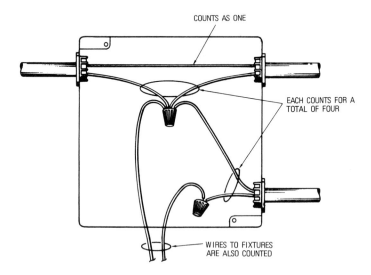

COUNTS AS ONE

EACH COUNTS FOR A
TOTAL OF FOUR

WIRES TO FIXTURES
ARE ALSO COUNTED

Fig. 370-1. Which conductors to count in junction box.

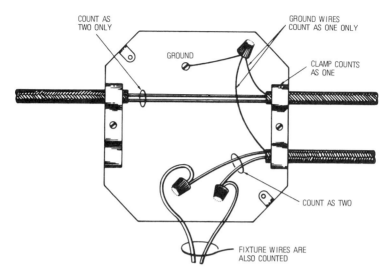

COUNT AS
TWO ONLY

GROUND

GROUND WIRES
COUNT AS ONE ONLY

CLAMP COUNTS
AS ONE

COUNT AS TWO

FIXTURE WIRES ARE
ALSO COUNTED

Fig. 370-2.   Grounding wire does not count.

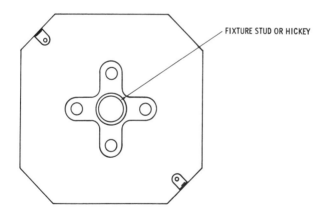

FIXTURE STUD OR HICKEY

Fig. 370-3.   Fixture stud or hickey counts as one conductor.

(2) There will be numerous occasions where Table 370-6(a) will not be applicable. In such cases, refer to Table 360-6(b) from which the number of conductors that will be permitted in the box can be calculated. The various wire sizes and the space that will be allowed per conductor are given. It is only necessary to calculate

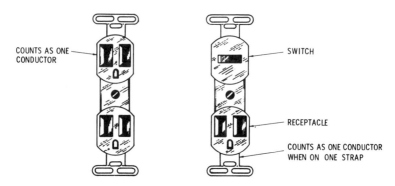

COUNTS AS ONE CONDUCTOR

SWITCH

RECEPTACLE

COUNTS AS ONE CONDUCTOR WHEN ON ONE STRAP

Fig. 370-4. How to count devices in figuring fill.

the cubic space in the box, and multiply by the free space within the box for each conductor. If the calculation exceeds the cubic size of the box, the next larger box will have to be used or an extension added.

(b) **Other Boxes.** Other boxes that are less than 100 cubic inches and are not covered in Table 370-6(a), such as conduit bodies having more than two conduit entries and nonmetallic boxes, are required to be durably marked when manufactured with their cubic-inch interior capacity. To find the maximum conductor allowed in these boxes, you use Table 370-6(b), and you are allowed to take the deductions provided for in Section 370-6(a)(1). These deductions for volume are based on the largest conductor entering the box. If boxes have a larger cubic-inch capacity than that which is designated in Table 370-6(a), their cubic-inch capacity shall be marked as was indicated in this section. The maximum allowable conductors to enter such a box may be figured using the volume allowed for each conductor as found in Table 370-6(b). Please refer to Tables 370-6(a) and 370-6(b) in your *NEC*.

(c) **Conduit Bodies.** If conduit bodies contain No. 6 or smaller conductors, the cross-sectional area of a conduit body shall be not less than twice the cross-sectional area of conduit entering the conduit body. You are referred to Table 1, Chapter 9 for conduit fill, and this will indicate the number allowed in the conduit body.

Explanation: From Table 4. Chapter 9, 1-inch conduit has a cross-sectional area of 0.86 square inches. If a 1-inch LB is used, the cross-sectional area of the LB shall be a minimum of $2 \times 0.86 = 1.72$ square inches. This of course would permit a larger LB to be used with reducing bushings at the threaded hubs, to fulfill the two times requirement.

Conduit bodies with less than three entries shall comply with Section 370-6(b); otherwise no taps or splices will be permitted and the conduit body shall be supported in a secure manner.

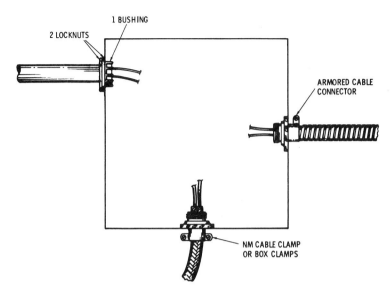

Fig. 370-5.   Connection of cables and conduit to boxes.

370-7. Conductors Entering Boxes, Conduit Bodies, or Fittings—

Care shall be exercised in protection of the conductors from abrasion where they enter the boxes or fittings. With conduit, this is accomplished by bushings or other approved devices. With NM cable, as may be seen in Fig. 370-5, the outer covering of the cable should protrude from the clamp to provide this protection. With armored cable, fiber bushings are to be inserted between the conductors and the armor to prevent any abrasion. The following shall be complied with:

(a) **Opening to Be Closed.** Where conductors enter any openings, they shall be properly closed. Where single conductors enter the boxes, loom covering is to be provided; with cable, cable clamps shall be used or the boxes provided with built-in cable clamps; with conduit, the locknuts and bushings will adequately close the openings.

(b) **Metal Boxes, Conduit Bodies, and Fittings.** When metal boxes, conduit bodies, or fittings are used with open wiring, proper bushings shall be used. In dry places, a flexible tubing may be used and extended from the last conductor support into the box and secured. See Fig. 370-6 on page 280.

Where a raceway or cable enters the box or fitting, the raceway or cable is to be properly secured to the box or fitting. With conduit, two locknuts and a bushing should be used. With armored cable, approved connectors shall be used. With NM cable, a connector or built-in clamps shall be used.

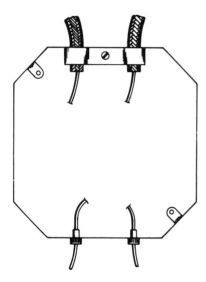

Fig. 370-6. Open wiring into boxes.

(c) **Nonmetallic Boxes.** Where nonmetallic boxes are used with either concealed knob-and-tube work or open wiring, the conductors shall pass through individual holes in the box. If flexible tubing is used over the conductor, it shall extend from the last conductor support into the hole in the box at least ¼ inch.

Where nonmetallic cable is used, it shall extend through the opening in the box at least ¼ inch. It is not required that individual conductors or cables be clamped if the individual conductors or cables are supported within 8 inches of the box. When nonmetallic conduit is used with nonmetallic boxes, the conduit shall be connected to the box by approved means.

Nonmetallic boxes shall be rated at the lowest temperature rating of the conductor that enters the nonmetallic box.

In all instances all permitted wiring methods shall be secured to the boxes.

(d) **Conductors No. 4 AWG or Larger.** Section 373-6(c) covers installation for these.

370-8. Unused Openings—Any unused openings of boxes, conduit bodies, or fittings, where the knockout has been removed, shall be effectively closed by an approved means which will afford equal protection to that of the original. Metal plugs or plates used to close the holes in nonmetallic boxes shall be recessed at least ¼ inch from the outer surface of the box.

370-9. Boxes Enclosing Flush Devices—See the *NEC*.

370-10. In Wall or Ceiling—This Section is much abused in the field. It is recommended that close attention be paid to this part to prevent fires from starting in walls and ceilings.

In walls and ceilings of concrete, tile, or other noncombustible materials, boxes and fittings are to be so installed that the front or outer edge of the box or fitting is not set back more than ¼ inch from the finished surface.

In walls or ceilings constructed of wood or other combustible materials, the outer or front edge of the box or fitting shall be flush with the finished surface or project therefrom. In the event of a short circuit or any arcing, the box or fitting will afford protection to the combustible materials. See Fig. 370-7.

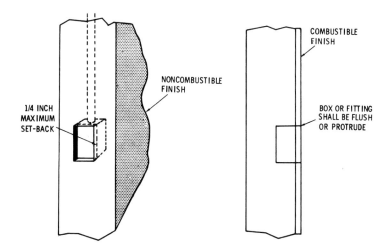

Fig. 370-7. Setback of boxes in walls and ceilings.

370-11. Repairing Plaster—See the *NEC*.

370-12. Exposed Surface Extensions—Exposed extensions from boxes or fittings are very often desirable or necessary. In making these extensions, there are a number of approved wiring methods which may be used, but a box extension ring or blank cover shall be used for attaching to the concealed wiring and shall be electrically and mechanically secured to the original box and extensions therefrom and shall be in accordance with the regulations as provided in other articles of Chapter 3.

370-13. Supports—See the *NEC*.

370-14. Depth of Outlet Boxes—In no case shall a box have a depth of less than ½ inch, and if flush devices are to be mounted in it, the depth shall be not less than ¹⁵⁄₁₆ inch.

370-15. Covers and Canopies—In completed installations each outlet box shall be provided with a cover unless a fixture canopy is used.

(a) **Nonmetallic or Metal Covers and Plates.** Either nonmetallic or metallic plates and covers may be used with nonmetallic boxes, but when metallic plates or covers are used, the grounding provisions of Section 250-42 will apply—it will be necessary to see that they are properly grounded.

Note: The **NEC** refers you to Sections 410-18(a) and 410-56(c) for metal faceplates.

As always, the Code is concerned with the practical side of things. Any metal part of a wiring system is subject to becoming energized, so should therefore be grounded whenever there is a possibility of anyone touching the device and a grounded surface at the same time. Concrete floors and walls are, as a rule, considered to be grounded surfaces, even if covered with block tile. See Section 250-42 in your *NEC*.

(b) **Exposed Combustible Wall or Ceiling Finish.** This paragraph is often overlooked. When mounted on combustible walls or ceilings, the fixture canopy or pan used, or the ceiling finish exposed between the edge of the canopy or pan and the outlet box, shall be covered with a noncombustible material. See Fig. 370-8.

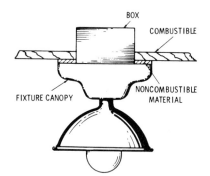

Fig. 370-8. Noncombustible material shall be installed between a canopy and a combustible ceiling.

(c) **Flexible Cord Pendants.** When outlet boxes or conduit fittings have covers through which flexible cords or pendants are to run, these holes shall be smooth, shall have bushings designed for the cord to pass through, and shall have well-rounded surfaces. Hard-rubber cord or rubber-type bushings shall not be used, as they will be subject to deterioration. Where the cord comes through the bushed hole in the cover, a suitable "electrician's" knot or some other suitable knot shall be provided above the plate to take the strain off the tap to the supply conductors.

370-17. Outlet Boxes.

(a) **Boxes at Lighting Fixture Outlets.** Any boxes used for lighting fixture outlets are to be designed for that purpose and all outlets used exclusively for lighting fixtures shall have the boxes designed or installed so that the lighting fixture may be attached. Attention should be given to the weight of the fixture. The provisions of Article 410 pertaining to the hanging of fixtures shall be complied with.

(b) **Floor Boxes.** Floor boxes especially approved for the purpose shall be used for receptacles located in the floor.

Exception: Standard listed types of flush receptacle boxes shall be permitted where receptacles are located in elevated floors of show windows or other locations when the authority having jurisdiction judges them to be free from physical damage, moisture and dirt.

(c) **Boxes at Fan Outlets.** Outlet boxes shall never be used for the support of ceiling-panel-type fans. They shall be attached by a secure means into a structural member of the ceiling.

Exception: If the boxes are listed for supporting ceiling fans, they may be used for the support of the fan.

This part should be adhered to as well as the jurisdiction to rule as to the approval of standard receptacle boxes, etc.

370-18. Pull and Junction Boxes—(a) through (d) below should be adhered to when boxes and conduit bodies are used for pull or junction boxes.

(a) **Minimum Size.** Where raceways ¾-inch trade size or larger are used to contain conductors No. 4 or larger, or for cables that contain conductors No. 4 or larger, the minimum dimensions of pull or junction boxes to be used with these raceways or cables is as follows:

(1) **Straight Pulls.** The width of a box for straight pull is governed by the size of conduits used and the space required for the locknuts and bushings. The length, however, will not be less than 8 times the trade size of the largest raceway. In Fig. 370-9, for example, there is a 4-inch conduit, a 2-inch conduit, and a 1-inch conduit. Therefore, the length will be 4 × 8, or a minimum of 32 inches in length, and the width will be approximately 12 inches to accommodate the locknuts and bushings without crowding.

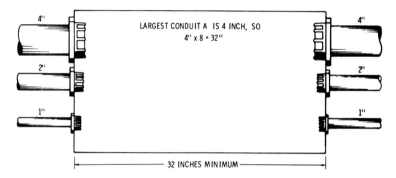

Fig. 370-9. Calculation of pull boxes for use without splices or taps.

(2) **Angle or U Pulls.** When angle or U pulls are made, the distance between the point where the raceway enters the box and the opposite wall shall be not less than six times the trade size diameter of the largest raceway. If more than one entry is made into the box, the distance just mentioned shall be increased by the sum of the diameters of all the other raceways that enter the same box in one row and on the same wall as the box. The row that provides the maximum distance shall be used.

Exception: If the entry into the box of the row of conduits is on a wall opposite the cover of the box, and if the distance from that wall to the cover meets the requirements of the column for one wire per terminal, as covered in Table 373-6(a).

When entries of raceways contain the same conductor, they shall be not less than six times the trade size diameter of the largest raceway.

In Fig. 370-10, the dimensions shown are minimum. It is very possible that the 30-inch figure will not agree with the diagonal figures; this will depend on the actual locations of the conduits. Nevertheless, the figures are minimum and, if necessary, a larger box will be required.

If cable size is transformed into raceway size in (a) (1) and (a) (2) above, you shall use what would be the minimum size raceway required to contain the size and number of the cable.

(3) Boxes of lesser dimensions than those required in subsections (1) and (2) may be used for installations of combinations of conductors which are less than the maximum conduit fill (of conduits being used) permitted in Table 1, Chapter 9, provided the box has been approved for and is permanently marked with the maximum number of conductors and the maximum AWG size permitted.

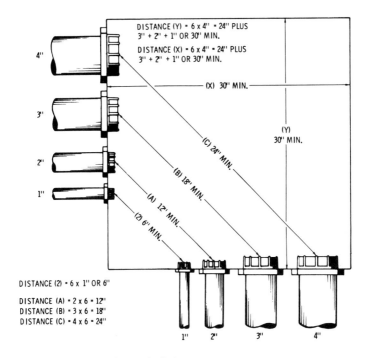

DISTANCE (Y) = 6 x 4" = 24" PLUS
3" + 2' + 1" OR 30" MIN.

DISTANCE (X) = 6 x 4" = 24" PLUS
3" + 2' + 1" OR 30" MIN.

(X) 30" MIN.

(Y)
30" MIN.

(C) 24" MIN.

(B) 18" MIN.

(A) 12" MIN.

(Z) 6" MIN.

4"

3"

2"

1"

DISTANCE (Z) = 6 x 1" OR 6"

DISTANCE (A) = 2 x 6 = 12"
DISTANCE (B) = 3 x 6 = 18"
DISTANCE (C) = 4 x 6 = 24"

1"   2'   3'   4"

Fig. 370-10. Junction box calculations.

Exception: On motors, the terminal size must comply with Section 430-12.

(b) **Conductors in Pull or Junction Boxes**—In pull or junction boxes having any dimension over 6 feet (1.83 m), it is necessary to either rack or cable the conductors. This is required not only to maintain some sort of support for the conductors, but it will also tend to keep the conductors of the same circuit together and, in this way, to keep magnetic induction to a minimum. This is especially important in circuits that carry heavy currents where magnetic induction may affect the voltage balance between phase. See Fig. 370-11.

Reference is made to Section 373-6(c) that requires insulated bushings or an equivalent insulation at terminations where No. 4 or larger conductors are used (see Fig. 370-12). These bushings may be fiber or plastic, a combination metal and plastic (where a grounding-type bushing is required), or fiber inserts.

(c) **Covers.** Covers shall be compatible with the box with which they are used. This covers pull boxes, conduit boxes, junction boxes, and

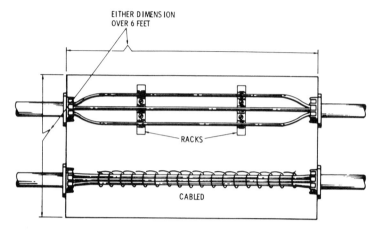

Fig. 370-11. Cabling or racking conductors in large boxes.

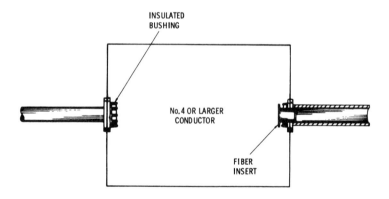

Fig. 370-12. Use of insulation at bushings.

fittings construction, and they shall all be suitably applicable for the condition of use. The requirements of Section 250-42 must be met where metal covers are used; in other words, where metal covers are used, the covers shall be effectively grounded. Covering is essential, in case a short circuit or ground fault should occur, to contain the sparks in the box or fitting.

(d) **Permanent Barriers.** When barriers are required in a box, each section made by the barrier is treated as a separate box.

370-19. Junction, Pull and Outlet Boxes to Be Accessible—All junction, pull, or outlet boxes shall be accessible without the necessity of removing any part of the building structure, paving, or sidewalk. It can be certain that an inspector will not consider a box buried in the ground and covered over as accessible. Junction, pull, and outlet boxes are there for a specific purpose—either for pulling in of conductors, for junctioning conductors, or for the connection of a device. Should it ever be necessary to rework the system, these boxes must be accessible. Boxes in accessible attics or crawl spaces are considered as accessible, as are boxes in drop ceilings with removable panels.

Exception: Listed boxes, where covered by gravel or light aggregate, or noncohesive granulated soil, are permitted if their location is marked so that they may be permanently marked and identified, and if they are located so that they may be easily excavated. Here again, protection against electrolysis in gravel and aggregate must be at least the minimum of any other type of covering, but added protection would not be amiss to ensure that the boxes are watertight against ground seepage.

C. Construction Specifications

The wireman is not too concerned in most cases with the construction specifications of boxes. He purchases approved boxes which will, of course, meet specifications. However, it sometimes becomes necessary to build or assemble a box to meet a certain purpose. Therefore, it is well to be aware of what these specifications are.

370-20. Metal Boxes, Conduit Bodies, and Fittings—Metal boxes, conduit bodies, and fittings shall conform to the following:

(a) **Corrosion-Resistant.** The covering of metal boxes, conduit bodies, and fittings, of course, shall be suitable for the conditions that prevail in the area in which they are used. They shall be protected by one of the following means (the one to be chosen shall be applicable for the conditions): (1) corrosion-resistant metal; (2) well galvanized; (3) enameled; or (4) otherwise properly coated.

Reference is made to Section 300-6 which prohibits the use of enamel in certain places. Also, coating with a conductive material is recommended, such as cadmium, tin, or zinc, since these will secure a better electrical connection.

(b) **Thickness of Metal.** See the *NEC*.

(c) **Metal Boxes Over 100 Cubic Inches.** See the *NEC*.

(d) **Grounding Provisions.** See the *NEC*.

370-21. Covers—See the *NEC*.

370-22. Bushings—See the *NEC*.

370-23. Nonmetallic Boxes—See the *NEC.*

370-24. Marking—The manufacturer's name or trademark shall be durably and plainly marked on all boxes, conduit bodies, covers, extension rings, plaster rings, etc.

D. Pull and Junction Boxes for Use on Systems Over 600 Volts, Nominal

370-50. General—Not only do the general requirements in Article 370 apply, but the rules in Sections 370-51 and 370-52 shall also specifically apply.

370-51. Size of Pull and Junction Boxes—The following will apply to the installation of conductors in pull and junction boxes, with adequate dimensions for their installation:

Note: The following is very essential in the installation of high-voltage cables. Most of them are shielded cables and great care must be taken so as not to disturb the shielding to any great extent during installation. Also there will be splices; since high-voltage splicing is a great deal different from low-voltage splicing a great deal more space is appropriate.

(a) **For Straight Pulls.** The length of the box shall be not less than 48 times the diameter of the conductor and insulation or cable entering the box. Remember, this figure of 48 times is a minimum, as in many instances, one may wish to increase this length for ease in handling of the cables and for splicing.

(b) **For Angle or U Pulls.** Between each conductor or cable that enters a box and the opposite wall of the box the distance shall be not less than 36 times the diameter of the outside of the largest cable or conductor. Where there are additional entries, the above distance shall be increased to the sum of the outside dimensions, over sheath, of the cables or conductor entries that enter through the same wall of the box.

Exception No. 1: Where the cables or conductors exist in the box, the 36 times the diameter required above on the entries may be reduced to 24 times the outside diameter of the cable and cable sheath or conductors.

Exception No. 2: If the provisions of Section 300-34 are followed, conductor or cable entries that enter the wall of the box opposite a removable cover are permitted.

Exception No. 3: Terminal housings on motors are required to conform to Section 430-12.

(c) **Removable Sides.** This requires that one or more sides of a pull box are to be removable.

370-52. Construction and Installation Requirements.

(a) **Corrosion Protection.** Some means must be used to make both the inside and outside of boxes corrosion-resistant. This may be accomplished by making them of material that is already corrosion-resistant or is suitable for such protection as enameling, galvanizing, plating, or other means. Of course, the authority having jurisdiction is the judge of whether the means of corrosion protection is adequate.

(b) **Passing Through Partitions.** Where cables or conductors pass through partitions, suitable means must be provided to prevent damage to the cable or conductors. This may be suitable bushings, shields, or fittings having smooth or rounded edges.

(c) **Complete Enclosure.** Provision shall be made to completely enclose conductors contained in boxes.

(d) **Wiring Is Accessible.** In accordance with Section 110-34, the boxes must be installed so that wiring is accessible without the necessity of removing any part of a building to get to the box. Adequate working space shall also be provided for working with conductors or cables after opening the box.

(e) **Suitable Covers.** Suitable covers must be installed to cover these boxes, and a means of securely fastening the cover in place shall be provided. If underground box covers weigh over 100 pounds, the weight of the cover shall be considered equivalent to fastening the cover in place. It is essential that a permanent marking be made on the outside of the box cover indicating "HIGH VOLTAGE." Half-inch-high block-type letters shall be used, and they shall be readily visible.

(f) **Suitable for Expected Handlings.** Both the box and cover must be made so that they will withstand any handling to which they may be subjected.

ARTICLE 373—CABINETS AND CUTOUT BOXES

373-1. Scope—This article covers the installation of cabinets, cutout boxes, meter socket enclosures, and their construction.

A. Installation

373-2. Damp or Wet Locations—Cabinets and cutout boxes used in wet or damp locations shall be suitable for the location and installed in such a manner that moisture is not likely to enter or accumulate in the enclosure.

The boxes for the cabinets must be mounted ¼ inch between the enclosure and the wall and any other type of members used for support. Only weatherproof cabinets and cutout boxes shall be used.

A recommendation that would be well to follow is: It is recommended that boxes of nonconductive material be used with nonmetallic sheathed cable when such cable is used in locations where moisture is likely to be present.

An interesting case involving this sort of installation concerned a 2-inch service mast which ran straight down to a service-entrance cabinet with branch circuit breakers included. The location was a turkey brooder house which had high humidity and was warm, but the outside temperature was below zero. The mast acted as a chimney drawing the warm moist air up and out of the interior. The moisture in the air condensed on the interior of the cold mast and continually dripped into the service-entrance equipment, causing a short which could have possibly developed into a fire. An inspector found the condition and required a seal-off next to the service-entrance equipment. This is mentioned because such an area might be overlooked as a damp location.

Note: You are referred to Section 300-6 of the *NEC* for protection against corrosion.

In hazardous (classified) locations, Articles 500 through 517 shall be conformed with.

373-3. Position in Wall—The requirements here are the same as for outlet boxes, namely that, in concrete, tile, or other noncombustible walls, the boxes or cabinets may be set back not to exceed ¼ inch from the finished surface, and on walls of combustible materials, they shall be flush with or project from the finished surface.

373-4. Unused Openings—See the *NEC*

373-5. Conductors Entering Cabinets or Cutout Boxes—All conductors entering cabinets or cutout boxes shall be protected from abrasion and shall meet the following requirements:

(a) **Openings to Be Closed.** You are required to properly close enterings through which conductors pass. In other words, where conduit is used, the hole in the cabinet or box shall be the proper size for the trade size of conduit used.

(b) **Metal Cabinets and Cutout Boxes.** When metal cutout boxes or cabinets are used with open wiring or knob-and-tube wiring, the conductors entering these boxes shall enter the metal by means of an approved insulating bushing, or you may use flexible insulating tubing that extends from the last support of the wiring and is firmly secured to the cabinet or cutout box.

(c) **Cables.** Each cable is required to be adequately secured to cabinets or cutout boxes.

373-6. Deflection of Conductors—This covers the deflection of conductors in cabinets and cutout boxes at terminals, or conductors entering or leaving cabinets and cutout boxes.

(a) **Width of Wiring Gutters.** Table 373-6(a) gives us the criteria by which conductors may be deflected in a cabinet or cutout box, which is the gutter width that is provided in these locations. The intent is not to injure the conductors or insulation in installation. The number of the conductors in parallel in accordance with Section 310-4 will be used to judge parallel conductors in cabinets or cutout boxes. (See the *NEC* for Table 373-6(a), Minimum Wire Bending Space at Terminals and Minimum Width of Wiring Gutters in Inches, and the note therewith.)

(b) **Wire Bending Space at Terminals.** The space for bending wiring to terminals is covered in (1) or (2) below:

(1) When the conductors do not enter or leave the enclosure through a wall that is opposite the terminal, Table 373-6(a) shall apply.

Exception No. 1: If conductors enter or leave an enclosure that is located opposite its terminal, Code permits said conductors to enter or leave the enclosure if the gutter is joined to a gutter adjacent thereto and if it has a width that conforms to Table 373-6(b). The gutter or enclosure or cutouts that we are covering here refers to the space that does not involve terminals or switches.

Exception No. 2: If a conductor is 300 MCM or less, it is permitted to enter or leave the enclosure that only contains a meter socket(s) through the wall opposite its terminal, and only if the terminal is the lay-in type and either (a) or (b) below are met:

(a) The terminal faces the opposite enclosure wall, but the offset may not be greater than 50 percent of the bending space required as specified in Table 373-6(a), or

(b) The terminal shall be turned in the enclosure, and the terminal is within a 45° angle facing directly to the enclosure wall.
   Note: This explains something about the offset. It is the distance on the enclosure wall from the center line of the terminal to a line that passes through the center of the opening in the enclosure.

(2) When a conductor enters or leaves the enclosure through a wall that is opposite this terminal, Table 373-6(b) shall be used.
   For removable (single-barrel) compression (crimp)-type lugs, bending space may be reduced as follows:

300MCM-750 MCM: 3 inches reduction
OAWG-259 MCM: 2 inches reduction

but reduction can only be applied to the extent that minimum wire bending space is reduced to 6 inches. In no case may the reduction to a value less than that in Table 373-6(a).

The above may seem confusing, but read it carefully and follow the instructions, for the results are highly important.

(c) **Insulated Fittings.** Where No. 4 or larger conductors that are ungrounded enter a raceway in a cabinet, pull box, junction box, or auxiliary gutter, protection for the conductors shall be provided by a fitting with a smooth and rounded insulating surface. This is usually in the form of an insulated bushing screwed on the raceway end. If the conductors are separated by an insulating material that is substantially and securely fastened in place, this may be used instead.

Exception: Threaded hubs may be mounted as part of the enclosure and the above fitting and insulation may be omitted, provided that the hub itself is smoothly rounded or flared where the conductors enter the enclosure.

None of the above permits conduit bushings to be entirely of insulating material securing the raceway. The temperature rating of the insulated conductors shall not be higher than the temperature rating of the insulating material used in the fitting or other material.

Insulated bushings and inserts are made in various forms. A metal bushing with a fiber insert which will lock into place may be used; an insulating bushing of insulating material in entirety may be used but a locknut installed ahead of it is a must; or bushings that are metal and have insulation incorporated as a part of the bushing may be used. See Fig. 373-1.

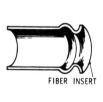
FIBER INSERT

INSULATION

METAL

Fig. 373-1. **Bushing insulation for No. 4 or larger conductors.**

373-7. Space in Enclosures—See the *NEC*.

373-8. Enclosures for Switches or Overcurrent Devices—This section has caused much discussion in the field and left much on the shoulders of the authority having jurisdiction to make the judgment as to adequate spaces within enclosures. (See the *NEC*.) The enclosures for overcurrent devices and switches may not be used as junction boxes, auxiliary gutters or raceways, for conductors tapping off or feeding through to other switches or overcurrent devices. See Figs. 373-2, 373-3, and 373-4.

Exception: Where adequate spacing is supplied so that the conductors do not fill over 40 percent of the cross-sectional area of the space and splices and taps are not permitted to fill more than 75 percent of any cross section.

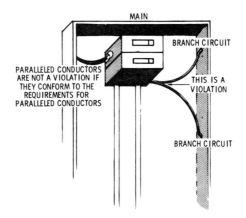

Fig. 373-2. Cabinets and cutout boxes shall not be used as junction boxes.

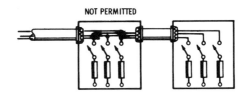

Fig. 373-3. Improper method of connecting more than one switch enclosure.

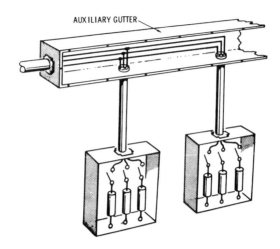

AUXILIARY GUTTER

Fig. 373-4. Proper manner of connecting more than one switch enclosure.

373-9. Side of Back Wiring Spaces or Gutters—Metal cabinets and cutout boxes are required to be furnished with adequate wiring space, auxiliary gutters, or special compartments for wiring as required by Section 373-11(c) and (d).

B. Construction Specifications

373-10. Material—See (a) through (c) below covering cabinets and cutout boxes:

(a) **Metal Cabinets and Cutout Boxes.** Cabinets and cutout boxes shall be coated inside and outside.

Note: For corrosion protection the *NEC* refers you to Section 300-6.

(b) **Strength.** Ample strength and rigidity must be incorporated in the design and construction of cabinets and cutout boxes. When these are made of sheet metal or metal without the coating, they shall have a thickness not less than 0.053 inch.

(c) **Nonmetallic Cabinets.** If nonmetallic cabinets are to be used, they must be approved or listed before they are installed.

373-11. Spacing—The mere fact that a switch enclosure is rated at X number of amperes does not mean that the space inside is adequate for the job. For instance, the enclosure might be designed for single-conductor installation but would be overcrowded if conductors were paralleled. Thus, the engineer, installer, and inspector must analyze the use to which it is to be put and see that the bending space conforms to Table 373-6(a). See the *NEC* for the balance of Section 373-11.

ARTICLE 374—AUXILIARY GUTTERS

374-1. Use—For all appearances, auxiliary gutters could, in a sense, be termed wireways (Article 362) or busways (Article 364). The main difference is the purpose for which they are to be used and some of the installation requirements. Auxiliary gutters are a supplemental wiring method to be used at meter centers, distribution centers, switchboards, and similar points of wiring systems. They may enclose conductors or busbars, but are never to be used to enclose switches, for overcurrent devices, for other appliances, or for other apparatus.

374-2. Extension Beyond Equipment—The only place where auxiliary gutters may be extended beyond a distance of 30 feet (9.14m) is for elevator work (Section 620-35). Whenever they extend beyond this 30-foot distance, they fall in the category of wireways or busways and come under The provisions of wireways (Article 362) and busways (Article 364). See Fig. 374-1.

374-3. Supports—Auxiliary gutters shall be securely fastened at intervals not to exceed 5 feet.

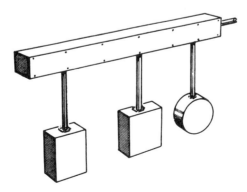

Fig. 374-1. Purpose of auxiliary gutters.

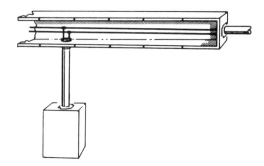

Fig. 374-2. Interior and construction of auxiliary gutters.

374-4. Covers—The covers shall be securely fastened to the gutter— this is usually done by means of screws.

Auxiliary gutters are troughs with a removable lid, and may be purchased in almost any length. The lid is usually fastened to the trough with screws (Fig. 374-2): When auxiliary gutters are used outdoors in damp or wet locations, they shall be weatherproof or waterproof, whichever is applicable.

374-5. Number of Conductors—The ruling is that auxiliary gutters shall contain no more than 30 current-carrying conductors at any cross section. However, there is no limit on the number of conductors used only for signal circuits or the number of controller conductors between a motor and its starter if these control wires are used only for starting duty. In addition, the number of conductors that may be installed in a gutter shall not exceed 20 percent fill, regardless of the use of the conductors.

Exception No. 1: Section 620-35 for use with elevators is an exception.

Exception No. 2: The conductors used for the following are not considered as current-carrying conductors:

(1) Signal circuits.
(2) Control conductors between motor starters when used for starting use duty only.

Exception No. 3: Correction factors are covered in Note 8(a) or Tables 310-16 through 310-31. There shall be no limitation on the number of current-carrying conductors. Instead, the sum of the cross-sectional area of all conductors is not to exceed 20 percent of the cross-sectional area of the auxiliary gutter.

Note: The NEC refers you to Tables 5, 6, 7, and 8, or Chapter 9 and the notes thereto at the beginning of Chapter 9.

374-6. Ampacity of Conductors—The ampacity of insulated aluminum and copper conductors is listed in Tables 310-16 and 310-31, respectively. Conductors in auxiliary gutters are not subject to Note 8(a) that accompanies these tables (30 or less) for derating. When copper bars are used in gutters, their ampacity is limited to 1000 amperes per square inch of the cross section of the bar. Aluminum is limited to 700 amperes per square inch cross section.

374-7. Clearance of Bare Live Parts—Bare conductors shall be securely and rigidly fastened, with adequate allowance made for contraction and expansion. This expansion and contraction may be provided for by various means, as long as the bars or bare conductors are mechanically secured.

The minimum clearance between bare current-carrying parts that are mounted on the same surface, but of opposite polarity, shall be 2 inches. There shall also be a minimum of 1 inch clearance between bare metal conductors (current-carrying) and the metal surfaces of the gutters.

374-8. Splices and Taps.

(a) **Within Gutters.** Splices and taps are permitted in gutters, but shall be made and insulated by approved methods only. They must be accessible by means of removable covers or doors. Not more than 75 percent of the area of the gutter shall be taken up by the conductors plus the taps and splices.

(b) **Bare Conductors.** Taps that are made from bare conductors (such as buses) shall leave the gutter opposite their point of terminal connection to the bus and the taps shall not come into contact with any bare current-carrying parts of opposite polarity.

(c) **Suitably Identified.** All taps from gutters shall be suitably identified as to the circuit or the equipment Which they supply. The Code does not spell out exactly how to do this, but the means of identifying the circuits or equipment supplied must meet the approval of the inspection authority. This could be done by tagging the leads in the gutter, but a very practical method is to mark the circuits served on the gutter lid. See Fig. 374-3 on page 298.

(d) **Overcurrent Protection.** Taps from conductors in a gutter are all subject to the provisions outlined in Section 240-21. In brief, Section 240-21 states that tap conductors not over ten feet in length shall have an ampacity of not less than the ampacity of the one or more circuits or loads that they supply. Taps not over 25 feet in length shall have an ampacity of at least one-third of the ampacity of the conductors to which they are tapped, and they shall terminate in a single set of fuses or circuit breakers which will limit the current to that of the tap conductors or less. There is considerably more to this "tap rule" in Article 240, but it will not be repeated here.

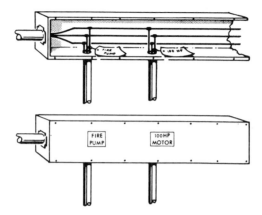

Fig. 374-3. Identifying circuits or loads from gutters.

374-9. Construction and Installation—Auxiliary gutters shall be constructed in accordance with the following:

(a) **Electrical and Mechanical Continuity.** Gutters shall be such that their installation will maintain electrical and mechanical continuity for the complete system. Mechanical and electrical security are two important points that are ever present in electrical wiring and must never be overlooked.

(b) **Substantial Construction.** The construction of gutters shall be such that a complete enclosure is provided for the conductors. Suitable protection from corrosion shall be provided both inside and outside the gutters. If corner joints are used, they shall be made tight to prevent entry of moisture, etc. If rivets or bolts are used in this construction of gutters, 12-inch spacing between rivets and bolts is the maximum allowed.

(c) **Smooth, Rounded Edges.** Protective means shall be applied any place where conductors may be subject to abrasion. In other words, bushings, shields, or other fittings necessary to protect the conductors shall be used at all joints, around bends, between gutters and cabinets or junction boxes, or at any other possible location where abrasion might occur. Insulation laying on the edge of metal may eventually cut through to the conductor because of weight, temperature, or vibration.

(d) **Deflected Insulated Conductor.** Section 373-6 and Table 373-6(a) will apply wherever insulated conductors are deflected within the auxiliary gutter, at the ends, or where conduit, fittings, or other raceways enter or leave the gutter, or at any point where the gutter is deflected more than 30 degrees.

(e) **Outdoor Use.** Only raintight auxiliary gutters shall be installed in wet locations.

ARTICLE 380—SWITCHES

A. Installation

380-1. Scope—This article applies to certain breakers used as switches, and to all switches, including switching devices.

380-2. Switch Connections.

(a) **Three-Way and Four-Way Switches.** With three-way and four-way switches, the connections shall be so made that the neutral or grounded conductor is not switched. If a metal raceway is used, the conductors shall be run so that both polarities are in the raceway in order to counteract inductance. See Fig. 380-1.

Exception: A grounding conductor shall not be required on switch loops. It is the author's opinion that a grounded conductor could be very appropriate where switches have plates mounted with metal screws, and metal plates shall be used in places that must be grounded. This is not a Code requirement.

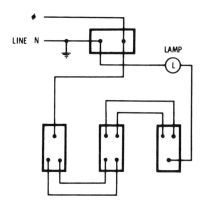

Fig. 380-1. The neutral on three- and four-way switching shall not be opened.

(b) **Grounded Conductors.** A grounding conductor must never be opened unless all other conductors associated with it are opened at the same time or before disconnecting the neutral or grounding conductor. In most instances, the grounded conductor is not disconnected, but with circuits going to or passing through gasoline dispensing islands, it is required that the neutral also be disconnected at the same time as the ungrounded conductor. See Section 514-5 in the *NEC*.

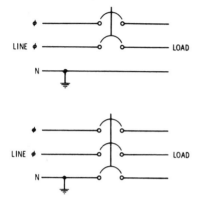

Fig. 380-2. A switch that opens the neutral shall simultaneously open the phase wires.

Fig. 380-2 shows two circuits; in one the grounded conductor is not disconnected, and in the other the grounded conductor is disconnected simultaneously with the ungrounded conductors. Note that the ground is on the supply side in each case so that the system is still grounded.

380-3. Enclosure—It is required that all switches and circuit breakers be enclosed in metal cabinets with externally operable handles, and the enclosure marked to indicate the position of the switch whether OFF or ON. Exceptions to this are pendant switches, surface-type snap switches, and open knife switches mounted on an open-face switchboard or panelboard.

Section 373-6 gave us the minimum bending space of terminals, and also includes the minimum gutter space provided in switch enclosures. See this section in the *NEC* for the space required.

380-4. Wet Locations—Section 373-2 covered cabinets and cutout boxes in damp or wet locations, and required a ¼-inch spacing between the cabinet and the mounting surface. The same applies to switches in wet locations and, if mounted out of doors, they are required to be in a weatherproof enclosure. Raintight is commonly acceptable if prevailing weather conditions are not such that they are endangered by the elements.

380-5. Time Switches, Flashers, and Similar Devices—Time switches, flashers, and similar devices are not required to be externally operable, but they shall be mounted in metal boxes or cabinets, except as follows:

Exception No. 1: Suitable barriers are required where switches are mounted on switchboards, control panels, or enclosures, if they are located so as to place any of the terminals within 6 inches of any manually adjustable clock dial or ON-OFF switches.

Exception No. 2: When enclosed in individual housings so that anyone can operate them if no live parts come in contact with them.

Where mounted in the open (Exception No. 1), they must meet all requirements of safety.

380-6. Position of Knife Switches—Single-throw knife switches shall be mounted in a position so that gravity will not tend to close the switch, but preferably so that they will tend to open. This ruling does not apply to double-throw switches, which may be mounted either vertically or horizontally as required.

(a) **Single-Throw Knife Switches.** Single-throw knife switches shall be mounted in a position so that gravity will not tend to close the switch. If single-throw switches that are approved for mounting in an inverted position, they must be provided with a locking device, which assures that they will stay in the open position.

(b) **Double-Throw Knife Switches.** Double-throw knife switches may be mounted vertically or horizontally, but if mounted vertically, they shall have a locking device to maintain the blades in the open position when in this position.

(c) **Connection of Knife Switches.** Knife switches, except those of the double-throw type, shall be so connected that when open the blades are dead. See Fig. 380-3. (Author's Note: If this is a fusible switch, the fuses shall also be dead when the switch is open. This is not a problem with modern switches as they would not be approved unless containing this feature. However, some older switches are not arranged in this manner.)

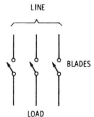

LINE

BLADES

LOAD

Fig. 380-3. Position of knife switches.

Exception: There may be times when the load side of the switch is connected to surface or equipment so that there may be a feedback from another source of power, thus energizing the open knifeblades or switch. If so, you are required to install immediately adjacent to the switches a sign reading, "WARNING—LOAD SIDE OF SWITCH MAY BE ENERGIZED BY BACKFEED."

380-7. Indicating—Switches and circuit breakers that are mounted enclosures for general use in motor circuits as described in Section 380-3 shall be clearly marked to indicate when they are in the OFF position and when they are in the ON position.

For handles of switches and circuit breakers that are operated vertically and not rotationally or horizontally, the switch shall be in the ON position when the handle is up. This does not apply to double-throw switches.

380-8. Accessibility and Grouping.

(a) **Location.** Switches and circuit breakers that are used as switches shall be mounted at a height that is readily accessible from the floor or working platform, and shall be so installed that the grip's center when in its highest point shall not exceed over 6 ½ feet.

Take note of the above. The 1975 *NEC* included the height of the handle for the first time; it is such that it may be reached by hand for opening. There are three important exceptions to the above to take care of impossible cases, where it is impossible to mount the handle as specified above.

Exception No. 1: Actually, this exception was covered early in the *NEC*. The point is that when switches are located on busways that are out of reach from the floor or platform, a suitable device such as a rope, chain, or an adequate stick shall be provided so that they can be accessed from the floor.

Exception No. 2: Motors and appliances and other equipment supplied by switches installed adjacent thereto may be located as specified above, if they are provided with portable means of operation for accessibility.

Exception No. 3: Isolating switches that are higher than 6 ½ feet may be operated by a hookstick.

(b) **Voltage Between Adjacent Switches.** Snap switches in outlet boxes are permitted to be ganged only when the voltage between live metal parts of adjacent switches does not exceed 300 volts, or unless they are installed in boxes equipped with permanently installed barriers between adjacent switches.

380-9. Faceplates for Flush-Mounted Snap Switches—Whenever flush snap switches are mounted on ungrounded boxes, the plates shall be of a nonconducting material in any location where they may be touched at the same time that contact can be made with grounded surfaces or any other conductive surface. Ferrous faceplates shall be at least 0.030 inch (0.762 mm) thick while nonferrous faceplates shall be at least 0.040 inch (1.016 mm) thick. Insulated faceplates shall be noncombustible and shall be at least 0.10 inch (2.54 mm) thick. If they are less than 0.10 inch (2.54 mm) thick, they shall be reinforced or formed to provide additional strength.

In other words, be certain that approved plates are used. Faceplates shall completely cover the opening in the wall surface.

380-10. Mounting of Snap Switches.

(a) **Surface-type.** See the *NEC*.

(b) **Box Mounted.** Boxes for snap switches as permitted in Section 370-10 are to be set back from the wall surface not more than ¼ inch, and shall use the plaster ears so that they seat firmly against the surface of the wall. Boxes that are mounted so that they are flush with the wall or at a slight projection from the wall shall be installed so that the mounting yoke or strap of the switch seats firmly against the box.

In installing boxes, wherever possible there shall be no extension of the box out from the wall surface. This is not a Code requirement, just good workmanship.

This is quite plain, but it might be well to return to Section 370-10. In walls of noncombustible materials, the boxes may be set back not to exceed ¼ inch, but on walls that are of combustible material, the boxes are to be set flush.

380-11. Circuit Breakers as Switches—A circuit breaker may be used as a switch provided that it has the same number of poles required by the switch to do the job. Thus, a single-pole breaker with a switched neutral may be used as a switch for simultaneously opening the hot and the neutral conductor feeding or passing through a gasoline dispensing island. A power operated circuit breaker capable of being opened by hand in the event of power failure shall be permitted to serve as a switch if it has the required number of poles. See Section 240-8. Also, the circuit breakers to be used as switches shall be approved for the purpose.

380-12. Grounding of Enclosures—It is mandatory that enclosures for switches or circuit breakers be grounded, except where accessible to qualified operators only. Article 250 sets forth the manner of grounding enclosures. This does not imply that enclosures for switches or circuit breakers of less than 150 volts to ground are not grounded, as in most cases this has been taken care of elsewhere. But it does make it mandatory to ground the enclosures of switches or circuit breakers on circuits of more than 150 volts to ground.

380-13. Knife Switches—The following sets forth the requirements of knife switches and the interrupting capacities as to sizes for amperages and voltages. Notice that nothing is stated about interrupting currents larger than the amperage of the switch. Unless marked, a knife switch is not intended to interrupt more than the rating of the switch. For example, a 200-ampere switch will interrupt 200 amperes, but a 200-ampere switch might be purchased that has an interrupting capacity of 8000 amperes. The intent is to show that there is a difference between the current-carrying ratings and the interrupting ratings of switches. Therefore, a switch that will interrupt more than the normal current-carrying rating of the switch will be so marked.

(a) **Isolation Switches.** Isolation switches are often used in faces in motors not in sight of their controller. For safety's sake, they are usually knife switches with no fuses. If they are rated at over 1200 amperes at 250 volts or less, or at 600 amperes at 251 to 600 volts, they are not to be opened while under load. They are for isolating only when working on machinery.

(b) **To Interrupt Currents.** Only circuit breakers or switches of special design shall be used for current interruption greater than 1200 amperes at 250 volts or less, or at 600 amperes at 251 to 600 volts.

(c) **General-Use Switches.** Knife switches rated lower than 1200 amperes at 250 volts or less, and 600 amperes at 251 to 600 volts, may be used as general-purpose switches and may be opened under load. Nothing, however, is mentioned of opening under fault currents. (See Article 100 for the definition of a general-use switch.)

(d) **Motor-Circuit Switches.** Reference is made to Article 100 for the definition of a motor-circuit switch in which percentages of load and horsepower ratings are mentioned. Knife-type switches may be used for motor switches.

380-14. Rating and Use of Snap Switches—These switches may be used within their rating, and as follows:

(a) **AC General-Use Snap Switch.** The following covers what form of general-use snap switch is suitable to use only on alternating currents when they control any of the following:

(1) If the ampere and voltage rating of the switch involved is not exceeded, they may be used for resistive and inductive loads, including electric discharge lamps.

(2) If they are for 120 volts and the ampere rating is not exceeded, they may be used with tungsten-filament lamps.

(3) If not to exceed 80 percent of the operating ampere rating of the switch, they may be used on motor loads.
General-use snap switches means the switches such as are general purpose switches in wall boxes or handy boxes.

(b) **AC-DC General-Use Snap Switch.** A form of general-use snap switch suitable for use on either ac or dc circuits for controlling the following:

(1) Resistive and inductive loads, if used where the ampere rating of the switch and the voltage supplied is not exceeded by the amperage and voltage of the resistive load. Resistive loads are similar

to dc loads and do not have an inductive kickback, which will cause the arcing common with inductive loads.

(2) Inductive type loads are not to load a switch over 50 percent of the ampere rating of the switch at the applied voltage. Switches when rated in horsepower may be used to control motor loads that are within the horsepower rating of the switch and the voltage applied. Note the percentage and the restrictions because of the inductive loads.

(3) Only "T" rated switches shall be used on tungsten-filament lamp loads, and they shall not exceed the rating of the "T" rated switch.

For noninductive loads other than tungsten-filament lamps, switches shall have an ampere rating not less than the ampere rating of the load. Noninductive loads are loads that have a 100 percent power factor. Induction is basically a load with a lagging power factor. However, the same effect would result when a capacitive load presented itself, but this would be a rather unusual case. Tungsten-filament lamps draw a heavy current on start.

Tungsten filaments draw heavy initial current for energizing the tungsten filament. Inductive loads include discharge lighting and all other inductive loads. Switches controlling signs and outline lighting should be selected according to the requirements of Section 600-2, and for controlling motors, Sections 430-83, 430-109, and 430-110.

Inductive loads, when opened, create a high-voltage kick caused by the collapsing flux with a resultant tendency to burn the contacts. High-amperage switches are the answer to this problem.

(c) **CO/ALR Snap Switches.** Snap switches of 20 amperes or less may be directly connected to either copper or aluminum conductors, but they shall be marked CO/ALR.

B. Construction Specifications

380-15. Marking—Switches shall be marked with the current rating, voltage rating, and maximum horsepower rating (if so rated).

380-16. 600-Volt Knife Switches—This is fundamentally a design factor, but it is important. When breaking currents over 200 amperes with 600-volt-rated knife switches, the switch blades shall have auxiliary contacts of a renewable or quick-break type, or they shall be of a type that will serve the equivalent purpose.

380-17. Fused Switches—Switches that are fused are not to have parallel fuses.

Note: The *NEC* refers us to Section 240-8, Exception.

380-18. Wiring Bending Space—Wiring bending spaces in switches shall meet the requirements of Section 380-3, and shall also meet Table 373-6(b) where spacings to the enclosure wall are opposite the line and load terminals.

ARTICLE 384—SWITCHBOARDS AND PANELBOARDS

384-1. Scope—Covered in this article are:

(1) All types of switches that are installed for lighting and power circuits; among these are distribution boards, panel boards, etc.

(2) Panels used for charging batteries supplied from light or power circuits.

Exception: Switchboards, if used only to control battery-operated signaling circuits.

384-2. Other Articles—As with many articles, the requirements of this article are often supplemented by others in the Code, such as Articles 240, 250, 370, 380, and any others that might apply. If switchboards or panelboards are to be located in hazardous (classified) areas they must meet the requirements of Article 500 through 517.

384-3. Support and Arrangement of Busbars and Conductors.

(a) **Conductors and Busbars on a Switchboard.** See the *NEC.*

(b) **Overheating and Inductive Effects.** See the *NEC.*

(c) **Used as Service Equipment.** Each switchboard, switchboard section, or panelboard used as service equipment may require a main bonding jumper sized as covered in Section 250-79(c) and placed within the service disconnecting section for connecting the grounded service conductor on the supply side of the disconnecting means. Bonding will be required to all sections of a switchboard to bond them together with an equipment grounding conductor, and this equipment grounding conductor shall be sized according to Table 250-95.

(d) **Load Terminals.** Load terminals in switchboards and panelboards shall be so located that it will be unnecessary to reach over phase busbars or conductors in order to make up the load connections.

(e) **High-Leg Marking.** When supplied by a 4-wire delta system and a mid-tap of one phase is grounded, the busbar or conductor having the higher voltage to ground is to be permanently marked by an outer finish of orange color or by any other effective means.

Refer to Fig. 210-3, which shows voltage relations on such a system. It will be noted that phase C has 208 volts to the neutral. This is the conductor with the higher voltage to ground which is being referred to and care must be exercised to keep from connecting 120 volt equipment to this phase and ground. This phase is commonly termed the "wild leg."

(f) **Phase Arrangement.** This is a much-needed Code requirement to achieve uniformity in phase lettering.

On 3-phase buses they shall be indicated as phase A, B, and C, beginning from front to back or top to bottom or left to right, as if viewed from the front of the switchboard or panelboard. The busbars "B" phase is to be the higher voltage ("wild leg") to ground the phase with. Busbar arrangements other than those above will be permitted if they are additions to existing installations, and shall be marked.

Exception: On 3-phase, 4-wire delta connected systems the same configuration of the phase shall be permitted as the metering equipment when single or multisection switchboards or panelboards are used for metering.

(g) **Minimum Wire-Bending Space.** The requirements of Section 373-6 cover the bending space at terminals, and also the minimum gutter space to be provided in switchboards and panel boards.

384-4. Installation—Equipment covered in this article is to be installed in a separate room or space used for no other purpose than installation of this equipment. The space that was described in Section 110-16 is the space required here. In addition the exclusively dedicated space must extend from the floor to the structure's ceiling, with a width and depth as required by the equipment. In this room there shall be no piping, air ducts, or any such items entering or passing through such spaces or rooms that are not required for the switchboard or panelboard.

It is impossible to include all of these rulings in one article, but many facts have been incorporated here as a matter of clarification and intent. Therefore, it is highly recommended that this article be thoroughly examined and understood.

Note: See the *NEC.*

Note: Installation of sprinkler systems to protect the electrical equipment is not prohibited.

Exception No. 1: If control equipment is required by the nature of the installation, or other rules applicable elsewhere in the Code, to be adjacent or within sight of machinery that it operates.

Exception No. 2: Electrical rooms or spaces that require ventilating heating or cooling or equipment are acceptable.

Exception No. 3: In industrial operations, equipment located throughout if isolated from foreign equipment by height or physical enclosures or covers that will provide adequate mechanical protection from any vehicle traffic or accidental contact by unauthorized persons, or spillage or leakage of pipe.

Exception No. 4: Outdoor electrical equipment may be located out of doors if it has weatherproof enclosures and is protected from accidental contact by unauthorized people or from vehicle traffic or accidental spillage or leakage from piping systems.

Author's Note: Some of these installations may require fencing.

A. Switchboards

384-5. Location of Switchboards—Switchboards which have any exposed live parts shall be installed in dry locations and accessible only to qualified persons and under the supervision of competent persons. The location of switchboards shall be such that the likelihood of damage from equipment or processes is kept to a minimum.

384-6. Wet Locations—Wherever switchboards are in a wet location, in or outside a building, they are required to be in a weatherproof enclosure and, if necessary, shall conform to Section 373-2 which requires a ¼-inch spacing from the surface on which they are mounted.

384-7. Location Relative to Easily Ignitible Material—All switch and panelboards shall be mounted away from readily ignitible materials. This section can be used in conjunction with Section 240-24(d).

If a combustible floor is used for mounting, protection shall be provided.

384-8. Clearances.

(a) **From Ceilings.** Unless there is an adequate fireproof ceiling, a switchboard shall not be installed closer than 3 feet from the ceiling.

Exception No. 1: Noncombustible shielding may be installed between the switchboard and ceiling.

Exception No. 2: Switchboard that is totally enclosed.

(b) **Around Switchboards.** Section 110-16, the provisions of which must be complied with for clearances around switchboards.

384-9. Conductor Insulation—When insulated conductors are used in switchboards, the insulation shall be flame-retardant and the voltage rating on the insulation shall be not less than the voltage that is applied to it and to any busbars or conductors with which it may come in contact.

384-10. Clearance for Conductors Entering Bus Enclosures—For conduits or raceways that enter a switchboard or a panelboard standing on the floor or similar enclosures, if they enter the enclosure at the bottom be sure to install the conductors in the enclosure so as To have sufficient space for the entering conduit or raceways. Following in the *NEC* is a table covering where conduit or raceways leave or enter below the busbars, supports for busbars, or any other obstruction. The conduit or raceway, including the fittings used, shall not rise in the enclosure more than 3 inches above the bottom of the enclosure.

384-11. Grounding Switchboard Frames—The grounding of all switchboard frames is mandatory except on frames of direct-current, single-polarity switchboards that are effectively insulated.

Exception: Single-polarity, direct-current frames of switchboards are not required to be grounded if they are effectively insulated.

384-12. Grounding of Instruments, Relays, Meters and Instrument Transformers on Switchboards—This is covered in Sections 250-121 through 250-125. In addition to other facts concerning grounding, the grounding conductor shall be no smaller than No. 12 copper.

B. Panelboards

384-13. General—Article 220 gives the facts necessary for computing the feeder loads to panelboards. After arriving at the feeder load, the panelboard shall have a rating not less than the minimum feeder size as calculated. All of the facts as to voltages, phase, capacity, etc., shall be plainly visible after installation. Most inspection authorities will also require the UL label. However, a UL label on an enclosure should not be construed to mean that it also applies to the devices installed therein. Each must have its own UL label.

384-14. Lighting and Appliance Branch-Circuit Panelboard—It is necessary that a distinction be made between lighting and appliance panelboards and power panelboards. Therefore, in this section, a lighting and appliance branch-circuit panelboard is defined as a panelboard which has more than 10 percent of its overcurrent devices rated at 30 amperes or less and for which neutral connections are provided.

384-15. Number of Overcurrent Devices on One Panelboard—The Code limits the number of overcurrent devices that are permitted in a lighting and appliance branch-circuit panelboard to forty-two. This number does not include the devices used as a main. In counting the devices, a double-pole overcurrent device is counted as two, and a three-pole overcurrent unit is counted as three. Each of these units is often counted as only one, which defeats the intent of this section. Older equipment often was made up with wafer-thin and piggyback breakers which made it possible to increase or even double the number of overcurrent devices in a panelboard. Thus, it might have been possible to install eighty-four breakers in a forty-two-breaker panel. The 1965 *NEC* took care of this possibility: The lighting and appliance branch-circuit panelboard to be approved must provide physical means to prevent more overcurrent devices to be installed than the panelboard was approved and listed for. The newer panels have ratings, such as 12-24, that mean it is designed for twelve full-size breakers or twenty-four piggyback breakers with provisions made for a bus ample to supply these. In this way, the number can be limited to the forty-two requirement.

A case of interest was where someone wanted to weld two forty-two-circuit panels together and run buses between them. The decision made, and rightly so, was that the UL label on the panelboard was for the panelboard as originally built, and that welding them together and the addition of the buses were not approved.

384-16. Overcurrent Protection.

(a) **Lighting and Appliance Branch-Circuit Panelboard Individually Protected.** If the combined rating of two panelboards is not exceeded, each lighting and appliance branch circuit panelboard may be individually protected by two main breakers or two sets of fuses.

This pertains to a feeder panel. As an example, a 100-ampere panel (one with 100-ampere buses) is fed by 200-ampere conductors and protected by 200-ampere overcurrent devices. In this case, the feeder panel is required to have a 100-ampere maximum main in it in order to give the proper protection.

A similar case involves a feeder panel with 100-ampere buses. The conductors feeding the panel are of 100-ampere capacity or larger, and are protected by a 100-ampere or smaller overcurrent protection at the source. In this case, it is not required to have a main in the feeder panel.

Author's Note: This has always been a little confusing to me, as attempts have sometimes been made to interpret it, for instance, where two circuit breakers are used as the means in the panel. One could be tripped off and the other still energized, causing injury. It is the responsibility of each inspection authority to see that this sort of thing does not happen.

Exception No. 1: Individual protection of the service-entrance panel for lighting and appliance branch-circuit panelboards is not required if the panelboard feeder at the service-entrance equipment has overcurrent protection that is not higher than the overcurrent protection for which the panelboard was rated.

Exception No. 2: This covers existing installations. Individual protection for lighting and appliance panelboards will not be required when the individual occupancy has service equipment supplying its panel boards. Please note that this exception applies to an individual residential occupancy only. Thus, a split-bus panel is permissible on service equipment in a single dwelling occupancy as long as it is limited to six operations and the 15- or 20-ampere branch-circuit bus is protected by an overcurrent device that will adequately protect these buses.

There is controversy on split-bus panels as to the size of the service-entrance conductors to be used. In a residence, and this is the only place split-bus panels are permitted, we might have a 2-pole, 50-ampere service for the range; a 2-pole, 40-ampere service for the dryer; a 2-pole, 30-ampere service for the water heater; and a 2-pole, 50-ampere service for the 15- and 20-ampere branch circuits. This would give us a total of 170 ampere as mains with the use of 100-ampere service-entrance conductors. Would the Code be met where there was a total of 170-ampere mains? It would be our interpretation that we have not met the Code requirements. Refer to Section 230-90.

Sometimes a conventional panelboard is installed which has lugs on the buses and a breaker is fed backwards as a main and the lugs are still intact. Inspection authorities will probably turn this down as there is a chance that the panelboard may be converted back to one without a main. They will probably accept it if the lugs are sawed off or otherwise fixed so that they may not be used later, but this will void the UL approval.

(b) **Snap Switches Rated 30 Amperes or Less.** See the *NEC*.

(c) **Continuous Load.** If the load is continuous for 3 hours or more, the load on any overcurrent device that is located in the panelboard shall not exceed 80 percent of the rating of the overcurrent device covering that particular circuit.

Exception: If the overcurrent device is approved for 100 percent rating on continuous loads, the load may be up to 100 percent of the overcurrent device rating.

(d) **Supplied Through a Transformer.** When a panelboard is supplied through a transformer, (a) and (b) above shall be located on the secondary side of the transformer.

Exception: If the load is supplied by a single phase 2-wire transformer with a single voltage, we may consider the secondary to be protected by the overcurrent devices in the primary or supply side of the transformer, provided the primary is protected as covered in Section 450-3(b) (1) and at a value that does not exceed the value determined by multiplying the transformer voltage ratio of the secondary-to-primary by the panelboard rating.

(e) **Delta Breakers.** A 3-phase disconnect shall never be connected to the buses of a panelboard having less than three buses.

384-17. Panelboards in Damp or Wet Locations—Reference is made to Section 373-2 which requires that panelboards in wet places shall be weatherproof, in damp locations shall be arranged to drain, and in both locations shall be installed with a ¼-inch air space back of them.

384-18. Enclosure—Panelboards shall be the dead front type, and may be mounted in cabinets or cutout boxes or other enclosures designed for the purpose.

Exception: Panelboards other than dead front panelboards that are externally operated are permitted where accessible only to qualified persons.

384-19. Relative Arrangement of Switches and Fuses—Panelboards having switches on the load side of any type of fuses shall not be installed except for use as service equipment as provided in Section 250-94. With fuses ahead of the switch, they would have to be replaced while still energized. Refer to Section 230-94 for any exceptions.

C. Construction Specifications

Most of these sections are not very applicable to installations, but are more for manufacturing of equipment.

384-20. Panels—See the *NEC*.

384-21. Busbars—See the *NEC*.

384-22. Protection of Instrument Circuits—See the *NEC*.

384-23. Components Parts—See the *NEC*.

384-24. Knife Switches—See the *NEC*.

384-25. Wire Bending Space—See the *NEC*.

384-26. Minimum Spacing—See the *NEC*.

384-27. Grounding of Panelboards—Panelboard cabinets shall be grounded in the manner specified in Article 250 or Section 384-3(c). An approved terminal bar for equipment grounding conductors shall be provided and secured inside of the cabinet for the attachment of all feeder and branch-circuit equipment grounding conductors, when the panelboard is used with nonmetallic raceway, cable wiring or where separate grounding conductors are provided. The terminal bar for the equipment grounding conductor is required to be bonded to the cabinet or panelboard frame or at the first disconnecting means in the system or for separately derived systems to the overcurrent device. It shall not be connected to the neutral bar of any of the equipment.

Exception No. 1: If as in Section 250-74, Exception No. 4 an isolated equipment grounding conductor is permitted, and insulated equipment grounding conductor shall be run with the other conductors and pass through the panelboard with no connection to the panelboard equipment grounding terminal bar.

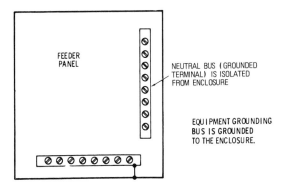

Fig. 384-1. Illustrating grounded grounding terminals on feeder panel.

Exception No. 2: As provided in Section 250-24, the equipment grounding conductors will be permitted to be connected to the neutral bar in separate buildings.

CHAPTER 4

Equipment for General Use

ARTICLE 400—FLEXIBLE CORDS AND CABLES

A. General

400-1. Scope— This article covers the general requirements for flexible cords and flexible cables, uses permitted, and the specifications of construction.

400-2. Other Articles—The requirements of this article are complemented by some of the applicable provisions of articles of this Code.

400-3. Suitability—Cables, cords, and fittings shall be used only in the proper locations and under proper conditions of usage.

Considerable information on flexible cords is included in this chapter of the *NEC*, a greater part being in the form of tables. Flexible cords are essential to the full utilization of electrical energy but are probably the most abused item in use today. A large part of the abuse comes from the use to which they are put by the general public and not by the electrical contractor or wireman.

400-4. Types—Cords of the several types shall conform to the descriptions of Table 400-4. Types of flexible cords other than those listed in Table 400-4 and uses for types listed in the table shall be the subject of special investigation and shall not be used before being approved. This is rather plain in that it is recognized that flexible cords are subject to many and varied usages, and that the responsibility of usages other than those specified by the *NEC* is given to the inspection authority involved. It would be impossible for a book such as the *NEC* to cover any and all usages to which flexible cords are put. (See the *NEC* for Table 400-4.)

Also refer to the notes under Table 400-4.

400-5. Ampacity of Flexible Cords and Cables—The allowable ampacity for cords and cables that do not have more than three current-carrying copper conductors is given in Table 400-5 of the *NEC*. If there are more than three current-carrying conductors in a cord or cable, the ampacity shall be reduced from the three current-carrying conductor cord ratings, and this is shown in the table following this paragraph in the *NEC*.

Be sure to take into consideration the notes that follow Table 400-5.

Refer to subheading C in Table 400-5. Here we find the ampacity for Type W cable, single-conductor, where the individual conductors are installed in raceways, and they shall also not be in physical contact with each other unless they do not exceed 24 inches in length when they pass through an enclosure wall.

In normal circumstances the neutral conductor carries only unbalanced current from the other hot conductors. If properly installed, the currents normally will be balanced in the three or more conductors, and if this applies, the neutral is not considered as a current-carrying conductor.

In a 4-wire, 3-phase wye-connected system, if a 3-wire circuit consists of only 2-phase wires and a neutral, the common conductor or neutral will carry approximately the same amount of current as the 2-phase conductors, and shall therefore be considered as a current-carrying conductor.

If in a 4-wire, 3-phase wye circuit a major part of the load consists of electric discharge lighting, or any data processing or similar equipment there will always be a third harmonic set up, causing currents in the neutral conductor. In these cases the neutral is always to be considered a current-carrying conductor.

Equipment grounding conductors are not considered current-carrying conductors, as they only take care of grounds that appear from phase conductors.

As was provided in Section 250-60, if a single conductor is only used for equipment grounding and unbalanced current (neutral) from the other conductors, it shall not be considered a current-carrying conductor when supplying such appliances as electric clothes dryers and electric ranges.

400-6. Marking—Marking is required for cords and cables by printed tags that are attached to the coil or carton containing the cords or cables. As required by Section 310-11(a), the tag shall designate the type of cord or cable, as SJ, SJE, SJO, SJEO, and other types of flexible cord, and G and W flexible cables shall be marked on the cable not more than 24 inches apart. The type, size, and number of conductors shall also be designated.

400-7. Uses Permitted.

(a) **Uses.** Refer to the *NEC* for the eleven different types of usage permitted, and additional sections that will apply with some of these uses.

In reference to the above, a few cases will be cited to give a general idea of the intent or uses that will be left up to the inspection authority. These are the author's opinions, and some inspection authorities will no doubt disagree.

In (7) might be included the use of portable shop equipment. Such equipment is essentially stationary but, by necessity, might have to be moved to other locations at times.

In (8) could be included a disposal unit, which so often is sold and installed by a plumber who will usually be called upon to repair it. If a flexible cord and plug is installed, the unit may be readily removed and any chance of reconnecting it to the wrong wires or mixing the equipment grounding conductor with the current-carrying conductors will be cut to a minimum. This, plus the fact that much time will be saved. The same is also true of ranges, dryers, washers, etc.

(b) **Attachment Plugs.** In the uses permitted in (a) (3), (a) (6), and (a) (8) of this section, which you are referred to in the *NEC*, the flexible cord must have an attachment plug for energizing from an outlet. There are many types of attachment plug for use, such as twisting type plugs, different voltage type plugs, etc. Refer to NEMA for configurations of the proper attachment plug to be used, and the proper place.

400-8. Uses Not Permitted.

(1) They shall not be substituted for a fixed wiring in a structure.

(2) They shall not be run through holes as the wiring between walls, ceilings, or floors.

(3) They shall not be run through doorways, windows, or other openings. If electrical connection is required, it shall be done by proper wiring methods.

(4) Only proper wiring methods shall be used for attaching to proper wiring surfaces, not cords.

(5) Cords shall not be used instead of proper wiring methods for concealed wire between building walls, ceilings, or floors.

400-9. Splices—This is important: During initial installation, flexible cord shall be installed in a continuous length and shall contain no splices or taps.

Hard service cords (flexible), if they are No. 14 or larger: repairs are permitted if the following conditions are met: (1) spliced in accordance with Section 110-14(b); (2) the completed splice retains the outer sheath properties, original flexibility, usage characteristics of the cord being spliced, the insulation. These above restrictions are plain, and in essence the cord will retain its original characteristics.

400-10. Pull at Joints and Terminals—When flexible cords are used, they shall be so connected and installed that there will be no tension on joints or terminals.

Note: There are many methods of preventing pull on cords. Some are by approved clamps on the attachment plug, using tape or fittings designed for the purpose.

400-11. In Show Windows and Show Cases—Flexible cords used in show windows and show cases shall be types S, SO, SE, SEO, SOO, SJ, SJE, SJO, SJEO, SJOO, ST, STO, STOO, SJT, SJTO, SJTOO, or AFS, which are heavy-duty cord types. There are two exceptions; where used for the wiring of chain-supported fixtures, and for supplying current to portable lamps and other merchandise for exhibition purposes, the cord may be other than those listed, but care should be exercised to secure safe cord of the proper type.

400-12. Minimum Size—The minimum size of flexible cord conductors is covered in Table 400-4.

400-13. Overcurrent Protection—As described in Section 240-4, you will often find cords smaller than wires covered in Table 310-16, which are permitted to be protected against overload by the installed overcurrent device. Some of these should be flexible cords smaller than No. 18 or tinsel cords. They may also include cords of similar characteristics or smaller size if approved for use with specific appliances.

400-14. Protection from Damage—If outlet boxes or similar enclosures are provided with holes for a cord to pass through the covers, these holes shall be protected with proper bushings or other approved fittings.

B. Construction Specifications

400-20. Labels—Factory testing and labeling shall be done before shipping flexible cords. Also look for the UL listing. The public very often interprets the UL label on a flexible cord as meaning that the appliance they are purchasing has been tested by UL. This is not the case. The appliance will also have a UL label attached, if it has been tested.

400-21. Nominal Insulation Thickness—The thickness of insulation covered in Table 400-4 for flexible cords and cables shall meet the specifications thereof.

400-22. Grounded-Conductor Identification—See the *NEC*.

400-23. Grounding-Conductor Identification—The aim of this Section is to point out the coloring methods used for the grounding conductor in flexible cords. The grounding conductor shall be identified by a continuous green covering, or by a green braid with a yellow stripe, so as to not mistake its purpose as being for grounding only. This conductor is never to be used as a current-carrying conductor.

400-24. Attachment Plugs—Section 250-59(a) and (b) covers attachment plugs that are equipped with a grounding terminal. If the flexible cord has an equipment grounding conductor, it shall be attached to this type of plug.

C. Portable Cables Over 600 Volts, Nominal

400-30. Scope—This part applies to multiconductor cables for connection to mobile and portable machinery or equipment that operates at over 600 volts, nominal.

400-31. Construction.

(a) **Conductors.** The minimum size of conductor that is permitted is No. 8 AWG copper or larger, and the conductors shall be of the flexible type (stranded).

(b) **Shields.** To confine the voltage stresses to the insulation, cables that operate at over 2000 volts shall bg of the shielded type.

(c) **Grounding Conductor(s)**—Grounding conductor(s) are to be provided. This grounding conductor shall not be less than the size required in Section 250-95.

400-32. Shielding—The shields mentioned in Section 400-31(b) shall be grounded.

400-33. Grounding—Part K of Article 250 (Grounding Conductor Connections) shall be followed in connection of grounding conductors.

400-34. Minimum Bending Radii—The minimum bending radii, especially on shielded cables, must be taken into account during installation and handling in service, in order to prevent damage to both the cable and the shielding.

400-35. Fittings—Cables may have to be connected together; if so, the connectors shall be of the locking type and provisions should be taken to prevent the opening or closing of these connectors while the cables are energized. Care also must be taken to eliminate tension at cable connections and terminations.

400-36. Splices and Terminations—Portable cables are not to be used with splices except where the splices are permanently molded and vulcanized types as covered in Section 110-14(b). Only qualified persons shall have access to terminals of high-voltage portable cables.

Portable high-voltage cables are usually used on sites where they may be easily damaged, and thus every precaution must be taken to prevent shorts, grounds and accidents.

ARTICLE 402—FIXTURE WIRES

402-1. Scope—This article deals with the general requirements and specifications for construction of fixture wires.

402-2. Other Articles—Fixture wire complies not only with this section, but with sections elsewhere dealing with fixture wires. Article 410 covers the usage of flexible wire in lighting fixtures.

402-3. Types—Table 402-3 in this article applies to fixture wires and their usage shall comply with the applicable parts of this table. Fixture wires are intended for fixture wiring and the application of same is covered in lighting fixtures Article 410. In Table 402-3, fixture wires are usable for 600 volts, nominal, unless not permissible as otherwise provided.

Note: As we have discovered before, thermoplastic insulation at minus 10°C (plus 14°F) requires special care and installation. Thermoplastic insulation is subject to deformation at normal temperatures where subjected to pressure. Thus, extra care must be exercised during installation, especially at points of support.

402-5. Ampacity of Fixture Wires—See Table 402-5 in the *NEC* for the ampacity of fixture wires and the note following.

The conductor insulation temperature rating shall not be less than specified in Table 402-3 of the *NEC* covering types of insulation.

Note: Temperature limitations of conductors is covered in Section 310-10.

402-6. Minimum Size—No conductor smaller than 18 AWG shall be used for fixture wires.

402-7. Number of Conductors in Conduit—Table 2 of Chapter 9 gives the number of fixture wires that may be pulled into a single run of conduit.

402-8. Grounded-Conductor Identification—The grounded conductor shall comply with the same requirements as the grounded conductor as for flexible cords and cables, in Article 400, Section 400-22(a) through (e).

402-9. Marking—Fixture wires require the same types of marking as was covered in Section 310-11(a).

(a) **Required Information.** See the *NEC*.

(b) **Method of Marking.** Thermoplastic insulated fixture wire shall be marked every 24 inches on the surface of the wire, and the marking shall be durable. All other fixture wire may be marked on the reel, coil, or carton.

402-10. Uses Permitted—See your *NEC*.

402-11. Uses Not Permitted—Branch circuits shall not use fixture wiring for the conductors.

Exception: There are some exceptions to the above. Section 725-16 allows it to be used in Class I circuits and, in fire protective signal circuits it may be used as covered in Section 760-16.

402-12. Overcurrent Protection—Section 240-4 specifies overcurrent protection that may be used for the protection of fixture wires.
Refer to Tables 400-5 and 402-5.

ARTICLE 410—LIGHTING FIXTURES, LAMPHOLDERS, LAMPS, RECEPTACLES, AND ROSETTES

A. General

410-1. Scope—Lighting fixtures, lampholders, pendants, receptacles, and rosettes, incandescent filament lamps, arc lamps, electric discharge lamps, the wiring and equipment forming a part of such lamps, fixtures, and lighting installations shall conform to the provisions of this Article, except as otherwise provided in this Code.

410-2. Application to Other Articles—Articles 500 through 517 cover hazardous (classified) locations, and all equipment with, and pertaining to, the fixtures in such locations shall meet the requirements of these Articles.

410-3. Live Parts—There shall be no live parts normally exposed on any fixture, lampholder, lamp, rosette, or receptacle, with the exception of cleat-type lampholders, rosettes, and receptacles which may have exposed live parts if they are at least 8 feet above the floor. Lampholders, receptacles, and switches that have live terminals exposed and accessible shall not be installed in metal canopies or in the open bases of portable table or floor lamps.

B. Fixture Locations

410-4. Fixtures in Specific Locations.

(a) **Wet and Damp Locations.** The installation of fixtures in all damp or wet locations shall be so done that water cannot enter or accumulate in the lampholders, wiring compartments, or any other electrical parts of the installation. Fixtures that are to be installed out of doors in damp or wet locations shall be marked "Suitable for Wet Locations." This should eliminate any haphazard installations that are exposed to moisture. All fixtures installed in wet or damp locations shall be marked "Suitable for Wet Locations" or "Suitable for Damp Locations."

Wet Locations: installations underground, in concrete slabs or masonry in direct contact with the earth, unprotected and exposed to weather, vehicle washing areas, and similar locations.

Damp Locations: interior locations protected from weather, but with moderate degrees of moisture, basements, some barns, some cold-storage warehouses, under canopies, marquees, roofed open porches, etc.

The *NEC* refers us to Article 680 for lighting fixtures in swimming pools, fountains, and similar locations.

(b) **Corrosive Locations.** If fixtures are installed in corrosive locations, they must be suitable and must be approved for such locations.

This will, of course, include any installation in atmospheres with corrosive ducts, gases, or liquids.

Note: Receptacles in fixtures were covered in Section 210-7.

(c) **In Ducts or Hoods.** Lighting fixtures may be installed in nonresidential occupancies, provided that they meet the conditions listed below.

(1) The fixtures used in commercial cooking hoods shall be installed so that the temperature limits of the material used are not exceeded by the temperatures encountered. Also, the fixtures have to be listed for such purposes.

(2) The construction of fixtures shall be such that the lamps and wiring compartments are not exposed to exhaust vapors, cooking vapors, grease, or oil. Thermal shock to diffusers shall be resisted.

(3) Parts of the surface of the fixture shall be smooth so that deposits shall not readily collect on them, and they can be easily cleaned. They shall also be resistant to corrosion, or additional protection shall be installed to protect them against corrosion. In order to facilitate cleaning and to prevent collection of grease, they must be of the smooth surface type.

(4) The wiring methods used to light these fixtures shall be exposed outside of the hood.

Note: The *NEC* refers you to Section 110-11.

(d) **Pendants.** In bathroom areas, no parts of pendants, hanging fixtures, or cord connected fixtures shall be within an area 3 feet measured horizontally and 8 feet vertically from the rim of the bathtub. This encompasses the entire bath area, including that directly over the tub.

410-5. Fixtures Near Combustible Material—The construction of fixtures shall be such, or they shall be so installed or equipped with shades or guards, so that any combustible materials in the immediate vicinity of the fixture will not be subject to a temperature more than 90°C (194°F). Combustible materials that are subject to higher temperatures will change in composition to a substitute that ignites very readily.

410-6. Fixtures Over Combustible Material—Lampholders that are installed over highly combustible materials shall not have a switch as a part of the lampholder, but shall be switched elsewhere and, unless an individual switch (located elsewhere) is used for each fixture, the lampholder shall be located at least 8 feet above the floor or otherwise located or guarded so the lamp may not be readily removed or damaged. See Figs. 410-1 and 410-2.

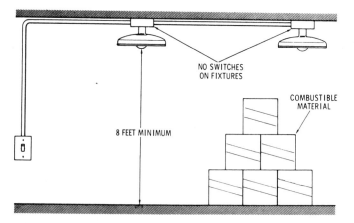

NO SWITCHES
ON FIXTURES

COMBUSTIBLE
MATERIAL

8 FEET MINIMUM

Fig. 410-1. Fixtures over combustibles must not have a switch as part of the fixture but must be switched elsewhere.

410-7. Fixtures in Show Windows—See the *NEC*.

410-8. Fixtures in Clothes Closets.

(a) **Definition.** Clothes closet areas are as follows:

(1) Areas immediately above shelves.

(2) An area where there is a clothes hanging rod on which combustible clothing is stored and which shall have the specific measurements found in the *NEC*.

(b) **Location.** If the conditions in (1) through (3) below are met, fixtures will be permitted to be installed in clothes closets under these conditions:

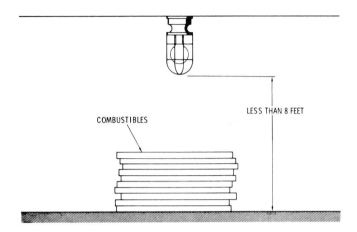

Fig. 410-2. Guarding and switching of fixtures over combustibles when fixture is less than 8 feet from the floor.

(1) Incandescent fixtures may be surface mounted on a wall above the door or on the ceiling. A minimum clearance of 18 inches must be maintained between the nearest point of a storage area and a fixture.

(2) If a minimum clearance of 6 inches is maintained, surface-mounted fluorescent fixtures may be mounted on the wall above a door or on the ceiling. This distance is to be measured from the maximum distance that the fixture projects from the ceiling or wall, to the nearest point of any storage area.

(3) Recessed fixtures with lenses that are flushed mounted or have solid diffusers installed on them may be installed in the ceiling or in the wall of a clothes closet, provided that the distance from the nearest point of storage area to the fixture in that storage area is at least 6 inches.

    The main point is that the lamp must not come into contact with any combustible material such as blankets or shoe boxes that may be on the shelf; also, that if the lamp explodes, hot filaments are not apt to set these items on fire.

Author's Note: Pendants are never to be mounted in clothes closets. This means that fixtures supported by cords, chains, or other devices are not permitted in clothes closets.

410-9. Space for Cove Lighting—See the *NEC*.

C. Provisions at Fixture Outlet Boxes, Canopies and Pans

410-10. Space for Conductors—Basically, this section refers to Article 370, which provides for the proper capacity in outlet boxes, canopies, and pans. The fundamental idea is that an adequate space must be provided so as not to crowd the fixture wires, the branch-circuit conductors, and their connecting devices.

410-11. Temperature Limit of Conductors in Outlet Boxes—A great many fixtures are of the enclosed type which will trap considerable heat. This Section provides that the fixtures be so constructed that the conductors are not subjected to a temperature higher than their rating. Often an outlet box is separated from the fixture proper by a short piece of flexible tubing through which high-temperature wire is run. This is done so that the wire with ordinary temperature insulation may be connected to the fixture conductors and not be overheated.

A common violation of the Code is in the use of an outlet box, which is an integral part of an incandescent lighting fixture, for the purpose of passing branch-circuit conductors through this outlet box. The only time that this is permissible is if the fixture and outlet box have been listed for this purpose. Look for the UL label.

410-12. Outlet Boxes to Be Covered—When an installation is complete, all outlet boxes shall be covered unless covered by a fixture canopy, lampholder, receptacle, rosette, or similar device.

410-13. Covering of Combustible Material at Outlet Boxes—Whenever a combustible wall or ceiling is exposed between the outlet box to which a fixture is connected and the canopy or pan of the fixture, the exposed part of the combustible material shall be covered with a noncombustible material. See Fig. 410-3.

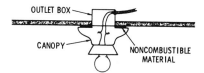

OUTLET BOX

CANOPY

NONCOMBUSTIBLE MATERIAL

Fig. 410-3. Method of installing a canopy larger than the outlet box.

410-14. Connection of Electric Discharge Lighting Fixtures—As a general rule, fluorescent fixtures that are supported independently of the outlet box are to be connected to the outlet box by metal raceways, metal-clad cable, or nonmetallic sheathed cable, not by flexible cords. When supported directly below the outlet box, however, this ruling may be waived and flexible cord used if there is no strain on the cord and if it will not be subjected to physical damage. When thus connected, the outer end of the cord shall terminate in an approved grounding-type plug or busway plug. See Section 410-30(c).

(a) **Independently of the Outlet Box.** Sometimes a fluorescent fixture may be located away from the outlet box to which it is connected. If this occurs, the connection shall be made with metal raceways, metal-clad cables, or with nonmetallic sheathed cables.

Exception: Section 410-30(b) and (c) allows some exceptions for connecting these fixtures.

(b) **Access to Boxes.** If electric discharge fixtures are mounted on unconcealed boxes, there shall be suitable openings in the back of the fixtures, or some other means of access to the box.

410-15. Supports.

(a) **General.** Secure supports shall be provided for all fixtures, lamp holders or rosettes, and receptacles. Any fixture that weighs over 6 pounds and is more than 16 inches in any dimension is not to be supported by the screw shell of the lampholder.

(b) **Metal Poles Supporting Lighting Fixtures.** Lighting fixtures are permitted to be installed in metal poles. Their supply conductors may also be enclosed, if the following conditions are met:

(1) The metal lamp pole shall have a handhole that is not less than 2 inches by 4 inches. The cover over the handhole shall be raintight. This will provide access within the pole or pole base for the supplying raceway or cables. If the raceway risers or cable are not installed within the pole, a threaded fitting or nipple must be brazed, welded, or tapped to the pole, and this shall be opposite the handhole.

(2) A place for grounding of the pole shall be provided that is accessible from the handhole.

(3) As provided in Section 250-91(b), any metal raceway or any other equipment grounding conductor is required to be bonded to the pole by means of equipment grounding conductors, thereby tying raceways, etc., of the pole together. They shall be sized according to Section 250-95.

(4) Section 300-19 covers the supporting of conductors that are run vertically. If the conductors are run vertically in a metal pole used as a raceway, they shall be supported as required by the aforementioned section.

Section 410-15(a) might cause some discussion, but the final decision is left up to the inspection authority. The one point that must be satisfied is that the fixture must be secure and not subject to a failure of the supporting device.

410-16. Means of Support.

(a) **Outlet Boxes.** Section 370-13 covers the support and methods of supporting outlet boxes. When a box is properly supported, it may be used to support fixtures weighing up to 50 pounds. Where not supported adequately, or where the fixture exceeds 50 pounds, the fixture shall be supported independently from the box.

(b) **Inspection.** Fixtures must be so installed that any connections between fixture conductors and circuit supplying conductors may be inspected.

Exception: Any lighting fixtures connected by cord and plug to an outlet.

(c) **Suspended Ceilings.** Lighting fixtures may be supported from the frames of suspended ceilings. The fixture shall be securely fastened to the frame by means of bolts, screws, or rivets. Clips that are made especially for clipping the lighting fixture to the ceiling frame may be used. The ceiling framing members must be attached to the building structure at appropriate intervals.

(d) **Fixture Studs.** If fixture studs are not a part of the fixture, it is necessary to install hickeys, tripods, and crowfeet, and these are to be made of steel or other material that has been suitable for such usage.

(e) **Insulating Joints.** Where there are insulated joints that are not designed to be mounted with screws or bolts, they shall have a metal casing insulating both screw connections.

(f) **Raceway Fittings.** When raceway fittings are used to support lighting fixtures, they must be capable of supporting the weight of the fixture assembly and the lamps.

(g) **Busways.** Section 364-12 covers fixtures that are permitted to be connected to busways.

E. Grounding

410-18. Exposed Fixture Parts.

(a) **With Exposed Conductive Parts.** When light fixtures that have exposed conductive parts and equipment that is directly wired to the fixture or attached thereto are supplied by a wiring method having an equipment grounding conductor, these exposed parts, etc., shall be grounded.

(b) **Made of Insulating Material.** When a fixture is directly wired or attached to a wiring method that has no means of equipment grounding, the fixture shall be made of nonconducting material and shall have no exposed conducting parts.

410-19. Equipment over 150 Volts to Ground.

(a) **Metal Fixtures.** Metal fixtures and transformers, and the enclosures used with a fixture on circuits operating at over 150 volts to ground, shall be grounded. This grounding shall be by means of an equipment grounding conductor tying in with the system grounding conductor.

(b) **Other Exposed Metal Parts.** Any exposed metal parts are required to be grounded, or, if insulated from ground or any conductive surface, they shall be accessible only to qualified persons.

Exception: For any tie wires for lamps, mounting screws, clips, or any other decorative metal bands that might be on the glass lamp space, there shall be at least 1 ½ inch clearance from these and the lamp terminals. If this is the case, grounding of these parts is not required.

410-20. Equipment Grounding Conductor Attachment—A place shall be provided for connecting the equipment grounding conductor to light fixtures that have exposed metal parts.

410-21. Methods of Grounding—As specified in Section 250-91(b), fixtures are to be considered grounded where they are mechanically connected to an equipment grounding conductor. The grounding conductor size shall be as covered in Section 250-95.

F. Wiring of Fixtures

410-22. Fixture Wiring—General—See the *NEC*.

410-23. Conductor Size—See the *NEC*.

410-24. Conductor Insulation—See the *NEC*.

410-25. Conductor for Certain Conditions—The information given in this section is basically for use in manufacturing of fixtures. However, it may be necessary to know what type of conductors to use as a replacement in repair work or to construct a special fixture that is not available commercially. Refer to the *NEC*.

410-27. Pendant Conductors for Incandescent Filament Lamps.

(a) **Support.** Pendant lampholders with permanently attached leads (commonly termed pigtail sockets) that are used for other than festoon wiring are to be hung by separate stranded rubber-covered conductors which are separately soldered to the circuit conductors. These rubber-covered conductors are not to support the lampholder; other means of support shall be used. See Fig. 410-4 on page 328.

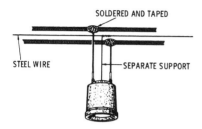

Fig. 410-4. Method of attaching pigtail sockets.

(b) **Size.** Conductors shall not be smaller than No. 14 for mogul-base or medium-base, screw-shell lampholders when used as pendant conductors. They shall not be smaller than No. 18 where used as pendant conductors for intermediate or candelabra-base lampholders.

Exception: Conductors smaller than No. 18 shall not be used for Christmas trees and decorative lighting systems. Conductors feeding these systems cannot, of course, be smaller than No. 14.

(c) **Twisted or Cabled.** If pendant conductors are longer than 3 feet, they shall be twisted together where not cabled in a listed assembly.

410-28. Protection of Conductors and Insulation.

(a) **Properly Secured.** The conductors shall be secured properly so there will be no cutting or abrading of the insulation of the conductors.

(b) **Protection Through Metal.** Whenever the conductors pass through a metal plate, protection from abrasion is required. This has been discussed above.

(c) **Fixture Stems.** There shall be no splices or taps when fixture stems or arms are used to carry the fixture conductors to the lamp.

(d) **Splices and Taps.** Splices and taps shall not be made on a lighting fixture, except where absolutely necessary.

Note: Section 110-14 gives approved methods for making connections.

(e) **Stranding.** Any movable or flexible parts, including fixture chains, shall be wired using stranded conductors.

(f) **Tension.** The weight of the fixture or movable parts shall not put tension on the conductors. When installing these conductors, fixtures, or movable parts, therefore, they shall be arranged so as not cause tension on these conductors.

410-29. Cord-Connected Showcases—Fixed showcases shall be permanently wired. Movable showcases may be wired by flexible cord running to a permanently installed receptacle. A group consisting of not more than

six such showcases may be connected to each other with flexible cord having a lock-type separable connection.

The installation of these showcases shall comply with (a) through (d) of this section:

(a) **Cord Requirements.** The flexible cord used shall be only of the hard-service type, and the conductors in this cord shall not be smaller than the branch-circuit conductors serving the receptacle. The flexible cord conductors shall have an ampacity equal to that of the branch-circuit overcurrent protection, and shall be equipped with an equipment grounding conductor.

Note: Table 250-95 gives the size of the equipment grounding conductor that shall be used.

(b) **Receptacles, Connectors, and Attachment Plugs.** All receptacles, connectors, and attachment plugs shall be rated 15 or 20 amperes, shall be of a type used for grounding, and shall be listed.

(c) **Support.** Flexible cord shall be securely fastened to showcases on the under side so that:

(1) None of the wiring is exposed to mechanical damage;

(2) Where more than one case is involved, they shall be not more than 2 inches apart and the distance from the first case to the receptacle shall be not more than 12 inches; and

(3) At the end of the group the free end of the cord in showcases shall have a female connection that is not permitted to extend beyond the case.

(d) **No Other Equipment.** No equipment, other than the showcase lighting equipment, shall be connected to the showcase wiring.

(e) **Secondary Circuit(s).** Where showcases are cord-connected, the secondary circuit(s) or discharge lighting shall be limited to one showcase.

410-30. Cord-Connected Lampholders and Fixtures.

(a) **Lampholders.** When a lampholder is attached to a flexible cord, it must be equipped with an insulated bushing. If by chance it is equipped with a pipe nipple and threaded, this pipe shall not be smaller than $\frac{3}{8}$-inch pipe size. It must be large enough for the cord to enter, and it shall be reamed or otherwise have all the burrs on the inside removed so that there will be no chance of damaging the cord insulation.

With plain pendant cord, $\frac{9}{32}$-inch busings may be used. Bushing holes $\frac{13}{32}$ inch in diameter may be used with reinforced cord.

(b) **Adjustable Fixtures.** Hard-usage cord or extra-hard-usage cord may be used on fixtures requiring adjusting or aiming after installation (such as, e.g., playing-field lighting). They are not required to have attachment plug and cord connector if the exposed cord is of the hard-usage or extra hard-usage type and the cord is not longer than that which would be required for maximum adjustment, and is not subject to strain or physical damage.

(c) **Electric-Discharge Fixtures.** Permission is granted to use cord-equipped electric-discharge fixtures below the outlet box, provided that the cord is entirely visible for its entire length outside the fixture. The cord shall not be subject to strain or physical damage. When these conditions are met, such cord-equipped fixtures shall terminate at the outer end of an attachment plug that is the grounding type or a busway plug.

If the requirements of Section 240-4 are met, electric-discharge fixtures that use mogul-base screw-shell lampholders may be permitted to connect to 50-ampere or less branch circuits or cords complying with the above. If these fixtures are connected by receptacles and attachment plugs, they may have an ampere rating less than that of the branch circuit supplying them, but in no case less than 125 percent of the full load current of the fixture.

Cord connectors are permitted to supply electric-discharge lighting fixtures that have flanged surface inlets. The inlet and connectors may be lower than the rating of the branch circuit, but the pendant shall not be lower than 125 percent of the full load current rating of the fixture.

410-31. Fixtures as Raceways—Fixtures in general are not intended to be used as raceways for circuit conductors unless they are specifically designed and listed for that purpose. There are three exceptions to this, but it must be remembered that the exceptions cover only the conductors of a single two-wire or multiwire branch circuit supplying these fixtures.

Exception No. 1: This exception is permitted only when the fixture has been listed for use as a raceway.

Exception No. 2: If fixtures are so designed as to be mounted in a continuous row that is end to end, or if they are connected by fittings that are recognized wiring methods, the conductors of a two-wire or multiwire branch circuit shall be permitted to carry the conductors straight through.

Exception No. 3: In Exception No. 2 above, one additional branch circuit that separately supplies one or more of the connected fixtures is permitted.

Note: The definition of multiwire circuits was covered in Article 100.

Branch-circuit conductors that come within 3 inches of the ballast of an electric-discharge lighting fixture shall be recognized for use at temperatures not lower than 90°C (194°F. Some of these types are RHH, THW, THHN, FEP, FEPB, SA, XHHW, and AVA.

G. Construction of Fixtures

See the *NEC*.

H. Installation of Lampholders

410-47. Screw-Shell Type—It has long been a common practice to use screw-shell type lampholders for other purposes than for lamps, such as the female end of an attachment plug, or a pigtail socket as a fuse holder, etc. These uses are all prohibited by the *NEC*. Screw-shell sockets are to be used as lampholders only.

410-48. Double-Pole Switched Lampholders—Where a lampholder is connected to the hot conductors of a multiwire branch circuit, the switching device of the lampholder shall simultaneously disconnect both conductors of the circuit. This can be readily understood considering that, whenever hot wires feed a circuit, if only one is opened it leaves the other one hot. The Code has provided for this dangerous condition by requiring that both hot conductors be opened simultaneously.

410-49. Lampholders in Wet or Damp Locations—See the *NEC*.

J. Construction of Lampholders

See the *NEC*.

K. Lamps and Auxiliary Equipment

410-53. Bases, Incandescent Lamps—Incandescent lamps for general use on lighting branch circuits are limited to not over 300 watts when used in medium-base lampholders. Mogul-base lampholders are limited to 1500-watt incandescent lamps. Special bases or other devices shall be used for incandescent lamps above 1500 watts.

410-54. Enclosures for Electric-Discharge Lamp Auxiliary Equipment—Resistors and regulators used with mercury-vapor lamps are sources of heat and shall be so treated by being installed in noncombustible cases and wired accordingly.

The switching device of auxiliary equipment when supplied by the hot legs of a circuit must disconnect all conductors simultaneously.

410-55. Arc Lamps—See the *NEC*.

L. Receptacles, Cord Connectors, and Attachment Plugs (Caps)

410-56. Rating and Type.

(a) **Receptacles.** Receptacles for attaching portable cords should be rated at not less than 15 amperes, 125 volts or 15 amperes, 250 volts. These are to be suitable only for lampholders. Notice that receptacles shall be of such a type that lamps cannot be screwed into them.

Exception: In nonresidential occupancy only, receptacles of 10 amperes, 250 volt rating used to supply equipment other than portable hand tools, portable hand lamps,or extension cords shall be permitted.

Author's Note: I have yet to find where a 10-ampere receptacle can be purchased; this does not mean, however, that they are not to be found.

(b) **CO/ALR Receptacles.** Any receptacles 20 amperes or less to which may be connected aluminum conductors are required to be a permanently marked CO/ALR. These of course may also be used for copper.

(c) **Faceplates.** See the *NEC.*

(d) **Position of Receptacle Faces.** Upon installation, receptacle faces shall be flush, or if mounted on insulating material, the faceplate of the insulating material shall project a minimum of .015 inch from metal faceplates. Faceplates shall be mounted after installation so that they completely cover the opening and seat against the mounting surface. If the mounting boxes for receptacles are set back of the wall surface, as was covered in Section 370-10, the receptacle shall be so installed that the yoke or strap on the receptacle shall be held rigidly at the surface of the wall. When boxes are mounted flush with the wall surface or project somewhat from the wall surface, the receptacle shall be mounted so that the yoke or strap on the receptacle will be well seated against the box or raised box cover.

(e) **Attachment Plugs.** 15 and 20 attachment plugs and connectors shall be so constructed that no current-carrying parts will be exposed, with the exception of the blades or pins. If, by necessity, the connections for the wires must be a part of the plug or connector, they must be covered.

A separate insulated disk which is mechanically secured will not be permitted. This applies to the fiber insulating disk that is slipped on the prongs of the plug.

(f) **Attachment Plug Ejector Mechanisms.** If attachment plugs have ejector mechanisms, they shall in no way affect the proper contact between the blades of the plug and the contacts of the receptacle.

(g) **Noninterchangeability.** This apparently refers to NEMA, plug and connector configurations, which prohibits interchangeable plugs and connectors and receptacles, so that only the proper parts will fit for the proper voltages and currents for which they were designed. Thus if properly installed, the wrong voltage equipment cannot be plugged into higher or lower voltages, etc.

Exception: T-slot receptacles or cord connectors that are rated 20 amperes are permitted to accept attachment plugs of the same voltage rating and a 15-ampere rating.

410-57. Receptacles in Damp or Wet Locations.

(a) **Damp Locations.** The enclosure for receptacles installed out of doors and protected from the weather, or installed in any other damp location, must be weatherproof when the receptacle is covered. This means that after the attachment plug is removed, the cover is automatically closed.

Receptacles that can be installed in wet locations are also suitable for damp locations. In damp or wet locations, the only sensible thing to do is to use GFCI's.

Receptacles located under roofs, open porches, canopies, or marquees, and the like, and not subjected to a beating rain or water runoff, including blowing snow, will be considered to be in a location protected from weather.

(b) **Wet Locations.** When receptacles are installed outdoors exposed to the weather or in any other wet location, they shall be in a weatherproof enclosure that shall not be affected when the receptacle is in use (that is, attachment plug cap inserted).

Exception: An enclosure that is weatherproof only when the self-closing receptacle cover is closed will be allowed to be used where the receptacle is installed outdoors. This is only when the receptacle is used for other than portable tools or other portable equipment, and they are not left connected to the outlet except for occasional use.

(c) **Protection for Floor Receptacles.** Floor receptacle standpipes must be high enough so that floor cleaning equipment can be used without damage to receptacles. It should be noted that Section 370-17 requires listed boxes where receptacles are located in the floor.

(d) **Flush Mounting with Faceplate.** An enclosure for outlets, if the box is installed flush with the wall surface, may be made weatherproof by using a weatherproof plate receptacle assembly that provides a watertight connection between the plate and the wall in which the box is recessed.

(e) **Installation.** If a receptacle outlet is installed outdoors, it shall be located so that accumulation of water is not likely to occur in the outlet cover or plate.

410-58. Grounding-Type Receptacles, Adapters, Cord Connectors, and Attachment Plugs.

(a) **Grounding Poles.** In addition to the circuit poles, on grounding-type receptacles, plugs and connectors there shall also be a pole for grounding purposes.

Exception: The cords shall have a grounding-type terminal in the attachment plugs, and the grounding pole of the receptacle shall be connected continuously for equipment grounding conductors. With portable hand-held, hand-guided, or hand-supported tools or appliances, the grounding plug on the equipment cords may be of the movable self-restoring type, if these are used only on circuits not over 150 volts between any two conductors nor over 150 volts between any conductor and ground.

Many hand-held tools are found with the grounding prong cut off of the attachment plug. These are put there for the protection of the personnel operating the tools.

(b) **Grounding-Pole Identification.** There shall be a means of connecting the grounding conductor to the grounding pole of grounding-type receptacles, adapters, cord connectors, and attachment plugs.

The grounding pole terminal shall be designated by one of the following:

(1) The grounding screw or nut shall be hexagonal and painted green, and shall be made so that it can not be easily removed.

(2) The wire connector body shall be pressure-connected in a green color.

(3) Where adapters are used, similar green devices for connection shall be used. The grounding adapter and ground terminal shall be a green-colored rigid ear, lug, or similar device. The grounding connection shall be so designed that it will not come into contact with a current-carrying conductor and either parts of the receptacle adapter or attachment plug. The adapter shall be polarized.

(4) When the terminal for the equipment grounding conductor is not visible and the wire is inserted into a hole where contact is made, the hole where the wire is to be inserted shall be marked with the word "green" or otherwise identified by a green color.

(c) **Grounding Terminal Use.** The grounding terminal or grounding-type device is intended only for grounding purposes and shall never be used for any other purpose.

(d) **Grounding-Pole Requirements.** The shape and/or length of grounding-type devices shall be so designed that the grounding poles of attachment plugs cannot be brought into contact with current-carrying parts of receptacles or cord connectors. The design of grounding-type attachment plugs shall be such that the ground connection is made before the current-carrying connections are made.

(e) **Use.** Grounding-type plugs shall be used only where an equipment grounding conductor is provided. A GFCI provides the protection. These are available on the market, and many electricians and servicemen carry them as part of their tools.

This makes it wrong to use the 2-wire plug-in adapter to convert to a 2-wire with ground plug-in.

M. Rosettes

410-59. Unapproved Types.

(a) **Fusible Rosettes.** This type of rosette shall not be used.

(b) **Separable Rosettes.** Rosettes that are separable shall be so constructed that it is impossible to put them back together with the wrong polarity.

410-60. Rosettes in Damp or Wet Places—See the *NEC*.

410-61. Rating—See the *NEC*.

410-62. Rosettes for Exposed Wiring—See the *NEC*.

410-63. Rosettes for Use with Boxes or Raceways—See the *NEC*.

N. Special Provisions for Flush and Recessed Fixtures

410-64. General—Fixtures installed in cavities of walls or ceilings shall be of a listed type. Sections 410-65 through 410-72 give information on the Code requirements.

410-65. Temperature.

(a) **Combustible Material.** It is very important that combustible materials adjacent to fixtures will not be subjected to temperatures of over 90°C (194°F).

(b) **Fire-Resistant Construction.** Fixtures that are recessed in fire-resistant material in a fire-resistant building may have allowable temperatures of more than 90°C (194°F) but not more than 150°C (302°F). In order that fixtures thus used are acceptable they shall be listed for this type service.

(c) **Recessed Incandescent Fixtures.** Recessed incandescent fixtures are required to be identified (listed) as having thermal protection. The heat produced by the incandescent fixture may start a fire, so the thermal protection shuts them off before this temperature is reached.

Exception No. 1: If the recessed fixture is identified for installation in poured concrete, it may be used.

Exception No. 2: If recessed fixtures are listed and identified for contact with thermal insulation.

410-66. Clearance and Installation.

(a) **Clearance.** On recessed lighting, the recessed part of the fixture enclosures, except at the point of support, is required to be spaced at least ½ inch from combustible materials.

Exception No. 1: Fixtures that are listed for installation in direct contact with the insulation are permitted.

Exception No. 2: Fluorescent fixtures installed recessed are not required to conform with (a) above.

(b) **Installation.** Thermal insulation is not permitted within 3 inches of the fixture enclosure wiring compartment, and may not be placed above the ballast. The insulation shall be so placed as to not stop free circulation of air.

Exception No. 1: There are some fixtures that are listed to be in direct contact with the insulation.

Exception No. 2: Fluorescent fixtures installed recessed are not required to conform with (b) above.

410-67. Wiring.

(a) **General.** Only conductors with insulation suitable for the temperatures that will be encountered shall be used.

(b) **Circuit Conductors.** Branch-circuit conductors that have insulation temperature rating suitable for the temperature they will encounter may be terminated in the fixture.

(c) **Tap conductors.** Tap connection conductors which have a temperature rating for that which will be encountered shall be run from the fixture terminal connection to an outlet or junction box placed at least 1 foot away from the fixture. Take note of "1 foot away," and don't forget: These tap conductors shall be in a suitable raceway that is at least 4 feet but not more than 6 feet long. This means that the box may be not less than 1 foot away from the fixture, but that a raceway shall be run to it that is not less than 4 feet nor more than 6 feet long.

A suitable raceway may include wiring methods found in Chapter 3. The reason for the 4-foot minimum length is to prevent the heat from traveling through too short a raceway. Type AF wire is not allowed as a branch-circuit conductor, but would be allowed for the fixture tap from a branch circuit into the fixture where the above method of connection is used.

P. Construction of Flush and Recessed Fixtures

These sections pertain mostly to the manufacturing of flush and recessed fixtures. However, attention is called to Section 410-70 which requires marking the fixture in ¼-inch letters or larger to indicate the maximum wattage bulb that may be used. Larger wattage lamps will produce a higher temperature than the fixture is designed for. Also refer to Section 410-71 which prohibits the use of solder. See part P of the *NEC* for total instructions.

Q. Special Provisions for Electric-Discharge Lighting Systems of 1000 Volts or Less

410-73. General.

(a) **Open-Circuit Voltage of 1000 Volts or Less.** With electric-discharge lighting that is designed for an open-circuit voltage of 1000 volts or less, the equipment used with such systems shall be of a type suitable for the service.

(b) **Considered as Alive.** The discharge lamp terminals are to be considered alive when any lamp terminal is connected to a circuit of over 300 volts.

(c) **Transformers of the Oil-Filled Type.** Oil-filled-type transformers are not permitted.

(d) **Additional Requirements.** In addition to requirements we have covered, lighting fixtures shall be required to comply with Part Q of this article.

(e) **Thermal Protection.** Fluorescent fixtures that are installed indoors are required to have thermal protection (Class P) built into the ballasts. If replacement of the ballasts is required, they shall be replaced only by ballasts having thermal (Class P) protection within them.

Exception to (e) above: Fluorescent fixtures with reactance ballasts do not require thermal protection.

(f) **Recessed High-Intensity Discharge Fixtures.** This type of fixture, where recessed, shall have ballasts integrally mounted to the fixture when installed indoors. If the ballasts have to be replaced in this type of fixture, a ballast with integral thermal protection shall be used.

410-74. Direct-Current Equipment—All discharge lighting equipment in this class that is designed for use on direct-current shall be so marked and the resistors and other equipment used shall be designed for direct-current operation. A fluorescent fixture designed for alternating current will not work on direct current.

410-75. Voltages—Dwelling Occupancies.

(a) **Open-Circuit Voltage Exceeding 1000 Volts.** Lighting equipment for dwelling occupancies is limited to an open-circuit voltage of not more than 1000 volts. Sometimes a request is made to use neon lighting in a residence. According to the Code, this type of lighting would be prohibited because the voltage will exceed 1000 volts in practically all cases.

(b) **Open-Circuit Voltage Exceeding 300 Volts.** Equipment having an open-circuit voltage over 300 volts is not to be installed in dwelling occupancies unless it is so designed that there will be no exposed parts when lamps are being replaced or removed.

410-76. Fixture Mounting.

(a) **Exposed Ballasts.** There are times when exposed ballasts or transformers are used. In such installations, they shall be so mounted that they do not come in contact with any combustible material.

(b) **Combustible Low-Density Cellulose Fiberboard.** Where a fixture containing a ballast is to be installed on combustible low-density cellulose fiberboard it shall, where surface mounted, be listed for direct mounting on this type of combustible material or it shall be 1½ inches from the surface of the fiberboard. Where such a fixture is partially or wholly recessed, the provisions of this article (Sections 410-64 through 410-72) shall apply.

Note: This covers combustible low-density cellulose fiberboards. Included shall be sheets, panels, and tiles, the density of which is 20 pounds per cubic foot or less. These fiberboards are formed of bonded plant fibers. Solid or laminated wood is not included, nor is fiberboard that has a density of over 20 pounds per cubic foot. It can be a material that has been properly treated with fire-retarding chemicals, and these fire-retarding chemicals shall be treated so that the flame spread in any place on this material shall not exceed 25. This will be determined by tests for surface burning characteristics of building materials, which appear in ANSI/ASTM E84-1984, Surface Burning Characteristics of Building Materials.

410-77. Equipment Not Integral with Fixture—See the *NEC*.

410-78. Autotransformers— This section is very similar to the requirements for autotransformers supplying branch circuits as covered in Section 210-9 except that this covers lighting. Autotransformers that are used as a part of a ballast for supplying lighting units and which raise the voltage to more than 300 volts shall be supplied only from a grounded system.

410-79. Switches—Section 380-14 covers snap switches. They are to meet the requirements of this section.

R. Special Provisions for Electric Discharge Lighting Systems of More than 1000 Volts

410-80. General.

(a) **Open-Circuit Voltage Exceeding 1000 Volts.** Only equipment that is of a type intended for such service shall be used on electric discharge lighting systems with an open-circuit voltage in excess of 1000 volts.

(b) **Considered as Alive.** All terminals are to be considered alive when connected to over 300 volts.

(c) **Additional Requirements.** Not only the general requirements for lighting fixtures apply but also comply with Part R of this article.

Signs and outline lighting are covered in Article 600.

410-81. Control.

(a) **Disconnection.** Fixtures and lamp installations may be controlled individually or in groups by switches or circuit breakers, but either shall open all of the ungrounded conductors of the primary circuit (the branch circuit supplying the fixtures or lamps).

(b) **Within Sight or Locked Type.** For protection, the switches or circuit breakers shall be located within sight of the fixtures or lamps, or shall be capable of being locked in an open position.

410-82. Lamp Terminals and Lampholders—Any fixture parts that must be removed for lamp replacement shall be hinged or fastened in an approved manner, and the lamps and lampholders, or both, shall be so designed that there will be no exposed live parts when lamps are being removed or replaced.

410-83. Transformer Ratings—The open-circuit rating of ballasts and transformers shall not exceed 15,000 volts, with an allowable 1000 volts on test in addition. The secondary current rating shall not exceed 120 milliamperes (0.120 ampere) when the open-circuit voltage to the ballast or transformer exceeds 7500 volts, and the secondary current shall not exceed 240 milliamperes (0.240 ampere) when the open-circuit voltage is 7500 watts or less.

410-84. Transformer Type—All transformers shall be enclosed and listed.

410-85. Transformer Secondary Connections.

(a) **High-Voltage Windings.** The high-voltage windings of transformers shall not be connected in parallel or series, with the exception that two transformers, each of which has one end of the high-voltage winding grounded and attached to the enclosure, may have the high-voltage windings connected in series to form the equivalent of a midpoint grounded transformer. See Figs. 410-5 and 410-6 on page 340.

(b) **Grounded Ends of Paralleled Transformers.** When transformers are paralleled, the grounded ends shall be connected by an insulating conductor that shall be no smaller than No. 14 AWG.

410-86. Transformer Locations—See the *NEC.*

410-87. Transformer Loading—The loading of the transformer should be such that there will not be a continuous over-voltage condition. At first

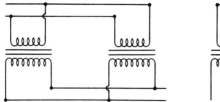 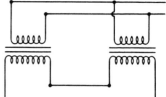

(A) High-voltage secondaries shall not be paralleled.

(B) High-voltage secondaries shall not be connected in series.

Fig. 410-5. These connections are prohibited on high-voltage lighting transformers.

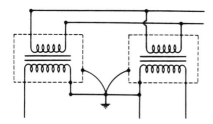

Fig. 410-6. A connection that is permissible on high-voltage lighting transformers.

glance this sounds odd, but these transformers are of the high-leakage reactance type and as the load increases the voltage increases to maintain the proper current. The lamp load should be properly balanced for the transformer being used.

410-88. Wiring Method. Secondary Conductors—See the *NEC*.

410-89. Lamp Supports—See Section 600-33.

410-90. Exposure to Damage—See the *NEC*.

410-91. Marking—See the *NEC*.

410-92. Switches—See the *NEC*.

S. Lighting Track

410-100. Definition—This is a manufactured track assembly designed to support and energize lighting fixtures that are capable of being readily moved to different positions on the track. Its length may be changed by adding or subtracting sections therefrom.

410-101. Installation.

(a) **Lighting Track.** Lighting track is to be permanently installed, and permanently connected to a branch circuit. Only fittings made for lighting track shall be installed thereon. There shall be no general-purpose receptacles installed on lighting track.

(b) **Connected Load.** As with any conductor the load on the lighting track shall not exceed the rating (ampacity) of the track. The rating of the branch-circuit supplying the lighting track shall not be greater than the rating of the lighting track.

(c) **Locations Not Permitted.** Lighting track is not permitted to be installed in the following locations:

(1) If it may be subjected to physical damage;

(2) In wet or damp locations;

(3) Where corrosive vapors exist;

(4) In storage battery rooms (the vapors there are corrosive);

(5) In hazardous (classified) locations—sparks may occur when fixtures are moved on the track;

(6) In concealed places;

(7) It shall not penetrate walls or partitions;

(8) Unless protected from physical damage, it shall not be located less than 5 feet above finished floors.

(d) **Support.** Only identified fittings shall be used on lighting track and they shall be designed for the specific lighting track on which they will be used. The fittings shall be securely fastened to the track. Polarization and grounding shall be maintained. They shall be designed to be suspended directly from the track.

410-102. Track Load—When calculating the branch circuits for the lighting track, each 2 foot or less length of lighting track shall be considered as 180 VA. If multiwire circuit track is installed and each section of the track is supplied by one portion of the multiwired circuit, it shall be considered that the load is evenly divided.

410-103. Heavy-Duty Track—Heavy-duty lighting track is considered and identified as exceeding 20 amperes. Each fitting used for attachment of heavy-duty lighting track is required to have individual overcurrent protection.

The above indicates to the author that when circuits are over 20 amperes to the lighting track, each individual lighting track over 20 amperes shall be supplied by an individual branch circuit.

410-104. Fastening—The lighting fixture track must be securely mounted so that it will handle the maximum load put on it after installation. Unless it is listed for supports at greater intervals of 4 feet or shorter length, it is required to have two supports. When installed in a single length of track, the individual supports shall be not more than 4 feet apart, and there shall be one additional support.

410-105. Construction Requirements—See the *NEC*.

ARTICLE 422—APPLIANCES

A. General

422-1. Scope—This article covers the installation of electric appliances in any occupancy. Equipment shall be of a type approved for the purpose and location.

422.2. Live Parts—The live parts of appliances shall be normally enclosed to avoid exposure to contact. This, however, cannot always be done, as in the case of toasters, grills, and the like.

422-3. Other Articles—Article 430 covers Motors. The requirements of this Article will amend and supersede portions of Article 430. Some other articles in the Code may also be applicable to this article. Hazardous (classified) locations must comply with Articles 500 through 517.

Article 440 will apply to appliances which contain hermetically sealed refrigeration motor-compressor(s), unless amended within this Article.

B. Branch-Circuit Requirements

422-5. Branch-Circuit Sizing—This section is not intended to apply to the conductors which are an integral part of an appliance. This section applies to the sizes of branch-circuit conductors which may be used without heating under the conditions specified in Article 210.

(a) **Individual Circuits.** The rating marked on the appliance shall be used in determining the individual branch-circuit rating to which it is connected. The branch-circuit rating shall not be lower than the rating on the appliance or an appliance that has a combination of loads, such as those you will find in Section 422-32.

Exception No. 1: Motor-operated appliances which do not have the ampacity of the branch circuit marked in the appliance shall be treated according to Part B of Article 430, covering this type of operation.

Exception No. 2: Appliances that are not motor operated shall have an overcurrent device rating of less than 125 percent of the marked rating on the appliance, if used for continuous loading. If the branch-circuit devices are rated for use at 100 percent of the rating, then the branch-circuit rating shall be not less than 100 percent of the marked rating.

Exception No. 3: Branch circuits to household cooking appliances have a special concession on rating. This is covered in accordance with Table 220-19 and the notes therewith.

(b) **Circuits Supplying Two or More Loads.** Section 210-23 gives us percentages to use on branch-circuit loading. So branch circuits supplying appliances and other loads shall conform to Section 210-23.

422-6. Branch-Circuit Overcurrent Protection—Section 240-3 gives us the necessary information for protecting branch circuits. When there is a protective device rating marked on an appliance, the branch-circuit overcurrent device rating shall not exceed the protective device rating marked on the appliance.

C. Installation of Appliances

422-7. General—Care must be taken to install all appliances in an approved manner.

422-8. Flexible Cords—Flexible cords used to connect heating appliances shall comply with the following:

(a) **Heater Cords.** This part defines the types of cords required for all smoothing irons and portable electrically heated appliances rated at more than 50 watts and that produce temperatures in excess of 121°C (250°F) on surfaces that the cord is likely to come in contact with. Table 400-4 lists cords for heating appliances, along with their temperature ranges and usages.

(b) **Other Heating Appliances.** All other portable heating appliances shall have cords that are listed in Table 400-4 and meet the requirements for the use to which they are put.

(c) **Other Appliances.** Flexible cord may be used for the following purposes: (1) If appliances are frequently interchanged or transmit noise or vibration; (2) If appliances are fastened in place, but have to be moved frequently for maintenance and repair. A good example of this is a garbage disposal. With a flexible cord connection, it merely has to be unplugged and thus the danger of a wrong connection upon reinstallation is largely avoided.

(d) **Specific Appliances.** (1) Kitchen waste disposals for use in households that are supplied by a Type S, SO, ST, STO, SJ, SJO, SJT, SJTO, SP-3, SPE-3, or SPT-3 three-conductor cord (one conductor for equipment grounding), terminated with an equipment grounding attachment plug shall be permitted if all the following conditions are met:

    a. The cord attached to the appliance is not less than 18 inches in length, nor more than 36 inches in length.

    b. Receptacles are so placed that they will not cause any damage to the flexible cord.

    c. The receptacles are so placed that they are accessible.

(2) For dwelling purposes, built-in dishwashers and trash compacters using the same type of cords specified in (1) above may be used, and the balance of (1) above also applies to (2).

    a. The length of the cord allowed shall be 3 to 4 feet.

    b. See b. of (1).

    c. The receptacle shall be mounted in the space where the appliance is located or immediately adjacent thereto.

    d. See c. of (1).

Exception: Listed kitchen waste disposals, dishwashers, or trash compactors, when protected by double insulation and so marked, are not required to have an equipment grounding conductor.

(3) Both the external cord and the internal wiring, supplying high-pressure spray washing machines, are required to have GFCI for protection for persons. The GFCI is to be listed for use with portable equipment, and may also be part of the attachment plug.

422-9. Cord and Plug-Connected Immersion Heaters—Portable immersion heaters are to be constructed and installed so that the current-carrying parts shall not come into contact with the substance into which they are immersed. This prohibits the type of immersion heaters which have open coils in contact with the liquid.

422-10. Protection of Combustible Material—All electrically heated appliances that, because of size, weight, or service, and that are intended to be used in fixed position, shall provide for ample protection from combustibles.

422-11. Stands for Cord- and Plug-Connected Appliances—All portable heating appliances, such as irons, that are intended to be used by applying them to combustible substances shall be provided with stands for support when actually not being used. These stands may be part of the appliance or a separate item.

422-12. Signals for Heated Appliances—This does not apply to appliances intended for residential use, but other electrically heated appliances that are applied to combustible articles shall have a signaling device unless the appliance has a temperature-limiting device.

422-13. Flatirons—All electrically heated smoothing irons shall be equipped with an identified temperature-limiting means, such as a thermostat.

422-14. Water Heaters.

(a) **Storage- and Instantaneous-Type Water Heaters.** In addition to control thermostat, temperature-limiting means to disconnect all ungrounded conductors are to be used on storage- or instant-type water heaters. They shall be so installed that they sense the maximum water temperature. The water heater must be either trip-free or of a type having replacement elements. This type is required to have a temperature and pressure relief valve, and shall be marked for such.

Exception: If the water heater supplies water at 180° F or 82° C or higher, or has a capacity of 60 kW or more, it shall be listed for this use; also water heaters of a capacity of one gallon or less and listed as being satisfactory for the such use.

It is almost universally a Code that there is to be a pressure and temperature relief valve installed on water heaters. The requirements above are in addition to this requirement. Some heaters in the past have provisions for opening only one ungrounded conductor by means of a thermostat. It is now required that all ungrounded conductors be opened by the thermostat. Often, if an element is shorted to ground, one side will open but the other side of the circuit will stay energized. Thus, current will go to ground, still producing heating of the water. By opening all ungrounded conductors, this problem will be eliminated.

(b) **Storage-Type Water Heaters.** With fixed storage-type water heaters having a capacity of 120 gallons or less, the branch circuit is required to be rated at not less than 125 percent of the water heater's nameplate rating.

Note: Sizing of the branch circuit is covered in Section 422-5(a), Exception No. 2.

422-15. Infrared Lamp Industrial Heating Appliances—See the *NEC*.

422-16. Grounding—Metal frames of portable, stationary and fixed electrically heated appliances, operating on circuits above 150 volts to ground, shall be grounded in the manner specified in Article 250; provided, however, that where this is impracticable, grounding may be omitted by special permission, in which case the frames shall be permanently and effectively insulated from the ground.

In rural areas especially, grounding the water heater frame to the same ground as the service entrance will have many burnouts due to lightning. This provision of grounding that requires the cold-water pipe to be bonded to a made electrode (when a made electrode is required) will automatically do much to prevent troubles that used to develop. Even when (by special permission) the equipment is not required to be grounded, the Code recommends that the frames be grounded in all cases. It will be recalled that the frames of ranges and dryers may be grounded to the neutral if the neutral is sized at No. 10 or larger. These are two cases in which this type of grounding is permitted. It does not apply to mobile homes or travel trailers.

Refrigerators and freezers shall comply with the requirements of Sections 250-42, 250-43, and 250-45. Electric ranges, wall-mounted ovens, counter-mounted cooking units, and clothes dryers shall comply with the requirements of Sections 250-57 and 250-60. This, of course, will not apply to mobile homes or travel trailers.

422-17. Wall-Mounted Ovens and Counter-Mounted Cooking Units.

(a) **Permitted to Be Cord- and Plug-Connected or Permanently Connected.** Wall-mounted ovens and counter-mounted cooking units are considered to be fixed appliances, and this includes the provisions for mounting and connection of the wiring. They may be cord- and plug-connected, or permanently connected.

(b) **Separable Connector or Plug and Receptacle Connector.** A separable connector or plug and receptacle combination in the supply line to a wall-mounted oven or counter-mounted cooking top shall not be considered as a disconnecting means, but only to be used as a means for ease of servicing. This means that it is not to be used as a disconnecting means as covered in Section 422-20. Also, it shall be approved for the temperature to which it might be subjected, especially since the space is limited in most cases.

422-18. Support of Ceiling Fans—Ceiling fans that are listed and do not weigh over 35 pounds—with or without added accessories—may be supported by outlet boxes that have been identified and listed for such use. The supporting of these boxes shall be as outlined in Sections 370-13 and 370-17.

422-19. Other Installation Methods—If appliances use methods of installation other than those covered in this Article 422, they will require special permission. You will recall that "special permission" is permission granted in writing by the authority having jurisdiction.

D. Control and Protection of Appliances

422-20. Disconnecting Means—Each appliance shall have some means for disconnecting all ungrounded conductors. These means for fixed, portable, and stationary appliances will be covered in the next few sections.

422-21. Disconnection of Permanently Connected Appliances.

(a) **Rated at Not Over 300 Volt Amperes or ⅛ Horsepower.** The branch-circuit overcurrent device may be used as a disconnecting means for appliances not over 300 volt amperes or ⅛ horsepower.

(b) **Permanently Connected Appliances of Greater Rating.** If the over-current protection device is readily accessible to the user, it may be used as the disconnecting means for permanently connected appliances that have greater ratings.

Note: Section 422-26 provides for motor-driven appliances using motors over ⅛ horsepower.

Exception: Section 422-24 covers disconnecting means when unit switches are used for appliances.

The above should not prevent the addition of a separable connection or a plug and receptacle approved for conditions as being installed as a means of serving the fixed appliance. They are not intended merely to be the disconnecting means.

422-22. Disconnection of Cord- and Plug-Connected Appliances —See the *NEC.*

422-24. Unit Switches as Disconnecting Means—See the *NEC.*

422-25. Switch and Circuit Breaker to Be Indicating—Switches or circuit breakers used as disconnecting means for appliances shall indicate whether they are in the open or closed position.

422-26. Disconnecting Means for Motor-Driven Appliances—When a switch or circuit breaker serves as the disconnecting means for a stationary or fixed motor-driven appliance or more than ⅛ horsepower, it shall be located within sight of the motor controller or shall be capable of being locked in the open position. It will be found that most inspection authorities will consider any distance over 50 feet as being out of sight. The intent of this part is to give safety on motor-driven appliances of over ⅛ horsepower during service work.

Exception: As required in Section 422-24(a), (b), (c), or (d), a switch or circuit breaker serving as the other disconnecting means is permitted to be out of sight from the appliance motor controller provided with unit switch(es). There shall be a marked OFF position on all such means of disconnecting the ungrounded conductor.

422-27. Overcurrent Protection.

(a) **Appliances.** See Sections 422-5 and 422-6. Appliances shall be protected against overcurrent as provided in (b) through (f) below and these two sections.

Exception: Part C of Article 430 requires that motor-operated appliances shall have overload protection provided. Part F of Article 440 covers the motors of hermetic refrigerant motor-compressors in air-conditioning or refrigerating equipment that shall be provided with overcurrent protection. When separate overcurrent devices are provided for an appliance, the data covering these overcurrent devices must be marked on the appliance. Sections 430-7 and 440-4 cover the minimum marking on such appliances.

(b) **Household-Type Appliance and Surface Heating Elements.** Table 220-19 lists the demand factors for residential ranges. Any residential range that has a demand factor of over 60 amperes (as calculated from this table) must have its power supply divided into two or more circuits, each of which is provided with overcurrent protection of not more than 50 amperes.

(c) **Infrared Lamp Commercial and Industrial Heating Appliances.** Infrared heating appliances shall be protected by overcurrent protection of not more than 50 amperes. This covers commercial and industrial heating appliances.

(d) **Open-Coil or Exposed Sheathed-Coil Types of Surface Heating Element in Commercial-Type Heating Appliances.** Exposed sheathed-coil or open-coil heating elements of surface-heating-type appliances shall be protected by overcurrent protection, and this heating device shall be not over 50 amperes.

(e) **Single Nonmotor-Operated Appliance.** When a branch circuit is supplying a single nonmotor-operated appliance, the rating of the overcurrent device is not to exceed the protective device rating marked on the appliance. If there is no marking on the appliance, the following specifications shall be met:

See the *NEC* for these ratings.

(f) **Electric Heating Appliances Employing Resistance-Type Heating Elements Rated More than 48 Amperes.** When electric heating appliances use resistive-type heating elements and they are rated more than 48 amperes, the heating elements must be subdivided. When subdivided, each subdivision shall be rated not more than 48 amperes and shall be protected by not over 60 amperes.

The supplementary overcurrent devices shall be: (1) supplied by the factory and in or on the heater enclosure, or it may be a separate assembly furnished by the heater manufacturer; (2) the overcurrent device must be accessible, but need not be readily accessible; (3) the overcurrent protection shall be suitable for branch-circuit protection.

The conductor that supplies the overcurrent protection for these heaters is a branch circuit.

Exception No. 1: In household equipment that is supplied by surface heating elements as covered in Section 422-27(b), and also in commercial-type heating appliances that were covered in Section 422-27(d).

Exception No. 2: Any commercial kitchen or cooking appliances using sheath-type heating elements that were not covered in Section 422-27(d) may be subdivided into circuits that shall not exceed 120 amperes, and the protection for such shall not be over 150 amperes if one of the following conditions is met:

a. The heating elements shall be a part of the equipment and shall be enclosed in the cooking element;

b. The enclosure is listed suitable and the elements are completely contained in the enclosure; or

c. If the vessel is ASME rated and stamped, elements may be contained therein.

Exception No. 3: Resistive-type elements that are mounted in water heaters or steam boilers and use resistive-type commercial heating elements, and the vessel that contains them is marked with an ASME rating and is stamped. A surface may be divided into a circuit not exceeding 120 amperes and protected at not more than 150 amperes.

E. Marking of Appliances

See the *NEC*. This part concerns primarily manufacturer's requirements. The markings must be on the appliances, so look for the UL label.

ARTICLE 424—FIXED ELECTRICAL SPACE HEATING EQUIPMENT

A. General

424-1. Scope—This article covers fixed equipment for space heating. The equipment may be heating cables, unit heaters, boilers, central systems, or other approved fixed heating equipment. Not covered in this article are process heating and room air conditioning.

424-2. Other Articles—This is basically the same requirement appearing in other articles of the Code to primarily indicate that heating equipment intended for use in hazardous (classified) locations must also comply with Articles 500 through 517. It also indicates that heating equipment employing a hermetic refrigerant motor-compressor must comply with Article 440.

Fixed electric space heating equipment incorporating a sealed (hermetic-type) motor-compressor shall comply with Article 440.

All other applicable portions of the Code shall apply.

424-3. Branch Circuits.

(a) **Branch-Circuit Requirements.** Branch circuits supplying two or more outlets for fixed heating equipment are limited to 15, 20, or 30 amperes. An individual branch circuit may supply any load.

There is an exception which says that branch circuits for fixed infrared heating equipment shall not be rated at more than 50 amperes. This covers other than residential occupancies.

(b) **Branch-Circuit Sizing.** For the sizing of overcurrent devices and branch-circuit conductors, for electrical space heating equipment (fixed), they shall be calculated on the basis of 125 percent of the total load of the heaters and motors if equipped with motors. Contactors, relays, thermostats, etc., that are rated at continuous load ratings of 100 percent may be used to supply the full rated load. See Section 210-22(c), Exception No. 2.

Sections 440-34 and 440-35 shall be used in computing the size of the branch-circuit conductors being used if the electric space heating equipment consists of a heat pump that is mechanical refrigeration with or without resistive elements.

The provisions of the above paragraph do not apply to conductors that supply part of an approved fixed electric space heating equipment.

B. Installation

424-9. General—Only approved methods of installation shall be used for all electrical space heating equipment.

424-10. Special Permission—Special permission shall be secured from the inspection authority to install fixed space heating systems employing methods of installation other than covered in this Article.

424-11. Supply Conductors—Some heating equipment will require high-temperature wiring for the connections. Any equipment which is not suitable for connection to conductors with 60°C insulation shall be clearly and permanently marked and this marking shall be plainly visible after installation.

424-12. Location.

(a) **Exposed to Severe Physical Damage.** Fixed electrical space heating equipment shall never be installed where it will be subject to physical damage. However, if subject to physical damage, it has to be adequately protected.

(b) **Damp and Wet Locations.** Only approved heaters and related equipment shall be installed in damp or wet locations. The construction and installation of these shall be such that water cannot enter or be allowed to accumulate in or on the electrical parts or duct work.

A Fine Print Note calls attention to Section 110-11. This is where equipment shall be covered during installation for protection.

424-13. Spacing from Combustible Materials—All fixed electrically heated appliances (heating equipment) that, because of size, weight, or service, are intended to be used in a fixed position shall be amply protected from combustibles. That is, unless they have been approved when installed in direct contact with combustible materials.

424-14. Grounding—Metal parts that are exposed and are a part of fixed electrical heating equipment shall be grounded as required in Article 250.

C. Control and Protection of Fixed Electric Space Heating Equipment

424-19. Disconnecting Means—All fixed electric space heating equipment shall have means provided to disconnect all of the ungrounded conductors to the heater, controller(s), and overcurrent device(s). Where heating equipment is supplied from more than one source, the disconnecting means shall be grouped and identified.

(a) **Heating Equipment with Supplementary Overcurrent Protection.** If supplementary overcurrent protection is in the enclosure of the disconnecting means for fixed electric space heating equipment, this disconnection equipment is required to be in sight on the supply side of a supplementary overcurrent device(s). It must also comply with either (1) or (2) below:

(1) **Heater Containing No Motor Rated Over ⅛ Horsepower.** The disconnecting means mentioned above or unit switches complementing Section 424-19(c) may be used as the required disconnecting means to both the heater and the motor controller(s) as permitted either under (a) or (b) below:
   a. The disconnecting means must be in sight of the motor controller(s) and the heater itself; or
   b. The disconnection means is the type that can be locked in the open position.

(2) **Heater Containing a Motor(s) Rated Over ⅛ Horsepower.** This covers motors used with heaters that are rated over ⅛ horsepower.
   a. If the disconnecting means is in sight of both the motor controller(s) and the heater, it will be permitted to serve as a disconnecting means for both.
   b. Switches for disconnecting means shall comply with Section 424-19(c). If they are not visible from the heater, a separate disconnecting means shall be installed, or the disconnecting means shall be capable of being locked in the open position.
   c. When the disconnecting means is not in sight of the motor controller location, the disconnecting means used shall comply with Section 430-102.
   d. Section 430-102(b) shall apply when the motor disconnect is not visible from the location of the motor controller.

(b) **Heating Equipment Without Supplementary Overcurrent Protection.** This covers heating equipment that does not have overcurrent protection.

(1) **Without Motor or with Motor Not Over ⅛ Horsepower.** When fixed heating equipment does not have a motor over ⅛ horsepower, it shall be permitted to use the branch-circuit switch or circuit breaker for the disconnecting means, if it is readily accessible for servicing.

(2) **Over ⅛ Horsepower.** If a motor over ⅛ horsepower is used in motor-driven electric space heating equipment, the disconnecting means shall be visible from the motor control.

Exception: Section 424-19(a) (2) provides an exception for the above.

(c) **Unit Switch(es) as Disconnecting Means.** If a disconnecting switch(es) for a unit has plainly marked the opposition that will disconnect all ungrounded conductors to the fixed heater, it shall be permitted to be the disconnecting means that this article requires, or other disconnecting means may be provided in the following occupancies:

(1) **Multifamily Dwellings.** In multifamily dwellings, the disconnecting means is required to be in the dwelling unit involved or on the same floor as the dwelling unit where the fixed heater is installed. The disconnecting means will also be permitted to have branch-circuit breakers supplying lamps and appliances.

(2) **Two-Family Dwellings.** In a two-family dwelling the disconnecting means may be installed on the inside or outside of the dwelling unit, supplying the dwelling in which the fixed heating is installed. In this case the disconnecting means may have overload protection, not only for the fixed heating protection, but also as protection for lamps and appliances.

(3) **One-Family Dwellings.** In a one-family dwelling, the disconnecting means for the dwelling may be the other disconnecting means. This disconnecting means, it is assumed, disconnects all the service to the one-family dwelling.

(4) **Other Occupancies.** In other occupancies, the fixed heater may have the branch-circuit switch or breaker. If it is readily accessible for providing service to the fixed heating, it shall be permitted as the other disconnecting means.

424-20. Thermostatically Controlled Switching Devices.

(a) **Serving as Both Controllers and Disconnecting Means.** Thermostatically controlled switches for controlling the temperature may be a combination thermostat, capable of being manually controlled, with a switch incorporated. This switch may be used if the following conditions are met:

(1) The thermostat must be marked with an OFF position and be able to open all current-carrying conductors.

(2) When placed in the OFF position, it shall manually open all ungrounded conductors.

(3) When the switch on the thermostat is set to the OFF position, the design must be such that the circuit cannot be energized automatically.

(4) It shall be located as covered in Section 424-19.

(b) **Thermostats that Do Not Directly Interrupt All Underground Conductors.** If the thermostat does not directly open all the underground conductors, and if the thermostat is operable by remote control, it is not required to meet the requirements of (a). Such devices shall not be used as the disconnecting means of the fixed heating.

424-21. Switch and Circuit Breaker to Be Indicating—Switches or circuit breakers used for disconnecting means for heating equipment shall indicate whether they are in the open or closed position.

424-22. Overcurrent Protection.

(a) **Branch-Circuit Devices.** Article 210 covering branch circuits goes into considerable detail on overcurrent protection. Heating equipment will generally be considered to have overcurrent protection when the conditions of Article 210 are met, with the exception of motor-driven heating equipment which comes under Articles 430 and 440.

(b) **Resistance Elements.** Any electric space heating equipment which draws a total of more than 48 amperes shall have the heating units subdivided so that each subdivided section will not draw more than 48 amperes; if it draws 48 amperes, it shall be protected by not more than 60 amperes overcurrent protection.

Exception: Section 424-72(a) covers the exception involved here.

(c) **Overcurrent Protective Devices.** Supplementary overcurrent protective devices that were used on subdivided loads specified in (b) above are covered in the following: (1) They shall be either factory installed within, on the heater enclosure itself, or they may be supplied as a separate assembly for use with that heater by the manufacturer; (2) Although required to be accessible, they are not required to be readily accessible; (3) These devices for overcurrent protection shall be suitable for use on branch circuits.

Note: This refers us to Section 240-10.

If cartridge fuses are used to provide the overcurrent protection, several subdivided loads may be served by the single disconnecting means.

Note: Refer to Section 240-40.

(d) **Branch-Circuit Conductors.** Any conductors supplying the supplementary overcurrent protection devices are branch-circuit conductors.

Exception: If the conditions following this paragraph are met for heaters rated at 50 kW or more, conductors used to supply the supplementary overcurrent devices, as covered in (c) above will not be permitted to be sized at less than 100 percent of the nameplate rating that is supplied on the heater. For this purpose, the following conditions shall be met:

   a. The heater shall have a marking giving the minimum size of conductors that may be used; and

   b. These conductors may not be smaller than the size of the conductors as marked on the nameplate of the heater; and

   c. There must be a device that is actuated by temperature to control the cycles of the operation of heating equipment.

(e) **Conductors for Subdivided Loads.** With wiring that is installed in the field, the conductors between the supplementary overcurrent devices and the heater are to be sized at not less than 125 percent of the load that is being served. Section 240-3 covers supplementary overcurrent protective devices that are covered in (c) above, and these conductors shall be protected in accordance with the aforementioned section.

Exception: With heaters that are rated at 50 kW or more, the ampacity of field-wired conductors allowed between the feeder and the supplementary overcurrent devices in no case shall be permitted to be less 100 percent of each subdivided circuit. This is permitted if all of the following conditions are met:

   a. See (a) of the exception to (d).
   b. See (b) of the exception to (d).
   c. See the *NEC.*

D. Marking of Heating Equipment

424-28. Nameplate—See the *NEC.*

424-29. Marking of Heating Elements—Heating elements that are replaceable in the field shall have the following markings on each heating element: volts and amperes, or volts and watts.

E. Electric Space Heating Cables

424-34. Heating Cable Construction—Heating cables are supplied by the manufacturer in a complete unit with 7-foot (2.13-m) nonheating leads. The nonheating leads shall not be cut off or shortened in any manner. See the next section. Also see Fig. 424-1.

Fig. 424-1. Nonheating leads shall be a minimum of 7 feet.

424-35. Marking of Heating Cables—Identifying name or identifying symbol, catalog rating number, the rating in volts and watts or in volts and amperes shall be marked on each heating cable.

Every heating cable length shall have a permanent marking on the nonheating lead, and this shall be located within 3 inches of the terminal end. The lead wires shall have distinctive colors to indicate the voltage at which they are to be used:

120 volts, nominal, yellow.
208 volts, nominal, blue.
240 volts, nominal, red.
277 volts, nominal, brown.

424-36. Clearances of Wiring in Ceilings—Wiring located above heated ceilings and in thermal insulation must be sized according to the temperature that it might be exposed to. Therefore, wiring above heated ceilings shall be located not less than 2 inches above the heated ceiling and, if it is in thermal insulation at this height, it shall be considered as being operated at an ambient temperature of 50°C. It will be necessary to refer to the correction.factors that accompany Tables 310-16 through 310-31 to find the correction factors for the ampacity of conductors at 50°C. Wiring above heated ceilings and located above thermal insulation having a minimum thickness of 2 inches will require no correction factor.

424-37. Location of Branch-Circuit and Feeder Wiring in Exterior Walls—The methods of wiring covered in Article 300 and Section 310-10 must be used for branch-circuit and feeders installed in exterior walls.

424-38. Area Restrictions.

(a) **Shall Not Extend Beyond the Room or Area.** Heating cables shall not, in any circumstance, extend beyond the room or area that is being heated. See Fig. 424-2 on page 356.

(b) **Uses Prohibited.** Heating cables shall not be installed in closets as over walls or partitions that extend to the ceiling, and they shall not be installed over cabinets. They may be installed in front of cabinets unless the ceiling above the cabinets is equal to their minimum horizontal dimensions. This takes into account the nearest cabinet edge to the room or area.

Exception: If they are embedded, a single run is permitted to pass over partitions.

CABLES NOT PERMITTED IN CLOSETS

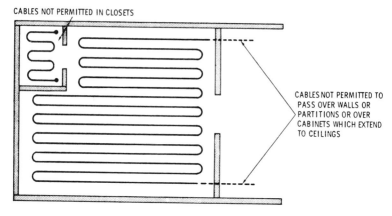

CABLES NOT PERMITTED TO PASS OVER WALLS OR PARTITIONS OR OVER CABINETS WHICH EXTEND TO CEILINGS

Fig. 424-2. Illustration showing where heating cables may and may not be installed in ceilings.

(c) **In Closet Ceilings as Low-Temperature Heat Source to Control Relative Humidity.** There are climates where humidity control is required in closets, but the prohibition of cables in closets is not intended to prohibit the use of low-temperature humidity controls in closets. See the *NEC*.

424-39. Clearance from Other Objects and Openings—There shall be a clearance of at least 8 inches from the edge of outlet and junction boxes that are to be used for mounting lighting fixtures.

Two inches (50.8 mm) shall be provided from recessed lighting fixtures and their trims, ventilating openings, and other such openings in room surfaces. Sufficient area shall be provided to assure that no heating cable or panel will be covered by other surface mounted lighting units. The temperature limits and overheating of the cable are involved in this instance. Therefore, the requirements of the section should be very carefully followed and, if in doubt, a little extra clearance should be given.

424-40. Splices—Splicing of cables is prohibited except where necessary due to breaks. Even then the length of the cable should not be altered as this will change the characteristics of the cable and the heat. It will be necessary to occasionally splice a break, but only approved methods shall be used.

424-41. Installation of Heating Cables on Dry Board, in Plaster and on Concrete Ceilings.

(a) **Shall Not Be Installed in Walls.** Heating cable shall not be installed in walls. It is not designed for this purpose and is strictly forbidden, with the exception that isolated runs of cable may run down a vertical surface to reach a drop ceiling.

(b) **Adjacent Runs.** Adjacent runs of heating cable shall be spaced not closer than 1½ inches on centers and have a wattage not to exceed 2¾ watts per square foot. See Fig. 424-3.

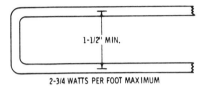

1-1/2" MIN.

2-3/4 WATTS PER FOOT MAXIMUM

Fig. 424-3. Heating cables installed in ceilings shall be placed at least 1 1/2 inches apart.

(c) **Surfaces to Be Applied.** Heating cables shall be applied only to gypsum board, plaster lath, or similar fire-resistant materials. If applied to the surface of metal lath or any other conducting material, there shall be a coat of plaster commonly known as a brown or scratch coat applied before the cable is installed. This coating of plaster shall entirely cover the metal lath or conducting surface. Also see Section 424-41(f).

(d) **Splices.** Splices to the nonheating leads shall have a 3-inch minimum after the splice is embedded in plaster or in dry board. The embedding shall be done in the same manner as with the feeding cable.

(e) **Ceiling surfaces.** On plastered ceilings, the entire surface shall have a finish coat of thermally noninsulating sand plaster or other approved coating which shall have a nominal thickness of ½ inch. Insulation (thermal) plaster shall not be used.

(f) **Secured.** The cable shall be fastened at intervals not to exceed 16 inches by means of taping, stapling, or plaster. Staples or metal fasteners which straddle the cable shall not be used with metal lath or other conducting surfaces. The fastening devices shall be of an approved type.

Exception: Heating cable shall be mounted so that it is not over 6 feet between mountings.

(g) **Dry Board Installations.** When dry board ceilings are used, the cable shall be installed and the entire ceiling below the cable shall be covered with gypsum board not exceeding ½ inch (12.7 mm) in thickness, but the voids between the two layers and around the cable shall be filled with a conducting plaster or other approved thermal conducting material so that the heat will readily transfer.

(h) **Free from Contact with Conductive Surfaces.** Heating cables shall not come in contact with metal or other conducting materials.

(i) **Joists.** When dry board applications are used, you must install the cable parallel to joists and leave a clearance of 2 ½ inches between centers of adjacent runs of cable. At times it is necessary to cross joists, but the cable crossing joists shall be kept to a minimum. Surface layers of heating cable and gypsum board shall be so mounted that nails or other types of fastener do not penetrate into the heating cable.

Note: When practical, heating cable shall cross joists only at the ends of the joist. This will reduce the chances of nails being driven into the heating cables.

424-42. Finished Ceilings—The question often arises as to whether

wallpaper or paint may be used over a ceiling that has heating cable. These materials have been used as finishes over heating cable since cables first were used in the late 1940's. This section gives formal recognition to painting or papering ceilings.

The above does not permit ceilings to be covered with decorative panels, or beams constructed of materials which have thermal insulating properties, such as wood, fiber, or plastic.

424-43. Installation of Nonheating Leads of Cables.

(a) **Free Nonheating Leads.** Only approved wiring methods shall be used for connecting the nonheating leads from a junction box at the heating leads to a location in the ceiling.

In these installations, single leads in raceways (conductors) or single or multiconductors Type UF, Type NMC, Type MI, or other approved conductors. Please note the absence of Type NM.

(b) **Leads in Junction Box.** Where the nonheating leads terminate in a junction box, there shall be not less than 6 inches of the nonheating leads free within the junction box. Also, the markings of the leads shall be visible in the junction box. This is highly important so that the heating cable can be identified.

(c) **Excess Leads.** Nonheating leads shall not be shortened. They shall either be fastened to the underside of the ceiling or embedded in plaster or other approved material, leaving a length sufficient to reach the junction box with not less than 6 inches of free lead remaining in the box.

424-44. Installation of Cables in Concrete or Poured Masonry

Floors—This section is for fixed indoor space heating and is not to be confused with Part J or ice and snow melting, which is covered in Article 426.

(a) **Watts per Linear Foot.** The wattage per foot of heating cable shall not exceed 16 ½ watts.

(b) **Spacing Between Adjacent Runs.** Runs of heating cable shall be not less than 1 inch on centers to adjacent heating cables.

(c) **Secured in Place.** Cables have to be secured in place while concrete or other finish material is being applied. Approved means, such as nonmetallic spreaders or frames, shall be used. Concrete floors often have expansion joints in them. Cables shall be so installed that they do not bridge an expansion joint unless they are protected so as to prevent damage to the cables due to expansion or contraction of the floor.

(d) **Spacings Between Heating Cable and Metal Embedded in the Floor.** There shall be some distance between heating cable and any metal embedded in the floor.

Exception: If the cable is metal-covered, it may come into contact with metal embedded in the floor. This includes MI heating cable, which is being extensively used.

(e) **Leads Protected.** Sleeving of the leads by means of rigid metal conduit, rigid nonmetallic conduit, intermediate metal conduit, or EMT shall be used for protection where the leads leave the floor.

(f) **Bushings or Approved Fittings.** The sleeves mentioned in (e) shall have bushings or other approved means used where the leads emerge within the floor slab to prevent damage to the cable.

424-45. Inspection and Tests—Great care shall be exercised in the installation of embedded heating cables to prevent any damage thereto. In addition, the installation is required to be inspected and approved before cables are covered or concealed. If MI cable is run, the insulation resistance to the metal covering should be Megger® tested.

After plastering ceilings or pouring floors, the cables shall be tested to see that the insulation resistance is within safe limits. A Megger® test should be made at about 500 volts.

F. Duct Heaters

424-57. General—This Part F covers heaters mounted in air ducts where they furnish a stream of air through the duct and where the air moving unit is not a part of the equipment design.

424-58. Identification—If heaters are installed in air ducts, they are required to be suitable for the installation. Look for the UL label, and check the installation instructions closely.

424-59. Air Flow—Air flow over the face of the heater must be adequate and uniform in accordance with the manufacturer's instructions. If the heaters are mounted within 4 feet of an air-moving device, heat pump, air conditioner, elbows, baffle plates, or other obstructions that might be present in the duct work and which might interfere with adequate and uniform air flow, it may be required to use turning vanes, pressure plates, or some other device on the inlet side of the duct heater to assure that the air flow will be uniform over the face of the heater.

424-60. Elevated Inlet Temperature—Many duct heaters are used with heat pumps or other sources of air that are above room temperature. The operation of the heater may not be the same with an elevated air temperature at the inlet as it would be with the inlet temperature at room temperature. Therefore, the heater shall be identified as suitable for use at the elevated temperatures.

424-61. Installation of Duct Heaters with Heat Pumps and Air Conditioners—A duct heater installed immediately adjacent to an air conditioner or heat pump under abnormal operating conditions could adversely affect electrical equipment in the heat pump or air conditioner. It has been found that the duct heater shall be mounted not less than 4 feet from such equipment, unless the duct heater has been identified as suitable for closer mounting and is so marked.

424-62. Condensation—Duct heaters that are also used with air conditioners or with other air-cooling equipment (such equipment will cause condensation of moisture) shall be identified as suitable for use with air conditioners (for example, a furnace that had air-conditioning installed within it).

424-63. Fan Circuit Interlock—A duct heater that operates in such a manner that the fan circuit is not energized with the first heating element might cycle on the high limit. This can cause an undue number of operations with the high limit to occur. Conceivably, in the course of years, the high limit might operate enough times to exceed the 100,000-cycle requirement and become erratic in its operation. By providing means to energize the fan circuit with the first heater circuit, we eliminate this potential problem.

424-64. Limit Controls—In order to prevent overheating, each duct heater is required to be provided with an integral approved automatic-reset temperature limiting control or controllers to de-energize the circuits if the temperature rises too high.

Also, an integral independent supplementary control must be provided with each duct heater that will disconnect a sufficient number of duct heaters and conductors to stop the flow of current. Such a device must be manually resettable or replaceable.

424-65. Location of Disconnecting Means—All control equipment for duct heaters shall be accessible and a disconnecting means provided which shall be installed at or within sight of the controllers for the heating units.

Exception: Section 424-19(a) gives an exception which is permitted.

424-66. Installation—See NFPA Pamphlets Nos. 90A and 90B. Also see the *NEC*.

G. Resistance-Type Boilers

424-70. Scope—This Part G covers resistance-type heating elements used in boilers. Electrode-type heating is not included here; that topic will be found under Part H.

424-71. Identification—Resistance-type boilers are required to be identified for this type of use.

424-72. Overcurrent Protection.

(a) **Boiler Employing Resistance-Type Immersion Heating Elements in an ASME Rated and Stamped Vessel.** Resistance-type immersion heating elements, covered by ASME, are to be stamped vessels. The heating elements shall be protected at not more than 150 amperes. If boilers are rated at more than 120 amperes, the heating units shall be subdivided so that each heating element load does not exceed 120 amperes.

Section 424-3(b) covers subdivided loads that are less than 120 amperes. The rating of the overcurrent protection devices are covered in that section.

(b) **Boiler Employing Resistance-Type Heating Elements Rated More than 48 Amperes and Not Contained in an ASME Rated and Stamped Vessel.** If the boiler is not an ASME rated and stamped vessel employing resistance-type heating elements, it shall have elements subdivided into not more than loads of 48 amperes and they shall not be protected by more than 60 amperes.

If such a boiler is rated at more than 48 amperes, the heating elements shall be subdivided into loads not to exceed 48 amperes.

If the load, when subdivided, is less than 48 amperes, the overcurrent protection device shall comply with Section 424-3(b).

(c) **Supplementary Overcurrent Protective Devices.** The supplementary overcurrent protective devices as required by Section 424-72(a) and (b) shall be:

(1) Factory installed within or on the boiler enclosure or provided as a separate assembly by the boiler manufacturer, and

(2) Accessible, but need not be readily accessible, and

(3) Suitable for branch-circuit protection.

See Section 240-40. If fuses are used to provide the overcurrent protection, a single disconnecting means may be used for the several subdivided circuits.

(d) **Conductors Supplying Supplementary Overcurrent Protective Devices.** The conductors supplying the supplementary overcurrent protection are considered branch-circuit conductors.

Exception: If all of the following conditions are met, where feeders are rated at 50 kW or more the conductors that supply the protective overcurrent device, as specified in (c) above, are permitted to be sized at not less than 100 percent of the nameplate rating of the heater:

a. If the minimum conductor size is marked on the heater; and
b. The conductors used are not smaller than those covered on the marking on the heater for minimum size; and
c. There must be a temperature- and pressure-operative device to control the operating cycles of the equipment.

(e) **Conductors for Subdivided Loads.** When field wiring of the conductors is done between the heater and the supplementary overcurrent device, the conductors shall be sized at not less 125 percent of the load that you are serving. Section 240-3 covers the protection of these conductors with the supplementary overcurrent protective devices specified in (c) above.

Exception: When heaters are 50 kW or more, the field-wired conductor ampacity from the feeder to the supplementary overcurrent device shall be not less than 100 percent of their individual subdivided circuits if all of the following conditions are met:

a. The heater must be marked with a minimum conductor size; and
b. The conductors shall not be smaller than the minimum marked size on the feeder; and
c. There is a temperature device that controls the cycles of the equipment operation.

424-73. Over-Temperature Limit Control—In addition to a temperature regulating system and other devices protecting the tank against excessive pressure, each boiler designed so there is no change in state of the heat transfer medium shall be equipped with a temperature sensitive limiting means. This shall be so installed that it limits the maximum liquid temperature and shall directly or indirectly disconnect all ungrounded conductors to the heating elements; thus a temperature sensitive relay device may open a magnetically controlled disconnecting means.

424-74. Over-Pressure Limit Control—Means shall be provided for a pressure regulating system and other devices protecting the tank against excessive pressure on each boiler so that in normal operation there is a change in state of the heat transfer medium from a liquid to a vapor. In addition to this, the boiler shall be equipped with a pressure sensing limiting device which shall be installed to limit pressure and directly or indirectly disconnect all ungrounded conductors to the heating elements.

424-75. Grounding—All metal parts that do not carry current shall be grounded as required by Article 250. A connection means shall be provided for the equipment grounding, and it is required to be sized in accordance with Table 250-95.

H. Electrode-Type Boilers

424-80. Scope.—Part H covers boilers heated by means of electrodes in the water. The voltage of the current passing between these electrodes shall not exceed 600 volts, nominal.

424-81. Identification—Electrode-type boilers are required to be identified where used as indicated, and shall be suitable for the installation involved.

424-82. Branch-Circuit Requirements—The overcurrent protection for conductors must be calculated as having 125 percent of the total load, with the exception of motors. A contactor or relay, if it has been approved for continuous service at 100 percent of its rating, shall supply its full-current-rated load. You are referred to Section 210-22(c), Exception No. 2. This section shall not apply to conductors when they are an integral part of an approved boiler.

Exception: See the *NEC*.

424-83. Over-Temperature Limit Control—In addition to a temperature regulating system and other devices protecting the tank against excessive pressure each boiler is designed so there is no change in state of the heat transfer medium, shall be equipped with a temperature sensitive limiting means. This shall be so installed that it limits the maximum pressure and shall directly or indirectly interrupt all current flow through the electrodes.

424-84. Over-Pressure Limit Control—Boilers used for making steam shall be equipped with pressure-sensitive limiting means, in order to limit the maximum pressure created in the boiler by the steam, and also directly or indirectly to interrupt the flow of electricity to the electrodes. This shall be in addition to a pressure-regulating system and other means of protecting the boiler from excessive pressure.

424-85. Grounding—On those boilers that are designed so that fault currents will not pass through the pressure vessel or boiler, and if the pressure vessel is isolated from the electrodes, all exposed metal parts, including the pressure vessel and supply and return piping, shall be grounded as required in Article 250.

For all other designs, the pressure vessel or boiler that contains the electrodes is required to be isolated and insulated from ground.

424-86. Markings—Marking will be required on all electrode-type boilers. The marking shall consist of the following:

(1) The name of the manufacturer;

(2) The normal rating in volts, amperes, and kW;

(3) The type of electrical supply of frequency, the number of phases required, and the number of wires required;

(4) The designation "Electrode-Type Boiler"; and

(5) The warning: "ALL POWER SUPPLIES SHALL BE DISCONNECTED BEFORE SERVICING, INCLUDING SERVICING THE PRESSURE VESSEL."

The location of the nameplate shall be such that it is visible after installation.

J. Electric Radiant Heating Panels and Heating Panel Sets

Cable and cable sets are not generically the same as heating panels and heating panel sets. The installations and wiring methods cannot be covered by the same Code requirements; the Code addresses this problem including them in this part. Previously, the inclusion of both radiant cable heating and radiant panel heating in Part E caused considerable confusion. The solution—adding a Part J—helps to clarify the requirements for each type of equipment.

424-90. Scope—This part shall apply to radiant heating panels and sets of heating panels.

424-91. Definitions.

(a) **Heating Panel.** Heating panels consist of a complete assembly. It shall be provided with a junction box or a length of flexible conduit so that it may be connected to the branch circuit.

(b) **Heating Panel Set.** A heating panel set may be of a rigid or nonrigid assembly, and shall be provided either with nonheating leads or a terminal junction assembly that has been identified as being suitable for the wiring system to which it is connected.

424-92 Markings—See the *NEC*.

424-93. Installation.

(a) **General.**

(1) Heating panels and heating panel sets shall be installed in accordance with the manufacturer's instructions.

(2) The heating portions:
   a. Shall not be installed in or behind locations where they would be subject to physical damage.
   b. Shall not be run above walls, partitions, cupboards, or any other similar portion of a structure that extends to the ceiling.
   c. Shall not be run in or through thermal insulation. However, they may be in contact with the surface of insulation. If run

in or through insulation, the heating qualities of the panels will be reduced and the panels will overheat.

(3) They shall not be installed less than 8 inches from any outlet box or junction box that will be used for the mounting of surface lighting fixtures. If recessed fixtures and trims are used, heating panels shall have a clearance of 2 inches from these or from ventilating openings and other such openings in the rooms. There shall be sufficient area allowed so that no heating panel or heating panel set will be covered by any surface-mounted unit causing overheating of the panel or panel sets.

If a heating panel is covered by a surface-mounted heating unit, the situation may be dangerous because of overheating, resulting in fire.

Exception: If heating panels are listed to be permitted to be mounted closer to the items described above, they may be installed at the distance marked in the listing.

(4) After installation and inspection of the heating panel or sets of heating panels, you are permitted to install a surface that has been identified and listed in the manufacturer's instructions as suitable for the installation. The surface shall be secured so that no nails or other fastenings can damage the heating panel or heating panel sets.

(5) Surfaces that were permitted in Section 424-93(a) (4) may be covered with paint, wallpaper, or other surfaces that have been listed and identified in the manufacturer's instructions as suitable for use.

It should be mentioned that there is an uncontrollable future danger of tenants or homeowners driving nails into walls with heat panels and contacting or breaking the heat cables in the heating panel.

(b) **Heating Panel Sets.**

(1) In installing heating panel sets, you are permitted to secure them to the lower face of the joists, or they may be mounted between joists, headings, or nailing strips.

(2) Heating panel sets are required to be mounted parallel to joists or nailing strips.

(3) Only the unheated portion of heating panel sets are permitted to be nailed or stapled in place. You shall not cut heating panel sets or nail them at points closer than ¼ inch to the elements. Nails, staples, etc., shall never be used where they penetrate current-carrying parts.

(4) Unless identified for cutting in an approved manner, heating panel sets shall be installed as complete units.

424-94. **Clearances of Wiring in Ceilings**—Any wiring above ceilings shall be spaced not less than 2 inches above the heated ceiling, and the ambient temperature at which they are to be operated shall be 50° C or 122° F. The ampacity of the ambient temperature shall be computed with the correction tables for ambient temperatures, as in Tables 310-16 through 310-31.

Exception: When wiring above the ceilings is located above thermal insulation, and the thermal insulation, and the thermal insulation is 2 inches or more in thickness, the wiring need not be corrected for temperature.

Author's Note: The material in Section 424-94 is, for all practical purposes, the same as covered previously for heat cables in ceilings.

424-95. Location of Branch-Circuit and Feeder Wiring in Walls.

(a) **Exterior Walls.** Wiring methods installed in exterior walls must comply with Article 300 and Section 310-10.

(b) **Interior Walls.** Wiring installed in interior walls behind heating panels and heating panel sets shall be considered to be operating at an ambient temperature of 40° C and 104° F. The ampacity shall be computed as covered in Tables 310-16 through 310-31. Besides interior walls, this covers interior partitions.

424-96. Connection to Branch-Circuit Conductors.

(a) **General.** The manufacturer's instructions must be complied with when heating panels or heating panel sets are assembled in the field for installation in one room or area.

(b) **Heating Panels.** Only wiring methods that are approved shall be used when connecting heating panels to branch-circuit wiring.

(c) **Heating Panel Sets.**

(1) Only identified wiring methods that are considered suitable for the purpose shall be used for connecting heating panel sets to branch-circuit wiring.

(2) The manufacturer's instructions shall be used on heating panel sets that are provided with terminal junction assemblies that have had the nonheating leads attached at the time of installation.

424-97. **Nonheating Leads**—It is permissible to cut nonheating lead of heating panels or heating panel sets to the required length. They shall meet the requirements for the installation of the wiring used as covered in Section 424-96. Nonheating leads are part of the heating panel or heating panel set and are not subject to the ampacity requirements covered in Section 424-3(b) for branch circuits. Remember too that there is a requirement in the Code for a minimum of 6 inches of conductors, including these leads, in junction boxes.

424-98. Installation in Concrete or Poured Masonry.

(a) **Maximum Heated Area.** The maximum wattage for heating panels or heating panel sets installed in concrete or poured masonry is 33 watts per square foot.

(b) **Secured in Place and Identified as Suitable.** The manufacturer's instructions shall specify the means of securing heating panels or heating panel sets in concrete or poured masonry. The means of securing shall also be identified for that use.

(c) **Expansion Joints.** Unless protected from expansion and contraction, heating panels and heating panel sets shall not bridge expansion joints.

(d) **Spacings.** Heating panels and panel sets shall not come in contact with metal embedded in the floor.

Exception: If the heating panels have a metal-clad covering that is grounded, they may be in contact with metal embedded in the floor.

(e) **Protection of Leads.** Rigid metal conduit, intermediate metal conduit, rigid nonmetallic conduit, EMT, or other approved means shall be used for leads to protect them where they leave the floor.

(f) **Brushings or Fittings Required.** Leads emerging within the floor shall have bushings or fittings that are approved.

424-99. Installation under Floor Covering.

(a) **Identification.** Any heating panels or heating panel sets to be installed under floor covering shall be identified and listed as suitable for that use.

(b) **Maximum Heated Area.** The maximum heated area in wattage for heating panels or heating panel sets installed under floor covering is 15 watts per square foot.

(c) **Installation.** Panels or panel sets that are listed for installation in the floor covering are to be installed only on a smooth and flat floor area as called for by the manufacturer's instructions, which shall also comply with the following:

See the *NEC* for the five conditions that must be met to cover the above.

ARTICLE 426—FIXED OUTDOOR ELECTRIC DE-ICING AND SNOW-MELTING EQUIPMENT

A. General

426-1. Scope —This article covers electrically energized heating systems and their installation.

(a) **Embedded.** Driveways, steps, and various other areas may have heating cable embedded.

(b) **Exposed.** Heating cable may be used for drainage systems, bridges, structures, and roofs, and they may be installed on other structures.

It is the author's opinion that where they are mounted in downspouts, in roofs, etc., they should be MI-heating cables, either copper or stainless steel, and the copper continuity of the equipment grounding system should be maintained. He would also go so far as to require that GFCI's supply these branch circuits.

426-2. Definitions—Refer to the *NEC*.

426-3. Application of Other Articles—As is true throughout the Code, this article must be in accord with parts of the Code unless specifically amended by this article. In particular, applications of the coverage of this Article for use in hazardous (classified) locations must comply with Articles 500 through 516.

When the outdoor heating, de-icing, and snow-melting equipment is used and is cord- and plug-connected, it shall be identified and installed as with Article 422.

It is the author's opinion that heating cable used for roofs, downspouts, steps, etc., should be controlled by a thermostat mounted where it is not exposed to direct heat from the sun, so that you need not depend upon people to turn it on and off when it is needed and not needed.

426-4. Branch-Circuit Sizing—The ampacity of branch circuit conductors used for these purposes and the rating of the overcurrent protection devices supplying this fixed outdoor de-icing and snow-melting equipment is to be not less than 125 percent of the maximum load to the heaters to which they are connected. See Section 240-3, Exception No. 1.

B. Installation

426-10. General —Equipment and materials used for installing fixed outdoor electric de-icing and snow-melting systems may be subject to many troubles and possible hazards, so extreme care should be taken in the installation and inspection to assure that the equipment and other installation materials are identified as being suitable for the use and installed according to the Code for:

(1) Chemical, thermal, and physical environment must all be considered, and

(2) The manufacturer's drawings and instructions must be followed in making the installation.

An actual incident that the author was involved in was the use of stainless steel MI heating cable. It was laid on the earth surface of steps, then precast concrete step tops were added. During the time that the cable was exposed it drew moisture, which was found by using a Biddle Meggar®. Upon further examination of the MI cable, it was found that there were places in the stainless steel covering that were not completely closed, so the installation was not approved until the MI cable was replaced with cable without leaks in the outer covering.

426-11. Use—The installation of de-icing and snow-melting heating equipment must be done in such a manner as to provide protection from physical damage.

426-12. Thermal Protection—De-icing and snow-melting electrical equipment that operate at temperatures exceeding 60°C (140°F) shall be guarded, thermally insulated, or otherwise isolated to prevent persons coming into contact with it.

426-13. Identification—De-icing and snow-melting equipment outdoors shall be identified as per location by posting signs or markings that are appropriate and clearly visible.

426-14. Special Permission—Special types of de-icing or snow-melting equipment which employ methods of construction or installation other than those covered by this Article shall not be used or installed unless special permission is granted in writing.

C. Resistance Heating Elements

426-20. Embedded De-Icing and Snow-Melting Equipment.

(a) **Watt Density.** The heater area shall have not more than 120 watts per square foot.

(b) **Spacing.** The spacing of the cable is dependent upon the rating of the de-icing cable, but it shall not be less than 1 inch on centers.

(c) **Cover.** Heating panel or cables shall be installed as follows:

(1) If installed in asphalt or concrete or other masonry, you are required to have at least 2 inches of masonry or asphalt, and the cable shall be at least 1 ½ inches below the surface of the masonry or asphalt or the installation of panels or other units; or

(2) They may be installed over other approved bases of masonry or asphalt and embedded with 3 ½ inches of the material, but they shall not be installed less than 1 ½ inches from the top surface; or

(3) If other forms of heating equipment have been specifically been listed for other forms of installation, then the installation shall be done only in the manner for which it has been investigated and listed.

(d) **Secured.** Frames or spacers shall be installed between cables for support while the masonry or asphalt is being applied over the cables.

(e) **Expansion and Contraction.** Added protection for expansion and contraction is required for cables, units, and panels that are installed on expansion joints on bridges.

426-21. Exposed De-Icing and Snow-Melting Equipment.

(a) **Secured.** Approved means must be used when installing heating unit assemblies so that they will be securely fastened to the surface.

(b) **Overtemperature.** In any place where heating elements are not in direct contact with the surface that they are heating, the design of the heating assembly shall be such that its temperature limitations are not exceeded.

(c) **Expansion and Contraction.** Expansion joints shall not be crossed with heating elements and assemblies unless provision is made for expansion and contraction.

(d) **Flexural Capability.** When heating is installed where structures are flexible, the heating assemblies must have a flexibility that is compatible with the structure.

426-22. Installation of Nonheating Leads for Embedded Equipment.

(a) **Grounding Sheath or Braid.** If the nonheating leads have a grounding sheath or braid, they may be embedded in masonry or asphalt in the same manner as heating cable without the need for additional protection.

(b) **Raceways.** All but 1 to 6 inches of nonheating leads of type TW, or cables with other approved types of insulation which do not have a grounding sheath or braid, shall be installed in conduit, intermediate metal conduit, EMT, or other raceway, and this conduit or other protection shall extend a minimum of 1 inch from the factory splice to the heating part of the cable to not more than 6 inches from the factory splice.

(c) **Bushings.** Insulated bushings shall be installed on the conduit, EMT, etc., in the masonry or asphalt where the cable emerges from the conduit.

(d) **Expansion and Contraction.** All leads shall be protected where buried in expansion joints; where they emerge from masonry or asphalt, they shall be installed in conduit, intermediate metal conduit, EMT, or other raceway.

(e) **Leads in Junction Boxes.** There shall be a minimum of 6 inches of nonheating leads left in junction boxes.

426-23. Installation of Nonheating Leads for Exposed Equipment.

(a) **Nonheating leads.** Power supplies to nonheating leads that are cold leads, supplying resistive elements, must be suitable for the temperature that they will encounter. Approved heaters that have attached nonheating leads are permitted to be shortened, provided the markings that were covered in Section 426-25 are kept on the nonheating leads. There must be not less than 6 inches of nonheating leads in the junction box.

(b) **Protection.** Rigid metal conduit, intermediate metal conduit, EMT, or any other approved means shall be supplied over the nonheating leads from the power supply.

426-24. Electrical Connection.

(a) **Heating Element Connection.** Only insulated connectors that are listed for the purpose shall be used to make connections to heating elements where factory connections are not supplied, when heating elements are embedded in masonry or asphalt or are on exposed surfaces.

(b) **Circuit Connections.** The nonheating leads may be spliced or terminations made according to Sections 110-14 and 300-15. This does not apply to connection to the heating element itself.

426-25. Marking—Factory-assembled heating units must be marked within 3 inches from the heating element on the nonheating lead at both ends. This permanent marking shall have identification symbol, catalog number, and rating in volts, watts, or in volts and amperes.

426-26. Corrosion Protection—Raceways made of ferrous or nonferrous cable, cable armor, cable sheaths, boxes, fittings, supports, and support hardware are permitted to be installed in concrete or direct contact with the earth. If the areas are subject to severe corrosive conditions, the material must be suitable for the conditions. Keep in mind that conduits, etc., are not corrosion-resistant in many types of earth.

It is up to the installer to prove to the authority having jurisdiction that the materials are adequately protected from corrosion.

426-27. Grounding.

(a) **Metal Parts.** All exposed metal parts of fixed outdoor electric de-icing and snow-melting equipment, raceways, boxes, etc., likely to become energized shall be grounded as required in Article 250.

(b) **Grounding Braid or Sheath.** The heating section of the cable, panel, or unit shall have a means for grounding, such as copper braid, lead, copper sheath, or other approved means.

(c) **Bonding and Grounding.** Any metal parts involved in cable or cable installations and likely to become energized shall be grounded. Table 250-95 shall be used to find the equipment grounding conductor size.

Author's Note: A very dangerous situation can exist when heat cables are installed in drainage gutters or downspouts such as on residences. This is done for the most part by do-it-yourselfers. Attention should be called to the fact that unless downspouts are properly grounded, as per Article 250, a dangerous situation may occur.

D. Impedance Heating

426-30. Personnel Protection—See the *NEC*.

426-31. Voltage Limitation—See the *NEC*.

426-32. Isolation Transformer—See the *NEC*.

426-33. Induced Currents—Section 300-20 covers current-carrying components.

426-34. Grounding—If impedance operated heating systems are operated at voltages over 30 and under 80 volts, they shall be grounded at specified points.

E. Skin Effect Heating

426-40. Conductor Ampacity—See the *NEC*.

426-41. Pull Boxes—See the *NEC*.

426-42. Single Conductor in Enclosure—See the *NEC*.

426-43. Corrosion Protection—See the *NEC*.

426-44. Grounding—See the *NEC*.

F. Control and Protection

426-50. Disconnecting Means.

(a) **Disconnection.** Disconnecting means which open all ungrounded conductors shall be used for de-icing and snow-melting equipment. Branch-circuit switches or circuit breakers may be used for this purpose if readily accessible and marked so as to indicate what position they are in. Never trust any circuit as being de-energized unless proper tests have been performed to assure you that they are open.

(b) **Cord- and Plug-Connected Equipment.** If attachment plugs or cord- and plug-connected equipment are factory installed and rated at 20 amperes or less and 150 volts or less to ground, the attachment plug may be used as a disconnecting means.

426-51. Controllers.

(a) **Temperature Controllers with OFF Position.** Temperature controllers with switching devices that indicate an OFF position and open all ungrounded conductors are not usable as a disconnecting means unless they have a positive lockout in the OFF position.

(b) **Temperature Controllers Without OFF Position.** Temperature control switching devices that do not open all ungrounded conductors are not required to serve as the disconnecting means.

(c) **Remote Temperature Controllers.** The requirements of Section 426-51(a) are not required to meet all the specifications in this section when they are used as a remote-control temperature-actuated device. Also, they are not permitted to be used as a disconnecting means.

(d) **Combined Switching Devices.** The following conditions shall apply when combined temperature-actuated devices and manually controlled switches serve both as the controller and the disconnecting means:

(1) When placed in the OFF position, the manually operated device will open all ungrounded conductors.

(2) The design shall be such that the heating elements cannot be energized when the manually operated device is in the OFF position.

(3) There shall be a positive lockout in the OFF position.

426-52. Overcurrent Protection— Section 426-4 of this article covers branch-circuit requirements. Fixed outdoor electric de-icing and snow-melting equipment shall be considered as protected against overcurrent when the preceding section is adhered to, remembering that this is considered as a continuous load and is subject to the 80 percent factor.

ARTICLE 427—FIXED ELECTRIC HEATING EQUIPMENT FOR PIPELINES AND VESSELS

A. General

427-1. Scope—This article covers the application of electrically energized systems of various types and how to install these systems on pipelines and/or vessels.

427-2. Definitions—For the purpose of this article:

Pipeline. The length of pipe, including the valves, pumping, strainers, control devices, and other equipment that carries fluids. The purpose is to maintain the fluid condition of fluids that may tend to congeal at lower temperatures.

Vessels. The portion of the system that holds the volume of the fluid that is to be carried by pipeline. They may be barrels, drums, or tanks. They may contain not only fluids, but other materials.

Integrated Heating Equipment. This composes the complete system and all components and vessels used by the heating elements, medium of transferring the heat, thermal insulation, barriers to keep out moisture the nonheating leads for connection to the source of supply, and any temperature controllers, warning signs, and all the electrical raceway fittings, etc., to connect the system to the source.

Resistance Heating Element. A separate element that generates the heat that is applied to the pipeline or vessel, either externally or internally.

Note: The resistive-type heaters may come in many forms: tubular heaters, strip heaters, heating cable, heating blankets, and immersion heating.

From the above definition it may readily be seen that there is a certain tie-in between Articles 426 and 427.

Impedance Heating System. A system in which the pipeline and vessels are fed from a dual-winding transformer to the pipeline of vessel wall, causing current to flow therein by direct connection to an ac source of voltage.

See Part D in Article 426.

Induction Heating System. Heat is generated in the pipeline of vessel walls by inductive current and the hysteresis effect of the alternating current in the pipeline of vessel wall. The ac current must be supplied from an externally and isolated ac field.

Skin Effect Heating System. The heating effect of a ferromagnetic envelope attached to the pipeline and/or vessel. The heat is generated on the inner surface of the ferromagnetic envelope.

Note: Electrically insulated conductors are routed through and connected to the envelope at the other end. The envelope and the insulated conductor must be connected to an ac voltage source that originates from a dual-winding transformer.

See Part E of Article 426.

427-3. Application of Other Articles—Article 422 covers cord-connected pipe heating assemblies intended for specific uses and approved for the purpose. Hazardous (classified) locations shall comply with Articles 500 through 516 for fixed pipeline and vessel heating equipment in such hazardous locations.

427-4. Branch-Circuit Sizing—As with other branch-circuit requirements for continuous loads, conductors and overcurrent devices that supply fixed electric pipeline and vessel heating equipment shall be calculated on the basis of 125 percent of the total load of the heaters. Section 240-3, Exception No. 1, covers rating or setting of overcurrent devices.

B. Installation

427-10. General—The chemical, thermal and physical environment involved by necessity requires that the equipment for pipeline and vessel shall be compatible with the aforestated problems.

The manufacturer's drawings and instructions shall be followed in the installation.

427-11. Use—Care must be taken in the installation of feeding equipment to protect it from physical damage.

427-12. Thermal Protection—Pipelines or vessels with external heating equipment that operate with a surface temperature of 60° C or 140° F shall be protected from personnel contacting it by thermal insulation.

427-13. Identification—The presence of electrically heated pipelines or vessels shall be made known by posting caution signs or by markings placed at intervals along the pipeline or vessel.

C. Resistance Heating Elements

427-14. Secured—Thermal insulation shall not be used as the method of securing the heating element assemblies to the surface that is being heated. Other means must be used.

427-15. Not in Direct Contact—Unless the heater assemblies are such that the temperature limits cannot be exceeded when the heating element is not in direct contact with the pipeline or vessel that is being heated, other means must be provided to prevent the temperature of the heating element from rising higher than that at which it should be operated.

427-16. Expansion and Contraction—Unless provision is made for expansion and contraction of the heating source, heating elements shall not be allowed to bridge expansion joints.

427-17. Flexural Capability—When installed on flexible pipelines, the flexibility of the heating element shall be compatible with the flexibility of the pipeline.

427-18. Power Supply Loads.

(a) **Nonheating Leads.** The nonheating leads from the power supply, which are also known as the cold leads, when used with resistance-type elements shall have insulation to withstand the temperatures with which they may come in contact. Nonheating leads that are factory assembled may be shortened, as was covered in Section 427-20, but there shall be not less than 6 inches of lead extending into the junction box.

(b) **Power Supply Lead Protection.** Rigid metal conduit, intermediate metal conduit, EMT, or other raceways that are listed as being suitable for this application shall be supplied for the protection of nonheating supply leads where they emerge from the electrically heated pipeline or vessel.

(c) **Interconnecting Leads.** The nonheating leads interconnecting with the heating leads are permitted to be covered by the thermal insulation in the same way as the heaters.

427-19. Electrical Connections.

(a) **Nonheating Interconnections.** Insulated identified connectors when properly installed, shall be used to make nonheating interconnections under thermal insulation.

(b) **Circuit Connections.** Splices and terminations outside thermal insulation shall be in a box or fitting in accordance with Sections 110-14 and 300-15.

427-20. Marking—Each factory-assembled heating unit shall be legibly marked within 3 inches of the end of each power supply nonheating lead with the permanent identification or symbol, catalog number, rating in volts and watts, or rating in volts and amperes.

427-21. Grounding—All exposed noncurrent-carrying metal parts of the electrical heating equipment shall be grounded as required by Article 250 if there is any possible chance of such parts becoming energized.

427-22. Equipment Protection—Heating equipment that is not metal covered is required to have ground-fault protection for the branch circuit supplying it.

D. Impedance Heating

427-25. Personnel Protection—Personnel protection, either by guarding or by insulation, shall be provided for all external portions of the pipeline and/or vessel that is being heated. If the insulation is exposed to the outside, it must be weatherproof.

427-26. Voltage Limitations—The voltage used for the heating shall not be greater than 30 volts AC.

Exception: This exception allows it to be greater than 30 volts, but not greater than 80 volts, when GFCI is provided.

427-27. Isolation Transformer—Dual-winding transformers that have a shield between the primary and secondary windings shall provide isolation between the heating system and the distribution system.

427-28. Induced Currents—You are referred to Section 300-20, which covers the installation of all current-carrying parts.

427-29. Grounding—When a heating system for pipeline or vessel operates at not less than 30 and not more than 80 volts, it shall be grounded at designated points, which should be described in the installation instructions supplied by the manufacturer.

427-30. Secondary Conductor Sizing—The ampacity of the current-carrying conductors from the transformer shall be rated at at least 30 percent of the load the heater will be using.

E. Induction Heating

427-35. Scope—Covered in this section is the installation of line frequency induction heating equipment that is used to heat pipelines and vessels and all their accessories.

Note: You are referred by Code to Article 665 for other applications of inductive heating.

427-36. Personnel Protection—The induction coils used for heating pipelines and vessels, and that operate at voltages greater than 30 volts AC, must be enclosed in nonmetallic raceways or in split metallic enclosures. These shall be either isolated or made inaccessible, to protect people in the area. The purpose of this split metallic enclosure is to keep heat being induced in the metallic enclosure, thereby allowing it to go to the pipeline or vessels.

427-37. Induced Current—To prevent induction into the metal that surrounds the area of mechanical equipment supports or structures, there shall be shielding, isolation, or insulation of the path that the induced currents might take other than the pipelines or vessels. The stray current paths shall be bonded to prevent arcing between them.

F. Skin Effect Heating

427-45. Conductor Ampacity—The ampacity of conductors that are electrically insulated inside ferromagnetic envelopes may be permitted to exceed values that appear in Article 310, provided that they be identified or listed for the purpose for which they are used.

427-46. Pull Boxes—Pull boxes used for pulling the electrically insulated conductors into ferromagnetic envelopes may be buried under the thermal insulation. This may be done only if these locations are permanently marked on the insulation jacket and on drawings. Pull boxes thus mounted out of doors shall have watertight construction.

427-47. Single Conductor in Enclosure—Section 300-20 will not apply where a single conductor is enclosed in ferromagnetic envelopes or other metal enclosures.

427-48. Grounding—Not only shall the ferromagnetic envelope be grounded at both ends, but it may be grounded at points in between the two ends as might be required in the design. All joints of ferromagnetic envelopes or enclosures shall be bonded so that the electrical continuity will be assured.

Skin effect heating systems are not required to comply with Section 250-26.

Note: You are referred to (d) of the section mentioned above.

G. Control and Protection

427-55. Disconnecting Means.

(a) **Switch or Circuit Breaker.** You are required to have a disconnecting means that opens all conductors to fixed electrical pipeline or vessel-heating equipment. For this purpose, the branch-circuit switch or circuit breakers may be used as the disconnecting means if they are readily accessible. However, on either means the position must be identified, and there shall be a positive means of locking it in the OFF position.

(b) **Cord- and Plug-Connected Equipment.** If the circuit does not exceed 20 amperes rating or 150 volts or less to ground, the factory-installed attachment cord and plug-connection is permitted to be used as the disconnecting means.

427-56. Controls.

(a) **Temperature Control with OFF Position.** If the temperature-controlling means has an OFF position that opens all ungrounded conductors and the OFF position is plainly indicated, these may not be used as the disconnecting means unless they are provided with a positive lockout on the OFF position of the control.

(b) **Temperature Control Without OFF Position.** Temperature-controlled devices that have an OFF position need not open all ungrounded conductors; neither shall it serve as disconnecting means.

(c) **Remote Temperature Controller.** Temperature control devices located in a remote position shall not be required to meet the requirements of Section 427-56(a) and (b), and shall not be used as a disconnection means.

(d) **Combined Switching Devices.** Switching devices that are a combination of temperature-actuated devices and manually controlled switches that serve both controllers and the disconnecting means must comply with the following conditions:

(1) When manually placed in the OFF position, they shall manually open all ungrounded conductors.

(2) The design shall be such that when thrown in the manually OFF position they will not automatically energize the system.

(3) A positive means shall be provided to lock it in an OFF position.

427-57. Overcurrent Protection—If Section 427-4 is complied with, heating equipment supplied by a branch circuit shall be considered as adequate protection by the overcurrent protection device.

ARTICLE 430—MOTORS, MOTOR CIRCUITS, AND CONTROLLERS

A. General

430-1. Motor Feeder and Branch Circuits—The articles in the NEC are divided into parts A, B, C, etc., each having a specific heading. This materially aids in finding the desired information. Once this key to the Code has been mastered, it will seldom be necessary to refer to the index. Article 440, which covers refrigerating and air-conditioning equipment, applies to this Article 430 as well.

Diagram 430-1 is an important key to finding the correct parts and what they cover in this article. Notice that the parts are indicated in the right-hand column. Thus, if the concern is with motor running overcurrent protection, notice that it refers to Part C, motor disconnecting means in Part H, and so on for each part of the circuit. This diagram is extremely helpful and is a prime example of the lengths taken to make the Code easy to use.

430-2. Adjustable Speed Drive Systems—The power conversion equipment, if fed from a branch circuit or feeder and including part of an adjustable speed drive system, is considered a part of the adjustable speed drive system, and the rating is to be based upon the power required by the conversion equipment. When the power conversion equipment supplies overcurrent protection for the motor, no additional overload protection is required.

It is permitted to have the disconnecting means in the line coming into the conversion equipment, and the rating of the line shall be not less than 115 percent of the input current rating of the conversion unit.

This could be such as solid state units to change the cycles or chop part of the wave forms to vary the speed of squirrel cage motors as necessary for the application.

430-3. Part-Winding Motors—Induction or synchronous motors that have a part-winding start are arranged so that at starting they energize this part at the primary (armature) winding. After starting, the remainder of the winding is energized in one or more steps. The purpose of this is to reduce the initial insurge of current until the motor accumulates some speed, developing a counter electric motor force. The inrush current at start is locked-rotor current, and is quite high. A standard part-winding-start induction motor is arranged so that only one half of its winding is energized at start; then, as it comes up to speed, the other half is energized, so both halves are energized and carry equal current. Hermetically sealed refrigerating motors are not considered standard part-winding-start motors.

Separate overload devices are used on the standard part-winding-start induction motor. This requires that each half of the motor winding has to be individually protected. This is covered in Sections 430-32 and 430-37. Each half of the winding has a trip current that is one half of the specified running current.

As specified in Section 430-52, each of the two motor windings shall have branch-circuit short-circuit and ground-fault protection that is to be not more than one half the currents mentioned in Section 430-52.

Exception: A single device with this one-half rating is permitted for both windings, provided that it will allow the motor to start. If a time-delay (dual-element) fuse is used as a single device for both windings, its rating is permitted if it does not exceed 150 percent of the motor full-load current.

430-5. Other Articles—See the *NEC.*

430-6. Ampacity and Motor Rating Determination—Ampacities shall be determined as follows:

(a) **General Motor Applications.** This part is very important and should be carefully read. Whenever the current rating of a motor is used for figuring the ampacity of conductors, switches, branch-circuit overcurrent devices, etc., the actual motor nameplate current rating shall not be used. Instead, Tables 430-147, 430-148, 430-149 and 430-150, which give full-load currents for direct-current motors, single-phase ac motors, two-phase ac motors, and three-phase ac motors, are used.

Separate motor overload protection is to be figured from the actual nameplate current rating. When a motor is marked in amperes instead of horsepower, the horsepower rating shall be assumed to correspond to the values given in Tables 430-147, 430-148, 430-149, and 430-150. At times, it may be necessary to interpolate to arrive at an intermediate horsepower rating.

Exception No. 1: Sections 430-22(a) and 430-52 cover multispeed motors.

Exception No. 2: When shaded-pole or permanent-split-capacitor-type fan or blower motors are applied on equipment, if the motor type is marked, the full-load current for the motor marked on the nameplate of the equipment where the fan or blower is being used shall be used instead of the horsepower rating of the motor where the amperage, to determine the rating of the disconnecting means and branch-circuit conductors, also the controller, the short-circuit branch-circuit and ground-fault protection as well as the separate overload protection. The amperage marked on the nameplate shall not be less than that marked on the fan or blower nameplate.

(b) **Torque Motors.** Torque motors are commonly designed for applications which require prolonged stalled torques or special running-torque characteristics such as being turned against the direction of rotation. Direct-current, single-phase or polyphase induction wound-rotor, polyphase induction, repulsion, repulsion-induction, universal and other motors can be designed as torque motors. A torque motor develops its maximum torque at locked rotor or stalled conditions. This information will make the following clearer to you.

The locked-rotor current is the rated current of a torque motor. Thus the nameplate current shall be used to determine the ampacity of the branch-circuit conductors covered in Sections 430-22 and 430-24, and the ampere rating of the motor overcurrent protection.

Note: See Section 430-83, Exception No. 3, and Section 430-110.

(c) **AC Adjustable Voltage Motors.** For motors used on adjustable alternating current, adjustable voltage, variable torque drive systems, etc., the maximum current marked on the motor and the controller nameplate shall be used for the amperage of the conductors or the amperage rating of the switches, branch-circuit short-circuits, and any ground fault protection used. Should the amperage not appear on the nameplate, the ampacity shall be determined on the basis of 150 percent of the values found in Tables 430-149 and 430-150.

430-7. Marking on Motors and Multimotor Equipment.

(a) **Usual Motor Applications.** The following information shall be marked on a motor:

(1) Manufacturer's name.

(2) The maximum motor amperes on shaded-pole and permanent-split-capacity motors is to be used when the motors run only at maximum speed. On multispeed motors the full-load current for each speed shall be marked.

(3) If it is an alternating current motor, the frequency and number phases shall be marked.

(4) The rated full-load speed is to be marked.

(5) The rated ambient temperature and the rated temperature rise of the insulation system class shall be marked.

(6) The time rating of use shall be marked, e.g., 5, 15, 30, or 60 minutes, or continuous if it is for continuous use.

(7) If a ⅛-horsepower motor or more, then the horsepower rating shall be given. On multispeed motors that are ⅛ horsepower or more, the horsepower rating for each speed shall be given, except for shaded-pole or permanent-split-capacitor motors at ⅛ horsepower or more. Arc welding motors are not required to be marked in horsepower.

(8) On alternating current motors that are rated ½ horsepower or more, the Code letter shall be given if they are alternating current motors, so that the motor can be replaced with a similar motor. Code letters shall be omitted on polyphase wound-rotor motors. See (b) below.

(9) If it is a wound-rotor induction motor, the full-load current and secondary voltage shall be given.

(10) On synchronous motors that are dc excited, the field current and voltage shall be given.

(11) The type of winding, whether straight shunt, stabilized shunt, compound, or series wound, if they are direct-current motors, shall be marked. Direct-current motors that are 7 inches or less in diameter and are fractional horsepower motors are not required to be marked.

(12) When a motor is provided with thermal protection that meets the requirements of Section 430-32(c) (2), it shall be marked "Thermally Protected." The abbreviated marking "T.P." may be used on motors that are thermally protected with a rating of 100 watts or less, provided they meet the requirements of Section 430-32(c) (2).

(13) When a motor complies with Section 430-32(c) (4), it shall be marked "Impedance Protected." If impedance protected motors are 100 watts or less and meet the requirements of Section 430-32(c) (4), the marking "Z.P." may be used.

(b) **Locked-Rotor Indicating Code Letters.** The Code letters marked on the motor nameplate show the kilovolt-ampere input per horsepower when the rotor is locked. These code letters are given in Table 430-7(b) and also used with Table 430-152 in determining branch-circuit overcurrent protection as provided in Section 430-52.

(1) Code letters shall be marked on multispeed motors and shall designate the locked-rotor kVA per horsepower. This will be for the locked-rotor current at the highest speed at which the motor may be started.

Exception: The locked-rotor current for kVA and horsepower shall be marked on multispeed motors.

(2) Single-speed motors that start on Y connection but run on delta connection are required to be marked with the locked-rotor kVA per horsepower for the Y connection. Y started motors are often used for large motors to cut down on the locked-rotor current to start them; as the current drops, they are automatically cut over to a delta connection, and this is where they run when in use.

(3) Dual-speed motors will have two locked-rotor current ratings and kVA per horsepower on the two different voltages. They are to be marked with the Code letter for the voltage that gives the highest locked-rotor rating and kVA per horsepower.

(4) Motors that have both a 60- and 50-hertz ratings shall be marked with the Code letter designating the locked-rotor current, and the kVA per horsepower will be for the 60 hertz.

(5) Motors that start on part winding shall have the Code letter that designates the locked-rotor kVA per horsepower that is based on the locked-rotor current for the full winding of the motor. Refer to Table 430-7(b), Locked-Rotor Indicating Code Letter.

(c) **Torque Motors.** Torque motors have a standstill-rated operation, so all of the markings as covered in (a) of this section will apply except that locked-rotor torque shall replace horsepower.

(d) **Multimotor and Combination Load Equipment.** See the *NEC*. This marking is needed for multimotor and combination load equipment because often the individual nameplates are visible after mounting. It may be very difficult for both the inspector and the installing contractor to determine which loads may or may not be in operation at the same time, and this is necessary to determine the minimum circuit ampacity and maximum rating of the circuit protective device required. Such information can best be furnished by the equipment builder who knows the conditions of operation, thereby minimizing the chance of errors in field calculations where the specific conditions may not be known.

See Section 430-8.

A considerable portion of the above applies to the manufacturer, but it is also very essential that the trade and inspectors know what and where to look. See Section 430-25 for the computation of the ampacity of the conductors.

430-8. Marking on Controllers—Controllers shall be marked as follows: (1) manufacturer's name or identification; (2) voltage; (3) current or horsepower rating; (4) any other data which might be necessary to indicate the proper application of the motor.

If a controller includes motor overload protection that satisfies the requirements for group application, the controller shall be marked with the following information: motor overload protection, ground-fault protection, and the maximum branch circuit short-circuit for use with such applications.

When instantaneous circuit breakers are used in combined controllers that have instantaneous trip, they are to be clearly marked on the circuit breaker to show the ampere settings on the trip adjustable elements.

Where a controller is built in as an integral part of a motor or of a motor-generator set, the controller need not be individually marked when the necessary data is on the motor nameplate.

430-9. Marking at Terminals—See the NEC.

430-10. Wiring Space in Enclosures.

(a) **General.** In Article 373 it was stated that switches were not intended to be used as junction boxes or wireways. This ruling also includes enclosures for controllers and disconnecting means for motors. Neither shall they be used as junction boxes or raceways for conductors feeding through or tapping off to other apparatus, unless they are specifically designed for this purpose. Other means, such as auxiliary gutters, junction boxes, etc., shall be used instead. See Section 373-8 for switch and overcurrent-device enclosures.

(b) **Wire Bending Space in Enclosures**—Table 430-10(b) gives the minimum bending space allowable in motor controllers. The measured distance, in the direction in which the wire leaves the terminal, is in a straight line from the end of a connector or lug to the wall or barrier. If alternate wire terminating means is substituted for other than that supplied by the manufacturer of the controller, it is required to be identified by the manufacturer (please note "by the manufacturer") for use in that controller, and the minimum wire bending space shall not be reduced. [See the NEC for Table 430-10(b).]

When a motor control center is used as the enclosure, Article 373 will apply to the minimum wire bending space.

430-11. Protection against Liquids—Motors that are mounted directly under or in locations where dripping or spraying oil, water, or other injurious liquids may occur shall be either suitably protected or designed for the existing conditions.

430-12 Motor Terminal Housings.

(a) **Material.** Motor terminal housings shall be made of substantial constructed metal.

Exception: Nonmetallic, nonburning housings will be permitted in other than hazardous (classified) locations. They shall be of substantial construction, and a grounding means on the motor inside the terminal housing shall be provided so that the equipment grounding conductor will properly ground the motor.

(b) **Dimensions and Space—Wire-to-Wire Connections.** Table 430-12(b) shall be used in terminal housing where wire-to-wire connections will be made. The minimum dimensions and usable volumes shall be in accordance with Table 430-12(b). See the *NEC* for this table and the note thereto.

(c) **Dimensions and Space—Fixed Terminal Connections.** See the *NEC* for Tables 430-12(c)(1) and (c)(2), where terminal housings enclose rigidly mounted motor terminals. These tables give the usable volumes so that the terminal housing shall be of sufficient size to provide minimum terminal spacings.

Incorporated in this section is Table 430-12(b), which gives the horsepower, minimum cover opening dimension, and minimum usable volume. Please note, however, that nothing is stated concerning the voltages of the motors. In part (c) we find two tables. Table 430-12(c)(1) gives the information necessary for terminal housings, enclosing rigidly mounted motor terminals, while Table 430-12(c)(2) lists the usable volumes. All this is information pertinent to the manufacturer and to the trade as well.

(d) **Large Wire or Factory Connections.** The foregoing provision covering the volumes of terminal housings is not to be considered applicable when the following is encountered: For motors at larger ratings and greater number of leads, if they have large wire sizes or if the motors are installed as part of factory-wired equipment so that no additional connections have to be made at the motor terminal housing, during the installation of such equipment it is required that the motor terminal housing be of adequate size for making the connections.

(e) **Equipment Grounding Connections.** With motor terminal housings or wire-to-wire connections, or fixed terminal connections, a means shall be provided as covered in Section 250-113 for attaching the equipment grounding conductor so as to ground the motor properly.

Exception: When the motor is part of factory-wired equipment, which is required to be grounded, and is without additional terminal connection provided in the motor terminal housing during the installation of such motor equipment, a separate means for motor grounding at the motor terminal housing will not be required.

430-13. Bushings—All conductors to the motor, including leads, shall be properly bushed to prevent abrasion and deterioration by oils, greases, or other contaminants. If conductors are exposed to deteriorating agents, you are referred to Section 310-8.

430-14. Location of Motors.

(a) **Ventilation and Maintenance.** Motors shall be located so as to give adequate ventilation and provide room for normal maintenance, such as greasing of bearings and changing of brushes.

(b) **Open Motors.** Open motors that have commutators or slip rings shall be so located that sparks from the brushes will not ignite combustibles. This does not prohibit the mounting of motors on wooden floors or supports.

430-16. Exposure to Dust Accumulations—Motors in locations where dust or flying materials will accumulate within the motor in such quantities as to interfere with the cooling and thereby cause dangerous temperatures shall be replaced with types that are suitable for the conditions. There are many types of motors designed to eliminate the accumulation of dust, dirt, etc. If extremely severe conditions exist, pipe-ventilated motors should be used or the motors located in reasonable dust-free rooms.

430-17. Highest Rated (Largest) Motor—Refer to the following sections for determining how to comply with them: 430-24, 430-53(b), and 430-53(c). The highest full-load current rating shall be considered the highest-rated motor. To determine the full-load current used to determine the highest-rated motor, the equivalent value shall correspond to the motor horsepower rating, and shall be selected from Tables 430-147, 430-148, 430-149, and 430-150.

You are advised that it might be possible in calculations to become fooled by the horsepower rating and find that you should, in fact, have taken the full-load currents instead.

430-18. Nominal Voltage of Rectifier Systems—The value of the rectified voltage derived from a system will be determined from the nominal voltage (ac) rectified.

Exception: If the nominal dc voltage from the rectifier exceeds the peak value of the ac voltage being rectified, it shall be used.

B. Motor Circuit Conductors

430-21. General—This Part B gives us the sizes of the conductor specified and capable of carrying the current encountered under specified conditions.

Exception: For volts over 600, nominal, you are referred to Section 430-124.

The provisions covering grounding in Article 250 and conductors in general in Article 310 are not intended to apply to conductors which form an integral part of equipment such as motors, motor controllers, etc. See Sections 300-1(b) and 310-1.

430-22. Single Motor.

(a) **General.** Branch-circuit conductors that supply a single motor shall have an ampacity of not less than 125 percent of the full-load current of the motor. Remember that the ampacity in Tables 430-147 through

430-150 will govern the branch-circuit conductor calculations and not the nameplate amperes.

When multispeed motors are used, the ampacity of branch-circuit conductors from the controller to the motor is to be based on the highest full-load current ratings. This will be shown on the motor nameplate. In selecting the ampacity of the branch-circuit conductors running between the controller and the motor, when they are to be energized for some particular speed of that multispeed motor, the current rating speed shall be used to determine selection of branch circuits between the controller and the motor.

Note: There is an example of this in Chapter 9 and in Example No. 8. Also see Diagram 430-1.

Exception No. 1: Table 430-22(a), Exception, shows the motor nameplate current rating. This shall be used for conductors to motors that are run for short periods of time, or for intermittent, periodic, or varying duty. This is to be followed except when the authority having jurisdiction gives permission for use with smaller conductors. Notice that there is a variation of from 85 percent to as high as 200 percent in Table 430-22(a). This is why it is necessary to use this table instead of the usual 125 percent.

Exception No. 2: When direct current supplies motors on a rectified source derived from a single-phase power supply, the ampacity of the conductors between the controller and the motor shall be not less than the full-load current rating. The percentage is covered below:

a. 190 percent ampacity is derived from a rectifier bridge of a half-wave single-phase ac.
b. When a full-wave rectifier is used from a single-phase, the percentage of ampacity is 150 percent.
   Refer Table 430-22(a), Exception, in your *NEC.*

(b) **Separate Terminal Enclosure.** The conductors between a stationary motor rated one horsepower or less, and the separate terminal enclosures permitted in Section 430-145(b) may be smaller than No. 14 but not smaller than No. 18, provided they have an ampacity as specified in Table 430-22(a) Exception.

430-23. Wound-Rotor Secondary.

(a) **Continuous Duty.** When a wound-rotor motor is used for continuous duty, the conductors that connect the wound-rotor to its controller shall have a rating of 125 percent ampacity for the full-load current of the secondary of the motor.

(b) **Other than Continuous Duty.** When wound-rotor motors are not used for continuous duty, the ampacity of the conductors from the secondary shall be not less than those specified in Table 430-22(a) exception.

(c) **Resistor Separate from Controller.** Table 430-23(c) gives the ampacity of the conductors where the controller is mounted separately from the secondary resistor. See Table 430-23(c), which will give the percentage of full-load secondary current, from which the ampacity of the conductor that may be used can be figured. Always remember that an oversized conductor is preferable to a conductor that is too small.

430-24. Conductors Supplying Several Motors—Conductors that supply several motors sometimes cause confusion. The basic rule is that 125 percent of the ampacity of the largest motor is taken, plus the ampacity (100 percent) of the other motors connected. This applies when there are two or more motors. It will be recalled that Tables 430-147 through 430-150 give the ampacity used for figuring conductor sizes.

Example: For four 3-phase, 230 volt motors, the following ratings would be used to figure the service-entrance conductors:

The preceding example will not apply when one or more motors are used on short-time, intermittent, periodic, or varying duty. In this case, 125 percent of the nameplate full-load current of the largest continuous-duty motor, or the highest current obtained by multiplying the applicable percentage of Table 430-22(a) Exception by the nameplate full-load current of the noncontinuous-duty motor (whichever is the larger), plus the nameplate full-load currents of the other motors, each multiplied by 100 percent or the applicable percentage of the Table, whichever is smaller.

Motor Size	Full Load Current (from Table 430-150)
25 hp	64
25 hp	64
5 hp	15
10 hp	28
	—
Total amperes	171
Plus 25% of 64	16
	—
Ampacity to use in figuring the conductors	187

Exception: If there is interlocking in the circuitry that will prevent starting of a second motor or a group of motors, The size of the conductor shall be determined from the largest motor or group of motors that is to be operated at any one time. See Chapter 9, Example 8.

Cases of interlocking, where only part of the motors may be operated at a given time, are often encountered. In such a case this is taken into consideration as the conductors will not be called upon to serve all motors at the same time.

430-25. Conductors Supplying Motors and Other Loads.

(a) **Combination Load.** When one or more motors is served from a circuit that also has a lighting and appliance load, the lighting and appliance load is computed from Article 220 or other applicable Sections. The conductors shall have sufficient ampacity to carry this appliance and lighting load as calculated, plus the motor-load ampacity as calculated for a single motor in Section 430-22 or for two or more motors in accordance with Section 430-24.

Exception: Section 424-3(b) governs the ampacity of conductors that supply a motor that is operated with electrical space heating equipment.

(b) **Multimotor and Combination-Load Equipment.** Section 430-7(d) covers the ampacity of conductors that supply multimotors and combination-load equipment. The ampacity shall not be less than the minimum ampacity that is marked on the equipment. Also, you must conform to the section mentioned.

430-26. Feeder Demand Factor—The authority enforcing the Code may grant special permission for feeder conductors to be of less capacity than specified in Sections 430-24 and 430-25 where motors operate on duty-cycle, intermittently, or where all motors do not operate at the same time.

The conductors shall have sufficient ampacity for the maximum load determined in accordance with the sizes and numbers of motors supplied and the characteristics of their loads.

430-27. Capacitors with Motors—Capacitors are used for power-factor correction and will change the current that the conductor will be required to carry. Figuring loads where capacitors are used on motors is covered in Sections 460-8, and 460-9.

430-28. Feeder Taps—The ampacity of feeder taps shall be not less than that required in Part B, and they shall terminate in a protective device for the branch circuit. In addition, they shall also be required to meet one of the following:

(1) They are to be enclosed either in a raceway not exceeding ten feet or in a controller.

(2) The ampacity of these conductors shall be at least one third the ampacity of the feeder conductors. They shall be protected from physical damage, and are not allowed to be over 25 feet in length.

(3) They may have the same ampacity as the feeder conductors.

Exception: Feeder Taps Over 25 Feet Long. If the feeder taps are supplying, e.g., a manufacturing area that is of a high-bay type (over 35 feet), conductors from the tap to a feeder are permitted to be over 25 feet in length, horizontally. The overall length to the feeder shall be not over 100 feet if the following conditions are met:

a. The feeder taps shall be at least one third the size of the feeder conductors.
b. A single circuit breaker or switch with fuses is used for termination of the tap conductors conforming with (1) Part D, if the tap is a branch circuit; (2) Part E, if the tap is a feeder.
c. The conductors must be installed in raceways and must not subjected to physical damage.
d. The taps must be continuous from end to end without splices.
e. The tap conductors shall not be smaller than No. 6 AWG copper, or if aluminum, shall not be smaller than No. 4 AWG. (Of course, they may be larger.)
f. At no point shall the conductors penetrate walls, floors, or ceilings.

430-39. Constant Voltage DC Motors—Power Resistors—When the conductors are connected to the motor controller, or to breaking resistors, and they are in the armature circuit, the ampacity shall be not less than that shown in Table 430-29, and the motor full-load current shall be used. When an armature-shunting resistor is used and the power resistor is used for acceleration conductors, you must calculate the ampacity by using both the total of the full-load motor current and the amperage of the armature-shunting resistor.

The ampacity of armature-shunt resistor conductors will be calculated from Table 430-29. Use the shunt resistor current as the full-load current.

See Table 430-9, Conductor Rating Factors for Power Resistors.

C. Motor and Branch-Circuit Overload Protection

430-31. General—This part gives the overload protection that is intended to protect the motors, the motor controllers, and the branch-circuit conductors from overheating due to motor overloads. When a motor controller continually trips, do not merely increase the size of the overload protection—there is something that is causing the trouble, such as low voltage, high voltage, high ambient temperatures, unbalanced voltages, or an overload on the motor. Take time to evaluate the cause and remedy the trouble.

Overload is defined as any current operating for a length of time such that it would cause damage or overheating of the motor involved. This does not include short circuits or ground faults. The Code sets up the maximum overcurrent protection that is permitted for various motors. This is a proven value and should be followed.

NFPA Standard for Centrifugal Pumps (No. 20) sets up provisions for overcurrent protection for equipment such as fire pumps, where the overcurrent would be the less of the hazards. The reference to NFPA No. 20 makes it a part of the *NEC*.

The provisions of motor circuits over 600 volts are covered in Part J. Part C does not apply to them.

430-32. Continuous-Duty Motors.

(a) **More than 1 Horsepower.** One of the following means shall be used to protect motors rated more than 1 horsepower and used for continuous duty:

(1) Separate overload devices for the motor shall be selected to trip by being rated at no more than the following percent of the current that appears on the motor nameplate for full-load current:

See the *NEC* for the percentage ratings.

Some modification of these values is permitted by Section 430-34.

Each section of a multispeed motor shall be considered separately.

If a separate overcurrent device is located so as not to carry the full current as stated on the motor nameplate, (such as for wye-delta starting), the proper percentage of current appropriate for either the selection or the setting of the overcurrent device must be clearly marked on the equipment involved, or come from a table from the manufacturer selecting the overcurrent value taken into consideration.

(2) A thermal integral protector supplied with the motor and approved for use with the motor it protects, will be acceptable if it prevents damage or overheating of the motor in case of overload and failure to start. In the case where there is a separate current-interrupting device, apart from the motor, and this device is actuated by the integral thermal device, it shall be arranged so that the interruption of the control circuit will interrupt the current to the windings. An example of this is a thermal protector built into the winding of a motor that interrupts the control current to a magnetic coil.

The trip current on thermally protected motors shall not be greater than the percentage of those that are given for full-load current in Tables 430-148, 430-149, and 430-150. See the *NEC* following this part for the percentages.

If the device opening the current is separate from the motor and its control circuit is operated by a protective device integral with the motor, it shall be such that the opening of the control circuit will interrupt the current to the motor.

(3) An overcurrent device as part of the motor that protects the motor from damage due to failure to start will be permitted if the motor is part of an approved assembly that normally is not subject to overloads.

(4) With motors larger than 1500 horsepower, a protective device shall be included that has embedded detectors that will cause the current to the motor to be interrupted if the temperature rises

higher than that marked on the nameplate when the motor is in an ambient temperature of 40° C.

(b) **One Horsepower or Less, Nonautomatically Started.**

(1) A motor of 1 horsepower or less used for continuous duty that is not permanently installed and that is nonautomatically started, if it is in sight from the controller location, may be protected by a device having overcurrent protection on the branch circuit that will protect it from overload, short-circuit, and ground-fault. The branch-circuit protective device is not to be larger than specified in this Article 430.

Exception: With any motor as described just above and operating at 120 volts, overload protection that is not greater than 20 amperes is permitted.

(2) This portion tells us that any motor located out of sight of the controller, and any motor rated at one horsepower or less which is permanently installed, have to be protected as in the next part (c).

(c) **One Horsepower or Less, Automatically Started.** Where a motor of 1 horsepower or less is started automatically, it is to be protected by one of the following means:

(1) It may have a separate overload device that responds to the motor current. Such a device shall have a trip rating that is no more than the following percentages applied to the motor nameplate full-load current rating: See the *NEC.*

On multispeed motors, each winding is considered separately, and modification of this rating will be permitted as covered in Section 430-34.

(2) An integral thermal protector approved for use with the motor will be considered as acceptable. This type of protector prevents damage or overheating of the motor in case of overload or failure to start. In the case where a separate current-interrupting device, apart from the motor, is actuated by the integral thermal device, it shall be arranged so that the interruption of the control circuit will interrupt the current to the motor windings.

(3) Overcurrent devices, when integral with the motor and protecting it against damage due to failure to start, are permitted (1) if the motor is part of an approved assembly that will not permit the motor to be subject to overloads, or (2) when the assembly is provided with other safety controls (such as the controls for safety from combustion on an oil burner) where they protect the motor against damage if it fails to start. If the motor assembly has safety controls for this protection of the motor, it shall be so marked on the nameplate of the assembly, where it will be visible after the assembly is installed.

(4) Motors that have a winding impedance high enough to prevent overheating due to failure to start will be considered as protected when complying with (b) of this section if they are manually started.

Note: A number of ac motors are less than ½₀ horsepower, including clock motors, series motors, etc., and also some larger motors such as torque motors all come within this classification. Split-phase motors have an automatic switch to disconnect the starting windings, and are not included.

(d) **Wound-Rotor Secondaries.** The secondary of wound-rotor motors for alternating current that includes conductors, controllers, resistors, and so forth shall be permitted to be protected by means of the motor overload protection.

430-33. Intermittent and Similar Duty—See the *NEC*.

430-34. Selection of Overload Relay—This Section allows for overload protection where the proper size devices are not available. Where the values specified for overload protection for a motor are not built to the standard sizes or ratings of fuses, nonadjustable circuit breakers, thermal cutouts, thermal relays, heating elements of thermal-trip motor switches, or possible settings of adjustable circuit breakers adequate to carry the load, the next higher size, rating, or setting may be used. Other types of motors shall not exceed 130 percent of their full-load current rating. In cases where the overcurrent protection is not shunted during starting time, it shall have sufficient delay to allow starting and acceleration of the load. See the *NEC*, which gives the percentages allowable for overcurrent protection.

430-35. Shunting During Starting Period.

(a) **Nonautomatically Started.** For a nonautomatically started motor the overload protection shall be permitted to be shunted or it is allowable to shunt or cut out the overload protection during start, providing that the shunting device cannot be left in use after starting and that the fuses or time-delay circuit breakers are rated or set so as not to exceed 400 percent of the full-load motor current and that these fuses or circuit breakers are not so located as to be in the circuit during starting.

(b) **Automatically Started.** It is not permissible to shunt or cut out overload protection on automatically started motors.

Exception: The overload protection may be shunted or cut out when starting automatically during the starting period where:

(1) The motor starting period is greater than the time delay of the available motor overload protective device, and

(2) Where a listed means is provided that:
  a. Senses the motor rotation and will automatically prevent the shunting or cutout if the motor fails to start, and

b. Limits the time of shunting of the overload protection or cutout to a point that is less than the locked rotor rating of the motor that you are protecting, and

c. Causes shutdown. You will have to restart the motor manually if running position has not been reached.

430-36. Fuses—In Which Conductor—If fuses are used for motor overload protection, a fuse shall be inserted in the ungrounded conductor.

Fuses shall also be inserted in the grounded conductor if the supply system is a 3-wire, 3-phase ac with one phase grounded.

In the past there has been much discussion over what is now covered in the Exception. This will clarify the matter. For instance, if the fuse were not in the grounded phase, serious results could occur when one phase opened on a 3-phase irrigation pump motor on a grounded phase delta system.

Not only does this apply to the above discussion, but also to a delta or wye, where one phase conductor is grounded.

430-37. Devices Other than Fuses—In Which Conductor—The Table 430-37 and its footnotes have been under discussion for a long time. The 1971 *NEC* straightened this out and you may just as well purchase all 3-phase starters with three overload units. See the *NEC*.

430-38. Number of Conductors Opened by Overload Device—Motor-running overload devices such as are located in the controller, other than fuses, thermal cutouts, or thermal protectors, are required to open simultaneously a sufficient number of ungrounded conductors so as to stop the flow of current into the motor.

430-39. Motor Controller as Overload Protection—Motor controllers may serve as overload devices for motors under the following conditions: (1) where the number of overload devices comply with Table 430-37; (2) where these units are operable both during starting and running when used with direct-current motors; (3) when in the running position when used with alternating-current motors. When nonautomatic motor controllers serve as the overload protection for motors, it is recommended that all ungrounded conductors be opened. Always follow Code recommendations.

It is clear that practically all three-phase motor installations shall have three overload units or other approved means for overload protection. Many inspection authorities will accept dual-element motor fuses as the other approved means if they are sized properly and the fuse box marked with a warning as to what the replacement is to be. In fact, these dual-element fuses are a very economical form of motor insurance in addition to the three overload units.

430-40. Thermal Cutouts and Overload Relays—If motor-running overload protection consisting of thermal cutouts, overload relays, and other devices for motor-running overload protection are not capable of opening short-circuits, then protection shall be required by means of fuses or circuit breakers, and the ratings or settings shall comply with Section 430-52 or where the same section covers motor short-circuit protection.

Exception No. 1: This allows for approved group installation and marked for the maximum size of fuse or inverse time circuit breaker by which they may be protected.

Exception No. 2: It is permitted to mark the nameplate of approved equipment that has thermal overcurrent or overload relays with the circuit-breaker ampere rating.

Note: See Section 430-52, which covers instantaneous trip circuit breakers for protection for motor short-circuits.

430-42. Motors on General Purpose Branch Circuits—Article 210 covers the connection of certain motors on general-purpose branch circuits but the overload protection of motors on general purpose branch circuits shall conform to the following:

(a) **Not Over 1 Horsepower.** One or more motors may be connected to general-purpose branch circuit without individual overload protection of the motor or motors provided the requirements of Section 430-32(b) and (c) and Section 430-53(a)(1) and (a)(2) are complied with.

(b) **Over 1 Horsepower.** Motors rated at over 1 horsepower, as covered in Section 430-53(a), may be connected to general-purpose branch circuits only where each motor has its own overload protection which meets the overload ratings specified in Section 430-32. Both the controller and the motor overload device shall be approved for group installation with the protective device of the branch circuit to which they are connected. See Section 430-53.

(c) **Cord- and Plug-Connected.** When a motor is connected to a branch circuit by means of a plug and receptacle, and it has no individual overload protection as allowed in Section 430-42(a), the rating of the plug and receptacle shall not exceed 15 amperes at 125 volts or 10 amperes at 250 volts.

Where a motor is connected to a branch circuit by means of a plug and receptacle and is used as a motor or motor-operated appliance, and also meets the requirements of Section 430-42(b), the overload device shall be an integral part of the motor or appliance. The rating of the plug and receptacle shall be assumed to determine the rating of the circuit to which the motor may be connected. See Section 210.

(d) **Time Delay.** Motors take considerable current on start. Therefore, it is required that branch-circuit overcurrent devices for motors shall have sufficient time delay to allow them to accelerate their load.

430-43. Automatic Restarting—Care shall be taken in installing motors that automatically restart after the overload protection trips. Such a protection device shall not be installed unless it is approved for use with the motor which it protects. When a motor can restart automatically after tripping, it shall be so installed that an injury to persons cannot result from its automatic starting.

430-44. Orderly Shutdown—Where a number of motors are used in conjunction with one another, if immediate shutdown occurs, the motor overload protective device(s) could and often does introduce additional or increased hazard(s) to a person(s), thus necessitating continued motor operation for safe shutdown of the equipment or process. The motor overcurrent sensing device(s) may be installed if they conform to provisions that were covered in Part C of this article, and shall be permitted to be installed through a supervised alarm so that immediate interruption to the motor circuits will not result and corrective action may be taken for an orderly shutdown.

D. Motor Branch Circuit Short-Circuit and Ground-Fault Protection

430-51. General—This part is intended to specify protection for branch-circuit conductors that supply motors, motor control apparatus, and the motors against overcurrent due to short circuits and ground faults. These provisions are in addition to or amendatory to the provisions of Article 240.

Devices provided for by Sections 210-8, 230-95, and 305-6 are not included in Part D as specified there.

See Part J, as the provisions of Part D do not apply to motor circuits over 600 volts, nominal.

Note: Refer to Example No. 8, Chapter 9.

430-52. Rating or Setting for Individual Motor Circuit—The motor branch circuit overcurrent device shall be capable of carrying the starting current of the motor. Short circuit and ground fault current will be considered as being taken care of when the overcurrent protection does not exceed values in Table 430-152. An instantaneous-trip circuit breaker (without time delay) shall be used only if it is adjustable, if it is a part of a combination controller that has overcurrent protection in each conductor, or if the combination has been approved.

In case the values for branch circuit protective devices determined by Table 430-152 do not correspond to the standard sizes or ratings of fuses, nonadjustable circuit breakers, or thermal devices, or possible settings of adjustable circuit breakers adequate to carry the load, the next higher size, rating or setting may be used. See Section 240-6 for standard ratings.

There are exceptions where the overcurrent protection as specified in Table 430-152 will not take care of the starting current of the motor.

Exception No. 1: If the values of the branch-circuit, short-circuit, and ground-fault protection devices determined from Table 430-152 do not conform to standard sizes or ratings of fuses, nonadjustable circuit breakers, or possible settings on adjustable circuit breakers—and they are capable of adequately carrying the load involved—then the next higher setting or rating will be permitted.

Exception No. 2: If the ratings shown in Table 430-152 are not sufficient for the starting current of the motor, then:

a. When no time delay fuses are used and do not exceed 600 amperes in rating, it shall be permitted to increase the fuse size up to 400 percent of the full-load current, but not over 400 percent.

b. Time-element fuses (dual-element) are not to exceed 225 percent of full-load current, but they may be increased to this percentage.

c. Inverse time-element breakers are to be permitted to be increased in rating. However, they shall not exceed (1) 400 percent of full-load current or 100 amperes or less; (2) they may be increased to 300 percent to a full-load current greater than 100 amperes.

d. Fuses of ratings from 601 to 6000 amperes will be permitted to be increased. However, in no case shall they exceed 300 percent of the full-load rating of the motor involved.

Exception No. 3: In accordance with Section 240-3, Exception No. 1, torque motor branch circuits are to be protected at the motor nameplate current rating.

Note: Standard rating of fuses and circuit breakers is given in Section 240-6 of the *NEC*.

If instantaneous trip breakers are not adjustable and are a part of the motor controller covering overload and also short-circuit and ground-fault protection for each of the conductors, a motor short-circuit protector shall be permitted in lieu of the listed devices in Table 430-152. This is where short-circuit protectors are a part of a combination controller that has both motor overload protection and short-circuit and ground-fault protection. These must be present in each conductor. There is a provision that they shall operate at not more than 1300 percent of the full-load motor current. Circuit breakers with instantaneous trip or motor short-circuit protectors shall be used only as part of the combination motor controller that provides protection that is coordinated to the motor branch-circuit overload short-circuit and ground-fault protection.

Exception: If the specified setting in Table 430-152 is found to be not sufficient for the starting current of the motor, the setting on an instantaneous trip circuit current may be increased, provided that in no instance shall it exceed 1300 percent of the motor full-load current rating.

You are required to use only one single short-circuit and ground-fault protective device for a multispeed motor for two or more windings of the motor. This is only when it is provided that the rating of the protective device is within the limits of the applicable percentage of the nameplate rating of the smaller windings protected.

When the short-circuit and ground-fault protective device ratings are shown in the manufacturer's overload relay table for use with the motor controller involved or as otherwise marked on the equipment, they shall not be allowed to exceed the highest values shown above.

Note: Refer to Chapter 9, Example 8, and Diagram 430-1.

In lieu of devices listed in Table 430-152, suitable fuses may be used instead for adjustable speed drive systems. This is only if markings for replacement are provided adjacent to the fuses.

Where maximum protective device ratings are shown in the manufacturer's heater table for use with a marked controller or are otherwise marked with the equipment, they shall not be exceeded even if higher values are allowed as shown above. See Example No. 8, Chapter 9, and Diagram 430-1 of the *NEC.*

430-53. Several Motors or Loads on One Branch Circuit—Under conditions specified in (a), (b), or (c) below, two or more motors or one or more motors shall be permitted to be run from the same branch circuit.

(a) **Not Over 1 Horsepower.** Two or more motors of 1 horsepower or less, that do not have a full-load rating of more than 6 amperes, may be used on branch circuits that are protected at not more than 20 amperes at 120 volts or less, or on branch circuits rated at not more than 15 amperes at 600 volts or less. Individual running overcurrent protection for these motors is not required unless specifically called for in Section 430-32.

Short-circuit and ground-fault protective devices for branch circuits shall have the ratings marked on any of the controllers, and this rating is not to be exceeded.

(b) **If Smallest Motor Protected.** If it is determined that the branch-circuit, short-circuit and ground-fault protective device will not open under the most severe normal operating conditions that might be encountered, and the branch-circuit protective device is not larger than allowed in Section 430-52, then two or more motors, each having individual running overcurrent protection, may be connected to one branch circuit.

(c) **Other Group Installation.** On two or more motors of any rating, or one or more motors plus other load(s), each motor is to have individual overcurrent protection, but they shall be permitted to be connected to one branch circuit where the motor controller(s) and the overcurrent device(s) are (1) a factory assembly, and the short-circuit ground-fault protective devices may be a part of the assembly or may be specified by marking the assembly and installing separately; or (2) the branch-circuit overload protection, short-circuit and ground-fault protection devices, and the motor controller(s) and motor overload device(s) are field-installed by use of a separate assembly that has been listed for this purpose, and are to be provided with the instructions from the manufacturer where the use with each other is provided; or (3) all the following conditions shall be met:

(1) Each motor overload device (listed for group installation) is to be tested with a specific maximum rating of the inverse circuit breaker or fuse.

(2) The motor controller used shall be listed to be used for group installation, and there shall be a specific maximum rating for the fuse or circuit breaker.

(3) Each circuit breaker shall be listed for group installation and shall be of the inverse-time-type breaker.

(4) The branch circuit using fuses or inverse-time circuit breakers is required to have a rating not exceeding that covered in Section 430-52. This rating is for the largest motor that is connected to the branch circuit; to this must be added the sum of full-load current ratings of the other motors involved, and is for the rating of other loads that are to be connected to the branch circuit. It shall be permitted to increase the maximum rating of fuses or circuit breakers to a value that is not over that permitted by Section 240-3, Exception No. 1, if the results of the calculation come to less than that of the supply conductors.

(5) These branch circuit fuses or inverse-time circuit breakers are not permitted to be larger than Section 430-40 allows for thermal cutouts or overload relay that is protecting the smallest motor of the group.

The *NEC* refers to Section 110-10.

(d) **Single Motor Taps.** With group installations of motors as described above, the conductors of any tap supplying a single motor shall comply with the following: (1) all the conductors to the motor shall have an ampacity of at least that of the branch-circuit conductors; (2) conductors to a motor shall not have an ampacity of less than one-third that of the branch-circuit conductors, meet the requirements of Section 430-22, which requires an ampacity of at least 125 percent that of the full-load current of the motor. The conductors to the motor-running protection shall not exceed 25 feet in length and shall be protected from physical damage.

Any tap supplying a single motor shall not be required to have an individual branch-circuit, short-circuit and ground-fault protective device, provided they comply with the conditions outlined above in this section.

430-54. Multimotor and Combination-Load Equipment—Multimotor and combination-load equipment is covered in Section 430-7(d). The rating of the branch-circuit short-circuit and ground-fault protective device for this purpose shall not exceed the rating on the equipment provided for this purpose.

430-55. Combined Overcurrent Protection—The overcurrent protection may be combined in one piece of equipment with the branch-circuit overcurrent protection and ground-fault protection, and motor-running overcurrent protection when the setting or rating of the devices provides the 115 percent and 125 percent overcurrent running protection as specified in Section 430-32.

430-56. Branch-Circuit Protective Devices—In Which Conductor—Overcurrent devices shall open all ungrounded conductors of the circuit as required in Section 240-20. They may also open the grounded conductor if it is opened simultaneously with the ungrounded conductors.

430-57. Size of Fuseholder—Where fuses are used in branch circuits for motor protection, the fuseholders shall not be smaller than required to accommodate fuses as specified by Section 430-152. An exception to this would be when time-delay fuses are used that have appropriate characteristics for motors, in which case the fuseholders may be smaller, but check to make certain that the switch and fuseholders are rated in a horsepower rating to accommodate the motor. Fuseholder adapters may be used to reduce the size of the fuseholder to adapt to the time-delay motor fuses, but this is not always the best policy as they may be easily removed and a larger size inserted. Check the horsepower rating of fusible switches. See the *NEC* for Exception.

430-58. Rating of Circuit Breaker—Sections 430-52 and 430-110 cover The current rating of a circuit breaker that is used for motor branch-circuit, short-circuit, and ground-fault protection.

E. Motor Feeder Short-Circuit and Ground-Fault Protection

430-61. General—The provisions of Part E specify overcurrent devices intended to protect feeder conductors supplying motors against overcurrents due to short-circuits or grounds.

Note: You are referred to Chapter 9, Example No. 8.

430-62. Rating or Setting Motor Load.

(a) **Specific Load.** A feeder that supplies a fixed motor load must be calculated as far as the conductor ampacity from Section 430-24, which allows a carrying capacity of 125 percent of the rating of the full-load current of the largest motor plus 100 percent of the full-load current rating of the other motors. This conductor shall further be protected by overcurrent protection which shall not be greater than allowed for the protection of the largest motor (as figured from Table 430-152, or Section 440-22(a) for hermetic refrigerand motor-compressors) plus the sums of the full-load current of the other motors.

If two motors of the same rating are used, only one is considered as the larger. This motor is then used to calculate the excess rating and the other motor the 100 percent rating.

Where two or more motors are started simultaneously, the feeder sizes and overcurrent protection must be figured accordingly and will require higher ratings. See Example No. 8 in Chapter 9.

(b) **Future Additions.** On such as large industrial plants, etc., for large capacity installations, heavy capacity feeders are usually or should be installed to provide for future additions of load, or changes which might be made. The rating or setting of the feeder protective devices shall be permitted to be based on the rated ampacity of the feeder conductors.

430-63. Rating or Setting—Power and Light Loads—Where a feeder carries a motor load in addition to lighting and/or appliance loads, the ampacity of the lighting and/or the appliance loads must be figured as in Articles 210 and 220. To this is added the capacity for the motor as figured in Section 430-52 or Section 430-62. These totals are combined to determine the ampacity of the feeder conductors and the overcurrent protection for the feeders.

F. Motor Control Circuits

430-71. General—This Part F applies to special conditions of motor control circuits, and thus applies to the general requirements.

Note: The *NEC* refers us to Section 430-9(b).

Definition of Motor Control Circuit: The control circuit of motor apparatus controlling the operation of the motor or system carries only the electrical signals that direct the controller to stop, go, jog, etc., and does not contain the main power of the circuit.

430-72. Overcurrent Protection.

(a) **General.** The control circuit that originates at the motor branch circuit by being tapped therefrom on the load side thereof and short-circuit and ground-fault protective device(s) functioning to control the motor(s) connected to that branch circuit shall be protected against overcurrent, complying with Section 430-72. The motor control circuit is not considered a branch circuit, and supplementary overcurrent protection separate from the branch-circuit overcurrent protection is used. A motor control circuit other than tapped control circuit is to be protected against that overcurrent that is covered in Section 725-12 or Section 725-35, whichever is applicable.

(b) **Conductor Protection.** The values specified in Column A of Table 430-72(b) shall not be exceeded for the overcurrent protection of the conductors.

Exception No. 1: When the control circuit conductors do not extend beyond the motor control equipment enclosure, they are required to have only short-circuit and ground-fault protection, and this can be covered by the motor branch-circuit, short-circuit, and ground-fault protective device(s), if the rating of the protective devices does not exceed the value as determined from Column B of Table 430-72(b).

Exception No. 2: When the control circuit conductors extend beyond the controller, they will be required to have only short-circuit and ground-fault protection. They may also be protected by the motor branch-circuit, short-circuit, and ground-fault protective devices when the ratings of the protective devices do not exceed those of Column C or Table 430-72(b).

Exception No. 3: When control conductors are supplied by a single phase transformer on the secondary side and have only a 2-wire single voltage secondary, they are permitted to be protected by the over-current protection on the primary side of the transformer. This is if they are provided by overcurrent protection not exceeding the value obtained by multiplying the appropriate minimum rating of the overcurrent device for the secondary conductor as provided in Table 430-72(b) by the secondary-to-primary voltage ratio. If the secondary conductors are other than 2-wire, they are not permitted to be protected by the primary overcurrent protection.

Exception No. 4: Control conductor circuits are only required to have short-circuit and ground-fault protection, and are permitted to be protected by the motor short-circuit and ground-fault protection device. Also, they are permitted to be protected by the branch-circuit protection to the motor that is short-circuit and ground-fault protected if the opening of the control circuit would cause a hazardous condition (as in a control circuit to a fire pump). See Table 430-72(b) and the notes following.

(c) **Control Circuit Transformer.** When a control circuit tranformer is used, this transformer protection is covered in Article 450.

Exception No. 1: If the control circuit transformer is rated at less than 50 VA and is a part of the motor control and located in the enclosure for the motor controller.

Exception No. 2: If the control circuit transformer current is less than 2 amperes, the overcurrent device on the primary side is not to exceed 500 percent of the primary current rating and may be used.

Exception No. 3: Refer to Section 725-11(a). This will cover transformers that supply Class 1 power limited circuits and transformers that supply Class 2 and Class 3 remote-control circuits. See Article 725, Part C, in your *NEC*.

Exception No. 4: If other means of protection is provided.

Exception No. 5: Where opening of the control circuit would create a hazard such as for a fire pump, etc., the overcurrent protection may be omitted.

430-73. Mechanical Protection of Conductor—Where damage to a control circuit would constitute a hazard, all conductors of such remote-control circuit shall be installed in a raceway or be otherwise suitably protected from physical damage outside the control device itself. Damage to control wiring might cause an important operation to stop, or might cause a machine to unintentionally start, causing a hazard.

Where one side of a motor control circuit is grounded, the control circuit shall be so arranged that an accidental ground other than the intended ground elsewhere in a circuit will not start the motor. Most circuits have a grounded conductor along with the ungrounded conductor. Extreme care should be exercised to connect the stop and start buttons of a magnetic starter so that it will not energize the magnetic coil and start the motor should one of the conductors become grounded. The same could very easily happen on an ungrounded 480-volt, three-phase circuit which uses a 115-volt grounded system to energize the controls. Grounding one side could cause the motor to start. This item is very important, but so often little attention is paid to the matter.

430-74. Disconnection.

(a) **General**—Motor control circuits are to be so arranged that if the disconnecting means is in open position, the control circuit will also be open. Two or more separate disconnecting means will be used. One will open the power to the motor controller itself, and the other(s) disconnecting means will open the motor controller circuit(s) permitting power supply. Where more than one disconnecting means is used, they shall be mounted adjacent to one another.

Author's Note: It is the author's recommendation that the two disconnecting means be marked indicating that both supply sources are disconnected when either of the disconnecting devices is opened.

Exception No. 1: If all the following conditions are met and if there are more than twelve motor control circuit conductors that are required to be disconnected, this exception permits the disconnecting means to be located elsewhere than immediately adjacent to each other:

a. Part K of this article will permit the live parts to be accessible only to qualified persons.

b. There shall be a warning sign posted on the door or enclosure cover on the outside of each disconnecting means that permits access to live parts of the motor control circuit(s). This warning shall indicate that the disconnecting means of the control are remote from the controller of the motor, giving the location and identification of each disconnect. If, as permitted in Sections 430-

132 and 430-133, live parts are not in equipment enclosures, an additional warning sign(s) is to be located so as to be visible to persons working in the area of the live parts.

Exception No. 2: The conditions of (a) and (b) of Exception No. 1 above shall be adhered to where the opening of one or more of the motor control circuit disconnects might result in an unsafe condition for personnel or property.

(b) **Control Transformer in Controller.** A transformer or other device is often used to obtain a reduced voltage for the control circuit and is located in the controller. Such a transformer or other device shall be connected to the load side of the disconnecting means for the control circuit, so that when the motor disconnecting means is opened, the control circuit is also de-energized.

G. Motor Controllers

430-81. General—The intent of Part G will be to cover suitable controllers for all motors.

(a) **Definition.** For the definition of "Controller," the *NEC* refers to Article 100. In this portion the purpose of a controller is any switch or other device that would normally be used to stop and start the motor by opening the motor control circuit.

(b) **Stationary Motor of ⅛ Horsepower or Less.** On motors less than ⅛ horsepower, where mounted stationary or continuously, the construction must be such that if they fail to start they do not burn out and the branch circuit to which they are connected will be the overload protection for them.

(c) **Portable Motor of ⅓ Horsepower or Less.** Motors of ⅓ horsepower or less may use a plug and receptacle and cord connection for a disconnecting means.

430-82. Controller Design.

(a) **Starting and Stopping.** Every motor controller shall be capable of both starting and stopping the motor which it controls. Controllers for alternating-current motors shall be capable of interrupting the stalled-rotor current. Stalled-rotor current was covered in the first part of this article. Recall that this current is much higher than the running current and, unless the controller is capable of interrupting this larger current, damage may result to the controller. Controller listings in catalogs show the horsepower rating and the voltage.

(b) **Autotransformer.** Autotransformer controllers are alternating-current devices which incorporate an autotransformer to reduce the voltage and increase the current at start. This will reduce the current drawn from the branch circuit at start.

Autotransformer controllers shall have an OFF, RUN, and at least one START position. More than one start position may be incorporated to accelerate the motor in steps. The design shall be such that the controller cannot remain in the start position, which would render the overcurrent protection inoperative.

(c) **Rheostats.** Rheostats shall conform to the following:

(1) Motor-starting rheostats shall be so designed that they will not remain in any of the starting positions or segments when the starting handle is released, but will return to the off position. In addition the design will be such that the first contact will not engage any part of the rheostat.

(2) Rheostats used as motor-starts on direct current which operate from a constant voltage supply are to be equipped with a device which, should the voltage drop, will release the starter before the motor speed has dropped to less than one-third of its normal speed.

430-83. Rating—Controllers shall be marked in horsepower and shall not be rated at less horsepower than the motor being served.

Exception No. 1: Stationary Motor of 2 Horsepower or Less. A general use switch may be used as a controller for motors rated at 2 horsepower or less and 300 volts or less, provided that it has a current rating of at least twice the full-load current rating of the motor with which it is to be used.

On ac circuits it is permissible to use an ac general-use snap switch, but not a general-use ac-dc snap switch, as the controller for motors of 2 horsepower or less and 300 volts or less, providing that the full-load current rating of the motor does not exceed 80 percent of the current rating of the snap switch.

Exception No. 2: Only inverse time circuit breakers rated in amperes shall be used in branch circuits supplying a controller. If this circuit breaker is also used for overload protection, it must conform to the parts of this article that govern overload protection.

Exception No. 3: Torque motors shall have a continous-duty and also a full-load current rating that is not less than the full-load rating marked on the motor. If the motor controller is rated in horsepower and not marked as covered above, you shall determine the ampere or the horsepower rating by using Tables 430-147, 430-148, 430-159, and 430-150.

430-84. Need Not Open All Conductors—Section 430-111 covers controllers that serve as both the controller and the disconnecting means, and these shall open all ungrounded conductors. Where the controller does not serve as both the controller and the disconnect, it need not open all of the conductors, but only those necessary to start and stop the motor.

430-85. In Grounded Conductors—There is nothing that prohibits the opening of the grounded conductor if one is used to supply a motor.

However, if the grounded conductor is opened, all ungrounded conductors shall be simultaneously opened.

430-87. Number of Motors Served by Each Controller—Each motor must have a separate controller.

Exception: Under one of the following conditions, a single controller of 600 volts or less shall not be rated less than the sum of the horsepower ratings of all the motors that are in a group, and they shall be permitted to be served by the group of motors as mentioned in the beginning of this paragraph:

    (a) A single machine or a piece of apparatus, such as metal or wood-working equipment, cranes, hoists, etc., might require several motors in its operation? in which case a single disconnecting means may serve all the motors. Other conditions of this Article, such as over-current protection, must also be met.

    (b) In Section 430-53(a), more than one motor was permitted to be protected by one overcurrent device if certain requirements as to current and voltage were met.

    (c) If a group of motors is located in a single room, and all are within sight of the disconnecting means, then a single disconnecting means may be used.

430-88. Adjustable-Speed Motors—Some motors, especially shunt and compound-wound dc motors, have speed adjustment controlled by the regulation of the field current. Where such is the case, the controller shall be so designed that the motor cannot be started with a weakened field unless the motor is specifically designed for such starting. Starting a motor with a weakened field is dangerous and may cause a current high enough to burn out the armature.

430-89. Speed Limitation—See the *NEC*.

430-90. Combination Fuseholder and Switch as Controller—When a combination fuseholder and switch is used as a motor controller, it shall be such that the fuseholder will permit only the size of fuse specified in Part C of this article covering overload protection. A fuseholder of larger capacity is permissible if fused down to proper value.

Exception: Where time-delay fuses that have the appropriate motor-starting characteristics are used, fuseholders that are smaller than those covered in Part C of this article will be permitted.

430-91. Motor Controller Enclosure Types—Table 430-91 gives the basis for the selection of enclosures in nonhazardous locations for specific purposes. These enclosures are not intended to be used for protection for the conditions such as condensation, icing, corrosion, or contamination that might be likely to occur in the enclosures or to enter through openings that are not sealed, or through the conduit. When any of these conditions exists, the installer or user is required to give it special consideration.

See the *NEC* for Table 430-91, Motor Controller Enclosure Selection Table.

H. Disconnection Means

430-101. General—The intent of Part H of this article is the requirement of the disconnecting means for the disconnection of motors and controllers from the circuit.

Note: Code refers us to Diagram 430-1.

Note: Identification of the disconnecting means will be found in Section 110-22.

430-102. Location.

(a) **Controller.** The disconnecting means shall be located in sight of the controller.

Exception No. 1: In circuits using over 600 volts for a motor, the disconnecting means will be permitted to be out of sight of the controller, if the controller is plainly marked with a warning label that gives the location and identifies the disconnecting means that can be locked in an open position.

Exception No. 2: Where a multimotor continuous process machine is used, a single disconnecting means is permitted to be located by the group of coordinated controls that are mounted and adjacent to each other.

(b) **Motor.** The disconnecting means is required to be mounted within sight of the motor and driven machinery.

Exception: As provided in Section 430-102(a), if the disconnecting means is capable of being locked in an OFF position, it may be out of sight of the motor.

A great many inspectors will probably require, and rightly so, that the disconnecting means be marked as to what motor-driven machinery it disconnects. They might also require a sign at the motor or machinery stating that the disconnecting means is to be locked in an open position. This is only common sense, in that the main purpose of this ruling is safety to anyone who might perform mechanical or electrical work on the motor or the driven machinery.

430-103. To Disconnect Both Motor and Controller—All ungrounded conductors to the motor and controller supply conductors shall be energized when the disconnecting means is in the OFF position. The disconnecting means shall be designed so that no pole can be operated independently. The disconnecting means may also be located in the control enclosure. See Section 430-113. This section covers those installations where energy is received from more than one source.

430-104. To Be Indicating—Any means of disconnection shall readily indicate whether it is OFF or ON.

430-105. Grounded Conductors—One pole of the disconnecting means may open the grounded conductors if one is used in the circuit. However, if it opens the grounded conductor, it shall also simultaneously open all conductors of the circuit.

430-106. Service Switch as Disconnecting Means—If the installation consists of only one motor, the service switch may be used as a disconnecting means if it meets all of the requirements of this article.

430-107. Readily Accessible—There shall be no obstructions in the way of ladders needed in the operation of the disconnecting means.

430-108. Every Switch—See the *NEC*.

430-109. Type—The motor circuit switch for motor disconnecting means shall be rated in horsepower. A noninterruptable switch or molded case switch is permitted.

Exception No. 1: When a motor is ⅛ horsepower or less and is mounted stationary, the branch-circuit overcurrent device shall be the disconnecting means.

Exception No. 2: See Exception No. 1 of Section 430-83.

Exception No. 3: If all of the following conditions are met for motors over 2 horsepower up to 100 horsepower, and if the separate disconnecting means that is required in an autotransformer type of controller is used for a motor, it may be a general-use switch if the following provisions are met:

a. A motor supplies a generator that is equipped with overload protection.
b. The controller (1) is capable of interupting the rotor-locked current; (2) has a nonvoltage release supplied; and (3) the motor is protected with overcurrent protection not exceeding 125 percent of the full-load current rating.
c. Separate fuses for an inverse time circuit breaker, if it is rated or set at not more than 150 percent of the full-load current rating of the motor, are provided in the branch circuit.

Exception No. 4: For direct-current stationary motors that are operated at over 40 horsepower on direct current or not rated at over a 100 horsepower on alternating current, general-purpose switches will be permitted as the isolating switch if they are plainly marked, "Do not open under load."

Exception No. 5: When motors are cord- and plug-connected, the attachment plug and receptacle shall be horsepower rated, and cord or receptacles of a lesser rating will not be permitted to serve as the disconnecting means. As covered in Section 422-22, a horsepower-rated attachment plug and receptacle will not be required, nor will it be required as covered in Section 440-63 for air conditioners.

Exception No. 6: A general-use switch is permitted as the disconnecting means for a torque motor.

430-110. Ampere Rating and Interrupting Capacity.

(a) **General.** The disconnecting means is required to have an interrupting capacity of at least 115 percent of the full-load rating of the motor, for motors, and circuits rated 600 volts, nominal, or less.

(b) **For Torque Motors.** The disconnecting means for a torque motor shall be at least 115 percent of the nameplate rating on the motor.

(c) **For Combination Loads.** The following will give a method of determining the disconnecting means size where two or more motors are used together or where one or more motors are in combination with other types of load such as resistance heaters. If the combined loads can come on at the same time, the signal disconnecting means shall be calculated by the ampere and the horsepower ratings of the combined loads.

(1) In determining the size of the disconnecting means, the sum of all currents, including the resistance loads at the full-load condition, and also at the locked-rotor condition, and the combined full-load current condition and combine locked-rotor current so obtained, shall be considered as follows:

From Table 430-148, 430-149, or 430-150 select the full-load current of each motor. The combination of these full-load currents plus the other loads added to them in amperes will determine the full-load current of the combined motor.

From Table 430-151, select the locked-rotor current equivalent for the horsepower rating of each motor. Locked-rotor current ratings are to be added to the other combined loads. If two or more motors and or other loads cannot be started simultaneously, the appropriate combinations will determine the combination locked-rotor rating and will be permitted to be used in making a decision on the locked-rotor current for the loads that come on simultaneously.

Exception: Where the total concurrent load or part of the load is a resistance load, and if the disconnecting means is a switch that is rated in horsepower and amperes, then the switch used may have a horsepower rating of not less than the total combined load of the ampere rating of the switch that is not less than the sum of the locked current and the motor(s) plus the resistance load.

(2) The ampere rating of the disconnecting switch is not allowed to be less than 115 percent of the total combination of all currents at the full-load condition as was determined above in (c) (1).

(3) For small motors that are not covered by Tables 430-147, 430-148, 430-149, or 430-150, the locked-rotor current may be assumed to be six times the full-load currents of the small motors.

430-111. Switch or Circuit Breaker as Both Controller and Disconnecting Means—See the *NEC*.

430-112. Motors Served by Single Disconnecting Means—See the *NEC*.

430-113. Energy from More than One Source—If equipment receives its energy from more than one source, such as the control circuit from an isolation transformer of a different voltage from that of the motor or from a dc source and the motor from an ac source, the disconnecting means for each source (and there must be a disconnecting means for each) shall be located adjacent to each other. Each source may have a separate disconnecting means.

Exception No. 1: If a motor receives power from more than one source, the disconnecting means that is used for the main power supply to the motor is not required to be located immediately next to that motor, but it must be capable of being locked in the open position.

Exception No. 2: If the control circuit is derived from a Class 2 circuit that is remote and conforms with Article 725, and this Class 2 circuit has not more than 30 volts and is isolated and ungrounded, a separate disconnecting means will be required.

J. Over 600 Volts, Nominal

430-121. General—This part covers motors and controllers operating at more than 600 volts. There are special hazards that are encountered at these voltages that must be taken into consideration. Other requirements for circuits and equipment that operate at over 600 volts will be covered in Article 710.

430-122. Marking on Controllers—The control voltage shall be marked on the controller in addition to the marking that was required in Section 430-8.

430-123. Conductor Enclosure Adjacent to Motors—Flexible metal conduit including liquidtight flexible metal conduit with listed fittings not exceeding 6 ft. in length shall be permitted to be used for raceway connection to the motor terminal housing. Be certain that if required the proper size equipment grounding conductor is also in the wiring methods mentioned above and size them according to Table 250-95. Many places in industry, the equipment grounding conductor may be required regardless of the Code requirement.

430-124. Size of Conductors—The setting at which the motor overload protective device(s) is set will determine that ampacity of the conductors supplying the motor.

430-125. Motor Circuit Overcurrent Protection.

(a) **General.** High-voltage circuits for each motor must include protection that is coordinated to interrupt automatically any overloads or fault currents in the motor, and also the control apparatus for the motor and the conductors to the motor.

Exception: When one particular motor is vital to the operation of the entire plant, and if the motor's failing to operate means greater hazards to persons, then there will be a sensing device(s) that will be permitted to operate a supervised annunciator alarm. These are permitted instead of interrupting the motor circuit.

(b) **Overload Protection.**

(1) A thermal protector within the motor, or external devices sensing the current, shall be used in each motor to prevent damage by overheating caused by motor overloads or failure to start.

(2) The overcurrent device protecting the motor is considered as protecting the secondary circuits of wound-rotor, alternating-current motors, including the controllers and resistors that are used in the secondary circuit and rated for that application.

(3) All ungrounded conductors shall be opened at the same time by the overload interrupting device.

(4) Devices to sense overload shall not automatically reset after tripping unless the resetting of the overload sensing device will not cause automatic restarting of the motor, or unless there can be no hazards to persons from the restarting of the motor or by the machinery it runs.

(c) **Fault-Current Protection.**

(1) The following means shall be used to provide fault-current protection in each motor circuit:
   a. The circuit breaker may be used if it is of suitable type and proper rating, and is so arranged that it can be serviced without causing a hazard. All ungrounded conductors are required to be opened at the same time by the circuit breaker. Internal or external sensing devices shall be permitted for the circuit breaker to sense fault currents.

b. Fuses arranged so that they cannot be serviced while energized may be used if of suitable type and rating and if they are placed in each ungrounded conductor. There shall be a suitable disconnecting means for the fuses, although they can also serve as the disconnecting means if listed for that use.

(2) Circuits shall not be automatically closed by fault-current interrupters.

Exception: This permits automatically closing if the opening was caused by a transient fault current, or if, in closing the circuit, it does not create a hazard to people.

(3) The same device may be used for overload and fault-current protection.

430-126. Rating of Motor Control Apparatus—The current at which the overload protective device(s) is set to trip basically determines the minimum ratings for motor controllers and motor branch-circuit disconnecting means. The rating of this equipment shall never be less than that of the overload protective device settings.

430-127. Disconnecting Means—The disconnecting means for a controller must be capable of being locked in the open position.

K. Protection of Live Parts—All Voltages

430-131. General—Part K requires that live parts be adequately protected from possible hazards.

430-132. Where Required—Any live parts exposed on motors or controllers that operate at 50 volts or more between terminals are required to be guarded from accidental contact by an enclosure, or by location as follows:

(a) They may be enclosed in a room or enclosure that is accessible only to qualified persons. The definition of "qualified person" in Article 100 is someone who is familiar with the operation and construction of the equipment and with any hazards that might be involved.

(b) They may be installed on a suitable balcony, gallery, or platform that is so elevated and arranged as to keep all unqualified persons away. An open stairway that is not barred or that does not have a gate would not comply.

(c) They shall be elevated 8 feet or more above the floor. This 8-foot requirement appears often in the code.

Exception: When commutators, collectors, and brush rigging on stationary motors are inside of the motor end brackets and are not conductively connected to a voltage of 150 volts to ground from the supply source. An example might be a wound-rotor motor.

430-133. Guards for Attendants—See the *NEC*.

L. Grounding All Voltages

430-141. General—This Part L covers the grounding of motors and controller frames to prevent voltages above ground in the event of accidental contact of the live parts and the frames. There are permissible conditions where insulation, isolation, or guarding will suffice instead of grounding the frames.

430-142. Stationary Motors—Under any of the following conditions, frames of stationary motors shall be grounded: (1) if connected to metal enclosed wiring; (2) if they are in wet locations and are not isolated or guarded; (3) if, as covered in Article 500 through 517 they are in a hazardous (classified) location; and (4) if any motor operates with terminals over 150 volts to ground.

If the frame of the motor is not grounded, it shall be effectively and permanently isolated from ground.

Other suitable precautions should be taken to keep persons from coming in contact with the ground, should a fault occur.

430-143. Portable Motors—Frames of motors (portable) that operate at more than 150 volts to ground are required to be either guarded or grounded. In Section 250-45(d), portable motors in other than residential occupancies were to be grounded where the location was of a damp or wet nature, or where persons might come into contact with grounded objects. An exception to this was that motors that operate at not more than 50 volts or are supplied by an isolation transformer did not need to be grounded. There was also a recommendation that motors that operate at more than 50 volts should be grounded.

Note: Portable appliances and other than residential occupancies will be found in Section 250-45(d).

Note: The grounding conductor color is covered in Section 250-59(b).

430-144. Controllers—Controller cases shall be grounded, regardless of voltage, except controllers attached to ungrounded portable equipment and lined covers of snap switches; that is, where the cover is properly insulated.

430-145. Method of Grounding—Grounding of motors and controllers shall conform to Article 250.

(a) **Grounding through Terminal Housings.** In Article 250, Type AC metal-clad cable or metal raceways was, in most cases (except in some hazardous installations), acceptable as a ground if properly installed. Where these types of wiring are used, a junction box shall be provided for the terminals of the motor, and the cable or raceway attached to this junction box as specified in Article 250.

Note: See the *NEC*, Section 430-12(e), for grounding and terminal housings.

(b) **Separation of Junction Box from Motor.** The junction box, as provided for in (a) above, may be separated from the motor a distance not to exceed 6 feet (1.83 m), provided that the leads to the motor are one of the following: (1) Type AC metal-clad cable; (2) armored cable; or (3) stranded leads enclosed in flexible metal conduit, liquid-tight flexible nonmetallic conduit, rigid or intermediate metal conduit, or in electrical metallic tubing no smaller than ⅜-inch trade size. Where stranded leads that are protected by one of the means above are used, they shall be no larger than No. 10, and all other requirements for conductors, as provided by the Code, shall be met.

(c) **Grounding of Controller Mounted Devices.** Instrument transformer secondaries and exposed noncurrent-carrying metal or other conductive parts or cases of instrument transformers, meters, instruments, and relays shall be grounded as specified in Sections 250-121 through 250-125.

See the *NEC* Part M for the following tables: Table 430-147, Full-Load Current in Amperes, Direct-Current Motors (the values of current at full-load are the average direct-current quantities for motors running at base speed); Table 430-148, Full-Load Current in Amperes for Single-Phase Alternating-Current Motors; Table 430-149, Full-Load Current for Two-Phase Alternating-Current Motors, 4-Wire; Table 430-150, Full-Load Current, Three-Phase Alternating-Current Motors (induction-type squirrel-cage, wound rotor type, and synchronous types at unity power factor); Table 430-151, Locked-Rotor Current Conversion (determined from horsepower and voltage rating—for use only with Sections 430-110, 440-12, and 440-41); Table 430-152, Maximum Rating or Setting of Motor Branch-Circuit Protective Devices (for all types of motors and also the Code letter on motors; gives the percent of full-load current for nontime delay fuses, dual-element (time-delay) fuses, instantaneous trip breakers, and inverse time breakers; be sure to observe the notes at the bottom of this table).

ARTICLE 440—AIR-CONDITIONING AND REFRIGERATING EQUIPMENT

A. General

440-1. Scope—This article covers electric motor-driven air-conditioning and refrigeration equipment, and the controllers and branch-circuits that supply this equipment. Included will be special considerations necessary to supply hermetic refrigerant motor-compressors. It takes into consideration an individual branch circuit that supplies hermetic refrigerant motor-compressors, and any air conditioning and/or refrigeration equipment supplied from an individual branch circuit.

440-2. Definitions.

Hermetic Refrigerant Motor-Compressor: Here the compressor and the motor are both enclosed in the same housing; therefore, they do not have a shaft extending out from a compressor to an external motor.

440-3. Other Articles.

(a) **Article 430.** Provisions in this article are in addition to or amendatory to Article 430 and other articles in the *NEC* which will apply unless modified by this article.

(b) **Articles 422, 424, or 430.** Air-conditioning and refrigeration equipment which employ conventional motors, instead of hermetic-type motors, will come under Articles 422, 424, or 430. This will include the following units when driven by conventional motors: refrigeration compressors, furnaces with air-conditioning equipment, fan-coil units, remote forced-air-cooled condensers, and remote commercial refrigerators.

(c) **Article 422.** The following items are considered as appliances and come under Article 422: room air conditioners, household refrigerators, household freezers, drinking-water coolers, and beverage dispensers.

(d) **Other Applicable Articles.** The applicable conditions follow for the circuits, controllers, and equipment as well as the hermetic refrigerant motor-compressor. Refer to the *NEC*, which lists places that require special installations.

440-4. Marking on Hermetic Refrigerant Motor-Compressor and Equipment.

(a) **Hermetic Refrigerant Motor-Compressor Nameplate.** On the hermetic refrigerant motor-compressor, a marking is required to be provided on the nameplate giving the manufacturer's name, trademark, or symbol and designating the identification, number of phase, voltage, and frequency. The rated load current is to be marked in amperes for the motor-compressor. It can be marked on the manufacturer's nameplate and the nameplate of the equipment on which the motor-compressor is to be used. Also marked on the motor compressor nameplate shall be the locked-rotor current for a single-phase motor-compressor that has a rated-load current of more than 9 amperes at 115 volts, or for 230-volt operation if more than 4.5 amperes. Polyphase motor-compressors shall be marked as such on the motor-compressor nameplate. Where there is a thermal protector that complies with Section 440-52(a) (2), the motor-compressor nameplate or the equipment nameplate shall be permanently marked "Thermally Protected." If a protective system complying with Section 440-52(a) (4) and (b) (4) is used and is also furnished as part of the equipment, the equipment nameplate shall be marked "Thermally Protected System." Where the protective system complies with Section 440-52(a) (4) and (b) (4), the equipment nameplate shall be marked to indicate that it is not supplied with the equipment, but must be used.

Note: The rated-load current of the refrigerant motor-compressor that is marked thereon is the result of full-load current when the motor compressor is operated at its rated load and the rated voltage and frequency that is marked for the equipment it serves.

(b) **Multimotor and Combination-Load Equipment.** Multimotor and combination-load equipment shall be provided with a visible nameplate marked with marker's name; rating in volts; frequency; number of phases; minimum circuit ampacity; and maximum rating of the branch-circuit short-circuit and ground-fault protective device rating. The ampacity calculations will be covered in Part D, a little later. Part C will cover ground-fault protection calculation. See the *NEC* for further details.

Exception No. 1: When suitable under the provisions of this article, multimotor and combination-load equipment that is equipped for a single 15- or 20-ampere connection at 120 volts, or connected to a 15-ampere source or a 208- or 240-volt single-phase branch circuit, shall be marked and be permitted.

Exception No. 2: Part G of this Article 440 covers room air conditioners.

(c) **Branch-Circuit Selection Current.** Sealed (hermetic-type) motor-compressors or equipment containing such compressor(s) in which the protective system, approved for use with the motor-compressor which it protects, permits continuous current in excess of the specified percentage of nameplate rated-load current given in Section 440-52(b)(2) or (b)(4) shall also be marked with a branch-circuit selection current that complies with Section 440-52(b)(2) or (b)(4). This marking shall be on the nameplate(s) where the rated-load current(s) appears.

Note: Definition: Value of amperes to be used in the selection of branch-circuit current instead of a rated full-load current shall be determined by the rating of the motor branch-circuit conductors, the controllers, the disconnecting means, and also the branch-circuit, short-circuit, and ground-fault protective devices, wherever the running overload protective device will permit sustained current that is more than is specified as the percentage of load current. The value of the branch-circuit selected current will always be equal to or greater than the marked rated full-load current.

440-5. Marking on Controllers—Controllers shall be marked with the maker's name, trademark, or symbol; identifying designation; voltage; phase; full-load current; locked-rotor current (or horsepower) rating; and any other pertinent information.

440-6. Ampacity and Rating—The rating of the equipment and the ampacity of the conductors selected from Tables 310-16 through 310-31, shall be arrived at as follows:

(a) **Hermetic Refrigerant Motor-Compressor.** For a sealed (hermetic-type) motor-compressor, the rated-load current marked on the nameplate of the equipment in which the motor-compressor is employed shall be used in determining the rating or ampacity of the disconnecting means, branch-circuit conductors, controller, ground-fault protection, and separate motor overload protection. If there is no rated-load current on the equipment nameplate, you shall use the rated-load on the compressor nameplate. For disconnecting means and controllers, see Sections 440-12 and 440-41.

Exception No. 1: Permits us to use the branch-circuit selection current when shown, instead of the rated-load current for determining the rating or ampacity of disconnecting means, branch-circuit conductors, controller size, branch-circuit protection, short-circuit protection, and ground-fault protection.

Exception No. 2: As covered in Section 440-22(b), it is permitted for the branch-circuit, short-circuit, and ground-fault cord- and plug-connected equipment to be used for the protection.

(b) **Multimotor Equipment.** If multimotor equipment employs shaded-pole or permanent split-capacitor-type fans that run blowers, the current for such motors that is marked on the nameplate of the equipment for which the fan or blower is used shall be the current used instead of the horsepower rating in determining the ampacity that is required for disconnecting means, branch-circuit conductors, controllers, the branch-circuit, short-circuit, and ground-fault protection, and also the separate overcurrent protection that is needed for this equipment. The marking that is on the nameplate or equipment is to be not less than the current marked on the fan or blower motor nameplate.

440-7. Highest Rated (Largest) Motor—In compliance with this article and with Sections 430-24, 430-53(b), and (c), and 430-62(a), the motor with the highest load-rated current is the largest motor. If there should be two or more motors of the same load-rating, only one is used. Any motors other than (hermetic-type) compressor motors, as were covered in Section 440-6(b), shall have their full-load current determined by using Tables 430-148, 430-149, or 430-150, using horsepower to determine full-load current, not the nameplate current-rating.

Exception: If it is so marked, then the branch-circuit selection current is to be used instead of the rated load current in determining the largest motor compressor.

440-8. Single Machine—Section 430-87 considers air-conditioning systems as a single machine. Section 430-87, Exception, and Section 430-112, Exception, stipulate that the motors need not be mounted adjacent to each other, but may be mounted remote to each other.

B. Disconnecting Means

440-11. General—The *NEC* refers you to Diagram 430-1. The intent of Part B is to require disconnecting means for air-conditioning and refrigeration equipment, including the motor and the compressor and controllers to be supplied from a circuit feeder.

440-12. Rating and Interrupting Capacity.

(a) **Hermetic Refrigerant Motor-Compressor.** In considering the rating of the disconnecting means that serves a hermetic refrigerant motor-compressor, it is to be considered as selected from the nameplate rated-load current or the branch-circuit current, whichever is greater, and locked-rotor current, respectively, of the motor-compressor as follows:

(1) The rating of the ampere shall be at least 115 percent of the rated-load current on the nameplate or the branch-circuit current, whichever is larger. This gives us a minimum, but on large units the 115 percent will not be of sufficient ampacity for opening under load.

(2) To determine the equivalent horsepower in complying with the requirements of Section 430-109, select the horsepower rating from Table 430-148, 430-149, or 430-150 corresponding to the rated-load current or branch-circuit selection current, whichever is greater, and also the horsepower rating from Table 430-151 corresponding to the locked-rotor current. See the *NEC* for the balance of this part.

The first three Tables mentioned, Tables 430-148, 430-149, and 430-150, cover horsepower to full-load current. These may also convert full-load current to horsepower. Table 430-151 gives us the locked-rotor conversion Table.

Hermetic-type motor-compressors usually do not have a horsepower rating on the nameplate, so we use the ampere rating and if amperes and horsepower rating do not correspond when we convert to horsepower, we use the next larger horsepower in the tables.

(b) **Combination Loads.** If one or more hermetic refrigerant motor-compressors are operated together, or other combinations of motors or loads such as resistive heaters are used with them, if the combination load can come on at the same time on a single disconnecting means, then the rating for the combined load shall be as follows:

(1) The disconnecting means shall be determined by the sum of the currents, such as: current of resistive load at rated load-current plus locked-rotor currents of the motor(s). The combined rated-load current and the combined locked-rotor current by summation of (a) and (b) to convert the ampacity as needed as if the combination were just one motor.

    a. Other than hermetic refrigerant motor-compressors and fans for blower motors, the full-load current to a horsepower rating to each motor, as covered in Section 440-6(b), is to be selected from Tables 430-148, 430-149, or 430-150. Of the sum of these currents and the motor-compressor rated-load current(s), or branch-circuit current(s), you are to use the greater. Also amperes of other loads, to obtain equivalent, will give the full-load current of the combined loads.

    b. Other than the hermetic refrigerant motor-compressor, the locked-rotor current equivalent to the horsepower rating of each motor shall be selected from Table 430-151, and for the fan and blower motors of the shaded-pole or permanent split-capacitor type that is marked with the locked-rotor current, the marked values shall be used. The locked-rotor current values of the motor-compressor locked-rotor current(s) and the rating in amperes of other loads shall be added to obtain the locked-rotor current for the combined load. Where two or more motors and or other loads cannot be started at the same time, the appropriate locked-rotor and rated-load currents and branch-circuit selection of current, whichever is greater, will be acceptable as the means for determining the equivalent locked-rotor current combinations that will operate at the same time.

    Exception: If part of the load is resistive and if the disconnecting means is rated in horsepower and amperage, the switch may have a horsepower rating that shall be not less than the combined load of the motor-compressor(s) and the other motors at locked-rotor current. If the amperage is equal to or greater than the locked-rotor plus the resistance load, it may be used.

(2) As referred to in Section 440-12(b) (1), the disconnecting means shall have an ampere rating that is at least 115 percent of the combination of all currents at the rated-load conditions.

(c) **Small Motor-Compressors.** For small motors that do not have locked-rotor current rating marked on the nameplate, or for small motors covered in Tables 430-147, 430-148, 430-149, or 430-150, the locked-rotor current shall be assumed to be six times the full-load current rating.

(d) **Every Switch.** The requirements of Section 440-12 shall be met wherever the disconnecting means in the refrigerant motor-compressor circuit is between the point of attachment to the heater and a point of connection to the refrigerant motor-compressor.

(e) **Disconnecting Means Rated in Excess of 100 Horsepower.** The provisions of Section 430-109 will apply when, as determined above, the rated-load or locked-rotor current indicates that the rating is in excess of 100 horsepower.

440-13. Cord-Connected Equipment—When room air conditioners, home refrigerators and freezers, drinking water coolers, and beverage dispensers are cord-connected, a cord, plug, or receptacle, which may be separable, will be permitted as the disconnecting means. For additional information on this, see Section 440-63.

440-14. Location—This is slightly different from some of Article 430, but you are referred to see Parts G and H of Article 430 for additional requirements. The disconnecting means shall be located within sight from the air-conditioning or refrigeration equipment and shall also be readily accessible. The disconnecting means is permitted to be installed within or on the refrigerating or air conditioning equipment.

Note: Additional requirements may be found in Parts G and H of Article 430.

C. Branch-Circuit Short-Circuit and Ground-Fault Protection

440-21. General—Part C covers devices that are intended to protect the branch-circuit conductors, control apparatus, and motors that serve hermetic refrigerant motor-compressors against overcurrent caused by short-circuits and grounds. They are also supplementary or amendatory of Article 240.

440-22. Application and Selection.

(a) **Rating or Setting for Individual Motor-Compressor.** The branch-circuit, short-circuit and ground-fault protective device of the motor-compressor shall be capable of handling the motor starting current, but shall not be over 175 percent of the motor's rated-load current or branch-circuit selection current, whichever is the greater; 15 amperes is the minimum size.

Should the above 175 percent be too small to take care of the starting current, this 175 percent may be increased to a maximum of 225 percent with the same stipulations.

(b) **Rating or Setting for Equipment.** The equipment branch-circuit short-circuit and ground-fault protective device shall be capable of carrying the starting current of the equipment. Where the hermetic refrigerant motor-compressor is the only load on the circuit, the protection shall conform with Section 440-22(a). Where the equipment incorporates more than one hermetic-refrigerant motor-compressor or a hermetic refrigerant motor-compressor and other motors or other loads, the equipment protection shall conform with Section 430-53 and the following: (Article 430 and Article 440 are closely tied together. Refer to Section 430-53 which will give you the information required.) Section 430-53 and the following cover short-circuit and ground-fault protection:

(1) If the hermetic-refrigerant motor-compressor is the larger load, the rating or setting of the protective device shall conform to Section 440-22(a) plus the rated-load current or branch-circuit selection current, whichever is the greater of the other smaller motor-compressor(s) and/or the rating of any other loads covered by this protective device. The values specified in Section 440-22(a) are not to exceed the rating and setting of the branch-circuit, short-circuit, and ground-fault protective device.

(2) Where a hermetic-refrigerant motor-compressor is not the largest load connected to the circuit, the rating or setting of the protective device shall not exceed a value equal to the sum of the rated-load current or branch-circuit selection current, whichever is greater, rating(s) for the motor-compressor(s) plus the value specified in Section 430-53(c)(4) where other motor loads are supplied in addition to the motor-compressor(s), or the value specified in Section 240-3 where only nonmotor loads are supplied in addition to the motor-compressor(s).

Exception No. 1: In many cases where the equipment will start and operate on a 15- or 20-ampere, 120-volt or a 15-ampere, 208- or 240-volt single-phase branch circuit, a 15- or 20-ampere overcurrent device may be used to protect the branch-circuit. Should the maximum branch-circuit, short-circuit, and ground-fault protective device rating be marked on the equipment that is less that these values, then the values of the overcurrent device in the branch circuit shall not exceed the values marked on the nameplate of the equipment.

Usually such equipment will have protective devices built into the unit itself.

Exception No. 2: On equipment not rated over 250 volts, such as household refrigerators, drinking water coolers, and beverage coolers, that has a nameplate marking for cord- and plug-connection, this nameplate rating is to be used for the branch-circuit device rating and, unless the nameplate is marked otherwise, this equipment is to be considered as single motor equipment.

(c) **Protective Device Rating Not to Exceed the Manufacturer's Values.** Where the maximum protective device ratings that will be shown on the manufacturer's heater table for use with a motor controller are less than the rating or setting as determined by Section 440-22(a) and (b), the manufacturer's values marked on the.equipment shall not be exceeded by the protective device rating.

D. Branch-Circuit Conductors

440-31. General—Conductor sizes are specified in Part D and in Articles 300 and 310. Conductors shall be of large enough ampacity to carry the motor current, without heating. Exception No. 1 of Section 440-5(a) modifies this specification.

The provision of Articles 300 and 310 do not cover the following: Integral conductors of motor, motor controllers and the like; and conductors which form an integral part of approved equipment. See Section 300-1(b) and 310-1.

440-32. Single Motor-Compressors—This is the same as for a single motor as covered in Article 430, that is, not less than 125 percent of either the motor-compressor rated-load current or the branch-circuit selection-current, whichever is greater.

440-33. Motor-Compressor(s) With or Without Additional Motor Loads—The ampacity of conductors supplying one or more motor-compressors, with or without additional motor loads shall be figured from the rated load or branch-circuit selection current ratings, whichever is the larger. The rated load shall be 125 percent of the full-load current of the highest rating of the largest motor or motor-compressor rating of the group, plus the full-load ratings of all of the other motors or motor-compressors in the group.

Exception No. 1: If the circuitry is interlocked to prevent starting and running of a second motor-compressor or group of motor-compressors, you will use the current value of the largest motor-compressor or, if a group of compressors can run together at a given time, the conductor size will be for this largest group of motor-compressors.

Exception No. 2: Part G of this Article 440 will cover room air conditioners.

440-34. Combination Load—For conductors that supply a motor-compressor load and also a lighting or appliance load, the computation was given in Article 220, and there are other articles that might apply. The conductors shall have sufficient ampacity to handle the lighting or appliance load in addition to the required ampacity for the motor-compressor load. This shall meet the requirements of Section 440-33, or, if for a single motor-compressor load, the requirements of Section 440-32.

Exception: Should the circuitry be so designed that the motor-compressor and other loads on the circuit cannot be operated at the same time, the conductor sizes will be determined by the motor-compressor(s) and any other loads that may be operated at the same time.

440-35. Multimotor and Combination-Load Equipment—For such equipment we use the minimum circuit ampacity marked on the equipment in accordance with Section 440-3(b), which need not be repeated here as it has just been covered.

E. Controllers for Motor-Compressors

440-41. Rating.

(a) **Motor-Compressor Controller.** The motor-compressor controller is required to have not only the continuous-duty full-load current, but also must have the locked-rotor current rating. This shall not be less than the load indicated on the nameplate-rated load current or the selected current for a branch-circuit, whichever is greater, and the locked-rotor current (you are referred to Sections 440-6 and 440-7) tied in with the locked-rotor current of the compressor. In case the controller for the motor is rated in horsepower but is without one or both of the foregoing current ratings required, the equivalent currents of the horsepower may be determined from ratings by using Tables 430-148, 430-149, or 430-150 to determine the equivalent full-load current. Table 430-151 will be used to determine the equivalent locked-rotor current.

This is basically no different from that for the conventional type of motor and the ampacity of the controller is determined in the same manner and with the use of the same tables.

(b) **Controller Serving More than One Load.** Where there is more than one motor-compressor or a motor-compressor and other loads, the controller rating shall be determined by the continuous-duty full-load current rating, and a locked-rotor rating of not less than the combined loads, as determined in accordance with Section 440-12(b).

F. Motor-Compressor and Branch-Circuit Overload Protection

440-51. General—See Section 240-3, Exception No. 3. This Part F is intended to cover devices that give protection to the motor compressor, the apparatus to control the motor, and the branch-circuit conductors. In this part, the main idea is to protect the motor from overload and excessive heating and/or failure to start.

Note: Overloading on electrically driven equipment can cause damage or overheating of the electrical system. Not included here are short circuits or ground faults.

440-52. Application and Selection.

(a) **Protection of Motor-Compressor.** Overloads or failure to start may be prevented by one of the following means:

(1) This tells us the separate overload relay shall be responsive to not over 140 percent of the motor-compressor rated-load current.

(2) A thermal protector built into the compressor-motor is acceptable, if it prevents damage from overheating due to overload or failure to start.

The current-interrupting device may be external and operated by a thermal device in the motor, provided that it is so arranged that the control circuit from the thermal device will cause interruption of current to the motor-compressor.

(3) Fuses or inverse time circuit breakers that respond to the motor current are permitted if they are not rated at more than 125 percent of the motor-compressor rated-load current. Time-delay shall be sufficient to take care of the starting current.

Either the motor-compressor or the equipment shall be marked with the maximum size of branch-circuit fuse or inverse time circuit-breaker rating.

(4) The protective system we are covering, whether furnished or supplied with the equipment, is intended to prevent overheating of the motor-compressor due to overload and failure to start. When the current interrupting device is not a part of the motor compressor and the control circuit is operated by a device that is not a part of the current interrupting equipment, it shall be arranged so that the control circuit results in the interruption of the current to the motor-compressor.

(b) **Protection of Motor-Compressor Control Apparatus and Branch-Circuit Conductors.** This portion explains that the motor-compressor controller(s), the disconnecting means and branch circuit conductors are to be protected from overcurrent due to motor overload or failure to start. It also gives us the means that we may use to accomplish this and tells us that these means may be the same device or system that protects the motor-compressor as called for in Section 440-52(a).

Exception: As provided in Sections 440-54 and 440-55, motor-compressors and equipment that operate from a 15- or 20-ampere single-phase branch circuit will be permitted.

(1) An overload relay that meets the requirements of (a)(1) of this section.

(2) As provided in Section 440-52(a)(2), the thermal protector applied in accordance with this section and that prevents continuous current in excess of 156 percent of the marked rated-load current or branch-circuit selection current.

(3) A fuse or inverse time circuit breaker that meets the requirements of (a)(3) of this Section.

(4) A protective system that meets the requirements of Section 440-52(a)(4) and that will not permit the current to be over 156 percent of the marked rating of load current or the selection of branch-circuit current.

440-53. Overload Relays—Relays or other devices for motor protection, which are not able to open short circuits, must be protected by fuses or inverse time circuit breakers, and the ratings of these shall be in accordance with Part C—that is, unless approved for group installation of part-winding motors. They shall be marked to indicate the maximum size of the fuse or of the inverse time circuit breaker that is used to protect them.

Exception: Fuses or inverse time circuit breakers shall permit the size marking on the nameplate of the approved equipment in which the overload relay or other overload device is used.

440-54. Motor-Compressors and Equipment on 15- or 20-Ampere Branch Circuit—Not Cord- and Attachment Plug-Connected—As permitted by Article 210,(a) and (b) below cover overload protection for motor-compressors and equipment used on 15- or 20-ampere 120-volt, or 15-ampere 208- or 240-volt single-phase branch circuits.

(a) **Overload Protection.** Motor compressor overload protection shall be selected as required by Section 440-52(a). The controller and motor overload protective device must be approved for the installation of short-circuit and fault-current protective devices. This is for the branch circuit that supplies the equipment.

(b) **Time Delay.** The branch circuit short-circuit or ground-fault protective device (usually fuse or circuit breaker), shall have a sufficient time delay to take care of the starting current.

440-55. Cord- and Attachment Plug-Connected Motor-Compressors and Equipment on 15- or 20-Ampere Branch Circuits—As permitted by Article 210(a), (b), and (c) below cover overload protection for motor-compressors and equipment that are cord- and attachment plug-connected and used on 15- or 20-ampere, 120-volt, or 15-ampere 208- or 240-volt, single-phase branch circuits.

(a) **Overload Protection.** See (a) above in Section 440-54.

(b) **Attachment Plug and Receptacle Rating.** Plug- and cord-connection to the receptacle shall not exceed 20 amperes at 125 volts or 15 amperes at 250 volts.

(c) **Time Delay.** See (b) above in Section 440-54.

G. Provisions for Room Air Conditioners

440-60. General—Electrically energized air conditioners that control both temperature and humidity are covered in Part G. Room air conditioners (which may or may not have provisions for heating) shall be considered to be of the alternating-current type of appliance that may be a window mounted, console, or in-the-wall type of installation located in the room that is to be conditioned and that uses a hermetic refrigerant motor-compressor(s). This Part G covers equipment not over 250 volts and single-phase. This type of equipment may be cord- and attachment plug-connected.

If the room air conditioner is 3-phase or operated at over 250 volts, it is required to be directly connected (not cord- and plug-connected) by methods that were covered in Chapter 3 and will be covered in this Part G.

440-61. Grounding—Sections 250-42, 250-43, and 250-45 cover the grounding of this type of equipment and room air conditioners shall be grounded in accordance with these sections.

440-62. Branch-Circuit Requirements.

(a) **Room Air Conditioner.** If the following conditions are met, a room air conditioner shall be considered a single motor unit when determining its branch-circuit requirements, provided all the following conditions are met:

(1) It is cord- and attachment plug-connected.

(2) Its rating is less than 40 amperes, single-phase and 250 volts.

(3) A nameplate rating of the air conditioner is shown rather than individual currents, and

(4) The rating of the branch-circuit, short-circuit, and ground-fault protective equipment shall not exceed the ampacity of the branch-circuit conductors or of the receptacles from which it is supplied.

As we are aware, a room air conditioner usually has the hermetic-type motor compressor as well as another fan motor or two.

(b) **Where No Other Loads Are Supplied.** If no other loads are supplied, the marked rating of cord- and attachment plug-connection is not permitted to exceed 80 percent of the branch circuit.

(c) **Where Lighting Units or Other Appliances Are Also Supplied.** The marked rating of the air conditioner is not to exceed 50 percent of the rating of the branch-circuit conductors, where lighting or other appliances are supplied from the same branch circuit.

440-63. Disconnecting Means—The room air conditioner operating at 250 volts or less may be cord- and plug- and receptacle-connected for single-phase air conditioners if (1) the manual controls for the air conditioner are readily accessible and within 6 feet of the floor, or (2) if a separate manually operated switch to control the air conditioner is mounted in sight of it.

440-64. Supply Cords—Flexible cords supplying room air conditioners shall be no longer than: (1) 10 feet for a nominal 120-volt rating, or (2) 6 feet for a nominal 208- or 240-volt rating.

ARTICLE 445—GENERATORS

See the *NEC*.

ARTICLE 450—TRANSFORMERS AND TRANSFORMER VAULTS
(Including Secondary Ties)

450-1. Scope—This article applies to the installation of all transformers with the following exceptions:

(1) Current transformers.

(2) Dry-type transformers which are a component part of apparatus and which conform to the requirements of this apparatus.

(3) Transformers for use with X-ray and high-frequency or electrostatic-coating apparatus.

(4) Transformers used with Class 2 and Class 3 circuits that comply with Article 725.

(5) Transformers for sign and outline lighting conforming to Article 600.

(6) Transformers for discharge lighting as covered in Article 410.

(7) Transformers used for power-limited fire protective signaling circuits that comply with Part C of Article 760.

(8) With transformers used for research, development, or testing, whether liquid-filled or dry type, proper safeguards must be provided for unqualified persons coming in contact with high-voltage terminals or conductors that are energized.

As covered in Articles 501 to 503, this article also covers transformers in hazardous (classified) locations.

A. General Provisions

450-2. Definitions.—This article covers as follows:
Transformer. "Transformer" means a single-transformer or polyphase transformer identified by a single nameplate, unless otherwise covered elsewhere in this article. See Section 450-6, for example.

450-3. Overcurrent Protection—In this section, the word "transformer" shall mean either a single transformer or a polyphase bank of two or three single-phase transformers operating together.

(a) **Transformers over 600 Volts, Nominal.**

(1) **Primary and Secondary.** Every transformer of over 600 volts, nominal, shall have primary and secondary overcurrent protective devices rated or set at not over the value shown in Table 450-3 (a) (1). See the *NEC*.

Exception No. 1: If the overcurrent fuse of a circuit breaker does not meet the standard ratings or settings, the next higher rating or setting is to be used.

Exception No. 2: See (a) (2) below.

(2) **Supervised Installations.** If maintenance and supervision is done only by qualified persons who will be monitoring and servicing the transformers and installation, overcurrent protection as provided in (a) (2)a. will be permitted.

(3) **Primary.** The term "primary" is often inferred in the field as being the high side and the term "secondary" as being the low side of the transformer. This is not the case, however. The primary is always the input side of a transformer and the secondary is always the output side. Thus voltage has nothing to do with the terms.

Each transformer is to be protected by an overcurrent device in the primary side. If the overcurrent protection is fuses, they shall be rated at not more than 250 percent of the rated primary current of the transformer. When circuit breakers are used they shall be set at not more than 300 percent of the rated primary current.

This overcurrent protection may be mounted in the vault, or at the transformer if identified for the purpose. It may also be mounted to protect the circuit supplying the transformer. Thus, in the case of a vault, it could be mounted out of doors on a pole, but a disconnecting means will have to be provided in the vault. See Fig. 450-1.

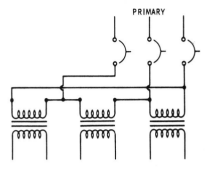

PRIMARY

Fig. 450-1. Overcurrent protection may be at the transformer or in the circuit supplying the transformer.

(b) **Transformers 600 Volts, Nominal, or Less.**

(1) **Primary.** An individual overcurrent device on the primary side of each transformer of 600 volts, nominal, or less shall be installed to protect the transformer. The rating or setting of this overcurrent device shall be rated or set at not more than 125 percent of the rated primary current of the transformer.

Exception No. 1: See Exception No. 1 of 450-3(a) (1).

Exception No. 2: Individual overcurrent devices are not required if the primary circuit overcurrent device provides the protection specified in this section.

Exception No. 3: See (a) (2)b. below.

b. **Primary and Secondary.** If a transformer with more than 600 volts, nominal, has an overcurrent device on the secondary, meets the rating, or is set to open at a value noted in Table 450-3(a) (2)b, or if the transformer is equipped with a thermal overload protection device installed by the manufacturer, overcurrent devices will not be required in the primary connection. The primary feeder overcurrent device shall be rated or set to open at no more than required in Table 450-3(a) (2)b. See the *NEC*.

Author's Note: The inrush current in charging a transformer primary winding wire exceeds the maximum current the transformer is designed to normally carry.

Exception No. 1: If the primary current of a transformer is 9 amperes or more, and 125 percent of this current does not show up in standard rating of fuse or nonadjustable circuit breakers, by Section 240-6, the next higher standard rating may be used. If the primary current is less than 9 amperes, the overcurrent device, if set at not more than 167 percent of the primary current, will be permitted to use the standard rating.

The primary overload protection device may have a setting at not more than 300 percent. This is permitted only where the primary current is less than 2 amperes.

Exception No. 2: If the primary circuit overcurrent protection provided in this section is used, an individual overcurrent device will not be required. This applies to where the feeder or branch circuit originates.

Exception No. 3: See (b) (2) below.

(2) **Primary and Secondary.** A transformer rated at 600 volts, nominal, or less, having an overcurrent device in the secondary that is rated or set at not to exceed 125 percent of the current rating of the secondary of the transformer, shall not be required to have an individual overcurrent device on the primary side, provided the primary feeder overcurrent is rated or set at not more than 250 percent of normal operating current of the primary of the transformer.

Many of these installations will be separately derived systems, which is still not as clear as the author feels it should be. First we have a 10-foot tap rule in Section 240-21 covering transformer secondaries and applicable rules governing same. Then in the same section, we have Exception No. 8, which governs the 15-foot rule. See (e) of Section 240-21. In Exception No. 2, covering the 10-foot tap rule, a note states: Lighting and branch-circuit panelboards are covered in Section 384-16(a). This requires secondary overcurrent devices. Consider all of these statements in making your decision on overcurrent secondary devices.

If a transformer of 600 volts, nominal, or less has been equipped with thermal overload protection by the manufacturer and is arranged to disconnect the primary current, the transformer primary will not be required to have an individual overcurrent device, provided that the feeder overcurrent device is rated or set at a current value of not over six times the rated current for the transformer with an impedance of not over 6 percent. If the transformer has an impedance rating of more than 6 percent but not over 10 percent, the rating of the overcurrent shall not be over four times the load of the rated current of the transformer.

There is more inrush current upon energizing a transformer, with lower impedance transformers.

Exception: If the secondary current rating of a transformer is 9 amperes or more and if 125 percent of the full-load current does not correspond to the rating of a fuse or a nonadjustable circuit breaker, you may use the higher standard rating described in Section 240-6.

When the secondary current is less than 9 amperes, and an overcurrent device of the circuit is not rated over 167 percent of this full-load current rating, the overcurrent device may be used.

(c) **Potential (Voltage) Transformers.** When installed indoors or enclosed, potential transformers are to be protected by primary fuses. To the author, it is just good practice to install protection for all potential transformers.

Note: The *NEC* refers you to Section 384-22.

450-4. Autotransformers 600 Volts, Nominal, or Less.

(a) **Overcurrent Protection.** Potential transformers of 600 volts or less must have individual overcurrent devices installed, and so must each ungrounded conductor on the input side of the autotransformer. These overcurrent devices shall be set at not more than 125 percent of the full-load current of the autotransformer. An overcurrent device is not to be installed in the shunt winding of an autotranformer (the winding that is common to both the primary and secondary circuits). See Diagram 450-54 in the *NEC*.

Exception: If the input rating of the current to the autotransformer is 9 amperes or more, and if 125 percent of this current does not meet the standard ratings for fuses and nonadjustable circuit breakers as covered in Section 240-6, the next higher standard rating will be permitted. If the rating of the input current to an autotransformer is less than 9 amperes, the overcurrent device rating or setting shall be not more than 167 percent of the input current rating for a full-load current.

(b) **Transformer Field-Connected as an Autotransformer.** An autotransformer shall be identified as such and for the use at higher voltage if the autotransformer is field-connected.

Note: The use of autotransformers is covered in Section 210-9.

450-5. Grounding Autotransformers—Many electrical systems are not grounded, especially older systems of 600 volts or less and many 2400-, 4800-, and 6900-volt systems. Also when it is desired to ground ungrounded existing delta systems, grounding autotransformers may be used to obtain a neutral. Grounding autotransformers such as the zigzag type may be used. The type most generally used is the 3 ø zigzag type transformer with no secondary winding. See Fig. 450-2 on page 432 for the schematic connections of such an autotransformer.

The impedance of the autotransformer to 3 ø currents is high so that there is no fault on the systems; only a small magnetizing current flows in the transformer winding. The transformer impedance to ground current, however, is low so that it allows high ground current to flow. The trans-

LINE LEADS

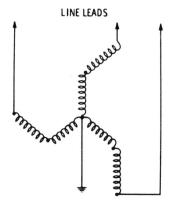

Fig. 450-2. Schematic diagram of a 3 φ zigzag grounding autotransformer.

former divides the ground current into three equal components; these currents are in phase with each other and flow in the three windings of the grounding autotransformer.

Due to the direction of the actual windings this tends to have equal division of the three lines and accounts for the low impedance of the transformer to ground currents. The above will give an idea of the operation and results of what Section 450-4 is covering.

Grounding autotransformers are to be zigzag or T-connected transformers connected to 3-phase, 3-wire systems that are ungrounded, the purpose of which is creating a 3-phase, 4-wire distribution system that will provide a neutral reference for grounding purposes. This kind of system shall have continuous phase currents and neutral current ratings.

Note: The current and the phase of an autotransformer shall be one third of the neutral current.

(a) **Three-Phase, 4-Wire System.** When a 3-phase, 3-wire autotransformer system is converted to a 3-phase, 4-wire system, the following conditions shall be met:

(1) **Connections.** The ungrounded phase conductors shall be connected directly and shall not be switched or provided with overcurrent protection that is independent of the main switch with a common-trip overcurrent protection for the 3-phase, 4-wire system.

(2) **Overcurrent Protection.** A device to provide sensing of overcurrent and a phase or phases is permitted if it causes a main switch or common-trip overcurrent protection, which was covered in (a) (1) above, to open should the load on the transformer reach or exceed 125 percent of a full-load continuous current per phase or neutral rating. The sensing device may be used to delay tripping for temporary overloads that are being sensed. The purpose of

this is to allow proper operation of branch or feeder protection in the 4-wire system.

(3) **Transformer Fault Sensing.** A sensing device for faults that will cause the opening of a main switch or common tripping of the overcurrent device on the 3-phase, 4-wire side of the system is to be provided to protect against single phasing or internal faults.

Note: You can accomplish this by using two subtractive-connected donut-type current transformers so installed that they sense and signal any unbalanced currents in the line current of 50 percent or more of the rated current of the autotransformer.

(4) **Rating.** The neutral current rating on an autotransformer system or 4-wire shall be sufficient to handle the unbalanced load.

(b) **Ground Reference for Fault Protection Devices.** The following requirements will be required where a grounding autotransformer is used to make available the intensity of ground-fault current for a ground-fault protective device on an ungrounded 3-phase, 3-wire system.

(1) **Rating.** The rating of the ground-fault autotransformer is to have continuous neutral current rating to cover specified ground-fault current.

(2) **Overcurrent Protection.** An overcurrent protection device of sufficient short-circuit rating to instantaneously open all ungrounded conductors when it operates shall be applied to the grounding transformer branch circuit and rated at a current not exceeding 125 percent of the load rating of autotransformers or 42 percent of the continuous current rating of any operated in the series-connected device and the neutral of the autotransformer connection. Delayed tripping will be permitted for temporary overcurrents where the proper operation of the ground tripping device that is responsible for tripping devices on the main system will be permitted, but the values shall not exceed the short-time rating of either the grounding autotransformer or any devices connected in series with a neutral connection.

(c) **Ground Reference for Damping Transitory Overvoltages.** Grounding is always advantageous in damping and limiting transitory overvoltages. Autotransformers used for this purpose shall be rated and connected in accordance with (a) (1) above.

450-6. Secondary Ties—A secondary tie is a circuit operating at 600 volts, nominal, or less connected between two phases and connecting two power sources or supplies, e.g. the secondary for two transformers. The connections will be permitted to use one or more conductors per phase.

Note: The word "transformer" used in this section, means either a single transformer or transformers operated as a bank.

This should not be confused with the definition of transformer given in Section 450-2.

(a) **Tie Circuits.** Article 240 covers overcurrent protection in general, and tie circuits shall be provided with overcurrent protection at each end as provided in Article 240.

Exceptions are under the conditions described in Section 450-6 (a)(1) and (a)(2), and in these cases the overcurrent protection may be in accordance with Section 450-6(a)(3).

(1) **Loads at Transformer Supply Points Only.** Where transformers are tied together (parallel) and connected by tie conductors that do not have overcurrent protection as per Article 240, the ampacity of the ties (connecting conductors) shall not be less than 67 percent of the rated secondary current of the largest transformer in the tie circuit. This applies where the loads are at the transformer supply points.

The paralleling of transformers is rather common, but great care should be taken to assure that the transformers are similar in all characteristics. If they are not, one transformer will attempt to take all the load. If the transformers are of equal capacity and similar characteristics, they would theoretically each take 50 percent of the load. The 67 percent allows for any difference in transformer sizes. See Fig. 450-3.

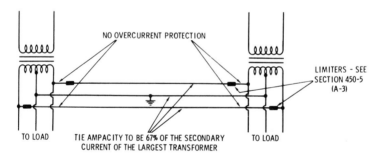

Fig. 450-3. Secondary ties.

(2) **Loads Connected Between Transformer Supply Points.** If Article 240 is not used where load is connected to the tie points between the supply points to the transformer, and overcurrent protection has not been provided as in the article stated above, the ampacity rating of the ties is to be not less than 100 percent current rating of the largest transformer connected in the secondary tie system. See (a)(4) below.

(3) **Tie Circuit Protection.** In Sections 450-6(a)(1) and (a)(2), both ends of each tie connection shall be equipped with a protective

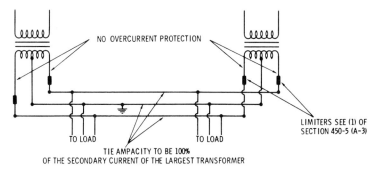

NO OVERCURRENT PROTECTION

LIMITERS SEE (1) OF
SECTION 450-5 (A-3)

TO LOAD   TO LOAD

TIE AMPACITY TO BE 100%
OF THE SECONDARY CURRENT OF THE LARGEST TRANSFORMER

Fig. 450-4.   Loads connected between transformer supply points.

device which will open at a predetermined temperature of the
tie conductor. This is to prevent damage to the tie conductor and
its insulation, and may consist of: (1) A limiter, which is a fusible
link cable connector (not a common fuse) designed for the insulation, conductor material, etc., on the tie conductors (ordinarily
a copper link enclosed in a protective covering); (2) a circuit breaker
actuated by devices having comparable characteristics to the above.
See Figs. 450-3 and 450-4.

(4) **Interconnection of Phase Conductors Between Transformer Supply Points.** When the tie consists of more than one conductor per
phase, the conductors of each phase shall be interconnected so
that a point of load supply will be established. Also, the protection
that was specified in (a)(3) above shall be required in each tie
conductor at this point.

Exception: Loads are permitted to be connected to each conductor of a paralleled conductor tie, but it is not required to
interconnect the conductors from each phase, or, without protection specified in (a)(3) above, at points for the load connection,
provided the tie conductors of each phase have a combined ampacity of not less than 133 percent of the rating of the secondary
current using the load of the largest transformer for this purpose
that is connected to the tie system. The total load of these taps
is not to exceed the rated current of the largest transformer; the
loads must be equally divided on each phase and on the individual
conductors of each phase as far as practical.

The use of multiple conductors on each phase and the requirement that loads do not have to tap both of the multiple conductors
of the same phase could possibly set up unbalanced currents in
the multiple conductors on the the same phase. This is taken care
of in the requirements that the combined capacity of the multiple
conductors on the same phase be rated at 133 percent of the

secondary current of the largest transformer. Limiters are necessary at the tap or connections to the transformers that are tied
together.

(5) **Tie Circuit Control.** If the operating voltage of secondary ties
exceeds 150 volts to ground, there shall be a switch ahead of the
limiters and tie conductors which will de-energize the tie conductors and the limiters. This switch shall meet the following
conditions: (1) the current rating of the switch shall not be less
than the current rating of the conductors connected to the switch;
(2) the switch shall be capable of opening its rated current; and
(3) the switch shall not open under the magnetic forces resulting
from short-circuit current.

(b) **Overcurrent Protection for Secondary Connections.** When secondary ties from transformers are used, there shall be an overcurrent
device in the secondary of each transformer that is rated or set at not
more than 250 percent of the rated secondary current of the transformer. In addition, there shall be a circuit breaker actuated by a
reverse-current relay, the breaker to be set at not more than the
rated secondary current of the transformer. The overcurrent protection takes care of overloads and shorts, while the reverse-current
relay and circuit breaker takes care of any reversal of current flow
into the transformer.

450-7. Parallel Operation—Section 450-6 covered ties for transformer
connections which, in essence, is a form of paralleling. However, this Section covers the actual paralleling of transformers. Paralleled transformers
may be switched as a unit provided that the overcurrent protection meets
the requirements of Section 450-3(a)(1) or 450-3(b)(2).

Anyone working with paralleled transformers or transformer tie circuits
should be extremely cautious that there are no feedbacks or other conditions
which would affect safety. In order to secure a balance of current between
paralleled transformers, all transformers should have characteristics that
are very much alike, such as voltage, impedance, etc. These pertinent facts
may be obtained from the manufacturer of the transformers.

450-8. Guarding—Transformers shall be guarded as follows:

(a) **Mechanical Protection.** When exposed to physical damage, transformers shall be protected to minimize damage from external causes.

(b) **Case or Enclosure.** Dry-type transformers are to be mounted in
noncombustible and moisture-resistant enclosures. Also, provision
must be made to prevent the accidental insertion of foreign material
from the outside into the enclosure.

(c) **Exposed Live Parts.** Sections 110-17 and 110-34 will apply to live
parts of transformers operating at 600 volts or less. Article 710 covers
transformers operating at voltages higher than 600 volts.

(d) **Voltage Warning.** Signs indicating the voltage of live exposed parts of transformers, or other suitable markings, shall be used in areas where transformers are located.

450-9. Ventilation—The ventilation shall be adequate to prevent a transformer temperature in excess of the values prescribed in ANSI/IEEE C57.12.00-1980.

450-10. Grounding—See the *NEC*.

450-11. Marking—Nameplates with the following information shall be provided for transformers: name of manufacturer; rated kilovolt-amperes; frequency; primary voltage; secondary voltage; amount and kind of insulating liquid (where used); impedance of transformers 25 kVA and larger.

The nameplate of each dry-type transformer shall include the temperature class for the insulation system.

450-12. Terminal Wiring Space—The bending space of fixed terminals of transformers of 600 volts or less, including terminals for both load and line connections, shall meet the specification as required in Section 373-6. The wiring space is covered in Table 370-6(b).

450-13. Location—Maintenance and inspection of transformers and transformer vaults shall be readily accessible to qualified personnel.

Exception No. 1: Dry transformers of 600 volts, nominal, or less are not required to be readily accessible if located in the open, on walls, columns, or structures.

This requirement has never been enforced throughout the country simply because transformers where readily accessible have in many cases been damaged. It would be far better to elevate dry-type transformers when they are installed. This would not cause any further problems where vaults are considered or required.

Exception No. 2: See the *NEC*. This clarifies the installation of dry-type transformers above drop-ceilings, where the hollow space is fire-resistant. The main requirement is that the ventilation must be sufficient to maintain temperatures not in excess of those prescribed in NFPA 251-1985. A limitation of 50 kVA and 600 volts is put on transformers thus installed.

It is impossible to cover everything pertaining to transformer locations in this section, so oil-insulated transformers are found in Sections 450-26, 450-27, and 450-71. Dry-type transformers are covered in Section 450-21, and askarel-insulated transformers in Section 450-25.

Note: The *NEC* refers you to ANSI/ASTM E119-83, and Fire Test of Building Construction and Materials, NFPA 251-1985.

Note: The location of different type transformers is covered in Part B of this article. Transformer vaults are covered in Section 450-41.

B. Specific Provision Applicable to Different Types of Transformer

450-21. Dry-Type Transformers Installed Indoors.

(a) **Not Over 112 ½ kVA.** Dry-type transformers of not over 112 ½ kVA that are mounted indoors shall be mounted at least 12 inches from combustible material unless there is a fire-resistant, heat-insulating barrier between the transformer and the wall, or unless the transformer has a rating of not over 600 volts, and, except for ventilation openings, is completely enclosed.

(b) **Over 112 ½ kVA.** Dry-type transformers of over 112 ½ kVA are to be installed in a fire-resistant room.

Exception No. 1 to (b): When the rating of a transformer is 80°C or higher and there is a fire-resistant barrier separating the transformer from combustible materials and the separation is by a fire-resistant, heat-insulating material, or is installed not less than 6 feet horizontally and 12 feet vertically from combustible material.

Exception No. 2 to (b): When the rise of a transformer is 80°C or higher rated, if the transformer is of ventilated construction and enclosed.

(c) **Over 35,000 Volts.** Transformers operating at 35,000 volts or higher must comply with Part C of this article covering installation in volts.

450-22. Dry-Type Transformers Installed Outdoors—Only weatherproof enclosures shall be used on transformers installed out of doors.

If the transformer exceeds 112 ½ kVA, it shall not be located within 12 inches of combustible materials in buildings.

450-23. Less-Flammable Liquid-Insulated Transformers—When liquid that is less flammable is used for insulation in transformers and listed as such, they shall be permitted to be installed without being in a vault in Types I and II buildings and in areas that contain no combustible materials, provided arrangements are made for a liquid-tight area, so that in case of leakage the liquid is confined to this area. Liquid shall have a fire point that is 300°C or more, and the installation shall comply with all restrictions provided for in the listing of the liquid. Such indoor transformers not meeting the liquid listing, or installed in other than Types I and II buildings, or in areas where combustible materials are stored, (1) will be required to have a fire-extinguishing system and a liquid confinement area, or (2) are to be installed in a vault complying with Part C of this article.

When transformers rated over 35,000 volts are to be installed indoors, a vault for this must be provided.

Section 450-27 covers safeguards for transformers installed out of doors, and they shall comply with the requirements thereof.

Note: In NFPA 220-1985 (ANSI) "Noncombustible" refers to Types I and II building construction, and the materials defined in the building are found in this NFPA code.

Note: "Listing" was defined in Article 100 of the *NEC*.

450-24. Nonflammable Fluid-Insulated Transformers—When transformers are filled for insulating with a dielectric fluid and this fluid is identified or listed as nonflammable, they shall be permitted to be installed indoors or out of doors. If over 35,000 volts when installed indoors, they must be installed in a vault. The dielectric fluid that is nonflammable for the purpose of this section is one that does not have a flash point or fire point and is not flammable in air.

450-25. Askarel-Insulated Transformers Installed Indoors—If askarel-insulated transformers are installed indoors and have a rating of over 25 kVA, they must be manufactured with a pressure relief vent, and if the area is poorly ventilated there must be other means provided for absorbing gases that would be generated by arcing inside the transformer case. The pressure-relief valve may also be connected to a chimney or other flue to carry the gases formed out of the building. Askarel-insulated transformers over 35,000 volts shall be installed in a vault.

Both askarel and the fumes from same are extremely toxic, so great care must be taken where askarel is used.

450-26. Oil-Insulated Transformers Installed Indoors—All oil-insulated transformers installed indoors are to be in vaults, with the following exceptions:

(1) **Not Over 112½ kVA Total Capacity.** The specifications for vaults in Part C of this article may be modified so that the vault may be constructed of reinforced concrete not less than 4 inches thick.

(2) **Not Over 600 Volts.** A vault is not necessary when the transformer rating is 600 volts or less, if the following conditions are met: Proper means are provided to prevent a transformer-oil fire from igniting other materials, and if the total transformer capacity in this location does not exceed 10 kVA if the section of the building in which they are installed is classified as combustible, or if the total transformer capacity is from 10 to 75 kVA and the surrounding structure is classified as fire-resistant.

(3) **Furnace Transformers.** Electric-furnace transformers that do not exceed 75 kVA need not be installed in a vault if the building or room is of fire-resistant construction and if a suitable drain or other means is provided for preventing an oil fire from spreading to combustible materials.

(4) **Detached Buildings.** A building detached from other buildings— that is, an entirely separate building or one which may be defined

as such by proper walls, etc.—may be used for transformers if neither the building nor its contents constitute a fire hazard to any other building or property, and the building where the transformer is located is used only to supply electric service and has an interior that is accessible only to qualified persons.

(5) **Oil Transformers without a Vault.** Oil-insulated transformers without a vault are permitted for portable or mobile surface mining equipment (such as electric excavators) provided each of the following conditions is met:

    a. Provision must be made for draining leaking fluid to the ground.

    b. Safeguards shall be used for the protection of persons.

    c. A steel barrier of ¼ inch minimum is provided to protect personnel.

450-27. Oil-Insulated Transformers Installed Outdoors—Oil-insulated transformers that are installed outdoors shall be installed so that no hazard to combustible materials, combustible buildings and parts of buildings, fire escapes, and door and window openings will exist in case of fire. These transformers may also be attached to or adjacent to buildings or combustible materials if precautions are taken to prevent fire hazards to the buildings or combustible materials. The following steps are recognized.

Some safeguards for hazards from transformer installations are as follows: space separations, automatic water spray stystems, fire-resistant barriers, and enclosures that will confine oil from a rupture in the transformer tank. One or more of these safeguards shall be used, depending upon the degree of hazard involved.

The enclosure for oil from a rupture may consist of fire-resistant dikes, curbed areas or basins, or trenches filled with porous crushed stone. A basin made of concrete and filled with coarse crushed stone will keep oil from seeping into the ground into underground water. Where the quantity of oil involved is such that removal of the oil is important, oil enclosures shall be provided with trap drains.

Note: For transformers mounted on poles, see the National Electrical Safety Code, ANSI C2-1984.

450-28. Modification of Transformers—If transformers are modified in existing installations in a way that changes the type of the transformer in any respect to Part B of this article, said transformer shall be marked to show the type of insulating liquid installed and what modifications were made to the transformer. All modifications shall comply with the requirements of that type of transformer.

C. Transformer Vaults

450-41. Location—Where practical, transformer vaults shall be located so that they will be ventilated to the outside air without the use of flues or ducts.

450-42. Walls, Roof and Floor—Reference is made in the fine print note to this section to standards covering building materials, construction, etc.

Transformer vaults shall have roofs and walls constructed of material adequate for structural conditions and with a minimum fire resistance of 3 hours. Floors in contact with the earth of concrete shall be less not than 4 inches thick, but if the floor is mounted above other space below, the structural strength of the floor shall be adequate to handle the load placed on it, and it shall have a minimum of 3 hours' fire resistance.

Note: NFPA 251-85 and ANSI/ASTM E119-83 contain added information for fire test of building materials.

Note: A typical 3-hour construction consists of 6 inches of reinforced concrete.

Exception: One-hour fire rating construction may be used, if the transformers are protected by automatic sprinklers, water spray, carbon dioxide, or halon.

450-43. Doorways

The following covers the protection of doorways and vault doorways.

(a) **Type of Door.** Doors for vaults are covered in the NFPA Standard for the Installation of Fire Doors and Windows, No. 80, and this is referenced in the fine print note. They shall be rated at 3 hours and be tight fitting, and the inspection authority may require a door on each side of the wall.

See Exception to Section 450-42.

(b) **Sills.** The door shall not extend completely to the floor, but a sill shall be provided which is high enough to take care of the oil from the largest transformer in the vault. In no case shall this door sill be less than 4 inches high.

(c) **Locks.** All doors shall be provided with locks which shall be kept locked so that access will be to qualified persons only. Latches and locks shall be such that they are readily opened from the inside of the vault. Many authorities require crash bars.

450-45. Ventilation Openings—When required by Section 450-8, openings for ventilation shall be provided as follows:

(a) **Location.** Openings used for ventilation of vaults shall be kept as far away as possible from doors, windows, and combustible material.

(b) **Arrangement.** Where vaults are ventilated by a natural circulation of air, the total area of the openings for ventilation may be divided, with half of the area at the floor level and the remainder in one or more openings in the roof or near the ceiling. All of the area required for ventilation may be supplied by one or more openings near or in the roof.

(c) **Size.** When vaults are ventilated directly to the outdoor area, and ducts or flues are not used, the net area of the ventilation openings (after deducting the area that the screen, gratings, or louvres occupy) shall not be less than 3 square inches per kVA of transformer capacity in the vault. For any vault with a transformer capacity of less than 50 kVA, the area of the ventilation opening shall not be less than 1 square foot.

(d) **Covering.** The covering for ventilation openings in vaults is left up to the inspection authority for the final decision, but they shall be covered with durable gratings, screens, or louvres. The final decision will be made to avoid unsafe conditions.

(e) **Dampers.** Dampers that possess a standard fire rating of not less 1½ hours shall be provided with automatic closing dampers that will respond to a vault fire.

Note: You are referred in the *NEC* to ANSI/UL 555-1972 for the standard for fire dampers.

(f) **Ducts.** Ventilating ducts are to be made of fire-resistant material.

When foreign systems cannot be avoided, access to them shall be other than the entry into the vault. Any leaks or other malfunction of the foreign systems shall not cause damage to the transformers and their equipment.

450-46. Drainage—If vaults have more than 100 kVA transformer capacity, they shall be provided with a drain or other means that will carry off any accumulation of water or oil that might accumulate in the vault, unless this is impracticable. The floor shall be sloped enough to aid in the drainage.

450-47. Water Pipes and Accessories—Systems foreign to the electrical system, such as pipes and ducts, shall not enter or pass through a transformer vault. Piping or other facilities for fire protection or cooling of transformers are not to be considered as being foreign to the electric system.

450-48. Storage in Vaults—Transformer vaults are just what the term implies, and are not to be used for material storage. This means that transformer vaults are only transformer vaults and not warehouses or storage areas. The vault is to be kept clear at all times—there is high voltage involved and safety is a very important factor.

ARTICLE 460—CAPACITORS

460-1. Scope—The installation of capacitors on electric circuits is covered in this article.

Surge capacitors are excluded from these requirements when they are a part of other apparatus and conform to the application for use on this apparatus.

Capacitors in hazardous (classified) locations are included in this article for installation therein, with some modification covered by Article 501 through 503.

460-2. Enclosing and Guarding.

(a) **Containing More than 3 Gallons of Flammable Liquid.** Capacitors shall be enclosed in vaults or outdoor fenced enclosures complying with Article 710 if they contain more than 3 gallons of flammable liquid.

(b) **Accidental Contact.** Capacitors are to be enclosed or properly guarded to keep persons from coming into contact with them or from bringing conductive materials in contact with them. This covers all energized parts, terminals, or buses associated with them.

Where capacitors are installed where they are accessible to authorized and qualified personnel, the above precautions may be omitted.

Exception: When accessible to qualified persons only, no additional guarding of the enclosures will be required.

A. 600 Volts, Nominal, and Under

460-6. Drainage of Stored Charge—Capacitors store up a charge of electricity and the larger sizes may be lethal. Therefore, it is necessary to provide some means of draining off this charge.

(a) **Time of Discharge.** The plates of the capacitor retain a charge of voltage. This is called residual charge, and it shall be reduced to 50 volts, nominal, or less. This shall occur in one minute after the capacitor has been disconnected from the source of supply.

(b) **Means of Discharge.** The means of discharging a capacitor (such as a resistor) may be permanently connected to the terminals of the capacitor, or the disconnecting means to the capacitor may be so arranged that, upon opening, the capacitor is automatically connected to some discharging means. A manual discharging means is prohibited. The windings of transformers, motors, or other equipment that are directly connected to capacitors without a switch will act as the discharging means for the capacitor.

460-8. Conductors.

(a) **Ampacity.** The two statements in this part are not to be confused. The ampacity of conductors to capacitors shall not be less than 135 percent of the rated current of the capacitor; power factor enters into this rating as the capacitors have a leading power factor. The ampacity of the conductors connecting the capacitor to the terminals of a motor or to motor circuit conductors shall not be less than one-third the ampacity of the motor circuit conductors, and not less than 135 percent of the rated current capacity of the capacitor.

(b) **Overcurrent Protection.**

(1) Each ungrounded conductor to each capacitor shall be provided with an overcurrent device.

Exception: When a capacitor is connected to the load side of a motor overcurrent protection device, a separate overcurrent device is not required for the capacitor.

(2) The overcurrent device protecting the capacitor shall be of as low an amperage as possible.

(c) **Disconnecting Means.**

(1) Each ungrounded conductor to each capacitor shall have a means of disconnecting.

Exception. A separate overcurrent device shall not be required for a capacitor connected on the load side of a motor overload protective device.

(2) All ungrounded conductors to capacitors shall be opened at the same time.

(3) The capacitors may be disconnected by their disconnecting means as a normal operating procedure.

(4) The disconnecting means shall have a rating not less than 135 percent of the capacitor rated current.

460-9. Rating or Setting of the Motor, Overload Device—Due to the fact that a capacitor connected to a motor through the motor overload devices (running protection devices), and also due to the fact that a capacitor in a motor circuit corrects the lagging power factor of the motor, the current to the motor will be less than that of the same motor if it did not have capacitors for power-factor correction.

Use Section 430-32 for calculating the rating or setting of the motor overload devices, but the actual value of current drawn by the motor must be used instead of the nameplate current, which will be less in value.

Section 430-22 applies to the rating of the conductors. This is not derated because of the capacitor but is used as if the capacitor were not in the circuit.

460-10. Grounding—See the *NEC*.

460-12. Marking—See the *NEC*

B. Over 600 Volts, Nominal

460-24. Switching.

(a) **Load Current.** The switches for capacitors shall be group-operated, and shall be capable of:

(1) Continuously carrying the current of the capacitor at 135 percent of the current rating of the capacitor installation.

(2) Interrupting the maximum continuous load current of each capacitor, capacitor bank, or capacitor installation when switched as a unit.

(3) Withstanding the inrush current, not only of one capacitor, but including currents contributed from adjacent capacitor installations.

(4) Carrying fault currents that occur on the capacitor side of the switch.

(b) **Isolation.**

(1) All sources of voltage to each capacitor, capacitor bank, or capacitor installation shall have a means installed to isolate sources of voltage from any of these that will be removed from service as a unit.

(2) The isolating means is required to have a gap that is visible in the electric circuit and is also adequate for the operating voltage.

(3) Isolating or disconnecting means for capacitors (that do not have the load interrupting rating on the nameplate) are required to be interlocked with the load interrupting device, or they shall be permanently marked with signs that are prominently displayed as required by Section 710-22. This is to prevent switching of load current.

(c) **Additional Requirements for Series Capacitors.** The switching sequence shall be done in a proper manner by one of the following: (1) isolating and bypass switches that are mechanically sequenced; (2) interlocks; or (3) the operating sequence shall be visibly displayed giving the procedures, and this shall be installed at the location of the switching.

460-25. Overcurrent Protection.

(a) **Provided to Detect and Interrupt Fault Current.** There shall be provided a means of detecting and interrupting fault currents, which may cause dangerous pressure within an individual capacitor.

(b) **Single-Phase or Multiphase Devices.** You may use either single-phase or multiphase devices for this purpose.

(c) **Protected Individually or in Groups.** Capacitors may be protected either singly or in groups.

(d) **Protective Devices Rated or Adjusted.** Capacitors or capacitor equipment shall have the protective devices either rated or adjusted so that they will operate within the safety zone limits for individual capacitors.

Exception: If the rating or adjustment of the protective devices is within the limits of Zones 1 or 2, it is required that the capacitors be isolated or enclosed.

Under no condition shall the maximum limits of Zone 2 be exceeded by the protective devices.

Note: The definition of Zones 1 and 2 may be found in the pamphlet standard for Shunt Power Capacitors, ANSI/IEEE 18-1980.

460-26. Indentification—There shall be a permanent nameplate on the capacitor giving the maker's name, rated voltage, frequency, kilovar or amperes, number of phases, number of gallons of liquid contained therein, and, if the liquid is flammable, whether listed as flammable.

460-27. Grounding—The grounding of capacitor neutrals and cases, if grounded, shall meet the grounding requirements of Article 250. Except where the capacitors are supported on a structure which is not intended to be grounded.

460-28. Means for Discharge.

(a) **Means to Reduce the Residual Voltage.** Capacitors hold a dangerous amount of electrical energy so a means shall be provided to reduce the stored energy of the capacitor to 50 volts or less within 5 minutes after the capacitor is disconnected from the power source.

(b) **Connection to Terminals.** The discharging as required in (a) may be accomplished by means of a permanently connected discharge circuit to the terminals of the capacitor or an automatic means of connection to the terminals of the capacitor bank may be used which immediately connects to the terminals after the disconnection of the capacitor bank from the source of supply.

The requirements of (a) above must be met if the windings of motors or other equipment are connected to capacitors without a switching device.

ARTICLE 470—RESISTORS AND REACTORS

For Rheostats, see Section 430-82.

A. 600 Volts, Nominal, and Under

See the *NEC*.

B. Over 600 Volts, Nominal

See the *NEC*.

ARTICLE 480—STORAGE BATTERIES

See the *NEC*.

CHAPTER 5

Special Occupancies

Articles 500 through 517 refer to hazardous areas and should be well understood by anyone concerned with the wiring in such locations. Such areas are dangerous from many standpoints and each has its own problems which require special methods for taking care of the electrical systems installed in these places.

ARTICLE 500—HAZARDOUS (CLASSIFIED) LOCATIONS

500-1. Scope—Articles 500 Through 503—It is the responsibility of the Code-enforcing authority to judge whether or not areas come under Articles 500 through 503 as indicated by the classifications indicated in these articles. These articles cover locations where fire or explosive hazards may exist to the following: flammable gases, vapors, liquids, combustible dusts, ignitible fibers, or flyings.

500-2. Location and General Requirements—Locations are classified as Class I, Class II, or Class III. The location is classified according to the properties and materials therein, such as flammable vapors, liquids, or gases, or combustible dust or fibers that may be present and could cause flammable concentrations, or the quantity of such. Where pyrophoric material are the only materials used or handled, they are not to be classified.

Note: A pyrophoric material is one that is capable of igniting spontaneously when exposed to air.

The intent is that each room, section, or area (including motor and generator rooms and rooms for enclosure of control equipment) shall be individually considered in determining the classification suitable for the conditions.

In judging of these areas and what equipment is allowable therein, the inspection authority refers to the Underwriter's Laboratories listings for the equipment that is installed in each area. All other wiring methods of the

Code are applicable except as modified by these articles covering hazardous areas.

The following terms will appear often; they are: approved; dustproof; dust-ignitionproof; dusttight; and explosionproof apparatus. Refer to Article 100 in the *NEC* for the definitions of these terms, except "dust-ignition proof," which is defined in Section 502-1.

Equipment and associated wiring approved as intrinsically safe may be installed in any hazardous location for which it is approved, and the provisions of Article 500-517 need not apply to such installation. Intrinsically safe equipment and wiring are incapable of releasing sufficient electrical energy under normal and abnormal conditions to cause ignition of a specific hazardous atmospheric mixture. Abnormal conditions will include accidental damage to any part of the equipment or wiring, insulation or other failure of electrical components, application of overvoltage, adjustment and maintenance operations, and other similar conditions.

In designing the wiring and selecting the equipment to use in a hazardous location, less expensive materials and equipment can often be used by relocation or by adequate ventilation, forced or otherwise. Anyone doing installation in hazardous areas, but more especially inspectors, should become familiar with other Codes published by the National Fire Protection Association, such as: Flammable and Combustible Liquids Code, NFPA 30-1984; Dry Cleaning Plants, NFPA 32-1975; Manufacture of Organic Coatings, NFPA 35-1982 (ANSI); Solvent Extraction Plants, NFPA 36-1985 (ANSI); Storage and Handling of Liquefied Petroleum Gases, NFPA 58-1986; Storage and Handling of Liquid Petroleum Gases at Utility Gas Plants, NFPA 59-1984; Classification of I Hazardous Locations for Electrical Installation in Chemical Plants, NFPA 497A-1986 (ANSI).

All references in the fine print notes intend to direct users of the Code to other NFPA Codes and standards. See *NEC* Section 110-1.

Designers and inspectors will find many items pertaining to the subjects covered in this chapter in many other of the NFPA Codes. These Codes will often assist in arriving at many decisions which must be made, especially by the inspector.

For electrical installations in hazardous areas where it is necessary to use threaded rigid metal conduit, the Code requires that the joints be made up wrenchtight—this applies to threaded joints and connections. Please note that the Code states wrenchtight and not pliertight. In addition, standard conduit dies which provide a taper of ¾-inch taper per foot shall be used. All of this amounts to the fact that, even though the proper equipment is used and the wiring methods are as required, a loose threaded connection, when subject to fault current, may spark and cause an explosion. Where it is impossible to make a proper threaded connection, the joint shall be bonded with a bonding jumper.

Note: Static electrical hazards are potentially very dangerous in some hazardous locations. See Recommended Practice on Static Electricity, NFPA 77-1983 (ANSI) for coverage.

Note: The standard electrical classification for laboratories using chemicals may be found in NFPA 45-1982.

500-3. Special Precaution—The intent of Articles 500 and 503 is that more than ordinary precaution must be exercised in the construction of equipment and the installation and maintenance of the entire wiring system for safe operation. This becomes the responsibility of all concerned in the matter.

The atmospheric mixtures of various gases, vapors, and dusts, and the hazard involved, depends upon the concentrations, temperatures, and many other things. It is impossible to cover all these variables here, but they may be found in the various NFPA Codes.

Note 1: Inspection authorities and users must use more than ordinary care in the installation or maintenance of wiring in hazardous conditions.

Note 2: Explosive conditions of gas vapors or dust vary greatly with specific materials that are involved in the determination of maximum pressure of explosion, the maximum distances for safe clearances between clamp joints in an enclosure, and the minimum temperature of explosive conditions in the atmospheric mixture with the gases that refers to Class I areas. Referring to Class II locations, including Groups E, F, and G, the classification involves the tightness of the joints of assembly and shaft openings to prevent entrance of dust in the dust-ignition-proof enclosure, the blanketing effect of layers of dust on the equipment that may cause overheating, electrical conductivity of the dust, and the ignition temperature of the dust. It is necessary, therefore, that equipment be approved not only for the class, but also for the specific group of the gas, vapor, or dust that will be present.

Note 3: Low ambient temperatures require special consideration. It may not be necessary to use explosionproof or dusttight equipment when temperatures are lower than $-25°$ C or $-13°$ F, but equipment must be suitable for low-temperature service. However, care must be taken, because if the ambient temperature rises, the temperature of flammable concentrations of vapors may not exist in the location that is classified Class I, Division I when the ambient temperature is normal.

Note 4: For testing purposes, approval, and the classification of areas, various air mixtures (not including oxygen-enriched) are grouped according to their characteristics, and facilities have been available for the testing of the equipment and approval for use in the following atmospheric groups. See the *NEC* for Notes 5 through 18.

(a) **Approval for Class and Properties.** Equipment in hazardous locations must be approved not only for the class of location in which it is to be used, but also for the explosive, combustible, and ignitible properties of the particular items involved, such as gas, vapor, dust, fiber, or flyings. In addition, Class I equipment is not permitted to have any surfaces that are exposed to the igniting temperature of the specific gas or vapor. Later you will find that lighting and painting booths require special installation. It is required that Class II equipment shall not have a higher temperature than that specified in Section 500-3(d). For Class III equipment, the maximum surface temperature specified by Section 503-1 shall not be exceeded.

When equipment is approved for Division 1 locations, permission is granted to use it in Division 2 locations when the class and group are the same.

Under normal operating conditions, the source of ignition is not encountered in Articles 501 through 503. If specifically permitted, general-purpose equipment or equipment in general-purpose enclosures will be permitted to be installed in Division 2 locations.

Motors are to be considered as operating steadily under full-load conditions unless otherwise specified.

If either flammable gases or combustible dusts might be present, the presence of both has to be considered when determining what the safe operating temperature of the electrical equipment is.

Note: The various atmospheric mixtures of gases, vapors, and dusts depend upon the characteristics of the materials involved.

(b) **Marking.** Approved equipment shall always be marked showing class, group, and operating temperature. This will be referenced to a 40°C ambient temperature.

For the balance of (b) and Table 500-3(b), refer to the *NEC*.

There shall be a marking on equipment that is approved for Class I and Class II that shows the maximum safe operating temperature. This operating temperature is determined by exposure to the combination of Class I and Class II conditions that occur simultaneously.

Exception No. 1: Operating temperature is not required to be marked on equipment such as junction boxes, conduits, and fittings when the temperature does not exceed 100°C or 212°F.

Exception No. 2: Marking indicating the group is not required for fixed lighting fixtures that are marked either Class I, Division 2 or Class II, Division 2.

Exception No. 3: It is not required that fixed general-purpose equipment be marked with a class, group, division, or operating temperature. In Class I locations this does not include fixed lighting fixtures that are acceptable for Class I, Division 2 locations.

Exception No. 4: Fixed dusttight equipment, not including fixed lighting fixtures, that is acceptable for use in Class II, Division 2 and Class III locations is not required to be marked with the class, group, division, or operating temperature.

See Table 500-3(b), Identification Numbers.

Note: For testing and approval, various atmospheric mixtures that are not oxygen enriched have been grouped according to their characteristics, and facilities have been available for testing and approving equipment for use in the atmospheric groups listed in Classification of Gases, Vapors, and Dusts if listed for use in Hazardous (Classified) Locations, NFPA 497M-1986. Since there is no consistent relationship between explosive properties and ignition temperatures, the two are independent requirements.

(c) **Class I Temperature.** The temperature marking specified in (b) above is not to exceed the ignition point of the specific vapor or gas encountered in that area. See the *NEC* for the balance of (c).

(d) **Class II Temperature.** The surface temperature specified in (b) and so marked is to be less than the ignition temperature of the type of dust, and it shall not be permitted in any case to be greater than the temperature given below for Groups E, F, and G. (See Classification of Gases, Vapors, and Dusts for Electrical Equipment in Hazardous (Classified) Locations, NFPA 497M-1986, for the specific minimum temperature of ignition for specific dust.)

Exception: When equipment is subject to overloads, they shall not exceed 150°C (302°F) in normal operation, and the ignition temperature of the dust shall not be in excess of 200°C (392°F), whichever is lower, when the installation is in a location that is classified due to the presence of carbonaceous dusts.

See the Table in the *NEC* at this point for maximum surface temperatures that were approved prior to this requirement.

500-4. Specific Occupancies—See Articles 510 to 517 inclusive for rules applying to garages, aircraft hangars, gasoline dispensing and service stations, bulk storage plants, spray application, dipping and coating processes and health care facilities.

500-5. Class I Locations—Locations in which flammable gases and vapors are or may be present in the air in sufficient quantity to produce an explosion or a mixture that is ignitible are Class I locations. Included in Class I locations are those that appear in (a) and (b) below:

(a) **Class I, Division 1.** This is a location: (1) in which under normal operating conditions there will be ignitible concentrations of flammable gases or vapors; or (2) in which concentrations of ignitible gases or vapors frequently exist during repair or maintenance or because of leakage; or (3) in which breakdown of operations that are faulty due to faulty equipment or processes could possibly release ignitible concentrations of flammable gases or vapors, and also at the same time cause the electrical equipment to fail.

Class I, Division 1 areas also include: (1) locations where volatile flammable liquids or liquefied flammable gases are transferred from one container to another. (2) interiors of spray booths; (3) areas in the vicinity of spraying and painting operations where volatile flammable solvents are used; (4) areas with open tanks or vats of volatile flammable liquids; (5) drying rooms or compartments for the evaporation f flammable solvents; (6) areas containing fat and oil extraction apparatus using volatile flammable solvents; (7) portions of cleaning and dyeing plants where hazardous liquids are used; (8) gas generator rooms and other portions of gas manufacturing plants where flammable gas may escape; (9) inadequately ventilated pump rooms for flammable gas or for volatile flammable liquids; (10) interiors of refrigerators or freezers in which volatile, flammable materials are stored in open, lightly stoppered, or easily ruptured containers; (11) any other locations where flammable vapors or gases are likely to occur in the course of normal operations.

(b) **Class I, Division 2.** A Class I, Division 2 location is a location: (1) in which volatile liquids or flammable gases may be handled, processed, or used, but where the liquids, vapors, or gases will be in closed containers or closed systems from which they normally would not escape except in the case of an accidental rupture or breakdown of equipment; or (2) in which positive mechanical ventilation would normally prevent concentrations of ignitible gases or vapors, or in which they may become hazardous locations due to failure of ventilation equipment; or (3) locations adjacent to Class I, Division 1 locations where ignitible concentrations of gases or vapors might occasionally pass into that area unless the adjacent area has a positive pressure of clean air, and safety guards for ventilation failure are provided.

The locations under this classification usually include those where volatile flammable liquids or flammable gases or vapors are used, but in the judgment of the Code-enforcing authority would become hazardous only in case of accident or unusual operations. In deciding whether or not this would be a Class I, Division 2 location, the Code-enforcing authority must take into account the quantity of hazardous materials that might escape in case of an accident, the records of similar locations with respect to fires and explosions, and any other condition which might affect the amount of hazard present or which could be present.

Piping that is without valves, checks, meters, and similar devices would not ordinarily be considered as being capable of introducing a hazard, neither would storage areas for hazardous liquids or of liquefied or compressed gases in sealed containers which would normally not be hazardous.

There are special instances where storage of material such as anesthetics is considered as Class I, Division 1 locations.

If conduits and their fittings have a single seal or barrier separating process fluids, they will be classified as Division 2 if the outside conduit and enclosures are in a nonhazardous area.

500-6. Class II Locations—The presence of combustible dust creates Class II locations and includes the following:

(a) **Class II, Division 1.** Class II, Division 1 locations are as follows: (1) Where combustible or explosive dusts are in the air when operating normally in quantities sufficient to cause an explosive or ignitible mixture; or (2) Where mechanical problems or any other abnormal operation of the machinery or equipment could possibly cause an explosive or ignitible mixture to be formed, and could also be the source of ignition through failure of electrical equipment or operational protection devices, or from some other cause; or (3) Places where mixtures of dusts in air of an electrical conducting nature may be present in hazardous quantities.

Also included in this classification are: (1) grain handling and storage plants; (2) rooms containing grinders or pulverizers, cleaners, graders, scalpers, open conveyors or spouts, open bins or hoppers, mixers or blenders, automatic or hopper scales, packing machinery, elevator heads and boots, stock distributors, dust and stock collectors (except all-metal collectors vented to the outside), and all similar dust producing machinery and equipment in grain processing plants, starch plants, sugar pulverizing plants, melting plants, hay grinding plants, and any other occupancy of a similar nature; (3) coal pulverizing plants, unless the pulverizing equipment is essentially tight; (4) all working areas were metal dusts and powders are produced, processed, handled, packed, or stored (except in tight containers); and (5) all other similar locations where combustible dust may, under normal operating conditions, be present in the air in sufficient quantities to produce explosive or ignitible mixtures.

(b) **Class II, Division 2.** This classification covers locations in which, during the normal operation of apparatus and equipment, combustible dust is not likely to be in suspension in the air in quantities sufficient to produce explosive or ignitible mixtures, but where deposits or accumulations of such dust may be of sufficient quantity to interfere with the safe dissipation of heat from electrical equipment and apparatus; or where such deposits or accumulations of dust on or in electrical equipment or apparatus may be ignited by sparks, arcs, or burning material from same.

The decision as to whether an area is a Class II, Division 1, or a Class II, Division 2 location is determined by the inspection authority. Such locations might include: (1) rooms containing closed spouts and conveyors; (2) closed bins or hoppers; (3) machines and equipment from which appreciable quantities of dust might escape under abnormal operating condition; (4) rooms adjacent to Class II locations; (5) rooms in which controls over suspension of dust in explosive or ignitible quantities is exercised; (6) warehouses and shipping rooms where dust-producing materials are stored; and (7) any similar location.

Note: The quantities of dust present and the adequacy of dust removal systems are both factors that should be considered in arriving at the classification of the location; it may result in an unclassified area.

Note: In areas such as where seed is handled, the quantity of dust that is deposited may be so low as not to require classification of that location.

500-7. Class III Locations—Class III locations include those where ignitible fibers or flyings are not likely to be in suspension in quantities likely to produce explosive or ignitible conditions, but in which they are present. The following are included in Class III locations.

(a) **Class III, Division 1.** Locations in which easily ignitible fibers or materials producing combustible flyings are handled, manufactured, or used. Such locations may include: (1) some parts of rayon and cotton or other textile mills; (2) combustible fiber manufacturing and processing plants; (3) cotton gins and cotton-seed mills; (4) flax processing plants; (5) clothing manufacturing plants; and (6) other establishments and industries involving similar hazards.

Included in easily ignitible fibers and flyings are rayon, cotton, cotton linters and cotton waste, sisal or henequen, istle, hemp and jute, tow, cocoa fiber, oakum, baled waste kapok, Spanish moss, excelsior, other similar materials, and sawmills and other woodworking locations.

(b) **Class III, Division 2.** Locations in which easily ignitible fibers are stored or handled (except in process of manufacture).

ARTICLE 501—CLASS I LOCATIONS

501-1. General—The general requirements of the Code covering wiring and the installation thereof and the provisions of Article 500 as classified under Section 500-5 will apply with the modifications covered in this article.

501-2. Transformers and Capacitors—It was stated in Articles 450 and 460 that transformers and capacitors in hazardous locations would also be affected by the Articles covering hazardous locations. The installation of transformers and capacitors shall conform to the following:

(a) **Class I, Division 1.** In Class I, Division 1 locations, transformers and capacitors shall conform to the following:

(1) **Containing a Liquid that Will Burn.** Transformers and capacitors containing a flammable liquid shall be installed only in vaults conforming to the provision in Part C of Article 450, Section 450-41 to 450-48 inclusive, but the following will also apply: (1) there shall be no door or other communicating opening between the vault and the hazardous area; (2) sufficient ventilation shall be provided to remove hazardous vapors or gases; all vent ducts and openings shall lead to a safe location outside of the building; vent ducts and openings shall be of sufficient size to relieve any explosive pressures that might occur in the vault; and all portions of vent ducts within the building shall be of reinforced concrete.

(2) **Not Containing a Liquid that Will Burn.** Transformers and capacitors that do not contain a flammable liquid shall: (1) be installed in vaults conforming to the requirements in (a)(1) above, or (2) be approved for explosionproof Class I locations.

(b) **Class I, Division 2.** Transformers and capacitors in Class I, Division 2 must comply with Sections 450-21 through 450-27.

501-3. Meters, Instruments and Relays—The installation of meters, instruments, and relays shall conform to the following:

(a) **Class I, Division 1.** Enclosures that are approved for Class I locations shall be used in Class I, Division 1 locations for meters, instruments and relays, including kilowatt-hour meters, instrument transformers and resistors, rectifiers and thermionic tubes. It should be determined that the Group Letter is applicable for the location.

Included in enclosures approved for Class I, Division 1 locations are (1) enclosures that are explosionproof, and (2) enclosures that have been purged and pressurized.

Note: The *NEC* refers you to NFPA 496-1982 (ANSI), Purged and Pressurized Enclosures for Electrical Equipment in Hazardous Locations.

(b) **Class I, Division 2.** The installation of meters, instruments, and relays in Class I, Division 2 locations shall conform to the following:

(1) **Contacts.** Switches and circuit breakers, and make and break contacts of push buttons, relays, and alarm bells or horns, shall have enclosures approved for Class I locations, unless general purpose enclosures are provided, and current interrupting contacts are:

a. Immersed in oil; or

b. Enclosed in a chamber hermetically sealed against the entrance of gases or vapors; or

c. In circuits that under normal conditions do not release enough energy to ignite the specific hazardous atmospheric mixture.

(2) **Resistors and Similar Equipment.** Resistors, resistant devices, thermionic tubes, and rectifiers, which are used in or in connection with meters, instruments and relays, shall conform to (a) above, except that enclosures may be of general purpose type when such equipment is without make and break or sliding contacts [other than as provided in (b)(1) above] and when the maximum operating temperature of any exposed surface will not exceed 80 percent of the ignition temperature in degrees Celsius of the gas or vapor involved.

(3) **Without Make-or-Break Contacts.** When the following do not have sliding or make and break contacts, the enclosure may be of a general-purpose type: Transformer windings, impedance coils, solenoids, or other windings.

(4) **General-Purpose Assemblies.** If an assembly is made up of parts for which general-purpose enclosures are acceptable as covered in (b) (1), (b) (2), and (b) (3) above, a single general-purpose enclosure will be acceptable for such an assembly. If such an assembly includes the equipment described in (b) (2) above, the maximum temperature at the surface of any component of this assembly must be clearly and permanently indicated or marked on the outside of the enclosure. As an alternative, equipment that is approved will be permitted to indicate the temperature range for which it is suitable, and shall be so marked. In doing this, use the identification numbers of Table 500-3(b).

(5) **Fuses.** Where general purpose enclosures are permitted under (b) (1), (b) (2), (b) (3), and (b) (4) above, fuses for overcurrent protection of the instrument circuits may be mounted in general purpose enclosures provided each such fuse is preceded by a switch conforming to (b) (1) above.

(6) **Connections.** To make it easier to replace process control instruments, they may be connected by means of a flexible cord, attachment plug, and receptacle, provided: (1) a switch that complies with (b) (1) above is provided so that the attachment plug will not depend upon the plug for interrupting current; (2) the current shall not exceed 3 amperes at 120 volts, nominal; (3) the flexible cord shall not be over 3 feet and shall be of a type approved for extra-hard usage, or hard usage if the location provides some protection; also, the attachment plug and receptacle must be of the locking type and grounding type; (4) no more than the necessary receptacles shall be provided; and (5) the receptacle has a label on it that warns against opening by unplugging while under load.

501-4. Wiring Methods—Wiring methods shall conform to the following:

(a) **Class I, Division 1:**

(1) Threaded rigid metal conduit.

(2) Threaded steel intermediate metal conduit.

(3) Type MI cable with termination fittings.

(4) Boxes, fittings, and joints shall be threaded connection to conduit or approved cable terminations.

(5) Threaded joints shall be made up of at least five full threads. This is to cool any escaping gases and to prevent loose joints which may cause sparking or arcs in case of fault.

(6) MI cable shall be installed and supported in a manner to prevent tensile stress at the termination fittings.

(7) The fittings in (3) shall be explosionproof.

(8) Flexible fittings shall be explosionproof and approved for Class I locations. Liquidtight flexible metal conduit is not permitted for this purpose.

(b) **Class I, Division 2:**

(1) Threaded rigid metal conduit.

(2) Threaded steel intermediate metal conduit.

(3) Enclosed, gasketed busways, and wireways.

(4) Type PLTC cable in accordance with the provisions of Article 725.

(5) Type MI, MC, MV, TC, or SNM cable shall be permitted to be installed in cable tray systems and shall be installed so as to prevent tensile stress at termination fittings.

(6) Boxes, fittings, and joints shall not be required to be explosion-proof, except as required in Sections 501-3(b) (1), 501-6(b)(1), and 501-14(b)(1).

Where provisions must be made for a flexible connection, as at motors, the following may be used, but additional grounding must be provided around these flexible connections: flexible metal fittings, flexible metal conduit with approved fittings, extra-hard usage flexible cord with approved bushed fittings and an extra grounding conductor, and liquidtight flexible metal conduit with approved fittings.

Exception: If there is wiring that under normal conditions cannot release sufficient energy to ignite a specific ignitible atmosphere mixture and if the wiring is opening, shorting, or grounding, it shall be permitted to use any of the wiring methods that would be used and allowed by the Code in ordinary locations.

For voltages over 600 volts and where adequately protected from physical damage, metallically shielded high voltage cable shall be acceptable in cable trays when installed in accordance with Article 318.

501-5. Sealing and Drainage—Seals are to be provided in conduit and cable systems to minimize the passage of gases or vapors from one portion of the system to another portion. Type MI cable is inherently sealed, but sealed fittings must be used at terminations to keep moisture and other liquids from entering the insulation of the MI cable. Seals in conduit and cable systems shall conform to (a) through (f) below.

Note: Seals must be provided in conduit and cable that enter from hazardous locations; this is to minimize the passing of gases or vapors and to prevent flames passing from one part of the electrical installation to another through the conduit. Where MI cable is used, such passage of gases or vapors is automatically prevented by the construction of the Type MI cable.

Caution to inspection authorities: Often in the field the wireman installs a seal and there forgets to go back and load it with a sealing compound; therefore, each seal should be thoroughly checked. Used seals shall not be reused, but discarded. Seals used to prevent the passage of liquids, gases, or vapors at a continuous differential pressure across the seal must be designed, tested, and listed especially for that purpose. Even with a very small pressure differential across the seal, the equivalent of only a few inches of water pressure, it is possible to have a slow passage of gas or vapor through a seal, and through the conductors passing through the seal. Section 501-5(e) (2) is referred to in the *NEC*. Highly corrosive liquids and vapors and temperature extremes can affect the ability of the seals to perform their intended function. Refer to Section 501-5(c) (2).

(a) **Conduit Seals, Class I, Division 1.** The location of seals for Class I, Division 1 is given in the following:

(1) In every run of conduit that enters enclosures, switches, circuit breakers, fuses, relays, resistors, and any apparatus that may produce sparks, arcs, or high temperature. These seals are to be located as close as practical to the enclosure but in no case shall be more than 18 inches away from the enclosure. The purpose of the seals is to keep from transmitting an explosion or to keep ignition from traveling between sections of the system. Seals are made for vertical and horizontal installation and are to be used only for the purpose for which they are designed. Thus, a vertical seal is not to be placed horizontally. See Fig. 501-1.

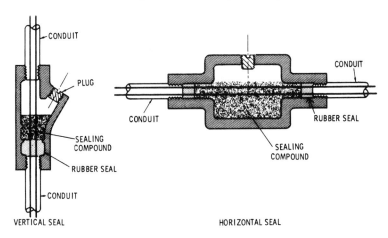

Fig. 501-1. Horizontal and vertical seals.

Exception: When conduit of 1 ½ inches or smaller enters an explosionproof enclosure that is used for switches, circuit breakers, fuses, relays, or any other equipment that may produce arcs or sparks, it will not be required to have seals if the parts that interrupt current are as follows:

    a. If the parts that cause the arcs or sparks are in a hermetically sealed chamber to stop the entrance of gas or vapors, or

    b. As permitted in Section 501-6(b) (1) (2), and are immersed in oil.

(2) **and** (3) When a conduit run of 2-inch conduit or larger enters an enclosure or fitting housing terminals, splices or taps, there shall be a seal within 18 inches of such enclosure or fitting. See Fig. 501-2. When two or more enclosures for which seals are required, as in Section 501-5(a)(1)(2), are connected by a nipple or conduit run which is no longer than 36 inches in length, only one seal will be required (Fig. 501-3). This will fulfill the requirement of not more than 18 inches from the enclosure. The Code suggests that you see the notes under Group B in the sixth fine-Print note that appears in Section 500-3.

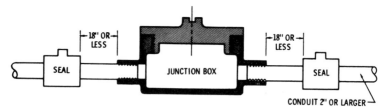

Fig. 501-2. Junction boxes with splices or taps shall have seals.

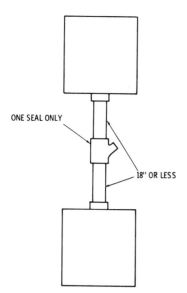

Fig. 501-3. One seal only on runs of 36 inches or less.

(4) Each conduit run leaving a Class I, Division 1 location shall have a seal at the point of leaving the hazardous area. This seal may be located on either side of the boundary, but there shall be no fitting, union, coupling, box, or any type of fitting between the seal and the nonhazardous area. See Fig. 501-4. This also applies to Class I, Division 2 locations.

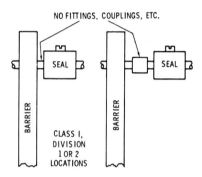

NO FITTINGS, COUPLINGS, ETC.

SEAL

SEAL

BARRIER

BARRIER

CLASS I, DIVISION 1 OR 2 LOCATIONS

Fig. 501-4. Location of seals when leaving Class I locations.

Exception: Unbroken conduit which passes completely through a Class I, Division 1 area with no fittings 12 inches beyond each boundary, providing that the termination points of the unbroken conduit are in nonhazardous areas, need not be sealed.

(b) **Conduit Seals, Class I, Division 2.** Below is given the location for installing seals in Class I, Division 2 locations:

(1) The wiring methods as outlined in Section 501-4(a) will apply. Also, seals shall be provided as in (a)(1), (a)(2), and (a)(3) above.

(2) The provisions that were covered in Section 501-5(a)(3) apply to Class I, Division 2 areas where conduit leaves that area and passes into a nonhazardous area.

Exception: Unbroken conduit which passes completely through a Class I, Division 2 area with no fittings 12 inches beyond each boundary, providing that the termination points of the unbroken conduit are in nonhazardous areas, need not be sealed.

(c) **Class I, Divisions 1 and 2.** Seals used in Class I, Divisions 1 and 2 locations shall conform to the following:

(1) **Fittings.** Enclosures for connections or equipment in all Class I locations shall be provided with approved seals. These may be an integral part of the enclosure or fitting or they may be a sealing fitting. For instance, most explosionproof lighting fixtures have the seal inherently built in, and curb junction boxes for use with gasoline dispensing islands may be purchased with a built-in provision to make a seal off from it.

(2) **Compound.** The compound used in seals shall not be affected by temperature or liquids that it might come into contact with. It shall be a compound that is approved for this purpose and shall have a melting point of not less than 93°C (200°F).

(3) **Thickness of Compound.** The sealing compound, when put into the seal, shall not be less than ⅝ inch thick and in no case shall it be less than the trade size of the conduit it is designed for. Thus, for a 1-inch conduit seal, the thickness of the compound shall not be less than 1 inch. If the conduit is ½ inch trade size, the thickness of the compound shall not be less than ⅝ inch.

(4) **Splices and Taps.** Splices and taps are not to be made within fittings that are made for sealing only, and neither shall boxes that are made only for taps and splices be used as a seal. There are, however, combinations available.

(5) **Assemblies.** When a separate compartment has an assembly of equipment that could produce arcs, sparks, or high temperatures, and this compartment is separate from another compartment that contains splices or taps, if a seal is provided for the conductors that pass from one compartment to the other, the entire assembly and the two compartments shall be approved for Class I locations. When conduit enters the compartment containing the splice and taps, seals shall be provided in that conduit in Class I, Division 1 locations. See (a) (2) above for where these are required.

(d) **Cable Seals, Class I, Division 1.** In Class I, Division 1 locations that have multiconductor cables installed in conduit, the cable is to be considered as a single conductor when the cable is capable of transmitting vapors or gases through its core. Sealing of these cables is covered in (a) above.

If cables have a gas/vapor-tight continuous sheath that is capable of transmitting gases or vapors by means of the cable core, they are required to be sealed in Division 1 locations. First the jacket and any other coverings must be removed, so that sealing compound can completely surround each individual conductor, and can also seal the outer jacket.

(e) **Cable Seals, Class I, Division 2.** The following information is for the location of cable seals in Class I, Division 1 locations:

(1) Cables are required to be sealed at the point where they enter enclosures that are approved for Class I locations. For the seal fittings, (b) (1) above must be complied with. Even though multiconductor cables are within a gas/vapor-tight continuous sheath that would allow transmission of gases or vapors through the cable core, they are required to be sealed in fittings approved for the purpose in Division 2 locations after the inside jacket is removed, so that the sealing compound completely surrounds each individual insulated conductor in such a way as to minimize the passage

of gases and vapors. Multiconductor cables in conduit shall be sealed as described in (d) above.

(2) If there is a gas/vapor-tight continuous sheath over the cable, and if the cable will not transmit gas or vapor through the cable core in any quantity that exceeds that which is permitted in seal fittings, it shall not be required to be sealed except as required in (e) (1) above. The minimum length of such a cable shall be not less than the length that limits the passing of gas/vapor to the rate permitted for seal fittings—.007 cubic feet per hour of air at a water pressure of 6 inches.

Note: ANSI/UL 886-1980 covers Outlet Boxes and Fitting for Use in Hazardous Locations.

Note: Interstices of the conductor strands are not included in the cable core.

(3) When the sheath of a cable is continuous and is gas/vapor-tight, yet is capable of transmitting gases or vapors through the core of the cable, sealing will not be required except as covered in (e) (1) above, unless the cable is attached to process equipment or to devices that may cause a pressure in excess of 6 inches of water to be exerted at the cable's end. If a greater pressure is transmitted, sealing, a barrier, or other means must be provided to prevent flammables from passing into an unclassified area.

Exception: A cable that has unbroken outer sheath will be allowed to pass in a continuous length to a Class I, Division 2 location without seals.

(4) If a gas/vapor-tight continuous sheath is installed over cable, it shall be sealed at the boundary of the Division 2 and nonhazardous location. This shall be done in such a way that the passage of gas and vapors into a nonhazardous location will be a minimum.

Note: Metal or nonmetallic material may be used for the sheath mentioned in (d) and (e) above.

(f) **Drainage.**

(1) **Control Equipment.** In control equipment where there is a possibility of liquid accumulating or vapor condensing and becoming trapped in the enclosure, provision shall be made for periodically draining off this liquid, and the draining means shall be of an approved type.

(2) **Motors and Generators.** The authority enforcing the Code has the responsibility of deciding where there is a probability of liquid or condensed vapor accumulating in motors and generators. If judged that there is this accumulation, the conduit system shall be arranged so as to minimize this possibility and, if a means of permitting periodic draining is judged necessary by the inspector,

such means shall be provided at the time of manufacture and shall be an integral part of the machine.

(3) **Canned Pumps, Process Connections, Etc.**, frequently depend on a single seal diaphragm or tube to prevent process fluids from entering the electrical conduit system. An additional approved seal or barrier shall be provided with an adequate drain between the seals in such a manner that leaks would be obvious.

501-6. Switches, Circuit Breakers, Motor Controllers and Fuses —Switches, circuit breakers, motor controllers and fuses shall conform to the following:

(a) **Class I, Division 1.** Class I, Division 1 locations shall have the switches, circuit breakers, motor controllers and fuses, including push buttons, relays, and similar devices in approved enclosures together with the apparatus enclosed therein approved for Class I locations.

(b) **Class I, Division 2.** Switches, circuit breakers, motor controllers, and fuses in Class I, Division 2 locations shall conform to the following:

(1) **Type Required.** Switches, circuit breakers, and motor controllers that are intended to interrupt current in the normal performance of the function for which they are installed shall be approved, along with the enclosures for same, for Class I locations. See Section 501-3(a). Exceptions to this are: (1) where the interruption of the current occurs within a chamber hermetically sealed against the entrance of gases and vapors; and (2) where the current-interrupting contacts are oil-immersed and the device is approved for locations of this class and division: 2-inch minimum immersion for power and 1-inch minimum immersion for control.

General-purpose oil-immersed circuit breakers and controllers may not completely confine the arc that might be produced under heavy overloads, so they shall be specifically approved for locations in Class I, Division 2 locations.

(2) **Isolating Switches.** Isolating switches need not have fuses included as they are not intended to be opened under load or to interrupt current. Their purpose is to isolate the equipment after the electricity is shut off by other means approved for that purpose, so they may be of The general-purpose type. Most inspectors prefer that they be marked "Do Not Open Under Load."

(3) **Fuses.** Except as provided in (b)(4) below, the following may be used for the protection of motors, appliances, and lamps: (1) If installed in enclosures approved for the purpose of location, cartridge fuses and plug fuses may be used if of the proper voltage for the job. (2) Some fuses have the operating element immersed in oil or other liquid, such as carbon tetrachloride. These may be used or they may be enclosed in hermetically sealed chambers sealed against the entrance of gases or vapors.

(4) **Fuses or Circuit Breakers for Overcurrent Protection.** When not more than ten sets of approved enclosed fuses, or not more than ten circuit breakers that are not intended to be used for switching, are installed for branch-circuit purposes or for feeder protection for only one room area or section of the Class I, Division 2 location, it is permitted to use general-purpose enclosures for these fuses or circuit breaker purposes. That is, if they are for protection only of circuits or feeders that are supplying lighting that is maintained in a fixed position.

Please note that this does not cover portable lamps. For the purpose of this part, three fuses on a three-phase system to protect the three ungrounded conductors is considered as a set. Also a single fuse to protect the ungrounded conductor of a single-phase circuit is considered as one set. Fuses which conform to (b)(3) above need not be counted in the 10 sets covered in this part. See the *NEC*.

(5) **Fuses Internal to Lighting Fixtures.** Lighting fixtures are permitted to have approved cartridge-type fuses in the fixture as supplementary protection.

501-7. Control Transformers and Resistors—Transformers, impedance coils and resistors used as or in conjunction with control equipment for motors, generators and appliances shall conform to the following:

(a) **Class I, Division 1.** Transformers, impedance coils, and resistors, together with their switching equipment, shall be provided with approved (explosionproof) enclosures for Class I, Division 1 locations in accordance with 501-3(a).

(b) **Class I, Division 2.** Control transformers and resistors used in Class I, Division 2 locations shall conform to the following:

(1) **Switching Mechanisms.** When these are used in conjunction with transformers, impedance coils, and resistors, switching mechanism shall meet the requirements of Section 501-6(b); in other words, shall be approved for Class I locations.

(2) **Coils and Windings.** If provided with adequate vents to take care of the prompt escape of gases or vapors that may enter the enclosure, transformers, solenoids, and impedance coils may be of the general-purpose type.

(3) **Resistors.** Resistors shall be enclosed, and the assembly is required to be approved for Class I locations, unless the resistance is nonvariable and the maximum operating temeperature in degrees Celsius does not exceed 80 percent of the temperature that will ignite the gas or vapor involved, or unless it has been tested and approved as being incapable of igniting the gas or vapor.

501-8. Motors and Generators—Motors and generators shall conform to the following:

(a) **Class I, Division 1.** Motors and generators used in Class I, Division 1 locations shall be: (1) explosionproof and approved for Class I locations; or (2) totally enclosed types with positive-pressure ventilation from a source of clean air and the air discharged into a safe area. (A totally enclosed motor is not necessarily an explosionproof motor.) The motor and ventilating fan must be interlocked electrically so that the motor cannot be started until the fan has purged the motor with air in a quantity of at least 10 times that volume of air in the motor. The interlock must also be arranged to stop the motor if the air source fails; or (3) a totally enclosed type, pressurized by a suitable and reliable source of inert gas with interlocking to stop the motor in the event that the gas pressure drops; or (4) it may be designed to be submerged in a liquid that is flammable only when it is vaporized and mixed with air, or in a gas or vapor where the pressure is greater than atmospheric pressure, and is flammable only when mixed with air; and the machine is designed to prevent starting until it has been purged with the liquid or gas to get rid of all air, and is also designed so that it will automatically be de-energized when the supply of liquid, gas, or vapor drops and the pressure is reduced to atmospheric pressure.

In (2) and (3), the operating temperature of any external surface of the motor shall not exceed 80 percent of the ignition temperature of the gases or vapors involved in the hazardous location. These temperatures are to be determined by ASTM test procedure (Designation D2155-69). Any device used to detect the rise in temperature shall be of an approved type. All auxiliary equipment used for ventilating or pressurizing must also be approved for the location.

(b) **Class I, Division 2.** Motors, generators, and other rotating electrical machinery used in Class I, Division 2 locations shall be approved for Class I locations (explosionproof) if they have: sliding contacts; centrifugal or other switching devices or mechanisms (including motor overcurrent, overloading and overtemperature devices); or integral resistance devices, either while starting or running, unless the sliding contacts or switching devices and resistance devices are provided for in enclosures approved for the location.

If operated at rated voltage, the exposed surface of space heaters that are installed to prevent condensation of moisture during periods of shutdown, the space heater shall not exceed 80 percent of the temperature in degrees Celsius that would ignite the gas or vapors involved.

The above rules do not prohibit the use of open-squirrel-cage, non-explosionproof motors that do not use brushes or switching mechanisms.

Note: The temperature of internal and external surfaces that may be exposed to flammable atmosphere must be considered.

501-9. Lighting Fixtures—Lighting fixtures must comply with (a) and (b) below.

(a) **Class I, Division 1.** In Class I, Division 1 locations, fixtures for lighting shall conform to the following:

(1) **Approved Fixtures.** All fixtures shall be approved for Class I, Division 1 locations and shall be approved as a complete unit with the maximum wattage of lamps that may be used plainly marked on them. Portable fixtures shall also be approved as a complete unit.

Many times in the field, explosionproof and dust-tight lighting fixtures are confused. They definitely are not the same. An explosionproof fixture has to contend primarily with explosions from within, so the glass enclosure must be thick and strong. While the temperature of operation is also a factor, it is not the same as with dust-tight fixtures. In dust-tight units, the operating temperature of the fixture is the important factor, so the glass will be thinner, but the enclosure will be larger so the heat will have more surface to dissipate from. Look for the Group Letter on the fixture and check with the atmospheric groups that are listed in the first part of Article 500.

(2) **Physical Damage.** The fixtures shall be protected from physical damage, either by guards or by location. The breaking of a lamp bulb might cause the hot filament to start an explosion or fire.

(3) **Pendant Fixtures.** Rigid metal conduit or threaded steel intermediate conduit stems shall be used to suspend pendant fixtures. The conduit shall have threaded joints and a set screw shall be provided to prevent loosening. Fixtures having stems longer than 12 inches may be installed in one of two ways: (1) The stems shall be securely supported at a height not to exceed 12 inches above the fixture; these supports shall secure the fixture laterally and shall be of a permanent nature. (2) An approved, explosionproof, flexible connector may be used if it is not more than 12 inches below the box or fitting which supports the fixture.

(4) **Supports.** Support boxes and fittings used to support fixtures shall be approved for the purpose and also be approved for Class I locations.

(b) **Class I, Division 2.** In Class I, Division 2 locations, lighting fixtures shall conform to the following:

(1) **Portable Lighting Equipment.** Portable lighting must comply with (a)(1) above. In other words, they shall be approved as a complete unit for Class I locations.

Exception: If portable lighting equipment is mounted on movable stands and flexible cord is used to connect them as in Section 501-11, they may be mounted in any position if they conform to Section 501-9(b) (2) below.

(2) **Fixed Lighting.** Fixed lighting fixtures shall be protected from physical damage by guards or by location. If there should be a danger of hot particles falling from lamps or fixtures, they shall be suitably guarded to prevent these hot particles falling into areas of concentrations of flammable gases or vapors. Where the lamps are of a size which might reach an operating temperature of more than 80 percent of the ignition temperature of the gases or vapors involved, as determined by ASTM test procedure (Designation D286-30), the fixtures shall conform to Section 501-9(a)(1).

(3) **Pendant Fixtures.** This is a repetition of (a)(3) above.

(4) **Switches.** Section 501-6(b)(1) covers switches that are a part of an assembled fixture or of an individual lampholder.

(5) **Starting Equipment.** The requirements of Section 501-7(b) shall be met for starting and control equipment used with electric discharge lighting. This section requires that they be in an approved enclosure, or that they are not capable of emitting sparks or arcs that will ignite or explode the gases or vapors in that area.

Exception: Thermal protection installed into a thermally protected ballast for fluorescent lighting must be used if approved for locations in this class and division.

501-10. Utilization Equipment—Utilization equipment, fixed or portable, shall conform to the following:

(a) **Class I, Division 1.** All utilization equipment, including electrically heated and motor-driven equipment, that is used in Class I, Division 1 locations, shall be approved for the location.

(b) **Class I, Division 2.** The following shall be complied with in Class I, Division 2 locations for all utilization equipment:

(1) **Heaters.** Either (a) or (b) below shall be conformed with for electrically heated utilization equipment:
a. When continuously energized at the maximum rated ambient temperature for the location, heaters shall not exceed 80 percent of the ignition temperature in degrees Celsius rating of the gas or vapor involved on any surface of the heater that is exposed to the gas or vapor. If no controller of temperature is used, the conditions apply if the heater is operated at 120 percent of the rated voltage used.

Exception: See Section 501-8(b), when motor-mounted space heaters are used to stop condensation.

b. Any heaters used shall be approved for Class I, Division 1 locations.

(2) Motors. Motors in this location will be treated the same as other motors, as explained in Section 501-8(b).

(3) Switches, Circuit Breakers, and Fuses. These were covered in Section 501-6(b).

501-11. Flexible Cords, Class I, Divisions 1 and 2—Flexible cord shall be used only for portable lighting fixtures or portable utilization equipment and the supply circuit fixed portion thereof, and where used: (1) the cord must be the type suitable for extra-hard usage; (2) it shall contain a grounding conductor complying with Section 400-23 in addition to the other conductors; (3) the connection to the supply conductors to terminals shall be done in an approved manner; (4) the cord shall be supported by clamps or other approved means so that there will be no tension on the terminal connections; and (5) wherever the cord enters boxes, fittings, or enclosures that are the explosionproof type, seals suitable for the purpose shall be used.

Exception: Sections 501-3(b) (6) and 501-4(b) will provide some exception for cords.

Submersible electric pumps that are provided with means of removing the pump without entering a wet-pit will be considered as portable utilization equipment.

Note: Section 501-13 covers flexible cords that may come in contact with liquids having a deteriorating effect on insulation.

501-12. Receptacles and Attachment Plugs, Class I, Divisions 1 and 2—Receptacles and plugs shall be of a type approved for Class I locations (explosionproof), and shall be equipped with a connection for a grounding conductor. The grounding conductor shall make connection first and the other terminals shall be so arranged that, upon insertion or removal, no sparks will result in ignition or explosion. Except as provided in Section 501-3(b)(6).

501-13. Conductor Insulation Class I, Divisions 1 and 2—Where condensed vapors or liquids may come in contact with the insulation on conductors or cords, the insulation shall be of an approved type for use in this location or the conductors shall be protected by a lead sheath or other approved means.

TW insulation, as such, is not approved for use where it will be exposed to gasoline. However, there is a TW wire with a nylon cover that is approved, as well as THWN and many others that go by the trade names of the manufacturer. The best method of finding out whether the insulation is approved for contact with any liquid is to refer to the Underwriter's Laboratories listing and check. If it was tested for this use, it will be there.

501-14. Signal, Alarm, Remote-Control and Communication Systems—Signal, alarm, remote-control and communication systems shall conform to the following:

(a) **Class I, Division 1.** All apparatus, equipment, etc., used in Class I, Division 1 locations for signaling systems, alarms, remote-control, and communications shall be approved for Class I locations, irrespective of the voltages that are involved. The wiring methods and sealing, as prescribed in Sections 501-4(a) and 501-5(a) and (c), shall apply to the installation of same. There are no exceptions.

(b) **Class I, Division 2.** The following will cover what must be complied with for signaling alarm, remote-control, and communication systems, and in Class I, Division 2 locations:

(1) **Contacts.** The enclosures for switches, circuit breakers, the make-and-break contacts of push buttons, relays, and alarm bells and horns shall be approved for Class I, Division 1 locations in accordance with Section 501-3(a).

Exception: You are permitted to used general-purpose enclosures, provided the interrupting contacts are as follow:
a. Immersed in oil, or
b. Enclosed within a chamber that is hermetically sealed to prevent gases or vapors from entering the chamber, or
c. Their circuits do not emit sufficient energy to cause ignition of specific atmospheric mixtures.

(2) **Resistors and Similar Equipment.** Resistors, resistance devices, thermionic tubes and rectifiers, shall meet the same requirements as covered in Section 501-3(b) (2).

(3) **Protectors.** The enclosures for lightning protective devices and for fuses may be of the general-purpose type.

(4) **Wiring and Sealing.** All wiring must conform to the requirements for Class I locations covered in Section 501-4(b) and the sealing shall conform to the requirements of Section 501-5(b) and (c).

501-15. Live Parts, Class I, Divisions 1 and 2—No live parts will be permitted where exposed.

501-16. Grounding, Class I, Divisions 1 and 2—Not only are wiring and equipment required to be grounded in Class I, Divisions 1 and 2 locations as specified in Article 250, but with the following additional requirements:

(a) **Bonding.** The locknut-bushing and double-locknut types of connection shall not be depended upon for proper bonding purposes, but bonding jumpers with listed fittings or other approved methods of bonding shall be required. This method of bonding applies to all intervening raceways, fittings, boxes, enclosures, etc., between the point of grounding of the service equipment in Class I locations.

(b) **Types of Equipment Grounding Conductors.** If the flexible metal conduit or liquidtight flexible metal conduit is used as permitted in Section 501-4(b), and if it is to be relied upon for the sole equipment grounding path, you are required to use an internal or external bonding jumper paralleled with each flexible conduit, and Section 250-79 shall be complied with.

501-17. Surge Protection, Class I, Divisions 1 and 2—Surge arresters are required, including their installation and connection, in compliance with Article 280. Also, if surge arresters are installed in Class I, Division 1 locations, The enclosure shall be suitable for the location.

ARTICLE 502—CLASS II LOCATIONS

502-1. General—In Section 500-6, Class II locations were covered and thoroughly outlined as to the coverage included in this classification. The general rules of the Code will apply to all Class II locations, with the exception that they are modified by this article.

It will be recalled that Class II locations were those areas where dusts were in suspension or otherwise present to the extent that they might be ignitible or explosive. The article covers that supplemental requirements in wiring installations which are necessary to take care of this hazardous condition. In dealing with this article, it should be remembered that most dusts in the proper suspension might become explosive. All of the dusts are not covered in the Code and it becomes the responsibility of the inspection authority to judge whether or not these dusts may be a problem and to what extent.

A few definitions that are applicable to these locations are as follows:

In this article "dust-ignitionproof" means that they will be enclosed in a way that will exclude amounts of dust that might affect performance or rating and that, when installed in compliance with the *NEC*, they will not permit arcs, sparks, or heat that might be generated or liberated in the enclosure to cause ignition of suspended or accumulated specified dusts that might occur in the vicinity of the enclosure.

One major problem of Class II locations is temperature. Equipment used in Class II locations must be capable of functioning at full rating without developing temperatures on the surface high enough to cause excessive dehydration or to cause the dust to carbonize, especially organic dust.

Note: Spontaneous combustion is likely to occur in dusts that are excessively dry or carbonized.

In the above, the answer is in the fact that not only will arcs and sparks cause explosions when dust is in suspension in the proper amounts in the atmosphere, but also the fact that the temperatures of ignition are very low, and when organic dusts are exposed to a high temperature over a prolonged period, the composition of the dust will change and, in most cases, the flash point will even be lowered.

Equipment and wiring defined in Article 100 as being explosionproof will not be required and will not be acceptable in Class II locations, except where approved for Class II locations.

The point here is that the explosion possibility may be taken care of, but the temperature also has to be considered, since many dusts have a lower flash point than gases or vapors in Class I locations. NFPA 497M mentioned in other parts concerning hazardous locations will give the flash points and other pertinent facts that will be encountered with dusts. Inspectors and anyone concerned with design and installation of wiring in these areas should be familiar with (or at least know where to find) the facts applicable to the conditions that might prevail.

Where Class II, Group E and F dusts with a resistance less than 10^5 ohm-centimeters are present in quantities that can be hazardous, they shall be in only Division 1 locations.

502-2. Transformers and Capacitors—The installation of transformers and capacitors shall conform to the following:

(a) **Class II, Division 1.** Transformers and capacitors in Class II, Division 1 locations shall meet the following conditions:

(1) **Containing Liquid that Will Burn.** Sections 450-41 through 450-48 covered transformer vaults. These requirements will apply to transformers in Class II locations that contain a liquid that will burn. In addition: (1) Any openings such as doors, etc., that communicate with the Division 1 locations are required to have self-closing firing doors, and these are to be on both sides of the wall; they shall be closely fitted so that they can close readily, and suitable seals shall be provided (such as weather stripping), to keep to a minimum the dust that enters into a vault; (2) any ducts or vents shall enter only into the outside air; and (3) suitable pressure relief openings shall communicate with the outside air and must be provided to relieve any pressures that might occur from an explosion in the vault and communicate this pressure to the outside air away from hazardous locations.

(2) **Not Containing Liquid that Will Burn.** Transformers and capacitors which contain a liquid that will not burn shall be installed in a transformer vault that conforms to the requirements of Sections 450-41 to 450-48 inclusive, or they shall be approved as a complete assembly, including terminal connections, for Class II locations.

(3) **Metal Dusts.** Transformers and capacitors shall not be installed in locations in which dust from magnesium, aluminum, aluminum bronze powders, or other metals of similar hazardous characteristics may be present. Recall that, in Section 500-6(a), electrically

conducting dusts from materials such as coal, charcoal, or coke were mentioned. Even though these are not considered as metallic dusts, it will be found that most inspection authorities will, in practically all cases, treat them as metal dusts.

(b) Class II, Division 2. Class II, Division 2 locations are treated as having a lesser hazard than Class II, Division 1 locations, and transformers and capacitors shall conform to the following:

(1) Containing Liquid that Will Burn. Transformers and capacitors containing a liquid that will burn, in Class II, Division 2 locations, shall conform to the requirements for transformer vaults as covered in Sections 450-41 to 450-48 inclusive.

(2) Containing Askarel. Transformers in excess of 25 kVA that contain askarel shall: (1) have a pressure-relief vent (these naturally must vent outdoors and away from hazardous areas); (2) either have a means of absorbing any gas that might be generated by arcing internally, or the pressure-relief vents must be connected to a chimney or other type of flue that will carry the gases outside the building; and (3) there shall be a space of not less than 6 inches left between the cases of the transformers and combustibles adjacent to it.

(3) Dry-Type Transformers. Vaults shall be used for dry-type transformers, or they shall: (1) be enclosed in tight metal enclosures without vents or any other openings (this means that they should be hermetically sealed), and operate at a voltage not to exceed 600 volts, nominal (including both the primary and secondary voltages).

502-4. Wiring Methods—Wiring methods shall comply with (a) and (b) below.

(a) Class II, Division I. The only two wiring methods approved for Class II, Division 1 locations are threaded rigid conduit, threaded steel intermediate metal conduit, or MI cable with fittings approved for the location and properly supported so that there will be no strain on the fittings.

(1) Fittings and Boxes. Fittings and boxes in which taps, joints, or terminal connections are made shall be designed to minimize the entrance of dust and they shall have threaded bosses and be equipped with telescoping or close-fitting covers; have other effective means to prevent the escape of sparks or burning materials; and have no openings (such as screw holes for attachment) through which, after installation, sparks or burning material might escape, or through which adjacent combustible materials might be ignited.

The above, in summary, states that all fittings and boxes shall be dust-tight and approved for Class II locations. See Fig. 502-1.

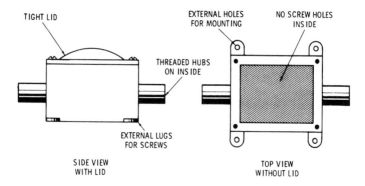

Fig. 502-1. Type of boxes for Class II locations.

(2) **Flexible Connections.** Flexible connections are often a necessity. When they are, the following types may be used, except where the dusts are of an electrical conducting nature, flexible metal conduit shall not be used and flexible cords shall be provided with dust-tight seals at both ends: dust-tight flexible connectors, liquidtight flexible metal conduit with approved fittings, or flexible cord approved for extra-hard usage and provided with bushed fittings.

When using the above methods, some precautions shall be required, such as a grounding conductor in flexible cords.

If flexible connections are subject to oil or corrosive conditions, the conductors shall be of a type having insulation for the condition, or a suitable sheath may be used to protect them.

(b) **Class II, Division 2.** For Class II, Division 2 locations, the following may be used for the wiring methods: rigid metal conduit, intermediate metal conduit, EMT, dusttight wireways, Type MI, MC, or SNM cables used with approved termination fittings, or Type PLTC or TC cables that are installed in ventilated channel-type cable trays. They shall be laid in a single layer, with a space not less than the diameter of the largest cable left between the cables.

Exception: You shall be permitted to use any methods that are suitable for ordinary wiring locations, provided that under normal conditions this wiring method cannot release sufficient energy to cause ignition of combustible dust fixtures by opening, shorting, or grounding.

(1) **Wireways, Fittings, and Boxes.** Wireways, their fittings, and boxes provided for taps, joints, or terminal connections must be of a design that will minimize the entrance of dust, and: (1) they shall be provided with telescoping or close-fitting covers or some other effective means that will prevent sparks or burning material from

escaping; and (2) there shall be no openings in the enclosure such as for attachment with screws that after mounting could allow sparks or burning material to escape or through which nearby ignitible material may be ignited. The screw holes for attachment should be in the metal part of the enclosure external to the inside of the enclosure.

(2) **Flexible Connections.** Where flexible connections are required, (a)(2) above will apply.

502-5. Sealing, Class II, Divisions 1 and 2—In the installation of a dust-ignition-proof enclosure and one that is not, there may be communication of dust between the two enclosures. The entrance of dust into the dust-ignition-proof enclosure must be prevented. This may be done by one of the following means: (1) by use of an effective and permanent seal, such as used in Class I locations; (2) by connection to a horizontal raceway that is not less than 10 feet in length; or (3) by means of a vertical raceway not less than 5 feet in length, which extends downward from the dust-ignition-proof enclosure. Note this carefully—if the raceway extends downward from the conventional enclosure, it will not meet the requirements.

If a raceway provides communication between an enclosure that is required to be dusttight and dust-ignition-proof and an enclosure that is located in an unclassified location, seals will not be required.

Where seals are used they are to be accessible. See Fig 502-2.

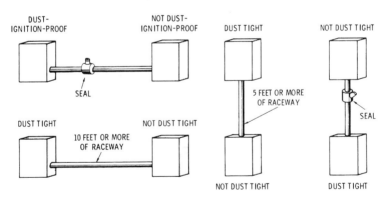

Fig. 502-2. Sealing in Class II locations.

502-6. Switches, Circuit Breakers, Motor Controllers and Fuses —Switches, circuit breakers, motor controllers and fuses shall conform to the following:

(a) **Class II, Division 1.** In Class II, Division 1 locations, the following will cover switches, circuit breakers, motor controllers, and fuses:

(1) **Type Required.** The emphasis of this part is on any device that is intended to interrupt a current, such as switches, circuit breakers, motor controllers and fuses. This also includes push buttons, relays, and similar devices installed in Class II, Division 1 locations. Mention is also made of dusts having an electrical conductive nature.

Such devices shall be installed in dust-ignition-proof enclosures and shall be approved for Class II locations. In this discussion it should be mentioned that there is an enclosure available for industrial use which is termed a dust-tight enclosure. However, to secure approval, the enclosure shall be listed for a hazardous location and classified by a Group number, as covered in Article 500. In this classification are included the following: (1) service and branch-circuit fuses, (2) switches and circuit breakers, and (3) motor controllers, including push-buttons, pilot switches, relays, motor overload protective devices, and switches, fuses, and circuit breakers for the control and protection of lighting and appliance circuits.

(2) **Isolating Switches.** Isolating switches do not need to contain fuses and are not intended to interrupt current. Their purpose is to isolate the conductors for working on motors and the equipment driven by the motors. When isolating switches are installed in locations that do not have dusts of an electrical-conducting nature, they shall be so designed as to minimize the entrance of dust, and shall: (1) have telescoping covers or close-fitting covers or any other means that will prevent the escape of sparks or burning material; and (2) have no holes within the enclosures for attaching enclosures with screws where, after installation, sparks or burning material could escape, or through which exterior accumulations of combustible materials or dust could be ignited.

It might be stated that, while not required by the Code, some insurance companies and some inspectors suggest that these and other sheet-metal enclosures be mounted on fire-proof material such as ¼-inch asbestos board. This is a relatively small expense which might pay large dividends.

(3) **Metal Dusts.** Where there are present dusts from magnesium, aluminum, or aluminum bronze powders, or any other metals with similarly hazardous characteristics, the enclosures shall be specifically approved for these locations that have fuses, switches, motor controllers, and circuit breakers.

(b) **Class II, Division 2.** Enclosures for switches, circuit breakers, motor controllers, including push buttons, relays, and similar devices for Class II, Division locations, shall be the same as required in Section 502-6(a)(2).

502-7. Control Transformers and Resistors—Transformers, solenoids, impedance coils and resistors used as or in conjunction with control

equipment for motors, generators and appliances shall conform to the following:

(a) **Class II, Division 1.** Dust-ignition-proof enclosures approved for Class II, Division 1 locations shall be required for transformers, solenoids, impedance coils, and resistors. There shall be no transformer impedance coil, or resistor installed in locations where dusts from magnesium, aluminum, aluminum bronze powders or other similar metal dusts are present unless the enclosures in which they are installed have been specifically approved for such a location.

(b) **Class II, Division 2.** Transformers or resistors in Class II, Division 2 locations must conform to the following:

(1) **Switching Mechanisms:** Section 502-6(a)(2) also applies here for switching mechanisms (including overcurrent devices) associated with control transformers, solenoids, impedance coils, and resistors. That section basically called for enclosures that were designed to minimize the entrance of dusts and to prevent sparks or burning material from escaping from the enclosure provided in dust-tight enclosure.

(2) **Coils and Windings.** When not located in the same enclosure with the switching mechanism, then control transformers, solenoids, and impedance coils are to be mounted in tight metal enclosures and shall have no ventilation openings.

(3) **Resistors.** Resistors become heated when current passes through them, so they are required to be mounted in dust-ignition-proof enclosures approved for Class II locations. The maximum operating temperature of the resistor shall not exceed 120°C (248°F) for nonadjustable resistors and resistors which are a part of an automatically timed starting sequence. In the case where the temperature does not exceed that just specified, the resistors may have enclosures conforming to (b)(2) above—that is, tight metal cases without ventilation openings.

502-8. Motors and Generators—Motors and generators shall conform to the following:

(a) **Class II, Division 1.** Motors, generators, and other rotating electrical machinery installed in Class II, Division 1 locations shall be:

(1) Shall be approved for Class II, Division 1 locations, or

(2) Totally enclosed and pipe-ventilated, meeting temperature requirements as in Section 502-1.

Motors, generators, or rotating electrical machinery located in areas where metal dust such as magnesium, aluminum, aluminum bronze, or similar dusts are present, shall not be installed unless they are specifically approved for such locations and are totally enclosed or totally enclosed and fan-cooled.

(b) **Class II, Division 2.** Motors, generators, and other rotating electrical equipment shall be totally enclosed and nonventilated in Class II, Division 2 locations, totally enclosed if pipe-ventilated, totally fan-cooled or dust-ignitionproof when the maximum full-load external temperature meets the requirements of Section 500-3(d) under normal operation in free air (not dust blanketed air), and shall have no external openings.

There are exceptions to this which may be granted if the authority having jurisdiction believes that the accumulations of nonconducting, nonabrasive dust will be moderate. They may also be granted if the machines may be easily reached for routine cleaning and maintenance. If these conditions are met and approval is given, the following may be installed:

(1) Standard open-type machines that do not have any sliding contacts, centrifugal switches, or any other type of switching mechanism, including overcurrent, overloading, and overtemperature devices, or built-in resistance devices.

(2) Standard open-type machines that have contacts, switching arrangements, or resistance devices may be enclosed in a tight metal housing that has no ventilating devices or openings.

(3) Squirrel cage–type textile motors that are self-cleaning.

The *NEC* is a very fair instrument placed in our hands, with permission granted in many instances to deviate from the strict portions, provided that we are sure that such deviations will not cause unsafe conditions. We must always consider what might happen after the inspection is made and ask ourselves if the same conditions will be lived up to.

502-9. Ventilating Piping—Vent pipes for motors, generators, or other rotating electrical machinery, or for enclosures for electrical apparatus, where it is permissible to use vents for these types of enclosures, shall: (1) be of a metal not lighter than No. 24 MSG; (2) be of other substantial noncombustible material; (3) lead directly out to clean air outside the building; (4) be screened to prevent the entrance of small animals or birds; (5) be protected from physical damage; and (6) be protected against rust and other corrosion.

In addition to the above, they shall conform to the following:

(a) **Class II, Division 1.** In Class II, Division 1 locations, vent pipes, including their connections to motors or to the dust-ignition-proof enclosures for other equipment or apparatus, shall be dusttight throughout their length. When metal pipes are used, they shall be: (1) riveted (or bolted) and soldered, (2) welded, or (3) rendered dusttight by some other equally effective means.

(b) **Class II, Division 2.** Ventilating pipes and their connections in Class II, Division 2 locations are to be sufficient to prevent entrance of appreciable quantities of dust into the ventilated equipment or enclosure. They shall also be installed so as to stop sparks, flames, or burning material that could possibly cause ignition of any dust accumulations or any combustibles that are in the vicinity. The metal pipes shall have lock seams and welded joints will be permitted, and when necessary to permit some flexibility, tight-fitting slip joints will be permitted for the connections to motors.

For metal pipes, the following may be used: lock seams, riveted joints, welded joints, or tight-fitting slip joints where some flexibility is necessary, as at motor connections.

502-10. Utilization Equipment—Utilization equipment, fixed and portable, shall conform to the following:

(a) **Class II, Division 1.** Utilization equipment, fixed and portable, located in Class II, Division 1 locations, also includes electrically heated and motor-driven equipment. They shall be dust-ignition-proof and approved for Class II, Division 1 locations. Where dusts from metals such as magnesium, aluminum, aluminum bronze powders, or other similar dust are present, the equipment shall be approved for these locations. This will be Group E equipment.

(b) **Class II, Division 2.** All utilization equipment used in Class II, Division 2 locations must comply with the following:

(1) **Heaters.** Only approved equipment for Class II locations will be permitted for electrically heated utilization equipment.

Exception: Radiant heating panels that are metal-enclosed are to be dusttight and marked in accordance with Section 500-3(d).

(2) **Motors.** The motors used on motor-driven utilization equipment must comply with Section 502-8(b). This section allowed some latitude and left up to the inspection authority to decide what was involved and the equipment permitted.

(3) **Switches, Circuit Breakers, and Fuses.** Enclosures used for switches, circuit breakers, and fuses must be approved for being dusttight.

(4) **Transformers, Impedance Coils and Resistors.** These shall conform to Section 502-7(b). There are three parts to this section, and it is suggested that it be read again.

502-11. Lighting Fixtures—Recall that in Class II locations the ignition of dusts can be caused by either sparks, arcs, or heat. Bear this in mind while reading the following:

(a) **Class II, Division 1.** In Class II, Division 1 locations, lighting fixtures for fixed and portable lighting shall conform to the following:

(1) **Approved Fixtures.** For Class II locations where ordinary dusts are present, the fixtures shall be approved and plainly marked. In locations where dusts from magnesium, aluminum, aluminum bronze, or similar metal dusts with hazardous characteristics are present, the fixtures shall be approved and so marked.

(2) **Physical Damage.** Suitable guards or suitable locations shall be provided for fixtures to protect against physical damage. "By location" means that they are to be mounted high enough so that they are not likely to be bumped or hit.

(3) **Pendant Fixtures.** Pendant fixtures shall be suspended by threaded rigid metal conduit stems, chains with approved fittings, other approved means threaded steel intermediate metal conduit. If the stems are longer than 12 inches, they shall either be rigidly braced laterally at a point not more than 12 inches above the lower end of the stem, or there shall be an approved flexible fitting or flexible connection used and these shall not be mounted more than 12 inches from the attachment to the supporting box or fitting.

The wiring shall be rigid conduit or, where necessary, a flexible rubber cord that is approved for hard usage may be used if it is sealed properly where attachments are made. The cord shall not support the fixture but shall be supported by other suitable means. Where stems are used, a set screw shall be provided to keep the stem from loosening.

(4) **Supports.** Lighting fixtures shall be supported by approved boxes, box assemblies, and fittings for Class II locations. Class II boxes and fittings, of course, are to be dusttight.

(b) **Class II, Division 2.** Lighting fixtures of Class II, Division 2 locations must comply with the following:

(1) **Portable Lighting Equipment.** Portable lighting equipment shall be approved for Class II locations and shall be plainly marked as such. Also, the maximum size of lamp that may be used in them shall also be plainly marked.

(2) **Fixed Lighting.** Fixed lighting shall be approved for Class II locations except, if not approved, they shall be enclosed to prevent an accumulation of dust on the lamps and to prevent the escape of sparks, burning material, or hot metal. Each fixture shall be plainly marked to indicate the maximum size lamp that may be used in the fixture and, when in use, the maximum temperature of the exposed surface shall not exceed 165°C (329°F) under normal use.

(3) **Physical Damage.** See the *NEC*.

(4) **Pendant Fixtures.** The requirements for pendant fixtures for Class II, Division 1 locations are practically the same as for pendant fixtures in Class II, Division 1. Please refer to (a)(3) above.

(5) **Electric-Discharge Lamps.** Section 502-7(b) gives the requirements to be complied with for starting and control equipment for discharge lighting.

502-12. Flexible Cords, Class II, Divisions 1 and 2—Flexible cords used in Class II, Divisions 1 and 2 must conform to the following: (1) the cord must be approved for extra-hard usage; (2) a grounding conductor complying with Section 400-23 shall be enclosed in the cord with the circuit conductors; (3) an approved manner for connecting the terminals to the supply conductors shall be used; (4) clamps or other suitable means of support causing no tension on the terminal connections shall be used; and (5) when flexible cords enter boxes or fittings that are required to be dust-ignitionproof, suitable seals to prevent the entrance of dust shall be used.

502-13. Receptacles and Attachment Plugs.

(a) **Class II, Division 1.** Plugs and receptacles for use in Class II, Division 1 locations shall be provided with a grounding conductor connection for the flexible cord and be dust-ignition-proof approved for Class II locations.

(b) **Class II, Division 2.** Plugs and receptacles for use in Class II, Division 2 locations shall be provided with a grounding conductor connection for the flexible cord and be so designed that connection to the supply circuit cannot be made or broken while live parts are exposed.

502-14. Signaling, Alarm, Remote-Control, and Communication Systems, Meters, Instruments, and Relays—Refer to Article 800, covering the rules governing the installation of communication circuits, and to the definition in Article 100.

The communication circuits will include telephone, telegraph, fire and burglar alarms, watchman, and sprinkler systems. Signal, alarm, remote-control, and local loudspeaker intercommunication systems shall conform to the following:

(a) **Class II, Division 1.** In this classification, they shall conform to the following:

(1) **Wiring Methods.** In any location where accidental damage or breakdown of insulation might cause arcs, sparks, or heating, the wiring method to be used shall be by rigid conduit, intermediate metal conduit, electrical metallic tubing, or type MI cable with approved fittings. The number of conductors to be installed in conduit or EMT is not the same for current-carrying conductors, but is only limited by the 40 percent fill requirement. This is to prevent damage to the insulation when pulling in the conductors. Flexible cord approved for extra-hard usage may be used where flexibility is required and where it will not be subject to physical damage.

(2) **Contacts.** Class II, Groups E, F, or G, as required, shall be the types of enclosures for switches, circuit breakers, relays, contactors, and fuses which may interrupt other than voice currents, and for current-breaking contacts for bells, horns, howlers, sirens, and other devices in which sparks or arcs may be produced. An exception to this is if the contacts are immersed in oil or when the interruption of current occurs within a sealed chamber; then the first part need not apply. The purpose of all this is to be certain that any sparks or arcs are isolated so that no ignition or explosion will occur.

(3) **Resistors and Similar Equipment.** Enclosures shall be approved for Class II locations where there are resistors, transformers, choke coils, rectifiers, thermionic tubes, or any other heat-generating equipment.

Exception: General-purpose enclosures may be used where resistors or similar equipment are immersed in oil or if the chambers enclosing them are so sealed as to prevent the entrance of dust.

(4) **Rotation Machinery.** Section 502-8(a) shall be compiled with for motors, generators, and other rotational electric machinery.

(5) **Combustible Electrically Conductive Dusts.** When the dust happens to be of a conductive nature, such as magnesium, aluminum, aluminum bronze, or metal of other similarly hazardous characteristics, all equipment shall be specifically approved for such conditions.

(6) **Metal Dusts.** See (a)(3) of Section 502-6.

(b) **Class II, Division 2.** The following shall be complied with where signaling, alarm, remote-control, and communication systems and meters, instruments, and relays are stored in Class II, Division 2 locations:

(1) **Contacts.** Enclosures for contacts in Class II, Division 2 locations shall either conform to the requirements for contacts in Class II, Division 1, as outlined in (a)(2) above, or be enclosed in tight metal enclosures that are designed to minimize the entrance of dust, and shall have telescoping of tight-fitting covers with no openings through which, after installation, sparks or burning materials might escape.

Exception: General-purpose enclosures will be permitted to be used in circuits that under normal operating conditions do not release sufficient energy to ignite a dust layer.

(2) **Transformers and Similar Equipment.** The windings of transformers and terminal connections of the transformers, choke coils, and similar equipment shall be enclosed in tight metal enclosures that do not have ventilating openings.

(3) **Resistors and Similar Equipment.** In the installation of resistors, resistance devices, thermionic tubes, and rectifiers in Class II, Division 2 locations, they shall either conform to the requirements in (a)(3) above, or thermionic tubes, nonadjustable resistors, or rectifiers which have a maximum operating temperature that will not exceed 120°C (248°F) may be installed in general-purpose type enclosures.

(4) **Rotating Machinery.** The same requirements apply to rotating machinery of this type as apply to other rotating machinery in Class II Division 2. See Section 502-8(b).

(5) **Wiring Methods.** Section 502-4(b) shall be complied with for the wiring methods.

502-15. Live Parts, Class II, Divisions 1 and 2—Live parts in Class II, Divisions 1 and 2 locations shall not be exposed.

502-16. Grounding, Class II, Divisions 1 and 2—Article 250 with the following additional requirements shall be required in Class II, Divisions 1 and 2 locations for grounding.

(a) **Bonding.** Locknut bushings and double-locknut types of contact are not to be the grounding means for bonding purposes, but bonding jumpers Used with the proper fittings or other approved type of bondings may be used. This includes the bonding type of bushing bonded to the enclosure.

Recall that the sheet-metal type of bonding clamp is not approved. Approved means of bonding are to be used not only in hazardous locations, but also in intervening raceways, fittings, boxes, enclosures, etc., between hazardous locations and the point of grounding for service equipment.

(b) **Types of Equipment Grounding Conductors.** Where, as permitted in Section 502-4, flexible conduit use is permitted, it shall be installed with internal or external bonding jumpers in parallel with each conduit if they comply with Section 250-79.

Exception: With liquidtight flexible metal conduit 6 feet or less in length, if the fittings used and the overcurrent protection is limited to 10 amperes or less and the load is not a power utilization type of load, the grounding jumper shall be permitted to be deleted in Class II, Division 2 locations.

502-17. Surge Protection, Class II, Divisions 1 and 2—Surge arresters, including installation and connection, are required to comply with Article 280. Also, surge arresters installed in Class II, Division 1 locations shall have enclosures suitable for this type of location.

The surge capacitors shall be of a type designed for the purpose. (See Fig. 502-3.) Take note that there is overcurrent protection in the capacitor circuit.

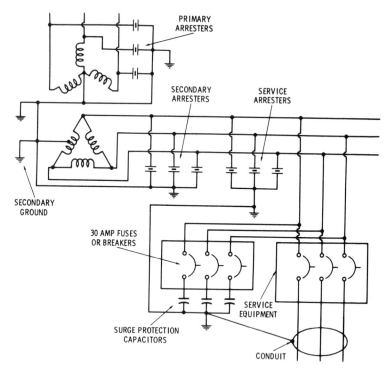

Fig. 502-3. Lightning and surge protection.

ARTICLE 503—CLASS III LOCATIONS

While Class III locations might be considered as having fewer hazards than Class I or II locations, the hazards are not to be minimized. Wherever there is a likelihood of fire or explosion, the hazard must be given the respect that is due it.

503-1. General—The general wiring and installation requirements of the Code apply to Class III locations as classified in Section 500-7, with the exceptions that are covered in this article.

Class III locations are areas in which fibers and flyings are present. The major item to remember is that the wiring equipment and apparatus shall operate at full rating without causing excessive dehydration or gradual carbonization of fibers or flyings. Any organic substance that is carbonized or very dry is susceptible to spontaneous combustion (ignition). The maximum surface temperature under operating conditions: (1) shall not exceed 165°C (329°F) for equipment not subject to overloading, and (2) shall not exceed 120°C (248°F) for motors, power transformers, etc., which may be overloaded.

Note: NFPA 505-1982 (ANSI) covers electric trucks.

503-2. Transformers and Capacitors, Class II, Divisions 1 and 2 —Refer to Section 502-2(b), which covers transformers and capacitors.

503-3. Wiring Methods—(a) and (b) below cover wiring methods:

(a) **Class III, Division 1.** Wiring methods in Class III, Division 1 shall be rigid metal conduit, rigid nonmetallic conduit, intermediate metal conduit, EMT, dusttight wireways, Type MI, MC, or SNM cables if approved fittings are used at terminations.

   (1) **Boxes and Fittings.** Only dusttight boxes and fittings shall be used.

   (2) **Flexible Connections.** If it is necessary to have flexible connections in dusttight locations, you shall use flexible connectors and liquidtight flexible metal conduits, and, of course, approved fittings are to be used. Extra-hard usage cord that is provided with bushed fittings may be used. An additional conductor for equipment grounding must be provided in the flexible cord, or other approved means may be used for the grounding purpose.

     Section 502-4(a)(2) approved dusttight flexible connectors, flexible metal conduit with approved fittings, or flexible cord approved for extra hard usage and with approved fittings and seals. Grounding conductors were also required for bonding.

(b) **Class III, Division 2.** Wiring methods shall be the same as for Class III, Division 2 locations covered in (a) above, with the exception that in sections, compartments, or areas used solely for storage and containing no machinery, open wiring on insulators conforming to the requirements of Article 320 may be used, but only on the condition that protection as required by Section 320-14 be provided where conductors are not run in roof spaces, and well out of reach of sources of physical damage. Section 320-14 provides for the protection of open wiring from physical damage.

503-4. Switches, Circuit Breakers, Motor Controllers and Fuses, Class III, Divisions 1 and 2—The items in the title of this section, and also including push buttons, relays, and similar devices, shall be in dusttight enclosures.

503-5. Control Transformers and Resistors, Class III, Divisions 1 and 2—The same requirements apply here as in Class II, Division 2 locations covered in Section 502-7(b). An exception to this is that, in Class III, Division 1 locations, if these devices are in the same enclosures with the switching devices of control equipment, and are only used for starting or for short time duty, the enclosure may have telescoping covers or other effective means for preventing the escape of sparks or burning material as covered in Section 503-1.

503-6. Motors and Generators, Class III, Divisions 1 and 2—Motors, generators, and other rotating machinery located in Class III, Divisions 1 and 2 locations shall be totally enclosed and nonventilated, or totally enclosed and pipe-ventilated, or totally enclosed and fan-cooled.

An exception to the above is that the Code-enforcing authority may accept the following if, in his judgment, there is only moderate accumulation of lint and flyings:

a. Squirrel-cage textile motors if they are self-cleaning.
b. Standard open-type machines that do not have open arcing contacts.
c. With standard open-type machines if the switching mechanisms or resistance devices are enclosed within tight housings without any openings for ventilation.

503-7. Ventilating Piping, Class III, Divisions 1 and 2—Ventilating piping for Class III, Divisions 1 and 2 that is used for motors, generators, or any other rotating electric machines, or used for enclosures for electrical equipment, shall be made of metal no lighter than No. 24 MSG or other noncombustible substantial materials, and shall be required to comply with the following: (1) ventilating pipes shall lead directly outside into clean air; (2) the other end of the ventilating pipe shall be screened to prevent the entrance of small animals and birds; and (3) it shall be protected from physical damage, rusting, or corrosive influences.

These ventilating pipes shall be tight enough for both the pipes and their connections to prevent the entrance of any small amounts of fibers or flyings into the ventilated equipment or enclosure and to prevent the escape of sparks, flames, or burning materials that could ignite accumulations of fibers or flyings or other nearby combustible materials. The pipe shall be of the lock seam type, and riveted or welded joints are to be used. It will be permitted to use tight-fitting slip joints where some flexibility is necessary in connections to motors.

503-8. Utilization Equipment, Class III, Divisions 1 and 2—Utilization equipment shall conform to the following:

(a) **Heaters.** Only approved electric heater utilization equipment will be allowed in Class III locations.

(b) **Motors.** Motors of motor-driven utilization equipment that is used in Class III locations are subject to the same requirements as for motors covered in Section 503-6. When motor-driven utilization equipment is readily movable from one location to another, it shall be required to meet the standards required for the most hazardous location in which it is to be used.

(c) **Switches, Circuit Breakers, Motor Controllers and Fuses.** Section 503-4 applies to switches, circuit breakers, motor controllers and fuses, and also to the same items used with utilization equipment.

503-9. Lighting Fixtures, Class III, Division 1 and 2—Lamps shall be installed in fixtures which shall conform to the following:

(a) **Fixed Lighting.** There shall be enclosures for fixed lamps and lampholders that shall: (1) be designed to minimize the entrance of fibers and flyings; (2) prevent the escape of sparks, burning materials, or hot metal; (3) be plainly marked for the maximum wattage lamp that shall be used; and (4) be capable of being used without exceeding a maximum exposed surface temperature of 165°C (329°F) under normal operating conditions.

(b) **Physical Damage.** Fixtures are to be either guarded or located so as not to be subject to physical damage.

(c) **Pendant Fixtures.** In the suspension of pendant fixtures the suspension stem will be threaded rigid metal conduit, or threaded intermediate metal conduit, equivalent sizes of threaded metal tubing, or chains that use approved fittings.

If the stem is longer than 12 inches (305 mm), it shall: be permanently and effectively supported laterally against displacement, and this bracing shall not be more than 12 inches (305 mm) above the lamp fixture; and have an approved flexible connector provided at a distance of not more than 12 inches (305 mm) from the point of attachment to the supporting box or fitting.

(d) **Portable Lighting Equipment.** Portable lighting equipment shall conform to all of the requirements of (a) above, and, in addition, shall: be provided with a handle; have a suitable guard for the lamp; and have a lampholder of the unswitched type, with no exposed metal parts, with no means for receiving an attachment plug, and with all exposed noncurrents carrying metal parts grounded.

503-10. Flexible Cords, Class III, Divisions 1 and 2—Flexible cords used in Class III, Divisions 1 and 2 locations must comply with the following: (1) must be approved for extra-heavy usage; (2) must contain an grounding conductor in addition to the conductors of the circuit in compliance with Section 400-23; (3) the connections to terminals or supply conductors shall be done in an approved manner; (4) they must be supported by clamps or other suitable means; and (5) there shall be a suitable means to prevent the entrance of fibers or flyings at the point where the cord enters boxes or fittings.

503-11. Receptacles and Attachment Plugs, Class III, Divisions 1 and 2—Receptacles and attachment plugs must be of the grounding type and shall be so designed as to allow only minimal accumulations of fibers or flyings and to prevent sparks of molten particles to escape.

Exception: If, in the opinion of the authority having jurisdiction, there will be only moderate accumulations of lint or flyings in the vicinity of the receptacle, and if the receptacle is readily accessible for cleaning, general-purpose grounding-type receptacles, if they are mounted so as to minimize the entry of fibers or flyings, may be allowed.

503-12. Signal, Alarm, Remote-Control and Local Loudspeaker Intercommunication Systems, Class III, Divisions 1 and 2—See the *NEC.*

503-13. Electric Cranes and Hoists, and Similar Equipment, Class III, Divisions 1 and 2—Where travelling cranes and hoists for handling materials and similar installed equipment operate over fibers or accumulations of flyings, they shall conform to the following:

(a) The power supply shall be isolated from all other systems (this may be done by isolation transformers) and shall be equipped with an acceptable ground detector that will: give an audible and visual alarm, maintaining the alarm as long as power is supplied to the system and the ground fault remains, and automatically de-energize the contact conductors in the case of a fault to ground.

(b) Contact conductors for cranes and hoists shall be so located or guarded as to be inaccessible to other than authorized persons and protect against accidental contact with foreign objects.

(c) Current collectors shall be so located or guarded so as to confine normal sparking and prevent the escape of sparks or hot particles. In order to reduce sparking, there shall be two or more separate contact surfaces for each contact conductor and a reliable means for keeping the contact conductors and current collectors free of accumulation of dust and of flyings and lint.

(d) Sections 503-4 and 503-5 covered various control equipment. The requirements of Sections 503-4 and 503-5 apply to control equipment for electric cranes, hoists and similar equipment in Class III, Division 1 and 2 locations.

503-14. Storage-Battery Charging Equipment, Class II, Divisions 1 and 2—Equipment for the charging of storage batteries shall be located in separate rooms, shall be built or lined with material that is substantially noncombustible and so constructed as to satisfactorily exclude flyings or lint, and shall be well ventilated.

Not only are the lint and flyings a problem, but so are the fumes from the batteries. Proper ventilation will also assist in taking care of these fumes.

503-15. Live Parts, Class III, Divisions 1 and 2—There shall be no live parts exposed in Class III locations, with the exception provided for in Section 503-13 pertaining to electric cranes and hoists.

503-16. Grounding, Class III, Divisions 1 and 2—Wiring and equipment in Class III, Divisions 1 and 2 shall be grounded as specified in Article 250 with the following additional requirements:

(a) **Bonding.** The locknut-bushing and double-locknut types of contact shall not be depended upon for bonding purposes, but bonding jumpers with the proper fittings or other approved means of bonding shall be used. This could be bonding-type bushings bonded to the enclosure. This means of bonding shall be required to apply to all intervening raceways, fittings, boxes, enclosures, etc., between the Class III locations and the point where the service equipment bonding begins.

(b) **Types of Equipment Grounding Conductor.** Where flexible metal conduit is used, as permitted in Section 503-3, it shall be installed with internal or external bonding jumpers in parallel with the flexible conduit and that meet the requirements of Section 250-79.

ARTICLE 510—HAZARDOUS (CLASSIFIED) LOCATIONS— SPECIFIC

510-1. Scope—Articles 501, 502 and 503 give the general requirements for Class I, II, and III locations. The Provisions of Articles 511 to 517 inclusive shall apply to occupancies or parts of occupancies which are hazardous because of atmospheric concentrations of hazardous gases, vapors, or liquids, or because of deposits or accumulations of materials which may be readily ignitible.

The intent of these articles is to assist Code-enforcing authorities in the classification of areas of locations with respect to hazardous conditions. These hazardous conditions may or may not require construction and equipment conforming to Articles 501, 502, and 503. They also set forth additional requirements that may be necessary in specific hazardous locations.

510-2. General—The general rules of the code shall apply to the installation of electric wiring and equipment for use in the occupancies covered within the scope of Articles 511 to 517 inclusive, and the inspection authority is responsible for judging with respect to the application of specific rules. These include:

Article 511—Commercial Garages, Repair and Storage
Article 513—Aircraft Hangars
Article 514—Gasoline Dispensing and Service Stations
Article 515—Bulk-Storage Plants
Article 516—Spray Application, Dipping and Coating Processes
Article 517—Health Care Facilities

It is recommended by the Code that the authorities enforcing the Code become familiar with the National Fire Protection Association's Standards that apply to occupancies included within the scope of Articles 511 to 517 inclusive. Not only should inspectors be familiar with these Codes and Standards, but anyone that designs or makes electrical installations should also be familiar with them. Some of the NFPA Standards involved are listed in Appendix A in the *NEC*. See also Section 90-3.

There are others that will be of great assistance in evaluating the hazards that might be involved, and these may be purchased from the National Fire Protection Association, Batterymarch Park, Quincy, MA 02269, in an 8-volume set that includes all standards. The individual Codes may also be purchased.

ARTICLE 511—COMMERCIAL GARAGES, REPAIR AND STORAGE

511-1. Scope—This article covers occupancies or locations that are used for service and repair in conjunction with self-propelled vehicles (including passenger automobiles, buses, trucks, tractors, etc.) where flammable liquids are used for fuel or power for operation.

Note: See the definition of garage in *NEC* Article 100.

511-2. Locations—Occupancies for flammable fuel that is transferred into vehicle fuel tanks will be covered in Article 514. Areas used exclusively for parking garages and parking or storage, and where no repair work is done except exchange of parts and routine maintenance that do not require the use of electrical equipment, open flame, or the use of volatile flammable liquids, are not classifed. There shall, however, be adequate ventilation to carry the exhaust fumes away from engines. (These last items are exceptions that one does not ordinarily meet.)

Note: Information on parking structures is covered in NFPA 88A-1985, and Repair Garages NFPA 88B-1985. See the definition of volatile flammable liquid in *NEC* Article 100.

511-3. Class I Locations—Classification under Article 500. This is for further clarification of this particular usage.

(a) **Up to a Level of 18 Inches Above the Floor.** The entire area of a floor up to a height of 18 inches above the floor is a Class I, Division 2 location, unless the enforcing agency determines that there is mechanical ventilation that will change the air completely four times every hour. Fig. 511-1 will assist in a clarification of the above.

(b) **Any Pit or Depression Below Floor Level.** Pits or depressions below floor level, but which extend up to the floor level, shall be considered as Class I, Division 1 locations, except that if the pit or depression is unventilated, the authority enforcing the Code may judge the area to be a Class I, Division 2 location. See Fig. 511-2.

Any pit or depression in which six air changes per hour are exhausted at the floor level of the pit shall be permitted to be judged by the enforcing agency to be a Class I, Division 2 location.

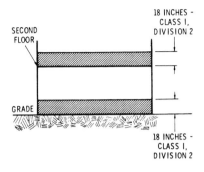

Fig. 511-1. Hazardous areas of commercial garages above grade level.

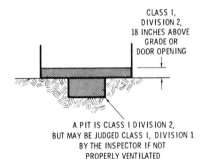

Fig. 511-2. Hazardous areas and classification of pits or depressions in garage floors.

In cases where there is adequate and positive ventilation of the floors below grade level, it is up to the inspection authority to classify the areas. He may judge the floors to be Class I, Division 2 up to a height of 18 inches above the floors, even though they are below grade level. It is not mandatory that he judge them this way, however. See Fig. 511-3.

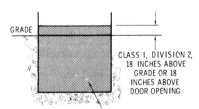

Fig. 511-3. Hazardous areas of commercial garages below grade level.

(c) **Areas Adjacent to Defined Locations with Positive Pressure Ventilation.** Areas adjacent to Class I, Division 2 locations in which there is no likelihood of hazardous vapors being released (such as stockrooms) are also Class I, Division 2 locations unless the floor of the adjacent area is elevated 18 inches above the floor of the hazardous area, or unless a separation between the two areas is provided by an 18-inch tight curb or partition.

Gasoline vapors are heavier than air and settle to the floor area. The intent here is that, since these vapors settle to the floor, they may be transmitted into other rooms which might look to be nonhazardous areas since there are no vapors likely to be released in that room. Transmittal of the hazardous vapors may be stopped by an elevated floor, tight curb, or a partition, each at least 18 inches high, between the two rooms.

(d) **Adjacent Areas by Special Permission.** Adjacent areas that are well ventilated or have different air pressure or physical spacing and where, in the opinion of the authority having jurisdiction, no ignition hazard exists, shall be classified as nonhazardous.

(e) **Fuel Dispensing Units.** When fuel dispensing units that handle other than petroleum gas, which is prohibited, are located in the building, you shall use Article 514 to govern the regulations for installation.

If mechanical ventilation is provided in the area where dispensing occurs, the controls shall be interlocked so that the dispenser cannot be operated without the ventilation equipment operating as described in Section 500-5(b).

(f) **Portable Lighting Equipment.** Portable lighting equipment such as extension cords and lamps is required to have a handle, lampholder, hook, and substantial guard, all attached to the lampholder handle. Exterior surfaces that are likely to come into contact with battery terminals, wiring terminals, or other objects shall be of a nonconducting material or shall be effectively insulated. Lampholders shall be of the unswitched type and shall have no plug-in for attachment plugs. The outer shell shall be of moulded composition or other material approved for the purpose. Metal-shell, lined lampholders, either of the switched or unswitched type, shall not be used.

Unless the lamp and cord are supported or arranged so that they cannot be used in hazardous areas classified in Section 511-3, they shall be of an approved type for hazardous locations.

511-4. Wiring and Equipment in Class I Locations—In hazardous locations as defined in Section 511-3, all of the requirements of Article 501 shall apply. The location will have to be judged either Class I, Division 1, or Class I, Division 2, and the wiring and equipment conform to the classification.

Raceways embedded in a masonry wall or buried beneath a floor shall be considered to be within the hazardous area above the floor if any connections or extensions lead into or through such areas.

As an example take the case of a garage at grade level with the doors opening at grade level. The classification would be Class I, Division 2 to a height of 18 inches above the floor. If all of the wiring and equipment is kept above the 18-inch height from the floor, EMT and general-duty equipment and devices can be used. If the wiring goes below the 18-inch point (possibly conduit is run in the floor slab), this part would be Class I, Division 2 and the wiring would have to meet the requirements of this classification, and would have to have seals above the 18-inch height to pass from the hazardous area into the nonhazardous area. Any equipment that is below the 18-inch level will also have to be approved for a Class I, Division 2 location.

511-5. Sealing—See the *NEC*.

511-6. Wiring in Spaces Above Class I Locations.

(a) **Fixed Wiring Above Class I Locations.** The only types of wiring permitted above hazardous areas are metal raceways, rigid nonmetallic conduit, electrical nonmetallic lubing, Types MI, TC, SNM, or MC cable. Cellular metal floor raceways may be used only to supply ceiling outlets or extensions to areas below the floor, outlets from the same shall not be connected above the floor.

(b) **Pendants.** Pendants must be approved for hard usage and the type of service for which they are to be used.

(c) **Grounded Conductors.** Circuits that supply pendants or portables are required to have a grounded conductor as covered in Article 200. With receptacles and attachment plug connectors or similar devices, the grounded conductor that carries current to the equipment supplied shall be attached to a polarized prong, and the grounded conductor shall be connected to the screw shell of the lampholder or to the grounded connection of the utilization equipment supplied.

In explanation, the standard 120-volt receptacle has two different length slots, but the majority of attachment plugs have both prongs the same width. The wider slot of the receptacle connects to the grounded (neutral) conductor of the circuit (the white screw). In garages, plugs that have two different width prongs are to be used. Thus, the attachment plug can only go into the receptacle one way. The neutral of the cord is attached to the wide prong and, if this is an extension cord with a portable lamp, the grounded conductor is

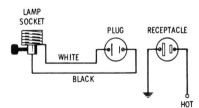

Fig. 511-4. Receptacles and attachment plugs.

to be connected to the screw shell of the lampholder. Thus, the polarity of the circuit can be maintained. (See Fig. 511-4, page 493.) Care shall also be taken to connect the grounded terminal of utilization equipment to the grounded conductor of the cord or circuits.

(d) **Attachment Plug Receptacles.** Attachment plugs and receptacles shall be above the Class I location or shall be of the approved type for Class I locations. From 18 inches down to the floor is the classified area.

511-7. Equipment Above Class I Locations.

(a) **Arcing Equipment.** If equipment is less than 12 feet above the floor level and is capable of producing arcs, sparks, or particles of hot metal such as cutouts, switches, charging panels, generators, motors, and other equipment (excluding receptacles, lamps, and lampholders) and has make-and-break or sliding contacts, they are to be of the totally enclosed type or so constructed as to prevent escape of sparks or hot metal particles.

(b) **Fixed Lighting.** Lamps and lampholders, mounted in a fixed location for lighting and mounted over lanes through which vehicles are ordinarily driven or where the fixtures may be exposed to physical damage, are to be located not less than 12 feet above floor level. An exception to this is that if the fixtures are of a totally enclosed type and are constructed so as to prevent the escape of sparks or hot metal particles, they may be located lower than 12 feet.

511-8. Battery Charging Equipment—Battery chargers and their control equipment, and the batteries that are being charged, are not to be located in areas classified in Section 511-3.

511-9. Electric Vehicle Charging.

(a) **Connections.** When flexible cords and connectors are used for charging, they shall be of the type that has been approved for extra-hard usage, and the ampacity of the conductors must be adequate to handle the charging current.

(b) **Connector Design and Location.** Connectors that are installed for disconnecting must be designed and installed so that they will disconnect easily at any position of the charging cable. Any live parts shall be guarded to prevent accidental contact. No connector shall be located in a Class I area, which was defined in Section 511-3.

(c) **Plug Connections to Vehicles.** If plugs are provided for direct connection, then Section 511-3 shall be adhered to so that the connection will not be in a Class I location, and if the cords are supplied from overhead, the lowest point of the plug shall be at least 6 inches above the floor. When the vehicle is equipped with an approved plug that may be readily disconnected and an automatic arrangement is provided for both cord and plug so they are not exposed to physical damage, no other connectors will be required in the cable at the outlet.

511-10. Ground-Fault Circuit-Interrupter Protection for Personnel—A ground-fault circuit-interrupter shall be installed for the protection of personnel in all 125-volt single-phase 15- and 20-ampere receptacles that are used for electrical connection to diagnostic equipment, electrical hand tools, and where portable lighting devices are used.

ARTICLE 513—AIRCRAFT HANGARS

513-1. Definition—This shall include occupancies that are used for storage or servicing of aircraft in which gasoline, jet fuels, or other volatile flammable fuels or flammable gases are used. Not included are locations used exclusively for aircraft which have never contained such volatile flammable gases or liquids and aircraft which have been drained or properly purged.

Note: See the definition of volatile flammable liquids in *NEC* Article 100.

513-2. Classification of Location—Classification under Article 500.

(a) **Below Floor Level.** Pits or depressions below the hangar floor level shall be considered as Class I, Division I locations, and this classification shall extend to the floor level. See Fig. 513-1.

(b) **Areas Not Cut Off or Ventilated.** The entire area of the hangar shall be considered as a Class I, Division 2 location to a height of 18 inches above the floor and shall also include adjacent areas into which the hazards may be communicated into unless suitably cut off from the hangar as described in (d) below. See Fig. 513-1.

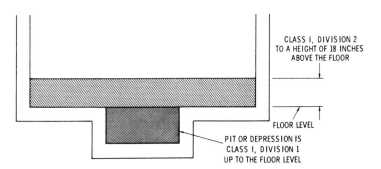

CLASS I, DIVISION 2
TO A HEIGHT OF 18 INCHES
ABOVE THE FLOOR

FLOOR LEVEL

PIT OR DEPRESSION IS
CLASS I, DIVISION 1
UP TO THE FLOOR LEVEL

Fig. 513-1. Hazardous areas in aircraft hangars.

(c) **Vicinity of Aircraft.** The area immediately adjacent to the aircraft shall be a Class I, Division 2 location. Such an area is defined as being within 5 feet horizontally from aircraft power plants, aircraft fuel tanks, or aircraft structures containing fuel. These locations shall extend from the floor level vertically to a level of 5 feet above the wings and above the engine enclosures.

(d) **Areas Suitably Cut Off and Ventilated.** See (b) above. Any adjacent area into which hazardous vapors are likely to be communicated or released, such as stockrooms and electrical control rooms, shall be a Class I, Division 2 location up to a height of 18 inches. These adjacent areas need not be classified as hazardous if they are effectively cut off from the hangar itself by walls or partitions and are adequately ventilated.

513-3. Wiring and Equipment in Class I Location—All wiring, whether portable or fixed, and all equipment that is located in the hazardous area of an aircraft hangar (hazardous as defined in Section 513-2) shall conform to the provisions of Article 501. If above the floor, the area shall be a Class I, Division 2 location, and if in our under the floor, the area shall be a Class I, Division 1 location. If any wiring is located in vaults, pits, or ducts, adequate drainage shall be provided, and the wiring shall not be placed in the same compartment with any service, with the exception that wiring may be placed in a duct with compressed air. Approved outlets, attachment plugs, and receptacles are to be used in Class I locations, or the design shall be such that they cannot be energized while the connection is being made or broken.

513-4. Wiring Not within Class I Locations.

(a) **Fixed Wiring.** With all of the fixed wiring that is installed in hangers—but not within Class I locations, which are defined in Section 513-2—the wiring methods shall be installed in metal raceways or type MI, TC, SNM, or MC cable may be used.

Exception: All wiring that is located in nonhazardous areas as defined in Section 513-2(d) is required to be of a type recognized in Chapter 3.

(b) **Pendants.** If flexible cords are used for pendants, they must be suitable for the location, and also approved for hard usage. Each cord must contain an equipment grounding conductor as well as the current-carrying conductors.

(c) **Portable Equipment.** Flexible cord may be used for portable utilization equipment and lamps, provided the flexible cord is approved for extra-hard usage. Included in such cord shall be a grounding conductor.

(d) **Grounded and Grounding Conductors.** When circuits supplying portables and pendants include a grounded conductor (Article 200), they shall have the following devices of the polarized type and the grounded conductor of the flexible cord shall be connected to the screw shell of any lampholder or to the grounded terminal of all utilization equipment: receptacles, attachment plugs, connectors, and similar devices.

Grounding continuity that is acceptable shall be provided between fixed raceways and the noncurrent-carrying parts (metallic) of pendant fixtures, portable lamps, portable and utilization equipment. This may be accomplished by bonding or attaching the grounding conductor to the fixed raceway system.

513-5. Equipment Not within Class I Locations.

(a) **Arcing Equipment.** In locations other than those described in Section 513-2, equipment which may produce arcs, sparks, or particles of hot metals, such as lamps and lampholders for fixed lighting, cutouts, switches, receptacles, charging panels, generators, motors, or other equipment having make-and-break or sliding contacts, shall be of such a type that the escape of sparks or hot metal particles will be prevented by being of the totally enclosed type, or so constructed as to prevent escape of sparks or hot metal particles. In areas described in Section 513-2(d), equipment may be of the general-purpose type.

(b) **Lampholders.** Metal-shell, fiber-lined-type lampholders are not permitted to be used for fixed incandescent lighting.

(c) **Portable Lighting Equipment.** Only portable lighting equipment that is approved for Use within a hangar shall be used.

(d) **Portable Equipment.** All portable utilization equipment that is or may be used in the hangar shall be of an approved and suitable type for use in Class I, Division 2 locations.

513-6. Stanchions, Rostrums, and Docks.

(a) **In Class I Locations.** Electrical wiring, outlets, and equipment, including lamps, that are attached to or on stanchions, rostrums, or docks that are either located or might be located in a Class I locations, as defined in Section 513-2(c), are required to meet the requirements of Class I, Division 2 locations.

(b) **Not in Class I Location.** Stanchions, rostrums, or docks which are not, or will not likely be, located in the hazardous areas defined in Section 513-2(c), shall not have wiring and equipment that conform to areas which are not classified as hazardous. The wiring for these areas was covered in Section 513-4, and the equipment for these areas was covered in Section 513-5. Exceptions to these requirements are as follows: (1) wiring and equipment that will be within the 18-inch classification above the floor shall be approved for Class I, Division 2 locations as covered in Section 513-6(a); and receptacles and attachment plugs shall be of the locking type that will not be readily pulled apart.

(c) **Mobile Type.** Mobile stanchions with electrical equipment which conforms to part (b) above shall carry at least one sign, permanently affixed to the stanchion, which shall read: "WARNING—KEEP 5 FEET CLEAR OF AIRCRAFT ENGINES AND FUEL TANK AREAS."

513-7. Sealing—Sealing in Class I locations was covered in Sections 501-5, 501-5(a), and 501-5(b)(2). The requirements of these sections shall apply to horizontal as well as to vertical boundaries of the hazardous areas. Raceways that are embedded in or under concrete will be in the same hazardous area that is above the floor when any connections lead into or through such areas. This will require seal-offs when connecting to enclosures where there is a possibility of arcs or sparks, or when going from a hazardous to a nonhazardous area.

513-8. Aircraft Electrical Systems—See the *NEC*.

513-9. Aircraft Battery—Charging and Equipment—It is not permitted to charge aircraft batteries while they are installed in the aircraft, if the aircraft is located in the hangar or partially located within the hangar.

Battery chargers and their control equipment, tables, racks, trays, and wiring must conform to the provisions of Article 480 and shall not be located in a hazardous area as defined in Section 513-2, but should be located in a separate building or in an area as defined in Section 513-2(d), that is an area suitably isolated from the hazardous area. Mobile chargers shall have at least one permanently affixed sign reading: "WARNING—KEEP 5 FEET CLEAR OF AIRCRAFT ENGINES AND FUEL TANK AREAS."

513-10. External Power Sources for Energizing Aircraft.

(a) **Not Less than 18 Inches Above Floor.** Aircraft energizers shall be so designed and mounted that all of the electrical equipment and fixed wiring will be at least 18 inches above the floor and will not be operated in a hazardous area as defined in Section 513-2(c).

(b) **Marking for Mobile Units.** Mobile energizers shall have at least one permanently affixed sign reading: "WARNING—KEEP 5 FEET CLEAR OF AIRCRAFT ENGINES AND FUEL TANK AREAS."

(c) **Cords.** Flexible cords used for aircraft energizers or ground support equipment shall be of an approved and an extra-hard-usage type; an equipment grounding conductor shall also be installed within the cord.

513-11. Mobile Servicing Equipment with Electric Components.

(a) **General.** Mobile servicing equipment that is not suitable for Class I, Division 2 locations shall be so designed and mounted that all fixed wiring and equipment will be at least 18 inches above the floor. This equipment includes vacuum cleaners, air compressors, air movers, and similar equipment. None of this equipment shall be operated in the hazardous areas which were defined in Section 513-2(c). All such equipment shall have at least one permanently affixed sign reading: "WARNING—KEEP 5 FEET CLEAR OF AIRCRAFT ENGINES AND FUEL TANK AREAS."

(b) **Cords and Connectors.** Flexible cords for mobile equipment shall be suitable for the type of service and be approved for extra-hard usage. They shall also include an equipment-grounding conductor. Receptacles and attachment plugs shall be suitable for the type of service and approved for the location in which they are installed. There shall also be a means of connecting the equipment-grounding conductor to the raceway system. This grounding may be accomplished in any approved manner.

(c) **Restricted Use.** No equipment shall be used or operated in areas where maintenance operations are likely to release flammable gases or vapors or flammable liquids unless the equipment is approved for Class I, Division 2 locations.

513-12. Grounding—All metal raceways and all noncurrent-carrying metal portions of fixed or portable equipment, irrespective of their operating voltages, are to be grounded as covered in Article 250.

ARTICLE 514—GASOLINE DISPENSING AND SERVICE STATIONS

514-1. Definition—This classification shall include locations where fuel is transferred to the fuel tanks of self-propelled vehicles, or to auxiliary tanks. The fuels referred to are gasoline or other volatile flammable liquids or liquefied flammable gases. A responsibility is placed on the inspection authority by the following part:

If the authority having jurisdiction is able to satisfactorily determine that flammable liquids have a flash point below 38°C (100°F), such as gasoline, will not be handled, he may classify such a location as nonhazardous.

Reference is also made to the NFPA Automotive and Marine Service Station Code, NFPA 30A-1984.

In practically every gasoline-dispensing location there are also lubritoriums, service rooms, repair rooms, offices, salesrooms, compressor rooms, storage rooms, rest rooms, and possibly a furnace room, as well as other areas that might be associated with a filling station. The wiring in these locations shall conform to Articles 510 and 511.

514-2. Class I Locations—Apply Table 514-2 where Class I liquids are stored, handled, or dispensed; it shall be used to delineate and classify service stations. An area beyond an unpierced wall, roof, or other solid partion shall not be classified as a Class I location. (Refer to the *NEC* for Table 514-2 and see Section 90-3.)

Figures 514-1 and 514-2 show the hazardous areas around a gasoline dispensing pump location. Figure 514-3 shows the hazardous area around vapor pipes.

This section was inserted in the Code because of the practice of dispensing such liquids as "white gasoline" from 55-gallon drums, etc., for special purposes. Please note that this is a hazard.

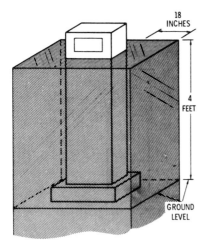

18 INCHES

4 FEET

GROUND LEVEL

Fig. 514-1. Hazardous areas around a gasoline dispenser.

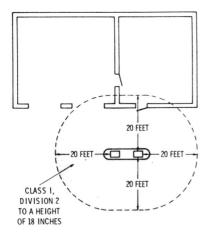

20 FEET

20 FEET — — 20 FEET

20 FEET

CLASS I, DIVISION 2 TO A HEIGHT OF 18 INCHES

Fig. 514-2. Hazardous areas around gasoline service stations.

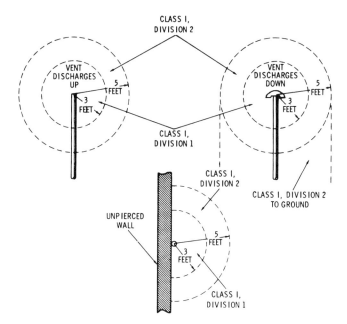

Fig. 514-3. Hazardous areas around vent pipes.

514-3. Wiring and Equipment within Class I Locations—Electrical equipment and wiring in the Class I, Division 1 and Class I, Division 2 locations, as defined in Section 514-2, shall be approved and suitable for these locations. The only wiring methods acceptable (see Article 501) are threaded rigid metal conduit, threaded steel intermediate metal conduit or, Type MI Cable. General-purpose devices and equipment are not permitted in these locations.

Section 501-13 states that conductors used in these locations shall be approved for the location. There are many conductors under various trade names that are approved for the location. These conductors have a nylon outer covering to protect them from gasoline. The Underwriter's Laboratories have a listing on the conductors that have been tested. TW wire, as such, is not approved. Also lead-covered cable may be used for the conductors, but is seldom used because of costs and the difficulty of pulling it into conduit.

Exception: Unless Section 514-8 permits.

514-4. Wiring and Equipment Above Class I Locations—Class I locations are defined in Section 514-2. Sections 511-6 and 511-7 cover wiring methods and equipment for use above Class I locations. These requirements apply to this article also. The only wiring methods recognized for use in these locations are metal raceways rigid nonmetallic, electrical nonmetallic tubing, or Type MI, TC, SNM, or MC cable.

514-5. Circuit Disconnects—Every circuit leading to or through a dispensing pump must be provided with a switch or other suitable means that disconnects all conductors at the same time from the source of supply to the pumps. This also includes the neutral conductor, if one is used.

Although this is very plain, it is often misinterpreted. The intent of the ruling is that, when the supply is disconnected from the source, there shall be no conductors connected that lead to or through a dispensing pump. There are various means of doing this. Special breakers are available that have a pigtail which ties to the neutral bus, and both the hot and the neutral will be disconnected when the breaker is in the "off" position. A double pole switch may also be used. See Fig. 514-4.

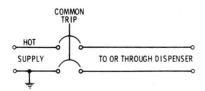

Fig. 514-4. **Neutral must also be switched to islands.**

514-6. Sealing.

(a) **At Dispenser.** A seal shall be provided in every conduit run that enters or leaves a dispenser or any enclosures or cavities that happen to be in direct communication with the dispenser. The sealing shall be the first fitting where the conduit leaves the earth or concrete."

This also is often misinterpreted. Notice the words "first fitting." This means exactly what it says. There is often an attempt to define a conduit coupling as not being a fitting, but this is not the case—it is a fitting.

All seals are to be readily accessible. Often someone attempts to install a seal at the edge of the hazardous area and bury it in the earth. This is not allowed. It shall be carried into the building or some other place out of the hazardous area and then installed. If, for instance, The seal goes into the service panel, and there is a hazardous area below the panel, the seal must be 18 inches or more above the floor, and there can be no fitting of any kind between the floor and the seal. See Fig. 514-5.

(b) **At Boundary.** Additional seals shall be provided as covered in Section 501-5. Section 501-5(a)(4) and 501-5(b)(2) will apply to both horizontal and vertical boundaries between the hazardous and nonhazardous areas.

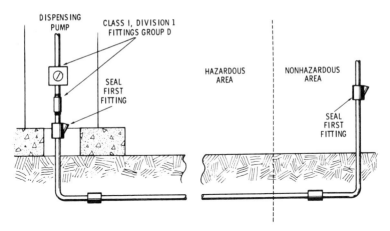

Fig. 514-5.   Seals required in gasoline service stations.

514-7. Grounding—All metal parts of the dispensing pump, metal raceways, and electrical equipment, regardless of voltage, shall be grounded as provided for in Article 250. This grounding will extend back to the service equipment and service ground. Care should be taken in grounding properly, for an accidental fault could cause a poor ground connection to arc and cause an explosion. See *NEC* Section 501-16.

514-8. Underground Wiring—The wiring installed underground shall be threaded rigid metal conduit or threaded steel intermediate metal conduit (remember that the soil conditions must be such as to prevent electrolysis from damaging the conduits; means should be used to protect the conduits). Any portion of the electrical wiring or equipment that is below the surface of Class I, Divisions 1 or 2 locations (See Table 514-2) will be considered to be in a Class I, Division 1 location extending to at least the point of emergence above grade. You are also referred to Section 300-5(a) Exception No. 3.

Exception No. 1: If MI cable is installed as per Article 330, it shall be permitted to be used.

Exception No. 2: If buried under not less than 2 feet of earth, rigid nonmetallic conduit that meetsthe requirements of Article 347 will be permitted to be used. When rigid nonmetallic conduit is used, threaded rigid conduit or threaded steel intermediate metal conduit is required to be used for the last 2 feet of the underground raceway; an equipment grounding conductor must be installed in the raceway for electrical continuity and grounding of the noncurrent-carrying metal parts.

Rigid nonmetallic conduit was added to the Code to take the place of metal conduit and thus relieve the problem of corrosion which might let fumes or gasoline into the conduit. The use of nonmetallic conduit in no way changes the sealing that is required, which remains the same. Metal conduit is still to be brought up into the dispenser or the nonhazardous location, as the case might be. This is necessary to prevent physical damage.

ARTICLE 515—BULK STORAGE PLANTS

515-1. Definition—This designation shall include locations where gasoline or other volatile flammable liquids are stored in tanks having an aggregate capacity of one carload or more, and from which such products are distributed (usually by tank truck).

515-2. Class I Locations—If Class I liquids are stored, handled, or dispensed, Table 515-2 shall be applied and shall also be used to describe and classify bulk storage plants. The classified area shall not extend beyond unpierced walls, roofs, floors, or other solid partitions.

See Table 515-2 in the *NEC* for the requirements. Also refer to Figs. 515-1 through 515-5.

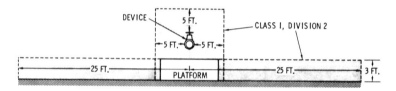

Fig. 515-1. Adequately ventilated indoor areas.

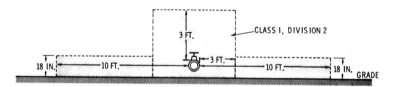

Fig. 515-2. Outdoor areas.

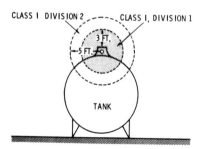

Fig. 515-3. Classification around vents.

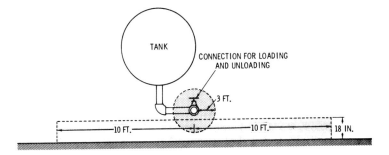

Fig. 515-4. Classification around bottom filler.

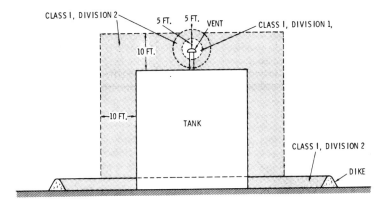

Fig. 515-5. Classification around vertical tank.

515-3. Wiring and Equipment Within Class I Locations—The hazardous areas for bulk storage plants are defined in Section 515-2. All wiring and equipment installed in these areas will be subject to the regulations of Article 501.

Exception: Section 515-5 requires this exception to be used.

515-4. Wiring and Equipment Above Class I Locations—The requirements of this Section are practically the same as for commercial garages. The main concern is sparks, arcs, or hot metal particles that might drop into the hazardous area and cause trouble. All fixed wiring above hazardous locations shall be in metal raceways or be Type MI, TC, SNM, or Type MC cable. Equipment which might produce arcs, sparks, or particles of hot metal, such as lamps and lampholders for fixed lighting, cutouts, switches, receptacles, motors, or other equipment having make-and-break or sliding contacts, shall be totally enclosed or so constructed as to prevent the escape of sparks or hot metal particles. Portable lamps or utilization equipment shall be approved and shall conform to the provisions of Article 501 for the most hazardous location in which they might be used.

515-5. Underground Wiring.

(a) **Wiring Method.** Underground wiring to and around aboveground storage tanks may be installed in threaded rigid metal conduit or threaded steel intermediate metal conduit. If buried not less than 2 feet deep, it may be installed in rigid nonmetallic conduit or duct. Direct burial cable may be installed if it is approved. One point that might come up here is (b) below; that is, the insulation shall conform to Section 501-13. This depends on whether or not there is a possible chance of the insulation being exposed to deteriorating agents.

If cable is used it must be enclosed in rigid or threaded steel intermediate metal conduit. This protection must begin at the lowest point and will be required to enclose the cable until it makes its connection to the aboveground raceway. Although not mentioned in the Code, buried cables entering conduits below ground are faced with a frost problem in cold climates. It is recommended that the conduit below ground level be in an ell shape so that the conductors will emerge horizontally through an insulated bushing on the end. Frost heave will not have a tendency to cut or abrade the insulation as much as if the conduit were merely a vertical run. Also, in a rocky ground, rocks may cut the insulation due to normal pressures and to frost heaval. Thus, direct burial cable should be protected below and above by a fine sand bed and covering. See Fig. 515-6.

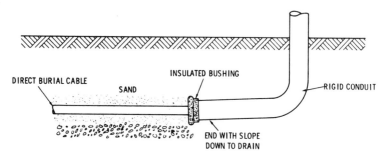

Fig. 515-6. Direct burial cable.

(b) **Insulation.** Section 501-13 gives the requirements that conductor insulation must meet. Recall that the insulation must be approved for exposure to vapors and liquids.

(c) **Nonmetallic Wiring.** When rigid nonmetallic conduit or cable that has a nonmetallic sheath is used, an equipment grounding conductor shall be included to maintain continuity of grounded raceway systems and for noncurrent-carrying parts.

This is standard procedure for practically all wiring in order to provide grounding protection for raceways and equipment where there is no raceway continuity. The grounding continuity must be complete back to the service equipment and the service ground. See *NEC* Section 501-16.

515-6. Sealing—Sealing shall be required in accordance with Section 501-5. Sealing requirements of Section 501-5(a)(4) and 501-5(b)(2) shall apply to both the horizontal and vertical boundaries of the location that is classified as a Class I location. Raceways that are buried under defined hazardous areas will be considered to be in the same classification or area.

515-7. Gasoline Dispensing—When gasoline is dispensed from a bulk-storage plant, this reverts to Article 514 which covers the dispensing of gasoline. All applicable requirements of that article shall be followed.

515-8. Grounding—See the *NEC*.

ARTICLE 516—SPRAY APPLICATION, DIPPING AND COATING PROCESSES

Two definite conditions must be kept in mind in this article. One is the vapors from spray application, dipping and coating processes and the storage of paints, lacquers, or other flammable finishes, and the other is the residues which accompany finishing processes.

Vapors can be coped with easier than the residues because the residues create a heat problem as well as the hazard created by the vapors. Bear this in mind while reading this article.

See Appendix A in the *NEC*.

516-1. Scope—This article covers the application of flammable liquids, combustible liquids, and combustible powders by spray operations done regularly at temperatures that will exceed their flash points. This may be done by dipping, coating, spraying, or other means.

Note: The NFPA 33-1985 (ANSI) gives further information covering these processes, including fire protection, the position of warning signs, and maintenance. The NFPA code called Spray Application Using Flammable and Combustible Materials, NFPA 34-1982 (ANSI), covers dipping and coating processes using flammable or combustible liquids. Additional information on ventilation is covered in NFPA 91-1983, Blower and Exhaust Systems, Dust, Stock, and Vapor Removal and Conveying.

516-2. Classification of Location—The classification is based on dangerous quantities, flammable vapors, combustible mists, dusts, residues, and deposits.

(a) **Class I or Class II, Division 1 Locations.** The following will outline the spaces that are to be considered Class I or Class II, Division 1 locations as applicable for the conditions involved.

(1) Unless specific provision is made in Section 516-3(d), the interiors of spray booths and rooms are classified.

(2) The interior of exhaust ducts, because they accumulate residues.

(3) Any other areas that are in the direct path of the spray operation.

(4) When dipping or coating operations are involved, the space that is within 5 feet in any direction from the vapor source, including a distance of 5 feet to the floor. The dip tank liquid surface shall be considered the vapor source. The vapor source shall be considered the liquid surface of the dip tank, the surface of the wetted drain boards, and the dipped object surface. The classified area shall be from the drain board surface or the wetted surface of the drain board, and shall extend from these surfaces to the floor.

(5) The whole of any pit that is within 25 feet of the vapor surface and extends beyond that distance will be classified Class I, Division 1 unless there is a vapor stop provided.

(b) **Class I or Class II, Division 2 Locations.** The areas covered below will be considered Class I or Class II, Division 2, whichever classification is applicable:

(1) When open spraying is used, all space outside, but within 20 feet horizontally and 10 feet vertically, is a Class I Division 1 location as defined in Section 516-2(a), if it is not separated by partitions.

(2) When spray and operations are conducted under a closed top that has an open front spray booth, a space shown in Fig. 2, and also a space within 3 feet in any direction from openings not including the open front or face. See the *NEC* for Fig. 2.

The following, as can be seen from Fig. 2, shall be Class I or Class II, Division 2, extending from the open face or front of the spray booth in conformance with the following:

a. If the spraying equipment is interlocked with the ventilating equipment so that it is impossible to spray if the ventilating equipment is not operating first, the space 5 feet out from the open face of a spray booth, and as shown in Figure 2A. See the *NEC* for Fig. 2A when ventilation is interlocked with spray equipment.

b. Should the spraying operation not be interlocked with the ventilating equipment, so that the spraying can be done without the ventilating equipment being in operation, the space shall extend 10 feet from the open face or front of a spray booth, which is shown in Fig. 2B. See the *NEC* for Fig. 2B when ventilation is not interlocked with spray equipment.

(3) Spray booths that have an open top 3 feet above the booth and 3 feet from other booth openings shall be considered as Class I or Class I, Division 2.

(4) When spray operations are confined to a spray booth or room, any space 3 feet in all directions from any openings into the spray area are to be considered Class I or Class II, Division 2, as may be seen in Fig. 3. See the *NEC* for Fig. 3.

(5) Fig. 4 illustrates dip tanks and drain boards, and other hazardous operations; all space beyond the limits for Class I, Division 1 and within 8 feet are defined in (a) (4) as being the vapor source. In addition, the vapor source that was defined in (a) (4) and shown in Fig. 4 shall cover all space to the floor to 3 feet above the floor, and it shall stand horizontally 25 feet from the vapor source.

(c) **Adjacent Locations.** If locations adjacent to Class I or Class II locations are cut off from them by tight partitions and have no communicating openings where hazardous vapors are likely to be released, they shall be classified as nonhazardous locations.

(d) **Nonhazardous Locations.** Locations utilizing drying, curing, or fusion apparatus may be judged nonhazardous by the authority enforcing the Code if (1) there is adequate positive mechanical ventilation provided to prevent the accumulation of concentrations of flammable vapors, and if (2) there are interlocks provided to de-energize all electrical equipment (other than Class I equipment) in the event of a failure of the ventilating equipment.

Note: See NFPA 86-1985 (ANSI), Ovens and Furnaces, Design, Location, and Equipment.

516-3. Wiring and Equipment in Class I Locations.

(a) **Wiring and Equipment—Vapors.** All electrical wiring and equipment located in a Class I location (where vapor only is contained and not residues), which was defined in Section 516-2, must comply with provisions of Article 501.

Article 501 covered Class I, Division 1 and 2 locations. Remember that such areas are in Group D. Group D covers gases and vapors but not deposits and residues. It will be found that no equipment is approved for use in spray booths for protection involving deposits and residues. For example, a motor may be approved for a Class I, Division 1, Group D location; but the motor cannot be mounted in an exhaust duct from a spray booth because of the deposits and residues from the spraying operation which are highly hazardous from a temperature standpoint. In addition, residues will deposit on the motor and cause a hazard. The same is true of lighting fixtures. A belt used to drive an exhaust fan creates a static electricity problem which must be remembered in designing the system. The NFPA states that the belt shall be enclosed in a nonferrous enclosure and that the fan shall be of nonferrous material. Even if the motor is mounted externally, it is possible to have gases or vapors come into contact With the motor, so it still must be approved for a Group D location.

(b) **Wiring and Equipment—Vapors and Residues.** Unless specifically approved for readily ignitible deposits and flammable vapor locations, no electrical equipment shall be installed or used in hazardous areas where it can be subjected to accumulations of readily ignitible deposits or residues, or subject to spontaneous heating and ignition of some residues, the likelihood of which will be greatly increased by rise in temperature. Type MI cable and wiring in threaded rigid metal conduit, or threaded steel intermediate metal conduit, will be permitted to be used in such locations.

(c) **Illumination.** Because there seem to be no lighting fixtures approved for deposits and residues, illumination of readily ignitible areas through panels of glass or other approved transparent or translucent material is permissible only where: (1) fixed lighting units are used as the source of illumination; (2) the panel effectively isolates the hazardous area from the area in which the lighting unit is located (see Fig. 516-1); (3) the lighting unit is approved specifically for a Class I, Division 1, Group D location; (4) the panel is of a material or is so protected that breakage will be unlikely; and (5) the arrangement is such that the normal accumulation of hazardous residues on the surface of the panel will not be raised to a dangerous temperature by radiation or conduction from the illumination source (see Fig. 516-1). The inspection authority must judge the hazard of the area in which lighting is mounted behind glass.

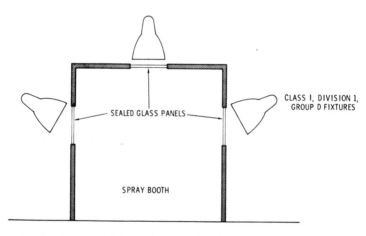

Fig. 516-1. Approved lighting for spray booths.

(d) **Portable Equipment.** Portable lamps and utilization equipment shall not be used in hazardous areas during the finishing operations. They may be used during cleaning or repair operations, but they shall be approved for Class I locations and all of the metal noncurrent-carrying parts shall be grounded.

Exception No. 1: If portable lamps are required in spaces not readily illuminated by the fixed lighting in the spraying area, the portable lamps shall be listed and approved type for Class I, Division 1 locations where there will be readily ignitible residues.

Exception No. 2: Where portable electric drying equipment is used for automobile finishing spray booths and the following requirements are met: (1) if its electrical connections are not located in the spray enclosure during spraying operations; (2) if electrical equipment within 18 inches of the floor is approved for Class I, Division 2 locations; (3) if the drying apparatus has all the metal parts electrically bonded and grounded; and (4) if interlocks are provided that will prevent the operation of spray equipment during the time that the drying equipment is within the spraying location; this will allow a three-minute purge of the area before the drying equipment is energized, and also shuts off drying apparatus if the ventilating system fails.

(e) **Electrostatic Equipment.** Only as provided in Section 516-4 will electrostatic spraying or detearing equipment be installed.

516-4. Fixed Electrostatic Equipment—For the requirements of this section, refer to the *NEC*.

516-5. Electrostatic Hand Spraying Equipment—For the requirements of this section, refer to the *NEC*.

516-6. Powder Coating—See the *NEC*.

516-7. Wiring and Equipment Above Class I and II Locations.

(a) **Wiring.** Fixed wiring above Class I and II locations shall be in metal raceways, rigid nonmetallic conduit, electrical nonmetallic tubing, or Types MC, MI, TC, or SNM cable. Cellular metal floor raceways will be permitted in the floor only to supply ceiling outlets or extensions to areas below the floor of the spray area or Class I or II location. Such floor raceways are not to have any connections that lead to or pass through Class I or II locations above the floor unless suitable seals are provided.

(b) **Equipment.** Equipment that may produce arcs, sparks, or hot metal particles, such as lamps, lampholders used for fixed lighting, cutouts, switches, receptacles, or any other type of electrical equipment that includes make-and-break or sliding contacts, if installed above Class I or II locations or above locations where freshly finished goods are to be handled, are required to be of the totally enclosed type, or the construction shall be such that it will be impossible for escaping sparks or hot metal particles to enter Class I or II locations.

516-8. Grounding—All metal raceways and noncurrent-carrying parts of either fixed or portable equipment shall be grounded as provided in Article 250, regardless of the voltage at which they are operated.

ARTICLE 517—HEALTH CARE FACILITIES
A. General

517-1. Scope —This article covers construction and installation of electrical wiring installed in health care facilities. See Appendix A in the *NEC.*

Note: Veterinary facilities are not included in this article.

Note: Refer to the information that concerns the performance, testing, and maintenance requirements for the health care facilities.

517-2. Definitions—This section gives necessary definitions that come into play with essential electrical systems for health care facilities.

Alternate Power Source. This may be one or more generator sets or battery systems, if the battery system is permitted for the location. The alternate power sources are intended to provide power during interruption of normal electrical service by the public utility electric service, and consist of generators on the premises.

Anesthetizing Location. These are areas in health care facilities that have been designated for administration of any flammable or non-flammable inhalation of any anesthetic agent in the course of examinations or treatments required for relative analgesia.

Critical Branch. This is a branch of an emergency system that may be feeders or branch circuits supplying energy for illumination, any special power circuits, and receptacles that are selected to serve these areas whose functioning is essential to patient care, and they are connected to an alternate power source by means of one or more transfer switches that energize from the temporary power source when the normal power source is interrupted.

Electrical Life Support Equipment. Any electrically powered equipment that is required to have continuous operation to maintain the patient's life.

Emergency System. Feeders to branch circuits that conform to Article 700 and are intended to supply power from an alternate source to a limited number of designated functions that are vital for the protection of life and for the patient's safety and must operate within 10 seconds of the interruption of the normal power source.

Equipment System. This consists of feeders or branch circuits arranged for delay manual or automatic connection to the power source. This ordinarily serves 3-phase power.

Essential Electrical System. A system supplying the alternate power source, all distribution systems, and ancillary equipment that have been designed to ensure electrical power continuity to designated areas and functions of a health care facility when the normal power source is disrupted. It shall also be designed to minimize disruption of power in the internal wiring system.

Exposed Conductive Surfaces. These surfaces are capable of carrying electrical current and are unprotected, not enclosed, and not guarded, permitting personal contact. Painting, anodizing, and similar coatings are not considered suitable insulation, unless they have been listed for that purpose.

Flammable Anesthetics. Gases or vapors such as fluroxene, cyclopropane, divinyl ether, ethyl chloride, ethyl ether, and ethylene, which can form flammable or explosive mixtures when combined with air, oxygen, or reducing gases such as nitrous oxide.

Flammable Anesthetizing Location. This is any area that has been designated to be used for the administration of any flammable inhalation anesthetic agents that will be used during normal examinations or treatment.

Hazard Current. A set of connections in the isolated power system where the total current could flow through a low impedance should it be connected between either the ground or an isolated conductor.
FAULT HAZARD CURRENT: The isolated systems that are hazardous current when all devices are connected except the line isolation monitor.
MONITOR HAZARD CURRENT: The line isolation monitor alone and its hazardous current.
TOTAL HAZARD CURRENT: The combined hazardous current in the preceding two definitions.

Health Care Facilities. These are buildings or parts of buildings that are not limited to occupancies such as: hospitals, nursing homes, residential care facilities, facilities for supervisory care, clinics, doctors' and dentists' offices, and ambulatory health care facilities that may be mobile or fixed.

Hospital. A building or a portion of a building that is used for medical, psychiatric, obstetrical, or surgical care and is open and maintained on a 24-hour basis having facilities for four or more inpatients. For the purpose of this article, hospitals include general hospitals, mental hospitals, tuberculosis hospitals, children's hospitals, and places providing inpatient care.

Isolated Power System. This consists of an isolation transformer or its equivalent and a monitor showing that it is isolated, and the circuit conductors are not to be grounded.

Isolation Transformer. Such a transformer consists of a primary and secondary winding that are physically separated, and that by induction couples the secondary to the feeders that are used to energize the primary winding.

Life Safety Branch. This consists of heaters and branch circuits that meet the requirements of Article 700 and the intent of which is to provide power needs adequate to secure the power source to the patients and personnel, and that shall automatically be connected to the alternate source of power upon interruption of the normal supply of power.

Line Isolation Monitor. This is a test instrument that is designated to give a continual check of the balanced and unbalanced impedance from each line of an isolated circuit to ground. It shall be equipped with a built-in test circuit that allows the alarm without adding leakage current hazard.

Note: This was formerly known as a "ground contact indicator."

Nursing Home. A building or portion thereof for lodging, boarding, and nursing care on a 24-hour basis for four or more persons, who because of their incapacity may be unable to provide for their own needs and safety unless aided by another person. Nursing homes, when used in this Code, will include nursing and convalescent homes in which there shall be skilled nursing facilities and immediate care facilities, and infirmary areas or homes for the aged.

Nurses' Stations. The location of a group of nurses that serve the needs of patients; also a point at which patients' calls are received and from which nurses are dispatched, where the nurses' notes are written and inpatient charts are maintained, and also where any medication is prepared to be distributed to patients. If more than one location is provided as a nursing unit, all these are to be included as part of the nurses' station.

Patient Equipment Grounding Point. In order to eliminate electromagnetic interference problems in grounding of electrical appliances serving patients, a jack or terminal bus is to serve as the collection point for redundant grounding of electric appliances.

Patient Vicinity. Patients are normally cared for in what is termed a patient vicinity. This is the space likely to be contacted by the patient or the attending person. A typical patient room shall contain space for the bed and its terminal location, and the space beyond the bed shall be not less than 6 feet horizontally and extend vertically not less than 7½ feet from the floor.

Psychiatric Hospital. This is a building that is used exclusively to give psychiatric care to four or more patients on a 24-hour basis.

Reference Grounding Point. This is a bus with terminals, and is the equipment grounding bus or an extension of it. It is a convenient place to connect grounding or bonding wires when needed.

Residential Custodial Care Facility. A building or part of one that provides boarding or lodging for four or more persons who are incapable of taking care of themselves because of age or physical or mental handicaps. Included here are facilities for taking care of the aged, nurseries (custodial care for children under six years of age), and for caring for the mentally retarded. If they do not provide lodging and board and day care facilities for the occupants, they are not to be classified as residential custodial care places.

Room Bonding Point. One or more grounding terminals are points that provide a place to ground exposed metal or conductive building circuits in a room.

Selected Receptacles. A minimal number of receptacles for use with appliances that under normal conditions are required for tasks in the room, and that are likely be used for the emergency treatment of patients.

Task Illumination. This is the minimum lighting required to conduct the necessary tasks in a given area. It also includes safe access to exits and supplies and equipment.

Therapeutic High-Frequency Diathermy Equipment. This is therapeutic induction and dielectric heating equipment operating high-frequency diathermy equipment.

Wet Location, Health Care Facility. An area for patients that is normally subjected to water on the floor, or where routine dousing or drenching of the work is required for housekeeping procedures. Places where liquids are accidentally spilled do not constitute wet locations.

517-3. General—The requirements that you will find under Parts C, D, and E apply not only to a building with a single function, but also to respective forms of occupancy within a building used for multifunctions (for example, a doctor's room located in a residential facility for custodial care would be required to meet the provisions of Part C).

B. Wiring Systems—General

517-6. Applicability—Part B applies to all health care facilities. For installations in these facilities that provide for patient care, services, or equipment, covered in other parts of this article shall also be required to comply with that part.

517-10. Wiring Methods—Wiring methods, except as modified in this article, shall comply with the appropriate requirements of Chapters 1 through 4 of the *NEC*. Wiring methods not permitted are found in Articles 331, 336, and 347, and shall not be used in those portions of health-care facilities that are for patient care areas.

517-11. Grounding of Receptacles and Fixed Electrical Equipment—In inpatient care areas, the grounding terminal of receptacles, all noncurrent-carrying surfaces that are conductive, and fixed electrical equipment that could possibly become energized and are subject to personnel contact, operating at over 100 volts, are to be grounded by an insulated copper conductor. Sizing the grounding conductor shall be done in accordance with Table 250-95, and it shall also be installed in metal raceways with the branch circuit supplying the fixed equipment or receptacles.

Exception No. 1: For Type MC, MI, or AC cable where an insulated grounding conductor is used, metal raceways are not required.

Exception No. 2: Metal faceplates will be permitted to be grounded. This may be done by means of metal mounting screw(s) securing the metal faceplate to a grounded outlet box or some device used for grounding.

Exception No. 3: Sections 336-2, 336-3, and 336-4 limit the use of type NM cable with an equipment-grounding conductor but are permitted for use in accordance with Parts C and D of Article 517.

517-13. Receptacles with Insulated Grounding Terminals—If receptacles have insulated grounding terminals as were permitted by Section 250-74, Exception No. 4, they must be identified so that the identification is still visible after installation.

Note: Care is very important in specifying such a system that uses insulated receptacle grounds, because the impedance of the grounding is controlled by the grounding wires, and no benefit is derived functionally from parallel grounding paths.

517-14. Ground-Fault Protection.

(a) **Feeders.** If ground-fault protection is provided to cover the operation of service disconnecting means as covered in Section 230-95, an additional step or ground-fault protection shall be provided at the next level of feeders from the original feeder, thus downstream from the load. This ground-fault protection consists of overcurrent devices and current transformers. Other equivalent protection that will cause the feeder to be disconnected may be used.

(b) **Selectivity.** Ground-fault protection for the service and disconnecting means shall be selective to the extent that such device and the feeder, and not the service device, will open if a ground-fault occurs on the load side of the feeder device. There shall be a six-cycle minimum differential between the service and the feeder tripping of the ground-fault. The time of operation of the disconnecting device must be considered when selecting time spread between these two bands so as to achieve 100 percent selectivity.

Note: Refer to Section 230-95 and the fine-print note there covering the transfer of alternate sources of protection.

(c) **Testing.** When equipment ground-fault protection is installed, each performance level is required to be tested to see that it conforms to (b) above.

C. Clinics, Medical and Dental Offices, Outpatient Facilities, and Other Health Care Facilities Not Covered in Parts D and E

517-30. Applicability—Not covered in Parts D and E are clinics, medical and dental offices, and outpatient facilities. Part C is applicable to portions of clinic, medical and dental offices, and outpatient facilities where patients are examined or treated. It is not applicable to offices, corridors, waiting rooms, etc.

517-31. Wiring, Grounding, and Receptacles—Sections 517-10 and 517-11 cover the wiring and grounding of receptacle installations.

517-32. Essential Electrical Systems

(a) **General.** With Section 517-30, in which the following are involved, the requirements of this Section 517-32 will apply to health-care facilities described in the previous section:

(1) Places where inhalation anesthetics are administered in any concentrations to patients, or

(2) Where electrical or electrically operated or mechanical life-supporting devices are required for patients.

(b) **Scope.** Essential electrical systems for these facilities shall be capable of supplying a limited amount of lighting and power that can maintain procedures essential for life and safety during any time That the normal electrical service has been interrupted for any reason.

(c) **Connections.** The essential electrical system shall have enough power supply for the following:

(1) Sufficient power for task illumination for safety of life and whatever is necessary for the safe cessation procedures in progress.

(2) All anesthesia and resuscitative equipment that is used in areas where anesthetics will be administered to patients shall include alarm and alerting devices.

Note: You are referred to the NFPA for Nonflammable Medical Gas Systems, NFPA 56F-1983 (ANSI), Chapters 3 and 6.

(3) All electrically operated and mechanical equipment in the areas that require the use of such equipment for the support of life and the procedures required therein.

(d) **Alternate Source of Power.**

(1) **Power Source.** The alternate power source is to be specifically designed for this purpose. It may be either the generator, the battery system, or a self-contained battery that is a part of the equipment being used.

(2) **System Capacity.** The alternate source of power shall be entirely independent of the normal source of power and separate therefrom. It shall also have the capacity to maintain the connected loads for at least 1 ½ hours after loss of the normal power.

(3) **System Operation.** This alternate source of power shall be arranged so that if the normal power source fails, the alternate source of power shall be on the line in 10 seconds or less.

Note: It is recommended that you see Health Care Facilities, NFPA 99-1984 (ANSI), Sections 8-5.5.2, for description of the switching operation with engine generator sets, or 8-5.5.3, for Description of Transfer Switch Operation with Battery Systems.

D. Nursing Homes and Residential Custodial Care Facilities

Note: The performance, maintenance, and testing of essential electrical systems to be used in nursing homes or residential custodial care facilities is covered in Health Care Facilities, NFPA 99-1984 (ANSI).

517-40. Applicability—Sections 517-42 through 517-47 of Part D and the requirements therein will apply to nursing homes and residential custodial care facilities.

Exception: In Parts C and E, any free-standing buildings other than those described in these parts of this article will be exempt from Sections 517-44 through 517-47.

a. It is used for admissions or discharges and does not preclude any provisions of care for any patient or resident who requires the need of sustained long-use electrical life-support equipment, and

b. There is no area for providing anesthesia for surgical treatment that requires them, and

c. It shall provide battery-operated systems or equipment that will operate for at least 1½ hours and that otherwise is covered in Section

700-12. It shall be capable of supplying lighting for exit lights, exit corridors, stairways, nursing stations, areas where medications are prepared, the boiler rooms, and any areas for communication. This equipment shall also supply power for alarm systems.

Note: Much essential information for this is contained in Life Safety Code, NFPA 101-1985 (ANSI).

517-41. Inpatient Hospital Care Facilities—Part E for hospitals shall apply to nursing homes and residential custodial care that provide hospital-type care for inpatients.

517-42. Facilities Contiguous with Hospitals—When a nursing home or residential care facility is part of a hospital, they shall be permitted to use the hospital's essential supply system.

517-43. Wiring, Grounding, and Receptacles—Sections 517-10 and 517-11 will cover wiring, grounding, and receptacles.

Exception: Sleeping areas for patients shall be wired according to Chapters 1 through 4 of the *NEC*.

517-44. Essential Electrical Systems.

(a) **General.** The essential electrical system in nursing homes and residential custodial care facilities shall consist of two separate branches, namely, the life safety branch and the critical branch. Both branches shall be capable of supplying a limited amount of lighting and power service, which is essential to protect life and ensure effective operation of the institution should normally supplied electrical service to said institution be interrupted for any reason. The installation and connections of essential electrical systems shall automatically take over if normal power fails and automatically be disconnected when normal power service is restored.

(b) **Transfer Switches.** The reliability, design, or load consideration shall determine the number of transfer switches used. There shall be one or more transfer switches in each branch of the essential electrical system. See the *NEC* for Diagrams 517-44(1) and 517-44(2). If the maximum demand does not exceed 150 kVA, one transfer switch may serve one or more branches of the facility of the electrical system.

Note: The *NEC* refers you to Health Care Facilities, NFPA 99-1984 (ANSI); for the description of transfer switching operations, it refers you to Section 8-4.5.2; the features of automatic transfer switches are also covered in Section 8-2.2.4; and you are referred in Section 8-2.2.4 for nonautomatic transfer switches.

(c) **Capacity of System.** The capacity of the essential electrical system shall be large enough so that all the requirements can be served at the same time.

(d) **Separation from Other Circuits.** The life safety branches must be kept entirely separate from the regular wiring and equipment and shall never enter the same raceways, boxes, or cabinets with other wiring except in the following:

(1) By necessity the two must meet in transfer switches,

(2) Two sources may supply exit and emergency lighting fixtures, or

(3) Two sources may be in a common junction box that is attached to exit emergency lighting fixtures.

The wiring of the critical branch circuits will be permitted to occupy the same raceways or cabinets that are not part of the life safety branch.

517-45. Automatic Connection to Life Safety Branch—Life safety branch shall be installed in connection with the alternate source of power supply in such a manner that all functions specified herein will be automatically restored to operation within 10 seconds after the interruption of the normal source of power. The following lighting, receptacles, and equipment shall be capable of being supplied from the life safety branch:

Note: The NEC terms the life safety branch as emergency systems; refer to Health Care Facilities, NFPA 99-1984 (ANSI).

(a) **Illumination of Means of Egress.** Means of egress shall be provided with illumination as necessary in passageways, stairways, landings, exit doors, and all ways of approach to exits. A means providing switching for patient corridor lighting from general-illumination circuits will be permitted, but only if only one circuit can be used at a given time.

Note: Refer to Life Safety Code NFPA 101-1985 (ANSI), Section 5-10.

(b) **Exit signs.** Exit directional signs and exit signs.

Note: You are referred to 5-11 of NFPA 101, which is referred to in the fine-print note to (a).

(c) **Alarm and Alerting Systems.** Alarm and alerting systems, including:

(1) Manually operated fire alarm stations, water flow alarm systems that are electrically connected with sprinkler systems, and alarms for fire or smoke that automatically detect products of combustion.

Note: Again the fine print: Life Safety Code, NFPA 101-1985 (ANSI), Sections 7-6, 12-3.4, and 12-3.5.

(2) Piping of nonflammable medical gases for alarms that are required to be used on them.

Note: The NEC refers to their Standard for Nonflammable Medical Gas Systems, NFPA 56F-1983 (ANSI).

(d) **Communication systems.** Where used for issuing instructions in emergency communication systems.

(e) **Dining and Recreation Areas.** Sufficient illumination to exits from dining and recreational areas.

(f) **Generator Set Location.** Illumination and selected receptacles in the generator location.

(g) **Elevator Cab Lighting, Control, and Communication Systems.** Elevator cab lighting, control, and communication systems may be connected to the nearby power systems.

Only functions listed in (a) through (g) shall be connected to the life safety branch.

517-46. Connection to Critical Branch—The critical branch shall be so installed and connected with the alternate source of power that equipment listed in Section 517-46(a) shall be automatically connected at appropriate intervals of time lag to put the life safety branch into operation. Equipment listed in 517-46(b) shall also be arranged either by delayed automatic action or by manual operation.

(a) **Delayed Automatic Connection.** Listed below is the equipment that shall be connected to the critical branch, and it is to be arranged for automatic delayed connection to the critical branch:

(1) Task illumination and receptacles that are in inpatient care areas:
   a. Areas where medication is prepared.
   b. Dispensing areas of pharmacies.
   c. Unless there is adequate lighting from corridor illumination, nurses' stations in this classification.

(2) Other equipment, including sump pumps required for the safe operation of major apparatus, and the control systems, including alarms.

(b) **Delayed Automatic or Manual Connection.** Listed below is the equipment that shall be connected to the critical branch. It shall be arranged for either delayed automatic or manual connection to the alternate power source:

(1) Any heat equipment that provides heat for the patient's room.

Exception: Under the following conditions, heating of the patient's room during disruption of the normal electrical source is not required:
   a. The design temperature outside is higher than $+20°$ F ($-6.7°$ C), or
   b. If the design temperature is lower than $+20°$ F ($-6.7°$ C), and where there is a selected room(s) provided to take care of all the needs of a confined patient, then only such a room(s) need to be heated, or

c. Where two sources of normal power can serve the facility as described in Section 517-47(c), fine-print note.

Note: If the outside design temperature is based on 97 ½ percent of the design values that are shown in Chapter 4 or the ASHRAE Handbook of Fundamentals (1981).

(2) **Elevator Service.** Where disruption of power would result in elevators stopping between floors, it is required to have a throwover facility that will temporarily allow the operation of any elevator so that passengers may be released. Lighting, control, and signal system requirements are covered in Section 517-45(g).

(3) More illumination receptacles and other equipment will be permitted to be connected only to the vertical branch.

517-47. Sources of Power.

(a) **Two Independent Sources of Power.** Essential electrical systems are required to have a minimum of two independent sources or power: normal power that ordinarily supplies the entire electrical system, and one or more alternate power sources to be used in the event of disruption of the normal power.

(b) **Alternate Source of Power.** A generator(s) that is driven by a prime mover(s) located on the premises may constitute the alternate source of power.

Exception No. 1: If the normal electrical supply is generated on the premises, the alternate source of power may be either an external source from utility service, or another generator.

Exception No. 2: In nursing homes and residential custodial care facilities that meet all the requirements to the exception-to Section 517-40 will be permitted the use of a battery system or self-contained battery that is a part of the equipment.

(c) **Location of Essential Electrical System Components.** Locations for the essential electrical system shall be carefully analyzed so that the effects of interruptions due to natural forces will be minimized (e.g. storms, floods, earthquakes, or hazards created by structures adjacent thereto or other activities). Careful consideration must also be given to normal electrical supplies that may be interrupted by similar causes, as well as disruptions of normal electrical services that may be caused by internal wiring or equipment failure.

Note: Facilities whose normal source of power is obtained from two or more central stations experience electrical service reliability that is greater than that of facilities whose normal supplies of power are served from only a single source. Such a source of electrical power consists of power supplied from two or more electrical generators or two or more electrical services supplied from separate utility distribution networks that have local power in the input sources and that are arranged so as to provide mechanical and electrical separation. This is so that a fault between the facilities and the generating source will not be likely to cause interruption of more than one of the service feeder facilities.

E. Hospitals

Note: See Health Care Facilities, NFPA 99-1984 (ANSI), which covers performance maintenance and testing that is required for essential electrical systems. See Standard for the Installation of Centrifugal Fire Pumps, NFPA 20-1983, covering the installation of centrifugal fire pumps.

Note: See Health Care Facilities, NFPA 99-1984 (ANSI), for additional information.

517-58. Applicability—Part E, Sections 517-60 through 517-65, applies to hospitals that require essential electrical systems.

Exception: Parts that are covered in Parts C and D for these facilities.

Note: See Health Care Facilities, NFPA 99-1984 (ANSI), for the needs of supplying essential electrical systems.

517-60. Essential Electrical Systems.

(a) **General.**

(1) In hospitals, essential electrical systems will be composed of two separate systems with capacity to supply limited amounts of lighting and power service for essential life safety and effective hospital operation during the period that the normal power service may be interrupted for any reason. These two systems will be the emergency system and the equipment system.

(2) The emergency systems are only for circuits necessary to life safety and to critical patient care. These are respectively designated as the life safety branch and the critical branch.

(3) Basic hospital operation and electrical equipment required for patient care are the equipment system.

(4) The number of transfer switches required is based on the reliability and design and the loads involved. One or more transfer switches may be used for each branch of the essential electrical systems. Refer to the *NEC* for Diagrams 517-60(1) and 517-60(2). If the demand on an essential electrical system has a maximum of 150 kVA, one transfer switch may serve one or more branch circuits of the facility.

Note: See the *NEC* here for the NFPA codes that will cover a number of features of these systems.

(b) **Wiring Requirements.**

(1) **Separation from Other Circuits.** You are required to keep the life safety branch and the physical branch of the emergency system entirely independent of all other wiring equipment. They are not to enter the same raceways boxes or cabinets with each other or with other wiring, with the following exceptions:

a. They both must be involved in transfer switches.
b. If emergency or exit lighting fixtures are supplied from two different circuits they must enter same, or
c. With a common junction box exit or emergency lighting fixture, there must be two different circuits involved.

When not a part of the emergency system, wiring of the equipment system will be allowed to occupy the same raceways, boxes, or cabinets as the other circuits.

(2) **Isolated Power Systems.** Isolated power systems that are installed in any of the areas in Section 517-63(a)(1) and (a)(2), with individual circuits serving no other loads, shall be used.

(3) **Mechanical Protection of the Emergency System.** The emergency systems of a hospital must be mechanically protected. This can be done by insulation and metallic raceways.

Exception No. 1: Cords used for flexibility, or serving power to appliances and other equipment utilizing electricity and connected to the emergency system, are not required to be enclosed in raceways.

Exception No. 2: Unless specified by Chapters 7 or 8, secondary circuits derived from the transformation for communication or signal circuits are not required to be encased in raceways.

Exception No. 3: See Section 510-101(b)(1) and (c)(1) for some special permissions for branch-circuit wiring.

(c) **Capacity of Systems.** Essential electrical systems are required to have adequate power to be capable of meeting the demand that could be imposed on them when all functions are in operation, and also for the equipment serve by each system and branch.

517-61. Emergency System.—The functions of patient care that depend on lighting or appliances that may be connected to the emergency system shall be divided into two required branches: the life safety branch and the critical branch, descriptions of which appear in Sections 517-62 and 517-63.

It is essential that the branches of the emergency system be installed and so connected to the alternate source of power that all functions necessary for them to perform as specified herein for the necessary emergency system must be automatically put into operation within 10 seconds after the interruption of the normal source of power.

517-62. Life Safety Branch—The following lighting, receptacles, and equipment shall be supplied from the life safety branch.

(a) **Illumination of Means of Egress.** The means of exit such as corridors, passageways, stairways, and landings at exits shall have illumination provided. Switching to change the patient corridor lighting in hospitals from general illumination to circuits for night illumination are permitted, but only one of two circuits can be selected, and it shall be made impossible for both circuits to be turned on at the same time.

Note: Life Safety Code, NFPA 101-1985 (ANSI), Section 5-10, has added information.

(b) **Exit Signs.** Exit lights and exit direction lights shall have sources of normal power and also the alternate source of power available.

Note: Life Safety Code, NFPA 101-1985 (ANSI), Section 5-11, has added information.

(c) **Alarm and Alerting Systems.** Life safety alarm and alert systems that include:

(1) Both automatic fire alarms and manually operated station.

(2) Sprinkler systems that have electric water-flow alarm devices in the system.

(3) Devices that will detect products of combustion and operate automatically for fire or smoke.

Note: see Life Safety Code, NFPA 101-1985 (ANSI), Sections 12-1 and 12-2.

(4) Piping for nonflammable medical gases where alarms are required for such systems.

Note: For additional information on Nonflammable Medical Gas Systems, see NFPA 56F-1983.

(d) **Communication Systems.** In hospitals, systems that are used to communicate instructions during emergency conditions.

(e) **Generator Set Location.** There shall be task illumination and receptacles that are selected for maintenance work and the generator set location.

(f) **Elevator Cab Lighting, Control, and Signal Systems.** Only those functions listed between (a) and (f) shall be permitted to be connected to the life safety branch.

517-63. Critical Branch.

(a) **Task Illumination and Selected Receptacles.**

(1) All receptacles, fixed equipment, and task illumination in anesthetizing locations.

(2) In special environments, the isolated power systems.

(3) Selected receptacles and illumination for patient care areas in:

See a. through g. in the *NEC*.

Refer to the *NEC* for 4 through 8, including a. through i.

(9) Special power circuits needed for effective hospital operation, such as additional task illumination, receptacles, and special power circuits needed for effective hospital operation. Also single-phase fractional horsepower motors used for exhaust fans, interlocked with the 3-phase motors, will be permitted to be connected to the critical branch circuit.

(b) **Subdivision of the Critical Branch.** Two or more circuits may be divided from the critical power branch.

Note: Analyzing the consequences is very important when supplying an area with only critical branch circuit power when failure occurs between the transfer switch and that area. It may be appropriate to supply normal and critical power by means from separate transfer switches.

517-64. Equipment System Connection to Alternate Power Source—Refer to the *NEC* for this, including (a) (1) through (3), the fine-print note, (b) (1), and the exception, which includes a. through c., fine-print note.

(2) Elevator(s) that are selected for the transfer of patients, surgical, obstetrical, and ground floors when normal power has been interrupted.

See the *NEC*, 517-46 (b)(2), Elevator Service.

(3) There shall be supply and exhaust ventilating systems in surgical and obstetrical delivery suites, in intensive care units, isolating rooms and emergency treatment spaces, and those areas constructed specifically for infection control laboratory fume hoods.

See the *NEC* for (4) through (8).

517-65. Sources of Power—It is recommended that this section be thoroughly covered in the *NEC*. Basically essential electrical systems shall have two sources of power available (minimum). One may be the normal source and the other may be the alternate source(s) for use when the normal power is interrupted, or may be a generator set(s) driven by a prime mover and located on the premises. Where normal power consists of generating unit(s) on the premises, the alternate source may be another generating set(s) or an external utility source.

Care must be exercised in the location of equipment to protect it from floods, fires, or icing. The electrical characteristics of the normal and emergency sources of power shall be compatible. Refer to the *NEC*.

Note: See the *NEC* Section 517-46 (c) (FPN) for this note.

F. Patient Care Areas

517-80. General—This section prescribes the performance criteria and/ or wiring methods to minimize shock hazards to patients in electrically susceptible patient areas. Potentials as low as 5 millivolts and currents of 10 microamperes can be hazardous to patients connected to instrument or probe.

Note: You are referred to Health Care Facilities, NFPA 99-1984 (ANSI)

(a) **Installation/Construction Criteria.** Part F covers the installation criteria and wiring methods that will minimize hazards by the maintenance of low voltage difference between conductive surfaces that are exposed and that could possibly become energized, and are accessible to the patient.

Note: It is very difficult to prevent the occurrence of a conductive or capacitive path, in health care facilities, from the patient's body to some grounded object, since this path can be established accidentally or through an instrument directly connected to the patient. Other surfaces that will conduct may make additional contact with the patient, or instruments that are connected to the patient might become possible sources of electrical currents that can be communicated to the patient's body. The hazard will be increased as more apparatus is used on the patient, requiring more precautions. Controlling the patient's shock hazard requires limiting the current that might flow in the circuit involving the patient's body. This can be accomplished by raising resistance of circuits that are conductive, which includes the patient, or by insulating surfaces that might become energized. This would be in addition to the reduction of the potential difference that can show up between exposed conductive surfaces in the patient vicinity, or by combining the different methods. Special problems will be created if there is an external conductive path to the patient's heart muscle. It could cause the patient to be electrocuted at a current level so low that additional protection is required in the design of the appliances, insulation of the catheter, and control of medical practice.

(b) **Patient Care Areas.** Areas in health control facilities where care is administered to the patient are classified as general care areas, critical care areas, and wet locations. It is up to the governing body of the facility to designate these areas according to the type of care that is anticipated for the patient and the following definitions of these types of area:

(1) Patient's bedrooms are general care areas, and so are examination rooms, treatment rooms, clinics, and similar areas where contact to the patient and ordinary appliances such as a nurse call system, electrical beds, examination lamps, and devices for entertainment will be evident. In such areas it may be the intent to connect the patient to electromedical devices (such as heating pads, electro-

cardiographs, drainage pumps, monitors, otoscopes, ophthalmo-scopes, and peripheral intravenous lines).

(2) Intensive care units, coronary care units, angiography laboratories, cardiac catheterization laboratories, delivery rooms, operating rooms, and similar areas are classified as critical care areas and requiring special care units.

(3) Areas that are normally subject to wet conditions, which could include standing water on the floor and routine dousing and drenching of the work area, are called wet locations. In ordinary housekeeping, incidental spillage of liquids does not define a wet location.

517-81. Grounding.

(a) **Methods.** Additional requirements for grounding other than what was covered in Section 517-11 are stipulated. Each branch circuit serving sufficient patient care area must be provided with ground path for fault-current. This is accomplished by installing rigid metal conduit, intermediate metal conduit, electrical metallic tubing, Type MI, MC, or AC cable if the AC cable's outer metal jack is an approved grounding means. The integrity of this ground path shall be verifiable. This can be established by running tests on it.

(b) **Performance.** This gives the maximum potential differences, which may exist between any two exposed conductive surfaces in the vicinity of the patient. The potential differences are checked at frequencies of 1000 hertz or less measured across a 1000-ohm resistor.

(1) **General Care Areas.** There shall be 500 mV when operating normally.

(2) **Critical Care Areas.** There shall be 40 mV when operating normally.

517-82. Panelboard Bonding—In normal and essential electrical system panelboards, the equipment grounding terminal is required to be bonded with an insulated continuous conductor, and this conductor shall be smaller than No. 10 AWG copper.

517-83. General Care Areas.

(a) **Patient Bed Location Branch Circuits.** Each patient bed location shall be supplied by at least two branch circuits, one of which originates in a normal supply system panelboard; it is required that all branch circuits served by the normal system must originate from the same panelboard.

Exception No. 1: It is not required that special purpose outlets to branch circuits be supplied from the same distribution panels This covers connections such as portable X-ray outlets.

Exception No. 2: Clinics, medical and dental offices, and outpatient facilities; psychiatric, substance abuse, and rehabilitation hospitals; the exception to Section 517-40 for nursing homes and residential custodial care facilities.

(b) **Patient Bed Location Receptacles.** Receptacles located by the patient's bed must be provided with a minimum of four single receptacles or two duplex receptacles. Each receptacle shall be grounded by the use of an insulated copper conductor in accordance with Table 250-95.

Exception No. 1: If the exception to Section 517-40 is met, the above will not apply to psychiatric, substance abuse, and rehabilitation hospitals.

Exception No. 2: Rooms that are used for psychiatric security are not required to have receptacles in the room.

517-84. Critical Care Areas.

(a) **Patient Bed Location Branch Circuits.** At each patient bed location supplied by at least two branch circuit, there shall be one or more circuits from the normal supply and one or more from the emergency supply. There is required to be at least one branch circuit from the emergency system. All branch circuits that originate from the original system may originate from a single panelboard; all branch circuits from the emergency supply shall be supplied from a single panelboard. The outlets that are supplied from the emergency service shall be marked to indicate the source of power, which panelboard it originates in, and the circuit in the panelboard that supplies them.

Exception: The branch circuits serving only special-purpose receptacles, or those in critical care areas, will be permitted to originate from other panelboards.

(b) **Patient Bed Location Receptacles.** Each patient bed location is required to be served with a minimum of six single or three duplex receptacles, and these are to be listed "Hospital Grade." Identification is required at each receptacle, and it is to be grounded to the reference grounding point by means of an insulated copper equipment grounding conductor.

(c) **Ground and Bonding, Patient Vicinity.**

(1) The patient equipment grounding source may be permitted at the patient's bed location; it may be grounded to the reference grounding point by means of copper-insulated conductor that is continuous, without splices; and it shall be no longer than No. 10 AWG. This conductor shall be run to the reference grounding point or be permanently connected to the grounding of a nearby receptacle for power. The patient's equipment grounding point, if supplied, shall be permitted to contain one or more jacks that are listed for the purpose.

(2) Fixed conductive surfaces, if they are likely to become energized and are in the patient's vicinity, shall be connected to the room bonding point and to the grounding point using a continuous copper conductor, conductive building structure members having conductance at least equal to AWG No. 10 copper. If bonding jumper conductors are installed, they shall be permitted to be arranged centrically or looped, as convenient.

Exception: Such items as surface-mounted towel racks, mirrors, and soap dispensers need not be connected to the room bonding point. If they are small in size and wall-mounted on conductive or large metal surfaces (such as windows and door frames) surfaces that are not likely to become energized, they need not be intentionally connected and grounded by connection to the room bonding point.

(3) The requirements in Section 517-84(c)(2) will not apply to bedside stands, overbed tables, chairs, portable IV poles, and small non-electrical devices such as trays, pitchers, bedpans, etc. The requirements in the section mentioned above do not apply to portable appliances or furniture.

(4) The bonding points of Section 517-84(c)(1) and (c)(2) may be combined into a single point.

(d) **Panelboard Grounding.** When an electrical distribution system that is grounded is used, if metallic feeder raceways or Type MC or MI cables are installed as the wiring method, the grounding of the switchboard or panelboard may be assured if one of the following means is used at each termination or junction point of a raceway or type MC or MI cable:

(1) A bonding bushing with a continuous copper jumper for bonding and sized in accordance with Section 250-95 where a locknut-bushing connection is used.

(2) Where there are threaded hubs or bosses at the termination at the enclosure connection of feeder raceways or Type MC or MI cables.

(3) Bonding-type locknuts or bushings or other approved means of bonding will be used.

(e) **Isolated Power System Grounding.** When an isolated ungrounded power source is used and limits first-fault current to a low amount, the conductor for grounding used with the secondary circuit will be allowed to be run outside of the enclosure of the power connector in the same circuit.

Note: Even though it is allowed to run the grounding conductor outside of the raceway, safety will be obtained if it is run in with the power conductors, and this will provide more protection in case of a second ground-fault.

(f) **Special Purpose Receptacle Grounding.** When special receptacles are used, e.g. for the purpose of mobile X-ray units, conductor for such special-purpose receptacles is to be run to the reference grounding points of branch-circuits for all locations likely to be served from such receptacles. If such a circuit is served by an isolated ungrounded system, the grounding conductor is not required to be run with the power conductors; the equipment grounding terminal or the special purpose receptacle shall, however, be connected to the reference grounding point.

517-90. Additional Protective Techniques—Refer to the *NEC* for coverage of this section.

G. Inhalation Anesthetizing Locations

Note: See Health Care Facilities, NFPA 99-1984, Chapters 3 and 4 (ANSI).

517-100. Anesthetizing Location Classifications.

(a) **Hazardous (Classified) Location.**

(1) Where flammable anesthetics are employed, the entire area is considered to be a Class I, Division 1 location, and this shall extend from the floor to 5 feet above the floor. The remaining area above the 5-foot level is considered to be above the hazardous (classified) locations.

(2) Any room or location in which flammable anesthetics or volatile flammable disinfecting agents will be stored is classified as a Class I, Division 1 location for the entire area of the room involved, including to the ceiling.

(b) **Other-than-Hazardous (Classified) Location.** Any inhalation anesthetizing areas that are designated only for the use of nonflammable anesthetizing agents will not be classified as hazardous (classified) locations.

517-101. Wiring and Equipment.

(a) **Within Hazardous Anesthetizing Locations.**

(1) With the hazardous (classified) locations that are referred to in Section 517-100, all fixed wiring and equipment and all portable equipment that operates at more than 10 volts between conductors is required to comply with the requirements of Sections 501-1 through 501-15 and Section 501-16(a) and (b) covering Class I, Division 1 locations. All equipment used therein shall be approved for hazardous atmospheres in that area.

(2) Where boxes, fittings, or enclosures are only partially mounted in a hazardous (classified) location(s), the entire location, including the box fittings or enclosures, shall be classified as hazardous.

(3) Receptacles and attachment plugs that are installed in hazardous areas shall be listed for use in Class I, Group C hazardous (classified) locations, and they shall be provided with connection to a grounding conductor.

(4) If flexible cords are required to be used in a hazardous area on lamps operating at 8 volts between conductors, the cord shall be of a type approved for extra-hard usage, and Table 400-4 shall be complied with. Also, an additional conductor for grounding will be installed in the cord.

(5) If a storage device such as a reel is used for flexible cord, the cord shall not be subjected to bending at a radius less than 3 inches.

Cords for use in anesthetizing locations for portable lamps and utilization equipment shall not be used for other purposes. General-purpose cords that are used elsewhere about the hospital should not be used in operating rooms. All cords should be inspected periodically and replaced (not repaired) when they show damage or wear.

(b) **Above Hazardous Anesthetizing Locations.**

(1) Wiring methods in hazardous areas are referred to in Section 517-100 and are to be installed in rigid metal conduit, EMT, intermediate metal conduit, Type MI cable, or Type MC cable when they employ a continuous gas and vaportight metal shield.

(2) Any installed equipment that is capable of producing arcs, sparks, or hot metals, which would be such as lamps and lampholders for fixed lighting, cutouts, switches, generators, or motors, etc., equipment that has make-and-break or sliding contacts is required To be of a totally enclosed type or so constructed as to prevent escape of sparks or hot metal particles.

Exception: See the *NEC.*

(3) Refer to Section 501-9(b) for surgical or other fixtures.

Exception No. 1: The temperature surfaces required in 501-9(b)(2) shall be limited as set forth in that section, and shall not apply.

Exception No. 2: Integral or pendant switches that are located above and cannot be lowered into the hazardous (classified) locations need not be of explosionproof type.

(4) Sections 501-5 and 501-(a)(4) covered approved seals; they shall be provided in conformance with these sections, in both horizontal and vertical boundaries of the hazardous classified locations.

Exception: When conduit penetrates a wall that forms a boundary of an anesthetizing location, seals shall be permitted to be located within 18 inches at the point where the conduit emerges from the wall forming the boundary of an anesthetizing location, provided all the following are met:

a. The junction box, switch, or receptacles are provided with a seal-off device between any arcing parts and the conduit.

b. There is no coupling of fittings in the conduit between the box and sealing fitting between the 18 inches and the box where the ceiling was installed.

(5) Plugs and receptacles shall be mounted above the hazardous area in anesthetizing locations. They must also be listed for hospital use and for the service at the prescribed voltage, frequency, rating, and number of conductors. They shall also have a means for connecting the grounding conductor. The above is applicable to plugs and receptacles that are 2-pole, 3-wire and the grounding type for use on single-phase 120-volt, nominal, as service.

(6) Plugs and receptacles to be mounted on 50-ampere and 60-ampere circuits of 250-volt ac for use with the medical equipment that is mounted above the hazardous (classified) locations are required to be so arranged that a 60-ampere receptacle will take either a 50- or 60-ampere attachment plug. Fifty-ampere receptacles must be designed to accept 60-ampere attachment plugs. These are to be 2-pole, 3-wire and shall be designed to be connected to a grounded insulated equipment grounding conductor (they shall be green insulation, or green with a yellow stripe) and the grounding conductor shall be attached to the grounding system.

(c) **Other-than-Hazardous Anesthetizing Locations.**

(1) If wiring serves other-than-hazardous (classified) locations that are defined in Section 517-100, it is required to be installed in rigid metal conduit, intermediate metal conduit, or EMT, or be used in Type MI, MC, or AC cable. The AC cable is required to have an insulated equipment grounding conductor.

Exception: If pendant receptacles that employ at least SJO or other equivalent cords, they shall be suspended not less than 6 feet from the floor.

(2) Attachment plugs and rectacles that are installed in other-than-hazardous (classified) locations shall be listed for use in hospital service and have the prescribed voltage, frequency, ampere rating, and shall also have the number of conductors that are to be used and a provision for connection of the equipment grounding conductor. These requirements apply to receptacles that are of the 2-pole, 3-wire grounding type and are to be used on 120-, 208-, or 240-volt, nominal, ac service.

(3) Plugs and receptacles rated 250-volt, 50-ampere and 60-ampere current rating ac that are for medical equipment to be used in other-than-hazardous (classified) locations shall be so made that the 60-ampere receptacle will accept either a 50-ampere or a 60-ampere plug. Fifty-ampere receptacles shall have a design that will not accept a 60-ampere plug. Requirements for the attach-

ment plug shall be 2-pole, 3-wire, the third connection shall be for the equipment grounding conductor, and the conductor to it shall be green or green with a yellow stripe and also shall be insulated, and this conductor shall be connected to the grounding conductor of the electrical system.

517-103. Grounding—In anesthetizing locations, it is required that all metallic raceways be grounded, as well as metal-sheathed cables and all noncurrent-carrying parts that are conductive portions of either portable or fixed electrical equipment.

Exception: When equipment operates at not over 10 volts between the conductors, it shall not be required to be grounded.

517-104. Circuits in Anesthetizing Locations.

(a) **Isolated Power Systems.**

(1) With the exception permitted in Section 517-104(c), every power circuit that is within or partially within an anesthetizing location, as was mentioned in Section 517-100, is required to be isolated from any distribution system other than that supplying anesthetizing locations. Every isolated power circuit is required to be controlled by a switch for disconnecting, and shall disconnect each isolated conductor. The isolating circuits shall be supplied from one or more isolating transformers that have no electrical connection between the primary and secondary windings, or they may be supplied by motor generator sets, or by suitable isolated batteries.

(2) The primaries of isolating transformers shall not operate at voltages exceeding 600 volts between conductors and shall be protected by overcurrent protection of proper size. The secondary of isolated systems shall not exceed 600 volts between conductors of every circuit, and all conductors, such as isolated secondaries, shall be ungrounded. They shall also be provided with an approved overcurrent device of the proper rating in each conductor. If circuits are supplied directly from batteries or from a motor generator set, the conductors shall be ungrounded and overcurrent proteciton shall be provided in the same fashion as transformer-supplied secondary circuits. When an electrostatic seal is present, it shall be connected to the reference grounding point.

(3) The isolating transformers, motor generator set, batteries and battery charges, and primary and/or secondary overcurrent protection devices are not permitted to be installed in a hazardous (classified) location. The requirements of Section 501-4 shall be used when the isolating secondary circuit wiring is extended into the hazardous anesthetizing location.

(4) An isolated branch circuit that supplies an anesthetizing location

will not be allowed to supply any other location. The insulation on the conductors on the secondary side of the isolated power supply must have a dielectric constant of 3.5 or less. If pulling compound increases the dielectric constant, it shall not be used on the secondary conductors of the isolated power supply.

(5) The identification of isolated conductors is required to be as follows:

See the *NEC*.

(b) Line Isolation Monitor.

(1) A continual operating line isolation monitor that indicates possible leakage or fault currents from any of the isolated conductors to ground shall be used in addition to the usual overcurrent protective devices that are required in isolated power systems. The design of this monitor shall be such that a green signal lamp is conspicuously visible to persons in the anesthetizing location. It remains lighted if the system is properly isolated from ground and there is a red signal lamp and also a audible warning signal, which can be remote if desired. These will be energized when the total hazardous current (which could result from resistive or capacitive current leakage) emanating from either isolated conductor to ground reaches a value of 5 milliamperes or slightly less when the line voltage conditions are nominal. The line isolation monitor shall not act where fault hazard current is less than 3.7 milliamperes. The isolating line alarm monitor is not to alarm when the total hazardous current is less than 5 milliamperes.

Exception: It will be permitted to be designed for operation at a lower threshold of total hazardous current. A line isolation monitor for such a system will be permitted to be approved, with the provision that the fault hazard current may be reduced, but not to less than 35 percent of the value of the hazardous current of the above section, and the monitor hazard current may also be reduced to not more than 50 percent of the alarm threshold value of the total hazard current as above.

Note: The systems in the section above provide little electric safety, and are to be used only in special applications.

(2) The internal impedance of a line isolation monitor shall be designed so that, when properly connected, the internal current can flow through the isolation monitor, and if any point of the system is grounded, shall be 1 milliampere.

Exception: Low-impedance type of line isolation monitor shall be permitted so that current through the monitor, when any point of the isolation system is grounded, will not exceed twice the alarm threshold value, and this shall be for a time period not exceeding 5 milliseconds.

Note: If the reduction of the monitor hazard current results in increased "not alarm" threshold hazard current, it will increase the circuit capacity.

(3) An ammeter that is calibrated for the total current of the system (contribution of the fault hazard current plus monitor hazard current) shall be mounted in a place that is plainly visible on the line isolation monitor, with the "alarm on" ampere zone located at approximately the center of the ammeter scale and visible to persons in the anesthetizing locations.

Exception: A line isolation monitor may be more than one unit that has a sensing section carried by cable to a separate display panel section where the alarm and/or text functions may be located.

(c) **Grounded Power Systems.**

(1) General-purpose lighting circuits connected to a normal ground service shall be installed in each operating room.

Exception: When connected to any alternate source of supply, as permitted in Section 700-12, that is separate from the service supplying the emergency service.

(2) When branch circuits supply only fixed therapeutic and diagnostic equipment that is permanently installed above the hazardous (classified) locations, it will be permitted to be supplied from a normally grounded single-or 3-phase system, provided: See the *NEC* for a. through d., including the exception of (2).

(3) Fixed lighting may be served from branch circuits that are supplied by normal grounded service provided. See the *NEC* for a. through d.

(4) Control stations for remote-control switching operating at 24 volts or less and installed on walls will be permitted to be installed in anesthetizing locations.

(5) Authorized isolated power centers and the primary feeder to them will be permitted to be located in an anesthetizing location if it is installed above that hazardous (classified) location or in another location that is not classified as hazardous.

517-105. Low-Voltage Equipment and Instruments—See the *NEC*.

H. Communications, Signaling Systems, Data Systems, Fire Protective Signaling Systems, and Low-Voltage Systems

517-120. Patient Care Areas—Patient care areas shall be provided with equivalent insulation, isolation, and grounding, as was required for electrical distribution systems, for communications, signaling systems, data system circuits, fire protective signaling systems, and low-voltage systems.

Note: There is an accepted alternate means for providing isolation for patient/nurse call systems; this is by use of nonelectrified signaling, control, or communication devices that may either be held or are within the reach of a patient.

Note: You are referred to Section 250-95 covering grounding requirements.

517-121. Other-than-Patient-Care Areas—See Articles 725, 760, and 800.

517-122. Signal Transmission Between Appliances.

(a) **General.** See Section 517-81. If there is a permanently installed signal cable from an appliance in a patient location to a remote appliance, it shall employ a signal transmission system that prevents grounding connection of the appliance.

(b) **Common Signal Grounding Wire.** If the appliances are all served from the same grounding point, grounding wires (i.e. the chassis ground for single-ended transmission) will be permitted for use between appliances located in the patient's vicinity.

K. X-ray Equipment

There is nothing in this part that can be construed as specifying safeguards from useful beam or stray X-ray radiation.

Note: Several classes of X-ray equipment covering radiation, safety, and performance requirements are regulated under Public Law 90-602. The enforcement of such regulations come under the Department of Health and Human Services.

Note: Refer to the (FPN) in the *NEC* at this point.

517-140. Definitions—Refer to your *NEC*.

517-141. Connection to Supply Circuit.

(a) **Fixed and Stationary Equipment.** The general requirements of this Code shall be used for fixed and stationary X-ray equipment.

Exception: X-ray equipment supplied or rated at 30 amperes or less shall be permitted to be supplied if extra-hard-usage cord is used and suitable plug and attachments are also used.

(b) **Portable, Mobile, and Transportable Equipment.** Individual branch circuits are not required for portable, mobile, and transportable medical X-ray equipment if it does not require over 60 amperes for operation.

(c) **Over 600-Volt Supply.** If X-rays are operated at over 600 volts, they must comply with Article 710.

517-142. Disconnecting Means.

(a) **Capacity.** A disconnecting means that has adequate capacity to provide at least 50 percent of the input required for momentary operation rating or 100 percent of the input required for long-term-time rating of the X-ray equipment, whichever is greater, shall be provided for disconnecting the supply circuit.

(b) **Location.** A disconnecting means shall be provided that is operable from a location that is easily accessible from the X-ray control.

(c) **Portable Equipment.** If portable equipment operates at 30 amperes or less and 120 volts, a grounding-type attachment plug and receptacle, with a rating that is appropriate for the load it is to carry, may be used as a disconnecting means.

517-143. Rating of Supply Conductors and Overcurrent Protection.

(a) **Diagnostic Equipment.**

(1) The ampacity of the branch-circuit conductors, and also the rating of the overcurrent devices protecting the branch circuit, are not permitted to be less than 50 percent when the diagnostic equipment is used only momentarily, or a 100-percent rating if used for a long time, whichever is greater.

(2) The ampacity of feeder conductors and the current rating of protective devices that supply two or more branch circuits supplying X-ray units, if the X-ray units are used only for momentary usage, shall not be less than 50 percent of each of the two largest diagnostic X-rays, plus 20 percent of the momentary ratings of any additional diagnostic X-ray units. Where simultaneous X-ray examinations are undertaken by X-ray units, the ampacity of the supply conductors and the overcurrent protective devices shall be 100 percent of the momentary rating of each X-ray unit.

Note: The minimum ampacity of branch circuits and feeder conductors from the circuit shall also be governed by the voltage regulation requirements. The manufacturer usually supplies specific information: minimum transformer and conductor sizes, the rating of the disconnecting means, and overcurrent protection.

(b) **Therapeutic Equipment.** The current rating shall be not less than the 100 percent of the rating of medical X-ray therapy equipment.

Note: The ampacity of branch circuit conductors and the ratings of overcurrent protection devices and disconnecting means for the protection of X-ray equipment are in most cases supplied by the manufacturer supplying the specific installation.

517-145. Control Circuit Conductors.

(a) **Number of Conductors in Raceway.** Section 300-17 will cover the number of control circuit conductors that are permitted to be installed in a raceway.

(b) **Minimum Size of Conductors.** As specified in Section 725-16, sizes No. 18 or No. 16 fixture wires are required. Flexible cords may be permitted for the circuits from control and operation of the X-ray and its auxiliary equipment if they are protected by 20-ampere or less overcurrent devices.

517-146. Equipment Installations—The equipment for use with new X-ray equipment for installation and for all used or reconditioned X-ray equipment that is moved and reinstalled at a new location shall be of an approved type.

517-148. Transformers and Capacitors.—It shall not be required to comply with Articles 450 and 460 for transformers and capacitors that are a part of X-ray equipment.

Capacitors shall either be grounded or mounted in insulating material.

517-151. Guarding and Grounding.

(a) **High-Voltage Parts.** All high-voltage parts of X-rays, including X-ray tubes, are to be mounted in grounded enclosures. You may use air, oil, or gas or other suitable insulation media to insulate the high-voltage components from the grounded enclosure. High-voltage shielding cables shall be used for connecting high-voltage equipment to X-ray tubes and any other high-voltage components that are required.

(b) **Low-Voltage Cables.** Oil-resistant insulation is required for low-voltage cables that are connected to oil-filled units when they are not completely sealed. This includes transformers, condensers, oil coolers, and high-voltage switches.

(c) **Noncurrent-Carrying Metal Parts.** Metal parts of X-rays and associated noncurrent-carrying equipment, such as controls, tables, X-ray tube supports, transformer tanks, shielded cables, X-ray tube heads, etc., are required to be grounded in a manner specified in Article 250, which may be modified by Section 517-11(a) and (b) under the criteria set forth in Section 517-81 covering critical care areas.

Exception: Battery-operated equipment is an exception.

Summary of Part G

Anesthetizing locations and anesthetic storage locations are susceptible to the smallest electrical discharge. The importance of this may be seen from the fact that all parts of the room and equipment, even though not connected to the electrical supply system, have been provided with precautionary measures. The tile on the floor is of a conductive type and is laid on metal grids that are grounded. Ground tests of the floor are laid on grounded metal grids recorded after installation and periodically retested.

Anyone working within an anesthetizing location is required to wear coverings over his shoes which are conductive and before entering the room he must stand on a resistance-testing machine to test the resistance to be certain that it is within allowable limits. The patient is grounded, furniture must meet the requirements for these locations, rubber hoses must meet conductive specifications, and all necessary precautions are taken to prevent any spark from occurring, even so far as to the type of garments that may be worn in the room. The NFPA Fire Codes should be in every engineer's, contractor's, and electrician's libraries. Inspectors should be especially well versed in the requirements that do not appear in the *NEC*.

Article 518—Places of Assembly

518-1. Scope—The coverage of this article includes all buildings or portions of buildings or structures that are designed and intended to be used for the assembly of 100 or more persons.

518-2. General Classifications—See the *NEC* for a list of places that could be used for the assembly of 100 or more persons.

Any room or space used for occupancy by less than 100 persons in a building used for other occupancy, even though incidental to such occupancy, shall be classed as part of the other occupancy, and shall be subject to the provisions applicable thereto.

If said building, part of building, or other structure has a projection booth or there is a stage platform where theatrical or musical productions are performed, whether these stages are fixed or portable, the wiring methods of the equipment and all the area and wiring used in the production, if not permanently installed, must comply with Article 520.

Note: It is very important that you use the NFPA Life Safety Code 101-1985 (ANSI), which contains the methods for determining how many occupants may be allowed in an area of assembly.

518-3. Other Articles.

(a) **Hazardous (Classified) Areas.** Hazardous (classified) areas located in any assembly place of occupancy must be installed in accordance with Article 500 covering hazardous (classified) locations.

(b) **Temporary Wiring.** In exhibition halls used for display booths, as in trade shows, any temporary wiring must be installed in accordance with Article 305—Temporary Wiring, except that approved flexible cables and cords will be permitted to be laid on the floors where they can be protected from contact by the general public.

(c) **Emergency Systems.** Article 700—Emergency Systems must be followed in the installation for control of emergency systems.

518-4. Wiring Methods—Wiring methods of the fixed type must be metal raceways, nonmetallic raceways if encased in not less than 2 inches of concrete, or Type MI or MC cable.

Exception No. 1: If the applicable building code does not require the buildings or portions thereof to be fire-rated construction by the applicable building code, nonmetallic-sheathed cable, Type AC cable, and rigid nonmetallic conduit will be permitted to be installed in those buildings or portions thereof.

Exception No. 2: As covered in Article 640—Sound Reproduction and Similar Equipment, in Article 800—Communication Circuits, and in Article 725 for Class 2 and Class 3 remote-control and signaling circuits, and in Article 760 for fire protection signaling circuits.

Note: Refer to the *NEC.*

ARTICLE 520—THEATERS AND SIMILAR LOCATIONS
A. General

520-1. Scope—This article covers buildings or portions of buildings that are used for motion picture projection, dramatic presentations, musicals, or similar purposes. It also applies to areas that incorporate assembly areas for motion picture and television studios.

520-2. Motion-Picture Projectors—See the *NEC.*

520-3. Sound Reproduction—See the *NEC.*

520-4. Wiring Methods—The fixed wiring method must be metal raceways, Type MI cable, or Type MC cable. Nonmetallic raceways which are encased in a minimum of 2 inches of concrete may be used.

Exception No. 1: See Article 640 for sound reproduction, Article 800 for communication circuits, and Article 725 for Class 2 and Class 3 remote-control and signaling circuits; and for fire protection signaling circuits, see Article 760.

Exception No. 2: Switchboards of the portable type, stage-set lighting, stage effects, and other wiring that is not maintained in a fixed locations but is portable, shall be permitted to be connected by flexible cords and cables as provided elsewhere in this article. The use of uninsulated staples or nails for securing these cords and cables in place will not be permitted.

520-5. Number of Conductors in Raceway—Table 1 of Chapter 9 governs the number of conductors for border or stage pocket circuits, or for remote-control conductors, which may be installed in any metal conduit, rigid nonmetallic conduit, or electrical metallic tubing. For auxiliary gutters or wireways, the sum of the cross-sectional areas of all of the conductors contained therein shall not exceed 20 percent of the interior cross-sectional area of the gutter or race-way. The limitation of thirty conductors covered in Sections 362-5 and 374-5 does not apply.

520-6. Enclosing and Guarding Live Parts—See the *NEC*.

520-7. Emergency Systems—See the *NEC*.

B. Fixed Stage Switchboard

520-21. Dead Front—See the *NEC*.

520-22. Guarding Back of Switchboard—See the *NEC*.

520-23. Control and Overcurrent Protection of Receptacle Circuits—See the *NEC*.

520-24. Metal Hood—See the *NEC*.

520-25. Dimmers—(a) through (d) below gives us the requirements for dimmers:

(a) **Disconnection and Overcurrent Protection.** When dimmers are installed in ungrounded conductors, the overcurrent for each dimmer shall not exceed 125 percent of the dimmer rating, and the dimmers shall be disconnected from all ungrounded conductors when the master or individual switch or circuit breaker supplying such dimmer is in an open position.

(b) **Resistance or Reactor-Type Dimmers.** It is permissible that resistance or reactor-type dimmers be placed in the grounded neutral conductor, but that they do not open the circuit. Resistance or series reactance dimmers may be placed in either the grounded or ungrounded conductor of the circuit.

   Where designed to open either the supply circuit to the dimmer, or the circuit that is controlled by it, the dimmer shall comply with Section 380-1 which requires that no switch shall open the grounded conductor unless the grounded conductor and ungrounded conductor or conductors are simultaneously opened.

(c) **Autotransformer-Type Dimmers.** Autotransformer-type dimmers shall be supplied by a source that does not exceed 150 volts, and the input and output grounds shall be common as provided for in Section 210-9.

(d) **Solid-State-Type Dimmers.** Circuits not exceeding 150 volts between two conductors may be used for solid-state dimmers, subject to the dimmer having approval for higher voltage operation. Where the grounded conductor supplies a dimmer, it is required to be common to the input and output circuits, and the dimmer chassis is to be connected to the equipment grounding conductor.

Note: Refer to Section 210-9 on circuits derived from autotransformers.

520-26. Type of Switchboard—Either one or both of the following may be used for stage switchboards.

(a) **Manual.** Handles mechanically linked to the control devices, such as dimmers and switches.

(b) **Remotely Controlled.** A pilot-type control console or panel is used to operate the devices that are electrically operated. The pilot control panels are required to be either part of the switchboard, or they may be permitted to be in another location.

(c) **Intermediate.** A switchboard that has interconnection is a secondary switchboard (patch panel), or it is a panelboard that is remote to the primary stage switchboard. Overcurrent protection shall be contained therein. If the branch circuit overcurrent protection is provided in the dimmer panel, the intermediate switchboard shall be permitted.

520-27. Stage Switchboard Feeders—The feeder used to supply the stage switchboards shall be one of the following:
Refer to the *NEC* for (a) through (c) of this section.

C. Stage Equipment—Fixed

520-41. Circuit Loads—Branch circuits that supply footlights, border lights, and proscenium sidelights shall not carry a load that exceeds 20 amperes. Where circuits have heavy-duty lampholders, an exception is made to provide for these, but the conditions in Article 210 that cover heavy-duty lampholders must be complied with.

520-42. Conductor Insulation—When wiring with connectors used for foot, border, proscenium, or portable strip lighting fixtues and any connector strips used with these, it is required that the installation be suitable for the temperature encountered. However, the conductors will be operated at not less 125° C or 257° F.

Note: Table 310-13 covers conductor types.

520-43. Footlights—See *NEC*. Notice in (b) that disappearing footlights shall be arranged so as to automatically disconnect from the circuit when they are in the closed position. Otherwise they would present a great fire hazard if energized while in the closed recess.

520-44. Borders and Proscenium Sidelights.

(a) **General.** General border and proscenium lights shall be: (1) constructed as specified in Section 520-43; (2) suitably stayed and supported; and (3) designed so that reflector flanges or other suitable guards are provided to protect the lamps from contact with other scenery or combustible material and give mechanical protection from injury that could be caused by accidental contact with the above.

(b) **Cables for Border Lights.** Only types S, SO, STO, or ST flexible cords shall be used to supply border lights. These flexible cords shall be suitably supported and used only where flexible conductors are necessary.

520-45. Receptacles—Receptacles shall be rated in amperes when used on stages for electrical equipment and fixtures.

(1) Continuous loads from receptacles shall not exceed 80 percent of the receptacle rating.

(2) If the load is noncontinuous, it shall not exceed 100 percent of the receptacle rating.

Article 310 shall be complied with for conductors supplying receptacles.

520-46. Connector Strips, Drop Boxes, and Stage Pockets—Receptacles shall comply with Section 520-45 when intended for use with portable stage lighting equipment and shall be mounted in suitable pockets or enclosures.

520-47. Lamps in Scene Docks—When lamps are used in scene docks, their location shall be such that they are protected from physical damage, and an air space is to be provided of not less than 2 inches between any combustible material and the lamps.

520-48. Curtain Motors—The conditions in (a) through (f) below are to be adhered to if curtain motors have brushes or sliding contacts:

(a) **Types.** They shall be of enclosed-pipe-ventilated, totally enclosed, or enclosed-fan-cooled type.

(b) **Separate Rooms or Housings.** They may be installed in separate rooms or housings, either of which is built of noncombustible material, and are to be constructed so as to exclude flyings or lint. There shall also be proper ventilation from a source of clean air.

(c) **Solid Metal Covers.** Motors with brushes or sliding contacts at the end of a motor are to be enclosed in solid metal covers.

(d) **Tight Metal Housings.** They may be enclosed in substantial housings that are tight and made of metal where there are brushes or sliding contacts.

(e) **Upper and Lower Half Enclosures.** The upper half of the brushes or sliding contacts at the end of the motor may be enclosed by means of a wire screen, or it may be perforated metal, but solid metal covers shall be used for the lower half.

(f) **Wire Screens or Perforated Metal.** They may have screens that are perforated metal installed at the commutator of the brush end, provided no dimension of openings in the wire screen or perforated metal exceeds .05 of an inch irrespective of the shape of the openings or of the material that is used to cover the openings.

520-49. Flue Damper Control—If stage flue dampers are opened by means of an electrical device, the circuit that operates the devices will normally be closed, and it is to be controlled by means of at least two switches for the operation. One of these switches is to be placed at the electrician's station, and the authority having jurisdiction will determine where the other switch is to be located. The operating devices shall be designed for the full voltage of the circuit to which it is connected; no resistance shall be inserted. The control device is to be located in the loft above the scenery, and it shall be enclosed in a tight metal enclosure that has a self-closing door.

D. Portable Switchboards on Stage

520-50. Road-Show Connection Panel. (A Type of Patch Panel)— This is a panel designed for a road show with connection to portable stage switchboards and portable lighting outlets by using supplementary circuits permanently installed. The panel, the supplementary circuits, and any outlets must meet the requirements of (a) through (d) below:

(a) **Load Circuits.** Grounding and polarized inlets of current and voltage rating that match the fixed load receptacle shall be connected only to circuits that meet the requirements of this.

(b) **Circuit Transfer.** If circuits are transferred between fixed and portable switchboards, they are required to have the line and neutral transferred at the same time.

(c) **Overcurrent Protection.** The devices that supply supplementary circuits shall be protected by branch-circuit overcurrent protective devices. Each supplementary circuit within the road-show connection panel and the theater is to be protected by branch-circuit overcurrent protective devices, the ampacity of which is required to be suitable and installed within the road-show connection panel.

(d) **Enclosure.** Article 384 covers the construction of the enclosures of panels.

520-51. Supply—Only outlets of sufficient voltage and ampere rating are to be used on portable switchboards. Only externally operable, enclosed fused switches or circuit breakers are to be used for these outlets, and they shall be mounted either on the stage or at the permanent switchboard in locations that are readily accessible from the stage floor. Provision shall be made for equipment grounding connections. If the neutral of a 3-phase,

4-wire system is used on a dimmer circuit system, the neutral shall be considered to be a current-carrying conductor.

520-52. Overcurrent Protection—Circuits originating from portable switchboards that directly supply equipment that contains incandescent lamps of not over 300 watts are to be protected by overcurrent protection devices having a rating or setting not exceeding 20 amperes. If overcurrent protection complies with Article 210, circuits for lampholders of over 300 watts will be permitted.

520-53. Construction and Feeders—Refer to the *NEC*.

E. Stage Equipment—Portable

For Sections 520-61 through 520-68, refer to the *NEC*.

F. Dressing Rooms

Refer to the *NEC*.

G. Grounding

520-81. Grounding—You are required to ground all metal raceways and metal-sheathed cables. Metal frames and enclosures of all equipment —including border lights and portable light fixtures—shall be grounded, and the grounding shall comply with Article 250.

ARTICLE 530—MOTION PICTURE AND TELEVISION STUDIOS AND SIMILAR LOCATIONS

Refer to the *NEC*.

ARTICLE 540—MOTION PICTURE PROJECTORS

This article is seldom used by the trade. Therefore, refer to the *NEC* for answers to any questions involving motion picture projectors.

ARTICLE 545—MANUFACTURED BUILDING

A. General

545-1. Scope—This article covers requirements for a manufactured building and/or building components as herein defined.

545-2. Other Articles—Wherever requirements of other articles of this Code and Article 545 differ, the requirements of Article 545 shall apply.

545-3. Definitions—There are a number of definitions in this section, for which reference to the *NEC* should be made, but since manufactured buildings are becoming a way of life, they will be mentioned here.

See the *NEC* definitions of the following: Manufactured Building, Building Component, Building System, and Closed Construction.

545-4. Wiring Methods.

(a) **Methods Permitted.** The wiring systems specifically intended and listed for manufactured buildings shall be permitted with listed fittings and with fittings listed for manufactured buildings. Otherwise all raceways and cable wiring methods included in this Code shall comply.

(b) **Securing Cables.** In closed construction, cables are permitted to be secured only at cabinets, boxes, or fittings, provided No. 10 AWG or smaller conductors are used, and they must be protected against physical damage. Requirements for this protection shall be found in Section 300-4.

Manufactured buildings will in many instances require inspection by the authority having jurisdiction in the area to which they are being installed. It would be suggested to check beforehand to find out local regulations covering such buildings.

545-5. Service-Entrance Conductors—This is one problem which must be controlled because of the electric utility line locations. The requirements of Article 230 must be met for service-entrance conductors, which must be routed from the service equipment to the point of attachment to the service. Reference is made to Section 310-10 for temperation of conductors.

545-6. Installation of Service-Entrance Conductors—From the preceding section one may readily see why: The service-entrance conductors are installed after the erection of the building.

Exception: Except where the point of attachment is known prior to manufacture.

545-7. Service Equipment Location—This is the same as required in Article 230. The service-entrance equipment must be made readily accessible at the point nearest to where the service conductors, either inside or outside the building, are attached.

545-8. Protection of Conductors and Equipment—Manufactured buildings are usually moved from place of manufacture in parts or as one unit and thus subjected to various strains and weather conditions:

The protection of exposed conductors and equipment must be provided during the process of manufacture, in transit, and during the construction of the building.

545-9. Outlet Boxes.

(a) **Other Dimensions.** Outlet boxes of dimensions other than those required in Table 370-6(a) will be permitted if they are identified, tested and listed to standards applicable.

(b) **Not Over 100 Cubic Inches.** Outlet boxes not over 100 cubic inches in size shall be mounted in closed construction affixed with approved anchors and clamps to provide rigid and secure installation.

545-10. Receptacle or Switch with Integral Enclosure—Receptacles and switches that are part of an enclosure and mounting means may be used where they have been identified, tested and listed for installation for standards that apply to them. Check with UL, NEMA, or ANSI.

545-11. Bonding and Grounding—Bonding and grounding are as important in manufactured buildings as in any other building. Panels and/or components of the building that come prewired must provide bonding and/ or grounding in accordance with Article 250, Parts E, F, and G, if it is likely that these parts may become energized.

545-12. Grounding Electrode Conductor—This is to be no different from the requirements of Part J of Article 250.

545-13. Component Interconnection—When intended to be concealed at time of assembly, fittings and conductors, if they have been identified, tested and listed for the standards to which they are applicable, will be permitted for on-site connection to modules or other building components. The fittings and connectors must be equal to the wiring method used in insulation, temperature rise, and withstanding of fault current, and shall be capable of withstanding vibrations or any minor motions that occur in the components of the manufactured building.

In a number of cases, manufactured buildings have concerned inspection authorities and some require inspection at the manufacturing site before being moved, as well as after set in place.

ARTICLE 547—AGRICULTURAL BUILDINGS

547-1. Scope—This article applies to agricultural buildings or parts of buildings that will be covered in (a) and (b) below:

(a) **Excessive Dust and Dust with Water.** This covers agricultural buildings where excessive dust or dust with water accumulate. These buildings contain areas that are totally enclosed and where poultry and livestock confinement systems are environmetally controlled, where feed dust, litter dust, including mineral feed particles, may accumulate, and also including enclosed areas of similar nature.

(b) **Corrosive Atmosphere.** Agricultural buildings in which a corrosive atmosphere exists are covered here. Such buildings include totally enclosed and environmentally controlled environmental areas: (1) where poultry and animal excrement may cause corrosive vapors; (2) where corrosive materials may combine with water; (3) the area is damp or wet, because periodic washing is required for cleaning and for sanitation by the use of water and cleaning agents; or (4) where similar conditions exist.

547-2. Other Articles—In agricultural buildings where conditions such as were covered in the previous section occur, the wiring installations may be made using applicable articles of the Code.

The above calls to the author's mind a turkey building where a general purpose service-entrance equipment was installed and a mast service. It was only a very short time until shorts and grounds occurred in the service equipment. This was due to the high humidity rising up the mast and condensing, causing water to run down on the circuit breakers. This was stopped by installing duct-seal at both the top and bottom of the mast.

547-3. General—When electrical equipment and devices are installed in compliance with provisions of this article, the installation shall be in such a manner that the equipment will be able to work at its full rating and not develop surface temperatures in excess of normal safe operation of the equipment or device.

547-4. Wiring Methods—With agricultural buildings described in 547-1(a) and (b), you may use Type UF, NMC, SNM, Copper SE, or other cables or raceways that will be suitable for the location, and if you use approved terminal fittings, these wiring methods may be employed. For Section 547-1(a), Article 320 and the wiring methods therein will be permitted. Buildings that are wired in accordance of Article 502 will be permitted. Securing of cables within 8 inches of each cabinet, box, or fitting is required.

Note: If raceway systems are exposed to widely varying temperatures, you shall refer to Sections 300-7 and 347-9 for their installation.

(a) **Boxes, Fittings, and Wiring Devices.** Compliance with Section 547-5 is required for all boxes and fittings.

(b) **Flexible Connections.** Where it becomes necessary to used wiring with some flexible connection and dusttight flexible connectors, liquidtight metal conduit or flexible cord that has been listed for hard usage may be used. All these wiring methods shall have fittings that are listed and identified.

547-5. Switches, Circuit Breakers, Controllers, and Fuses—When the parts in the title of this section, including pushbuttons, relays, and similar devices, are used in Section 547-1(a) and (b), they are to be provided with weatherproof, corrosion-resistant enclosure. They shall be designed to minimize the entrance of dust, water, and corrosive elements, and shall be equipped with close-fitting lids or telescoping covers.

547-6. Motors—Motors or other operational machinery must be equipped so that they are totally enclosed, or must be designed to keep the entrance of dust, moisture, or corrosive particles to a minimum.

547-7. Lighting Fixtures—When installed in agricultural buildings covered in Section 547-1, lighting fixtures installed must meet the following requirements:

(a) **Minimize the Entrance of Dust.** Design of the installed lighting fixtures must be such as to keep the entrance to a minimum of dust, foreign material, corrosive material, and moisture.

(b) **Exposed to Physical Damage.** If exposed to physical damage, the lighting fixture must have suitable guards for protection.

(c) **Exposed to Water.** If they are exposed to water and condensation and cleaning or water solutions used to clean the building, lighting fixtures shall be watertight.

547-8. Grounding, Bonding, and Equipotential Plane.

(a) Grounding and Bonding. Article 250 must be complied with for grounding and bonding.

Note: Section 250-21 covers current that would be objectionable passing over the grounding conductors.

Exception: If all the following conditions are met, it will not be required to have a main bonding jumper at a distribution panelboard when the buildings house livestock or poultry:

a. The same owner must own the buildings and premises wiring.
b. Run with the supply conductors shall be an equipment grounding conductor that is the same size as the supply conductors.
c. There shall be a service disconnecting means at the point of distribution to these buildings.
d. The service-entrance equipment and equipment grounding conductor are to be bonded together.
e. An approved grounding electrode must be provided; it shall also be connected to the equipment grounding conductor in the distribution panelboard.

(b) **Concrete Embedded Elements.** Either wire mesh or other conductive elements that are provided in the concrete floor of locations where animals are confined shall provide a plane of equipotential, and it shall be bonded to the grounding electrode system. The bonding conductor shall be only copper that is insulated, covered, or bare, and shall not be smaller than No. 8 AWG. The bonding of the equipment grounding conductor shall be connected to the wire mesh or conductive elements by means of pressure connectors or clamps. These are required to be of brass, copper, copper alloy, or equally substantial approved means.

Equipotential Plane: An area where wire mesh or other conductive elements are embedded in the concrete and bonded to all adjacent equipment, structures, or surfaces that are conductive and are connected to the grounding system. This is required to prevent a difference of potential from occurring in the plane.

Note: If wire mesh or other conductive grid embedded in concrete floor or platform is bonded to the electrical grounding system, should livestock make contact between the connected floor or platform and the equivalent or metal structure, They will be less likely to be exposed to a potential that will change the behavior or the productivity of the animal.

(c) **Separate Equipment Grounding Conductor.** As described in Section 547-1(a) and (b) and covering the agricultural buildings described there, any noncurrent-carrying equipment, raceways, or other enclosures that might accidentally be grounded are required to be grounded by a copper equipment grounding conductor. This shall be installed to the equipment and the building disconnection means. If this equipment grounding conductor is installed underground, it is required to be insulated or covered.

Note: When grounding electrode systems have lower resistances than those required in Article 250, Part H, this will also reduce any potential differences within the livestock areas.

ARTICLE 550—MOBILE HOMES AND MOBILE HOME PARKS

550-1. Scope—This article covers electrical conductors and equipment that are installed in or on mobile homes and conductors from the mobile homes to a supply of electricity, and includes the installation of electrical wiring fixtures, equipment, and other portions related to electrical installations within the mobile home park up to the mobile home. If service-entrance conductors do not exist, then the mobile home service equipment shall be used.

(Do not let this confuse you, as the service equipment, as will be seen in Section 550-4, shall be located adjacent to, and not in or on, the mobile home.)

Mobile homes have caused much discussion by Code panels and inspection authorities in general. They are built and sold to the public as a complete unit with the walls in place. Thus, local inspection authorities cannot really check to see that the wiring meets the Code requirements. Underwriter's Laboratories have a labeling service that is available to mobile-home manufacturers and the mobile homes come from such factories with the label on them. However, these seem to be in the minority. Some inspection authorities demand an inspection before the units are allowed in their jurisdictional area. Others find that some manufacturers ask for local inspection and label their product accordingly to show that a local inspection has been made, feeling that the public is entitled to purchase a mobile home with adequate and safe wiring. These local labels are often accepted by other inspection authorities.

Another problem that faces inspection authorities is that so often the wheels are removed and the mobile home is set on a permanent foundation. Local laws will govern whether it stays a mobile home or not. In many localities it may stay a mobile home as long as a license is purchased annually for a mobile home.

There is also a popular mobile home that is built in two or more mobile sections which are hauled to the location and bolted together to become a large home.

These problems cannot be covered by the *National Electrical Code*; they are problems to be answered by local rulings and laws.

550-2. Definitions—There are a number of definitions included which cover mobile homes. They will not be repeated, so refer to the *NEC*; however, the headings will be given:

1. Appliance, Fixed
2. Appliances, Portable
3. Appliance, Stationary
4. Distribution Panelboard
5. Feeder Assembly
6. Laundry Area
7. Mobile Home
8. Mobile Home Accessory Building or Structure
9. Mobile Home Lot
10. Mobile Home Park
11. Mobile Home Service Equipment
12. Park Electrical Wiring Systems

As stated previously, the following is given: Basically, the local authority enforcing the Code is interested that:

(1) Mobile homes and the electrical panel therein is basically a feeder panel, and that the neutral bus is isolated from the panel enclosure and the equipment grounding. This must be taken care of by an extra conductor for grounding purposes only from the source of supply through the cord or cords supplying the home. See Figs. 550-1 and 550-2.

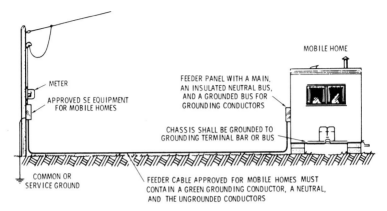

Fig. 550-1. Pole-mounted service-entrance equipment for mobile-home use with the feeder cable above ground.

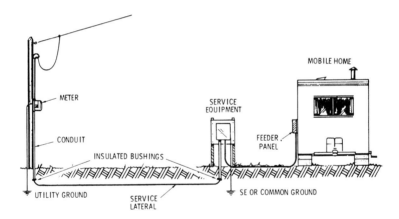

Fig. 550-2. Underground service lateral for use with a mobile home.

(2) If there are two cords supplying the home, the two panels must be treated as entirely separate panels and not interconnected.

(3) Supply cord or cords shall be no longer than 36½ feet and no less than 20 feet in length.

(4) Where the calculated load exceeds 100 amperes, or where a permanent feeder is used as a supply, four permanently installed conductors, one being identified as the grounding conductor as required by Code, must be used. See Figs. 550-3 and 550-4.

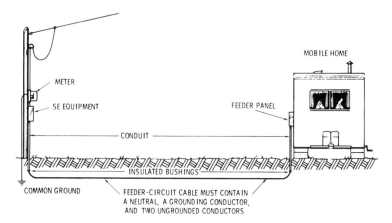

Fig. 550-3. Pole-mounted service-entrance equipment for mobile-home use with the feeder cable buried.

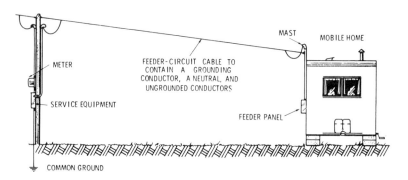

Fig. 550-4. An overhead feeder-cable installation to supply power to a mobile home.

(5) Grounding of both electrical and nonelectrical metal parts in a mobile home is through connection to a grounding bus in the mobile-home distribution panel. The grounding bus is grounded through the green colored conductor in the supply cord or the feeder wiring to the service ground in the service-entrance equipment located adjacent to the mobile-home location. Note this last part. Neither the frame of the mobile home nor the frame of any appliance may be connected to the neutral conductor in the mobile home.

(6) The chassis shall be grounded. The grounding conductor may be solid or stranded, insulated or bare, and shall be an armored grounding conductor or routed in conduit if it is No. 8 AWG. The conductor,

if No. 6 AWG or larger, may be run without metal covering. The grounding conductor shall be connected between the distribution panel grounding terminal and a terminal on the chassis. Grounding terminals shall be of the solderless type and approved for the wire size employed.

In summary, the distribution panel of a mobile home is not service-entrance equipment. It is, in essence, a feeder panel. The service-entrance equipment is located adjacent to the mobile home. When a mobile home is located and installed as a permanent home, then the picture changes and the necessary alterations must be made in the wiring system to meet the requirements of the Code for a permanent home.

Note under definition of Mobile Home that it is designed to be used as a dwelling unit(s) without a permanent foundation. This rules out a mobile home as a "prefabricated" or "module home."

550-3. Other Articles—If requirements of other articles of the *NEC* differ from Article 550, the requirements of Article 550 will take precedence and apply.

550-4. General Requirements.

(a) **Mobile Home Not Intended as a Dwelling Unit.** When a mobile home is not intended as a dwelling unit—for example, one that is used primarily for sleeping purposes or for contractors' on-site offices for a construction job, for dormitories, dressing rooms in mobile studios, banks, clinics, mobile stores, or for exhibiting and demonstrating of merchandise or machinery—it will not be required to meet the provisions of this article pertaining to the number of capacity of the circuits required. All other applicable requirements in this article must be followed if a mobile home of the type mentioned above is provided with an electrical installation that will be energized from a 120-volt or 120/240-volt ac power system. If a different voltage is required, either by available power supply systems or design, adjustments must be made to meet the requirements of other articles and sections covering the voltage used.

(b) **In Other than Mobile Home Parks.** Mobile homes, if they are installed in other than regular mobile home parks, are required to comply with the provisions of this article.

(c) **Connection to Wiring System.** The provisions of this article apply to mobile homes that will be connected to a wiring system rated 120/240 volts, nominal, 3-wire ac, with a grounded neutral.

(d) **Listed or Labeled.** The electrical materials, including devices, appliances, fittings, and other equipment, are required to be listed or labeled. This must be done by a qualified testing agency, and the installation and connection of same shall be done in an approved manner.

Refer to the *NEC* for complete coverage of this article.

A. Mobile Homes

550-5. Power Supply.

(a) **Service Equipment.** The service equipment for a mobile home is required to be located adjacent to the mobile home and shall not be mounted in or on the mobile home. The power supply to the mobile home shall be a feeder assembly from the adjacent service equipment, and it shall consist of not more than one listed 50-ampere mobile home power-supply cord that has a molded cap that is part of the cord on the permanently installed feeder.

Exception: If the mobile home has been factory equipped with gas- or oil-fired central heating equipment and cooking appliances, the mobile home shall be permitted to be supplied with a power-supply cord that is listed and rated at 40 amperes.

(b) **Power-Supply Cord.** If a power-supply cord goes to the mobile home, it shall be permanently attached to the distribution panel or a junction box that is a permanently connected distribution panelboard, and the free end of this cord is to be terminated with an attachment plug cap.

Cords that use adapters and pigtail end extension cords and similar items shall not be shipped with a mobile home or attached thereto.

A clamp or other device that is suitable to afford strain relief for the cord shall be used at the distribution panelboard knockout. The purpose of this is to prevent strain to the terminals when the power cord is handled in a normal manner.

The cord must be a listed type and include four conductors, one of which is to be identified by a continuous green color or a continuous green color with one or more yellow stripes. This conductor shall be used for the grounding conductor.

(c) **Attachment Plug Cap.** The attachment plug cap shall be a 3-pole, 4-wire, grounding type that is rated at 50 amperes, 125/250 volts, such as is shown in the *NEC* in Fig. 550-5(c), and that is intended for use with 50-ampere 125/250-volt receptacles. The attachment plug shall be molded of butyl rubber, neoprene, or other materials that have been found to be suitable for this purpose, and the plug shall be molded to the flexible cord in such a manner that it adheres tightly to the cord where the attachment plug enters the receptacle cap. When a right-angle cap is required, the configuration is required to be such that the grounding member is furthest from the cord.

Note: Complete details may be seen in the *NEC* in Fig. 550-5(c).

For the balance of this section, refer to the *NEC*.

550-6. Disconnecting Means and Branch-Circuit Protective Equipment—See the *NEC*.

550-7. Branch Circuits—See the *NEC*.

550-8. Receptacle Outlets—See the *NEC*.

550-9. Fixtures and Appliances—See the *NEC*.

550-10. Wiring Methods and Materials—See the *NEC*.

550-11. Grounding—See the *NEC*.

550-12. Testing—See the *NEC*.

550-13. Calculations—See the *NEC*.

550-14. Interconnection of Multiple Section Mobile Home Units—See the *NEC*.

550-15. Outdoor Outlets, Fixtures, Air-Cooling Equipment, Etc.—See the *NEC*.

B. MOBILE HOME PARKS

550-21. Distribution System—See the *NEC*.

550-22. Calculated Load—See the *NEC*.

550-23. Mobile Home Service Equipment—See the *NEC*.

550-24. Feeder—See the *NEC*.

ARTICLE 551—RECREATIONAL VEHICLES AND RECREATIONAL VEHICLE PARKS

Part A applies to wiring systems used in the vehicles. Part B applies to recreational vehicle park wiring systems and includes: type of distribution, receptacles, load calculations, lot service equipment, and installation requirements for overhead and underground conductors.

It appears that any authority having jurisdiction over the enforcement of the *National Electrical Code* has a very comprehensive guide for inspection and enforcement of the *NEC* in regard to recreational vehicles and parks. See the *NEC* for coverage of this article.

ARTICLE 553—FLOATING BUILDINGS

See the *NEC*.

ARTICLE 555—MARINAS AND BOATYARDS

These areas have the possibility of becoming very hazardous from an electrical aspect. In wiring marinas and boatyards, be sure that you follow the prescribed methods outlined in the *NEC*.

CHAPTER 6

Special Equipment

ARTICLE 600—ELECTRIC SIGNS AND OUTLINE LIGHTING

Refer to the *NEC* for coverage of this article.

ARTICLE 604—MANUFACTURED WIRING SYSTEMS

Refer to the *NEC* for coverage of this article.

ARTICLE 605—OFFICE FURNISHINGS
(Consisting of Lighting Accessories and Wired Partitions)

605-1. Scope—Lighting accessories, electrical equipment, and the wiring used to connect same, which may be installed in relocatable wired partitions, are covered by this article.

Office areas use many relocatable partitions so that areas of work may be relocated as business conditions change.

605-2. General—Only identified and suitable wiring systems shall be used to provide power for lighting accessories and appliances where supplied by wired partitions, and these partitions shall not extend from the floor to the ceiling.

(a) **Use.** As provided by this article, these assemblies shall be installed and used only as covered here.

(b) **Other Articles.** All other articles of the Code shall apply, unless modified by this article.

(c) **Hazardous (Classified) Locations.** When they are used in hazardous (classified) locations, manufactured wiring systems shall conform to Articles 500 through 517 in addition to the requirements of this article.

605-3. Wireways—The installation of conductors and their connections is to be contained within wiring channels that are made of metal or other material that is suitable for the conditions of use. There shall be no projections or other conditions that might damage the insulation of the conductors.

Wireways for this purpose often contain a divider so that telephone wire and electrical conductors may be run in the same wireway but are entirely separated. Drop ceilings are usually used and connections to the regular wiring system above the ceiling are used to connect the wireway, but only approved wiring methods shall be used for this connection.

Note: Flexible cords are not to be used as conductors in these partitions.

605-4. Partition Interconnections—The electrical connection between partitions shall be flexible assembly identified for use with wired partitions.

Exception: It will be permitted to use flexible cords between partitions if all the following conditions are met:

(a) The cords are extra-hard usage type.
(b) The partitions are mechanically contiguous.
(c) The flexible cord in no case is longer than 2 feet; it may be up to 2 feet long if necessary for maximum positioning of the partitions.
(d) The cord is terminated with an attachment plug and cord connector, and provision is made for strain relief.

605-5. Lighting Accessories—The following conditions must be met, and the lighting equipment is required to be listed and identified for use with wired partitions.

(a) **Support.** There shall be means for secure attachment or support provided.

(b) **Connection.** If cord- and plug-connections are provided, the cord that is used for this application and its length shall be suitable, but the length shall not exceed 9 feet in length. Cords no smaller than No. 18 AWG shall contain an equipment grounding conductor, and the cord shall be of hard-usage type. Any connections by other means must be identified and suitable for the conditions for which it is used.

(c) **Receptacle Outlet.** There shall be no convenience receptacles included in a lighting fixture.

605-6. Fixed-Type Partitions—If partitions are wired and are secured to the building surface, they are required to be permanently connected to the building surface, and one of the means covered in Chapter 3 shall be used for wires.

605-7. Free-Standing-Type Partitions—One of the wiring methods covered in Chapter 3 may use partitions that are of free-standing type and will be permanently connected to the building electrical system.

605-8. Free-Standing-Type Partitions, Cord- and Plug-Connected —Individual partitions that are of a free-standing type, or groups of individual partitions that are electrically connected, mechanically contiguous, and do not exceed 30 feet when assembled, may be permitted to be connected to the electrical system of the building by means of a single flexible cord and plug, provided all the following conditions are met:

(a) **Flexible Power Supply Cord.** The flexible supply for the power is required to be extra-hard-usage type cord and shall be No. 12 AWG or larger conductors and include an equipment grounding conductor, and the length of the flexible cord connection shall not exceed 2 feet.

(b) **Receptacle Supplying Power.** Receptacle(s) are to be supplied with power by a separate circuit that is not used to supply any other loads, but only the panels themselves, and the receptacle shall not be over 12 inches from the panel to which it is connected.

(c) **Receptacle Outlets, Maximum.** Individual partitions and groups of partitions that are interconnected shall not be allowed to contain more than thirteen 15-ampere, 125-volt receptacle outlets.

(d) **Multiwire Circuits Not Permitted.** Individual panels or groups of panels that are interconnected shall not be permitted to have multiwire circuits installed in them.

Note: You are referred to Section 210-4, which will cover circuits that supply partitions in Sections 605-6 and 605-7.

ARTICLE 610—CRANES AND HOISTS

Refer to the *NEC* for coverage of this article.

ARTICLE 620—ELEVATORS, DUMBWAITERS, ESCALATORS, AND MOVING WALKS

Refer to the *NEC* for coverage of this article.

ARTICLE 630—ELECTRIC WELDERS

Refer to the *NEC* for coverage of this article.

ARTICLE 640—SOUND-RECORDING AND SIMILAR EQUIPMENT

Refer to the *NEC* for coverage of this article.

ARTICLE 645—ELECTRONIC DATA PROCESSING SYSTEMS

Refer to the *NEC* for coverage of this article.

ARTICLE 650—ORGANS

Refer to the *NEC* for coverage of this article.

ARTICLE 660—X-RAY EQUIPMENT

Refer to the *NEC* for coverage of this article.

ARTICLE 665—INDUCTION AND DIELECTRIC HEATING EQUIPMENT

Refer to the *NEC* for coverage of this article.

ARTICLE 668—ELECTROLYTIC CELLS

Refer to the *NEC* for coverage of this article.

ARTICLE 669—ELECTROPLATING

Refer to the *NEC* for coverage of this article.

ARTICLE 670—INDUSTRIAL MACHINERY

Refer to the *NEC* for coverage of this article.

ARTICLE 675—ELECTRICALLY DRIVEN AND CONTROLLED IRRIGATION MACHINES

This article was new in the 1975 edition of the *NEC*. Basically most of these pivot in a circle from a source of irrigation water supply, usually supplied from a pump supplying water from an irrigation ditch or a ground-water well supplying water from a pumping source.

Some are electrically propelled, some are water propelled, but electrically controlled, so that they may be kept in line, over rough ground, but any that I have seen use electrical controls at least and many are driven by electric motors.

Refer to the *NEC* for coverage.

ARTICLE 680—SWIMMING POOLS, FOUNTAINS, AND SIMILAR INSTALLATIONS

A. General

Due to the large usage of underwater lighting and other electrical equipment in conjunction with swimming pools, this has become a very important article in the Code. The water and conductivity of wet surfaces around the pool have become a very serious hazard, and in designing or installing electrical installations in such locations, special precautions should be taken at all times.

680-1. Scope—This article covers the construction and installation of wiring for equipment that will be either in or adjacent to all swimming, wading, therapeutic, and decorated pools, fountains, hot tubs, spas, and hydromassage bathtubs, and this will be irrespective of whether they are of a permanent nature or can be stored; it also pertains to the metal auxiliary equipment. This will cover pumps, filters, ladders, and any other similar equipment in or near the water.

Note: The term "pool" as used in this article includes swimming, wading, and permanently installed therapeutic pools. "Fountains" as used in this article includes fountains, ornamental pools, display pools, and reflection pools.

680-2. Approval of Equipment—All electrical equipment that may be installed in the water or the walls or decks of pools, fountains, and similar installations are required to be installed according to this article. Underwriter's Laboratories approval is practically universally accepted for this equipment.

680-3. Other Articles—The requirements of Chapters 1 to 4, inclusive, are applicable to wiring of swimming pools with the exception of the modifications in this Article which are necessary due to the hazards involved.

Note: You are referred to Section 370-13 for the junction boxes, Section 347-3 for rigid nonmetallic conduit, and Article 720 for low-voltage lighting.

680-4. Definitions—The *NEC* covers definitions in this section. The following definitions are covered:

(1) Dry-Niche Lighting Fixture

(2) Forming Shell

(3) Hydro Massage Bathtub

(4) Permanently Installed Decorative Fountains and Reflection Pools

(5) Permanently Installed Swimming, Wading, and Therapeutic Pools

(6) Pool Cover, Electrically Operated

(7) Spa or Hot Tub

(8) Storable Swimming or Wading Pools

(9) Wet-Niche Lighting Fixtures

680-5. Transformers and Ground-Fault Circuit-Interrupters.

(a) **Transformers.** Transformers and their enclosures that supply fixtures shall be identified for the purpose. The transformers of the two-winding type with a grounded metal barrier between the primary and secondary windings shall be used. Check the green UL listing book to be certain that the one you use has been approved.

(b) **Ground-Fault Circuit Interrupters.** Self-contained units may be used for ground-fault circuit-interruption, or circuit-breaker types may be used, or receptacle types, or any other type that might be approved for such usage.

(c) **Wiring.** All conductors on the load side of ground-fault circuit-interrupters or transformers shall be kept entirely separate from all other wiring and equipment. This is in reference, for this equipment used to comply with Section 680-20(a)(1).

Exception No. 1: Ground-fault circuit interrupters are allowed to be installed in a panelboard even though it contains some circuits that are not protected by ground-fault circuit interrupters.

Exception No. 2: If the supply conductors are of the feed-through, receptacle type, you will be permitted to install them in the same enclosure ground-fault circuit interrupters.

Exception No. 3: The load side conductors from a ground-fault circuit-interrupter may occupy conduit, boxes, or enclosures where conductors in those items are also protected by ground-fault circuit interrupters.

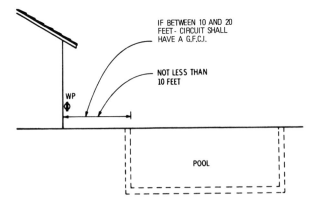

Fig. 680-1. Location and protection of all outside receptacles.

680-6. Receptacles, Lighting Fixtures, Lighting Outlets, and Switching Devices.

(a) Receptacles.

(1) Any receptacles on the property are required to be mounted at least 10 feet away from the inside walls of the pool.

Exception: Receptacle(s) installed to supply power to water-pump motor(s) for a pool that is permanently installed, as permitted in Section 680-7, shall be permitted to be installed between 5 and 10 feet from the inside walls of the pool. They shall be single receptacles, of the locking type and grounding type. It is also required that they be protected by GFCI's.

(2) At dwelling unit(s) with a permanently installed pool, there shall be at least one 125-volt convenience receptacle, and this is to be located at a distance of at least 10 feet and not more than 20 feet from the inside of the wall of the pool.

(3) Ground-fault circuit interrupters, as covered in Section 210-8(a)(3), will be required for lighting fixtures and outlets that are located within 20 feet of the inside walls of the pool.

Note: The distance is determined for the above dimensions by measuring the shortest path of a supply cord of an appliance that will be connected to the receptacle. This path is followed without piercing a floor, wall, ceiling, or doorway that has either hinged or sliding doors, any window openings, or any other effective barrier.

Note: Section 400-8(3) prohibits cord wiring where it is run through a window, doorway, or similiar opening.

(b) Lighting Fixtures and Lighting Outlets.

(1) No lighting fixtures or lighting outlets are to be installed over the pool or over the area extending 5 feet in a horizontal direction from the inside walls of the pool unless they are a minimum of 12 feet above the maximum water level.

Exception No. 1: If there are existing lighting fixtures or outlets that are located less than 5 feet from the inside walls of the pool in a horizontal direction, they shall be at least 5 feet above the surface of the maximum level of the water and must be rigidly attached to the existing structure.

Exception No. 2: The limitation of Section 680-6(b)(1) will not apply to indoor pool areas if all the following conditions are met: (1) they shall be the totally enclosed type of fixture; (2) a GFCI shall be installed in the branch circuit that is supplying the fixture(s); and (3) the distance from the bottom of the fixture to the maximum water level shall be not less than 7 ½ feet.

(2) Where lighting fixtures and lighting outlets are installed in the area extending between 5 feet and 10 feet from the inside walls of the pool, a GFCI shall be used unless they are installed 5 feet above the maximum water level and are rigidly and securely attached to the structure adjacent to or enclosing the pool.

(3) As set forth in Section 680-7, any cord- and plug-connected lighting fixtures shall meet these specifications, as would any other plug- and cord-connected equipment when installed within 6 feet at any point measured radially on the surface of the water.

(c) **Switching Devices.** Any switching devices on the property shall be located a minimum of 5 feet from the inside walls of the pool, unless they are separated from the pool by a solid fence or other permanent type of barrier.

680-7. Cord- and Plug-Connected Equipment—Whether fixed or stationary, any equipment rated 20 amperes or less, not including underwater lighting installed permanently in the pool, will be permitted to be connected by a flexible cord to aid in disconnection and removal for maintenance and repair. For other than storable pools, the flexible cord shall not exceed 3 feet in length, the cord must contain a copper equipment-grounding conductor that shall not be smaller than No. 12, and a grounding type attachment plug shall be used.

Note: For flexible cords used for connection, see Section 680-25(e).

680-8. Overhead Conductor Clearances—The following parts of pools are not to be placed under existing service-drop conductors or any other open-type overhead wiring; nor shall such type of wiring be installed above any of the following: (1) pools, including the area extending 10 feet horizontally from the inside wall of the pool; (2) structures designed for diving; or (3) platforms, towers, or stands used for observation.

Exception No. 1: Structures covered in (1) through (3) above will be permitted under untility-owned, -operated, and -maintained supply lines or service drops—if the following clearances are provided: See the table here in the *NEC*, the (FPN), and Fig. 680-8, Exception No. 1.

Exception No. 2: Utility-owned, -operated, and -maintained communication conductors, community antenna system coaxial cables that comply with Article 820, and the supporting messengers for the cable shall be permitted to at a height not less than 10 feet above swimming and wading pools, diving structures, diving stands, towers, or platforms.

Note: For clearances not covered by this section, you are referred to Sections 225-18 and 225-19.

680-9. Electric Pool Water Heaters—Electric water heaters for pools shall have the heating elements subdivided so that the load on each element is not over 48 amperes and the protection for that circuit shall not be more than 60 amperes.

The branch-circuit conductor's ampacity and the rating or setting of the overcurrent devices shall be not less than 125 percent of the total rating on the nameplate.

680-10. Underground Wiring Location—Any underground wiring going to the pool is not permitted to be installed under the pool or the area extending 5 feet horizontally from the inside wall of the pool.

Exception No. 1: Wiring that is necessary for the operation of the pool equipment, as permitted by this article, may be permitted within this area.

Exception No. 2: If, due to space limitations, the wiring cannot be limited to within 5 feet or more from the pool, this wiring may be in rigid metal conduit, intermediate metal conduit, or nonmetallic raceway systems. The metal conduit shall be suitable for the location, and corrosive resistant. Refer to the exceptions to Section 300-5(a) that shall not apply.

680-11. Equipment Rooms and Pits—It is not permitted to install electrical equipment in rooms or pits that are not provided with adequate drainage to prevent water accumulation under normal operation, or for filter maintenance.

B. Permanently Installed Pools

680-20. Underwater Lighting Fixtures.

(a) **General.** The following paragraphs (a) through (c) in this section apply to underwater lighting fixtures that are below the normal water level in the pool.

(1) Lighting fixtures that are supplied either from a branch circuit or by a transformer that comply with the requirements of Section 680-5(a) are to be designed so that, when the fixture is properly installed without a GFCI, there will be no likelihood of shock conditions with any probable combinations of fault conditions when the pool is in normal use. Relamping is not covered here.

There shall also be a GFCI installed in the branch circuit that supplies the fixtures that operate at more than 15 volts between conductors so that there is no possiblity of a shock hazard during relamping. The GFCI shall be installed is such a way that there is no likely shock hazard with any fault-condition combination involving a person in a conductive path from any ungrounded part of the branch circuit or the fixture to ground.

This requirement shall be complied with by the use of an approved underwater lighting fixture and with the installation of a GFCI in the branch circuit.

(2) No lighting fixtures shall be installed that require over 150 volts between conductors.

(3) Underwater lighting fixtures are to be installed with the top of the fixture at least 18 inches below normal water level of the pool. If the lighting fixture faces upward, it shall be properly guarded to prevent contact by a person. See Fig. 680-2.

Exception: Lighting fixtures shall be permitted if they have been identified for use at a depth of not less than 4 inches below the water level of the pool.

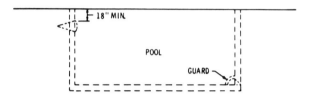

Fig. 680-2. Installation of fixtures below water level.

(4) Submerged lighting fixtures that depend upon submergence for proper operation are required to be inherently protected against hazardous overheating when not submerged.

(b) **Wet-Niche Fixtures.**

(1) An approved forming shell of metal shall be installed for mounting the wet-niche underwater fixtures, and this shall be equipped with threads for entries of conduit.

Conduit shall run from the forming shell to a suitable junction box or other enclosure located as covered in Section 680-21. The conduit shall be rigid metal conduit, intermediate metal conduit, or rigid nonmetallic conduit.

Metal conduit shall be made of brass or other corrosive-resistant metal.

If rigid nonmetallic conduit is used and insulated, copper conductor of size No. 8 AWG is required to be installed in the nonmetallic conduit, and it shall have provisions for terminating in the forming shell, junction box, transformer, or GFCI enclosure. The No. 8 conductor shall be terminated in the forming shell, and it shall be encapsulated or covered by a listed potting compound, the purpose of which is to protect such connection from any possible deteriorating effect of the pool water. Metal parts of the lighting fixture and forming shell in contact with the water in the pool are required to be of brass or other approved corrosion-resistant metal.

(2) The end of a flexible-cord jacket and the flexible-cord conductor terminations within a fixture are required to be covered with, or encapsulated in, a suitable potting compound; this is to prevent

the entry of water through the fixture, the cord, or its conductors. In addition thereto, the grounding connection within a fixture shall be similarly treated to protect such connection from any deteriorating effects that the pool water might have in the event of water entering into the fixture.

(3) The fixture is required to be bonded and secured to the forming shell by means of a positive locking device that ensures there will be low-resistance contact, and that requires a tool to remove the fixture for the forming shell.

(c) **Dry-Niche Fixtures.** Dry-niche lighting fixtures shall be provided with: (1) some provision for draining water, and (2) a means for connecting the equipment grounding conductor for each conduit entry.

Rigid metal conduit, intermediate metal conduit, or rigid non-metallic conduit, which has been approved, must be installed from the fixture to the service equipment or panelboard. A junction box is not required, but if one is used, it shall not be required to be elevated or located as specified in Section 680-21(a)(4), provided the fixture is specifically identified for the purpose.

Junction boxes mounted above the grade of finished walkways around the pool shall not be located in the walkway unless afforded additional protection such as location under diving boards, adjacent to fixed structures, or the like.

The purpose of this ruling is easy to understand. Junction boxes shall be so located as not to cause a stumbling hazard. The area around the pool is always wet and slippery—if installed without protection, the boxes might be a great hazard and likely to cause falls.

Exception: If installed in or on buildings, EMT may be used to protect conductors.

680-21. Junction Boxes and Enclosures for Transformers or Ground-Fault Circuit Interrupters.

(a) **Junction Boxes.** When the conduit is connected directly to the forming shell, a junction box connected to the conduit shall be:

(1) Required to have threaded hubs or bosses; and

(2) The junction box shall be made of copper, brass, suitable plastic, or any other material that is corrosion resistant and approved for the purpose; and

(3) The electrical continuity must be maintained between every metal conduit and the grounding terminals. This shall be by means of copper, brass, or any other approved noncorrosive metal that is part of the box; and

(4) Junction boxes are to be located not less than 8 inches measured from the bottom of the box to the ground level, pool deck, or

maximum water level. The greater of these distances is to be used, and the location shall be not less than 4 feet from the inside wall of the pool unless separated from the pool by a solid fence, wall, or other permanent barrier. See Fig. 680-3.

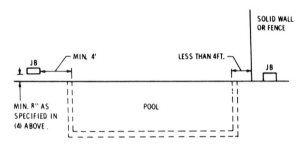

Fig. 680-3.   Junction box placement where walls or fence are used.

Exception: When lighting systems operate at 15 volts or less, a flush junction box on the deck may be used if:

a. Prevention of moisture entering the box may be accomplished by using an approved potting compound to fill the box; and

b. The flush deck box is not less than 4 feet from the inside edge of the pool.

(b) **Other Enclosures.** Enclosures such as for a transformer, GFCI, or similar device that connects to a conduit extending directly to the forming shell shall be:

(1) See (a)(1) of this section.

(2) Provided with an approved seal, such as duct seal, at the conduit connection; this prevents circulation of air between conduit and enclosures; and

(3) and (4) See (a)(3) and (a)(4), but replace box with enclosure.

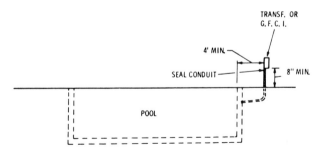

Fig. 680-4.   Showing conduit seal.

(c) **Protection.** Junction boxes and enclosures mounted above the finished walkway grade around the pool shall not be located in the walkway unless protected in addition by being, e.g., located under diving boards or adjacent to fixed structures, etc.

The purpose of this ruling is easy to understand. Junction boxes shall be so located as not to cause a stumbling hazard. The area around the pool is always wet and slippery; if installed without protection, the boxes might be a great hazard and likely to cause falls.

(d) **Grounding Terminals.** When junction boxes, transformer enclosures, and GFCI's enclosures are connected to a conduit that extends directly to the forming shell, they shall be provided with a number of grounding terminals and there shall be at least one more grounding terminal than there are conduit entries.

(e) **Strain Relief.** The termination of a flexible cord for underwater lighting fixtures within the junction box, transformer enclosure, GFCI enclosure, or other enclosures shall be provided with some means of approved strain relief.

680-22. Bonding.

Note: The intent of this subsection, in requiring No. 8 or larger solid copper bonding conductors is that it is not required to be extended or attached to any remote panelboard, Servicing equipment, or any electrode. It is only employed to eliminate voltage gradient that could occur in the pool area as prescribed.

(a) **Bonded Parts.** The following parts shall be bonded together:

(1) All metal parts used in the pool structure, including reinforcing metal of the pool shell, coping stones, and deck.

(2) All forming shells.

(3) All metal fittings within or attached to the pool structure.

(4) Metal parts of the electrical system equipment that are associated with the pool water circulating system, and including the pump motors.

(5) Metal parts associated with pool covers, including electric motors.

(6) Any metal conduit or piping, including all metal parts that are within 5 feet of the inside walls of the pool when there is not a permanent barrier separating them from the pool.

See Fig. 680-5 on page 572.

Exception No. 1: Special welding or clamping is not required to bond rebar in the pool, but it may be bonded by steel tie wires considered suitable for bonding reinforcing steel.

Exception No. 2: Bolted or welded metal structural parts of walls with reinforcing steel will be permitted as a common bonding grid

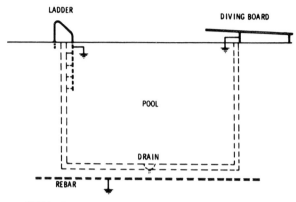

GROUND METAL PARTS, REBAR, LADDER, RAILS,
DIVING BOARDS, DRAINS, OTHER PARTS & EQUIPMENT.

Fig. 680-5. Bonding all metal equipment together by using solid copper wire.

for nonelectrical connection. They can be made as specified in Section 250-113.

Exception No. 3: Metal parts that are not more than 4 inches in dimension and do not penetrate the interior of the pool structure more than 1 inch are not required to be bonded.

(b) **Common Bonding Grid.** All these parts are to be of common bonding grid connected with solid copper conductor that is insulated, covered, or bare, and shall not be smaller than No. 8 AWG. The connection may be made by pressure connectors or clamps made of brass, copper, or copper alloy. The common bonding grid shall be as follows:

(1) Where the structural reinforcing steel of a concrete pool have been bonded together by the usual steel tie wires or equivalent; or

(2) If the wall is bolted or welded; or

(3) With the copper solid wire connection, which shall not be smaller than No. 8 AWG, it may be insulated, covered, or bare.

(c) **Pool Water Heaters.** In pool water heaters with a rating of more than 50 amperes that have specific instructions regarding bonding or grounding, only the parts designated to be bonded shall be bonded, and only those parts that are designated to be grounded shall be grounded.

680-23. Underwater Audio Equipment—Audio systems for underwater use shall be approved for the purpose.

(a) **Speakers.** They are to mounted in an approved metal forming shell, and the front shall be enclosed by a captive metal screen, or the equivalent, that is bonded to the forming shell by means of a positive locking device so that a low-resistance contact is ensured and a special tool is required to open the installation to service the speaker. The forming shell must be recessed in the wall or the floor of the pool.

(b) **Wiring Methods.** Rigid metal conduit, or intermediate metal conduit that is made of brass or other identified corrosive-resistant metal, or rigid nonmetallic conduit may be used to extend from the speaker enclosure forming shell to a suitable junction box or other enclosure. Section 680-21 covers this. If rigid nonmetallic conduit is used, No. 8 AWG copper conductor, which is insulated, is required to be installed in the conduit and provisions shall be made for terminations in the forming shell and the junction box. In the forming shell the termination of the No. 8 conductor shall be covered or encapsulated in a suitable potting compound to protect against possible deterioration of the terminal by the pool water.

(c) **Forming Shell and Metal Screen.** Both the forming shell and the metal screen shall be of brass or other approved metal that is corrosion resistant.

680-24. Grounding—Grounding is required for the following equipment: (1) wet-niche lighting fixtures underwater; (2) dry-niche lighting fixtures installed underwater; (3) any equipment located within 5 feet of the inside of the pool wall; (4) all equipment that is associated with the recirculation of the pool water; (5) junction boxes; (6) transformer enclosures; (7) GFCI's; (8) panelboard that is not part of the service-entrance equipment, but that supplies any electrical equipment associated with the pool.

680-25. Methods of Grounding.

(a) **General.** The following provisions apply to the grounding of underwater lighting fixtures, junction boxes, metal transformer enclosures, panelboards, motors, and all other electrical equipment and enclosures.

(b) **Pool Lighting Fixtures and Related Equipment.** See the *NEC*, starting with (b) of this section. See Figs. 680-6 and 680-7 on page 574.

680-26. Electrically Operated Pool Covers—See the *NEC*.

680-27. Deck Area Heating—This section will apply to pool deck areas, and will include the covered pool when electrical comfort heating units are installed within 20 feet of the inside of the pool.

(a) **Unit Heaters.** If unit heaters are used, they are to be rigidly mounted to the structure and must be totally enclosed or of a guarded type. They shall not be mounted over the pool nor over the area around the pool that within 5 feet horizontally of the inside wall of the pool.

(b) **Permanently Wired Radiant Heaters.** If radiant electric heaters are used, they must be securely and suitably guarded and fastened to

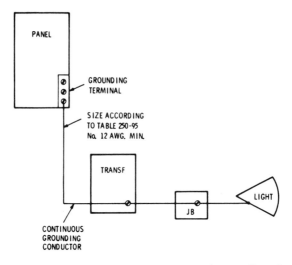

Fig. 680-6. Grounding all electrical equipment to the panelboard.

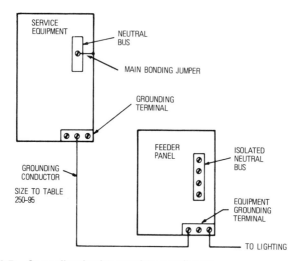

Fig. 680-7. Grounding feeder panel to panelboard.

their mounting devices. They shall not be mounted over the pool or within 5 feet from the inside wall of the pool, and shall be mounted not less than 12 feet vertically above the pool deck unless approval for other type of mounting is given.

(c) **Radiant Heat Cables Not Permitted.** No radiant heaters will be permitted to be mounted in or under the deck.

C. Storage Pools

680-30. Pumps—See the *NEC*.

680-31. Ground-Fault Circuit-Interrupters Required—See the *NEC*.

D. Spas and Hot Tubs

680-40. Outdoor Installation—The provisions of Parts A and B cover a spa or hot tub installed outdoors.

Exception No. 1: This allows the exemption covered in 680-22 for metal bands or hoops used to secure the wooden staves.

Exception No. 2: You will be permitted to use a cord- and plug-connection if its package is listed for such use, but the cord shall be no longer than 15 feet and shall be protected by GFCI.

Exception No. 3: It shall be permitted for metal-to-metal bonding on a common frame.

680-41. Indoor Installations—Spas and hot tubs that are installed indoors must meet the requirements of this part, and the wiring connections to same shall comply with Chapter 3.

Exception: Listed packaged units that are rated 20 amperes or less will be permitted to be cord- and plug-connected to facilitate removal and disconnection for maintenance and repair.

(a) **Receptacles.**

(1) Receptacles that are mounted or are located on the property shall be at least 5 feet from the inside of the spa or the hot tub.

(2) GFCI shall be used to protect 120-volt receptacles that are located within 10 feet of the inside wall of the spa or hot tub.

Note: The distances covered above are to be the shortest path that the supply cord for the appliance to be connected to the receptacle would follow. Piercing a floor, wall, or ceiling of a building or other effective barrier is not permitted.

(3) GFCI's must be used on receptacles that provide the power for the hot tub or spa.

(b) **Lighting Fixtures and Lighting Outlets.**

(1) Any lighting fixtures or outlets over the spa or hot tub or that are within 5 feet of the inside wall of the spa or hot tub are to be a

minimum of 7½ feet above the maximum level of the water, and shall be protected by GFCI's.

Exception No. 1: If lighting fixtures and outlets are located a minimum of 12 feet above the maximum water level, they shall not require a GFCI for protection.

Exception No. 2: Lighting fixtures meeting a. or b. below, and protected by a GFCI, will be permitted to be installed less than 7 feet 6 inches over a spa or hot tub:

a. They must have a glass or plastic lens and shall be recessed, and the trim shall be of a nonmetallic material that is permitted to be used in wet locations.

b. If they are surface-mounted, fixtures shall be equipped with a glass or plastic globe and nonmetallic body recognized for use in wet locations.

(2) The provisions of Part B of this article must be complied with for underwater lighting fixtures.

(c) **Wall Switches.** Wall switches are required to be mounted at least 5 feet away from the inside of the spa or hot tub.

(d) **Bonding.** Listed below are the parts that shall be bonded together:

(1) All metal fittings, when attached to or within the spa or hot tub structure.

(2) All metal parts of any of the electrical equipment used with the spa or hot tub for water circulating systems, and including pump motors.

(3) If not separated from the spa by a suitable barrier, metal conduit and piping that are within 5 feet horizontally from the inside of the spa or hot tub.

(4) Unless a permanent barrier is installed, all metal surfaces that are within 5 feet of the spa or hot tub.

(5) Any electrical device or controls that are not used in association with the hot tub or spa are to be maintained at a minimum distance of 5 feet from such units, or shall be bonded to the spa or hot tub system.

(e) **Methods of Bonding.** Any of the following means may be used for bonding of all metal parts associated with the spa or hot tub: the interconnection of threaded metal piping and fittings, metal-to-metal mounting when on a common base or frame, or the use of a copper bonding jumper that shall not be smaller than No. 8 solid and may be insulated, covered, or bare.

(f) **Grounding.** Grounding is required on the following:

(1) Any electrical equipment that might be located within 5 feet of the inside of the spa or hot tub.

(2) The electrical equipment used with a circulation system of the spa or hot tub.

(g) **Methods of Grounding.**

(1) Article 250 must be complied with for grounding all electrical equipment, and methods covered in Chapter 3 shall be used for connecting wiring.

(2) If equipment is connected by means of a flexible cord, the equipment grounding conductor in the cord shall be connected to the metal part of the assembly.

(h) **Electric Water Heaters.** Spa or hot tub electric water heaters are required to listed and to have the heating elements subdivided into loads that will not exceed 48 amperes, and they shall be protected by not more than 60 ampere overcurrent devices.

The branch-circuit conductor's ampacity and the rating or setting of the overcurrent protection devices is required to be not less than 125 percent of the total load listed on the nameplate.

E. Fountains

680-50. General—Water fountains were defined in 680-4, and this Part E shall apply to water fountains having water common to the pool.

Exception: Part E does not cover self-contained portable fountains that are no larger than 5 feet in any dimension.

680-51. Lighting Fixtures, Submersible Pumps, and Other Submersible Equipment.

(a) **Ground-Fault Circuit Interrupter.** A GFCI is required to be installed in the branch circuit that supplies fountain equipment.

Exception: If a circuit of 15 volts or less is supplied by a transformer that complies with Section 680-5(a), a GFCI will not be required for equipment operation. It will be recalled that this type of transformer that has two windings and a grounded metal barrier between the windings must also be an approved type.

(b) **Operating Voltage.** Lighting fixtures shall be installed for operation at 150 volts or less between conductors. Submersible pumps and any other submersible equipment shall operate at 300 volts or less between conductors.

(c) **Lighting Fixture Lenses.** Lighting fixtures shall be installed so that the top of the lens is below the normal water level of the fountain, unless they are approved for above-water-level locations. A lighting fixture facing upward must have the lens properly and adequately guarded to prevent contact by persons.

(d) **Overheating Protection.** A low-water cutoff or other approved means if the water level drops below the normal level shall be provided for electrical equipment which depends upon submersion for protection against overheating.

(e) **Wiring.** Equipment shall be provided with threaded conduit entries, or with flexible cords. The exposed cord is not permitted to be over 10 feet in length. If the cords extend beyond the fountain perimeter, they are to be enclosed in approved wiring enclosures. Any metal parts or equipment That make contact with the water are to be of brass or other corrosion-resistant metal.

(f) **Servicing.** All equipment used in the fountain shall be capable of being removed from the water for relamping or any normal maintenance. Fixtures are not permitted to be permanently embedded in the fountain structure so that the water level has to be lowered or the fountain drained when the relamping or maintenance is required.

(g) **Stability.** Equipment are required to be inherently stable, or securely fastened in place.

680-52. Junction Boxes and Other Enclosures.

(a) **General.** When junction boxes or other enclosures are installed for other than underwater installation, they are required to comply with Section 680-21 (a) (1), (2), (3), and (b), (c), and (d).

(b) **Underwater Junction Boxes and Other Underwater Enclosures.** Junction boxes and other underwater enclosures immersed in water or exposed to water spray shall comply with the following: (1) shall be equipped with provisions for threaded conduit entries or compression glands or seals for cord entry; (2) shall be copper, brass, or other approved corrosion-resistant material; (3) shall be located below the water level in the fountain wall or floor. An approved potting compound shall be used to fill the box to prevent the entry of moisture; and (4) when the junction box is supported only by the conduit, the conduit shall be of copper, brass, or other approved corrosion-resistant metal. When the box is fed by nonmetallic conduit, it shall have additional supports and fasteners of copper, brass, or other approved corrosion-resistant material. The box must be firmly attached to the supports or directly to the fountain surface and bonded as required.

Note: Refer to Section 370-13 covering this type of enclosures.

680-53. Bonding—All metal piping associated with the fountain is required to bonded to the equipment grounding conductor of the branch-circuit supply power to the fountain.

Note: The sizing of these equipment grounding conductors is covered in Section 250-95.

680-54. Grounding—The following equipment is required to be grounded: (1) all electrical equipment mounted within the fountain or within 5 feet of the inside wall of the fountain; (2) all equipment that is a part of the recirculating system of the fountain water; (3) panelboards that are not a part of the service equipment that supply power to any of the equipment involved with the fountain.

680-55. Methods of Grounding.

(a) **Applied Provisions.** Section 680-25 will apply, but this excludes paragraph (e) of that section.

(b) **Supplied by a Flexible Cord.** Any equipment that is supplied by flexible cords is required to have noncurrent-carrying exposed metal parts grounded, and this shall be by means of an insulated copper equipment grounding conductor that is integral to the wiring of the cord. This grounding conductor is required to be connected to a grounding terminal in the supply junction box, transformer enclosure, or any other enclosure.

680-56. Cord- and Plug-Connected Equipment.

(a) **Ground-Fault Circuit Interrupter.** GFCIs are required on all electrical equipment, and include power supplied by cords.

(b) **Cord Type.** Type SO or ST flexible cords shall be used when they are exposed to water.

(c) **Sealing.** Suitable potting compound must be used to prevent water entering the equipment through the cord or its conductors; this shall be done by covers or potting compound wherever the flexible cord jacket and flexible cord conductor terminate in equipment. Also, in addition to the above, the equipment grounding conductor is to be similarly treated to protect it from possible deterioration from water entering the equipment.

(d) **Terminations.** Permanent connection of flexible cord may be used, except that grounding-type receptacles and attachment plugs shall be permitted for aiding in removal or disconnection for repair and maintenance of equipment not located in any water-containing part of a fountain.

F. Therapeutic Pools and Tubs in Health Care Facilities

680-60. General—See Section 517 for definition of health care facilities. This Part F is intended to cover pools and tubs in health care facilities. Portable therapeutic appliances shall comply with Article 422.

680-61. Permanently Installed Therapeutic Pools—Parts A and B or this article shall be complied with for therapeutic pools that are constructed in or on the ground or that may be located in a building in a manner so that the pool can not be readily taken apart.

Exception: If lighting fixtures are of the totally enclosed type, the limitation put on them in Section 680-6(b)(1) will not be applicable.

680-62. Therapeutic Tubs (Hydrotherapeutic Tanks)—If patients are treated in therapeutic tanks that are not easily moved from one place to another in the normal sequence of use, or if they are fastened or otherwise secured to a particular location, including associated piping systems, they shall comply with this part.

(a) **Ground Fault Circuit-Interrupter.** GFCI's shall be used for the protection of all therapeutic equipment.

Exception: Compliance with Section 250-45 is required for portable therapeutic appliances.

(b) **Bonding.** You are required to bond the following parts listed below. See the *NEC* for (1) through (5).

(c) **Methods of Bonding.** The metal parts that are associated with therapeutic tubs are to be bonded by methods as follows: the interconnection of threaded metal piping and fittings; metal-to-metal contact mounting on a common base or frame; connections made by suitable metal clamps; or by solid copper bonding jumpers, insulated, covered, or bare, that are not smaller than No. 8 AWG.

(d) **Grounding.** The equipment below shall be grounded:

(1) Any electrical equipment located 5 feet or less from the inside of the tub.

(2) All electrical equipment that in any way is associated with the circulating system in the tub.

(e) **Methods of Grounding.**

(1) Article 250 spells out how electrical equipment shall be grounded, and the connections are covered in Chapter 3.

(2) With fixed metal parts of the assembly that are supplied by flexible cord, the grounding conductor of the cord shall be used for the grounding purpose.

(f) **Receptacles.** Any receptacle that is within 5 feet of a therapeutic tub is required to be protected by a GFCI.

680-63. Lighting Fixtures—Totally enclosed lighting fixtures are required when installed near therapeutic tub area.

G. Hydromassage Bathtubs

680-70. Protection—A GFCI shall be used to supply hydromassage bathtubs and their associated electrical components.

680-71. Other Electric Equipment—The requirements of Chapters 1 through 4 in the *NEC* cover the installation of equipment in a bathroom applying to fixed lighting, switches, receptacles, and other electrical equipment that is located in the same room and area, but may not be directly associated with a hydromassage bathtub.

ARTICLE 685—INTEGRATED ELECTRICAL SYSTEMS
A. General

685-1. Scope—Integrated electrical systems, but not unit equipment that is not integrated with other unit equipment, is covered by this article. In an integrated system, it is essential that an orderly shutdown of the equipment occurs in industrial operations where one unit of the operation depends on other unit(s) for their proper operation. Thus the following conditions must be met: (1) in order to keep hazards to personnel and damage to the equipment low, an orderly shutdown is required; (2) there must be qualified persons to service the system and maintain and supervise it properly; (3) the authority having jurisdiction is assured that effective safety guards are acceptable.

685-2. Application of Other Articles—In this Code, other articles contain information which will apply to an orderly shutdown in addition to the information contained in this article or are modifications of them.

See the *NEC* for a list of applicable sections for integrated systems.

B. Orderly Shutdown

685-10. Location of Overcurrent Devices In or On Premises—Overcurrent devices that are necessary for the operation of integrated circuits are allowed to be installed at heights that are accessible for security of operation to nonqualified personnel.

685-12. Direct-Current System Grounding—Two-wire dc circuits will be permitted to be ungrounded.

685-14. Ungrounded Control Circuits—For the purpose of control, operational continuity of service is required. If the voltage of the control circuits is 150 volts or less, they may be supplied from separately derived systems and shall not be required to be grounded.

ARTICLE 690—SOLAR PHOTOVOLTAIC SYSTEMS

Solar photovoltaic systems is not exactly a new method of power generation, but much progress is being made. It has been used for many years in photolight meters to measure light intensity by photoelectric cells. Street lights and yard lights, etc., have been turned on and off by the same means, that is, a cell that gives off a voltage when exposed to light.

As with the beginning of all advancement, photovoltaic cells are being improvised, and numbers of these cells are connected in series, parallel, or series and parallel to produce larger current supplies and higher voltages. The current produced is direct current, which, in turn, in most cases must be changed to alternating current and electronically changed to 60 hertz.

It is the author's opinion that Article 690 of the *NEC* covers the subject in a very fine manner. (See the *NE* for coverage of this article.)

CHAPTER 7

Special Conditions

ARTICLE 700—EMERGENCY SYSTEMS

A. General

There are now three articles on emergency systems; so in applying the regulations that cover, be certain you have the applicable article(s): Article 700, 701, and 702.

700-1. Scope—This article applies to design for electrical safety, installation, operation, and maintenance. The specific application is emergency systems made up of circuits and equipment the intent of which is to supply, distribute, and control electricity for illumination and/or power that will be required if the normal service of electricity is interrupted.

Emergency systems are those systems legally required and classed as emergency by municipal, state, or federal or any other codes, or any other governmental agencies under whose jurisdiction they may come. The intent is that these emergency systems automatically supply electricity for illumination and power to areas designated to require emergency power. If the normal supply of power is interrupted for any reason at all, then the emergency system takes over to distribute and control power and illumination that is required for safety to human life.

Note: Further information on the installation of emergency systems is covered in Article 517.

Note: More information on performance and maintenance required of emergency systems will be found in Health Care Facilities, NFPA 99-1984 (ANSI).

Note: Emergency systems are quite often installed in places of assembly to provide illumination in the event of a normal power outage so that there will be a means of safe exit and panic control in those buildings that may be occupied by a large number of persons, such as hotels, theaters, sports arenas, health care facilities, etc. Emergency systems may supply power for ventilation that may be essential for sustaining life, for fire protection and alarm systems, elevators, fire pumps, public safety communications, or industrial processes where interruption of current could cause serious life, safety, or health hazards.

Note: See Life Safety Code NFPA 101-1985 (ANSI) for specifications where emergency lighting is required for safety.

Note: Further information on emergency and standby power systems and their performance will be found in Emergency and Standby Power Systems, NFPA 110-1985.

Reference is made to NFPA Life Safety Code (NFPA No. 101) for specification of locations where emergency lighting is considered essential to life safety.

700-2. Application of Other Articles—The requirements of the *National Electrical Code* as covered elsewhere in the Code are applicable, except where modified by this article.

700-3. Equipment Approval—Approval of all equipment is required when used on emergency systems.

700-4. Tests and Maintenance.

(a) **Conduct and Witness Test.** The authority having jurisdiction should inspect the emergency system upon installation, and periodically thereafter.

(b) **Tested Periodically.** In order to assure proper operation of an emergency system, the authority that has jurisdiction shall require periodic tests to be conducted on the system to assure its maintenance in proper operating condition.

(c) **Battery System Maintenance.** The authority having jurisdiction shall require periodic maintenance on battery systems and unit equipment, including batteries used for starting or ignition on auxiliary engines.

(d) **Written Record.** Records of tests are to be kept in writing, and shall cover maintenance and operation of same.

(e) **Testing Under Load.** This requires a means of testing lighting and power emergency systems while they are Under actual maximum load conditions.

700-5. Capacity.

(a) **Capacity and Rating.** The capacity of the emergency system shall be adequate to handle the requirements of all the equipment to be operated simultaneously.

(b) **Selective Load Pickup and Load Shedding.** The alternate power source may supply emergency service, legally required standby, and other optional standby system loads where automatic selection of pickup and shedding of power is provided as needed to ensure that adequate power is available to (1) emergency circuits; (2) legally required standby circuits; and (3) the optional standby circuit, and it shall be done in this order of priority.

Note: The test requirements of Section 700-4(b) are covered for the load shaving operation to satisfy test requirements when all conditions are met as covered in Section 700-4.

A portable or temporary alternate source of power must be available whenever the emergency generator has to be taken out of service for major maintenance.

700-6. Transfer Equipment—The transfer equipment is required to be automatic and to be identified for emergency service only, or to be approved by the authority having jurisdiction. In installing the transfer equipment, it shall be so designed and installed that accidental transfers —interconnecting the normal and the emergency source—cannot result in any operation of the transfer equipment. You are referred to Section 230-83.

A means for isolating the transfer switch is permitted. If isolation switches are provided, accidental parallel operations shall be avoided.

700-7. Signals—For the following purposes, audible and visible signaling devices shall be used where practicable:

(a) **Derangement.** To give warning of a derangement or nonfunctioning of the emergency or auxiliary system.

(b) **Carrying Load.** To indicate if the batteries or generator are ready to carry the load if it becomes necessary for the emergency or auxiliary system to take over.

(c) **Not Functioning.** To indicate if the battery charger is functioning properly. The batteries and their condition should also be checked —this will come under the periodic checks required to be taken and written up in the log that is kept of the auxiliary or emergency system.

(d) **Ground Fault.** In solidly grounded wye emergency systems that are more than 150 volts to ground, protective devices rated at 1000 amperes or more are used to indicate a ground-fault. The sensor to indicate the ground-fault signal device shall be mounted ahead of the disconnecting means for the emergency source, and the maximum setting of this sensing devices shall be for a ground-fault current of 1200 amperes. Instructions shall be issued for the required action to take in case indicated ground-fault shall be located at or near the sensor location.

Code refers you to NFPA 110-1985 (ANSI) for signals for generator sets.

700-8. Signs—A sign shall be posted at the service-entrance equipment indicating the type and location of the on-site emergency power source.

B. Circuit Wiring

700-9. Wiring, Emergency System.

(a) **Identification.** All boxes and enclosures that contain emergency circuits are to be marked so that they will be easily identified as being a part of the emergency circuit.

(b) **Wiring.** Emergency source wiring, including its source of disconnecting overcurrent protection supplying the emergency load, is to be kept entirely separate from all other wiring and equipment, raceways, cables, and cabinets that contain other than emergency wiring.

Exception No. 1: Wiring in transfer equipment enclosures.

Exception No. 2: Exit for emergency lighting fixtures that are supplied from two sources.

Exception No. 3: Common junction boxes for exit lights and emergency lighting when supplied by two sources of power.

Exception No. 4: Two or more circuits supplied by the same emergency power may be run in the same raceway.

Exception No. 5: In a common junction box attached to a unit equipment, and which contains only the branch circuit supplying that equipment and the emergency circuit supplied by the unit equipment.

C. Sources of Power

700-12. General Requirements—The same types of emergency systems might not be suitable on all cases. The conditions must be evaluated as to whether the emergency system will be needed for a long period of time or a short period of time, and how much capacity the emergency system must have to supply the emergency demands. For example, the exit lights in a theater may be only needed for a period long enough to assure lighting while the theater is being emptied. In the case of interruption of service to a hospital goer, whether from within or without, the emergency system might be required to furnish a large amount of power for a long period of time. Each particular condition requires a thorough evaluation of the possible needs, the type of system, and its capacity, etc., and the requirements of the Code.

Whether the emergency system is for only one building or a group of buildings, it is required that the emergency service is in operation not to exceed 10 seconds after the failure of the normal source of power.

The emergency supply system, in addition to meeting the requirements of this section, shall also be permitted to consist of one or more of the types of system that are covered in (a) through (e) below. Unit equipment that is covered in Section 700-12(f) shall satisfy the requirements of this article. In selecting an emergency source of power, the occupancy and the type of service required must be considered: whether it is for short duration, as for the evacuation of a theater, or for longer durations, supplying light and power for indefinite periods of failure of power from either inside or outside the building.

In designing and installing emergency systems, consideration shall be given to minimizing hazards that could result and cause a total failure due to floods, fires, icing, and vandalism.

Each case of designing the emergency system must be individually evaluated as to the conditions and requirement for the particular installation.

(a) **Storage Battery.** Storage batteries may be used for a source of emergency power supply in some systems if suitably rated and have capacity to supply and maintain total load for a period of 1 ½ hours without the voltage falling below 87 ½ percent of normal.

Whether the batteries are acid or alkali, they shall be designed and constructed to meet the requirements of the emergency service and shall be compatible with the charger used to recharge them.

Automotive-type batteries are not to be used. If the battery container is of a sealed type, it does not have to be transparent. With the lead-acid-type battery that requires water additions, the container must be transparent or translucent. It is required to provide an automatic battery charger to keep the batteries fully charged.

(b) **Generator Set.**

(1) A generator is supplied by a prime mover that will be accepted by the jurisdiction having authority, and it is sized as covered in Section 700-5. It is required to have automatic starting of the prime mover when the normal source of power fails, and is required to have a transfer switch for all electrical equipment in the emergency circuit. To prevent immediate retransfer in cases of short-time restoring of the normal source of power, a time-delay feature allowing for a 15-minute setting shall be provided.

(2) Internal combustion engines used for prime movers are required to have an on-site fuel supply that will function at full demand for not less than 2 hours of operation.

(3) Prime movers shall not rely solely upon public utility gas systems for the fuel supply. Automatic transferring means shall be provided for transferring from one fuel supply to another when a dual fuel supply is used.

Exception: When acceptable to the authority having jurisdiction, it shall be permitted to use other than on-site fuels when there is a low probability of the failure of both the on-site fuel delivery system and the power from the outside electrical utility company.

(4) If a storage battery is used for control or signal power or as a means of starting prime movers, it shall be required to be suitable for that type of service and shall be equipped with an automatic charging means in the generator set.

(5) When an emergency generator requires more than 10 seconds to develop power, an auxiliary power supply will be acceptable to energize the emergency system until the regular generator is capable of picking up the load.

(c) **Uninterruptible Power Supplies.** Uninterruptible power supplies providing power for the emergency system, must comply with the applicable provisions of Section 700-12(a) and (b).

(d) **Separate Service.** If acceptable to the authority having jurisdiction, a second service will be permitted. This separate service shall comply with Article 230 and shall have a separate surface drop or lateral that is widely separated, both electrically and physically, from the normal service, in order to minimize the simultaneous interruption of the supply of services.

(e) **Connection Ahead of Service Disconnecting Means.** If acceptable to the authority having jurisdiction, connections may be made at, but not within, the main service disconnecting means. The emergency service is required to be sufficiently separated from the normal service disconnection means so as to prevent simultaneous interruption of the service when there is an occurrence within the building or group of buildings.

Note: Equipment that may be connected ahead of the disconnecting means was covered in Section 230-82.

(f) **Unit Equipment.** Unit equipment for individual emergency illumination shall consist of: (1) a rechargeable battery, often a unit system with a triple charger and lamps attached to the charger and hung in various locations; (2) a means of charging the battery; (3) provisions for attaching one or more lamps on equipment, and it is also permitted to have terminals for connecting lamps in remote locations; and (4) a relay device designed to energize the lamps immediately upon failure of the supply to the unit equipment. The batteries are required to be suitable for maintaining the supply at not less than 87 ½ percent of the normal battery voltage for the total load of lamps attached thereto and for a period of at least 1 ½ hours, or the equipment shall supply and maintain at least 60 percent of the emergency lighting for a period of at least 1 ½ hours. The supply batteries, whether alkali or acid type, shall be designed and constructed to meet the requirements of the emergency service.

This unit equipment is to be permanently installed and not portable, and all the wiring to the unit shall be done by wiring methods covered in Chapter 3. Flexible cord may be used if it does not exceed 3 feet in length. The branch circuit supplying the emergency units shall be the same branch circuit that supplies the normal lighting in that area, and it shall be connected ahead of any local switches controlling regular lighting. Emergency illumination fixtures, which are to obtain power from the unit equipment, are to be wired to the unit equipment by one of the wiring methods covered in Section 700-9 and Article 300.

Exception: In a separate area, which is uninterrupted and is supplied by a minimum of three lighting circuits, you may install a branch circuit for the unit equipment provided it originates from the same panelboard as do the normal lighting circuits, but this separate branch circuit shall be provided with a lock-on feature.

D. Emergency Circuits for Lighting and Power

700-15. Loads on Emergency Branch Circuits—No loads, except those specifically required for the emergency service, shall be connected to or supplied from the emergency supply. Emergency equipment is not intended to take care of the entire load unless designed for this purpose.

700-16. Emergency Illumination—Emergency illumination includes means of egress lighting and auxiliary illumination required for the safe evacuation of a building or buildings. This illumination should also supply sufficient light for the purposes for which it is intended. Many new structures are being built without provisions for illumination from the outside daylight. This condition makes it even more important to have an emergency source of illumination to supply sufficient lighting for the evacuation of the building or buildings. This has been experienced in outrages that covered a large area.

Emergency lighting systems shall be so designed and installed that the failure of an individual lighting element, which could be the burnout of a bulb, will not leave in total darkness any space required to have emergency illumination. The burning out of an individual lamp would not, in most cases, cause total interruption of the lighting source in any one area since most areas are supplied by more than one lamp, but there are installations where this is possible.

There are battery-operated self-contained units which have a trickle charger to keep the battery fully charged. If these are installed, they should be on the emergency supply circuit so that if a breaker should trip or a fuse blow on the regular circuit, the battery could still charge and the unit be operable until the malfunction is corrected.

700-17. Circuits for Emergency Lighting—Emergency lighting branch circuits are required to be installed and supplied from a source of power complying with Section 700-12, if the normal power supply is interrupted. These installations shall supply one of the following: (1) an emergency lighting supply that is independent of the general lighting supply and has provisions for automatically transferring emergency light if the general lighting supply is interrupted, or (2) two or more complete and separate systems with independent power supply, each system supplying enough current for the purpose of emergency lighting. If both lighting systems are used for regular lighting purposes and both systems are kept lighted, there shall be means provided for automatically energizing one system if the other system fails. Either or both systems will be permitted for automatic energizing of either system upon failure of the other. Both or either of the systems shall be part of the general lighting system of the projected occupancy if circuits supplying lights for emergency illumination are installed as permitted by other sections of this article.

700-18. Circuits for Emergency Power—With branch circuits supplying equipment classed as emergency, there shall be an emergency supply source to which this load will automatically transfer in the event of loss of the normal power supply.

E. Control Emergency Lighting Circuits

700-20. Switch Requirements—The switch or switches that control emergency circuits are to be accessible only to qualified persons or persons authorized to have control of these circuits.

Exception No. 1: When two or more single-throw switches are connected in parallel and control a single circuit, at least one of these switches shall be accessible to authorized persons. This means that switches for control of emergency lighting may be paralleled but, if they are, one must be accessible only to authorized persons.

Exception No. 2: There may be additional switches in addition to the one that is controlled by authorized persons, but they shall be arranged so that the unauthorized person may put the lighting into operation but will not be able to disconnect it.

Switches connected in series, or three-and four-way switches shall not be used.

700-21. Switch Location—See the *NEC*.

700-22. Exterior Lights—Lights mounted outside a building that are not required to be turned on when there is sufficient illumination by daylight are permitted to be actuated by an automatic light-actuating device after dark.

F. Overcurrent Protection

700-25. Accessibility—Only authorized persons shall have access to overcurrent devices in emergency circuits. This will prevent tampering or interference with the operation of the emergency circuits.

Note: The reliability of emergency systems can be ensured if the fuses and circuits provided for overcurrent protection are coordinated so that selective clearance of fault-currents is assured.

700-26. Ground-Fault Protection of Equipment—The alternate source that supplies emergency systems is not required to have ground-fault protection of equipment.

ARTICLE 701—LEGALLY REQUIRED STANDBY SYSTEMS
A. General

701-1. Scope—This article covers the electrical safety and design, installation, operation, and maintenance of standby systems consisting of circuits and equipment intended to supply distributing and controlling electricity to facilities that are legally required to have standby power to cover illumination and/or power should there be an interruption in the normal source of power.

The systems in this article involve only those that are permanently installed in their entirety and that also include the normal power source.

Note: See Health Care Facilities, NFPA 99-1984 (ANSI), for additional information.

Note: See Emergency and Standby Power Systems, NFPA 110-1985, for further information covering the performance of emergency standby systems.

701-2. Legally Required Standby Systems—Legally required standby systems are those required by municipal, state, federal, or by other codes, or any governmental agency having jurisdiction over same, the intent of which is to supply power to selected loads (other than those classified as emergency systems) in the event that the normal power source fails.

Note: Typical installations of legally required standby systems are for operation to serve loads for such as heating, refrigerator systems, communication systems, ventilation and smoke removal systems, sewage disposal, and industrial processes, which, if normal operation of the normal power supply fails, could create hazards or hinder rescue or fire fighting operations.

Many industrial buildings must be designed for eliminating dust entrance and thus may not have windows. Therefore, some emergency lighting is required for such things as exit lights and lighting exit corridors.

701-3. Application of Other Articles—Except as modified by this article, all other articles of the Code shall be applied.

701-4. Equipment Approval—All equipment shall be listed or approved for this Article. This includes approval by the jurisdiction having authority.

701-5. Tests and Maintenance for Legally Required Standby Systems.

(a) **Conduct or Witness Test.** The authority having jurisdiction shall conduct or witness a test when the installation is completed.

(b) **Tested Periodically.** Systems are to be periodically inspected on a schedule approved by the authority having jurisdiction. This is to ensure their maintenance in proper condition for operation.

(c) **Battery Systems Maintenance.** When batteries are used for starting or ignition of the prime movers, periodic maintenance is to be required by the authority having jurisdiction.

(d) **Written Record.** A permanent written record must be kept of all these tests and maintenance.

(e) **Testing Under Load.** Legally required standby systems shall have means provided for testing under load conditions.

This gives the authority having jurisdiction the right to make repeated inspections to cover the purpose of this article.

701-6. Capacity and Rating—A legally required standby system shall have adequate capacity and rating for supplying all equipment intended to be operated at one time.

The alternate power source may be permitted to supply legally required standby and optional standby system loads, when these loads are automatically picked up for load shedding so as to ensure power to the legally required standby circuits.

701-7. Transfer Equipment—Automatic transfer equipment shall be identified or approved for standby use by the authority having jurisdiction. The automatic transfer systems equipment must be so designed that no accidental interconnection of the normal and alternate sources of supply will occur in the operation of any transfer equipment.

Again, the authority having jurisdiction must approve this transfer equipment.

Isolation equipment may be used to isolate the transfer equipment. If isolation equipment is used, inadvertent parallel operation shall be avoided.

701-8. Signals—Where possible, audible and visual signal devices are to be provided for the following purposes:

(a) **Derangement.** To notify any derangement of the standby source.

(b) **Carrying Load.** To show that the standby source is carrying the load.

(c) **Not Functioning.** Should the battery charger fail to function, it will cause an alarm.

Note: See Emergency and Standby Power Systems, NFPA 110 (ANSI), which covers signals for generator sets.

701-9. Signs—Signs shall be located at the service entrance to indicate the type and location of the legally required on-site standby power source.

B. Circuit Wiring

701-10. Legally Required Standby Systems—Legally standby service will be permitted to occupy the same raceways, cables, boxes, and cabinets with other general wiring.

C. Sources of Power

Much of this section is very similar to Section 700-12 in the preceding article.
Refer to the *NEC* for Section 701-11.

D. Overcurrent Protection

This is the same as Sections 700-25 and 700-26.

701-15. Accessibility—Only authorized persons shall have access to overcurrent devices in emergency circuits. This will prevent tampering or interference with the operation of the emergency circuits.

Note: The reliability of emergency systems can ensure that if the fuses and circuits provided for overcurrent protection are coordinated so that selective clearance of fault currents is assured.

701-17. Ground-Fault Protection of Equipment—The alternate source that supplies emergency systems is not required to have ground-fault protection of equipment.

ARTICLE 702—OPTIONAL STANDBY SYSTEMS
A. General

702-1. Scope—Optional standby installation operations are covered in this article.
This covers only those standby systems that are permanently installed in place, and also includes the prime mover.

702-2. Optional Standby Systems—Optional standby systems are intended only for the protection of business or property and do not include places where life safety is dependant on performance of the system. They may be operated manually or automatically.

With brownouts and blackouts over the country, many individuals and especially farms and milking operations, may have a standby source of power to eliminate losses from power outages.

Note: This type of system is typically installed to provide an alternate source of electrical power for facilities such as industrial and commercial buildings, farms and residences, heating or refrigeration systems, data processing and communication systems, and industrial processes, which, if stopped during a power outage, could cause serious interruption to the process or damage to the product, etc.

702-3. Application of Other Articles—As with most special conditions other Articles of this Code shall apply unless specifically exempted by this Article.

702-4. Equipment Approval—All equipment shall be listed or approved for this Article. This includes approval by the authority having jurisdiction.

702-5. Capacity—Optional standby systems shall have capacity and rating adequate to supply all the equipment intended to be operated at one time.

Note: They are needed to supply loads selected by the user.

702-6. Transfer Equipment—Transfer equipment need only be suitable for its intended use, and designed and installed so as to prevent accidental connection with normal or alternate sources of power.

Again, the authority having jurisdiction must approve of this transfer equipment.

702-7. Signals—For the following purposes, audible or visible signals may be installed:

(a) **Derangement.** To indicate derangement of the optional source of power.

(b) **Carrying.** To indicate that the optional source of power is carrying the load.

702-8. Signs—A sign must be placed at the service-entrance equipment stating the type and location of the optional power source.

B. Circuit Wiring

702-9. Wiring Optional Standby Systems—The wiring from the optional standby equipment is allowed to be in the same raceways, cables, boxes, cabinets as other general wiring.

ARTICLE 705—INTERCONNECTED ELECTRIC POWER PRODUCTION SOURCES

705-1. Scope—This article covers one or more sources of power that will operate in parallel with the primary souce(s) of power.

Note: The primary source of power could be a utility supply or such other sources as on-site electric power source(s).

705-2. Definition—The following definition applies for the purpose of this article:

Interactive System. Any source of electric power system that is operating in parallel and is also capable of delivering power to the primary source of the supply system.

705-3. Other Articles—Interconnected systems shall comply not only with this article, but with applicable requirements of the following articles: See the *NEC*.

705-10. Directory—A permanent plaque or directory must be installed at every electric service and also at all the electrical power production sources that can be interconnected, and they shall denote all sources of electrical power on the premises.

Exception: If a large number of these production services is involved, they shall be designated by groups.

Since interconnected electrical power sources are rarely encountered in most wiring installations, I refer you to the *NEC* for the balance of this article.

ARTICLE 710—OVER 600 VOLTS, NOMINAL

This article covers general requirements for installations with voltages over 600 volts, nominal. It is suggested that information concerning the particular equipment or the conductors used be obtained from the manufacturer of the product and that their recommendations be closely followed.

In dealing with equipment and conductors used with voltages over 600 volts, it will be found that they are not generally listed by Underwriter's Laboratories. In designing and approving high-voltage equipment and conductors, the National Electrical Manufacturers Association specifications should be secured. These specifications will be found extremely helpful for this type of work.

A. General

710-1. Scope—This article is intended to give the general requirements to be used on all circuits and equipment operated at more than 600 volts, nominal.

710-2. Other Articles—On specific types of installation, other articles must be used. Refer to the *NEC*.

710-3. Wiring Methods.

(a) **Aboveground Conductors.** Conductors that are installed aboveground are to be installed in rigid metal conduit and intermediate metal conduit, in cable trays, as busways, as cablebus, in rigid nonmetallic conduit, in other raceways suitable for handling the higher voltage conductors, or they may be run as open runs of metal-clad cable if suitable for the use and pupose.

Open runs of nonmetallic-sheathed cable, bare conductors, or busbars will be permitted only where the locations are suitable or accessible to qualified persons only.

(b) **Underground Conductors.** When run underground, it is required that the cables are suitable and approved for the voltages and conditions under which the underground conductors are installed.

Section 310-7 must be complied with where direct burial cables are used.

If the conductors meet the requirements of Table 710-3(b), they will be permitted to be used for direct burial, or they can be installed in raceways that have been identified for the usage, and shall meet the depths required by the above table.

High-voltage cables that are not shielded may be installed in rigid metal conduit, in intermediate metal conduit, or in rigid nonmetallic conduit, but these raceways must be encased in not less than 3 inches of concrete.

Author's Note: A number of 13,800-volt conductors were installed in a common trench with specially made concrete supports under and above each layer to maintain a spacing between the conduits. Then they were encased in 2,500-pound concrete having a 7-inch slump and not larger than ⅜-inch aggregate, so that they would be totally enclosed from the bottom between conduits, etc., with concrete, and the concrete was dyed red so that any digger in the vicinity who came across the concrete would be aware of danger.

Exception No. 1: Nonshielded cable may be installed in Type MC cable if the metallic sheath of the MC cable is grounded and the grounding path is effective and meets the requirement of Section 250-51.

Exception No. 2: You may use lead sheath cable with nonshielded conductor if the lead is properly grounded through a path that meets the requirements of Section 250-51. See the *NEC* for Table 710-3(b), which covers minimum cover requirements, and see the five exceptions following this table.

(1) **Protection From Damage.** When the cable emerges from the ground, the conductors shall be protected by enclosing them in

an approved raceway. If the raceways are installed on poles, they are required to be rigid metal conduit, intermediate metal conduit, Schedule 80 PVC, or other equivalent raceway. This shall extend from the ground line to a point up the pole to a minimum of 8 feet above the finished grade. If they enter a building, the conductors must be protected by approved enclosures starting from the ground line to the entrance, and if the enclosures are metallic, they shall be properly grounded.

(2) **Splices.** It is permissible on direct burial cables to splice or tap without the use of splice boxes; however, splices and taps must be installed by the use of suitable materials. They shall be watertight, and also must be protected from mechanical damage. If the cables are shielded, continuity must be made from the shielding across splices and taps.

In the use of this section, the manufacturer's specifications should be carefully adhered to when terminating or splicing high-voltage cables. The metallic or other static voltage shield on cables shall be stripped back to a safe distance according to the voltage of the circuit and the manufacturer's specifications.

A suitable termination shall be made at potheads or joints. This termination may bg one of many various forms as described in the specifications of the cable for the purpose of stress reduction at the termination of the shield. The metallic shielding tape shall be grounded.

Many high-voltage cables have a conductive tape over the conductor insulation. This is often a cloth tape impregnated with graphite. The graphite residue that might be left on the insulation must be carefully removed by approved methods or there will be a leakage across the insulation and a subsequent breakdown.

The dielectric stresses involved may be seen in Fig. 710-1. These stresses pinpoint back to the termination of the shielding and cause undue strain at that point, with accompanying flashovers or breakdowns. The purpose of stress cones, potheads, terminators, etc., is to spread these stresses out and not let them concentrate at one spot on the cable.

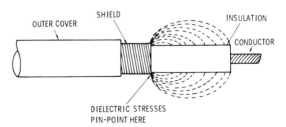

Fig. 710-1. Dielectric stresses in a shielded cable.

(3) **Backfill.** If the backfill material contains large rocks, paving materials, cinders, large or sharply angular substances, or corrosive materials, they are not to be placed in the excavation because they may cause damage to raceways, cables, etc. They may also prevent adequate compaction of the backfill and cause corrosion of the raceways, cables, or other structures.

The prevention of physical damage for the protection of the cable or raceway may be granular or suitable sleeves. Sand makes a nice subbase and fill, immediately above, before other backfill materials.

(4) **Raceway Seal.** Where raceway feeds underground and enters a building, suitable compound shall be used to seal it so as to prevent the entrances of gases or moisture, otherwise it must be so arranged as to keep moisture from contacting live parts.

Often when duct banks are installed, extra ducts are installed for future use. These should be capped to keep out rodents as well as moisture.

(c) **Busbars.** Either copper or aluminum may be used for busbars.

710-4. Braid-Covered Insulated Conductors—Open Installation—

The following applies to open runs of braid-covered insulated conductors: The braid shall be flame-retardant. If not flame-retardant, the braid shall be made flame-retardant with a saturant for this purpose. The braid shall be stripped back a safe distance at the conductor terminal, according to the operating voltage. This distance should not be less than 1 inch per kilovolt (1000 volts) if practical. (The voltage is the conductor-to-ground voltage of the circuit.)

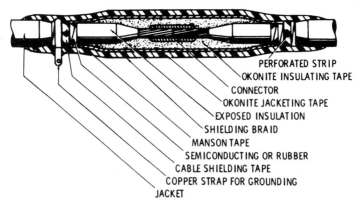

PERFORATED STRIP
OKONITE INSULATING TAPE
CONNECTOR
OKONITE JACKETING TAPE
EXPOSED INSULATION
SHIELDING BRAID
MANSON TAPE
SEMICONDUCTING OR RUBBER
CABLE SHIELDING TAPE
COPPER STRAP FOR GROUNDING
JACKET

Fig. 710-2. A straight-through splice of high-voltage shielded cable.

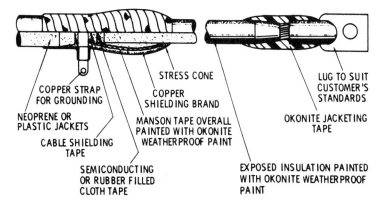

Fig. 710-3. Termination of shielded high-voltage cable, showing proper shielding, etc.

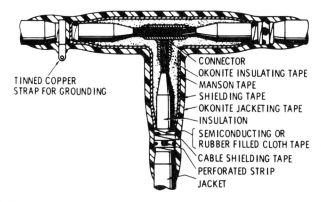

Fig. 710-4. Tee-splice of high-voltage cable, showing how properly made and properly shielded.

710-6. Insulation Shielding—Depending upon the voltage of the circuit, metallic and semiconducting shielding on the cable shall be removed. A means of reducing stress from factory-applied shielding shall be provided. (See Fig. 710-10.)

It is required that metallic shielding parts of the cable, whether they be tapes, wires, braids, or combinations of any of these, and the semiconducting components along with them shall be grounded.

Splices and terminations of shielded high-voltage cables are not always understood as to the importance of being properly made. Figures 701-2, 701-3, and 710-4 were sent to the author by Ronald W. Dearwater, District

Manager of the Okonite Co., Denver, Colorado, for publication in this book. They illustrate how splices and terminations are properly made up to eliminate the damaging electrical stresses set up as shown in Fig. 710-1.

710-7. Grounding—Applicable provisions of Article 250 shall be used for the grounding, wiring, and equipment installations.

710-8. Moisture or Mechanical Protection for Metal-Sheathed Cables—See Figs. 710-2, 710-3, and 710-4, which illustrate where cable emerges from its metal sheath or where protection from moisture or corrosive damage is required. Installation of the conductors must be protected.

710-9. Protection of Service Equipment, Metal-Enclosed Power Switchgear, and Industrial Control Assemblies—Any pipes or ducts that are not related to the electrical installation and that require periodic maintenance or whose malfunction would endanger the operation of the electrical system shall not be permitted to be located in the vicinity of service equipment, metal-enclosed power switchgear, or industrial control assemblies. Protection shall be provided where necessary to prevent damage from condensation, leaks, or breaks in foreign systems. If the pipes are installed for the protection of electrical equipment, they shall not be considered foreign objects.

B. Equipment—General Provisions

710-11. Indoor Installations—You are referred to Section 110-31(a).

710-12. Outdoor Installations—You are referred to Section 110-31(b).

710-13. Metal-Enclosed Equipment—You are referred to Section 110-31(c).

710-14. Oil-Filled Equipment—Other than transformers, covered in Article 450, the installation of other electrical equipment containing more than 10 gallons of flammable oil for each unit is required to comply with Parts B and C of Article 450.

C. Equipment—Specific Provisions

Note: For special types of installation, you are referred to Section 710-2.

710-20. Overcurrent Protection—One of the following means of supplying overcurrent protection shall be used for each ungrounded conductor:

(a) **Overcurrent Relays and Current Transformers.** When circuit breakers are used on 3-phase circuits for overcurrent protection, there shall be a minimum of three overcurrent relays, each operated from a separate current transformer.

Exception No. 1: On a 3-phase, 3-wire circuit, the overcurrent relay in the current transformer's residual circuit will be permitted to do away with one of the phase relays.

Exception No. 2: When operated from a current transformer that links all phases of the 3-phase, 3-Wire circuit, the overcurrent relay is permitted to replace one of the phase conductor current transformers and a residual relay.

(b) **Fuses.** It is required to have a fuse connected in series with each ungrounded conductor.

710-21. Circuit Interrupting Devices

(a) **Circuit Breakers.**

(1) Indoor installations shall consist of metal-enclosed units or fire-resistant cell-mounted units except that open mounting of circuit breakers is permissible in locations accessible to qualified persons only.

Exception: In locations accessible to qualified persons only, open circuit breakers may be mounted.

(2) When oil-filled transformers are used, circuit breakers shall be either located outside the transformer vault or be capable of operation from outside the vault.

(3) Any adjacent readily combustible structures or materials shall be safeguarded in an approved manner when oil circuit breakers are used.

(4) The following equipment or operating characteristics shall be used with circuit breakers. Refer to the *NEC* for these, which include a. through f.

(5) The continuous current rating of a circuit breaker shall be not less than the continuous circuit that may pass through the circuit breaker.

(6) The maximum fault current that a circuit breaker may be required to interrupt shall be covered by a circuit breaker with a rating of this amount of fault current, and it shall include any contribution to the circuit from other sources of energy.

(7) The circuit breaker that is used for closing a circuit shall have not less than the maximum assymetrical fault current into which the circuit breaker can be closed.

(8) The momentary rating of the circuit breaker shall not be less than the maximum amount of assymetrical fault current available at the point of installation.

(9) The maximum voltage rating of the circuit determines the maximum voltage of the circuit breaker.

(b) **Power Fuses and Fuseholders.**

(1) **Use.** When fuses are used to protect conductors and equipment, a fuse shall be placed in each ungrounded conductor. Two fuses in parallel will be allowed to protect the same load provided that both fuses have the same rating and are installed in an approved common mounting, and the connections between the paralleled fuses shall be such as to divide the current equally. Unless approved for such usage, ventilated power fuses are not to be used indoors, underground, or in metal enclosures.

(2) **Interrupting Rating.** The interrupting rating of the power fuses shall not be less than the maximum fault current that fuse are intended to interrupt, including all sources of other energy.

(3) **Voltage Rating.** The maximum voltage of the circuit determines the maximum voltage rating of power fuses. Fuses having a minimum operating voltage are not to be used for supplying circuits below the minimum rating of the fuse.

(4) **Indentification of Fuse Mounting and Fuse Units.** The mountings for the fuses and the fuse units shall be identified by a permanent legible nameplate that shows not only the manufacturer's type or designation, but also the continuous current rating, the maximum voltage rating, and the current interruption rating.

(5) **Fuses.** If fuses expel flame when the circuit is opened, their design and arrangement shall be such that they will operate properly without causing any harm to persons or property.

(6) **Fuseholders.** All fuseholders must be so designed that they are in open position and will be de-energized while replacing a blown fuse.

Exception: If they are designed so that only qualified persons replace them by the use of approved equipment designed for the purpose, they may be replaced without de-energizing the fuse-holder.

(7) **High-Voltage Fuses.** When metal switchgear and substations use high-voltage fuses, they must be designed to be operated by a gang disconnecting switch. Fuses are to be isolated from the circuits either by using a switch between the fuses or by means of a roll-out switch and fuse construction. A switch must be of the load-interrupting type, unless either mechanical or electrical interlocks are provided with load-interrupting devices so as to reduce the interrupting possibility of the switch.

Exception: For the disconnecting means, more than one switch will be permitted for one set of fuses if the switches are provided so that more than one set of supply conductors are connected. An interlocking device shall be provided so that access to the fuses can only be gained when all switches are open. A conspicuous sign shall be placed at the fuses reading: "WARNING—FUSES MAY BE ENERGIZED FROM MORE THAN ONE SOURCE."

(c) **Distribution Cutouts and Fuse Links—Expulsion Type.** Refer to your *NEC* for (1) through (7).

(d) **Oil-Filled Cutouts.**

(1) **Continuous Current Rating.** The oil-filled cutouts shall have a continuous current rating that shall not be less than the maximum continuous current that will pass through the cutout.

(2) **Interrupting Rating.** The interrupting rating of oil-filled cutouts shall meet the maximum fault current, or greater, that the cutout will be required to interrupt. This rating will include contributions from any other sources of energy.

(3) **Voltage Rating.** The maximum voltage rating of an oil-filled cutout shall be at least the maximum voltage of the circuit it serves.

(4) **Fault-Closing Rating.** The fault-closing rating of the oil-filled switch rating shall be at least the maximum assymetrical fault current that can occur at the cutout location unless there are interlocks or suitable procedures that can prevent the possibility of closing into a fault.

(5) **Identification.** There shall be a permanent and legible nameplate on all oil-filled cutouts that show the rating of the continuous current, the maximum voltage, and the amount of current it will interrupt.

(6) **Fuse Links.** There shall be a legible identification that shows the rated continuous current on fuse links. This shall be a permanent rating.

(7) **Location.** The location of cutouts shall be readily accessible and the top of a cutout shall be not over 5 feet above the floor or platform.

(8) **Enclosure.** To prevent contact with nonshielded cables or any energized parts of oil-filled cutouts, suitable barriers or enclosures shall be installed.

(e) **Load Interrupters.** Switches that will interrupt load may be installed provided suitable fuses or circuit breakers are used along with these devices so that they may interrupt fault currents. Where these devices are used in combination, the electrical coordination between them shall be such that they will safely withstand the effects of closing, carrying, or interrupting all currents. This includes the assigned maximum short-circuit rating.

Where more than one switch is installed and has interconnected load terminals that will provide alternate connections to different supply conductors, it is required that each switch be provided with a conspicuous sign reading: "WARNING SWITCH MAY BE EN-ERGIZED BY BACKFEED."

(1) **Continuous Current Rating.** Interrupting switches shall have continuous current rating that is equal to or greater than the maximum current that can occur at the point of installation.

(2) **Voltage Rating.** The maximum voltage rating of cutouts shall be equal to or greater than the maximum voltage of the circuit involved.

(3) **Identification.** Cutouts used for distribution are required to have on their body or on the door or fuse tube a legible nameplate or other identification showing manufacturer's type or designation, maximum voltage rating, continuous current rating, and also their current interrupting rating.

(4) **Switching of Conductors.** The mechanism for switching is to be arranged to be operated from a location that will not expose the operator to energized parts, and it must open all ungrounded conductors on the same circuit at the same instant by means of only one operation. Arrangement must be provided to lock switches in the open position. Metal-enclosed switches are required to be operated from outside the enclosure.

(5) **Stored Energy for Opening.** The energizing storing apparatus will be permitted to be left uncharged after the switch has been closed, provided that by a single movement of the operating handle, it charges the operator and opens the switch.

(6) **Supply Terminals.** All supply terminals that supply fuse-interrupted switches are required to be at the top of the enclosure for the switch.

Exception: If there is a barrier provided in the enclosure, so installed as to prevent persons from accidentally contacting the energized parts or dropping tools or fuses into the energized parts, the supply terminals shall not be required to be at the top of the switch enclosure.

710-22. Isolating Means—Means shall be provided so that any item of the equipment may be completely isolated. It is not necessary to use isolation switches if there are other means for de-energizing the equipment for inspection and repairs. These could be drawout-type, metal-enclosed switchgear, or removable truck panels.

A sign warning against opening under load will be required on isolating switches not on interlock with circuit-interrupting device that have been approved.

A fuse and fuseholder will be permitted as an isolating switch if designed for the purpose.

710-23. Voltage Regulators—Proper switching sequence for regulators must be ensured by the use of one of the following: (1) regular bypass switches that are mechanically sequenced; (2) interlocks that are mechanically operated; or (3) instructions for switching procedure that are prominently displayed at the switching location.

710-24. Metal-Enclosed Power Switchgear and Industrial Control Assemblies—Check the *NEC* for information contained in this section from (a) through (p).

D. Installations Accessible to Qualified Persons Only

710-31. Enclosure for Electrical Installations—An enclosure in an electrical installation accessible to qualified persons only is defined as being considered an electrical installation in a vault, a closet, or in an area surrounded by a wall, screen, or fence, access to which is controlled by a lock and key or other approved means, and accessible only to qualified persons. (See Section 110-31.) The height of the wall, screen, or fence shall not be less than eight feet over-all, except if the enclosure is provided with an equal degree of isolation. In designing the enclosure for a given case, consideration shall be given to the nature and the degree of hazard involved. Article 450 covers minimum construction requirements for oil-filled transformers. Isolation by elevation is covered in Sections 710-11 and 710-34.

710-32. Circuit Conductors—Circuit conductors may be installed in raceways, cable trays, as metal-clad cable, as bare wire cable, and buses, or as nonmetallic sheathed cables or conductors as provided in Sections 710-3 through 710-6. When bare live conductors are installed, they shall conform to Sections 710-33 and 710-34.

In the installation of conductors that carry high-voltage, the sizing of bare conductors must be done with consideration for corona effects.

Insulators, their mountings, and conductor attachments, when used as supports for single-conductor and busbars, shall be capable of safely withstanding the magnetic forces which will result between two or more conductors in the event of a fault current being imposed on them. The magnetic forces tend to push the conductors apart. The magnitude of the force depends upon the amount of short-circuit current involved, the spacing, etc.

If open runs of lead-sheathed cables are used, they shall be protected from physical damage and electrolysis of the sheath.

710-33. Minimum Space Separation—This section deals with interior wiring design and construction. It does not apply to the space separation provided in electrical apparatus and wiring devices.

Table 710-33 in the *NEC* lists the minimum indoor air separation between bare live conductors and between such conductors and adjacent surfaces. These are the minimum values—the spacing may be greater but not less than the spacing shown in the table. (See Table 710-33. Minimum Clearance of Live Parts.)

710-34. Work Space and Guarding—You are referred to Section 110-34.

E. Mobile and Portable Equipment

Much of Part E is covered in previous sections of this article, so instead of repeating it we refer you to Part E in the National Electrical Code.

High-voltage equipment is, of course, subject to hazards and therefore only qualified persons should work on it; they will know the proper respect to show it. Grounding is extremely important. The author's suggestion is that all grounds be thoroughly checked for ground resistance and also periodic inspections made to be certain the grounding is intact.

F. Tunnel Installations

710-51. General.

(a) **Covered.** This part applies to installation and use of high-voltage distribution and utilization power equipment that is portable and mobile such as substations, cars, trailers, mobile shovels, draglines, hoists, drills, dredges, compressors, pumps, conveyors, underground excavators, etc.

(b **Other Articles.** The requirements of this part shall bg in addition to other articles, such as Articles 100 through 710 of this Code. Grounding requires special attention; see Article 250.

(c) **Protection Against Physical Damage.** All conductors and cables used in tunnels shall be located so that they are above the tunnel floor, and they must be thoroughly located and guarded so that they will not be subject to physical damage.

710-52. Overcurrent Protection—Article 430 covers the protection of motor-operated equipment from overcurrent. Transformers are to be protected as covered in Article 450.

710-53. Conductors—Conductors installed in tunnels for high voltage shall be installed as in (1) metal conduit or other metal raceways; (2) they may be installed in Type MC cable; or (3) if approved, they may be installed in other types of cable. Cables that are multiconductor, if approved for the service, may be a portable type supplying mobile equipment.

710-54. Bonding and Equipment Grounding Conductors—Great care must be exercised in bonding and equipment grounding, for personnel safety.

(a) **Grounding and Bonding.** Nonenergized metal parts of the electrical equipment and metal raceways and the cable sheath are required to be effectively grounded and bonded to all metal rails and pipes, not only at the portal, but at intervals not exceeding 1000 feet throughout the tunnel.

This is very important, as the best grounds will no doubt be encountered outside the tunnel, and thus extra paths are provided to this point.

(b) **Equipment Grounding Conductor.** Inside the metal raceway, or inside the multiconductor cable jacket, an equipment grounding conductor shall be run with the circuit conductors. This equipment grounding conductor will be permitted to be insulated or bare.

710-55. Transformers, Switches, and Electric Equipment—It is required that all transformers, switches, motor controllers, motors, rectifiers, and other equipment installed below ground shall be protected from physical damage by location or guarding.

710-56. Energized Parts—Any bare terminals or electrical equipment, including transformers, switches, motor controllers, etc., are to be enclosed to protect persons from accidental contact.

710-57. Ventilation System Controls—When venitilation equipment is used, it shall be so installed that the ventilation may be reversed, as during the summer air will probably be going out of the tunnel and in the winter, going into the tunnel.

710-58. Disconnecting Means—A switching device that conforms to requirements of Articles 430 and 450 is to be installed at each transformer or motor location for the purpose of disconnecting the transformer or motor. This switching device shall open all ungrounded conductors at the same time.

710-59. Enclosures—Any enclosure used in a tunnel shall be dripproof or submersible as may be required by environmental conditions. Neither switch nor contactor enclosures are permitted to be used as junction boxes or raceways for conductors feeding through or tapping off at those locations to other switches, unless specially designed equipment is provided that is adequate for the purpose.

710-60. Grounding—Article 250 covers the grounding of tunnel equipment.

G. Electrode-Type Boilers

See the *NEC*, Sections 710-70 through 710-74.

ARTICLE 720—CIRCUITS AND EQUIPMENT OPERATING AT LESS THAN 50 VOLTS

This article covers the installations that operate at less than 50 volts, either direct current or alternating current, with the exception of coverage of low voltage systems below 50 volts as covered in Articles 650, 725, and 760. Refer to the *NEC*.

ARTICLE 725—CLASS 1, CLASS 2, AND CLASS 3 REMOTE-CONTROL, SIGNALING, AND POWER-LIMITED CIRCUITS

Refer to the *NEC*.

ARTICLE 760—FIRE PROTECTIVE SIGNALING SYSTEMS
A. Scope and General

This article was new with the 1975 edition of the *NEC* and it will not be necessary to repeat it here, but your attention should be called to Section 760-1.

760-1. Scope—Covered in this article is equipment for fire alarms and fire alarm signal systems that operate at 600 volts, nominal, or less.

Note: Refer to following NFPA Codes:

NFPA 71-1982—Central Station Signaling Systems.
NFPA 72A-1985—Local Protective Signaling Systems.
NFPA 72B-1986—Auxiliary Protective Signaling Systems.
NFPA 72C-1986—Remote Station Protective Signaling Systems.
NFPA 72D-1986—Proprietary Protective Signaling Systems.
NFPA 72E-1984—Automatic Fire Detectors.
NFPA 74-1984—Household Fire Warning Equipment.

Note: Article 725 defines Class 1, 2, and 3 circuits.

The preceding standards should be purchased from the NFPA by anyone involved with the installation or maintenance of fire protection signaling systems. See the *NEC* for coverage of this article.

ARTICLE 770—OPTICAL FIBER CABLES

Optical fiber cables are being used with great success for control, signaling and communication purposes. Optical fiber cables get involved with electrical cables, or are sometimes pulled in raceway with electric cables so they definitely belong in the *NEC*.

770-1. Scope—This article applies to the installation of optical fiber cables along with electrical conductors. It does not cover the construction or installation of optical fiber cables, except in installations that are covered in this article.

770-2. Other Articles—(a) and (b) below covers equipment:

(a) You are referred to Section 300-21 covering the spread of fire or products of combustion.

(b) **Duct, Plenums, and Other Air-Handling Spaces.** Section 300-22 covers the installation of optical fiber cables in plenums, ducts, or any other air-handling equipment.

Exception to (b): Section 770-6(c) gives an exception to (b).

770-3. Optical Fiber Cables—By the transmission of light through optical fiber cables, they can be used for control, signaling, and communication.

770-4. Types—There are three types of optical fiber cable:

(a) **Nonconductive.** These cables do not contain any metallic members or other materials that conduct electricity.

(b) **Conductive.** These cables are noncurrent-carrying, but have conductive members such as metallic strength members and metallic vapor barriers.

(c) **Hybrid.** These carry optical fiber cables and also current-carrying conductors; they may be classified as electrical cables according to the type of electrical conductors.

770-5. Optical Fibers and Electrical Conductors.

(a) **With Conductors for Electric Light, Power, or Class 1 Circuits.** Optical fiber will be permitted in the same hybrid cable for use in electric lighting, power, or Class 1 circuits provided they operate at 600 volts or less, and only where optical fibers and the electrical conductors are associated. Nonconductive optical fiber cables will be permitted to occupy the same raceway or cable tray with conductors for light and power, or Class 1 circuits rated 600 volts or less. Conductors in hybrid optical fiber cables are not permitted to be in the same raceway as cable tray for electrical light or power or Class 1 circuits.

Nonconductive optical fiber cables shall not be allowed to occupy the same cabinet, panel, or any other enclosure that houses electrical terminations for electrical light and power or Class 1 circuits.

Exception No. 1: If nonconductive optical fiber cables are functionally associated with the light, power, or Class 1 circuits, they may occupy the same cabinet, panel, outlet box, etc.

Exception No. 2: If nonconductive optical fiber cables are installed in either factory- or field-assembly control centers, the optical fiber cables will be permitted to occupy the same panel, outlet box, or similar enclosure.

Exception No. 3: In industrial locations where maintenance and supervision ensures that only qualified persons will be servicing the installation, nonconductive optical fiber cables will be permitted to be with circuits exceeding 600 volts.

Section 300-17 covers the installation of optical fiber cables in raceways.

(b) **With Other Conductors.** If any of the following are complied with, optical fiber cables shall be permitted in the same cable, and conductive and nonconductive fiber cables shall be permitted in the same raceway, cable tray, or enclosure with other conductors:

(1) If in compliance with Article 725, Class 2 and 3 remote-control signaling and power-limiting circuits may be installed.

(2) If in compliance with Article 760, signaling systems that are power-limited for fire protective use are permitted.

(3) If in compliance with Article 800, communication circuits are permitted.

(4) If in compliance with Article 820, distribution systems for community antenna for television and radio will be permitted.

(c) **Grounding.** Noncurrent-carrying conductive parts of optical fiber cables shall be grounded and meet the requirements of Article 250.

770-6. Fire Resistance of Cables.

(a) **Wiring Within Buildings.** When installed in buildings, optical fiber cables shall bg Type OFC or OFN and be listed as resistive to the spread of fire. This requirement will become effective on July 1, 1988. If optical fiber cables run vertically in a shaft, Section 770-6(b) will apply, and if cables are installed in ducts, plenums, or other air-handling spaces, refer to Section 770-6(c), which will apply. Types OFCR and OPNR cables are listed for use in vertical runs as covered in Section 770-6(b) and if Types OFCP and OFNP cables are listed for use in ducts, plenums, or any other air-handling space and comply with Section 770-6(c), they will be permitted to be used as requirements of this section.

Note: UL 1581, termed the vertical tray flame test, is one method of checking the spread of fire for optical fiber cables.

Exception No. 1: If optical fiber cables are enclosed in raceways or noncombustible tubing, they may be used in the above locations.

Exception No. 2: If the cable does not exceed 10 feet in nonconcealed spaces.

(b) **In Vertical Runs.** Optical fiber cables shall be Type OFCR or OFNR when run vertically in a shaft and listed as having fire-resistant characteristics that are capable of preventing the spread of fire from floor to floor. Types OFCP and OFNP cables, which are listed for use in ducts, plenums, and other air-handling areas as covered in Section 770-6(c), shall meet the requirements of this section.

Exception: They are permitted if encased in noncombustible tubing, or the shaft in which they are located is fireproof shaft having firestops at each floor.

(c) **In Ducts, Plenums, and Other Air-Handling Spaces.** Optical fiber cables shall comply with Section 300-22 as to installation methods where they are installed in ducts, plenums, or other spaces used to handle environmental air.

Exception: Types OFCP and OFNP optical fiber cables that have been listed as having adequate fire resistance and a low smoke-producing characteristic will be permitted for ducts and plenums as described in Section 300-22(b) and other spaces used for environmental air as described in Section 300-22(c).

Note: One method of establishing low-smoke-producing cables to a value that is acceptable is covered in NFPA 262-1985, which tests to a maximum of 0.5 peak optical density and a maximum optical density of 0.15. Another similar fire-resistance test for cables is covered in the NFPA 262-1985 test, and can be defined as having a maximum allowable flame travel for a distance of 5 feet.

770-7. Grounding of Entrance Cables—Where the noncurrent-carrying members of optical fiber cable are exposed to hostile contact with light or power conductors, they are to be grounded or interrupted as close as possible to the entrance by using an insulating joint or equivalent device.
    The point of emergence from an exterior wall, concrete floor slab, or from a rigid metal conduit or an intermediate metal conduit, grounded in accordance with Article 250, shall be considered for this section as the point of entrance.

770-8. Cable Marking—Table 770-8 covers the marking of listed optical fiber cables. See Table 770-8, Cable Markings in the *NEC.*

ARTICLE 780—CLOSED-LOOP AND PROGRAMMED POWER DISTRIBUTION

Refer to the *NEC.*

Chapter 8

Communications Systems

ARTICLE 800—COMMUNICATION CIRCUITS

Refer to the *NEC* for coverage of this article.

ARTICLE 810—RADIO AND TELEVISION EQUIPMENT

Refer to the *NEC* for coverage of this article.

ARTICLE 820—COMMUNITY ANTENNA TELEVISION AND RADIO DISTRIBUTION SYSTEMS

Refer to the *NEC* for coverage of this article.

Chapter 9

Tables and Examples

This chapter contains many tables and examples which have been referred to in this text by notations to see the *NEC*. Tables and changes will not appear here since we are asking you to use this book in conjunction with the 1987 *National Electrical Code*.

APPENDIX A

Refer to the *NEC*.

Index

Agricultural buildings (Article 547), 548-551
  grounding, bonding, and equipotential plane, 550-551
  lighting fixtures, 550
  motors, 550
  other articles, 549
  scope, 548-549
  switches, circuit breakers, controllers, and fuses, 550
  wiring methods, 549
Air-conditioning and refrigerating equipment (Article 440), 414-427
  ampacity and rating, 417
  branch-circuit conductors, 422-423
  branch-circuit protection, 420-422
  controllers for motor-compressors, 423
  cord-connected equipment, 420
  definitions, 415
  disconnecting means, 418-420

  ground-fault protection, 420-422
  highest rated motor, 417-418
  location, 420
  marking, 415-417
  motor compressors, 422, 423, 425-426
  other articles, 415
  overload protection, 423-426
  rating and interrupting capacity, 418-420
  room air-conditioners, 426-427
  scope, 414-415
  short-circuit protection, 420-422
  single machine, 418
Aircraft hangars (Article 513), 495-499
  aircraft battery-charging and equipment, 498
  classification of location, 495-496
  definition, 495
  equipment not within class I location, 497
  external power sources for energizing aircraft, 498

Aircraft hangars (Cont.)
  grounding, 499
  mobile servicing equipment,
    498-499
  sealing, 498
  stanchions, rostrums, and docks,
    497-498
  wiring and equipment in class I
    location, 496
  wiring not within class I
    location, 496-497
Appliances (Article 422), 342-349
  branch-circuit overcurrent
    protection, 343
  branch-circuit requirements,
    342-343
  ceiling fans, 346
  control and protection, 346-349
  cooking appliances, 346
  disconnection, 346-347
  flatirons, 344
  flexible cords, 343-344
  grounding, 345-346
  heated appliances, 344
  heating appliances, 348-349
  immersion heaters, 344
  installation, 343-346
  live parts, 342
  marking, 349
  other articles, 342
  overcurrent protection, 343,
    347-349
  protection of combustible
    material, 344
  scope, 342
  stands, 344
  water heaters, 345
Armored cable Type AC (Article
    333), 213-216
  attics, 215-216
  bends, 215
  boxes and fittings, 215
  conductors, 214-215
  construction, 214
  definition, 214
  exposed work, 215
  marking, 215
  other articles, 214
  supports, 215

  through studs, joists, and
    rafters, 215
Auxiliary gutters (Article 374), 295-
    299
  ampacity of conductors, 297
  clearance of bare live parts, 297
  construction and installation,
    298-299
  covers, 296
  extension beyond equipment,
    295
  number of conductors, 296
  splices and taps, 297
  supports, 295
  use, 295

Boatyards, Marinas and (Article
    555), 558
Branch circuits (Article 210), 26-44
  circuits derived from
    autotransformers, 34-35
  classifications, 27
  color code for branch circuits,
    30-31
  conductors—minimum ampacity
    and size, 36-37
  dwelling unit receptacle outlets,
    41-43
  general provisions, 26-36
  ground-fault protection for
    personnel, 33-34
  guest rooms, 43-44
  lighting outlets, 44
  maximum loads, 38-39
  multiwire branch circuits, 27-30
  other articles, 27
  outlet devices, 38
  outlets, 40-44
  overcurrent protection, 37-38
  permissible loads, 39-40
  ratings, 36-40
  receptacles and cord connectors,
    32-33
  rooftop heating, air-conditioning,
    and refrigeration equipment
    outlet, 44
  scope, 26
  show windows, 44

summary, 40
ungrounded conductors tapped
    from grounded systems, 36
voltage limitations, 31-32
Branch-circuit and feeder
    calculations (Article 220), 48-
    61
    additional loads, 59
    additional loads to existing
        installations, 59
    appliance load—dwelling units,
        54
    branch circuits required, 50-51
    computation of branch circuits,
        48-50
    dwelling units, 58-59
    electric clothes dryers, 54
    electric ranges and cooking
        appliances—dwelling units, 54
    farm loads, 61
    feeder neutral load, 55-58
    feeders, 51-58
    fixed electric space heating, 53
    kitchen equipment—other than
        dwelling units, 54-55
    laundry loads—dwelling unit, 53
    lighting, general, 52
    motors, 53
    multifamily dwelling, 59-60
    noncoincidental loads, 55
    optional calculations, 58-61
    receptacle loads—nondwelling
        units, 53
    schools, 60
    scope, 48
    show-window lighting, 52
    small appliance and laundry
        loads—dwelling unit, 53
    two dwelling units, 60
    voltages, 48
Branch circuits and feeders,
    outside (Article 225), see
    Outside branch circuits and
    feeders
Bulk storage plants (Article 515),
    504-507
    class I locations, 504
    definition, 504
    gasoline dispensing, 507

sealing, 507
underground wiring, 506-507
wiring and equipment above
    class I locations, 505-506
wiring and equipment within
    class I locations, 505
Busways (Article 364), 269-274
    branch circuits, 272
    branches from, 271
    dead ends, 271
    definition, 269
    feeders and subfeeders, 271
    length of busways, 272
    other articles, 270
    over 600 volts, 272-274
    overcurrent protection, 271, 272
    reduction in size, 272
    scope, 269
    subfeeder, 271, 272
    supports, 270
    through walls and floors, 270-271
    use, 270

Cabinets and cutout boxes (Article
    373), 289-295
    conductors entering, 290-291
    construction specifications, 294-
        295
    damp or wet locations, 289-290
    deflection of conductors, 291-292
    enclosures for switches or
        overcurrent devices, 293
    installation, 289-294
    position in wall, 290
    scope, 289
    side of back wiring spaces or
        gutters, 294
Cable trays (Article 318), 181-193
    ampacity of cables, 191-192, 193
    cable installation, 187-188
    grounding, 187
    installation, 183-185
    number of cables 2001 volts or
        over, 192-193
    number of cables rated 2000
        volts or less, 188-192
    scope, 181
    uses not permitted, 182
    uses permitted, 181-182

Capacitors (Article 460), 442-446
  600 volts and under, 443-444
  conductors, 443
  drainage of stored charge, 443
  enclosing and guarding, 443
  grounding, 446
  over 600 volts, 445-446
  overcurrent protection, 445-446
  overload device, 444
  scope, 442-443
Cellular concrete floor raceways
  (Article 358), 265
Cellular metal floor raceways
  (Article 356), 262-265
  definition, 262
  installation, 263-265
  other articles, 263
  use, 263
Circuits, and equipment operating
  at less than 50 volts (Article
  720), 607
Class I locations (Article 501), 448,
  452-453, 455-471, 493-494,
  496, 499-502, 504-506, 509-
  512
  conductor insulation, 469
  control transformers and
    resistors, 465
  flexible cords, 469
  grounding, 470-471
  lighting fixtures, 467-468
  live parts, 470
  meters, instruments, and relays,
    456-457
  motors and generators, 466-467
  receptacles and attachment
    plugs, 469
  scope, 448
  sealing and drainage, 458-464
  signal, alarm, remote-control,
    and communication systems,
    470
  surge protection, 471
  switches, circuit breakers, motor
    controllers, and fuses, 464-465
  transformers and capacitors, 455-
    456
  utilization equipment, 468-469
  wiring methods, 457-458

Class II locations (Article 502),
  453-455, 471-483, 511-512
  control transformers and
    resistors, 476-477
  flexible cords, 481
  grounding, 483
  lighting fixtures, 479-481
  live parts, 483
  meters, instruments, and relays,
    481-483
  motors and generators, 477-478
  receptacles and attachment
    plugs, 481
  scope, 448
  sealing, 475
  signaling, alarm, remote-control,
    and communication systems,
    481-483
  surge protection, 483
  switches, circuit breakers, motor
    controllers, and fuses, 475-476
  transformers and capacitors, 472-
    473
  utilization equipment, 479
  ventilation pumps, 478-479
  wiring methods, 473-475
Class III locations (Article 503),
  453, 484-489
  control transformers and
    resistors, 485-486
  electric cranes and hoists, 488
  flexible cords, 487
  grounding, 488-489
  lighting fixtures, 487
  live parts, 488
  motors and generators, 486
  receptacles and attachment
    plugs, 487-488
  scope, 448
  storage-battery charging
    equipment, 488
  switches, circuit breakers, motor
    controllers, and fuses, 485
  transformers and capacitors, 485
  utilization equipment, 486
  ventilating piping, 486
  wiring methods, 485
Commercial garages, repair and
  storage (Article 511), 490-495

battery charging equipment, 494
class I locations, 490-493
electric vehicle charging, 494-495
equipment above class I locations, 494
ground-fault circuit-interrupter protection for personnel, 495
locations, 490
scope, 490
wiring and equipment in class I locations, 492-493
wiring in spaces above class I locations, 493-494
Concealed knob-and-tube wiring (Article 324), 198-201
attics and roof spaces, 199-200
boxes, 201
clearance from piping, exposed conductors, etc., 199
conductor clearance, 199
other articles, 199
splices, 201
switches, 201
through walls, floors, etc., 199
tie wires, 199
uses not permitted, 199
uses permitted, 199
Conductors for general wiring (Article 310), 172-181
ampacity, 179-181
conductors in parallel, 175-176
constructions and applications, 178
corrosive conditions, 176
identification, 177-178
insulated, 173
material, 173, 179
minimum size conductors, 174-175
scope, 172-173
shielding, 175-176
stranded conductors, 173
temperature limitation, 176
Cutout boxes, *see* Cabinets and cutout boxes

Definitions (Article 100), 7
De-icing equipment, *see* Fixed

outdoor electric de-icing and snow-melting equipment
Electrical metallic tubing (Article 348), 245-247
Electrical nonmetallic tubing (Article 331), 211-213
installation, 212-213
other articles, 211-212
uses not permitted, 212
uses permitted, 212
Electrically driven and controlled irrigation machines (Article 675), 562
Emergency systems (Article 700), 583-591
capacity, 584-585
control emergency lighting circuits, 590
emergency circuits for lighting and power, 589-590
equipment approval, 584
other articles, 584
overcurrent protection, 590-591
power sources, 586-589
scope, 583-584
signals, 585-586
tests and maintenance, 584
transfer equipment, 585
wiring, 586

Feeder calculations, *see* Branch-circuit and feeder calculations
Feeders (Article 215), 45-48
diagrams of feeders, 46
feeder conductor grounding means, 46-47
feeders with common neutral, 46
ground-fault protection for personnel, 48
identifying conductor with higher voltage to ground, 47-48
minimum rating and size, 45-46
overcurrent protection, 46
scope, 45
ungrounded conductors tapped from grounded systems, 47

Fire protective signaling systems
(Article 760), 608
Fixed electric heating equipment
for pipelines and vessels
(Article 427), 373-379
branch-circuit sizing, 375
control and protection, 378-379
definitions, 374
impedance heating, 376
induction heating, 377
installation, 375
other articles, 374-375
personnel protection, 376, 377
resistance heating elements,
375-376
scope, 373
skin effect heating, 377-378
Fixed electrical space heating
equipment (Article 424), 349-
367
area restrictions, 355-356
branch circuits, 349-350, 362,
366
clearances, 355, 356, 366
in concrete or poured masonry,
367
connection to branch-circuit
conductors, 366
control and protection, 351-354
definitions, 364
disconnection, 351-352
duct heaters, 359-360
electric radiant heating panels
and heating panel sets, 364-
367
electrode-type boilers, 362-364
feeder wiring in walls, 366
grounding, 351, 362, 363
heating cables, 354-359
inspection and tests, 359
installation, 350-351, 356-359,
360, 364-365, 367
location, 350, 355
marking, 354, 355, 363-364
nonheating leads, 366
other articles, 349
overcurrent protection, 353-354,
361-362
resistance-type boilers, 361-362
scope, 349
splices, 356
under floor covering, 367
Fixed outdoor electric de-icing and
snow-melting equipment
(Article 426), 367-373
branch-circuit sizing, 368
control and protection, 372-373
corrosion protection, 371
disconnection, 372-373
electrical connection, 371
embedded equipment, 369-370
exposed equipment, 370
grounding, 371-372
identification, 369
impedance heating, 372
installation, 368-369, 370-371
marking, 371
other articles, 368
overcurrent protection, 373
resistance heating elements,
369-372
scope, 367-368
special permission, 369
thermal protection, 369
use, 369
Fixture wires (Article 402), 319-
320
Flat cable assemblies (Article 363),
267-269
Flat conductor cable Type FCC
(Article 328), 203-208
branch-circuit ratings, 206
construction, 207-208
definitions, 203-204
installation, 206-207
other articles, 204
scope, 203
uses not permitted, 206
uses permitted, 205-206
Flexible cords and cables (Article
400). 314-318
ampacity, 315
attachment plugs, 318
construction specifications, 317-
318
grounding-conductor
identification, 317
insulation thickness, 317

labels, 317
marking, 315
minimum size, 317
other articles, 314
overcurrent protection, 317
portable cables over 600 volts,
318
protection from damage, 317
pull at joints and terminals, 316-
317
scope, 314
show windows and cases, 317
splices, 316
suitability, 314
types, 314
uses not permitted, 316
uses permitted, 315
Flexible metal conduit (Article
350), 249-250
Flexible metallic tubing (Article
349), 247-249
Fountains (Article 680), 577-579

Garages, *see* Commercial garages,
repair and storage
Gasoline dispensing and service
stations (Article 514), 499-504
circuit disconnects, 502
class I locations, 499-500
definition, 499
grounding, 503
sealing, 502
underground wiring, 503-504
wiring and equipment above
class I locations, 501-502
wiring and equipment within
class I locations, 501
Grounded conductors, use and
identification of (Article 200),
22-26
connection to grounded system,
22-23
general, 22
identification of terminals, 23
identifying grounded
conductors, 23
scope, 22
use of white or natural gray
color, 24

Grounding (Article 250), 112-152
alternating-current circuits and
systems, 113-122
bonding, 131-138
circuit and system, 112-117
circuits not to be grounded, 116-
117
clean surfaces, 150
clothes dryers, 130
common grounding electrode,
128
common service supplied
buildings, 119-120
conductor to be grounded, 120
cord- and plug-connected
equipment, 129-130
derived neutral systems, 151
direct-current systems, 112-113,
117
equipment, 123-125, 128-130
equipment grounding conductor
connections, 125-127
fixed grounding, 128-129
generators, portable and vehicle-
mounted, 116
grounded circuit conductor, 130-
131
grounding conductor
connections, 148-150
grounding conductors, 143-147
grounding connections, location
of, 117-122
grounding electrode conductor,
143-146
grounding electrode system,
138-143
grounding methods, 125-131
grounding path, 127
hazardous (classified) locations,
136
high-impedance grounded
neutral system connections,
122
high-voltage systems and
circuits, 151-152
installation, 144-146
instrument transformer circuits,
150-151
less than 50 volts, 113-116

Grounding (Article 250) *(Cont.)*
  lightning rods, 143
  meters, 151
  multiple circuit connections, 131
  neutral systems, 122
  number required, 152
  objectionable current over
    grounding conductors, 117
  one kv and over, 151-152
  other articles, 112
  outline lighting, 147
  over 250 volts, 135-136
  piping systems, 137-138
  point of connection, 117
  protection of attachment, 150
  ranges, 130
  receptacle grounding terminal,
    connection to box, 133-134
  relays, 151
  resistance of made electrodes,
    141-143
  scope, 112
  separately derived systems, 120-
    122
  service cable, metal armor or
    tape of, 133
  service equipment, 131-133
  service-supplied AC systems,
    117-119
  underground service cable, 128
Gutters, auxiliary, *see* Auxiliary
  gutters

Hazardous areas (Articles 500-517),
  448, 452, 489
  See also Hazardous (classified)
    locations
Hazardous (classified) locations
  (Article 500), 448-455
  class I locations, 452-453
  class II locations, 453-455
  class III locations, 455
  location and general
    requirements, 448-449
  marking, 451-452
  scope, 448
  special precaution, 450-452
Hazardous (classified) locations—
  specific (Article 510), 489-490

Health care facilities (Article 517),
  512-540
  clinics, 517-518
  communications and signaling
    systems, 536-537
  data systems, 536-537
  definitions, 512-515
  dental offices, 517-518
  emergency system, 524
  fire protective signalling
    systems, 536-537
  hospitals, 523-526
  inhalation anesthetizing
    locations, 531-536, 539-540
  low-voltage systems, 536-537
  medical offices, 517-518
  nursing homes, 518-523
  outpatient facilities, 517-518
  patient care areas, 527-531, 536-
    537
  residential custodial care
    facilities, 518-523
  scope, 512
  wiring systems, 515-517
  X-ray equipment, 537-539
Heating equipment
  for pipelines and vessels, *see*
    Fixed electric heating
    equipment for pipelines and
    vessels
  space heating, *see* Fixed
    electrical space heating
    equipment
Hot tubs (Article 680), 575-577
Hydromassage bathtubs (Article
  680), 580-581
Hydrotherapeutic tanks (Article
  680), 579-581

Insulators, open wiring on (Article
  320), 193-194
Integrated electrical systems
  (Article 685), 581
Integrated gas spacer cable Type
  IGS (Article 325), 201-202
Interconnected electrical power
  production sources (Article
  705), 595

Intermediate metal conduit (Article 345), 235-237
Irrigation machines, electrically driven and controlled (Article 675), 562

Lampholders, see Lighting fixtures, lampholders, lamps, receptacles, and rosettes
Lamps, see Lighting fixtures, lampholders, lamps, receptacles, and rosettes
Legally required standby system (Article 701), 591-593
Less than 50 volts (Article 720), 607
Lighting fixtures, lampholders, lamps, receptacles, and rosettes (Article 410), 320-342
    attachment plugs, 331-334
    autotransformers, 338
    auxiliary equipment, 331
    caps, 331-334
    clearance, 335-336
    clothes closets, 322-323
    conductors for certain conditions, 327
    connection of electric discharge lighting fixtures, 324-325
    construction of flush and recessed fixtures, 336
    cord-connected, 328-330
    cord connectors, 331-334
    covering, 324
    damp or wet locations, 333
    definition, 340
    direct-current equipment, 337
    electric discharge lamps, 324-325, 331
    electric discharge lighting, 337-340
    fastening, 342
    fixture locations, 320-323
    fixture mounting, 338
    fixture outlet boxes, canopies, pans, 324-326
    fixtures as raceways, 330
    flush fixtures, 335-336
    grounding, 326-327
    grounding poles, 333-334
    grounding terminal, 334
    incandescent filament lamps, 327-328
    incandescent lamps, 331
    installation, 331, 335-336, 341
    lamp supports, 340
    lamp terminals, 339
    lampholders, cord-connected, 329-330
    lampholders, installation, 331
    lighting track, 340-342
    live parts, 320
    other articles, 320
    outlet boxes to be covered, 324
    receptacles, 331-334
    recessed fixtures, 335-336
    rosettes, 335
    scope, 320
    showcases, 328-329
    space for conductors, 324
    supports, 325-326
    switches, 338
    temperature, 335
    temperature limit of conductors, 324
    transformers, 339-340
    voltages—dwelling occupancies, 337
    wiring, 336
    wiring of fixtures, 327-330
Liquidtight flexible metal conduit (Article 351), 250-253
Liquidtight flexible nonmetallic conduit (Article 351), 250, 251, 253-254

Manufactured building (Article 545), 546-548
Marinas and boatyards (Article 555), 558
Medium voltage cable Type MV (Article 326), 202-203
Messenger-supported wiring (Article 321), 197-198
Metal-clad cable Type MC (Article 334), 216-218

Mineral-insulated metal-sheathed
cable Type MI (Article 330),
208-211
construction specifications, 211
definition, 208
installation, 209-211
other articles, 209
uses not permitted, 209
uses permitted, 209
Mobile homes and mobile home
parks (Article 550), 551-557
definitions, 552-555
general requirements, 555
other articles, 555
power supply, 556
scope, 551-552
Motors, motor circuits, and
controllers (Article 430), 379-
414
adjustable speed drive systems,
379-380
adjustable-speed motors, 406
ampacity, 380-381
ampere rating and interrupting
capacity, 409-410
automatic restarting, 395-396
bushings, 385
capacitors with motors, 389
circuit breakers, 400
conductor enclosure, 410
conductors, 388, 389, 410-411
constant voltage DC motors-
power resistors, 390
continuous-duty motors, 391-393
controllers, 413
disconnection, 403-404, 407-410,
412
dust, 386
energy from more than one
source, 410
feeder demand factor, 389
feeder taps, 389-390
fuseholders, 400
fuses, 394
ground-fault protection, 396-401
grounding, 413-414
highest rated motor, 386
location, 385-386
marking, 381-384, 410

mechanical protection of
conductor, 403
motor circuit conductors, 386-
390
motor circuit overcurrent
protection, 411-412
motor control circuits, 401-404
motor controllers, 404-407
motor feeder, 379, 400-401
motor rating, 380-381
motor terminal housings, 384-
385
motors on general purpose
branch circuits, 395
nominal voltage or rectifier
systems, 386
orderly shutdown, 396
over 600 volts, 410-412
overcurrent protection, 400,
401-403, 411-412
overload protection, 390-396
part-winding motors, 380
portable motors, 413
protection against liquids, 384
protection of live parts, 412-413
protection of motor feeder, 400-
401
rating of motor control, 412
short-circuit protection, 396-401
single motor, 386-387
stationary motors, 413
thermal cutouts, 394-395
wiring spaces in enclosures, 384
wound-rotor secondary, 387-388,
393
Multioutlet assembly (Article 353),
256-258

National Electrical Code (NEC)
arrangement, 3
definitions (Article 100), 7
enforcement, 3-4
examination of equipment for
safety, 4
formal interpretations, 4
introduction (Article 90), 1-5
mandatory rules and explanatory
material, 9
metric units of measurement, 5

purpose, 1-2
scope, 2-3
size of conductors, 268
wiring planning, 4-5
See also Requirements for
electrical installations
Nonmetallic extensions (Article
342), 229-234
definitions, 229
fittings, 231
installation, 232-234
marking, 234
other article, 230
splices and taps, 231
uses not permitted, 231
uses permitted, 230
Nonmetallic-sheathed cable Types
NM and NMC (Article 336),
218-222
construction specifications, 221-
222
installation, 220-221
other articles, 219
uses not permitted, 219-220
uses permitted, 219

Office furnishings (Article 605),
558-561
Open wiring on insulators (Article
320), 193-194
Optical fiber cables (Article 770),
608-611
Optional standby systems (Article
702), 593-594
Outlet, device, pull, and junction
boxes, conduit bodies, and
fittings (Article 370), 274-289
accessibility, 287
conductors entering boxes,
conduit bodies, or fittings,
279-280
construction specifications, 287-
288
covers and canopies, 282-283
damp or wet locations, 275
depth in outlet boxes, 282
exposed surface extensions, 281
installation, 275-287
marking, 288

metal boxes, 275
metal boxes, conduit bodies, and
fittings, 287
nonmetallic boxes, 274
number of conductors, 275-278
outlet boxes, 283
over 600 volts, 288-289
pull and junction boxes, 283-286
round boxes, 274
scope, 274
unused openings, 280
wall or ceiling, 281
Outside branch circuits and
feeders (Article 225), 61-68
calculation of load, 62
circuit exits and entrances, 64
clearance from ground, 65
clearances from buildings, 65-67
conductor covering, 62
disconnection, 63
festoon supports, 64
lighting equipment installed
outdoors, 63
location of outdoor lamps, 67
means of attachment to building,
65
mechanical protection of
conductors, 67
multiconductor cables, 67
open-conductor spacings, 64
outdoor lampholders, 67
overcurrent protection, 63
point of attachment to buildings,
64-65
scope, 61-62
size of conductors, 62-63
support over buildings, 64
underground circuits, 67
wiring on buildings, 63-64
Over 600 volts, nominal (Article
710), 595-607
braid-covered insulated
conductors, 598
circuit conductors, 605
circuit interrupting devices, 601-
604
electrode-type boilers, 607
enclosure for electrical
installations, 605

Over 600 volts, nominal *(Cont.)*
 equipment, 600-601
 grounding, 600
 indoor installations, 600
 installations accessible to
  qualified persons only, 605
 insulation shielding, 599-600
 isolating means, 604
 metal-enclosed equipment, 600
 minimum space separation, 605
 mobile and portable equipment,
  606
 moisture or mechanical
  protection, 600
 outdoor installations, 600
 overcurrent protection, 600-601
 protection, 600
 scope, 595
 tunnel installations, 606-607
 voltage regulators, 604-605
 wiring methods, 596-598
 work space and guarding, 605
Overcurrent protection (Article
  240), 98-112
 adapters, 108-110
 branch circuits, 112
 circuit breakers, 111
 circuit breakers in parallel, 100
 conductors, 99-100
 damp or wet locations, 107-108
 disconnecting and guarding, 108
 electrical system coordination,
  101
 enclosures, 107-108
 equipment, 99
 feeders, 111-112
 fixture wires and cords, 100
 fuseholders, 108-111
 fuses, 108-111
 grounded conductors, 106
 location, 101-107
 over 600 volts, 111-112
 scope, 98
 standard ampere rating, 100
 supplementary, 100
 thermal cutouts, 108
 thermal devices, 100
 ungrounded conductors, 101-102
 vertical position, 108

Panelboards, *see* Switchboards and
 panelboards
Pipelines, heating equipment for,
 see Fixed electric heating
 equipment for pipelines and
 vessels
Places of assembly (Article 518),
 540-541
Power and control tray cable Type
 TC (Article 340), 228-229
Power production sources,
 interconnected electric
 (Article 705), 595

Receptacles, *see* Lighting fixtures,
 lampholders, lamps,
 receptacles, and rosettes
Recreational vehicles and
 recreational vehicle parks
 (Article 551), 557
Refrigerating equipment, *see* Air-
 conditioning and refrigerating
 equipment
Requirements for electrical
 installations (Article 110), 9-21
 approval, 9
 arcing parts, 17
 bolts, 13
 circuit impedance, 11
 conductors, 10
 deteriorating agents, 11
 electrical connections, 12-15
 enclosure for electrical
  installations, 18-19
 entrance and access to work
  space, 16, 19
 examination, identification,
  installation, and use of
  equipment, 9-10
 guarding of live parts, 16-17
 identification of disconnecting
  means, 17
 insulation, 10
 interrupting capacity, 11
 light and power from railway
  conductors, 17
 mandatory rules, 9
 mechanical execution of work,
  11-12

mounting and cooling of equipment, 12
over 600 volts, nominal, 17-21
screw fit, 12
screws, 13
voltages, 10
wiring methods, 10-11
work space about equipment, 15-16, 19
work space and guarding, 19-20
Resistors and reactors (Article 470), 446-447
Rheostats (Section 430-82, Article 470), 446
Rigid metal conduit (Article 346), 237-242
construction specifications, 241-242
installation, 238-241
other articles, 238
use, 237-238
Rigid nonmetallic conduit (Article 347), 242-245
description, 242
installations, 244-245
other articles, 344
uses not permitted, 243-244
uses permitted, 242-243
Rosettes, see Lighting fixtures, lampholders, lamps, receptacles, and rosettes

Service-entrance cables Types SE and USE (Article 338), 223-226
definition, 223-224
installation methods, 226
marking, 226
uses permitted, 224-225
Service stations, see Gasoline dispensing and service stations
Services (Article 230), 68-98
attachment, means of, 73
attachment, point of, 73
clearances, 71-73
connections at service head, 79-81
disconnecting means, 84-91, 97-98

enclosed or guarded equipment, 81-82
ground-fault protection, 94-96
grounding and bonding equipment, 82
insulation, 70-71, 74, 75-76
isolating switches, 97
mounting supports, 78
not supplied through other buildings, 69-70
number of services, 68-69
overcurrent protection, 92-96,98
overhead services, 70-74
overhead supply, 70-74
protection against damage, 74, 77-78
raceways to drain, 79
scope, 68
service conductors, 96
service-entrance conductors, 75-81, 96-97
service equipment, 81-96
services exceeding 600 volts, 96-98
short-circuit current, 84
size and rating, 71, 74
supports, over buildings, 74
supports, service masts as, 74
surge/lightning arresters, 98
terminations at service equipment, 81
transfer equipment, 90
underground service-lateral conductors, 74
warning signs, 97
wiring methods for 600 volts or less, 76-77
working space, 82
Shielded nonmetallic-sheathed cable type SNM (Article 337), 222-223
Snow-melting equipment, see Fixed outdoor de-icing and snow melting equipment
Solar photovoltaic systems (Article 690), 581-582
Space heating equipment, see Fixed electrical space heating equipment

Spas (Article 680), 575-577
Spray application, dipping and
coating processes (Article
516), 507-512
classification of location, 507-509
grounding, 512
scope, 507
wiring and equipment above
class I and II locations, 511-
512
wiring and equipment in class I
locations, 509-511
Standby system
legally required (Article 701),
591-593
optional (Article 702), 593-594
Storage plants, bulk, see Bulk
storage plants
Surface metal raceways (Article
352), 254-255
Surface nonmetallic raceways
(Article 352), 256
Surge arresters (Article 280), 152-
154
Swimming pools, fountains, and
similar installations (Article
680), 563-581
approval of equipment, 563
bonding, 571-572
cord- and plug-connected
equipment, 566
deck area heating, 573-575
definitions, 563-564
electric pool water heaters, 566-
567
equipment rooms and pits, 567
fountains, 577-579
grounding, 573
hot tubs, 575-577
hydromassage bathtubs, 580-581
junction boxes and enclosures
for ground-fault circuit
interrupters, 569-571
other articles, 563
overhead conductor clearances,
566
permanently installed pools,
567-575
receptacles, lighting fixtures,

lighting outlets, and switching
devices, 565-566
scope, 563
spas and hot tubs, 575-577
therapeutic pools and tubs in
health care facilities, 579-580
transformers and ground-fault
circuit-interrupters, 564
underground wiring location,
567
underwater audio equipment,
572-573
underwater lighting fixtures,
567-569
Switchboards and panelboards
(Article 384), 306-313
appliance panelboard, 309
arrangement of switches and
fuses, 312
clearances, 308-309
construction specifications, 312-
313
damp or wet locations, 308, 311
enclosure, 312
grounding, 309, 312-313
installation, 307-308
lighting panelboard, 309
location, 308
other articles, 306
overcurrent devices, 309-310
overcurrent protection, 310-311
panelboards, 309-312
scope, 306
support of busbars and
conductors, 306-307
switchboards, 308-309
Switches (Article 380), 299-306
600-volt knife switches, 305
accessibility and grouping, 302
circuit breakers as, 303
construction specifications, 305-
306
enclosure, 300
fused switches, 305
grounding of enclosures, 303
indicating, 301
knife switches, 301, 303-304,
305
marking, 305

mounting snap switches, 303
rating, 304-305
scope, 299
snap switches, 302-303, 304-305
switch connections, 299
time switches, flashers, etc.,
    300-301
wet locations, 300
wire bending space, 306

Temporary wiring (Article 305),
    170-172
Theaters and similar locations
    (Article 520), 541-546
connector strips, drop boxes,
    and stage pockets, 544
curtain motors, 544-545
flue damper control, 545
grounding, 546
lamps in scene docks, 544
number of conductors in
    raceway, 541-542
portable switchboards on stage,
    545-546
receptacles, 544
scope, 541
stage equipment—portable, 546
wiring methods, 541
Therapeutic pools (Article 680),
    579-580
Transformers and transformer
    vaults (Article 450), 427-442
Askarel-insulated transformers,
    439
autotransformers, 431-433
definitions, 428
doorways, 441
drainage, 442
dry-type transformers, 438
grounding autotransformers,
    431-433
guarding, 436-437
liquid-insulated transformers,
    438-439
location, 437, 440
marking, 437
modification of transformers, 440
nonflammable fluid-insulated
    transformers, 439

oil-insulated transformers, 439-
    440
overcurrent protection, 428-431
parallel operation, 436
scope, 427-428
secondary ties, 433-436
storage in vaults, 442
terminal wiring space, 437
transformer vaults, 440-442
ventilation, 437, 441-442
water pipes and accessories, 442

Underfloor raceways (Article 364),
    258-262
connections to cabinets and wall
    outlets, 262
covering, 259-260
dead ends, 261
discontinued outlets, 261
inserts, 262
junction boxes, 262
laid in straight lines, 261
markers at ends, 261
maximum number of
    conductors, 260
other articles, 258
size of conductors, 260
splices and taps, 260-261
use, 258
Underground feeder and branch-
    circuit cable Type UF (Article
    339), 226-228
Underplaster extensions (Article
    344), 234-235
Use and identification of grounded
    conductors, see Grounded
    conductors, use and
    identification of

Vessels, heating equipment for,
    see Fixed electric heating
    equipment for pipelines and
    vessels
Voltages less than 50 volts (Article
    720), 607
Voltages over 600 volts (Article
    710), see Over 600 volts,
    nominal

Wiring methods (Article 300), 155-170
  air-handling spaces, 167-169
  boxes and fittings, 164-165
  conductor bending radius, 169
  conductor in raceway, 166
  conductor length at outlets and
    switch points, 164
  conductors, 156-157
  conductors of different systems,
    169
  covers required, 169
  ducts, 167-169
  fire spread, 167
  grounding, 163, 170
  installation of conductors with
    other systems, 162-163
  limitations, 155
  mechanical continuity-raceways
    and cables, 164
  metal enclosures, 163, 167
  metal raceways, 163, 167
  over 600 volts, 169-170
  protection against corrosion,
    161-162
  protection against induction
    heating, 169-170
  protection against physical
    damage, 157-158
  raceway or cable to open or
    concealed wiring, 166
  raceways exposed to different
    temperatures, 162
  scope, 155
  securing and supporting, 163
  supporting conductors, 166-167
  underground installations, 158-
    161
Wireways (Article 362), 265-267

About the Author . . .

Roland Palmquist has been active in the electrical field since 1928. He was associated with the Engineering Department of the Public Service Company of Colorado; manager of the Public Service Company of Colorado at Ovid and at Windsor, Colorado, for a total of 15 years; owned and operated Palmquist Electric at Windsor, Colorado, for 17 years; and was for many years inspector in charge of District D, NE Colorado, for the Colorado State Electrical Board. He is presently retired from the Kodak Colorado Division, Area 1, Engineering Facilities.

A member of the electrical section of the National Fire Protection Association, Mr. Palmquist served two years as chairman of the Rocky Mountain Chapter of the International Association of Electrical Inspectors, serving on the Executive Committee or Program Committee.

Mr. Palmquist currently writes articles for the I.A.E.I. News. He is author of Audel's *House Wiring*, Audel's *Electrical Course for Apprentices and Journeymen*, and has revised Audel's *Answers to Blueprint Reading, Questions and Answers for Electricians Examinations*, and *Wiring Diagrams for Light and Power*.

AUDEL®

**Over a Century of Excellence
for the Professional
and
Vocational Trades and the Crafts**

**Order now from your local bookstore
or use the convenient order form at
the back of this book.**

AUDEL

These fully illustrated, up-to-date guides and manuals mean a better job done for mechanics, engineers, electricians, plumbers, carpenters, and all skilled workers.

Contents

Electrical II
Machine Shop and Mechanical Trades III
Plumbing IV
Heating, Ventilating and Air Conditioning IV
Pneumatics and Hydraulics V
Carpentry and Construction V
Woodworking VI
Maintenance and Repair VI
Automotive and Engines VII
Drafting VII
Hobbies VII
Macmillan Practical Arts Library VIII

Fractional Horsepower Electric Motors

Rex Miller and Mark Richard Miller
5½ x 8¼   Hardcover   436 pp.   285 illus.
ISBN: 0-672-23410-6 $15.95

Fully illustrated guide to small-to-moderate-size electric motors in home appliances and industrial equipment: • terminology • repair tools and supplies • small DC and universal motors • split-phase, capacitor-start, shaded pole, and special motors • commutators and brushes • shafts and bearings • switches and relays • armatures • stators • modification and replacement of motors.

Electrical

House Wiring sixth edition
Roland E. Palmquist
5½ x 8 ¼ Hardcover   256 pp.   150 illus.
ISBN: 0-672-23404-1 $14.95

Rules and regulations of the current National Electrical Code® for residential wiring, fully explained and illustrated: • basis for load calculations • calculations for dwellings • services • nonmetallic-sheathed cable • underground feeder and branch-circuit cable • metal-clad cable • circuits required for dwellings • boxes and fittings • receptacle spacing • mobile homes • wiring for electric house heating.

Practical Electricity fourth edition
Robert G. Middleton; revised by L. Donald Meyers
5½ x 8¼   Hardcover   504 pp.   335 illus.
ISBN: 0-02-584561-6 $14.95

Complete, concise handbook on the principles of electricity and their practical application: • magnetism and electricity • conductors and insulators • circuits • electromagnetic induction • alternating current • electric lighting and lighting calculations • basic house wiring • electric heating • generating stations and substations.

II

Guide to the 1987 Electrical Code®
Roland E. Palmquist
5½ × 8¼   Hardcover   664 pp.   225 illus.
ISBN: 0-02-594560-2 $19.95

Authoritative guide to the National Electrical Code® for all electricians, contractors, inspectors, and homeowners: • terms and regulations for wiring design and protection • wiring methods and materials • equipment for general use • special occupancies • special equipment and conditions • and communication systems.

Mathematics for Electricians and Electronics Technicians
Rex Miller
5½ x 8¼   Hardcover   312 pp.   115 illus.
ISBN: 0-8161-1700-4 $14.95

Mathematical concepts, formulas, and problem solving in electricity and electronics: • resistors and resistance • circuits • meters • alternating current and inductance • alternating current and capacitance • impedance and phase angles • resonance in circuits • special-purpose circuits. Includes mathematical problems and solutions.

Electric Motors
Edwin P. Anderson; revised by Rex Miller
5½ x 8¼   Hardcover   656 pp.   405 illus.
ISBN: 0-672-23376-2 $14.95

Complete guide to installation, maintenance, and repair of all types of electric motors: • AC generators • synchronous motors • squirrel-cage motors • wound rotor motors • DC motors • fractional-horsepower motors • magnetic contractors • motor testing and maintenance • motor calculations • meters • wiring diagrams • armature windings • DC armature rewinding procedure • and stator and coil winding.

Home Appliance Servicing fourth edition
Edwin P. Anderson; revised by Rex Miller
5½ x 8¼   Hardcover   640 pp.   345 illus.
ISBN: 0-672-23379-7 $15.95

Step-by-step illustrated instruction on all types of household appliances: • irons • toasters • roasters and broilers • electric coffee makers • space heaters • water heaters • electric ranges and microwave ovens • mixers and blenders • fans and blowers • vacuum cleaners and floor polishers • washers and dryers • dishwashers and garbage disposals • refrigerators • air conditioners and dehumidifiers.

Television Service Manual

fifth edition

Robert G. Middleton; revised by Joseph G. Barrile

5¹⁄₂ x 8¹⁄₄   Hardcover   512 pp.   395 illus.
ISBN: 0-672-23395-9 $16.95

Practical up-to-date guide to all aspects of television transmission and reception, for both black and white and color receivers: • step-by-step maintenance and repair • broadcasting • transmission • receivers • antennas and transmission lines • interference • RF tuners • the video channel • circuits • power supplies • alignment • test equipment.

Electrical Course for Apprentices and Journeymen

second edition

Roland E. Palmquist

5¹⁄₂ x 8¹⁄₄   Hardcover   478 pp.   290 illus.
ISBN:0-672-23393-2 $14.95

Practical course on operational theory and applications for training and re-training in school or on the job: • electricity and matter • units and definitions • electrical symbols • magnets and magnetic fields • capacitors • resistance • electromagnetism • instruments and measurements • alternating currents • DC generators • circuits • transformers • motors • grounding and ground testing.

Questions and Answers for Electricians Examinations ninth edition

Roland E. Palmquist

5¹⁄₂ x 8¹⁄₄   Hardcover   320 pp.   110 illus.
ISBN: 0-02-594691-9 $18.95

Based on the current National Electrical Code®, a review of exams for apprentice, journeyman, and master, with explanations of principles underlying each test subject: • Ohm's Law and other formulas • power and power factors • lighting • branch circuits and feeders • transformer principles and connections • wiring • batteries and rectification • voltage generation • motors • ground and ground testing.

Machine Shop and Mechanical Trades

Machinists Library

fourth edition   3 vols
Rex Miller
5¹⁄₂ x 8¹⁄₄   Hardcover   1,352 pp.   1,120 illus.
ISBN: 0-672-23380-0 $52.85

Indispensable three-volume reference for machinists, tool and die makers, machine operators, metal workers, and those with home workshops.

Volume I, Basic Machine Shop
5¹⁄₂ x 8¹⁄₄   Hardcover   392 pp.   375 illus.
ISBN: 0-672-23381-9 $17.95

• Blueprint reading • benchwork • layout and measurement • sheet-metal hand tools and machines • cutting tools • drills • reamers • taps • threading dies • milling machine cutters, arbors, collets, and adapters.

Volume II, Machine Shop
5¹⁄₂ x 8¹⁄₄   Hardcover 528 pp.   445 illus
ISBN: 0-672-23382-7 $19.95

• Power saws • machine tool operations • drilling machines • boring • lathes • automatic screw machine • milling • metal spinning.

Volume III, Toolmakers Handy Book
5¹⁄₂ x 8¹⁄₄   Hardcover   432 pp.   300 illus.
ISBN: 0-672-23683-5 $14.95

• Layout work • jigs and fixtures • gears and gear cutting • dies and diemaking • toolmaking operations • heat-treating furnaces • induction heating • furnace brazing • cold-treating process.

Mathematics for Mechanical Technicians and Technologists

John D. Bies
5¹⁄₂ x 8¹⁄₄   Hardcover   392 pp.   190 illus.
ISBN: 0-02-510620-1 $17.95

Practical sourcebook of concepts, formulas, and problem solving in industrial and mechanical technology: • basic and complex mechanics • strength of materials • fluidics • cams and gears • machine elements • machining operations • management controls • economics in machining • facility and human resources management.

Millwrights and Mechanics Guide

third edition
Carl A. Nelson
5¹⁄₂ x 8¹⁄₄   Hardcover   1,040 pp.   880 illus.
ISBN: 0-672-23373-8 $24.95

Most comprehensive and authoritative guide available for millwrights and mechanics at all levels of work or supervision: • drawing and sketching

• machinery and equipment installation • principles of mechanical power transmission • V-belt drives • flat belts • gears • chain drives • couplings • bearings • structural steel • screw threads • mechanical fasteners • pipe fittings and valves • carpentry • sheet-metal work • blacksmithing • rigging • electricity • welding • pumps • portable power tools • mensuration and mechanical calculations.

Welders Guide third edition

James E. Brumbaugh
5¹⁄₂ x 8 ¹⁄₄   Hardcover   960 pp.   615 illus.
ISBN: 0-672-23374-6 $23.95

Practical, concise manual on theory, operation, and maintenance of all welding machines: • gas welding equipment, supplies, and process • arc welding equipment, supplies, and process • TIG and MIG welding • submerged-arc and other shielded-arc welding processes • resistance, thermit, and stud welding • solders and soldering • brazing and braze welding • welding plastics • safety and health measures • symbols and definitions • testing and inspecting welds. Terminology and definitions as standardized by American Welding Society.

Welder/Fitters Guide

John P. Stewart
8¹⁄₂ x 11   Paperback   160 pp.   195 illus.
ISBN: 0-672-23325-8 $7.95

Step-by-step instruction for welder/fitters during training or on the job: • basic assembly tools and aids • improving blueprint reading skills • marking and alignment techniques • using basic tools • simple work practices • guide to fabricating weldments • avoiding mistakes • exercises in blueprint reading • clamping devices • introduction to using hydraulic jacks • safety in weld fabrication plants • common welding shop terms.

Sheet Metal Work

John D. Bies
5¹⁄₂ x 8¹⁄₄   Hardcover   456 pp.   215 illus.
ISBN: 0-8161-1706-3 $19.95

On-the-job sheet metal guide for manufacturing, construction, and home workshops: • mathematics for sheet metal work • principles of drafting • concepts of sheet metal drawing • sheet metal standards, specifications, and materials • safety practices • layout • shear cutting • holes • bending and folding • forming operations • notching and clipping • metal spinning • mechanical fastening • soldering and brazing • welding • surface preparation and finishes • production processes.

Power Plant Engineers Guide

third edition
Frank D. Graham; revised by Charlie Buffington
5½ x 8¼ Hardcover 960 pp. 530 illus.
ISBN: 0-672-23329-0 $27.50

All-inclusive question-and-answer guide to steam and diesel-power engines: • fuels • heat • combustion • types of boilers • shell or fire-tube boiler construction • strength of boiler materials • boiler calculations • boiler fixtures, fittings, and attachments • boiler feed pumps • condensers • cooling ponds and cooling towers • boiler installation, startup, operation, maintenance and repair • oil, gas, and waste-fuel burners • steam turbines • air compressors • plant safety.

Mechanical Trades Pocket Manual

second edition
Carl A. Nelson
4 x 6 Paperback 364 pp. 255 illus.
ISBN: 0-672-23378-9 $10.95

Comprehensive handbook of essentials, pocket-sized to fit in the tool box: • mechanical and isometric drawing • machinery installation and assembly • belts • drives • gears • couplings • screw threads • mechanical fasteners • packing and seals • bearings • portable power tools • welding • rigging • piping • automatic sprinkler systems • carpentry • stair layout • electricity • shop geometry and trigonometry.

Plumbing

Plumbers and Pipe Fitters Library

third edition 3 vols
Charles N. McConnell; revised by Tom Philbin
5½x8¼ Hardcover 952 pp. 560 illus.
ISBN: 0-672-23384-3 $34.95

Comprehensive three-volume set with up-to-date information for master plumbers, journeymen, apprentices, engineers, and those in building trades.

Volume 1, Materials, Tools, Roughing-In
5½ x 8¼ Hardcover 304 pp. 240 illus.
ISBN: 0-672-23385-1 $12.95

• Materials • tools • pipe fitting • pipe joints • blueprints • fixtures • valves and faucets.

Volume 2, Welding, Heating, Air Conditioning
5½ x 8¼ Hardcover 384 pp. 220 illus.
ISBN: 0-672-23386-x $13.95

• Brazing and welding • planning a heating system • steam heating systems • hot water heating systems • boiler fittings • fuel-oil tank installation • gas piping • air conditioning.

Volume 3, Water Supply, Drainage, Calculations
5½ x 8¼ Hardcover 264 pp. 100 illus.
ISBN: 0-672-23387-8 $12.95

• Drainage and venting • sewage disposal • soldering • lead work • mathematics and physics for plumbers and pipe fitters.

Home Plumbing Handbook

third edition
Charles N. McConnell
8½ x 11 Paperback 200 pp. 100 illus.
ISBN: 0-672-23413-0 $13.95

Clear, concise, up-to-date fully illustrated guide to home plumbing installation and repair: • repairing and replacing faucets • repairing toilet tanks • repairing a trip-lever bath drain • dealing with stopped-up drains • working with copper tubing • measuring and cutting pipe • PVC and CPVC pipe and fittings • installing a garbage disposals • replacing dishwashers • repairing and replacing water heaters • installing or resetting toilets • caulking around plumbing fixtures and tile • water conditioning • working with cast-iron soil pipe • septic tanks and disposal fields • private water systems.

The Plumbers Handbook

seventh edition
Joseph P. Almond, Sr.
4 x 6 Paperback 352 pp. 170 illus.
ISBN: 0-672-23419-x $10.95

Comprehensive, handy guide for plumbers, pipe fitters, and apprentices that fits in the tool box or pocket: • plumbing tools • how to read blueprints • heating systems • water supply • fixtures, valves, and fittings • working drawings • roughing and repair • outside sewage lift station • pipes and pipelines • vents, drain lines, and septic systems • lead work • silver brazing and soft soldering • plumbing systems • abbreviations, definitions, symbols, and formulas.

Questions and Answers for Plumbers Examinations

second edition
Jules Oravetz
5½ x 8¼ Paperback 256 pp. 145 illus.
ISBN: 0-8161-1703-9 $9.95

Practical, fully illustrated study guide to licensing exams for apprentice, journeyman, or master plumber: • definitions, specifications, and regulations set by National Bureau of Standards and by various state codes

• basic plumbing installation • drawings and typical plumbing system layout • mathematics • materials and fittings • joints and connections • traps, cleanouts, and backwater valves • fixtures • drainage, vents, and vent piping • water supply and distribution • plastic pipe and fittings • steam and hot water heating.

HVAC

Air Conditioning: Home and Commercial

third edition
Edwin P. Anderson; revised by Rex Miller
5½ x 8¼ Hardcover 528 pp. 180 illus.
ISBN: 0-672-23397-5 $15.95

Complete guide to construction, installation, operation, maintenance, and repair of home, commercial, and industrial air conditioning systems, with troubleshooting charts: • heat leakage • ventilation requirements • room air conditioners • refrigerants • compressors • condensing equipment • evaporators • water-cooling systems • central air conditioning • automobile air conditioning • motors and motor control.

Heating, Ventilating and Air Conditioning Library

second edition 3 vols
James E. Brumbaugh
5½ x 8¼ Hardcover 1,840 pp. 1,275 illus.
ISBN: 0-672-23388-6 $53.85

Authoritative three-volume reference for those who install, operate, maintain, and repair HVAC equipment commercially, industrially, or at home. Each volume fully illustrated with photographs, drawings, tables and charts.

Volume I, Heating Fundamentals, Furnaces, Boilers, Boiler Conversions
5½ x 8¼ Hardcover 405 illus.
ISBN: 0-672-23389-4 $17.95

• Insulation principles • heating calculations • fuels • warm-air, hot water, steam, and electrical heating systems • gas-fired, oil-fired, coal-fired, and electric-fired furnaces • boilers and boiler fittings • boiler and furnace conversion.

Volume II, Oil, Gas and Coal Burners, Controls, Ducts, Piping, Valves
5½ x 8¼ Hardcover 592 pp. 455 illus.
ISBN: 0-672-23390-8 $17.95

• Coal firing methods • thermostats and humidistats • gas and oil controls and other automatic controls •

ducts and duct systems • pipes, pipe fittings, and piping details • valves and valve installation • steam and hot-water line controls.

Volume III, Radiant Heating, Water Heaters, Ventilation, Air Conditioning, Heat Pumps, Air Cleaners

5 1/2 x 8 1/4   Hardcover   592 pp.   415 illus.
ISBN: 0-672-23391-6 $17.95
• Radiators, convectors, and unit heaters • fireplaces, stoves, and chimneys • ventilation principles • fan selection and operation • air conditioning equipment • humidifiers and dehumidifiers • air cleaners and filters.

Oil Burners fourth edition
Edwin M. Field
5 1/2 x 8 1/4   Hardcover   360 pp.   170 illus.
ISBN: 0-672-23394-0 $15.95

Up-to-date sourcebook on the construction, installation, operation, testing, servicing, and repair of all types of oil burners, both industrial and domestic: • general electrical hookup and wiring diagrams of automatic control systems • ignition system • high-voltage transportation • operational sequence of limit controls, thermostats, and various relays • combustion chambers • drafts • chimneys • drive couplings • fans or blowers • burner nozzles • fuel pumps.

Refrigeration: Home and Commercial second edition
Edwin P. Anderson; revised by Rex Miller
5 1/2 x 8 1/4   Hardcover   768 pp.   285 illus.
ISBN: 0-672-23396-7 $19.95

Practical, comprehensive reference for technicians, plant engineers, and homeowners on the installation, operation, servicing, and repair of everything from single refrigeration units to commercial and industrial systems: • refrigerants • compressors • thermoelectric cooling • service equipment and tools • cabinet maintenance and repairs • compressor lubrication systems • brine systems • supermarket and grocery refrigeration • locker plants • fans and blowers • piping • heat leakage • refrigeration-load calculations.

Pneumatics and Hydraulics

Hydraulics for Off-the-Road Equipment second edition
Harry L. Stewart; revised by Tom Philbin
5 1/2 x 8 1/4   Hardcover   256 pp.   175 illus.
ISBN: 0-8161-1701-2 $13.95

Complete reference manual for those who own and operate heavy equipment and for engineers, designers, installation and maintenance technicians, and shop mechanics: • hydraulic pumps, accumulators, and motors • force components • filters and filtration, lines and fittings, and fluids • hydrostatic transmissions • maintenance • troubleshooting.

Pneumatics and Hydraulics fourth edition
Harry L. Stewart; revised by Tom Philbin
5 1/2 x 8 1/4   Hardcover   512 pp.   315 illus.
ISBN: 0-672-23412-2 $19.95

Practical guide to the principles and applications of fluid power for engineers, designers, process planners, tool men, shop foremen, and mechanics: • pressure, work and power • general features of machines • hydraulic and pneumatic symbols • pressure boosters • air compressors and accessories • hydraulic power devices • hydraulic fluids • piping • air filters, pressure regulators, and lubricators • flow and pressure controls • pneumatic motors and tools • rotary hydraulic motors and hydraulic transmissions • pneumatic circuits • hydraulic circuits • servo systems.

Pumps fourth edition
Harry L. Stewart; revised by Tom Philbin
5 1/2 x 8 1/4   Hardcover   508 pp.   360 illus.
ISBN: 0-672-23400-9 $15.95

Comprehensive guide for operators, engineers, maintenance workers, inspectors, superintendents, and mechanics on principles and day-to-day operations of pumps: • centrifugal, rotary, reciprocating, and special service pumps • hydraulic accumulators • power transmission • hydraulic power tools • hydraulic cylinders • control valves • hydraulic fluids • fluid lines and fittings.

Carpentry and Construction

Carpenters and Builders Library
fifth edition 4 vols
John E. Ball; revised by Tom Philbin
5 1/2 x 8 1/4   Hardcover   1,224 pp.   1,010 illus.
ISBN: 0-672-23369-x $43.95
Also available in a new boxed set at no extra cost:
ISBN: 0-02-506450-9 $43.95

These profusely illustrated volumes, available in a handsome boxed edition, have set the professional standard for carpenters, joiners, and woodworkers.

Volume 1, Tools, Steel Square, Joinery
5 1/2 x 8 1/4   Hardcover   384 pp.   345 illus.
ISBN: 0-672-23365-7 $10.95
• Woods • nails • screws • bolts • the workbench • tools • using the steel square • joints and joinery • cabinetmaking joints • wood patternmaking • and kitchen cabinet construction.

Volume 2, Builders Math, Plans, Specifications
5 1/2 x 8 1/4   Hardcover   304 pp.   205 illus.
ISBN: 0-672-23366-5 $10.95
• Surveying • strength of timbers • practical drawing • architectural drawing • barn construction • small house construction • and home workshop layout.

Volume 3, Layouts, Foundations, Framing
5 1/2 x 8 1/4   Hardcover   272 pp.   215 illus.
ISBN: 0-672-23367-3 $10.95
• Foundations • concrete forms • concrete block construction • framing, girders and sills • skylights • porches and patios • chimneys, fireplaces, and stoves • insulation • solar energy and paneling.

Volume 4, Millwork, Power Tools, Painting
5 1/2 x 8 1/4   Hardcover   344 pp.   245 illus.
ISBN: 0-672-23368-1 $10.95
• Roofing, miter work • doors • windows, sheathing and siding • stairs • flooring • table saws, band saws, and jigsaws • wood lathes • sanders and combination tools • portable power tools • painting.

Complete Building Construction
second edition
John Phelps; revised by Tom Philbin
5 1/2 x 8 1/4   Hardcover   744 pp.   645 illus.
ISBN: 0-672-23377-0 $19.95

Comprehensive guide to constructing a frame or brick building from the footings to the ridge: • laying out building and excavation lines • making concrete forms and pouring fittings and foundation • making concrete slabs, walks, and driveways • laying concrete block, brick, and tile • building chimneys and fireplaces • framing, siding, and roofing • insulating • finishing the inside • building stairs • installing windows • hanging doors.

Complete Roofing Handbook

James E. Brumbaugh
5½ x 8¼ Hardcover 536 pp. 510 illus.
ISBN: 0-02-517850-4 $29.95

Authoritative text and highly detailed drawings and photographs,on all aspects of roofing: • types of roofs • roofing and reroofing • roof and attic insulation and ventilation • skylights and roof openings • dormer construction • roof flashing details • shingles • roll roofing • built-up roofing • roofing with wood shingles and shakes • slate and tile roofing • installing gutters and downspouts • listings of professional and trade associations and roofing manufacturers.

Complete Siding Handbook

James E. Brumbaugh
5½ x 8¼ Hardcover 512 pp. 450 illus.
ISBN: 0-02-517880-6 $23.95

Companion to *Complete Roofing Handbook*, with step-by-step instructions and drawings on every aspect of siding: • sidewalls and siding • wall preparation • wood board siding • plywood panel and lap siding • hardboard panel and lap siding • wood shingle and shake siding • aluminum and steel siding • vinyl siding • exterior paints and stains • refinishing of siding, gutter and downspout systems • listings of professional and trade associations and siding manufacturers.

Masons and Builders Library

second edition 2 vols
Louis M. Dezettel; revised by Tom Philbin
5½ x 8¼ Hardcover 688 pp. 500 illus.
ISBN: 0-672-23401-7 $27.95

Two-volume set on practical instruction in all aspects of materials and methods of bricklaying and masonry: • brick • mortar • tools • bonding • corners, openings, and arches • chimneys and fireplaces • structural clay tile and glass block • brick walks, floors, and terraces • repair and maintenance • plasterboard and plaster • stone and rock masonry • reading blueprints.

Volume 1, Concrete, Block, Tile, Terrazzo
5½ x 8¼ Hardcover 304 pp. 190 illus.
ISBN: 0-672-23402-5 $13.95

Volume 2, Bricklaying, Plastering, Rock Masonry, Clay Tile
5½ x 8¼ Hardcover 384 pp. 310 illus.
ISBN: 0-672-23403-3 $13.95

Woodworking

Woodworking and Cabinetmaking

F. Richard Boller
5½ x 8¼ Hardcover 360 pp. 455 illus.
ISBN: 0-02-512800-0 $18.95

Compact one-volume guide to the essentials of all aspects of woodworking: • properties of softwoods, hardwoods, plywood, and composition wood • design, function, appearance, and structure • project planning • hand tools • machines • portable electric tools • construction • the home workshop • and the projects themselves – stereo cabinet, speaker cabinets, bookcase, desk, platform bed, kitchen cabinets, bathroom vanity.

Wood Furniture: Finishing, Refinishing, Repairing second edition

James E. Brumbaugh
5½ x 8¼ Hardcover 352 pp. 185 illus.
ISBN: 0-672-23409-2 $12.95

Complete, fully illustrated guide to repairing furniture and to finishing and refinishing wood surfaces for professional woodworkers and do-it-yourselfers: • tools and supplies • types of wood • veneering • inlaying • repairing, restoring, and stripping • wood preparation • staining • shellac, varnish, lacquer, paint and enamel, and oil and wax finishes • antiquing • gilding and bronzing • decorating furniture.

Maintenance and Repair

Building Maintenance second edition

Jules Oravetz
5½ x 8¼ Hardcover 384 pp. 210 illus.
ISBN: 0-672-23278-2 $9.95

Complete information on professional maintenance procedures used in office, educational, and commercial buildings: • painting and decorating • plumbing and pipe fitting

• concrete and masonry • carpentry • roofing • glazing and caulking • sheet metal • electricity • air conditioning and refrigeration • insect and rodent control • heating • maintenance management • custodial practices.

Gardening, Landscaping and Grounds Maintenance

third edition
Jules Oravetz
5½ x 8¼ Hardcover 424 pp. 340 illus.
ISBN: 0-672-23417-3 $15.95

Practical information for those who maintain lawns, gardens, and industrial, municipal, and estate grounds: • flowers, vegetables, berries, and house plants • greenhouses • lawns • hedges and vines • flowering shrubs and trees • shade, fruit and nut trees • evergreens • bird sanctuaries • fences • insect and rodent control • weed and brush control • roads, walks, and pavements • drainage • maintenance equipment • golf course planning and maintenance.

Home Maintenance and Repair: Walls, Ceilings and Floors

Gary D. Branson
8½ x 11 Paperback 80 pp. 80 illus.
ISBN: 0-672-23281-2 $6.95

Do-it-yourselfer's step-by-step guide to interior remodeling with professional results: • general maintenance • wallboard installation and repair • wallboard taping • plaster repair • texture paints • wallpaper techniques • paneling • sound control • ceiling tile • bath tile • energy conservation.

Painting and Decorating

Rex Miller and Glenn E. Baker
5½ x 8¼ Hardcover 464 pp. 325 illus.
ISBN: 0-672-23405-x $18.95

Practical guide for painters, decorators, and homeowners to the most up-to-date materials and techniques: • job planning • tools and equipment needed • finishing materials • surface preparation • applying paint and stains · decorating with coverings • repairs and maintenance • color and decorating principles.

Tree Care ^{second edition}
John M. Haller
8½ x 11   Paperback   224 pp.   305 illus.
ISBN: 0-02-062870-6 $16.95

New edition of a standard in the field, for growers, nursery owners, foresters, landscapers, and homeowners: • planting • pruning • fertilizing • bracing and cabling • wound repair • grafting • spraying • disease and insect management • coping with environmental damage • removal • structure and physiology • recreational use.

Upholstering
updated
James E. Brumbaugh
5½ x 8¼   Hardcover   400 pp.   380 illus.
ISBN: 0-672-23372-x $15.95

Essentials of upholstering for professional, apprentice, and hobbyist: • furniture styles • tools and equipment • stripping • frame construction and repairs • finishing and refinishing wood surfaces • webbing • springs • burlap, stuffing, and muslin • pattern layout • cushions • foam padding • covers • channels and tufts • padded seats and slip seats • fabrics • plastics • furniture care.

Automotive and Engines

Diesel Engine Manual ^{fourth edition}
Perry O. Black; revised by William E. Scahill
5½ x 8¼   Hardcover   512 pp.   255 illus.
ISBN: 0-672-23371-1 $15.95

Detailed guide for mechanics, students, and others to all aspects of typical two- and four-cycle engines: • operating principles • fuel oil • diesel injection pumps • basic Mercedes diesels • diesel engine cylinders • lubrication • cooling systems • horsepower • engine-room procedures • diesel engine installation • automotive diesel engine • marine diesel engine • diesel electrical power plant • diesel engine service.

Gas Engine Manual ^{third edition}
Edwin P. Anderson; revised by Charles G. Facklam
5½ x 8¼   Hardcover   424 pp.   225 illus.
ISBN: 0-8161-1707-1 $12.95

Indispensable sourcebook for those who operate, maintain, and repair gas engines of all types and sizes: • fundamentals and classifications of engines · engine parts • pistons • crankshafts • valves • lubrication, cooling, fuel, ignition, emission

control and electrical systems • engine tune-up • servicing of pistons and piston rings, cylinder blocks, connecting rods and crankshafts, valves and valve gears, carburetors, and electrical systems.

Small Gasoline Engines
Rex Miller and Mark Richard Miller
5½ x 8¼   Hardcover   640 pp.   525 illus.
ISBN: 0-672-23414-9 $16.95

Practical information for those who repair, maintain, and overhaul two- and four-cycle engines – with emphasis on one-cylinder motors – including lawn mowers, edgers, grass sweepers, snowblowers, emergency electrical generators, outboard motors, and other equipment up to ten horsepower: • carburetors, emission controls, and ignition systems • starting systems • hand tools • safety • power generation • engine operations • lubrication systems • power drivers • preventive maintenance • step-by-step overhauling procedures • troubleshooting • testing and inspection • cylinder block servicing.

Truck Guide Library ^{3 vols}
James E. Brumbaugh
5½ x 8¼   Hardcover   2,144 pp.   1,715 illus.
ISBN: 0-672-23392-4 $45.95

Three-volume comprehensive and profusely illustrated reference on truck operation and maintenance.

Volume 1, Engines
5½ x 8¼   Hardcover   416 pp.   290 illus.
ISBN: 0-672-23356-8 $16.95

• Basic components · engine operating principles • troubleshooting • cylinder blocks • connecting rods, pistons, and rings • crankshafts, main bearings, and flywheels • camshafts and valve trains • engine valves.

Volume 2, Engine Auxiliary Systems
5½ x 8¼   Hardcover   704 pp.   520 illus.
ISBN: 0-672-23357-6 $16.95

• Battery and electrical systems • spark plugs • ignition systems, charging and starting systems • lubricating, cooling, and fuel systems • carburetors and governors • diesel systems • exhaust and emission-control systems.

Volume 3, Transmissions, Steering, and Brakes
5½ x 8¼   Hardcover   1,024 pp.   905 illus.
ISBN: 0-672-23406-8 $16.95

• Clutches • manual, auxiliary, and automatic transmissions • frame and suspension systems • differentials and axles, manual and power steering • front-end alignment • hydraulic, power, and air brakes • wheels and tires • trailers.

Drafting

Answers on Blueprint Reading
fourth edition
Roland E. Palmquist; revised by Thomas J. Morrisey
5½ x 8¼   Hardcover   320 pp.   275 illus.
ISBN: 0-8161-1704-7 $12.95

Complete question-and-answer instruction manual on blueprints of machines and tools, electrical systems, and architecture: • drafting scale • drafting instruments • conventional lines and representations • pictorial drawings • geometry of drafting • orthographic and working drawings • surfaces • detail drawing • sketching • map and topographical drawings • graphic symbols • architectural drawings • electrical blueprints • computer-aided design and drafting. Also included is an appendix of measurements • metric conversions • screw threads and tap drill sizes • number and letter sizes of drills with decimal equivalents • double depth of threads • tapers and angles.

Hobbies

Complete Course in Stained Glass
Pepe Mendez
8½ x 11   Paperback   80 pp.   50 illus.
ISBN: 0-672-23287-1 $8.95

Guide to the tools, materials, and techniques of the art of stained glass, with ten fully illustrated lessons: • how to cut glass • cartoon and pattern drawing • assembling and cementing • making lamps using various techniques • electrical components for completing lamps • sources of materials • glossary of terminology and techniques of stained glasswork.

Macmillan Practical Arts Library
Books for and by the Craftsman

World Woods in Color

W.A. Lincoln
7 × 10   Hardcover   300 pages
300 photos
ISBN: 0-02-572350-2 $38.41

Large full-color photographs show the natural grain and features of nearly 300 woods: • commercial and botanical names • physical characteristics, mechanical properties, seasoning, working properties, durability, and uses • the height, diameter, bark, and places of distribution of each tree • indexing of botanical, trade, commercial, local, and family names • a full bibliography of publications on timber study and identification.

The Woodworker's Bible

Alf Martensson
8 × 10   Paperback   288 pages   900 illus.
ISBN: 0-02-011940-2 $13.95

For the craftsperson familiar with basic carpentry skills, a guide to creating professional-quality furniture, cabinetry, and objects d'art in the home workshop: • techniques and expert advice on fine craftsmanship whether tooled by hand or machine • joint-making • assembling to ensure fit • finishes. Author, who lives in London and runs a workshop called Woodstock, has also written. *The Book of Furnituremaking.*

Cabinetmaking: The Professional Approach

Alan Peters
8½ × 11   Hardcover   208 pages   175 illus.
(8 pp. color)
ISBN: 0-02-596200-0 $28.00

A unique guide to all aspects of professional furniture making, from an English master craftsman: • the Cotswold School and the birth of the furniture movement • setting up a professional shop • equipment • finance and business efficiency • furniture design • working to commission • batch production, training, and techniques • plans for nine projects.

The Woodturner's Art: Fundamentals and Projects

Ron Roszkiewicz
8 × 10   Hardcover   256 pages   300 illus.
ISBN: 0-02-605250-4 $28.80

A master woodturner shows how to design and create increasingly difficult projects step-by-step in this book suitable for the beginner and the more advanced student: • spindle and faceplate turning • tools • techniques • classic turnings from various historical periods • more than 30 types of projects including boxes, furniture, vases, and candlesticks • making duplicates • projects using combinations of techniques and more than one kind of wood. Author has also written *The Woodturner's Companion.*

Cabinetmaking and Millwork

John L. Feirer
7⅛ × 9½   Hardcover   992 pages
2,350 illus. (32 pp. in color)
ISBN: 0-02-537350-1 $47.50

The classic on cabinetmaking that covers in detail all of the materials, tools, machines, and processes used in building cabinets and interiors, the production of furniture, and other work of the finish carpenter and millwright • fixed installations such as paneling, built-ins, and cabinets • movable wood products such as furniture and fixtures • which woods to use, and why and how to use them in the interiors of homes and commercial buildings • metrics and plastics in furniture construction.

Carpentry and Building Construction

John L. Feirer and Gilbert R. Hutchings
7½ × 9½   hardcover   1,120 pages
2,000 photos (8 pp. in color)
ISBN: 0-02-537360-9 $50.00

A classic by Feirer on each detail of modern construction: • the various machines, tools, and equipment from which the builder can choose • laying of a foundation • building frames for each part of a building • details of interior and exterior work • painting and finishing • reading plans • chimneys and fireplaces • ventilation • assembling prefabricated houses.